MILITARY SMALL ARMS

OF THE 20th CENTURY

7th Edition

Ian V. Hogg & John S. Weeks

About Our Covers.....

Front Cover - The Thompson submachine gun, in several models, served the U.S. military and the military arms of other nations. Below, the German MP40 submachine gun and Colt's new M4 carbine.

Back Cover - Legendary U.S. arms of the WWII era. Top, the Browning Automatic Rifle (BAR); M1 Garand rifle; Thompson submachine gun and the M3 submachine gun, also known as the "Grease Gun".

These illustrations were made possible through the generous assistance of Charles Justmann, Bob Pucci, Ray Farrell and Colt's Manufacturing Company, Inc. -- and we thank them.

Published by

krause publications

700 E. State Street • Iola, WI 54990-0001
Telephone: 715/445-2214
Web: www.krause.com

To place an order or receive our free catalog, call 800-258-0929.
For editorial comment and further information,
use our regular business telephone at (715) 445-2214.

Library of Congress Catalog Number: 73-83466
ISBN: 0-87341-824-7

Printed in the United States of America

CONTENTS

PREFACE

A TURBULENT CENTURY

From South Africa in 1900 to the Balkans in 1999, not a year has passed in the 20th century which has not seen, somewhere, men at war. Only in one year—1964—was no British soldier killed in combat, and scarcely any country has not been touched by war to some degree. And to make war, man needs weapons.

Lovers of conspiracy theories stand this on its head and tell us that it is the availability of weapons which causes war, that the evil armaments barons have waxed fat on warfare by selling arms to all sides. If this was the case, we should see some mighty armaments empires ruling the world by now, but the fact remains that the number of armaments firms which existed in 1900 and still exist today can be counted on the fingers, while the number which have gone bankrupt is legion. Men made war before firearms were invented, and if every firearm vanished overnight they would still be at war tomorrow, with spears and catapults. Ever since the 14th century, war has driven the development of firearms as soldiers have demanded better weapons for waging war, and the civilian development and employment of firearms has followed in its wake.

And in no century has the development of military firearms moved with such speed and complexity as in the twentieth; in 1900 the standard arm of the soldier was a bolt-action repeating rifle capable of taking effect at 2000 yards range, there were probably less than a thousand automatic machine guns in existence, and the heavy revolver was the standard side-arm. There were no submachine guns, no light machine guns, no anti-tank rifles. The automatic pistol was a commercial novelty being delicately explored by the military and blackpowder was still in use as the propellant charge in many smaller armies.

Today's infantryman carries a lightweight assault rifle, capable of automatic fire; he has a light machine gun in his squad, and heavy machine guns to provide supporting fire. The automatic pistol has virtually replaced the revolver in military use. The submachine gun has reached its zenith and declined in military importance, while the anti-tank rifle came and went almost within a single generation and the anti-materiel rifle has just begun to gain acceptance. The caseless cartridge has been perfected, together with weapons to fire it. Electro-optical sights provide the soldier with the capability of firing accurately throughout the entire day and night, and the technology of mass-production has made it possible to

manufacture weapons faster than they can be worn out. And the purpose of this book is to record and tabulate that development. Not as a glorification of war: like most professional soldiers I have seen sufficient of war to have seen beyond the glory to the bloody chaos which lies behind it. My purpose is simply to demonstrate the technical development of weapons as mechanical devices and show how mechanical ingenuity has overcome what often appeared to be insuperable difficulties. It also shows how the development of weapons has interacted with tactical theories and practices, and how the one has affected the other. And finally, in my view at any rate, it shows how the 'learning curve' of weapons development has approached a degree of perfection which is going to be very difficult and expensive to improve. I very much doubt if the 21st century will see an advance in design and technology comparable to what we have passed through in the twentieth.

It is now almost exactly 30 years since the late Colonel John Weeks and I began assembling data for the first edition of this book in the summer of 1969. It was published in 1973, which indicates the magnitude of our task. John fell ill in 1981 and died on New Year's Day 1983, as we were preparing for the 5th Edition, but his name is still on the cover and many of his photographs and some of his original text, notably on anti-tank rifles, are still in this present edition. The amount of material has almost doubled in the past thirty years, such has been the growth and development of small arms, and in this seventh and final edition I have attempted to bring back into the book much that had to be dropped from previous editions because of space restrictions. This will obviously be the last edition, since between now and the Millennium it is unlikely that any new firearms will appear and be adopted by a military force, and therefore I have been at pains to include as much as possible in order to make this a definitive work of reference. There are, undoubtedly, a few very minor weapons which have escaped; there are, equally undoubtedly, a handful of new weapons included which will probably turn out to be non-starters; only time will tell.

Ian V. Hogg
Upton-upon-Severn
June 1999

ACKNOWLEDGEMENTS

IN THE COURSE of preparing the various editions of this book, the authors have sought the assistance of many individuals, manufacturers, museums and official agencies. Most responded handsomely, sending literature, photographs and information concerning the various weapons. It is with gratitude, therefore, that we record our thanks to the following:

AAI Corporation, Baltimore, USA

Accuracy International, Portsmouth, England

Mr. Johan Adler

Sr. Gaetano Paolo Agnini

Mr. John A. Anderson

Armi Benelli SpA, Urbino, Italy

Armscor, Pretoria, South Africa

Mr. Per Arvidsson

Astra-Unceta y Cia, Guernica, Spain

Barrett Firearms Mfg. Inc., Murfreesboro, USA

Pietro Beretta SpA, Gardone VT, Italy

V- Bernadelli SpA, Gardone VT, Italy

Bofors Ordnance (formerly FFV), EskilstLina, Sweden

Breda Mecanica Bresciana SpA, Brescia, Italy

Browning SA, Liege, Belgium

M. Raymond Caranta

Ceska Zbrojovka, Uhersky Brod, Czech Republic

Chartered Firearms Industries, Singapore

China North Industries Corp., Beijing, China

Colt Firearms, Hartford, USA

A.J.Cormack

Daewoo Precision Industries, Inchon, South Korea

Diemaco Inc., Kitchener, Ontario, Canada

The late Dr. Edward C. Ezell

Firearms Department, West Midlands Constabulary, Birmingham, England

Fabrica Militar de Armas Portatiles 'Domingo Matheu', Rosario, Argentine

FAMAE, Santiago, Chile

Federal Directorate of Supply & Procurement, Belgrade, Yugoslavia

FEG Arms & Gas Appliances Factory, Budapest, Hungary

Mr. Abraham Flateau

FN Herstall SA, Liege, Belgium

Luigi Franchi SpA, Fornaci, Italy

Col. (Retd) Uzi Gal

Terry J Gander

GE Aerospace, Burlington, Vt.,

GIAT, Versailles-Satory, France

Gibbs Rifle Co.,

Glock GmbH, Deutsche-Wagram, Austria

Heckler & Koch GmbH, Oberndorf/Neckar, Germany

Heckler & Koch Inc., Sterling, USA

Hellenic Arms Industry (EBO) SA, Athens, Greece

Howa Machinery Co., Aichi, Japan

IMBEL, Sao Paulo, Brazil

INDEP, Lisbon, Portugal

Indian State Arms Factory, Kanpur, India

Israel Military Industries, Ramat Hasharon, Israel

Sphinx AG, Solothurn, Switzerland

Jack Krcma

M. Jacques Lennaerts

Liarna-Gabilondo y Cia SA, Vitoria, Spain

Lyttletori Engineering Works, Lyttleton, South Africa

MSgt J.W. Maddock, USMC

Makina ve Kimya EidListrisi Kurumo, Ankara, Turkey

Dott. Ing. France Manassero

Mauser-Werke AG, Oberndorf/Neckar, Germany

Mekanika Industrio e Cornercio Lda, Rio de Janiero, Brazil

Productos Mendoza SA. Mexico

Mr. James Mongello

Mr. Tom Nelson

Norsk Forsvarsteknologi AS, Kongsberg, Norway

Ronaldo S Olive

Omori Factory, Minebea Co.. Tokyo, Japan

Parker-Hale Ltd, Birmingham, England

Herr Karl Pawlas

Col. Des Radmore

Ramo Inc, Nashville, USA

Mme Chantal Regibeau

Remington Arms, Bridgeport, USA

Rheinmetall GmbH, Dusseldorf, Germany

Royal Military College of' Science, Shrivenham, England

Royal Ordnance ple, Guns & Vehicles Division, Nottingham, England

Saco Defense Inc., Saco, USA

Sako Ltd., Jyvaskyla, Finland

Empresa Naciorial Santa Barbara, Madrid, Spain

School of Infantry Museum, Warminster, England

SIG, Neuhausen-Rheinfalls, Switzerland

Sima-Cifar, Callao, Peru

SITES SpA, Turin, Italy

Mr. John Slough

Smith & Wesson Inc., Springfield, USA

Socimi SpA, Milan, Italy

Herr Wolfgang Stadler

Star-Bonifacio Echeverria y Cia, Eibar, Spain

Steyr-Mannlicher GmbH, Steyr, Austria

The late Mr. Eugene Stoner

Sturm, Ruger & Co., Prescott, USA

Sumitomo Heavy Industries, Tokyo, Japan

Fratelli Tanfoglio SpA, Gardone VT, Italy

J. David Truby

Dr. Martin Tuma

US Infantry Museum, Fort Benning, USA

US Marine Corps Museum, Quantico, USA

Våpensmia AS, Dokka, Norway

The late Mr. Stephen K. Vogel

Mr. John Walter

Carl Walther Waffenfabrik, Ulm a.d. Donau, Germany

G.S.Wardell, Chief Engineer, Lysaghts Works Pty Ltd

Dr. Ingo Weise

Mr. H. J. Woodend, Curator of the MoD Pattern Room, ROF Nottingham, England

Zastava Arms, Belgrade, Yugoslavia

Dipl.Tng Fritz Zeyher

The majority of the photographs from the collections of the Pattern Room, the School of Infantry Museum and the Royal Military College of Science were photographed by the authors, who greatly value the permission granted by the various governing bodies to photograph the weapons in their care, and especial thanks are due to Mr. H. J. Woodend for his assistance in this respect. Other photographs have been provided by the various manufacturers, and our thanks are extended to them for their cooperation.

Principles Of Operation

The following notes are offered as a means of explaining the operations of the various types of weapon covered in the body of the book. This avoids the necessity of repeating the same cycle of operations half-a-dozen times on the same page, and it forms a useful introduction to firearms for those coming fresh to the subject.

To an engineer, a gun is simply a heat engine in which fuel is burned in order to produce useful energy. In a typical heat engine—such as a motor-cycle engine—there is a cylinder with a piston. Air and petroleum vapor are introduced into the cylinder and ignited, the piston is forced down the cylinder by the expansion of hot gas, and by means of a crank it produces motion in the gearbox and thence to the back wheel.

The gun has a cylinder - which we call the barrel - and a piston, which we call the bullet. We introduce fuel—in the shape of the propellant powder—and ignite it, by means of a cap, and the expansion of gases drives the bullet down the barrel. The only difference is that this piston is not connected to anything but delivers its energy directly when it reaches the target.

The barrel is divided into three sections: the chamber, the throat (or lead) and the bore.

The chamber is where the round of ammunition is placed before firing, and it is therefore shaped to suit the particular cartridge in use. It has to withstand a considerable pressure and an equally considerable amount of heat. When a round is fired the propellant burns very rapidly and produces about 14,000 times its volume of gas. Pressure and heat build up very quickly, and within half a thousandth of a second the temperature is close to 2,700 C and the pressure in a NATO 7.62mm cartridge has risen to 22.3 tons/in^2. It is therefore necessary to close the rear of the chamber, which is done by using some form of bolt or breechblock. The breech unit is bored to permit passage of a firing pin or striker, the function of which is to give a sharp blow to the primer cap in the base of the cartridge case and so ignite the propellant.

The propellant gas must be prevented from leaking out of the chamber, so that all its energy drives the bullet, and the sealing of the breech is done by the cartridge case. This expands slightly under the gas pressure, forming a tight seal in the chamber, but contracts as soon as the bullet has left the bore and the pressure drops. Without this contraction it would be impossible to remove the empty case. In weapons where the breech begins to open before the pressure has dropped, there is a danger of the case sticking so firmly to the chamber wall that the head, or part of the rim, can be torn off the case by the extractor, leaving the damaged case in the chamber. This can be avoided by coating the case with oil or grease before loading it, or by cutting thin grooves along about two-thirds of the length of the chamber walls so that some of the propellant gas can get to the outside of the case and so equalize the pressure inside and outside, preventing sticking.

The chamber leads forward into **the bore**, which in almost all modern weapons is rifled. As the chamber converts into the bore, there is a conical section which guides the bullet into the rifling, and in this conical section the rifling grooves gradually commence. But the bore is actually measured from the point where the rifling grooves reach their full depth, and that short conical section is **the throat** (or lead pronounced 'leed' because it 'leads in' to the bore)

The rifling consists of a number of grooves cut spirally into the interior surface of the bore. The number and depth of the grooves is a question almost of preference between makers, but the rapidity of twist dictates the rate at which the bullet will spin when it emerges from the muzzle. This stabilizes the bullet along its longitudinal axis by imparting to it gyroscopic stability which resists efforts to change its direction. The ideal shape, weight and diameter of the bullet are fixed by the laws of external ballistics. The function of the barrel is therefore threefold: it guides the bullet in the required direction, it gives the bullet velocity by containing the expanding gases which force the bullet forward, and it imparts a rotary stabilizing effect by spinning the bullet.

The Operating Cycle.

The bolt or breech-block closes the breech opening and is generally locked in place until the chamber pressure is reduced to a safe level, after which the breech can be opened either by hand or by some automatic means. If an extractor is attached to the bolt-head, the empty case can be withdrawn and subsequently ejected from the weapon, and as the bolt goes backward it can be made to compress a spring - thus storing energy which can be subsequently used to drive the bolt forward again. The bolt can also be made to cock a firing mechanism. On its way forward the bolt can strip a round from a magazine, push it into the chamber, and support the base of the round (usually by locking the bolt to the barrel or the receiver). The energy stored in a spring during the cocking action can then be used to drive a pin into the primer.

This series of operations takes place every time a weapon is fired, and the sequence may be performed either by hand or by an automatic mechanism. It is generally referred to as the **'operating cycle'** and is summarized thus:

1: Chambering;
2: Locking (supporting the base of the cartridge case);
3: Firing;
4: Unlocking (removing the support to the base of the cartridge case);
5: Extraction;
6: Ejection;
7: Cocking;
8: Feeding.

These portions of the cycle need not necessarily take place in this order; cocking, for example, could occur before unlocking or before extraction, but all small arms have to go through the cycle regardless of its precise order (provided they use conventional metallic cartridges).

MANUALLY-OPERATED WEAPONS

SINGLE SHOT WEAPONS

The fundamental requirement in any firearm is to get the cartridge into the weapon so that it can be fired, and once the idea of loading at the breech began to appear practical, with the invention of some sort of self-contained cartridge, so mechanical ingenuity began to make an appearance. Most of the early breech closing systems depended upon a substantial block of metal, but for military use, and certainly so in the 20th century, the bolt action system became almost universal. There are two basic systems, the turnbolt and the straight-pull bolt.

The Turnbolt Action

Perhaps some industrial archaeologist could tell us when the common turnbolt was first applied to securing doors, though its origins appear to be lost in the mists of what lawyers call 'time immemorial. However, we can with some certainty say who first applied the principle to a firearm; this was Nicholas von Dreyse, who invented the 'Needle Gun' for the Prussian Army in 1838.

The needle gun acquired its name from the long and thin firing pin which passed through the bolt and was impelled by a spring so as to pass clear through the paper cartridge and strike a percussion cap attached to the base of the bullet. The bolt was a tubular piece of metal, with a handle on the side, for all the world like the common door bolt. It was hollow, and contained an inner sleeve and the firing pin and its spring, We need not concern ourselves too deeply with the action of cocking and releasing the striker; what interests us here is the locking of the bolt and the sealing of the chamber against the rearward escape of powder gas—the 'obturation', to use the correct technical term. Locking was done by simply turning the bolt handle down in front of a lug formed in the receiver or body of the rifle. Obturation was obtained by simply grinding the face of the bolt to a conical form and the rear of the chamber to a mating cone, so that the bolt fitted into the chamber tightly. The locking lug being slightly inclined, the more the bolt handle turned down, the tighter the bolt was pushed into the chamber.

Once the self-contained cartridge appeared, the design became simpler in some respects, more difficult in others. There was no need for a long needle-like firing pin now that the cap was at the base of the cartridge case, but with the increasing power of successive cartridge designs the locking system had to be improved and became more complicated. The usual method was to form the head of the bolt with lugs which would pass through slots formed in the chamber or the receiver and could then be turned through an angle so as to fit tightly behind the lugs formed between these slots. At the same time the bolt handle passed down into a recess in front of some sort of lug, giving additional safety, and in many designs a long guide rib on the bolt was provided with a suitable recess in the gun body into which it moved as the bolt was rotated to lock. All of which meant more and very precise machining and more nooks and corners for the soldier to clean.

The turnbolt is operated, as the name suggests, by grasping the bolt handle and lifting it so as to rotate the body of the bolt and unlock it; the bolt is then drawn back, a cartridge inserted into the feedway, the bolt pushed back so as to drive the cartridge into the chamber, and then the handle turned down again to lock. The movement of the bolt has, of course, cocked the firing pin ready to fire.

A variation on the turnbolt system appeared in the 1990s on a Swiss sniping rifle; here the rotation of the bolt handle turns a sleeve inside the bolt body which has shaped cams on it, and these cams force radial wedges out from the bolt to lock into recesses in the gun body. Lifting the bolt handle withdraws the wedges and allows the bolt to be drawn back. One advantage of this is that the rotary movement of the bolt handle is much less than the usual 90°, and the bolt itself does not rotate.

The Straight-Pull Bolt action

The straight-pull bolt, on the other hand, demands no lifting of the bolt handle; you simply grasp it and pull it straight back. What happens then depends upon the system in use; either the bolt rotates or it does not. In cases where the bolt rotates the actual locking mechanism is exactly the same as for a turnbolt, but the method of rotating the bolt is different. The withdrawal of the bolt handle causes a stud, attached to the handle, to ride in a spiral groove in the bolt body, so that the bolt is rotated to unlock. Once unlocked the groove stops, the lug pulls, and the body of the bolt is drawn back with the handle. There are other ways, but they are all variations of this simple theme.

If the bolt does not rotate, then the locking is done by means of a substantial wedge beneath the bolt which is lodged in front of a solid cross-piece in the gun body. Pulling on the bolt handle lifts this lug clear of the cross-piece and then withdraws the bolt.

Argument still rages between theorists on the subject of placement of the locking lugs on the bolt. In theory, the forward lug, locking directly into the chamber, is best since it provided a solid support for the cartridge and places no stress on the body of the gun. On the other hand, rear lugs, locking into the receiver or body, places stress upon the body and demand more robust construction and hence more weight. There is also the argument that front lugs demand full closure before rotation can commence, and full opening rotation before withdrawal can commence; rear lugs can be shaped so that the rotation can begin before the bolt is completely closed or the round completely chambered, and the opening rotation can also begin the withdrawal. Hence rear-locked bolts tend to be faster to operate than front-locked. The classic example of this is the Mauser (front lug) bolt compared with the Lee (rear lug) bolt; a Lee-Enfield, in the hands of a trained soldier, can produce a rate of fire far higher than any Mauser bolt.

As to the relative accuracy of front and rear lugs, which is really at the heart of the argument, theoretically the front lug will give better accuracy since the bolt cannot move; whereas the body of a rear lug bolt can be compressed and hence introduce vibrations and stresses which interfere with accuracy. These are probably very valid arguments if you are trying to put a bullet into a one-inch circle at two miles range, but they lose much of their force when you come down to a four-hundred yard snap shot against a running figure behind a low hedge in the rain.

The Repeating Rifle

Once the breech-loading rifle was an accepted fact of life, the next step was to provide it with some sort of built-in ammunition supply, so that the business of loading each individual cartridge was speeded up. The man could load up some sort of 'magazine' and then fire them off without delay between shots. This, of course, put the fear of God up the older generals; the men would obviously blaze off every round as soon as they saw the enemy and then have nothing left when the enemy put in his assault. This attitude belied their own faith in discipline, because in the armies of the latter 19th century discipline was such that nobody fired anything until he was told. Nevertheless, this belief led to a demand for some sort of 'cut-off' device which would lock the magazine out of action and make the soldier load each round singly, keeping his full magazine for the more desperate moments of battle.

The first magazines were tubular, lying beneath the barrel, and with a spring to push the cartridge backwards towards the breech, where they were lifted up and aligned with the chamber by some mechanism connected to the breech opening arrangement. This was moderately satisfactory in the days of large cartridges and soft lead bullets, but when compound bullets with hard and pointed tips began to appear, there was a considerable danger that with the tip of a bullet resting against the cap of the next round in the tube, the shock of recoil could cause the two to come into contact with sufficient violence to explode the cartridge. This was distressing enough for the man holding the rifle, but it was generally made more distressing because the explosion of one cartridge usually set off the rest of the magazine. So the tubular magazine fell under a cloud once smaller calibers and pointed bullets began to appear.

The tube magazine therefore ceased to be used in military calibers, though it is still to be found in wide use in sporting arms. The box magazine which replaced it is just what it says, a metal box which usually hangs down below the receiver just behind the chamber. As the bolt moves back, a spring in the bottom of the box pushed up the cartridges so that the top one protrudes into the 'feedway' in front of the bolt. It is restrained by lips on the magazine so that it is not free to leave the magazine until assisted by the bolt moving forward; this pushes on the cartridge and eases it forward, clear of the restraining lips, whereupon it moves up and aligns with the chamber and the bolt rams it in. The bolt then closes, the gun is fired, and on opening the bolt an extractor pulls out the case and an ejector flings it clear of the breech.

The box magazine can be attached at any convenient angle, but in manually operated weapons they are almost always beneath the receiver, either a removable box or an integral box, one which forms part of the receiver structure. There are also idiosyncratic magazines such as the Schoenauer rotary spool and the side-loading Krag-Jorgensen, but these are in the minority. Magazines which attach at the side or at the top of the weapon are not seen on manually-operated weapons because they are invariably adopted in an effort to provide a greater capacity than can be achieved beneath the receiver, and this argues an automatic weapon. Moreover they introduce problems of balance and sighting which are not insoluble but which a certainly not worth introducing on a simple manual weapon.

AUTOMATIC WEAPONS

The idea of a weapon which could be loaded and fired mechanically, and much faster than it could be hand-loaded, is one which had been pursued since the earliest days of firearms, resulting in some fairly hair-raising ideas being tried out at various times. But until the self-contained metallic cartridge was a practical reality, no method of automatic fire was really possible. The earliest mechanical machine guns attempted to get around this by pre-loading steel 'chambers' and firing these in succession, but they were scarcely practical. Only with the metallic cartridge could the Gatling, the Gardner, the Nordenfelt and the Mitralleuse be made into weapons worth taking into battle.

The limitation of these weapons was not so much the rate of fire—the Gatling system can support rates of up to 6000 rounds per minute—but the more prosaic fact of lack of accuracy due to the shaking about the weapon got because of the vigorous operating of a hand crank or lever. No matter how good the support or carriage might be, some shaking was inevitable and the bullets were consequently scattered over a considerable area. If the weapon could be powered independently of any outside agency, this disturbance would cease and the weapon would become more effective.

The gun may be a heat engine but it is not a particularly efficient one; about 40 percent of the energy developed by the propellant powder is dissipated as muzzle blast, and about 30 percent as heat, which leaves only 30 percent actually pushing the bullet out of the barrel. Various people in search of an automatic weapon observed the wasted energy of the muzzle blast, others of the recoil thrust or 'kick' felt when firing, and began to wonder whether these effects might not be put to use rather than simply being left to happen. Maxim was the first to succeed; he tamed the recoil; then Browning turned the muzzle blast to good effect; and finally Bergmann devised the simple blowback system. And, one way or another, every automatic weapon devised in this century has used one or other of those fundamental forces. In the broadest terms, therefore, we have three basic systems of automatic operation; Blowback, Gas and Recoil.

BLOWBACK OPERATION

The blowback operation of a small arm can be defined as 'a method of operation in which the energy required to carry out the cycle of operations is supplied to the bolt by the backward movement of the cartridge case caused by the gas pressure'.

The actual operation of the blowback system is uncomplicated. The gas pressure exerted on the base of the case drives the unlocked bolt to the rear, while the empty case pushes itself out of the chamber and is ejected from the gun. The return spring, which has absorbed energy, then drives the bolt forwards to feed a round from the magazine. The round is chambered and when the trigger is operated, the weapon is fired. The drawback to the blowback system is that it can only be used with relatively low-powered cartridges, so that the bullet is out of the barrel and the chamber pressure has dropped to a safe level before the impulse delivered by the cartridge case had started to move the breech block. It is also desirable to have short, straight-sided pistol cartridges rather than long, thin, bottle-necked cartridges, since the former extract cleanly and do not tend to stick to the chamber walls. Once the power of the cartridge is increased, so are the problems; it is feasible to put a massive breech-block and powerful recoil spring into a weapon—the Schwarzlose machine gun is a case in point—but the result is not often practical, and using a powerful rifle cartridge in a blowback weapon usually leads to difficult extraction, stretched cases, bulged cases, and even separated cases—where the head pulls completely off the body of the case and a monumental jam then occurs as the new round gets forced into the remains of the previous case. For use with military weapons, therefore, the blowback system has to become a more sophisticated arrangement.

Blowback with advanced primer ignition (API). Instead of firing from a stationary bolt, the bolt in this case is moving forward when the primer is struck. This means that the forward momentum of the bolt must be arrested by the firing impulse before the bolt can be driven back. As a result, the force available to accelerate the bolt backwards is reduced, which means that a lighter block can be used. This saves weight and it also has an effect upon the rate of fire, since the lighter block accelerates more rapidly. A good example of this principle is the Sten gun; in the Sten submachine gun the cap is struck by the fixed firing pin while the bolt still has 0.003-inch to travel to the breech face. The propellant immediately burns and the pressure in the case increases. Peak pressure is reached when the case is still 0.0018-inch from the breech, and the block continues forward to touch the breech face with minimum velocity before starting back. It can be seen from this simple explanation that the design of these parts is a delicate matter, and the success of the whole operation of the weapon depends to a great extent upon two features, the first being the mass of the bolt and its spring force, and the second, the characteristics of the ammunition.

One small disadvantage to API is the fact that the gun must always fire from an open bolt, which means that on pulling the trigger there is a delay while the bolt travels forward to the breech, and this delay—together with the attendant bolt movement—is not conducive to an accurate delivery of the first shot. Some training is also required before the firer becomes accustomed to the pause after pulling the trigger and to the shift of center of gravity as the bolt runs forward.

For submachine-guns it is rare to supply more than one type of ammunition, and where this has been done in the past it has not been mixed. If ammunition of different characteristics is mixed and fed into a gun working on an advanced primer ignition system it can lead to difficulties, for the bolt has to be balanced to one particular type of round, and another type may easily have quite different chamber pressures and bullet weights. If the two are fed alternately the motion of the bolt is likely to become upset; the gun may stop firing, or the action of the bolt may become progressively more violent until something breaks. Both these actions have happened with trial guns.

Delayed, hesitation, or retarded blowback. Although advanced primer ignition represents a saving of weight in the breechblock compared to a pure blowback system, it can only be used in small-caliber submachine guns and very heavy 20mm cannon carried on heavy mountings. It is not suitable for a rifle-caliber weapon because not only is the breech mechanism heavy but, by the nature of its construction, it must be an open-bolt firing system which, as we have just seen, leads to inaccuracy.

To be able to use a rifle-caliber weapon and to have one of an acceptable weight, a system known as 'delayed blowback' has been adopted. The essence of the system is that the breechblock is delayed in its backward travel while the projectile is in the bore and thereafter the momentum imparted by the cartridge explosion is utilized to carry out the cycle of operations. It must be remembered that pressure in the region of 6ton/in^2 exists at the muzzle of a rifle firing a 7.62mm NATO round, and this takes about 0.005-second (5 milliseconds) to decay. This pressure is quite adequate to produce the required bolt velocity, but arrangements must be made to delay the speed of breech opening so that (while the bullet is in the bore) the case cannot drive the bolt backward to expose enough unsupported brass to produce a case-head separation. There are many current examples of this system, most of which use some simple arrangement incorporating a mechanical disadvantage system although a few utilize gas forces.

The essential part of the delayed blowback design is that it must not be uniform in its action, as it must impose the maximum restraint on the movement of the bolt immediately after firing—yet as soon as the pressure drops off, the mechanism must allow the bolt to move with progressively increasing freedom as it accelerates backwards.

Most modern versions of this system use a two-part bolt and some form of restraint. The restraint acts upon the bolt itself, which rides in a carrier, to which it is connected by some means giving a mechanical disadvantage to the bolt. In other words, a very small movement of the bolt is turned into a large movement of the carrier, so requiring a large force to act on the bolt if the carrier is to be moved. The restrainers work in the same way. A very small movement of the bolt is turned into a much larger movement of the restrainers, and since the restrainers are held in place by strong springs or inclined cam surfaces, this means that the bolt has to exert a very large force indeed to move them out of engagement.

What happens on firing is as follows: the bolt face takes the full force of the chamber pressure, acting through the cartridge base. This force is enough to move the restraints out of engagement, but due to the leverages and distances that the restraints have to travel, the process takes a finite amount of time and does not release the bolt until the bullet has left the muzzle. However, while the bullet is still in the bore, the bolt does actually move a tiny amount, and in so doing it either takes the case with it, or it allows the case wall to stretch and

push the base back on to the bolt face. This means that during the time that pressure is high in the barrel, a part of the cartridge case is clear of the breech and unsupported, and what can then happen is that the unsupported part bulges out. This frequently occurs with the French FA-MAS rifle although it does not seem to affect its operation in any way.

When the bullet has left the muzzle and the restraint has been removed, the bolt is held forward only by the carrier, which is being pushed by the return spring. The pressure is still sufficient to throw the bolt back with dangerous force, so it is arranged that it has to accelerate the heavier carrier, using another mechanical disadvantage system, This acceleration effectively removes the remaining kinetic energy in the bolt, and it and the carrier move backwards together, compressing the return spring. In the German G3 rifle, the restraint is formed by two rollers which are forced outwards into recesses in the body. As these rollers are forced inwards by the bolt, they also accelerate the carrier, and so neatly perform two functions at once.

Locked-breech blowback or locked-breech, blowback-assisted.

The principal defect of the blowback system for high-powered arms is the question of extracting the empty case. We have seen that there is a movement of the bolt and a consequent stretching of the case which, unless kept to a minimum, is liable to result in torn rims or even separated cases. A favorite remedy of desperate designers is to oil the cartridge case, by one means or another. Another is to flute the chamber and so equalize the gas pressure in and outside the case. A third method, which retains most of the simplicity of the blowback system but locks the breech solidly until the chamber pressure drops, is this mixture of locked and blowback functioning. This system has been used in varying ways in the past. The breechblock is locked to the body at the time of firing and so the block itself can be of a minimum weight and size. After the point of maximum pressure has passed, the breech is unlocked and the remainder of the cycle of operations is carried out by simple blowback—usually referred to as 'residual breech pressure'. The method of breech unlocking may be achieved either by gas or by recoil but it must be emphasized that of the eight parts of the cycle of operation, seven are carried out by energy obtained from simple blowback. Only the unlocking process depends on some other system.

GAS OPERATION

In all automatic weapons the fundamental source of operating energy is the high-pressure gas created by the explosion of the propellant charge. This is true in a general sense of guns operated by the blowback system, the recoil system, or any other system of true automatic operation, but in spite of this fact the term 'gas operation' is reserved for a particular type of operating system in which the pressure of the gases is employed in a specific way.

In a typical gun which uses the system of gas operation, an opening or 'port' is provided in the wall of the barrel. When the bullet has passed this opening, some of the following high-pressure gas passes through the port to act upon a piston or some similar device for converting the pressure of the gas into thrust. This thrust is then utilized through a suitable mechanism to provide the energy necessary for performing the automatic functions required in sustained fire.

The gas-powered operating mechanism can take many forms, but the most commonly used device consists of a simple gas cylinder and a piston which is driven rearward to transfer its energy to the bolt by direct impact. In some cases the piston may be driven forward instead of rearward, but this does not involve any significant change in the principle of operation.

Even the nature of the member which is acted upon by the gas pressure is subject to great variation. Instead of being a conventional piston, this member can be in the form of a sleeve, a slide, or any other device arranged to receive an impulse from the gas pressure.

The methods used for transferring energy from the piston to the gun mechanism are also extremely diverse both in form and function. Instead of transmitting energy directly to the bolt, the piston itself sometimes moves through a very short stroke and transfers its energy by striking an intermediate rod or lever. Large numbers of devices have been designed to minimize the shock involved in the energy transfer through the use of levers, links or cams. In certain instances, the shock of transfer is reduced by causing the piston to load intermediate springs which subsequently transfer their stored energy to the mechanism with greater smoothness.

The principles involved in gas operation can be outlined by considering the general character of the pressures and forces which result from the firing of the cartridge in an elementary gun provided with a gas port and a piston. Immediately after the cartridge is fired, the bolt is rigidly locked to the barrel in order to support the base of the cartridge case against the thrust produced by the ignition of the propellant charge. This force acting on the base of the bullet drives it forward and produces an equal and opposite reaction which drives the entire gun backwards. As soon as the projectile has passed the gas port, the high-pressure gas behind the projectile starts to flow into the gas cylinder and to build up a pressure against the piston. For any given barrel and cartridge the rate at which this pressure builds up depends on a number of factors: these are complex and will not be discussed here, but it should be noted that the amount of gas which ordinarily flows into the cylinder is extremely small and has no significant effect on the bullet's muzzle velocity.

After the bullet has left the muzzle, the pressure in the barrel rapidly decreases and the pressure in the gas cylinder follows suit. All this is very quick, it happens within four or five thousandths of a second, so the piston is given a driving force for only a short time. The effect is to give the piston a sharp blow which accelerates it quickly, rather like a hammer hitting a nail. Owing to the short time in which the pressure acts and the necessity to have the breechblock locked while there is pressure in the bore, the force exerted on the piston cannot be used directly to drive the bolt back, but can only be employed to accelerate the piston mass; the kinetic energy so acquired is later used to carry out the automatic cycle. The amount of energy stored in the piston as the result of the applied impulse is determined by the mass of the piston: the lighter the piston, the greater becomes the energy produced by a given impulse. Thus the conditions of pressure, the location of the gas port, the size and shape of the orifice, the piston area and the piston mass all have an influence on the amount of energy derived from the action of the piston. By proper selection and control of these factors the piston energy can be regulated, so that low values or very high values of energy can be achieved at will. It is comparatively easy under practical conditions to achieve extremely high values of piston energy in gas-opened guns, but unless the gas operation is carefully controlled, the action of the piston may be so violent that it can literally smash the breech mechanism.

TYPES OF GAS OPERATION. Over the years, the design of gas-operated guns has crystallized into three distinct categories: long-stroke piston types, short-stroke piston types, and direct gas action types. Other systems, however, have been mooted in the past, some of which have seen experimental use.

Long-stroke piston. In this, the piston is attached directly to the breechblock and controls the block throughout the automatic cycle. The piston is of necessity massive and therefore comparatively slow-moving, moving the entire length of the bolt stroke. This means that the energy available, although adequate, is not excessive. Since the piston is either permanently fixed to the bolt—as in the FN-MAG—or holds the bolt as in the Bren, there are small impact shocks and energy losses when the piston is accelerated.

Short-stroke piston. In a short-stroke piston design, the piston itself generally has a short movement: possibly no more than 0.5-inch (12.7mm). The piston weighs less than 1oz (28.4gm) and so receives an impulsive blow which rapidly accelerates it. It is in contact with an actuating lever of light weight which is connected to the bolt, and the actuating lever absorbs the energy of the piston thereafter passing it to the bolt. This system is very suitable for rifles and is usually found in this application.

Direct gas action. In this method of operation, the gas tapped from the barrel is led back along a tube which enters an expansion chamber formed in the bolt carrier. The carrier is blown to the rear and unlocks the bolt from the barrel, or in some designs, from the body of the weapon, and carries it rearward. This system is used in the French Fusil MAS Mle 49 and also in the ArmaLite ARI5/MI6 series of rifles. The system usually leads to a light weapon, but there are greater chances of fouling than with other systems owing to the deposition of the products of combustion in the gas tube.

Despite the wide use of gas operation, there are drawbacks to it. These can be best summarized under three headings, fouling, fumes and barrel changing. Fouling occurs because the gas is led through ports to the cylinder, or to the bolt carrier. As the fouling builds up, the gas flow is restricted and the rate of fire slows down. This is usually overcome by arranging to have varying sizes of hole in the gas port, adjustable by the firer. Fumes occur because the cylinder vents to atmosphere, and in a vehicle this is hazardous if it happens inside the crew compartment. Barrel changing is more difficult with gas operation, though by no means impossible, since changing the barrel means making a break in the cylinder at some point.

RECOIL OPERATION

In the recoil system provision is made for locking the bolt to the barrel and these parts are mounted in the gun body so that they can slide to the rear. The gun is fired with the bolt locked to the barrel, and these parts remain locked together as they are thrust back by the pressure resulting from the explosion of the cartridge. In some guns the energy derived from this motion is used to perform the entire cycle of operations; in others, the energy derived from recoil may only perform certain functions in the cycle or may merely supplement the energy derived from another system of operation.

The distinguishing characteristic of the recoil system is that the energy used for operation is obtained from the recoil movement of the barrel and bolt while these parts are locked together. In a gun operated purely by recoil, the bolt remains locked to the barrel until the chamber pressure has become zero and therefore there are no problems (such as are encountered in blowback) resulting from movement of the cartridge case under pressure, and lubrication of the ammunition is unnecessary. The number of different machine-gun designs employing recoil operation is large and an examination of these will reveal an extreme diversity of mechanical detail and functional arrangements, but in spite of these only two recoil-operated weapons can be found in employment today—the various models derived from Browning's 1917 gun, and the Russian KPV—and the KPV could almost be called a delayed blowback. The other classic recoil-operated design was the Maxim and its derivations the Parabellum and the Vickers, but it is doubtful if any of this family are still in military service.

Nevertheless, every recoil-actuated design can be placed in one of two basic subclasses: long recoil or short recoil.

Long recoil operation.

Long recoil is a system of operation in which energy for operating the gun mechanism is obtained from a recoil movement which is greater than the overall length of the complete cartridge.

The cycle starts with a cartridge in the chamber and the bolt locked to the barrel. When the cartridge is fired, the barrel and bolt recoil together, and during this phase the retardation offered by the springs is relatively small: the only significant factor in limiting the recoil acceleration is the mass of the recoiling parts. The resistance of the springs gradually slows the recoiling mass until it stops at the extreme position and starts forward again. At this point the bolt is still locked to the barrel. The moment the barrel starts to move forward, it unlocks the bolt (which now stays at the fully recoiled position) and the barrel goes forward pulling itself off the case which stays held by the extractor against the face of the bolt until forced away by the ejector. When the barrel is almost at its fully run-out position, it operates a catch which releases the bolt. The bolt now moves forward faster than the barrel and catches it, at the same time feeding a fresh round into the breech. The breech locks at run-out and the bolt then trips the sear to release the striker and start the cycle afresh. The barrel gains a good deal of kinetic energy while 'running-out' (moving forward), and this is absorbed by large buffers at the forward end of the body. Some of the bolt energy is dissipated through these buffers also, but not necessarily all, since it is sometimes possible to arrange that the next round is fired before all the bolt energy is dissipated.

In general, the long recoil system is better suited to the larger calibers of cannon and certain types of shotgun, weapons which are not touched upon in this book. The greatest drawback to the system for the small arms designer is that the sequence of operations is wasteful of time. Throughout the recoil movement nothing happens beyond recoil, and this can be considered to be time essentially wasted. All the automatic actions have to happen on the forward stroke, and even then slowly, for the first part of the barrel movement is only used to extract the case. Ejection and feeding cannot begin until the barrel is well forward, and firing is delayed until the barrel is at rest after having run out. For these reasons the long recoil system only lends itself to low rates of fire. Where these are no handicap it does offer some advantages; the recoil energy is comparatively low, since most of it is employed in accelerating the mass of the barrel and bolt, and since this energy can be absorbed during the time of rearward movement of the mass, it can be kept within reasonable limits.

Short recoil operation. In a short recoil weapon, the bolt remains locked to the barrel for only a portion of the recoil stroke. After unlocking occurs, the barrel can move only a short distance with the bolt until it is stopped. The bolt continues to move to the rear, completing this movement by virtue of the momentum it possessed at the time of unlocking (although it may receive additional momentum through the action of a mechanical device, known as an accelerator, which transfers some of the energy of the barrel to the bolt). In either case the rearward motion of the bolt continues until the opening is sufficient for feeding and the bolt is then moved forward to close and lock the breech. In some guns the bolt pushes the barrel back to the firing position, in others the return motion of the barrel is accomplished independently before the bolt closes.

The outstanding feature of the short recoil system of operation is that, by proper design, high rates of fire can be attained. The bolt is unlocked without unnecessary delay as soon as the bullet has left the muzzle and then the bolt, which is already moving with considerable rearward velocity, is propelled to the rear at even greater velocity by the combined effects of the accelerator and residual breech pressure. With this, the recoil movement of the bolt, and its return to battery, are accomplished in a very short time.

The amount of energy available to operate a recoil system is relatively small, and guns using the short recoil principle are sometimes near to the limits of working when in mud or dust. One means of increasing the useful power is by means of muzzle boosters, or recoil intensifiers. These work by trapping some of the muzzle blast and using it to apply a heavy thrust to the front face of the barrel. This additional thrust causes the recoiling parts to have a higher velocity and hence a higher rate of fire. It alternatively overcomes the retarding effect of dust and dirt. It is important not to have too powerful a muzzle booster, since this can lead to violent recoil, and so to excessive pounding of the moving parts.

A further difficulty with the system is that it does not lend itself easily to adjustments for varying rates of fire, or for varying power in the ammunition. The Maxim series could be adjusted in their rates of fire by varying the tension in the return spring, but this is a relatively clumsy method, albeit a convenient one. In this respect of adjustment, the recoil system of operation is at a disadvantage when compared to the popular gas systems; the system does not entirely compensate for this drawback by its more compact dimensions and light working parts.

EXTERNALLY-POWERED SYSTEMS

The earliest mechanical machine guns were 'externally powered' by the gunner turning a crank; today the phrase means guns powered by an electric motor and thus weapons which form the armament of some vehicle such as an armored fighting vehicle or a helicopter which can supply the necessary power.

The return to mechanical guns began with the well-known electrification of the Gatling gun to produce the 20mm Vulcan cannon, and the principle was then extended to produce 7.62mm and 5.56mm versions. The attraction of these weapons was, of course, the high rate of fire, but there was another attraction too: the fact that a misfired cartridge would not stop the weapon. With a mechanical gun the misfired round is simply cycled through the system and ejected along with the empty cases. Admittedly, should the misfire turn out to be a slow hangfire, then the results can be embarrassing, but this is such a rare event that it can be discounted for all practical purposes.

Where the high rate of fire of the Gatling system is not required, the problem simply becomes one of moving a bolt backwards and forwards by mechanical means, and the first to be adopted was the Chain Gun. In this weapon a loop of endless chain lies in the bottom of the gun body, and a lug attached to one link of the chain drives the bolt. Thus, if we consider the gun body as a rectangle with a loop of chain running around its four sides; as the lug runs forward down one side, it drives the bolt forward to chamber the round. As the chain crosses the gun body behind the breech the breech is locked and the round fired. The lug now runs up the other side of the body, withdrawing the bolt, and then crosses the back of the body, holding the bolt to the rear for a brief pause and allowing air to pass through the barrel

The same effect can be achieved by putting a lug on the bolt and rotating a shaft with a spiral groove in it, engaging with the lug. When the shaft is revolved, so the bolt is driven backwards and forwards by the action of the spiral groove. This has been done on a number of French 20mm cannon.

One of the secondary, and perhaps questionable, advantages of these systems is that by simply regulating the voltage and therefore the speed of the drive motor, the rate of fire can be adjusted within quite wide limits. Whether this has any practical value is open to discussion.

BREECH LOCKING

Breech locking is the function of the mechanism which supports the cartridge case on firing. The object is to ensure that the cartridge case is positively supported by a locked mechanism until the gas pressure has fallen to a safe level (in automatic weapons) or until it is desired to remove the case in a manually-operated mechanism. There are too many different kinds of locking mechanism in use to be covered in a brief survey such as this, and so some of the most common types have been singled out for description. Almost all systems will be found to be closely related to one of the following:

1: rotating bolts.
2: tilting breech-blocks.
3: lug systems.
4: toggle systems.
5. non-ramming breech-blocks.
6: revolver systems.

The first four mechanisms employ breech-blocks which move along the prolonged axis of the barrel and are therefore able to ram the round and extract the case in addition to their more obvious functions, but by doing so they demand a certain length of space behind the breech in which to operate. The cramped confinement of a turret has led the designers of the 30mm Rarden cannon and the M73 machine-gun to revive a rare type of locking system, the non-ramming breechblock.

1: Rotating bolts. The bolt is pushed forward manually to ram the round and then the handle is turned into a recess in the receiver body to lock; lugs are generally added to the bolt for greater locking strength. No rearward travel is wasted in unlocking, because the bolt is turned and there is no significant axial movement. The same basic principle applies to automatic weapons; light machine-gun bolts are usually hollow with a cam-slot cut in them. The piston post engages in this and rotates the bolt by pressure on one face or the other; locking is achieved by lugs as on the bolt-action rifle.

The great majority of modern automatic rifles and light machine guns use the bolt-and-carrier system popularized by the Kalashnikov and ArmaLite designs. Here the weapon has a box-like bolt carrier riding on rods or surfaces in the receiver, and usually driven by a piston—though direct gas impingement is also common. Inside the carrier lies the bolt, with its separate firing pin. A lug in the carrier engages in a spiral slot in the bolt so that as the carrier is driven to the rear by gas action, so the lug rides in the spiral and rotates the bolt to unlock and then withdraws it to extract and eject the spent case. The rearward movement of the carrier loads a return spring and also cocks a hammer mechanism. On the forward stroke the bolt carries a fresh round into the chamber and then closes the breech; further forward movement of the carrier rotates the bolt to lock. In some designs the locking rotation of the bolt also aligns or otherwise frees the firing pin so that should there be a mechanical fault allowing it to be struck by the hammer before the bolt is locker, it cannot go forward to fire the round.

2: Tilting breech-blocks. The tilting-block system is strong and simple, and well suited to single-shot or automatic weapons. The best known and most common examples are found in Czech ZB series, the British Bren light machine-gun and the Browning Automatic Rifle. In these weapons the piston extension tends to raise the breechblock during forward travel, and when the block stops at the face of the breech, the ramp forces the locking shoulder into a recess in the body and locks the action. At the same time, the face of the breechblock is

'squared-up' to the breech. Unlocking is achieved by the piston withdrawing the locking shoulder and thus freeing the block so that the continued rearward movement of the piston can withdraw it, opening the breech and extracting the empty case. The direction in which the bolt tilts is immaterial—it can move vertically or horizontally according to the designer's whim—but it always pivots on its forward edges.

3: Lug systems. Lugs comprise the largest and most varied group; with these, the breechblock does not turn, but a lug or lugs move into and out of engagement with it. The block is usually roughly rectangular in shape and the lugs are hinged to it—generally at the forward end. The following descriptions will probably be sufficient to show the remarkable variety and ingenuity of designs in this group. It will be seen that, in general, the masses (and thus inertia) of the moving parts are low, so permitting high accelerations and high rates of fire.

German Kar 43. This is a gas-operated semiautomatic rifle introduced in 1943. The locking action is performed by the forward edges of the enlarged portion of the striker forcing the front end of the locking lugs outward into recesses in the receiver. Unlocking is done by the gas piston driving the striker to the rear, so that the rear edges of the enlarged portion strike the rear ends of the lugs and, by leverage, force the front ends out of engagement with the recesses and into a flush position in the bolt. There is no actual pivot, but the design allows the lugs to swing in their housings. It is a compact and efficient unit.

Russian Degtyarev system. This is another simple design, based on Friberg's design of c.1872, improved in 1907 by Kjellman. The two struts are hinged in recesses in the bolt at their forward end and are forced outwards by the striker to lock into the body. The struts are withdrawn by cams on the piston extension which act on studs machined on each strut. After withdrawing the lugs, the piston extension then carries the bolt to the rear.

4. Toggle systems. Toggle-locking systems are obsolete, and are no longer seen in military service. Toggle locks have only ever been used with recoil-operated weapons, but the action is rather slow and complicated; the principle is similar to a 'knee joint', which when bent is easily bent further, but when straight is rigid.

A source of weakness with toggle systems is the number of joints, all of which can wear, and the long stress path in the body. The system was utilized by the Parabellum pistol, the Maxim machine gun and the Vickers machine gun (both often gas-assisted), the Parabellum light machine gun and the Fürrer (Swiss) designs.

It is worth noting that a toggle can also be used as the delaying element in a delayed blowback system, arranged so that it unfolds at a mechanical disadvantage. Examples of this include the Pedersen rifle and the Schwarzlose machine gun. Perhaps the prime drawback of toggle systems is that they are generally highly sensitive to their ammunition; they are designed around a specific cartridge, and any changes in the properties of the cartridge will affect the operation of the weapon. Parabellum (Luger) pistols perform flawlessly with pre-1945 German service specification ammunition, but tend to be erratic in their operation when fed with modern submachine gun rounds.

5. Non-ramming breech-blocks. These are rare and have usually been forced upon the designer by some powerful influence. In the case of the most famous system, that of the Madsen machine gun, it was probably adopted as a means of evading patents. In its few modern applications it has usually been adopted as a method of reducing the inboard length of an automatic weapon intended to be mounted in an armored vehicle, an example being the US M73 tank machine gun. The non-ramming block can be extremely compact, but it requires an external mechanism to feed the rounds and sometimes to eject them. This system theoretically allows a higher rate of fire because the moving parts are light and the movement small.

Martini hinged block. This is the simplest method of all for breech closure, but it becomes hopelessly complicated when it is required to load successive rounds. It is, in fact, purely a single-shot system to which a number of parts have to be added, at a considerable cost in complexity, to produce an automatic weapon. The Madsen machine gun was the only successful application.

M73 sliding block. This was no more than a miniature version of an artillery-type sliding breechblock, opened and closed by a system of cams and studs actuated by the recoil of the barrel. The M73 was of 7.62mm caliber and so the masses of the working parts were comparatively low. The breechblock moved horizontally in the barrel extension. The ramming mechanism was quite complicated and ingenious.

The system adopted by Steyr for their Advanced Combat Rifle in the late 1980s might also be considered as a non-ramming block system, although it is a world apart from the Madsen and the M73. In the Steyr system the chamber is a separate item which commences its operating cycle lying beneath the axis of the barrel. A cartridge is rammed into this chamber which then rises to align with the barrel and a standing breech. The round is fired, the chamber drops out of alignment, and the next round is rammed in, driving the empty cartridge case out of the front of the chamber. It relies on an entirely unconventional round of ammunition, plastic-cased and side-primed; it would not be possible with a conventional round.

6: Revolver systems. This is a somewhat ambiguous term since the revolving principle can be applied to firearms in distinctly different ways. The most common application is that used in the revolver pistol, where a revolving cylinder containing a number of chambers is positioned behind a fixed barrel. A chamber is aligned with the barrel and locked in place, and the round is fired. The cylinder is then unlocked and rotated to bring the next loaded chamber into alignment, locked, and fired. Once all the chambers have been fired they must be emptied of the spent cases and reloaded. But in fact this typical revolver system was developed from an earlier system, the 'pepperbox' pistol in which a cluster of barrels, pre-loaded with powder and ball, were revolved and fired in turn. Having rendered that system obsolete by the adoption of the separate chamber it was then revived by the famous Dr. Gatling for his revolving machine gun in the 1860s. Again it fell into disuse, to be revived again in the 1940s when the power-driven Gatling principle was applied to the 20mm Vulcan cannon and then to a number of weapons of smaller caliber, some of which will be found in the machine gun section of this book.

In the multi-barreled weapons such as the Vulcan and Mini-Guns, the system differs in that an entire cluster of barrels revolves around a central axis. The chambers are contained within a cylindrical housing which has cam tracks cut on the inner surface, in which lugs on the bolts in each breech are engaged. As the barrels revolve, the cam tracks cause the bolts to open and close, and the design is such that as a barrel reaches the uppermost position its bolt is open and a cartridge is fed into the feedway. As the barrel continues moving round the circle the bolt is closed during the downward arc, the striker is released at the bottom-most point, and the bolt is opened and the case extracted and ejected during the upward arc so that it reaches the top once more with the breech open.

The advantage of this type of weapon is that the cyclic rate of fire can be great—up to 6000 rounds per minute or more—but in a six-barrel weapon each barrel spends five-sixths of the time cooling down and each barrel fires at only 1000 rounds per minute. A drawback is that when the trigger is released the cluster of barrels continues to revolve due to its momentum, and complex arrangements to stop the ammunition supply very promptly have to be made.

A different application of the revolving principle can be seen in the 'revolver cannon' or 'revolver gun' used for some designs of aircraft cannon and machine gun which use a form of revolving cylinder to strip the cartridge from its belt and present it to the chamber in a series of stages rather than in one complex and violent action. The Russian designer Shpitalny was particularly fond of this system, and examples can be seen on the DShK 38, ShKAS and ShVAK machine guns.

CASELESS CARTRIDGE WEAPONS

Weapons designed to use caseless cartridges—cartridges which consist simply of a block of propellant with a bullet embedded in one end and a combustible cap in the other—adhere to the general rules laid out above insofar as their operation is concerned, but produce two problems of their own. The first is the need to seal the breech, in the absence of a cartridge case, and the second is the problem of overheating the chamber due, again, to the absence of a cartridge case and its heat-absorbing property. The latter problem lies in the realm of the ammunition designer, and has been overcome by taking a fresh look at the composition of the propellant and moving away from the conventional nitro-cellulose compounds to a formula based on a denatured high explosive of the Hexogen family. The danger from an overheated chamber is that loading a naked propellant charge into it could (and did) cause premature ignition—or cook-off. The new type of propellant, devised by Dynamit Nobel for the Heckler & Koch G11 rifle, raises the ignition temperature by some 100 C and thus the round is not in the chamber long enough to reach ignition temperature before the breech is closed and the round is fired.

Sealing the breech, though, is the province of the gun designer, and in the G11 (which is, to date, the only proven successful caseless design) it was done by making the chamber in a circular block rotating in a circular housing and providing the block with flap-type seals which 'wipe' around the inside of the housing. (Heckler & Koch engineers will doubtless say that this is a gross simplification, and so it is, but the principle is there. It is not so grossly simplified as the explanation offered me by a German senior officer who observed that "It is just like the Wankel engine on my old Audi.")

A deviant form of caseless cartridge is the liquid propellant gun, in which the bullet is loaded and rammed into the rifling, after which a combustible liquid is injected into the chamber and ignited. The subsequent explosion drives the bullet from the gun. The propellant may be of various types—plain combustibles ignited by a spark, hypergolic substances which spontaneously ignite when they are simultaneously injected into the gun chamber, mystic liquids which explode when stimulated by an electrical field—the possibilities are endless. But they all involve carrying a supply of some highly nervous chemicals and supplying them to the weapon; such a procedure might be feasible in a self-propelled artillery piece, but it seems highly improbable in a shoulder arm.

MILITARY PISTOLS

IN 1900 THE standard military sidearm was the revolver, usually of a large caliber in the region of 11.5mm/45-caliber, and provided with a large lead bullet which would more or less guarantee stopping an adversary no matter where it struck. Exceptions to this were those armies where the revolver was more of a status symbol than a serious fighting weapon, in which case the weapon had to be lighter and less cumbersome lest it pull the uniform or equipment out of shape, and the preferred solution was to use the same caliber as the service rifle so as to economize on barrel manufacture. The ballisticians were, as ever, ready to prove that a light bullet moving quickly could deliver the same blow as a heavy bullet moving slowly. The British and Americans and others who had been involved in fighting unsophisticated but determined enemies who had not read the ballistic bulletins begged to differ.

The revolver, in 1900, was more or less at the zenith of its development. The products of Colt, Smith & Wesson, Webley and Nagant of that period have never been surpassed in either excellence of finish or precision of manufacture, except in some rare cases of hand-made luxury weapons. What advances there have been in revolver manufacture have been directed towards producing them more cheaply in order to keep their price competitive; there have been one or two attempts to devise a new revolver—the Mateba or the Dardick spring to mind—but these found little favor in the commercial market and no favor at all in the military one. One is irresistibly reminded of the well-known maxim 'If it ain't broke, don't fix it.' The revolver ain't broke and it don't need fixin.

The automatic pistol, in 1900, was fighting to gain acceptance. The only examples then available were the Borchardt, the Mauser c/96, and a handful of blowback designs from Schmeisser via Th. Bergmann. The blowbacks, in 6.5mm and similar low-powered calibers, were never going to interest the military or supplant heavy revolvers. The Borchardt was too cumbersome and temperamental, and the Mausers appeared to be effective but, well, let's wait and see, you never know with these new-fangled inventions, time will tell...and similar well-known phrases. The Swiss, however, were prepared to gamble, if the pistol designers paid attention to what they wanted; in response to that, Luger took the Borchardt design and transformed it from a

toolroom prodigy into a practical combat pistol. Not, it is true, of the caliber which three-quarters of the world's armies wanted, but that could come later; at least the automatic pistol had gotten a foot into the military door. Not a very substantial foot, and not a door of primary importance, but it was a start.

The acceptance by the Swiss led other armies to revise their opinions; the Swiss may not have been the most warlike of nations, but they were respected for their technical ability, and if they were prepared to gamble on the automatic principle, then the thing must be worth a second look. Provided that the caliber was not less than 11mm/45-caliber, of course. Few tried and fewer succeeded, the most famous of whom was John Browning and his Colt M1911 45-caliber pistol adopted by the US forces (and later by the Norwegians). Browning, as usual, got it exactly right; a simple and robust design, accurate and reliable, and of a caliber which satisfied the most reactionary of the military. Britain was similarly successful with the Webley & Scott, but this was less widely adopted, and considerably less aesthetic in its appearance.

World War I brought few conclusions; the revolver supporters were strengthened in their conviction that only a simple machine like a revolver could withstand the rigors of active service, and the automatic pistol group were quick to point out that most of the automatic pistol designs were equally successful; the ones which failed were generally wartime expedients and not pistols which had been slowly and certainly developed in peacetime for specific military use.

The immediate post-war period saw very little attention paid to pistols; the BSA company in Britain attempted to produce a 40-caliber weapon firing a powerful belted cartridge, but trying to promote such a weapon in 1920 was a bad psychological move—everybody had had enough of war and weapons.

Not until the 1930s did any major power make a move, and then the Soviet Army adopted the Tokarev pistol; which, for all that Tokarev may have been awarded this medal or that order, remained a Colt M1911 with a distinct Russian accent. The only innovative item was the placing of the mainspring and hammer mechanism in a separate removable module, simplifying assembly and maintenance. But John Browning was

still ahead; as far back as 1918 he had started on an improved design of pistol, which he offered to Fabrique Nationale of Belgium, and after his death in 1926 FN continued to develop his idea. They delayed marketing it until the worst effects of the 1929 Wall Street Crash were over and produced their new 'Browning High Power' in 1935. The same year saw designs from Finland, France and Poland. After a break, 1938 saw two new pistols which might well be said to represent the best and the worst of contemporary design—the Walther P-38, which is still being manufactured 60 years later, and the Czech vz/38 which barely survived the war before being discarded.

Once again, war had little effect on pistol design in the 1939-45 period; the combatants had more pressing things on their minds than pistols. But it did nudge the British Army into looking again at the automatic pistol, when, under British auspices, the Browning High-Power was put into production in Canada. This, in the first instance, was to provide pistols for China, who had adopted the design in 1936 and wanted more of them, but once their demands were satisfied, production was diverted to the British and Canadian armies, and the Browning gained a foothold. The Luger-Parabellum finally ended its long run, eclipsed by the Walther P-38, and this, in the long term, meant that a number of armies which had hitherto used the Luger were going to be looking for a replacement. Among them were the Swiss; even though they had their own production line for the Luger, they could see the writing on the wall, and during the war years there was some very serious research on pistol design carried out in Switzerland, culminating in the SIG design of 1948, a design which is still, fifty years later, probably the finest automatic pistol currently on the market.

After 1945 there was not the mad rush to disarmament and pacifism that had been seen in the post-WWI period, but, even so, there was little happening on the pistol front; again, the protagonists had bigger things on their minds and drawing boards. But in the 1960s, when prosperity began to spread and idle hands looked for mischief, the terrorist—under various names—began to make his (or her) mark. Police forces which had hitherto carried a 32-caliber or 7.65mm pistol with the same cartridge in the chamber from one year's end to another suddenly found themselves confronted with criminals wielding assault rifles and submachine guns. Heavier pistols were adopted, training was revamped, and the police decided that automatic pistols needed redesigning. They were not prepared to accept the military standard practice of carrying a loaded and cocked pistol at all times, and this was quite understandable. But they demanded a pistol which could be brought into action without delays and without fumbling around with safety catches or cocking levers or pulling back slides or, indeed, anything more than the simple act of draw and pull the trigger, as had been the practice with revolvers.

The result of this demand was an upheaval in pistol design which occupied most of the 1980s and has still not completely died down. The challenge was to produce a design which was instantly ready to fire when required to do so, but completely incapable of firing if dropped or mishandled. The solution lay in such things as automatic firing pin safety systems, in which the firing pin is not aligned with the hammer until the last few degrees of trigger movement; de-cocking levers which permit lowering the hammer safety onto a loaded chamber (protected by the aforesaid automatic firing pin safety) and allying this with a double action trigger so that a simple pull would cock the hammer, align the firing pin and then release the hammer to fire.

Different designers had different ways of doing these things, but by the 1990s these were universal features of virtually every modern pistol. The other significant design feature was the increasing use of synthetic materials—plastic, carbon fiber and so forth—in the construction of the frame and/or slide. In the early days this was not always a success, but as the designers and makers gained experience in the new materials, so the manufacture improved and today such materials are an accepted fact. In the early days, too, there was a good deal of to-do by the press over the prospect of a 'plastic pistol' which would be completely invisible to the X-ray eye of the airport baggage checker. Once the design wizards have solved the problem of making a plastic barrel, firing plastic cartridges and bullets and using plastic return springs, we may have a problem; but not yet, Oh Lord, not yet.

ARGENTINA

• Ballester Molina
Hispano Argentine Fabrica de Automoviles SA, Buenos Aires
45 ACP

The Argentine Government, after having used the Mannlicher M1905 pistol for some years, adopted the Colt M1911 pistol under the title 'Pistola Automatica Modelo 1916'. This was later augmented by supplies of the M1911A1 under the title 'Modelo 1927'. Production of the M1927, with technical assistance from the Colt factory, was eventually begun in Argentina, and continued there for many years.

It was ultimately decided to develop a local variation of the Colt pattern and this subsequently appeared as the Ballester Molina (known also as the 'Hafdasa' from the contraction of the maker's name—both titles appeared on the slide). It is a virtual copy of the Colt M1911 and seen from a distance, the two are practically indistinguishable. The Ballester Molina differs in the form of the hammer and in the absence of a grip safety; the trigger is pivoted at the top rather than sliding, and there is a different notching of the slide's finger grips. The construction is that of the Colt, utilizing the Browning locked-breech system in which ribs on the barrel top surface engage with slots formed in the slide, together with a swinging link mounted beneath the breech and tied to the frame. There are subtle variations in the formation of butt and grips, and the pistol seems to suit a small hand better than the Colt; it is of inferior finish compared to the Colt, although apparently similarly reliable. A

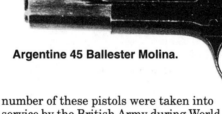

Argentine 45 Ballester Molina.

number of these pistols were taken into service by the British Army during World War II, notably for issue to clandestine units.

Length: 9.00in (228mm). **Weight unloaded:** 2lb 8oz (1130g). **Barrel:** 5.00in (127mm), 6 grooves, right-hand twist. **Magazine:** 7-round detachable box. **Muzzle velocity:** c.860 ft/sec (262 m/sec).

AUSTRIA-HUNGARY/ AUSTRIA

• Mannlicher Model 1901 and Model 1905
Osterreichische Waffenfabrik-Gesellschaft, Steyr
7.63mm Mannlicher

Like all the Mannlicher designs made by Steyr, the Model 1900 is a weapon of excellent workmanship, balance and finish which deserved a better success than it attained.

The operation is unique; it is a delayed blowback pistol in which the delay is imposed by a heavy spring and cam bearing against the recoiling slide, so that the initial movement of the slide has to overcome the spring's resistance, so producing sufficient delay for the bullet to leave the muzzle. The magazine, like several other Steyr designs of the time, was a fixed unit inside the pistol grip and was loaded by pulling back the slide and inserting a charger of cartridges, then pressing them down into the magazine. A release catch on the side of the frame allowed the magazine to be emptied without having to operate the slide more than once.

These pistols exhibit minor differences due to small modifications and improvements being added from time to time. Early models were made by Von Dreyse at Sommerda and carry the Von Dreyse marks but manufacture at Steyr began in 1901 and the pistols are so marked. Early models have the rear sight on the barrel above the chamber, while later models mounted it on the rear of the slide so as to give a longer sight radius. Final production took place in 1905 and large numbers of this model were adopted by the Argentine Army, marked with the Argentine crest and 'Md 1905'. It is believed that just over 10,000 of the 1901 model, in its various forms, were made.

Austrian 7.63mm Mannlicher Model 1905.

Length: 9.68in (246mm). **Weight unloaded:** 2lb 0oz (910g). **Barrel:** 6.18in (155mm), 4 grooves, right-hand twist. **Magazine:** 8-round integral box. **Muzzle velocity:** c.1025 ft/sec (313 m/sec).

• Mannlicher Selbstladepistole Model 1903
Osterreichische Waffenfabrik-Gesellschaft Steyr
7.65mm Mannlicher

Originally designed in 1896, this weapon, in common with the earlier Mannlicher pistols, is a delight to the eye and perfectly finished of the finest materials, although it is a good deal more scarce than the earlier guns. Like the 1901 design it was in competition with the Mauser for military acceptance, but although it was tried by several armies none ever adopted it as an official service weapon. The design uses a locked breech of the prop-up type, with a concealed internal hammer, and the cartridge was almost identical to the more common and more powerful 7.63mm Mauser round. The pistol was generally turned down on grounds of its unreliability, which was due to insufficiently strong manufacture for such a powerful cartridge; the lock and firing mechanism, in particular, were too highly stressed. It was also unusual in having a double-pressure trigger, rather like a military rifle, and this, with the stock attachment found on some examples, made the M1903 an above-average stock-fitted pistol for long range shooting. A few were made with extra-long barrels and long-range tan-gent sights, and some were permanently fitted with shoulder-stocks, possibly for evaluation as cavalry carbines, but the few which were made appear to have survived solely as hunting weapons.

Length: 11.00in (279mm). **Weight unloaded:** 2lb 4oz (1020g). **Barrel:** 4.50in (114mm), 6 grooves, right-hand twist. **Magazine:** 6-round integral box. **Muzzle velocity:** c.1180 ft/sec (360 m/sec).

• Roth-Steyr M07
Osterreichische Waffenfabrik-Gesellschaft, Steyr
8x18.5mm Roth M7

The Roth-Steyr holds the distinction of being the first self-loading pistol ever to be adopted by a major army, having been taken into service by the Austro-Hungarian cavalry in 1908. It was later used to some extent by early Austro-Hungarian aviators, from which it became known unofficially as the 'Flieger-Pistole'. Although long obsolete it continued to be used by elements of the Italian Army until the early 1940s and some are still in use in obscure corners of the Balkans to this day and ammunition is still manufactured from time to time. The cartridge is unique to this pistol and was never used in any other weapon.

The Model '07 uses a most involved system of locking based upon a rotating barrel. The bolt undoubtedly qualifies as the original 'telescoped bolt' since the front portion is hollow and surrounds the entire length of the barrel inside the tubular frame. On firing, bolt and barrel move back together for about 12mm, during which time cam grooves on the bolt rotate the barrel through 90 degrees. The barrel is then halted and the bolt is free to recoil, ejecting the spent case and reloading on its return stroke. As the bolt closes up so it revolves the barrel to lock the breech and then barrel and bolt run forward into the firing position. The second unusual thing is the firing system. The operation of the bolt, either by hand or by firing, part-cocks the striker, and the cocking movement is completed by pulling the trigger, which first draws back the firing pin to full-cock and then releases it. This system is said to have been demanded by the cavalry so that there was less likelihood of an inadvertent discharge of a fully-cocked pistol by a trooper on a skittish horse. Add to this a fixed integral box magazine which has to be loaded through the open action by means of a 10-round charger, and you have a somewhat idiosyncratic pistol. Nevertheless, some 90,000 were made before production stopped in the middle 1920s, and although odd in appearance they were well-made and reliable weapons.

Length: 9.18in (233mm). **Weight unloaded:** 2lb 4oz (1020g). **Barrel:** 5.18in (131mm), 4 grooves, right-hand twist. **Magazine:** 10-round integral box. **Muzzle velocity:** c.1050 ft/sec (320 m/sec).

Austrian 8mm Roth-Steyr Model 1907.

Austrian 7.65mm Mannlicher Model 1903.

Steyr 7.65mm M1909, based on Pieper's patents.

• Steyr Model 1908
Osterreichische Waffenfabrik-Gesell-schaft, Steyr
7.65mm automatic pistol (32 ACP)

This peculiar weapon was designed by the Pieper company of Liege, who also manufactured a small number under their own name, but the principal manufacture was done at Steyr and the gun was issued in some numbers to the Austrian police. Some later saw emergency service in World War I.

It appears to be a highly ingenious design until careful thought robs the unusual features of some of their attraction. In the first place, the gun has a thumb-catch on the left side which, when pressed, allows the barrel to hinge forward so that a cartridge can be loaded directly into the chamber. This movement also disconnects the above-barrel recoil spring from the breechblock so that the block can be drawn back and pushed forward to cock the internal hammer—but this should only be done when the magazine is either empty or withdrawn, otherwise the action feeds the top round out of the magazine and on to the ground. There is no extractor fitted as the design relies on residual gas pressure to blow out the spent case as it drives the breechblock back, until the ejector deflects the case through the side port. This means that ammunition malfunctions—especially misfires or stuck cases—cannot be cleared by operating the slide since this will only try to load a fresh round and compound the mischief. Pieper had a habit of coming up with odd designs, but it is a little surprising to find that Steyr should bother producing one of them.

Length: 6.38in (162mm). **Weight unloaded:** 1lb 6oz (620g). **Barrel:** 3.63in (92mm), 6 grooves, right-hand twist. **Magazine:** 7-round detachable box. **Muzzle velocity:** c.900 ft/sec (274 m/sec).

• Steyr M12 ('Steyr-Hahn,)
Osterreichische Waffenfabrik-Gesell-schaft, Steyr
9x23mm Steyr M12; 9mm Parabellum

This became the Austro-Hungarian side-arm for elements other than cavalry in 1912. Like the Roth-Steyr, it used a rotating barrel to lock the breech, but the system was much simpler, using a conventional type of slide. Barrel and slide recoiled together for a short distance, during which lugs on the barrel engaged in cam grooves on the frame to turn the barrel through 20 degrees. This disengaged an upper lug from a groove in the slide, so that the barrel halted and the slide was free to recoil. The motion was reversed on the return of the slide. As with other Steyr designs the magazine is an integral box, loaded by means of a charger, and the cartridge is a unique and powerful 9mm cartridge. The 'Steyr-Hahn' (Steyr with hammer—since it used an external hammer instead of the striker of the earlier design) was made in considerable numbers between 1911 and 1918, and was adopted in Romania and Chile as well as being sold commercially. It remained the standard Austrian pistol after 1918, and when the Austrian Army was absorbed into the Wehrmacht in 1938 some 200,000 or so were re-barreled to 9mm Parabellum so as to standardize with the German Army ammunition system. These are marked 'P-08' on the left side of the slide. Although the grip is somewhat square to the frame, the Model 1912 is an excellent pistol, strong and reliable, and it is possible that had it been made originally in a more common caliber it would have achieved greater success.

Length: 8.50in (216mm). **Weight unloaded:** 2lb 3oz (990g). **Barrel:** 5.10in (128mm), 4 grooves, right-hand twist. **Magazine:** 8-round fixed. **Muzzle velocity:** c.1100 ft/sec (335 m/sec).

• Steyr GB
Steyr-Daimler-Puch AG, Steyr Austria
9mm Parabellum

The Steyr GB was a delayed blowback pistol, the delay being obtained by tapping a small amount of gas from the chamber and leading it to the interior of the slide, where it entered an annular expansion chamber formed by the slide surrounding the barrel. Here the pressure built up resisted the opening action of the slide for a long enough period to allow the bullet to clear the barrel and the breech pressure to drop to a safe level. The system is akin to that pioneered by Barnitske of Gustloff-werke in the VG1-5 Volkssturmgewehr and in the Volkspistole. The trigger mechanism was double action, using an external hammer, and the barrel was rifled in the polygonal form, which is also that used by Heckler & Koch in their P9 pistol.

Developed in the mid-1970s and originally known as the Pi 18, this pistol was first developed with the option of automatic fire; used with a stock and a 36-round extended magazine it could function as a form of submachine-gun. This option, however, was soon dropped. It was then made under license in the USA by Rogac Inc., and sold as the LES P-18. Unfortunately the quality control was poor, the pistol acquired a reputation for malfunction, and the license was rescinded. Steyr then made some modifi-

9mm Steyr-Hahn M1912 with its 9x23mm cartridge.

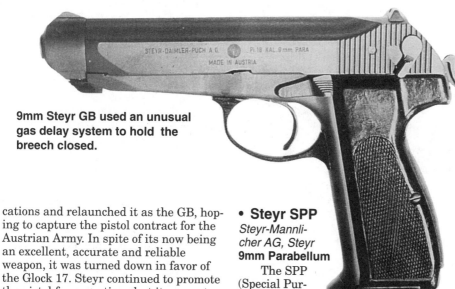

9mm Steyr GB used an unusual gas delay system to hold the breech closed.

cations and relaunched it as the GB, hoping to capture the pistol contract for the Austrian Army. In spite of its now being an excellent, accurate and reliable weapon, it was turned down in favor of the Glock 17. Steyr continued to promote the pistol for some time, but it was not adopted in any numbers by any military force and production ended in 1989.

Length: 8.5in (216mm). **Weight unloaded:** 1lb 14oz (840g). **Barrel.** 5.35in (136mm), 4 grooves, right-hand twist, polygonal. **Magazine:** 18-round detachable box. **Muzzle velocity:** c.1275 ft/sec (388 m/sec).

• Steyr SPP
Steyr-Mannlicher AG, Steyr
9mm Parabellum

The SPP (Special Purpose Pistol) is a semi-automatic version of the TMP (Tactical Machine Pistol) submachine gun. It uses the same synthetic frame and receiver and operates in the same delayed blowback mode by means of a rotating barrel. The principal difference is that the pistol has no forward handgrip and a slightly

greater length of exposed barrel and jacket in front of the receiver.

Length: 12.68in (322mm). **Weight unloaded:** 2lb 14oz (1300g). **Barrel:** 5.12in (130mm); 6 grooves, right-hand twist. **Magazine:** 15- or 30-round detachable box. **Muzzle velocity:** c.1246 ft/sec (380 m/sec).

• Glock Model 17 Pistol
Glock GmbH, Deutsch Wagram,
9mm Parabellum

This pistol was adopted by the Austrian Army in 1983, 25,000 being ordered. It is a recoil-operated semi-automatic, using a cam-controlled dropping barrel to lock slide and barrel together. Firing is by means of a striker controlled by the trigger; the first 5mm of trigger travel cocks the striker and releases the firing pin lock, and the next 2.5mm of travel releases the striker. The pressure required to actuate the trigger can be adjusted. There is no manual safety catch since the integral firing pin lock will prevent the pistol firing unless the trigger is properly operated. The Glock 17 is of simple design, there being only 32 components including the magazine.

The **Model 17L** is similar to the basic Model 17 but has a longer barrel, for target shooting. The **Model 17C** is also similar to the Model 17 but has an integrated muzzle compensator which is claimed to reduce muzzle climb by up to 30 percent.

Length: 7.40in (188mm). **Weight unloaded:** 1lb 7oz (625g). **Barrel:** 4.49in (114mm); 6 grooves, polygonal, right-hand twist. **Magazine:** 17-round detachable box. **Muzzle velocity:** c.1263 ft/sec (385 m/sec).

• Glock 18 and 18C
Glock GmbH, Deutsche Wagram
9mm Parabellum

The Glock Model 18 was basically the same as the Model 17 but with a selective fire capability, allowing automatic fire or single shots, and an enlarged magazine. For obvious reasons the principal mechanical components of the Models 17 and 18 are not interchangeable, and its sale is restricted to official bodies.

The Model 18 was replaced in production by the Model 18C; this is exactly the same but for the provision of a muzzle compensator. Four slots in the muzzle and a slot in the slide allow an upward escape of gas and thus helps to keep the weapon stable, particularly when firing in the automatic mode.

Length: 7.32in (186mm). **Weight unloaded:** 1lb 5oz (586g). **Barrel:** 4.49in (114mm); 6 grooves, polygonal, right-hand twist. **Magazine:** 17- or 19-round detachable box. **Muzzle velocity:** c.1115 ft/sec (340 m/sec).

The Steyr Special Purpose Pistol.

The Glock Model 17L, showing the safety spur on the trigger.

The Glock 18 is a full-automatic pistol and demands a large magazine.

The Glock 45 Model 21.

• Glock 19, 19C
Glock GmbH, Deutsche Wagram
9mm Parabellum

These are simple compact versions of the Model 17 and 17C; except for the dimensions they are to the same design and many of the component parts are interchangeable.

Length: 6.85in (174mm). **Weight unloaded:** 1lb 5oz (595g). **Barrel:** 4.49in (102mm); 6 grooves, polygonal, right-hand twist. **Magazine:** 17-round detachable box. **Muzzle velocity:** c.1148 ft/sec (350 m/sec).

• Other Glock models

Glock offers a selection of pistol models which are essentially the same as the Models 17 and 19 but in different chambering. Based on the Model 17 are the Models 20 (10mm Auto), 21 (45 ACP), and 22 (40 S&W). The Model 23 (40 S&W) is based on the compact Model 19.

In 1995 a number of 'sub-compact' models were introduced. These are still to the same mechanical design as the Model 17 but are smaller than the Model 19. They comprise the Model 26 (9mm Parabellum), Model 27 (40 S&W), Model 28 (380 ACP/9mm Short), Model 19 (10mm Auto) and Model 30 (45 ACP).

(Model 26)
Length: 6.30in (160mm).
Weight unloaded: 1lb 7oz (650g). **Barrel:** 3.46in (88mm); 6 grooves, polygonal, right-hand twist. **Magazine:** 10-round detachable box. **Muzzle velocity:** c.1115 ft/sec (340 m/sec).

BELGIUM

• Browning Model 1900
Fabrique Nationale d'Armes de Guerre, Herstal -lez-Liege
7.65x17SR Browning (32 ACP)

The Model 1900 was the first Browning design to be manufactured by Fabrique Nationale of Herstal, the result of experimental models of 1898 and 1899 and the beginning of a long association between the inventor and the company.

The mechanism is unusual in having the recoil spring in a tube above the barrel, connected to the reciprocating breechblock by a lever in such a fashion as to double as the firing spring and the recoil spring; an elegant engineering solution and also keeping the parts to a minimum. The barrel is fixed to the frame; the slide and

John Browning's first successful pistol, the 1900 'Old Model'.

The workings of the Browning 1900, showing how the return spring doubles as the striker spring.

breechblock are driven back on firing, pulling on the recoil spring. As the slide returns, the striker is held cocked by the sear, placing the recoil spring under additional compression to give the necessary motive power to the striker.

Although produced in vast numbers, the 1900 type was little used as a military weapon, as most armies of the time were a little suspicious of the self-loading pistol and more than a little contemptuous of such a small caliber as a combat loading. Some guns are, however, known to have been used by the armies of Tsarist Russia, Belgium and—possibly—Holland. If for nothing else, it earns its place in the annals of the century for being the weapon used by Gavrilo Princip to assassinate the Archduke Ferdinand in Sarajevo, thus precipitating World War I.

Length: 6.75in (170mm). **Weight unloaded:** 1lb 6oz (620g). **Barrel:** 4.00in (101mm), 6 grooves, right-hand twist. **Magazine:** 7-round detachable box. **Muzzle velocity:** c.950 ft/sec (290 m/sec).

• Browning Model 1903
Fabrique Nationale d'Armes de Guerre, Herstal-lez-Liege
9x20SR Browning Long

This is the Belgian-made version of the John Browning design which was also produced in the USA as the Colt 32 ACP and 380 ACP pistols. Blowback operation is used, which sounds dangerous in this caliber, but the weapon is chambered for the 'long Browning' cartridge which although slightly longer than the 9mm Parabellum is actually somewhat weaker. A robust and accurate pistol, the Mle 03 was widely adopted in Europe as a military and police weapon and large numbers are still in use. It is the weapon responsible for the fact that the word 'Browning' is, in French common parlance, synonymous with the words 'automatic pistol'. The armies of Sweden, Serbia and Turkey were among those to whom the Mle 1903

The Browning 1910 streamlined the shape by putting the return spring around the barrel.

was issued; some of the Swedish weapons (known as the Pistol m/1907) were manufactured by Husqvarna Vapenfabrik under a license granted by Fabrique Nationale, and numbers of these are still in use.

Due to the peculiar Spanish patent laws of the time, the Model 1903 was pirated there in vast quantities from 1905 to 1936, since it was a simple design which lent itself to manufacture by small companies. Fully 75 percent of automatic pistols made in Spain prior to 1936 were copies of either the M1903 or M1906 Browning pistols.

Length: 8.00in (203mm). **Weight unloaded:** 2lb 1oz (910g). **Barrel:** 5.00in (127mm), 6 grooves, right-hand twist. **Magazine:** 7-round detachable box. **Muzzle velocity:** c.1050 ft/sec (320 m/sec).

• Browning Model 1910
Fabrique Nationale d'Armes de Guerre, Herstal-lez-Liege
7.65mm Browning (32 ACP)
9x17mm Browning Short (380 ACP)

This model is variously referred to as the 1910 or the 1912, having been designed in 1910 and first marketed in 1912; it was a considerable improvement on the 1900 model and served as a pattern for several imitations and copies.

The most important feature lies in the mounting of the recoil spring around the barrel, giving the weapon a light and handy appearance. A grip safety is fitted, acting on the sear since the pistol is striker-fired.

The Browning 1910 was extensively sold commercially and widely adopted in Europe as a police pistol. It was also frequently purchased by military officers as a personal weapon and was used in small numbers by many armies, as a second-line weapon to augment their normal issues. Manufacture continued, in reduced numbers, until the 1960s.

Length: 6.00in (152mm). **Weight unloaded:** 1lb 5oz (600g). **Barrel:** 3.50in (89mm), 6 grooves, right-hand twist. **Magazine:** 7-round detachable box. **Muzzle velocity:** c.925 ft/sec (282 m/sec).

• Browning Model 1922 (or 10/22)
Fabrique Nationale d'Armes de Guerre, Herstal-lez-Liege
9x17mm Browning Short (380 ACP), 7.65x17SR Browning (32 ACP)

This pistol owes its existence to a 1923 request by the Yugoslavian government for a pistol with a 114mm barrel and an 8-round magazine capacity. The quickest solution was simply to take the 1910 pattern and extend the barrel by one inch (25mm) to improve the accuracy and extend the frame to increase the magazine's cartridge capacity. The existing design of slide was modified to accept an extension nosepiece attached by a bayonet joint in a praiseworthy attempt to utilize existing machine tools and components, a technique pioneered by Walther some years earlier in a similar conversion.

This weapon, in 9mm Short or 7.65mm chambering, was widely adopted

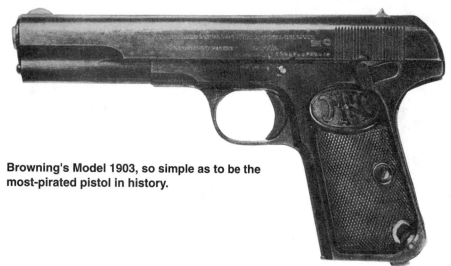

Browning's Model 1903, so simple as to be the most-pirated pistol in history.

The Browning 1922 was simply a stretched 1910.

for use by military and police forces all over Europe and was also adopted in 1940 as a substitute standard weapon issued to the German Luftwaffe as the Pistole 626(b). The weapon is striker-fired and a grip safety is fitted. The armies of Holland, Yugoslavia, France, Greece and Turkey numbered among those equipped with the Mle 22 pistols.

Length: 7.00in (178mm). **Weight unloaded:** 1lb 9oz (730g). **Barrel:** 4.50in (114mm), 6 grooves, right-hand twist. **Magazine:** 9-round detachable box. **Muzzle velocity:** c.875 ft/sec (266 m/sec) (9mm Short).

• Browning High-Power or GP35
Fabrique Nationale d'Armes de Guerre, Herstal-lez-Liege
9 mm Parabellum

Frequently called 'John Browning's last design', this pistol was originally

developed by him between 1914 and 1926, when he died; after that it was taken over by Dieudonné Saive, FN's chief designer, who was responsible for turning it into a hammer-fired weapon (instead of Browning's striker) and giving it a 13-shot double-row magazine. Due to the Depression it was not put into production until 1935, whereupon it was adopted by Belgium, Latvia, Lithuania and China, but no more than about 35,000 were made before the outbreak of war. In 1940 the FN factory was commandeered by the Germans and the pistol was thereafter manufactured for the German Army as the Pistole 640(b). The design was smuggled to Britain and put into production in Canada for the Canadian and Chinese armies, and was also adopted by the British Army for Commando and Airborne forces. After the war FN went back into production and it was formally adopted by the British Army in 1954 to replace their 38-caliber revolver. After this some 55 other countries adopted the pistol.

The GP35 is the logical step from Browning's Colt M1911 design. He changed the trigger system to use a sear bar in the slide, and replaced the Colt's swinging link with a shaped cam, but the action, that of dropping the barrel out of engagement with the slide, is the same. Early models came in two forms; one with fixed sights, the other with an optimistic tangent sight marked to 500 meters and an attachable shoulder stock. The latter was favored by the Chinese, but was not used to any extent elsewhere and was dropped soon after production was resumed in 1947.

The High-Power has proved a highly reliable and serviceable pistol in military

The modern version of the M1935 with fixed sights.

John Browning's last design: the 1935 'High Power' pistol, with the original adjustable tangent rear-sight.

The early Browning pistols were provided with a wooden holster-stock and had the butt grip grooved to fit.

hands; commercial models for target shooting were also made, but these were not widely adopted because the trigger mechanism did not lend itself easily to fine tuning.

Length: 7.75in (197mm). **Weight unloaded:** 2lb 3oz (990g). **Barrel:** 4.65in (118mm), 4 grooves, right-hand twist. **Magazine:** 13-round detachable box. **Muzzle velocity:** c.1110 ft/sec (335 m/sec).

• FN 140DA
Fabrique Nationale, Herstal-lez-Liege
7.65xl7SR Browning (32 ACP)

Resemblance between this and the Beretta 81/84 types is no coincidence; the FN pistol is a slightly modified Beretta 81 with a spur hammer rather than a ring hammer, and an all-enveloping slide with ejection port rather than the usual Beretta open-topped slide. Another difference is the placing of the safety catch on the slide, where it can be operated from either side, so that the pistol can be used by right- or left-handed shooters.

The Beretta Model 84 (in 9mm Short/380 ACP chambering) is also modified in this way and is sold in the USA as the 'Browning BDA Pistol'. For relevant data, see under Beretta Models 81 and 84.

• Browning Double Action
Fabrique Nationale, Herstal-lez-Liege
9mm Parabellum

This was introduced in the mid-1980s and closely resembled the GP35 Model (above) except for the shape of the triggerguard. The lockwork was double action, and could easily be converted to single-action if required. There was a de-cocking lever on both sides of the frame, and the magazine catch, normally

on the left, could be switched to the right side quite easily. An automatic firing pin safety unit prevented movement of the firing pin unless the trigger was properly operated; the final movement of the trigger unlocked the firing pin and then released the hammer.

The intention was to compete with the spate of double-action pistols then appearing on the market, but unfortunately FN ran into some severe production and quality control problems at that time and the pistol failed to sell. Production ceased in 1987.

Length: 7.87in (200mm). **Weight unloaded:** 1lb 14oz (850g). **Barrel:** 4.65in (118mm), 4 grooves, right-hand twist. **Magazine:** 14-round detachable box. **Muzzle velocity:** c.1110 ft/sec(335 m/sec).

The Compact version of the Double Action family, with the standard-length magazine in place.

• Browning Compact
Fabrique Nationale, Herstal-lez-Liege
9mm Parabellum

This was a reduced-size version of the double-action pistol which could also be provided with single-action lockwork if required. The mechanism was the same as that of the double-action described above, but the slide was shortened by 27mm and the butt by 37mm and a short magazine fitted; a standard magazine could also be fitted, though this canceled out the advantages of the compact design. It was also possible to mount the compact slide and barrel on a standard

The short-lived Browning Double-Action of 1980.

The 7.65mm FN 140DA is actually a licensed Beretta 84.

frame, to produce a medium-sized pistol. None of these designs prospered, and few of the compact and medium weapons were ever made.

Length: 6.8in (173mm). **Weight unloaded:** 1lb 9oz (710g). **Barrel:** 3.78in (96mm), 4 grooves, right-hand twist. **Magazine:** 7-round detachable box. **Muzzle velocity:** c.1000 ft/sec (328 m/sec).

• Browning Mk 2
Fabrique Nationale, Herstal-lez-Liege
9mm Parabellum

This was a slightly improved version of the original GP35 pistol, introduced in the early 1980s. It adopted an ambidextrous safety catch, a new design of grip, wider sights and an anti-glare finish. It was purchased by a number of military forces, but in relatively small numbers and in the face of very strong competition from more modern designs. There were also complaints of failures from some quarters, which led FN to withdraw it in 1987 and set about retooling their production line and developing the Mark 3 (below). The dimensions and data are exactly the same as those for the GP35.

• Browning Mk 3 and 3S
FN Herstal SA (Mk 3)
Browning SA (Mk 3S)
9mm Parabellum

These pistols were introduced in January 1989 and were essentially the Browning Mk 2 but manufactured to a higher standard, using new computer-controlled machinery, and with new dimensions of the frame and slide and a redimensioned ejection port. The rear sight was now mounted in a dovetailed slot which was to the same dimensions as that of the Target GP35, so that owners wishing to improve the sights could easily have the target sights fitted. There were also recesses for the addition of Tritium night sighting spots alongside the rear sight and in the front sight blade. The safety catch was ambidextrous and the grips were newly designed to a better anatomical shape. The Mark 3 was the standard single-action weapon; the Mark 3S was a special version produced for police use and incorporated an automatic firing pin safety system in which the firing pin is positively locked against any movement except during the final pressure of the trigger. A mechanism linked to the sear bar then releases the firing pin in time for it to be struck by the falling hammer. The Mark 3S was produced under the Browning name,

The Browning Mark 3 is the High Power with ambidextrous safety and built on new computer-controlled machinery.

since in late 1988 the company was reorganized into two sections: FN Herstal SA dealt with military business, while Browning SA attended to police and commercial sales. Within six months of its announcement, 25,000 of the Mark 3S had been sold to European police forces.

• FN BDA 9
FN Herstal SA
9mm Parabellum

The BDA 9 is a further development of the High-Power and functions in the same way, differing in having a double-action trigger and a hammer decocking lever in place of the safety catch. The decocking lever is duplicated on both sides of the frame and can thus be used with either hand. The magazine release is normally fitted for right-hand use but can easily be removed and reversed to suit left-handed use. The pistol is loaded in the usual manner by pulling back and releasing the slide. It can then be fired or, by pressing the de-cocking lever, the hammer can be lowered. Operation of the lever inserts a safety device between the hammer and the firing pin, and a braking lever slows down the hammer's fall. There is also an automatic firing pin safety system which keeps the firing pin securely locked except during the final movement of the trigger when firing. Once the hammer has been lowered the pistol can be carried with a round in the chamber in perfect safety and can be instantly fired by simply pulling the trigger through.

Length: 7.87in (200mm). **Weight empty:** 1lb 15oz (905g). **Barrel:** 4.65in (118mm), 6 grooves, right-hand twist. **Magazine:** 14-shot detachable box. **Muzzle velocity:** 1,148 ft/sec (350 m/sec).

The Browning Mark 2 reverted to single action and was simply an up-to-date M1935.

The BDA9 is the High Power updated to double action.

6 grooves, right-hand twist. **Magazine:** 14-shot detachable box. **Muzzle velocity:** 1,148 ft/sec (350 m/sec).

• FN Five-seveN
FN Herstal SA, Liege.
5.7x28mm

This is a self-cocking semi-automatic firing the same cartridge as the P-90 personal defense weapon (described in the Submachine Gun section). The trigger action is rather unusual in that pressure on the trigger first loads the firing pin spring and then releases the firing pin. Unless the trigger is pressed, the firing

• FN BDAO
FN Herstal SA
9mm Parabellum

The BDAO is the same as the BDA9 except that it is self-cocking only (or double-action only, as you prefer) and for that reason there is no cocking spur on the hammer. As the slide goes forward after cocking, and after each shot, so the hammer follows it but is arrested before it can strike the firing pin. An automatic firing pin safety system ensures that the pistol cannot fire unless the trigger is pulled completely through to the full-cock position, so that accidental discharges are practically impossible.

Length: 7.87ln (200mm). **Weight empty:** 1lb 14oz (870g). **Barrel:** 4.65in (118mm),

The Five-seveN field-stripped; don't be fooled by the lug, this is a delayed blowback pistol.

The FN Five-seveN fires a new high-velocity cartridge to give long range and superior penetration.

The FN Five-seveN with silencer fitted.

pin is never under any sort of pressure, and thus there is no safety catch of the normal type.

Surprisingly, for a weapon of such power, the Five-seveN operates on the delayed blowback principle. The slide carries two notches on its under-surface. Set into the frame is a cross-shaft carrying two connected lugs. The barrel is a loose fit in the slide, and when the barrel and slide are assembled to the frame, a slotted lug beneath the chamber is so placed that the slot lines up with the cross-shaft. On firing, the pressure in the chamber forces the bullet up the barrel, and the friction and torque of the bullet's movement tends to thrust the barrel forward. At the same time the gas pressure forces the cartridge case back and puts pressure on the slide to move to the rear. Barrel and slide move rearward together about 3mm, at which point the slide notches engage the upstanding lugs on the cross shaft and the slide is halted as the bullet leaves the barrel, so the friction and torque cease and the barrel is free to move backwards. This causes the slotted lug to move over the cross shaft and rotate it so that the twin lugs disengage from the notches in the slide, allowing the slide to continue moving rearwards to perform the usual extraction and reloading cycle while the barrel remains stationary. It all sounds very complicated but works with perfect efficiency.

The cartridge is considerably longer than the average pistol round, but the grip nevertheless fits the hand well and the recoil impulse is somewhat less than a 9mm Parabellum cartridge, so that the weapon is easily controlled. Introduced in 1995, it remains to be seen whether the Five-seveN makes an impact on the military market.

Length: 7.8in (208mm). **Weight:** 2lbs 5oz (618g). **Barrel:** 4.42in (122.5mm). **Magazine:** 20-round detachable box. **Muzzle velocity:** c.2133 ft/sec (650 m/sec).

• FN Barracuda Revolver
Fabrique Nationale, Herstal-lez-Liege
357 Magnum, 38 Special, 9mm Parabellum

This represented Fabrique Nationale's first and only venture into revolver manufacture. It was a solid-frame double-action revolver with side-opening cylinder. In standard form it fired 357 Magnum or 38 Special cartridges, but a special replacement cylinder was available, which permitted the use of 9mm Parabellum rounds. It was adopted in small numbers by various police and military security units, but it appeared at a time when double-action automatic pis-

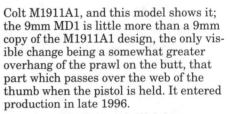

Imbel 9mm GC-MD1 is based on the Colt M1911A1 design.

tols with larger magazine capacity were appearing in ever-greater numbers and was thus denied a market which it might have had ten or fifteen years earlier. Manufacture ceased in 1989.

It might be noted that in 1990 FN bought Manurhin, the French pistol manufacturer, with the intention of marketing their revolver designs under the FN name, but shortly thereafter they were taken over by Giat and the proposed venture came to nothing.

Length: 7.8in (200 mm). **Weight:** 2lbs 5oz (1000g). **Barrel:** 3in (76mm), 6 grooves, right-hand twist. **Magazine:** 6-chambered cylinder. **Muzzle velocity:** c.1180 ft/sec (360 m/sec).

BRAZIL

• IMBEL 9GC-MD1
Industria do Materiel Belico de Brasil, Vila Estrela, Piquete-SP
9mm Parabellum

IMBEL got their start in pistol manufacturing by licensed production of the

Colt M1911A1, and this model shows it; the 9mm MD1 is little more than a 9mm copy of the M1911A1 design, the only visible change being a somewhat greater overhang of the prawl on the butt, that part which passes over the web of the thumb when the pistol is held. It entered production in late 1996.

Length: 8.50in (216mm). **Weight unloaded:** 2lb 1oz (940g). **Barrel:** 5.03in (128mm); 6 grooves, polygonal, right-hand twist. **Magazine:** 17-round detachable box. **Muzzle velocity:** c.1115 ft/sec (340 m/sec).

• IMBEL 45GC-MD1
Industria do Materiel Belico de Brasil, Vila Estrela, Piquete-SP
45 ACP

This is another M1911A1 copy, this time in the original caliber; it differs in the same way as the 9mm version, the rear overhang being greater, and is said to have been redesigned specifically for production on computer-controlled machinery.

Length: 8.50in (216mm). **Weight unloaded:** 2lb 14oz (1300g). **Barrel:** 5.03in (128mm); 6 grooves, polygonal, right-hand twist. **Magazine:** 14-round detachable box. **Muzzle velocity:** c.787 ft/sec (240 m/sec).

• IMBEL 45UC-MD1, MD2
Industria do Materiel Belico de Brasil, Vila Estrela, Piquete-SP
45 ACP

This is a compact version of the 45GC-MD1. The design generally follows that of the MD1 but with a serrated ring hammer instead of a spur type, and a shorter barrel. The MD2 version has eight holes in the muzzle end of the barrel aligned with two slots in the slide, one on each side of the front sight. These act as a muzzle brake and reduce the recoil as well as acting as a muzzle compensator to keep the barrel down when firing.

Length: 7.0in (178mm). **Weight unloaded:** 2lb 1oz (940g). **Barrel:** 3.23in (82mm); 6 grooves, polygonal, right-hand twist. **Magazine:** 7-round detachable box. **Muzzle velocity:** c.722 ft/sec (220 m/sec).

9mm FN Barracuda revolver.

The Imbel compact 45 MD1 (1) and MD2 (2) pistols.

CHINA (PEOPLE'S REPUBLIC)

• Pistol Type 51
State arsenals
7.62x25mm Soviet M30

This is simply a Chinese-made copy of the Soviet Tokarev TT-33 automatic pistol. The only observable difference lies in the external machining, the finger-grip grooves on the slide being narrow and more numerous than on the original Soviet models.

• Pistol Type 64
State arsenals
7.65x17mm Type 64

The Type 64 is a most unusual design. Basically it is a simple blowback pistol, but with the refinement of a permanently-fitted Maxim silencer as part of the basic construction. The frame unit carries the cylindrical silencer, formed of a wire mesh cylinder surrounded by perforated metal sleeves and containing a number of rubber discs through which the bullet passes; the result is to trap the gases emerging from the end of the short barrel and, by the internal baffling, reduce their eventual emergent velocity so that little or no noise results.

The rear section of the frame carries a short reciprocating slide which functions in the usual way to reload the pistol and carry the firing pin and extractor. However, this slide has a rotating-lug bolt head which, when optimum silence is required, can be turned by a manual catch so as to lock the slide to the receiver. Thus, on firing, there is no noisy movement of the slide, and after firing, at some convenient time and place, when noise is no longer important, the slide can be unlocked and drawn back by hand to extract and eject the spent case and reload. When a lesser degree of silence is acceptable, the manual catch can be pushed across to hold the bolt lugs out of engagement, where-upon the slide functions in the normal blowback fashion.

It should be noted that the cartridge used with this pistol is unique; although of the same appearance and nominal dimensions as the common 7.65mm ACP round, it is in fact rimless instead of semi-rimmed, and appears to be loaded to a somewhat lower velocity. Normal 7.65mm ACP will not chamber in this pistol and cannot be used.

Length: 13.00in (330mm). **Weight unloaded:** 2lb 12oz (1240g). **Barrel:** 4.9in (124mm). **Magazine:** 8-round detachable box. **Muzzle velocity:** c.900 ft/sec (275 m/sec).

• 7.65mm Type 67
State arsenals
7.65x17mm Type 64

The Type 67 pistol is an improved version of the Type 64 described above. The improvement is simply a matter of

China Type 64 silenced pistol.

Chinese type 67 is simply an improved version of the 64 with a more efficient silencer.

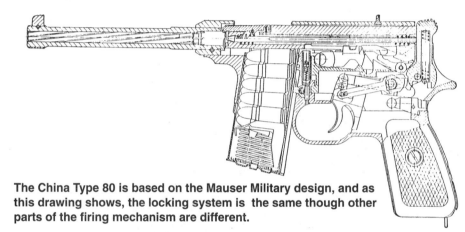

The China Type 80 is based on the Mauser Military design, and as this drawing shows, the locking system is the same though other parts of the firing mechanism are different.

China's Type 59 is a copy of the Russian Makarov.

making the silencer in a cylindrical form, more slender and lighter than that of the Type 64, which makes the pistol easier to carry in a holster and better balanced.

The mechanism is exactly the same, and there are some minor changes in the assembly of the internal parts of the silencer though the system of operation remains the same.

Length: 8.6in (225mm). **Weight unloaded:** 2.25lb (1020g). **Barrel:** 3.5in (89mm). **Magazine:** 9-shot detachable box. **Muzzle velocity:** 594 ft/sec (181 m/sec).

• 7.62mm Machine Pistol Type 80
State arsenals
7.62x25mm Soviet M30

The design of this pistol is based upon that of the Mauser Model 712 (System Westinger) 'Schnellfeuerpistole' of 1932-36, several thousand of which were sold to China. The Type 80 uses the same basic mechanism, an internal reciprocating bolt which locks to the barrel extension by means of lugs and an external hammer striking a firing pin in the bolt. The magazine is ahead of the trigger-guard in Mauser style but is removable and is noticeably sloped forward, probably to improve the feed. The grip angle has also been improved and there are minor changes in the external contours. A clip-on telescopic buttstock is provided, as is a bayonet, and with the stock attached the weapon is said to give good accuracy to a range of 150 meters.

Length: 11.81in (300mm) (without stock). **Weight unloaded:** 2.43lb (1100g). **Barrel:** not known. **Magazine:** 10- or 20-shot detachable box. **Cyclic rate:** not known. **Muzzle velocity:** 1,542 ft/sec (470 m/sec).

• 9mm Pistol Type 59
State arsenals
9mm Makarov

Apart from small differences in weight and dimensions, the Type 59 pistol is a copy of the Soviet Makarov PM pistol, a blowback design with double action derived from the Walther PP. It is standard issue in the Chinese armed forces and is also offered for export.

Length: 6.37in (162mm). **Weight unloaded:** 1.61lb (730g). **Barrel:** 3.68in (93.5mm). **Magazine:** 8-shot detachable box. **Muzzle velocity:** 1,030 ft/sec (314 m/sec).

CROATIA

• HS-95
RH-ALAN, Zagreb
9mm Parabellum

This pistol was first seen briefly in 1991, marketed as the 'CZ99' by Zastava

The Croatian HS-95 first appeared as the Zastava CZ89 and appears to have been copied from the SIG designs.

CZECHOSLOVAKIA

- ## Pistol vz/22

- ## Pistol vz/24
Ceskoslovenska Zbrojovka, Brno (vz/22)
Ceska Zbrojovka, Prague (vz/24)
9mm Browning Short (380 ACP)

These pistols were the earliest of a number of designs manufactured in Czechoslovakia to the designs of Josef Nickl, who had been employed by Waffenfabrik Mauser and for whom in 1916 he had designed the vz/22 as the 'Nickl-Pistole' in 9mm Parabellum caliber, for which a locked breech was necessary. After the war Nickl was sent to Czechoslovakia to assist in setting up rifle manufacture there, and interested the Czechs in his pistol, which Mauser had turned down. The Czechs adopted it, but in 9mm Short caliber. Hence, although using a low-powered cartridge, the vz/22 uses a locked breech dependent upon the rotation of the barrel for locking and unlocking. There is, of

Arms of Yugoslavia. The subsequent civil upheaval closed down communications with that country and nothing more was heard of the pistol until it reappeared in 1995 with some cosmetic changes and a new owner. It seems to have leaned heavily on the SIG 220 series for its inspiration, using a similar double-action and decocking system though with a rather more rounded contour to the butt. The mechanism is also similar, using the Browning cam and locking into the ejection opening and with an automatic firing pin safety. It is apparently issued to Croatian army personnel and is also offered for export.

Length: 7.09in (180mm). **Weight unloaded:** 2lb 3oz (990g). **Barrel:** 4.0in (102mm); 6 grooves, polygonal, right-hand twist. **Magazine:** 15-round detachable box. **Muzzle velocity:** c.1115 ft/sec (340 m/sec).

The Nickl pistol or vz/22 was a locked breech design firing the 98mm Short cartridge.

The vz/24 was an improved version of the Nickl pistol. Note that like all CZ pistols of the period, it bore the actual year of manufacture—'CZ27'—on the slide, which can cause some confusion.

course, no necessity for locking in 9mm Short caliber and the later vz/27 (32 ACP) reverted to blowback principles. In general terms the vz/22 had no particular virtues, though it was a sound weapon of first-class quality, and many are still in use.

The 1924 design, also in 9mm Short and also a locked-breech weapon, is no more than a logical development of the vz/22. Assembly is slightly more easy, a magazine safety has been added and, on the later models, the wooden butt grip based on the original Mauser type was replaced by one of hard rubber and bearing the CZ monogram.

Length: 6.00in (152mm). **Weight unloaded:** 1lb 8oz (700g). **Barrel:** 3.55in (91mm), 6 grooves, right-hand twist. **Magazine:** 8-round detachable box. **Muzzle velocity:** c.970 ft/sec (295 m/sec).

• Pistol vz/27
Ceska Zbrojovka, Prague
7.65x17SR Browning (32 ACP)

The vz/27 is the successor to the vz/22 and vz/24, and it is generally encountered as a 7.65mm blowback pistol with the barrel attached to the frame by ribs in the Browning fashion. An earlier experimental design, the vz/26, was also made (generally found in 9mm Short caliber) in which the barrel and the breech are locked together on firing by the same rotating barrel system used on the vz/24. Certainly there is no requirement for breech locking in either caliber. The external difference between the two vz/27 variations lies in the cutting of the finger-grip grooves in the slide: the blowback model has vertical grooves while the locked-breech model has the grooves obliquely inclined. The locked-breech models also have a magazine safety which prevents the trigger from being moved unless the magazine is in place. Early models have butt grips of wood and

are marked on the top rib 'CESKA ZBROJOVKA AS V PRAZE', while later models made after the German occupation are inscribed 'BÖHMISCHE WAFFENFABRIK PRAG' and in many cases have plastic butt grips. The German weapons, known as the Pistole 27(t), are often found in a slightly simplified form. Production of the vz/27 was resumed after 1948, such output being distinguishable by the marking 'NARODNI PODNIK'.

Length: 6.25in (158mm). **Weight unloaded:** 1 lb 9oz (700g). **Barrel:** 3.90in (100mm), 6 grooves, right-hand twist. **Magazine:** 8-round detachable box. **Muzzle velocity:** c.920 ft/sec (280 m/sec) (7.65mm ACP).

• Pistol vz/38
Ceska Zbrojovka, Prague
9mm Browning Short (380 ACP)

This is a terrible weapon and there seems to be no good reason for its existence; it is clumsy to hold and point and the lockwork is double-action only, so that accurate shooting is out of the question. It scores in only one respect as it is perhaps one of the easiest pistols to strip and clean, since the simple release of a catch allows the barrel and slide to hinge up at the muzzle so that the slide can be pulled from the barrel. The pistol is of good manufacture, well finished in good material.

While some authorities have claimed that this pistol is chambered for a special

version of the 9mm Short cartridge developed by the Czech Government for military use only, we have neither seen the cartridge in question nor even any official record of its existence—and all the specimens of this pistol so far examined seem to function quite satisfactorily with the standard 9mm Short round. A few examples with a conventional sear and a hammer grooved for manual cocking have also been noted.

Length: 8.11 in (206mm). **Weight unloaded:** 2lb 1oz (940g). **Barrel:** 4.65in (118mm), 6 grooves, right-hand twist. **Magazine:** 8-round detachable box. **Muzzle Velocity:** c.980 ft/sec (299 m/sec).

• Pistol vz/50 and 50/70
Ceska Zbrojovka, Strakonice
7.65x17SR Browning (32 ACP)

This is no more than a slightly modified Walther Model PP, and the modification seems to have been done for the sake of it since it adds nothing to the functioning. There is a slight difference in the shape of the frame and the triggerguard, the grip is changed slightly and the contour of the hammer is also different from the original Walther pattern. The biggest change is in the repositioning of the safety catch on the left side of the frame instead of on the slide. In this position it works directly on the lock-work instead of demanding some rather complex machining and fitting of operating pins in the slide, which simplifies manufac-

The vz/38; the catch above the trigger unlocks the slide and barrel to hinge open at the front end for stripping and cleaning.

The vz/27 was a logical progression from the vz/24 by removing the locked breech and making it a blowback. Note that the finger grips on the slide are now vertical, a useful identification feature.

A simple blowback, the vz/50 was basically a copy of the Walther PP.

The CZ75 was a commercial venture, but it soon made a name for itself around the world and was adopted by many police and paramilitary forces.

ture if nothing else. The double-action lockwork of the Walther is retained.

Length: 6.60in (167mm). **Weight unloaded:** 1lb 7.5oz (660g). **Barrel:** 3.75in (94mm), 6 grooves, right-hand twist. **Magazine:** 8-round detachable box. **Muzzle velocity:** c.920 ft/sec (280 m/sec).

• Pistol vz/52
Ceska Zbrojovka, Strakonice
7.62x25mm vz/30 (Soviet M30)

The vz/52 is a considerable improvement over its immediate predecessors, although it is notable that there still seems to be evidence of Mauser design techniques just as there were on pre-war pistols. It is a recoil-operated pistol with an unusual locking system. Chambered for the 7.62mm Soviet pistol cartridge (which is virtually the 7.63mm Mauser round), a locking system is very necessary and the design is loosely based on a Mauser patent of 1910, modified along lines first developed in Poland and later incorporated into the MG42 machine gun. Two rollers lock the barrel and slide together during a short recoil stroke and are then cammed out of engagement with the slide, permitting the slide to recoil fully, extract, return and chamber a fresh round. As the new round is chambered, the slide and barrel move forward and the locking rollers are once more forced into engagement.

Neat, strong and elegant as the system is, it seems unnecessarily complex when compared with Browning designs, though the vz/52 is probably the smoothest-shooting pistol of any using the 7.62mm Tokarev cartridge.

Length: 8.25in (209mm). **Weight unloaded:** 1lb 15oz (880g). **Barrel:** 4.7in (120mm), 4 grooves, right-hand twist. **Magazine:** 8-round detachable box. **Muzzle velocity:** c.1300 ft/sec (396 m/sec).

• Pistol CZ75
Ceska Zbrojovka, Uhersky Brod
9mm Parabellum

This pistol, introduced in 1975, rapidly acquired a reputation for accuracy and reliability. Chambered for the 9mm Parabellum cartridge, it was obviously not intended for Czech service use but for export, and it achieved considerable success. It was also widely copied and license-built in other countries, notably as the original ITM pistol in Switzerland, the Springfield P9 in the USA, and the Tanfoglio in Italy. It is a recoil-operated weapon, using the usual modification of the Colt swinging link breech lock in which the link is replaced by a shaped cam beneath the breech. The firing lock is double action, similar to that of the Walther P38, but the safety catch is well-positioned on the left of the frame and locks the hammer linkage. The magazine is a double-column type which holds 15 rounds.

Length: 8.25in (209.5mm). **Weight unloaded:** 2lb 3oz (1000g). **Barrel:** 4.8in (122mm). **Magazine:** 15-round detachable box. **Muzzle velocity:** c.1110 ft/sec (338 m/sec).

• Pistol CZ75 Automatic
Ceska Zbrojovka, Uhersky Brod
9mm Parabellum

This is CZ vz/75 modified to permit full-automatic fire. It also has a fitting on the frame, ahead of the triggerguard which allows a laser sight to be fitted or, perhaps more practical, a loaded magazine to be inserted upsidedown to act as a forward grip and also add some weight to the front end of the weapon to prevent it from leaping into the air when fired at 1,000 rounds per minute. Two versions exist; the standard model is generally of the same appear-

The unusual CZ 75 Automatic fires full-auto and uses a spare magazine as a front grip to keep the gun steady when firing. The slotted muzzle also helps.

The CZ 100 is the most recent CZ product and introduces synthetic materials and self-cocking operation.

The vz/83 is more or less a Czech version of the Russian Makarov.

ance as the vz/75. A second model has a longer barrel and an extension on the slide provided with slots to act as a muzzle-brake/compensator. An extended 25-round magazine is also available.

Length, standard model: 8.11in (206mm); extended model: 9.88in (251mm). **Weight unloaded**, standard: 2lb 4oz (1020g); extended: 2lb 11oz (1230g). **Barrel**, standard: 4.72in (120mm); extended: 6.49in (165mm); 6 grooves, right-hand twist. **Magazine:** 15- or 25-round detachable box. **Cyclic rate:** 1000 rds/min. **Muzzle velocity:** c.1214 ft/sec (370 m/sec).

• Pistol vz/83
Ceska Zbrojovka, Uhersky Brod
7.65x17SR Browning and 9x18mm Police

The vz/83 is a conventional design of a fixed-barrel blowback type. It is fitted with ambidextrous safety catch and magazine release, and the double-action lockwork includes a safety device by which the hammer is positively blocked until the final movement of the trigger squeeze. Dismantling is achieved by springing the triggerguard down, where it is held by a catch, and an interlock ensures that the pistol cannot be dismantled until the magazine has been removed and the magazine cannot be replaced unless the triggerguard is closed and locked into the frame.

Length: 6.51in (173mm). **Weight unloaded:** 1lb 7oz (650g). **Barrel:** 3.78in

(96mm), 6 grooves, right-hand twist. **Magazine:** 15-round detachable box (7.65mm); 12-round detachable box (9mm). **Muzzle velocity:** 1050 ft/sec (320 m/sec) (7.65mm); 1115 ft/sec (340 m/sec) (9mm).

• Pistol CZ-85
Ceska Zbrojovka, Uhersky Brod
9mm Parabellum

This is an updated version of the CZ75 in which the general appearance has been retained but the safety catch and slide stop have been duplicated on both sides for ambidextrous operation. Minor changes to the internals have been made to improve reliability, and the top of the slide is ribbed to reduce shine. Models with fixed or adjustable sights are available.

Length: 8.11in (206mm). **Weight unloaded:** 2lb3oz (1000g). **Barrel:** 4.74in (120mm), 6 grooves, right-hand twist. **Magazine:** 15-round detachable box. **Muzzle velocity:** c.1180 ft/sec (360 m/sec).

• Pistol CZ100/101
Ceska Zbrojovka, Uhersky Brod
9mm Parabellum or 40 S&W

Introduced in 1995 this chunky pistol brings synthetic materials into CZ construction. Slide and frame use plastics and steel; the pistol is a self-cocker, the firing system being under no tension unless the trigger is pulled. There is an automatic firing pin safety device. An unusual protrusion on the top of the slide, just behind the ejection port, is intended to permit one-handed cocking by simply placing this part against a hard surface and pushing down on the grip so that the slide is forced back to

load the first round. The action is the usual Browning cam, locking the chamber top into the ejection port. A laser sight can be fitted into rails provided in the front of the frame.

The Model 101 is similar but has a smaller magazine capacity: 7 rounds of 9mm or 6 rounds of 40-caliber.

(CZ100)

Length: 6.96in (177mm). **Weight unloaded:** 1lb 7oz (645g). **Barrel:** 3.74in (95mm). **Magazine:** 13-round (9mm) or 10-round (.40) detachable box. **Muzzle velocity:** c. 1115 ft/sec (340 m/sec) (9mm); 950 ft/sec (290 m/sec) (.40).

DENMARK

• Pistol Model 1910, Model 1910/21
Ancien Etablissements Pieper, Herstal-lez-Liege, Belgium; Haerens Tøjhus, Copenhagen
9x23mm Bergmann-Bayard M10

This weapon is one of the many designs produced by Theodor Bergmann in the early years of the century, although he only manufactured a very small number—perhaps no more than 1,800—and in 1907 the manufacturing rights and existing parts were acquired by Pieper. Originally known as the Bergmann 'Mars', Pieper renamed it the Bayard Model 1910, but such was the influence of its inventor's name that it is invariably known as the Bergmann-Bayard. Bergmann had initially begun supplying the Spanish Government in 1905 and this contract was thereafter fulfilled by Pieper, although

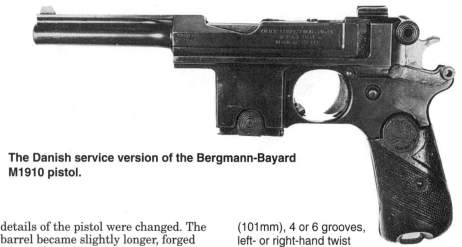

The Danish service version of the Bergmann-Bayard M1910 pistol.

details of the pistol were changed. The barrel became slightly longer, forged integrally with the barrel extension, and the rifling was changed from the original 4-groove right-hand twist to 6-groove left-hand twist. The pistol was later adopted in small numbers by the Greek Army.

The layout of the pistol, although vaguely reminiscent of the Mauser c/96, is a logical development of earlier Bergmann designs and owes nothing to Mauser. The great difference between this weapon and its forerunners is its utilization of a much more powerful cartridge, and a positive breech locking system. The bolt is locked by a plate beneath, which engages in slots in the bolt and is supported by a ramp on the frame. On firing, the barrel and bolt recoil slightly until this lockplate rides down the ramp and unlocks the bolt, which is then free to move back while the barrel is held. Another refinement absent from earlier Bergmann pistols is a firing-pin withdrawal spring which keeps the point of the pin inside the bolt during loading.

After having been tested by various governments in a variety of calibers, the pistol was adopted in 1911 by the Danish Army as the Pistol m/10, made under contract by Pieper. Supply was terminated by World War I and in 1922 the Danes decided to make their own; the indigenous product differed from the original Pieper issues by the use of large wooden or plastic grips and by having the lock cover-plate retained by a screw instead of by a spring catch. They were marked 'm 1910/21' with Danish inscriptions, although some of the original Pieper models were reworked to 1921 standard by the addition of the new plastic grips and these were also marked m 1910/21' (although they still bore the original Belgian markings).

Length: 10.0in (254mm). **Weight unloaded:** 2lb 4oz (1020g). **Barrel:** 4.00in (101mm), 4 or 6 grooves, left- or right-hand twist (see above). **Magazine:** 6- or 10-round detachable box. **Muzzle velocity:** c.1300 ft/sec (395 m/sec).

EGYPT

• Pistol Tokagypt 58
Fémaru és Szerszámgépgyár NV, Budapest, Hungary
9mm Parabellum

This is no more than an improved copy of the Soviet TT33 (Tokarev) pistol manufactured by FEG of Budapest in 9mm Parabellum for use by Egyptian military forces. The external improvements on the original design are no more than skin deep—a better shaped plastic one-piece butt grip is provided, and a better quality of finish and manufacture than that usually found on the native Soviet products is also apparent. But a safety catch was added and the caliber changed to 9mm Parabellum, resulting in a very practical weapon. However, the Egyptian army expressed dissatisfaction with the weapon and the contract was terminated before completion. Those pistols which had been delivered were transferred to the Egyptian police force.

Length: 7.65in (194mm). **Weight unloaded:** 1lb 15oz (910g). **Barrel:** 4.50in (114mm), 6 grooves, right-hand twist. **Magazine:** 7-round detachable box. **Muzzle velocity:** c.1150 ft/sec (350 m/sec).

FINLAND

• Pistol M35 Lahti
Valtion Kivääritehdas (VKT), Jyväskylä
9mm Parabellum

The Lahti pistol, often simply known as the L35, takes its name from the designer of the weapon, Aimo Lahti. The weapon was adopted as the official pistol of the Finnish Army in 1935, replacing the Pistol m/23 (a Parabellum), and was later adopted by Sweden as the Pistol m/40. The L35 is exceptionally well made and finished, and is particularly well sealed against the ingress of dirt; as a result it is remarkably reliable in arctic conditions, although a little heavy by modern standards. An unusual design feature of the Lahti is the provision of an accelerator, a device more usually associated with a machine gun in which it is utilized to increase the fire-rate. In this pistol, however, the accelerator is specifically intended to ensure operation of the action in sub-zero temperatures. It is impossible to strip the gun completely for cleaning or for repairs without the services of a trained armorer and access to a workshop, but it should be said that the likelihood of components

The Tokagypt was a Tokarev in 9mm Parabellum chambering, for the Egyptian armed forces.

The Finnish Lahti M35 9mm pistol has a Luger shape but a Bergmann mechanism.

breaking or wearing out is so remote that the armies in which the pistols serve are obviously prepared to discount the chances.

Length: 9.68in (245mm). **Weight unloaded:** 2lb 11oz (1220g). **Barrel:** 4.18in (105mm), 6 grooves, right-hand twist. **Magazine:** 8-round detachable box. **Muzzle velocity:** c.1150 ft/sec (350 m/sec).

FRANCE

• Pistol Modele 1892 ('Modele d'Ordonnance' or 'Lebel')
Various State-owned factories
8x27R Reglementaire Mle 92

The Modele 1892 is sometimes known as the 'Lebel', although it is questionable whether Nicolas Lebel had anything to do with the design and development of this weapon. The Mle 92 was introduced to the French Army in 1893 and remained in use until 1945 as the French had meanwhile failed to design and issue a suitable self-loading pistol other than the Modéle 1935. The revolver is a relatively simple double-action, six-chambered design, using a lock mechanism similar to that employed by the Italian 1889 design. It was built on a solid frame with a cylinder which swung out to the right for loading, a feature of arguable usefulness as most shooters are right-handed. One of the better features of the Mle 92 was that the left sideplate could be unlocked and swung forward to expose the lock and trigger mechanism for repair or cleaning, and one of the defects lay in the small and under-powered cartridge.

Length: 9.36in (236mm). **Weight unloaded:** 1lb 14oz (840g). **Barrel:** 4.60in (117mm), 6 grooves, right-hand twist. **Magazine:** 6-round cylinder. **Muzzle velocity:** c.750 ft/sec (228 m/sec).

• Le Français Militaire, Model 1928
Société Francaise d'Armes et Cycles, Saint-Etienne
9x20SR Browning Long

The 1928 'Militaire' Le Français is the senior model of a series of pistols of similar design made by SFAC of Saint-Etienne and it embodies a number of novel and distinctive design features.

The pistol operates on the blowback system, but has the recoil spring augmented by a leverage device which also functions as a recoil buffer. The barrel pivots downwards through about 15° to permit cleaning and loading single rounds, and withdrawing the magazine automatically unlocks the barrel and allows it to tip forward. The lockwork is self-cocking and there is no provision for the slide to be manually operated.

To operate the Le Français the magazine is inserted in the normal fashion; at the bottom of the magazine an external loop or clip holds an additional round which is removed and, with the barrel tipped forward, inserted into the chamber. The barrel is then closed. Pulling the trigger will now fire that round, because of the self-cocking lock, and the blowback action extracts and reloads from the magazine in the usual way. The firing mechanism is hammerless and the

The French M1892 with the frame opened and grip removed to reveal the inner workings.

The French M1892 'Model d'Ordonnance' revolver.

The Le Francais 'Military Model', so-called in the hope of selling it to the French Army. They refused it but it became a popular police weapon.

striker does not actually cock until the trigger is drawn back to fire the round. The only defect in the system is that the slide closes on an empty chamber after the last round has been fired, and the firer is given no warning.

Alternatively, after inserting the magazine, it can be withdrawn about 0.25in (6mm) and locked there, clear of the slide. The pistol can now be loaded with single rounds, the first into the tipped barrel and subsequent rounds by releasing the barrel (by using the barrel catch) to reload. This allows a slow fire to be kept up, with a full magazine in hand for emergencies. Much the same system had been used earlier on the Webley and Scott automatic pistol and, of course, it was a common feature in bolt-action military rifles.

Introduced early in 1929, the Le Française failed to catch on, though it is an interesting example of what might have been; perhaps it was a little too unusual in its concept and, by that time, the 9mm Browning Long cartridge was considered too weak to be practical.

Length: 8.00in (203mm). **Weight unloaded:** 2lb 6oz (1070g). **Barrel:** 5.5in (134mm), 6 grooves, right-hand twist. **Magazine:** 8-round detachable box. **Muzzle velocity:** c.1000 ft/sec (305 m/sec).

• Pistolet Automatique Modele 1935A

• Pistolet Automatique Modele 1935S

Manufacture d'Armes de Chatellerault (MAC), Manufacture d'Armes de Saint-Etienne (MAS), Manufacture d'Armes de Tulle (MAT), Société Alsacienne de Constructions Mechaniques (SACM) and Societe d'Applications Generals, Electriques et Mechaniques (SAGEM) **7.65x19.5mm Longue**

Taking the Colt 45 ACP 1911A1 as a starting point, Charles Petter of SACM made a number of improvements and embodied them in this French service pistol. The principal differences lie in the system of housing the recoil spring, the use of a single, wide locking rib on top of the barrel, the provision of a magazine safety and a safety catch on the slide, and the fitting of the hammer and lockwork in a separate sub-assembly. As the title implies, it was adopted in 1935 and put into manufacture, though with no great urgency.

In 1938, the French Army were alarmed at the slow issue of the M1935 pistol and pressed for greater production. It was, though, a slow production job, and for this reason it was slightly redesigned to make it easier and quicker to manufacture. The new design, known as the 1935S, was manufactured at the arsenals of Chatellerault, St.-Etienne and Tulle and at the SAGEM factory and differs from the 1935A in that it reversed the barrel locking system by forming the lug on the undersurface of the slide-top and the recess in the material of the barrel. This model is recognizable by the straight butt and slightly protruding barrel muzzle, whereas the original model—the M1935A—has the butt curved to bet-

The Model 35S was a more utilitarian version, redesigned for faster production.

The Petter-designed SACM Modele 35A was an elegant weapon.

The MAS 50 was more or less the SACM redesigned in 9mm Parabellum caliber.

ter suit the hand, and has the muzzle flush with the front end of the slide.

These weapons are little known and rarely seen. They are, moreover, of only academic interest outside France as they are chambered for the 7.65mm Longue automatic pistol cartridge peculiar to the French Army.

Length: 7.45in (189mm). **Weight unloaded:** 1lb 10oz (730g). **Barrel:** 4.30in (109mm), 4 grooves, right-hand twist. **Magazine:** 8-round detachable box. **Muzzle velocity:** c.1000 ft/sec (305 m/sec).

• Pistolet Automatique Modele 1950
Manufacture d'Armes de Saint-Etienne
9mm Parabellum

The French never seem to have excelled in weapon design until after World War II. The only pre-war pistol of any merit was more or less copied from earlier Browning designs and chambered for an odd and ineffective round, but after the war, work began on a pistol which was ultimately adopted as the Modele 1950. The weapon is, once again, basically the Colt M1911AI/Mle 1935A in 9mm Parabellum caliber, but with some small changes, the most important of which is in the matter of safety.

A cross-bolt safety catch, as used in the 1935 Petter-designed pistol, is retained in the Mle 50 and replaces the frame-mounted catch of the Colt. This was a sensible move in a way, since the users would have become used to the earlier system and, since the use of safety catches is largely instinctive, leaving it in a familiar place would obviate retraining. A magazine safety is also fitted, to prevent firing the round in the chamber when the magazine is removed; this is one of those features which looks good on a specification sheet or sales brochure but which is of dubious utility in a combat pistol.

Length: 7.60n (192mm). **Weight unloaded:** 1lb 8oz (680g). **Barrel:** 4.40in (112mm), 4 grooves, right-hand twist.

Magazine: 9-round detachable box. **Muzzle velocity:** c. 1100 ft/sec (335 m/sec).

• Pistole Automatique MAS-G1
Manufacture d'Armes de Saint-Etienne, St.-Etienne
9mm Parabellum

The PA-MAS G-1 is actually the Beretta Model 92G manufactured under license at St Etienne. It was originally adopted by the Gendarmerie Nationale (hence the letter G), then by the French Air Force, and its adoption by the French Army should be announced by the time this book is in print.

The PA-MAS G-1 is similar to the Beretta 92F model but has a decocking lever only, instead of the more usual safety/decocking combination. When the decocking lever has been pressed and the hammer lowered, releasing the lever

allows it to spring back to the normal position, and the pistol can be fired by simply pulling through on the trigger.
Length: 8.54n (217mm). **Weight unloaded:** 2lb 2oz (960g). **Barrel:** 4.92in (125mm), 4 grooves, right-hand twist. **Magazine:** 15-round detachable box. **Muzzle velocity:** c.1138 ft/sec (347 m/sec).

• MAB PA-15
Manufacture d'Armes Automatiques Bayonne, Bayonne
9mm Parabellum

For reasons which doubtless seemed good at the time, the French ceased production of their Model 1950 pistol in or around 1970. As a result, when more pistols were needed in the latter 1970s they had no in-house capability and had to turn to a commercial manufacturer.

The Manufacture d'Armes Bayonne had manufactured pistols since 1921, principally under the name 'Unique', and the PA-15 was essentially a militarized version of their commercial 'Unique Modéle R Para'. In its original form the Modéle R fired the 7.65mm ACP cartridge, and upgrading it to handle 9mm Parabellum demanded some form of breech locking. In order to make as few manufacturing changes as possible it was decided to adopt a form of delayed blowback operation similar to that employed in the Savage pistol. The barrel is mounted in the frame so as to be free to rotate but not recoil; a cam on the barrel engages in a curved track in the slide. Recoil of the slide attempts to rotate the barrel by forcing the cam to conform to the curved track, but this is resisted by the initial gas pressure and the rotational torque of the bullet in the rifling. This is sufficient to hold the breech closed until the bullet is clear of the muzzle and

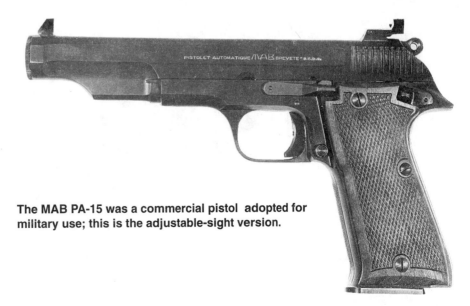

The MAB PA-15 was a commercial pistol adopted for military use; this is the adjustable-sight version.

the breech pressure has dropped, where-upon the barrel is free to rotate and the slide can move back in the usual manner.

The standard PA-15 carries a 15-shot magazine in the butt; a small number of a variant known as the **PA-8** exist, using an 8-shot magazine. This is, in fact, the commercial 'R Para' with military acceptance marks. A Modéle **PAPF-1** also exists; this has the barrel and slide lengthened and is fitted with an adjustable rear sight. It is used solely as a target pistol.

The Manufacture d'Armes de Bay-onne went out of business in the late 1980s and manufacture of the pistol ceased. It has been reported that the pis-tol, or a copy, was to be put into produc-tion in former Yugoslavia in 1991, but it is uncertain whether any serious produc-tion ever got under way.

Length: 8.0in (203mm). **Weight unloaded:** 2lb 6oz (1070g). **Barrel:** 4.6in (117mm), 4 grooves, right-hand twist. **Magazine:** 15-round detachable box. **Muzzle velocity:** c.1150 ft/sec (350 m/sec).

• Manurhin MR 73 Revolver
Manufacture de Machines du Haut-Rhin (Manurhin), Mulhouse
357 Magnum, 38 Special. (9mm Parabellum with special cylinder)

The MR 73 is a revolver which is intended to fulfill the requirements of a wide range of users. With a long target barrel it is a precision pistol for competi-tive shooting, with the shorter barrels it becomes a military and police weapon. The design is carefully thought out and incorporates some interesting features, particularly in regard to safety and trig-ger operation. In general terms the revolver is a solid-frame, swing-out cylin-der, double action type. The outer con-tours are smoothed and the front sight is

The German M1879 Trooper's revolver was a pecu-liarly old-fashioned weapon, but it was robust.

sloped to allow for easy drawing from a pocket or holster. The barrel is cold-ham-mered—unusual in a pistol. There is the usual flat mainspring operating the ham-mer, but the trigger is controlled by a separate flat spring which is strong enough to overcome the first one. This second spring works on a roller to decrease friction and its main purpose is to move the trigger forward after firing and to move the safety block up to pre-vent the hammer reaching the primer of the cartridge. The roller acts on this spring in such a way as to produce a prac-tically constant pressure, so giving a steady pull on the trigger; this valuable asset was protected by patents. By changing the cylinder, rimless 9mm ammunition can be loaded, the change taking no more than a minute or two.

High quality materials were used throughout the manufacture of this pistol resulting in an excellent but somewhat expensive weapon. It undoubtedly was attractive to police and private users but it failed to gain any significant military acceptance.

Length: (2.5in barrel); 7.67in (195mm). **Weight unloaded:** 1lb 15oz (880g). **Barrel:** 2.50in (63.5mm), 6 grooves, right-hand twist. **Magazine:** 6-round cylinder. **Muzzle velocity:** variable, according to caliber.

GERMANY (PRE-1945)

• Reichs-Commissions-Revolver, Modell 1879 and Modell 1883
Various manufacturers, including V. C. Schilling & Cie, Spangenberg & Sauer, C. G. Haenel & Cie (all of Suhl), Gebrüder Mauser & Cie, Oberndorf-am-Neckar, and Königlich Gewehrfabrik Erfurt.
10.6x25R German Ordnance

These revolvers were the designs approved by the various commissions which were charged in the late 1870s with providing new weapons for the German Army. In view of the number of advanced revolver designs appearing at that time the Reichs-revolver was remarkably con-servative, reflecting the viewpoint of most contemporary military authorities.

The two models differed only in bar-rel length, the M79 (also known as the 'Trooper' or 'Cavalry' model) having a 7-inch (178mm) barrel and the M83 (also known as the 'Officer' or 'Infantry' model) having a 5-inch (127mm) barrel. Apart from that, they were solid-frame sin-gle-action non-ejecting six-shot revolvers of robust construction. Loading was done through a gate on the right side, and the hammer could be pulled to half-cock to release the cylinder. Unloading—or eject-ing spent cases—was done by withdraw-ing the cylinder axis-pin and removing the cylinder, then using the axis-pin or a suitable rod to punch out the cases.

Although superseded in 1908 by the Parabellum, numbers of these weapons remained in second-line service through-out World War I and sufficient remained in private hands to make it worth one manufacturer's while to market commer-cial 10.6mm ammunition until 1939.

(Modell 1879)
Length: 12.20in (310mm). **Weight unloaded:** 2lb 5oz (1040g). **Barrel:** 7.20in (183mm), 6 grooves, right-hand twist. **Magazine:** 6-round cylinder. **Muzzle velocity:** c.670 ft/sec (205 m/sec).

Manurhin MR73, a popular French police pistol.

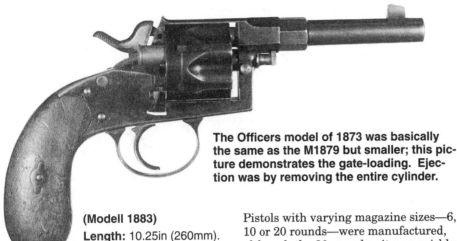

The Officers model of 1873 was basically the same as the M1879 but smaller; this picture demonstrates the gate-loading. Ejection was by removing the entire cylinder.

(Modell 1883)

Length: 10.25in (260mm). **Weight unloaded:** 2lb 1oz (940g). **Barrel:** 4.96in (126mm), 6 grooves, right-hand twist. **Magazine:** 6-round cylinder. **Muzzle velocity:** c.640 ft/sec (195 m/sec).

• Mauser-Selbstladepistole Construction 96 (c/96)

Waffenfabrik Mauser AG, Oberndorf-am-Neckar

7.63x25mm Mauser

The Mauser-Selbstladepistole c/96 was apparently invented by the three Federle brothers, employees of the Mauserwerke, probably in 1894, and patented in 1895 in the name of Peter-Paul Mauser. The prototype, chambered for the 7.65mm Borchardt round with a 10-round magazine and a spur hammer, was completed in the first months of 1895 and first fired on 15 March. The rest of 1895 was spent testing the prototypes in conditions of the utmost secrecy until in January 1896 Mauser announced that his company was ready to begin the manufacture of 'pre-production' pistols, about 110 of which were manufactured in nine months—including guns chambered for the 7.65mm Borchardt cartridge—with magazines of 6, 10 and 20 rounds, and a very small number of 6mm specimens with 10-round magazines. (Apart from its design number—DWM 414—nothing is known of this mysterious 6mm cartridge.) The magazines, all of which were integral with the frame, were loaded through the top of the action from chargers.

True production began in October of 1896, when the design was finalized around the 7.63mm Mauser cartridge which was in reality no more than a 7.65mm Borchardt in which the charge was increased and the bullet more securely anchored, for it had been found that the recoil of the c/96 was extremely hard on the ammunition held in the magazine and tended to loosen the bullets.

Pistols with varying magazine sizes—6, 10 or 20 rounds—were manufactured, although the 20-round unit was quickly discontinued as being too cumbersome.

At the beginning of 1897 a mechanical change was made when a supplementary locking lug was added to the underside of the bolt and several minor modifications were made to the mechanism, particularly in the method of supporting and guiding the mainspring housing.

The C96 failed to attract the favorable attention of the German military authorities, and with the emergence of the Parabellum, Mauser's chances receded. Pistols were, however, supplied to the Italian Navy and to Turkey and Russia. Almost all c/96 pistols were capable of being fitted to a hollowed wooden shoulder stock/holster, with which they were often supplied.

Length: 12.25in (312mm). **Weight unloaded:** 2lb 12oz (1250g). **Barrel:** 5.50in (139mm), 6 grooves, right-hand twist (4 grooves in early weapons numbered below c.100000). **Magazine:** 6-, 10- or 20-round integral box. **Muzzle velocity:** c.1450 ft/sec (442 m/sec).

• Pistol c/96 mit Sicherung c/02.

In 1902, Mauser attempted to improve the c/96 by patenting a revised form of safety device - the so-called *'gelenksicherung'* or 'hammer safety'- which consisted of a lever on the left side of the hammer. This safety lever could be used for single-hand cocking, which was a virtual

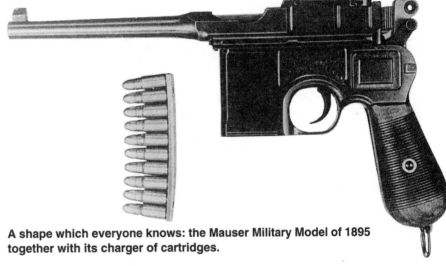

A shape which everyone knows: the Mauser Military Model of 1895 together with its charger of cartridges.

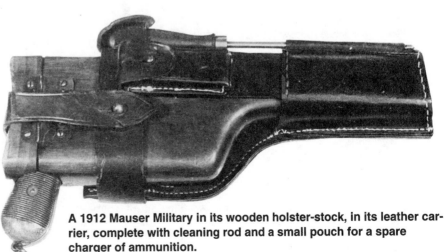

A 1912 Mauser Military in its wooden holster-stock, in its leather carrier, complete with cleaning rod and a small pouch for a spare charger of ammunition.

impossibility with the standard pistol hammer (designed for cocking against a horseman's saddle), and although the hammer could still be dropped in the 'safe' position the lever blocked the hammer nose from the striker.

• Pistol c/96 mit kurzer Anszieher, c/1905

In 1905 Mauser modified the c/96 by the addition of a shorter extractor, a small hammer which no longer obscured the rear sight when resting on the striker, and a two-lug firing pin retainer. It must be noted that transitional models exist with similar features, but still possessing the old long extractor.

• Pistol c/96 mit Sicherung neuer Art, c/1912

This 'new type safety'—'*Sicherung neuer Art*'—could only be applied when the hammer was manually retracted from contact with the sear; those pistols with the older pattern of safety device could have it applied regardless of the position of the hammer. Pistols fitted with this safety had the entwined letters 'NS' on their rear surface.

The 'Bolo Mauser' was simply a standard Mauser with a short barrel to comply with the Versailles treaty, and sold to Russia.

• Pistol c/96, 9mm Parabellum, 1915

During World War I the German authorities soon realized that they were in desperate need of small arms of every description, and that it would be most useful if the c/96 pistol could be made available in 9mm Parabellum. As a result of investigations made in mid-1915 by the Gewehr-Prüfungs-Commission, Mauser began the production of 150,000 c/96 pistols in the desired caliber; the weapons were marked on the grips with a large red-stained figure '9', although there are some in existence with black staining. Some guns first chambered for Mauser's 9mm Export cartridge—which had a longer case than the 9mm Parabellum—are thought to have been rebarreled for the latter caliber.

• 'Bolo-Model'

The so-called 'Bolo' pistols were made in c.1920 and supplied in large numbers to Soviet Russia ('Bolshevik'—hence 'Bolo'). The principal difference was the fitting of a 3.88-inch (99mm) barrel in order to comply with the provisions of the Treaty of Versailles. The term is, however, often misapplied, being given loosely to any short-barreled Mauser of any age.

• Pistol M711

A version of the basic c/96 manufactured c.1930, the 7.63mm M711 was provided with detachable magazines of 10, 20 and 40 rounds. A semi-automatic contemporary of the Schnellfeuerpistolen, it saw no military application.

• Pistol M30 with Universal-Safety

This was a 7.63mm 10-round magazine version of the c/96 strengthened and fitted with a new pattern of safety similar in basic principle to the Sicherung c/02, although it did not permit one-hand cocking. The safety could be applied with one hand, and effectively blocked the striker, which meant that the hammer could be dropped in safety on a loaded chamber. Pistols of this type were supplied to Norway and China.

• Pistol M30 'Schnellfeuer System Nickl'

Sometimes called the M712, this was the first full-automatic machine pistol to

The 1912 Mauser had an improved safety system but was otherwise the same as earlier models.

The 'Red Nine' Mauser, so-called from the red-filled figure 9 carved in the butt to indicate that it is chambered for the 9mm Parabellum cartridge. The two chargers show the difference between the 7.63mm and 9mm ammunition.

be manufactured by Mauser, to the patents of Josef Nickl. One thousand pistols of this type were delivered to China in 1931, where the market was being flooded by similar but cheaper weapons emanating from Spain, and about 100 were supplied to Yugoslavia in 1933-34 as the 'Model S'.

Few of this class of weapon can be considered as anything other than aberrations; without suitable shoulder stocks they climb much too rapidly in full-automatic and are extremely wasteful of ammunition. But of the many designs which have appeared, this Mauser is one of the few worth serious consideration, since its combination of stock, long barrel and high velocity ammunition made it an effective weapon in the hands of an experienced shot. The Nickl design can be recognized by the short, straight, selector lever on the left side of the frame.

• Pistol M36, 'Schnellfeuer System Westinger'

The 1936 pattern, made to the designs of a Mauser engineer named Karl Westinger, was introduced as a belated attempt to win back some of the machine pistol market which had been flooded by Mauser's cheap Spanish competitors. Notwithstanding sales of some Westinger pistols (which were offered in both 7.63mm Mauser and 9mm Parabellum calibres) to China, the war intervened before the pistol had time to become a commercial success, and Mauser's remaining stock were taken into use by the German Army. This Westinger pattern is recognizable by the diamond-shaped selector switch on the left side of the frame.

• Schwarzlose Model 1898
A- W. Schwarzlose GmbH Berlin
7.65x25mm Borchardt

Andreas Schwarzlose was an ingenious and versatile designer who patented a wide variety of weapons in the period 1892 to 1912. This pistol was the

The Schwarzlose 'Standart' of 1898, an ingenious, elegant, but unsuccessful design.

first of his many designs to be produced in any quantity, but unfortunately it arrived on the market shortly after the Mauser c/96, and less than 1,000 were actually made. It suffered by comparison with extant weapons and was consequently not commercially successful. The remaining stocks were apparently sold by an enterprising Berlin salesman to the Russian revolutionary movement of 1905, but the shipment was intercepted by the Russian authorities; the pistols were then distributed to the frontier police and similar official bodies and hence specimens of this pistol were more common in Russia than elsewhere.

The locking system is a turning bolt opened by a stud in a fixed guide ring riding in a helical groove in the bolt. This rotates and unlocks the bolt during recoil, after which the bolt reciprocates in the normal way, ejecting on the rearward stroke and reloading on its return. The Schwarzlose also ranks among the first designs to incorporate a hold-open device. The pistol is well-balanced and fits the hand excellently, but the mechanism was complicated and turned out to be unreliable unless maintained in a perfect condition. A further complication was that the cartridge was dimensionally similar to, but weaker than, the 7.63mm Mauser cartridge, and in consequence users who inadvertently loaded the Mauser cartridge usually regretted it.

Length: 10.75in (273mm). **Weight unloaded:** 2lb 1oz (940g). **Barrel:** 6.43in (163mm), 4 grooves, right-hand twist.

Magazine: 7-round detachable box. **Muzzle velocity:** c.1400 ft/sec (426 m/sec).

• Parabellum Pistols, 1898-1945
Deutsche Waffen-und-Munitions-fabrik, Berlin (originally)
7.65 Parabellum, 9mm Parabellum

The history and development of the Parabellum pistol is an involved affair itself the subject of several specialized studies—and much of it is only of marginal interest to these pages. As a result only essential detail is included here.

The Parabellum was a direct descendant of the Borchardt pistol, designed in 1893 by Hugo Borchardt and placed on the market in the following year by Ludwig Loewe & Cie of Berlin. For its time, this strange-looking gun was a revelation, but within three years, improved pistols began to appear (notably the Mauser c/96) and sales of the Borchardt rapidly declined until, in c.1898-9, production was discontinued.

There were, however, sufficient good features of the M93 to warrant continued development, although Hugo Borchardt had become disenchanted with the design (or perhaps he thought it to be incapable of further improvement). In any event, the succeeding designs were the work of Georg Luger, of the newly-formed Deutsche Waffen-und-Munitionsfabrik. Luger's first patents were granted in 1898 and covered a transitional pistol representing a halfway stage between the Borchardt and the perfected Parabellum, which appeared in 1900 when it was adopted by the Swiss as the 'Parabellum-Pistol, System Borchardt-Luger, Model 1900'.

The variations which followed upon the success of the 1900 pattern pistol—and there were many—made use of the same operating principle but with minor alterations. Luger was a champion of recoil operation, and his pistol made use of the rearward-moving barrel to break open a toggle-lock by moving the center of the pivot above the line of the bore. This permitted the lock to continue to

The Mauser 712 or 'Schnellfeuerpistole' was a full-automatic selective fire version with a removable magazine.

break upwards as the breechblock moved directly towards the rear of the receiver, compressing the return spring (in a housing at the rear of the handgrip) as it did so. The compressed spring then returned the breechblock to its position behind the barrel and as the block returned so the entire barrel-receiver assembly—which was capable of about 6mm free movement before being brought to rest—returned to the firing position, locking the toggle by ensuring that the center of the pivot lay below the centerline of the bore. The mechanism was well made of the finest materials then available, with the result that in the Parabellum, DWM had one of the finest automatic pistols of its day; there were faults in the design, it is true—especially in the pattern of the trigger mechanism (although it was adequate for military purposes)—and the fact that the gun's feed was a little delicate in operation. This stemmed from the recoil action which, although it was capable of smoothly handling powerful cartridges, returned the mechanism to battery by weak spring pressure; with cartridges loaded to a slightly lower pressure than normal, it was possible for the breechblock to recoil insufficiently far to clear the top cartridge in the magazine, from which position it either returned to an empty chamber or jammed against the base of the cartridge case. Provided the pistol was used with the regulation German Pistole Patrone '08 cartridge, it gave little trouble, but firing cartridges of foreign origin or of different ballistic characteristics could provoke malfunctions. The Parabellum, however, served the German Army (and several others) well through two world wars, and although theoretically replaced after 1941 by the Walther Pistole '38 the earlier weapon was never entirely displaced in German service until 1945.

• 7.65mm Parabellum Model 1900

After 1906 occasionally known as the 'old Model', the 1900 was the original pistol chambered for Luger's 7.65mm bottle-neck cartridge. It was adopted by the Swiss and extensively tested by various other countries. The pistol was fitted with a grip safety at the rear of the handgrip, which had to be depressed by the hand before the gun could fire, and a manual safety lever was placed on the left rear side of the receiver where it could easily be operated by the thumb. The toggle unit was partially cut away at the rear and a toggle-lock was fitted into the right toggle finger-grip. This was a spring catch which engaged in a slot in

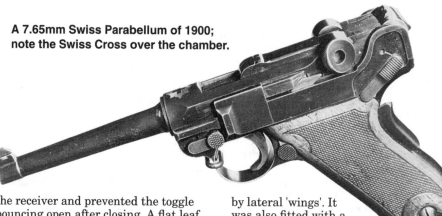

A 7.65mm Swiss Parabellum of 1900; note the Swiss Cross over the chamber.

the receiver and prevented the toggle bouncing open after closing. A flat leaf spring in the rear of the handgrip acted on the breech toggle through an intermediate crank; when the later coil-spring guns were introduced, the leaf-spring guns were christened *'alterer Art'* (old pattern) or *'alterer Modell'* (old model) as a means of distinguishing the two types.

Length: 8.31 in (211mm). **Weight unloaded:** 1lb 14oz (840g). **Barrel:** 4.90in (122mm), 4 grooves, right-hand twist. **Magazine:** 8-round detachable box. **Muzzle velocity:** c.1150 ft/sec (350 m/sec).

• 9mm Parabellum Pistole 1902

The 1902 pattern was the first of Luger's pistols to use his 9mm Parabellum cartridge, which had been developed in 1901 from the 7.65mm type; in a moment of genius, Georg Luger had removed the bottleneck from his cartridge to provide a straight-cased 9mm round, whose heavier bullet went some way to allay the objections of the authorities who were not convinced that the 7.65mm Parabellum bullet had sufficient stopping power. Luger's solution also had the important advantage of using the same case base size as the 7.65mm round, which meant that, ultimately, most of the existing machine facilities and spare parts could be used in the modified guns. Although few 9mm guns—which are usually known as the 'M'02'—were produced, the pattern provided adequate development for the later P'08. The gun was mechanically similar to the 1900 design (from which it could be readily distinguished by the heavier barrel) and had a cut-away toggle, a toggle-lock and a leaf recoil spring.

• 9mm Parabellum Marine Model 1904

The M04 was the first Parabellum to be adopted by a branch of the German armed forces, being taken into service by the Imperial Navy. The original pistol was in 9mm caliber with a longer barrel than the standard army P'08 of later years, and it could be quickly recognized by the two-position rear sight protected

by lateral 'wings'. It was also fitted with a lug at the bottom of the backstrap to which a shoulder-stock could be attached to increase accuracy at longer ranges. Mechanically, the M04 was an interesting transitional variety which represented a midstage between the *'alterer Modell'* and the *'neuer Modell'* as it married the leaf recoil spring and the toggle-lock with a new type of toggle finger grip which, flat sided, was only partially knurled about its circumference; the opportunity was also taken to add a combined extractor/loaded chamber indicator to the breechblock. This, which later appeared as a feature of the 'new' models, showed the word 'GELADEN' when a round had been chambered. Very few M04 pistols seem to have survived.

Length: 10.50in (267mm). **Weight unloaded:** 2lb 2oz (960g). **Barrel:** 6.00in (152mm), 4 grooves, right-hand twist. **Magazine:** 8-round detachable box. **Muzzle velocity:** c.1200 ft/sec (366 m/sec).

• 9mm Parabellum Marine Pistol Model 1904, system of 1906

Although still known to the German navy as the M'04, a modified version of the navy pistol was introduced in 1906; in accordance with the new patterns of the same year, the leaf recoil spring was eliminated in favor of a coil-spring and the toggle-lock was discarded.

• 9mm Parabellum Marine Pistole Model 1904, system of 1908

The 1908 variation of the M'04 was the navy's equivalent of the army P'08, from which it differed only in the length of the barrel and in the sighting arrangements.

• 7.65mm and 9mm Parabellum Pistols, *'neuer Art'*, 1906

The patterns of 1906 replaced the leaf recoil spring with one of coil type and eliminated the toggle-lock device which on previous models had appeared on the right toggle finger-grip. Experience had shown that since the toggle locked itself over-center, the additional lock was

The 1906 Parabellum looks similar to its predecessors but has the coil mainspring inside the butt instead of the earlier leaf spring.

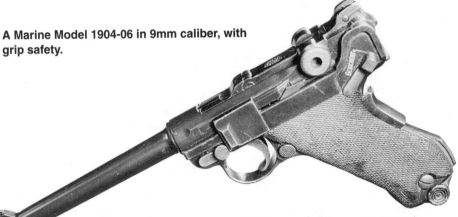

A Marine Model 1904-06 in 9mm caliber, with grip safety.

superfluous. All guns produced to the modified system were filled with the patented extractor/loaded chamber indicator which had first appeared on the naval pistol of 1904, and all made use of the grip safety. Two basic types were offered in this new range: the 7.65mm pistol was really the pattern of 1900, modified by the addition of the new spring and toggle unit, and the 9mm version was a revision of the gun of 1902.

• 9mm Parabellum Pistole Model 1908 (P'08)

The model of 1908, usually known simply as the P'08 (from the German Army's contraction of 'Pistole '08'), is undoubtedly the most famous of all the Luger-designed pistols. It was based on the 9mm Pistole 'neuer Art' of two years previous, with the elimination of the grip safety mechanism and a revision of the manual safety catch which, as a result, moved downwards (instead of upwards) to the 'safe' position, at which point an extension on the lever rose to lock the sear. The original production came from Deutsche Waffen-und-Munitionsfabriken, but in 1914, guns began to appear from the Königlich Gewehrfabrik Erfurt—the government arsenal at Erfurt in Thuringia. At about the same time, the opportunity was taken of adding a shoulder-stock lug to the butt and a hold-open device to the magazine follower.

The P'08 had a long production life, surviving as it did the provisions of the Treaty of Versailles; apart from various post-war commercial production emanating from such firms as Simson & Cie of Suhl, who had acquired the Erfurt arse-

nal tools, production arrangements passed in 1928 to Mauser-Werke AG of Oberndorf, although weapons continued to be produced under the DWM trademark until 1933-4—possibly for reasons of secrecy. P08 pistols were also manufactured in Suhl by Heinrich Krieghoff Waffenwerk, who purchased the tooling from Simson when the latter firm folded in 1934, and produced 10,000 P'08 for the German Air Force.

Over 6,000 Parabellum pistols were also assembled in 1920-21 by the British firm Vickers-Armstrong & Co Ltd, at Crayford; these were supplied as parts by DWM, assembled and finished by Vickers, and then shipped to Holland for the Netherlands East Indies Army. This roundabout procedure was due to the restrictions of the Versailles Treaty. The

Swiss arsenal at Bern also made many for the Swiss Army, and some were also produced for commercial sale.

By 1936, it was realized that the days of the P08 were almost over and in the following year possible replacements appeared in the form of the Mauser HSv (of which all too little is known), and the Walther Armee Pistole and Heeres Pistole. It was eventually decided that the Walther Heeres Pistole should be adopted as the Pistole 38, and that the Pistole '08 would be gradually replaced.

In July of 1941, Mauser-Werke began production of the P38, and in June of the following year they manufactured the last P08 pistols, the last batch of which were accepted by the Wehrmacht in November. The P08 nevertheless remained in widespread service until the war's end, as production of the P38 never reached a quantity which would completely supplant it.

Length: 8.75in (223mm). **Weight unloaded:** 1lb 15oz (970g). **Barrel:** 4.00in (102mm), 6 grooves, right-hand twist. **Magazine:** 8-round detachable box. **Muzzle velocity:** c.1150 ft/sec (350 m/sec).

The definitive Luger—the German Army's Pistole '08 served from 1908 to 1945.

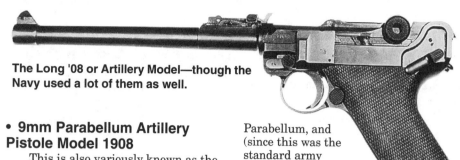

The Long '08 or Artillery Model—though the Navy used a lot of them as well.

• 9mm Parabellum Artillery Pistole Model 1908

This is also variously known as the 'Artillery Model 1914', the 'Model 1917' and the 'Long '08'. Development began in 1911 and the weapon was intended to arm artillerymen, airmen and some fortress troops. Production began in February 1914 and orders for 144,000 were placed with DWM and Erfurt, though there is no record of exactly how many were actually produced. The Artillery Model 1908 was a standard Pistole '08 with a 190mm (7.5in) barrel carrying a tangent-leaf rear sight. The fitting of this sight demanded that a lateral step had to be cut into the barrel ring at the front of the frame, and this modification was applied to all frames made in Erfurt, so that it also appears on Erfurt Pistole '08 production of the period. The sight was graduated, rather optimistically, to 800 meters range. A drum or 'snail' magazine which held 32 rounds was introduced in 1917, though the standard box magazine could still be used. The provision of a flat board type of shoulder stock which could be fitted to the butt converted the weapon to a light carbine.

In service, the magazines proved troublesome and unwieldy, but they continued in use until the Armistice and were also used on the Bergmann MP18 submachine guns. It was found that the original conical flat-nosed bullet cartridges were ill-suited to the helical magazine and showed a tendency to jam. At more or less the same time there was some doubt about the legality of the flat-nosed bullet *vis-à-vis* the Hague Convention, and so a round-nosed bullet was developed to counter these troubles; this bullet then became the military standard.

Length: 12.24in (311mm). **Weight unloaded:** 2lb 5oz (1050g). **Barrel:** 7.50in (190mm), 6 grooves, right-hand twist. **Magazine:** 8-round detachable box or 32-round helical 'snail' magazine. **Muzzle velocity:** c.1250 ft/sec (38l m/sec).

• Dreyse 'Heeres-Selbstlade-Pistole'

Rheinische Metallwaaren. und Maschinenfabrik AG, Sömmerda
9mm Parabellum

The Dreyse was one of the first commercial pistols to be produced in 9mm Parabellum, and (since this was the standard army round) small numbers were used by officers and soldiers alike during World War I, although it was never accepted as an official weapon and no more than 1,850 were actually produced. The gun was also employed by police and other para-military organizations in Germany.

It resembles the earlier 7.65mm Dreyse design in appearance, but has an unusual feature in that the recoil spring can be disconnected for cocking. This is necessary since the pistol is of the blowback type; to handle the powerful 9mm cartridge the recoil spring has to be extremely strong, making cocking in the normal way—pulling the slide back against the spring—very difficult. To cock the Dreyse, the knurled grips which form the rear sight are gripped and pulled up to unlock the top rib, which disconnects the slide from the recoil spring and allows the slide to be pulled back and pushed forward, chambering a cartridge and cocking the striker. With the breech closed, the rib is replaced, re-engaging the recoil spring, and the gun is ready to be fired.

Another unusual feature of design is that the striker spring is not fully compressed when the gun is cocked, additional pressure being applied when the trigger is pulled. Many 9mm Dreyse pistols found today have the locking lugs somewhat worn, and firing the pistol is a trifle hazardous, since the rib can jump open and the slide can then recoil violently, with unfortunate results to the pistol and, in extreme cases, to the firer.

Length: 8.12in (206mm). **Weight unloaded:** 2lb 5oz (1050g). **Barrel:** 5.00in (126mm), 6 grooves, right-hand twist. **Magazine:** 8-round detachable box. **Muzzle velocity:** c.1200 ft/sec (366 m/sec).

• Langenhan 'Army Pistol' (also known as the 'FL Selbstladepistole)

Fritz Langenhan & Cie, Suhl
7.65x17SR Browning (32 ACP)

Originally designed as a commercial weapon, this pistol was adopted by the German Army during World War I as a substitute standard weapon and the entire production went into military service. It is a blowback weapon, accurate and handy to use but of peculiar construction. The breechblock is a separate unit held in the slide by a stirrup-lock which forms the rear sight, and which is itself retained by a large screw at the rear of the block. The frame is cut away on the right side so that the breechblock is only supported on the left. Provided that the mating surfaces are unworn, and the lock screw is secure, the pistol works well, but once wear takes place the lockscrew and stirrup tend to loosen during firing and there is a considerable danger that, after twenty or thirty rounds, the breechblock might be blown into the firer's face.

The Dreyse was an ingenious attempt to make a blowback pistol in 9mm Parabellum caliber; but the army didn't like it.

The Langenhan 'Armee Pistole' as a 7.65mm emergency issue, with a somewhat unsafe mechanism.

Length: 6.60in (168mm). **Weight unloaded:** 1lb 7oz (650g). **Barrel:** 4.15in (105mm), 4 grooves, right-hand twist. **Magazine:** 8-round detachable box. **Muzzle velocity:** c.925 ft/sec (281 m/sec).

• Sauer 'Behörden Model'
J P Sauer & Sohn, Suhl
7.65x17SR Browning (32 ACP)

This blowback pistol, used by military and civil police in Germany in the 1930s and 1940s, is sometimes referred to as the *'Behörden'* ('Authorities') model. It is generally the same as the 1913 pattern (the so-called 'Old Model') with a more rounded butt and a redesigned trigger mechanism. The breechblock is a separate unit held in the rear of the slide and retained by a large knurled cap. A signal pin is fitted in the breechblock which protrudes through the rear of the cap when a cartridge is chambered, and some models were equipped with a tiny 'grip safety' fitted into the front surface of the trigger.

Length: 5.75in (146mm). **Weight unloaded:** 1lb 6oz (620g). **Barrel:** 3.03in (77mm), 6 grooves, right-hand twist. **Magazine:** 7-round detachable box. **Muzzle velocity:** c.900 ft/sec (274 m/sec).

• Walther Model PP
Carl Walther Waffenfabrik AG, Zella-Mehlis
Various calibers

This pistol, introduced in 1929, was a radical improvement on anything which had gone before. It was the first totally successful self-loading pistol which incorporated a double-action trigger mechanism, and it exhibited a clean and streamlined shape. It was originally produced as a police pistol—hence the initials PP (for Polizei- Pistole)—for holster use by uniformed officers, and it was later employed by the German services in large numbers. Originally developed in 7.65mm Browning caliber, models were also made in 22 Long Rifle, 6.35mm ACP (rare) and 9mm Short chambering, all of which are almost identical in external appearance. An uncomplicated blowback weapon, an interesting innovation found in the centerfire models was the provision of a signal pin which floated in the slide and pressed on the rim of the chambered round so that the end of the pin protruded just above the hammer and gave a visual and tactile indication that the weapon was loaded. Another unusual feature was the safety catch on the slide which, when applied, moved the firing pin into a safe position and then dropped the hammer, so that all that was necessary to fire was a long pull on the trigger to raise and release the hammer.

After World War II, this pistol was copied, with or without permission, in several countries. It was manufactured commercially, under license, by Manurhin of France until 1954, when Walther once more entered the firearms business, and it has been in continuous manufacture ever since.

In c.1931-3, Walther produced an enlarged blowback version of the PP in 9mm Parabellum for possible military adoption, which they called the MP (Military Pistol); it was not successful, the army being reluctant to adopt a blowback weapon.

Length: 6.38in (162mm). **Weight unloaded:** 1lb 9oz (710g). **Barrel:** 3.35in (85mm), 6 grooves, right- hand twist. **Magazine:** 8-round detachable box. **Muzzle velocity:** c.950 ft/sec (289 m/sec).

• Walther Model PPK
Carl Walther Waffenfabrik AG, Zelia-Mehlis
Various calibers

The Walther PPK is a smaller edition of the PP, intended to be issued to plain clothes police (Pistole, Polizei-Kriminale) and hence easily concealed. In mechanism and construction it is almost identical with the PP, the only differences lying in the dimensions and construction of the butt. On the PP, the butt frame is forged to shape, with two separate side-pieces of plastic. On the PPK, the frame forging is a simple rectangle and the plastic grip is a one-piece wrap-around component which produces the final shape. Like the Model PP, the PPK can be found in 22 Long Rifle, 6.35mm, 7.65mm and 9mm Short calibers, although the 7.65mm is by far the

The Sauer 'Berhorden Model' was widely used by German police in the 1930s.

The Walther Brothers: Top, the PP pistol, below the PPK.

The Walther PP and PPK with grips removed to show the difference in frame construction.

The Mauser 7.65mm M1934, heavier and more bulky than most of the competition, was more pleasant to fire.

The Walther Model 6 was simply an enlarged version of one of their commercial blowback pistols, firing the 9mm Parabellum cartridge. It was not popular.

most common and only a few 6.35mm pistols seem to have been made.

Length: 5.83in (148mm). **Weight unloaded:** 1lb 5oz (590g). **Barrel:** 3.15in (80mm), 6 grooves, right-hand twist. **Magazine:** 7-round detachable box. **Muzzle Velocity:** c.950 ft/sec (289 m/sec).

• Walther Model 6
Carl Walther Waffenfabrik AG, Zella-Mehlis
9x19mm Parabellum

The firm of Carl Walther had been manufacturing automatic pistols since 1908 and, in response to a 1915 request from the German Army, they produced an enlarged version of their commercial Model 4 as a military weapon. The resulting Model 6 is a blowback weapon, and since the caliber is 9mm Parabellum it leads to the use of a heavy slide and a very strong recoil spring to withstand the heavier forces. Very few of these pistols were made and manufacture was discontinued in 1917.

Length: 8.25in (210mm). **Weight unloaded:** 2lb 2oz (960g). **Barrel:** 4.75in (121mm). 4 grooves, right-hand twist. **Magazine:** 8-round detachable box. **Muzzle velocity:** c.1100 ft/sec (335 m/sec).

• Mauser Model 1934
Mauser-Werke AG, Oberndorf-am-Neckar
7.65x17SR Browning

The Model 34, known sometimes as the *'Mauser-Pistole alterer Art'* to distinguish it from the HSc, was a cleaned-up version of a design which had first appeared in 1910. Although looking rather more of a nineteenth-century product than most of its contemporaries, it was a sound pistol, immaculately finished, and it shoots well. Of the blowback variety, the assembly is such that the barrel can be removed for cleaning without disturbing the rest of the weapon. A typical example of Mauser craftsmanship is the butt grip, a one-piece wrap-around unit usually carved from wood (though sometimes of hard rubber) and fitted with the utmost precision. This pistol was originally produced as a commercial weapon, with the possibility of adoption by various European police forces. In this application it was successful but on the outbreak of war in 1939 it was taken into military service as a substitute standard pistol and largely issued to the German navy and air force; many of the examples found today bear the markings of one or other of these services.

Length: 6.25in (159mm). **Weight unloaded:** 1lb 5oz (600g). **Barrel:** 3.40in (87mm); 6 grooves, right-hand twist. **Magazine:** 8-round detachable box. **Muzzle velocity:** c.975 ft/sec (297 m/sec).

• Beholla
Becker & Hollander, Suhl (as Beholla).
Stendawerke GmbH, Suhl (as Stenda)
Gering & Co, Arnstadt (as Leonhardt).
August Menz, Suhl (As Menta)
7.65x17SR Browning (32 ACP)

This simple and sturdy blowback pistol was designed just prior to World War I

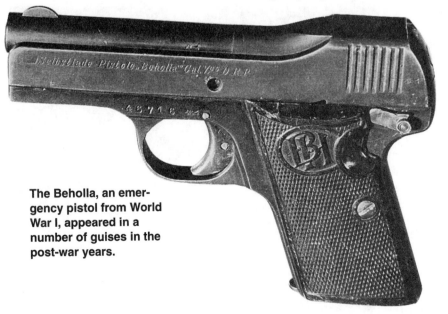

The Beholla, an emergency pistol from World War I, appeared in a number of guises in the post-war years.

by Stenda, with the intention of marketing it commercially. Before these plans got under way, the war began and the German army began demanding supplies of pistols. Since the standard Pistole '08 could not be produced fast enough, the Beholla was selected as a substitute standard weapon for staff officers and others whose pistol had no need to be of the same heavy caliber as the combat pattern. Manufacture was contracted to a number of companies and the design will be found bearing the names 'Beholla', 'Menta', 'Stenda' or 'Leonhardt', depending upon the manufacturer.

The design is quite simple, leading to rapid manufacture and a trouble-free life, but it is remarkable in that the gun cannot be dismantled without using a vise and a tool kit. A hole in the slide gives access to a locking pin which has to be driven out with a drift before dismantling can begin. With this removed, the slide is locked back and the barrel driven from its mounting with a hammer, after which the rest of the weapon can be stripped.

Manufacture for military use ceased in 1918, but Menz and Stendawerke produced it commercially from 1919 to 1926, while the Gering company acquired a host of Beholla spares and assembled them for sale as the 'Leonhardt' in the same period. So many thousands were made that they are still relatively common.

Length: 5.50in (140mm). **Weight unloaded:** 1lb 6oz (640g). **Barrel:** 2.88in (73mm), 6 grooves, right-hand twist. **Magazine:** 7-round detachable box. **Muzzle velocity:** c.900 ft/sec (274 m/sec).

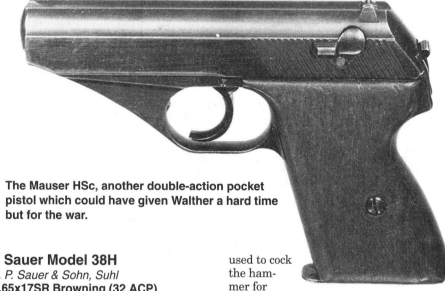

The Mauser HSc, another double-action pocket pistol which could have given Walther a hard time but for the war.

• Sauer Model 38H
J. P. Sauer & Sohn, Suhl
7.65x17SR Browning (32 ACP)

This is a vastly different weapon from anything which had previously come from Sauer, and it is undoubtedly among the best of its kind. But for World War II it might well have been a considerable commercial success, although almost the entire production was taken over by the army and Luftwaffe and manufacture ended with the close of the war.

The Model 38H is a blowback pistol of conventional pattern, but of superior design and heavier than most of its contemporaries, giving it good shooting qualities. It has a double-action trigger mechanism plus an unusual thumb-operated catch just behind the trigger which will release the internal hammer under control and allow it to be safely lowered on a loaded chamber. This lever can also be used to cock the hammer for deliberate single-action fire. When the hammer is down, a straight pull on the trigger will cock and fire if speed is more important than accuracy. A manual safety (omitted on specimens produced in 1944-5) was also provided.

Length: 6.75in (171mm). **Weight unloaded:** 1 lb 9oz (700g). **Barrel:** 3.27in (83mm), 4 grooves, right- hand twist. **Magazine:** 8-round detachable box. **Muzzle velocity:** c.900 ft/sec (274 m/sec).

• Mauser Model HSc
Mauser-Werke AG, Oberndorf-am-Neckar
7.65x17SR Browning (32 ACP)

The Mauser HSc was introduced in c. 1938-9 as a commercial venture (having been preceded by three experimental designs HS, HSa and HSb of 1935-7) and represented a considerable advance in design. It is a double-action blowback pistol and of very streamlined and clean appearance. The hammer is concealed within the slide, leaving only a small lip protruding sufficiently to allow it to be thumb-cocked, and the safety catch on the slide is unusual in that it lifts the entire firing pin into its recess and takes it out of alignment with the hammer, a most positive form of safety.

Though produced as a commercial venture, the HSc was taken into service for use by the German Navy and Air force in considerable numbers during World War II. A slightly improved version was commercially produced after the war until the mid-1970s, when Mauser licensed production to an Italian company.

Length: 6.00in (152mm). **Weight unloaded:** 1lb 5oz (600kg). **Barrel:** 3.38in (86mm), 6 grooves, right-hand twist. **Magazine:** 8-round detachable box. **Muzzle velocity:** c.960 ft/sec (29l m/sec).

The Sauer 38H might have given Walther some severe competition but the war prevented commercial sales and all were absorbed by the military.

Replacing the Luger in German service, the Walther P-38 is still in production.

• Pistole 38 (P38), (now known as Pistole 1 (P1)

Carl Walther Waffenfabrik, then of Zella-Mehlis, now of Ulm; and others
9mm Parabellum

In 1936-7, the Walther concern developed their double-action Model AP or *'Armeepistole'* as a potential military weapon. This made use of a locked breech and a concealed hammer, but when submitted to the army for approval the pistol was returned with a request that a visible external hammer be substituted lot the internal one. This was done, and the pistol was formally adopted in 1940 as the Pistole 38, the desire for which was brought about by the army's request for a more modern service pistol, easier and cheaper to manufacture than the old Parabellum-system Pistole 08.

In its early days (1937-8), a number of what later became the P38 were sold under the trade name *'Heerespistole'* or 'HP', some of which were marketed in 7.65mm Parabellum in addition to those in 9mm Parabellum, and experimental guns were also produced in 45 ACP and 38 Super. Military demands soon absorbed Walther's entire production capabilities and so the commercial guns are now rarely encountered.

Breech locking is performed by a wedge-shaped locking block beneath the breech; when the pistol is fired, the barrel and the slide recoil together for a short distance until the locking block is driven down to disengage the slide and halt the barrel. The P38 is fitted with a double-action trigger mechanism —in common with Walther's earlier PP and PPK designs—and a signal pin protrudes from the slide to indicate that the weapon is loaded.

The demands of wartime ultimately proved to be more than Walther could handle, and various other companies were impressed into the manufacture of the P38. Among them were Waffenfabrik Mauser AG of Oberndorf, who assembled complete pistols and whose first deliveries were made in 1941, and Spreewerke GmbH of Berlin. Use was also made by the Germans of the various arms factories in occupied countries, including Fabrique Nationale d'Armes de Guerre (Liege, Belgium), Waffenwerke Brünn (Brno, Czechoslovakia) and Ceska Zbrojovka (Strakonice, Czechoslovakia), to manufacture certain vital components.

Walther resumed production of the P38 in 1957, and it was again adopted as the Bundeswehr's official sidearm under the new designation of Pistole 1. It was also used in Austria for several years, until replaced by the Glock, and in other armies, and a number of pre-war commercial specimens were purchased in 1939 by the Swedish Army with the intention of adopting it as their service 'Pistol m/39', but the outbreak of war put an end to that idea.

Length: 8.38in (213mm). **Weight unloaded:** 2lb 2oz (960g). **Barrel:** 5.00in (127mm), 6 grooves, right-hand twist. **Magazine:** 8-round detachable box. **Muzzle velocity:** c.1150 ft/sec (350 m/sec).

• Volkspistol

Gustloffwerke, Suhl (?)
9x19mm Parabellum

This weapon, which existed only in prototype form, appears to be a late 1944 design intended for cheap production and issue to the Volkssturm towards the end of World War II. The specimen bears no markings and it cannot be attributed to any particular maker with any certainty, but examination points to it having been a development of the Gustloffwerke, since it operates on a delayed blowback system similar to that developed by the Gustloff designer Barnetski for the Volksgewehr rifle. Gas is tapped from the chamber and directed into the slide to delay the breech opening.

Firing the 9mm Parabellum cartridge, the general construction with a fixed barrel and a lift-off slide is reminiscent of Walther design and the magazine is the standard P-38 component. A smooth-bore extension is fitted to the end of the barrel, probably in order to extend the pressure/space curve and ensure that the delayed blowback operation gives sufficient delay.

Length: 11.25in (286mm). **Weight unloaded:** 2lb 2oz (960g). **Barrel:** 5.13in (130mm), 6 grooves, right-hand twist. **Magazine:** 8-round detachable box. **Muzzle velocity:** c.1250 ft/sec (381m/sec).

GERMANY (FEDERAL REPUBLIC)

• Heckler & Koch P9 and P9S

Heckler & Koch GmbH, Oberndorf-am-Neckar
9mm Parabellum, 7.65mm Parabellum

The P9 pistol uses the same roller-locked delayed blowback system of operation as is found in the Heckler & Koch series of rifles. It is hammer-fired, the hammer being concealed within the frame, and a thumb-operated hammer release and recocking lever is provided on the left side of the pistol; by using this lever the hammer can be lowered under control or cocked to allow single action firing. The P9 model offers the single-action mode only, while the P9S has a double-action lock whereby the first

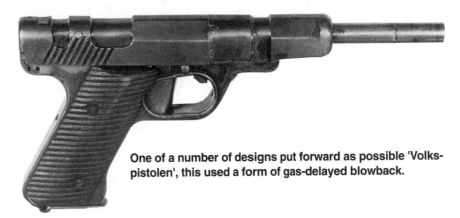

One of a number of designs put forward as possible 'Volkspistolen', this used a form of gas-delayed blowback.

The Heckler & Koch P9 had more success on the commercial market than on the military.

round can be firing by pulling through on the trigger.

The barrel introduced the Heckler & Koch 'polygonal bore' in which the four grooves are merged into the bore diameter so that the resultant cross-section of the bore resembles a flattened circle; this, it was claimed, reduced bullet deformation and improved velocity by offering less resistance to the passage of the bullet.

While the P9 and P9S were basically conceived as military pistols, and were taken into use by the German Border Police and other police forces, it was also offered as a potential competition pistol. Alternative barrel lengths of 5 and 5.5-inch were available, together with muzzle balance weights, adjustable sights, a trigger stop and fine adjustment of the trigger travel.

Length: 7.56in (192mm). **Weight unloaded:** 2lb 0oz (950g). **Barrel:** 4.0in (102mm), 4 grooves, right-hand, polygonal.

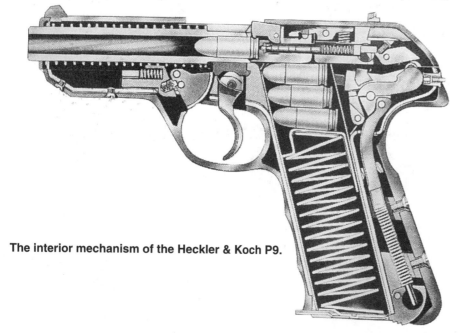

The interior mechanism of the Heckler & Koch P9.

Magazine: 9-round detachable box (7.65mm = 8 rounds). **Muzzle velocity:** c. 1150 ft/sec (350 m/sec) (7.65: 1200/370).

• Heckler & Koch VP-70
Heckler & Koch GmbH, Oberndorf-am-Neckar
9mm Parabellum

This is a blowback pistol with some unusual features. The magazine, in the butt, carries the remarkable number of 18 rounds, and the pistol can only be fired in the self-cocking mode, by means of a striker. Pulling the trigger first cocks and then releases the striker, and the

trigger movement gives a distinct 'first pressure' as the cocking action takes place, where upon further pressure fires the cartridge. This system removes most of the objection to double-action-only systems since it allows a steady aim to be taken and the minimum disturbance of aim at the point of striker release. Since this self-cocking system allows the pistol to be carried loaded quite safely, a safety catch is not normally fitted, but one could be provided (a push-button behind the trigger) if the purchaser so desired.

A holster-stock unit could be fitted; once this was done, a connection with the lockwork allowed the firing of single shots or three-round bursts for each operation of the trigger. This burst facility, another innovative idea, removed the principal objections to the conversion of a pistol into a submachine gun; in such cases only the first few rounds normally have any effect on the target, after which the gun climbs uncontrollably. The Heckler & Koch burst facility ensured that the first few rounds of the burst were the only ones, so that accuracy in automatic fire was guaranteed.

The VP-70 is also of interest in that it used the most modern approach to manufacturing; the receiver is of plastic, with a molded-in barrel support, a construction which is easy to make, resistant to damage, and demanding the minimum maintenance in the field.

The pistol enjoyed commercial sales to African and Asian countries and was adopted by a few military forces, but it was never as successful as the company had hoped and production ceased in the mid-1980s.

Length: 8.03in (204mm). **Weight unloaded:** 1lb 13oz (920g). **Barrel:** 4.57in (116mm). **Magazine:** 18-round detachable box. **Muzzle velocity:** c.1180 ft/sec (360 m/sec).

• Heckler & Koch P7
Heckler & Koch GmbH, Oberndorf-am-Neckar
9mm Parabellum

The P7 family was developed to satisfy a demand from the Federal German Police for a pistol which would be entirely safe to carry loaded but which could be brought into action with the minimum delay. This requirement has been satisfied by the adoption of a cocking lever which forms the front edge of the grip. Assuming the pistol to be empty, with the slide held open after the last shot, on inserting the magazine and squeezing the grip, the slide is released to run forward and chamber a round. Squeezing the grip will now cock the firing pin and pulling the trigger will release the firing pin and fire a shot.

The action will cycle in the normal way and the pistol is recocked on recoil. As soon as the grip is released the firing pin is uncocked and the trigger is no longer connected to the firing pin, so that the pistol is entirely safe. As a result, there is no other safety device fitted. In order to fire the 9mm Parabellum cartridge safely, a gas-actuated delayed blowback system is used. Beneath the breech is a short cylinder connected to the barrel by a gas port. In the front end of this cylinder is a piston connected to the front end of the slide. There is a return spring around the barrel. On firing, some of the propellant gas passes into the cylinder at high pressure and forces against the piston, thus resisting the rearward movement of the piston and the slide. Once the bullet has left the barrel, the trapped gas can leak back into the barrel and the piston can move back freely, allowing the slide to move back and reload the pistol on its forward stroke.

There were four distinct members of the P7 family. The P7M8 and P7Ml3 are as described, differing only in their magazine capacities of 8 and 13 rounds respectively. The P7K3 is a simple blowback pistol chambered for the 9mm Short cartridge; there is no gas delay system employed, and there are conversion kits allowing it to be changed so as to fire 22LR or 7.65mm ACP cartridges. The P7M7 was a heavy pistol chambered for the 45 ACP cartridge; instead of a gas delay there was an oil buffer delay system using similar components but relying upon the piston forcing its way into a cylinder filled with oil to provide the desired delay. This also acted to soak up a good deal of the recoil energy, making the P7M7 a very pleasant pistol to shoot. After reviewing the market, however, the company decided against production of this particular model.

(P7Ml3)

Length: 6.73in (171mm). **Weight unloaded:** 1lb 13oz (800g). **Barrel:** 4.13in (105mm), polygonal rifling, right-hand twist. **Magazine:** 8- or 13-round detachable box. **Muzzle velocity:** c.1150 ft/sec (350 m/sec).

• Heckler & Koch USP

Heckler & Koch Gmbh, Oberndorf-am-Neckar
Various calibers

The USP (Universal Self-loading Pistol) was designed with the intention of incorporating all the various features which military and law enforcement agencies appeared to find vital, and was introduced in 1993. It uses the Browning cam system of breech locking, together with a patented recoil-reduction system which

The plastic-framed VP-70.

The VP 70 with its butt attached, converting it into a three-round burst submachine gun.

The original Heckler & Koch P7, showing the front squeeze-grip which has to be held in to make the pistol work.

A 1993 production USP pistol in 40 S&W caliber.

forms part of the recoil spring and buffer assembly. The frame is of a polymer synthetic material, and metal components are given an anti-corrosion finish.

The pistol was originally designed and produced in 40 Smith & Wesson caliber, after which variants in 45 ACP and 9x19mm Parabellum were produced. All models have a wide variety of options covering the presence or absence of a manual safety catch, of a decocking lever, self-cocking only, double action, and ambidextrous controls.

(40 S&W Model)

Length: 7.64in (194mm). **Weight unloaded:** 1lb 11oz (780g). **Barrel:** 4.25in (108mm), polygonal rifling, right-hand twist. **Magazine:** 13-round detachable box. **Muzzle velocity:** c.935 ft/sec (285 m/sec).

• Heckler & Koch Pistol P-11

Heckler & Koch GmbH, Oberndorf-am-Neckar
7.62x36mm Special

The existence of this pistol had been known since the early 1980s, but it was not until 1997 that it was formally acknowledged and some details made public. It is a special weapon for underwater use by frogmen and similar operators, and it is reputed to be used by the German GSG9, British SBS and US SEALs among others, though none of them will actually confirm this. There is a strong suspicion that the similar Soviet weapon was actually based upon this German design, development of which began in the middle 1970s.

The pistol is actually little more than a butt, trigger and socket-like frame. A pre-loaded five-barrel module is slipped into the socket, thus completing the weapon. The five barrels are loaded with a special cartridge which uses an electric primer activated by a battery in the grip, and is loaded with a slender dart-like finned projectile. Pulling the trigger fires the barrels in sequence, launching the darts. When the last of the five barrels has been fired, the entire empty module is removed and discarded and a fresh module loaded.

Length: 7.87in (200mm). **Weight loaded:** 2lb 10oz (1200g). **Barrel:** not known, but said to be rifled. **Magazine:** 5-round detachable module. **Muzzle velocity:** not known, but lethal range about 15m under water.

• Walther Pistole 5

Carl Walther Waffenfabrik, Ulm-a-d-Donau
9x19mm Parabellum

Introduced in 1979 this is virtually an updated version of the P38, using the same breech locking system and double-action trigger. The safety arrange-

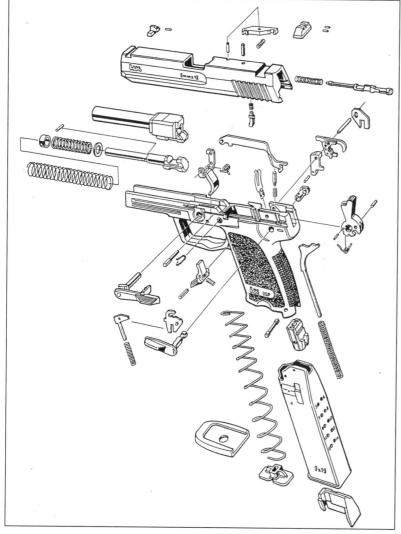

An exploded diagram of the Heckler & Koch USP pistol.

The Walther P5 uses the same mechanism as the P38 but in a more compact form.

ments have, however, been considerably altered. The safety catch is now on the left side of the frame and functions primarily as a decocking lever, providing safety as an adjunct. Safety is provided automatically by the firing pin having a degree of vertical movement within its housing. It is normally pressed down by a spring into a position where its forward movement is prevented by an abutment on the pin contacting a lug on the slide. In this position the exposed head of the firing pin is aligned with a recess in the face of the hammer so that even should the hammer fall, it would not exert any pressure on the firing pin. Only when the trigger is pressed will a trip lever be actuated, first to lift the firing pin up in its housing to disengage it from the lock, and secondly to release the hammer so that it can fall and strike the pin.

The P5 is also produced in 7.65mm Parabellum and 9x21mm IMI chambering to special order. It was adopted by the

Netherlands Police, by several German police forces and the Portuguese and Nigerian Armies among others.

Length: 7.10in (180mm). **Weight unloaded:** 1lb 12oz (795g). **Barrel:** 3.54in (90mm), 6 grooves, right-hand twist. **Magazine:** 8-round detachable box. **Muzzle velocity:** c.1150 ft/sec (350 m/sec).

• Walther P5 Compact
Carl Walther Waffenfabrik, Ulm-a-d-Donau
9x19mm Parabellum

The P5 Compact is basically the same as the P5 described above, except that it is shorter and lighter, of a size and shape making it more convenient for concealment. A new lateral magazine release is fitted, and the frame is of light alloy in order to save weight.

Length: 6.65in (169mm). **Weight unloaded:** 1lb 12oz (780g). **Barrel:** 3.11in (79mm), 6 grooves, right-hand twist. **Magazine:** 8-round detachable box. **Muzzle velocity:** c.1150 ft/sec (350 m/sec).

• Walther P1A1
Carl Walther Waffenfabrik, Ulm-a-d-Donau
9x19mm Parabellum

The P1A1 was announced in 1989 and was an improved version of the P5. The principal change was the adoption of a cross-bolt safety catch upon the slide which was pushed to the left for 'fire' and the right for 'safe'. This operated upon the firing pin; when pushed to safe the bolt forced the firing pin down, aligning it with a recess in the face of the hammer and locking against a lug in the slide. Should the hammer fall, the firing pin would not be struck. Except for being shorter in overall length, the dimensions, etc., of the P1A1 were the same as those of the P5. In spite of this apparent improvement, sales were disappointing and the P1A1 was withdrawn from pro-

The Walther P5 Compact.

The Walther P1A1 tried to improve on the P5; it didn't.

The Walther P88 dropped the Walther wedge lock and adopted the Browning cam system of locking.

unloaded: 2lb 0oz (900g). **Barrel:** 4.02in (102mm), 6 grooves, right-hand twist. **Magazine:** 15-round detachable box. **Muzzle velocity:** c.1150 ft/sec (350 m/sec).

• Walther P88 Compact
Carl Walther Waffenfabrik, Ulm-a-d-Donau
9x19mm Parabellum, 9x21mm IMI

As might be assumed from the name, this is a shorter version of the P88 which, apparently being more popular, replaced the P88 in production in 1996. It uses the same decocking/safety system and the same automatic firing pin safety, and it is also available in 9x21mm IMI chambering for competition shooting.

Length: 7.13in (181mm). **Weight unloaded:** 1lb 13oz (822g). **Barrel:** 3.82in (97mm), 6 grooves, right-hand twist. **Magazine:** 14- or 16-round detachable box. **Muzzle velocity:** c.1214 ft/sec (370 m/sec).

GREAT BRITAIN

• The Webley Revolvers
Webley & Scott Limited, Birmingham
455-caliber British Service

The manufacturer of this pistol design, Webley, underwent three changes of name during the period in which these weapons were made. The company traded under the name Philip Webley & Son until 1897, when the name changed to the Webley & Scott Revolver and Arms Company Limited. In 1906 the concern became Webley & Scott Limited.

Pistol, Webley, Mark 1 (introduced in November 1887)

This revolver was officially described as 'six chambered, top-opening with automatic extraction'. The butt was of the shape commonly called 'bird's head' and had a lanyard ring. The frame was locked by the familiar Webley stirrup lock mechanism.

Length: 10.25in (260mm). **Weight**

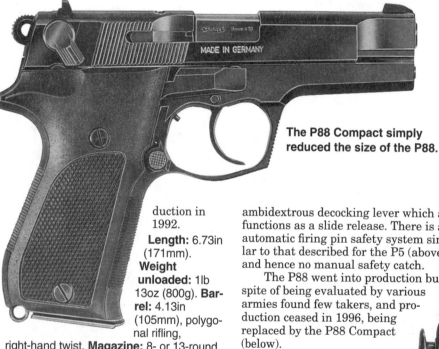

The P88 Compact simply reduced the size of the P88.

duction in 1992.
Length: 6.73in (171mm). **Weight unloaded:** 1lb 13oz (800g). **Barrel:** 4.13in (105mm), polygonal rifling, right-hand twist. **Magazine:** 8- or 13-round detachable box. **Muzzle velocity:** c.1150 ft/sec (350 m/sec).

• Walther P88
Carl Walther Waffenfabrik, Ulm-a-d-Donau
9x19mm Parabellum

This appeared in 1988 and is a considerable departure from previous Walther practice, abandoning the wedge lock and adopting the familiar Colt/Browning dropping barrel controlled by a cam and locking into the slide by means of a squared section around the chamber fitting into the ejection port. It is a double-action hammer-fired weapon with an ambidextrous decocking lever which also functions as a slide release. There is an automatic firing pin safety system similar to that described for the P5 (above), and hence no manual safety catch.

The P88 went into production but in spite of being evaluated by various armies found few takers, and production ceased in 1996, being replaced by the P88 Compact (below).
Length: 7.36in (187mm). **Weight**

Webley's first military revolver, the Mark 1 of 1887.

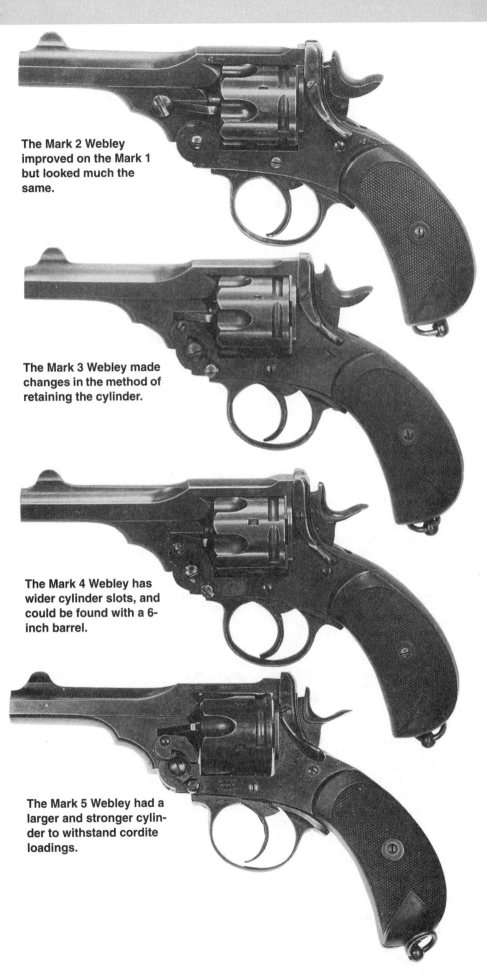

The Mark 2 Webley improved on the Mark 1 but looked much the same.

The Mark 3 Webley made changes in the method of retaining the cylinder.

The Mark 4 Webley has wider cylinder slots, and could be found with a 6-inch barrel.

The Mark 5 Webley had a larger and stronger cylinder to withstand cordite loadings.

unloaded: 2lb 3oz (992g). **Barrel:** 4.00in (101mm), 6 grooves, right-hand twist. **Magazine:** 6-round cylinder. **Muzzle velocity:** c.600 ft/sec (183 m/sec).

Pistol, Webley, Mark I* (October 1894)

Upon repair or refurbishing of the Mark I models, a hardened steel plate was added to the standing breech in order to approximate the design of the Mark 2. The head of the butt grip was rounded off and the thumb-pieces on the stirrup-lock were made smaller.

Pistol, Webley, Mark 2 (October 1894)

This model differed from the Mark I in the following respects: a hardened steel plate was used on the breech to lessen erosion, the hammer was strengthened, the grip was of a more rounded shape, slight changes were made in the extractor components, the hammer catch spring was spiral instead of V-shaped, and the stirrup-lock thumb-pieces were smaller.

Pistol, Webley, Mark 3 (October 1897)

The Mark 3 was basically the same as the Mark 2, but the attachment of cylinder to frame was improved and a cam was fitted to unlock the cylinder for removal. In 1905 a number of revolvers of this pattern were fitted with 6-inch (152mm) barrels 'to meet the requirements of officers and cadets desiring to purchase such pistols from store'.

Pistol, Webley, Mark 4 (July 1899)

The Mark 4 differed from Mark 3 in that the steel was of different quality, the trigger stop was raised and the slots in the cylinder made wider, the ratchet teeth of the extractor were case-hardened and the hammer was made lighter. As in the case of the Mark 3, 1905 saw a quantity produced with the 6-inch (152mm) barrel for sale to officers.

Pistol, Webley, Mark 5 (December 1913)

This differed from the Mark 4 in having the cylinder of larger diameter (in order to better withstand the higher pressures due to cordite-loaded cartridges) and rounded on the rear edge and the body modified to suit. Fitted as standard with a 4-inch (102mm) barrel, the weapon weighed 2lb 3.5oz (1010g).

Pistol, Webley, Mark I** (April 1915)

Intended for Naval Service, this is the conversion, on repair, of the Mark I or I * produced by fitting a Mark 4 barrel and a Mark 5 cylinder.

Pistol, Webley, Mark 2* (April 1915)

Not an officially approved nomenclature, this designation arose by virtue of a number of Mark 2 pistols being fitted with Mark 4 hammers and having (*) stamped erroneously after the number on the barrel strap.

Pistol, Webley, Mark 2** (April 1915)

Similar to the Mark I**, a conversion of the Mark 2 by fitting the Mark 4 barrel and Mark 5 cylinder.

Pistol, Webley, 6-inch barrel, Mark I**(June 1915)

A fine example of how convoluted British nomenclature could get. This is another wartime naval expedient in which, when undergoing repair, Mark 1 or I* pistols had the 6-inch barrels approved for Marks 4 or 5 pistols fitted, together with a removable front sight and a Mark 5 cylinder.

Pistol, Webley, 6-inch barrel, Mark 2** (June 1915)

A similar naval expedient to the foregoing model, in this case the repair of Mark 2 pistols by fitting the 6-inch barrel, removable front sight and Mark 5 cylinder.

Pistol, Webley, 6-Inch barrel, Mark 5 (May 1915)

This model is identical to the Mark 5 but with the original 4-inch barrel replaced by a 6-inch barrel carrying a removable front sight attached with a fixing screw. The revolver weighs 2lb 5.5oz (1063g).

Pistol, Webley, 6-inch barrel, Mark 6 (May 1915)

It differs from the Mark 5 in having a barrel 2 inches longer fitted with a removable blade front sight, a different and more square-cut grip, and a number of the components redesigned to facilitate more rapid production—thus making them special to this particular mark of pistol.

Length: 11.25in (286mm). **Weight unloaded:** 2lb 7oz (1105g). **Barrel:** 6.00in (152mm), 7 grooves, right-hand twist. **Magazine:** 6-round cylinder. **Muzzle velocity:** c.650 ft/sec (199 m/sec).

It is interesting to note that while all these pistols are generally described as being of 455-caliber (11.60mm), their actual caliber has always been 0.441-inch (1.20mm).

• The Webley-Fosbery Automatic Revolver

Webley & Scott Revolver and Arms Company Limited, Birmingham
455-caliber British Service

This weapon, the design of which was based on the 1896 patents of Col. G V Fosbery, VC, is in a class of its own—an 'automatic revolver' in which the force of recoil drives the barrel and cylinder unit back over the frame, cocks the hammer, and returns the unit by spring power to the firing position. During this movement

The ultimate Webley was the Mark 6, with 6-inch barrel and squared-end butt.

The Webley-Fosbery, the only successful automatic revolver.

a fixed stud on the frame is engaged in the grooves on the cylinder and the movement causes the cylinder to be rotated one-twelfth of a revolution during each stroke, thus completing one-sixth of a turn in the complete recoil cycle and hence indexing a fresh chamber in front of the hammer.

The Webley-Fosbery was never officially accepted into military service but it was tolerated insofar as, prior to the approval of the 38-caliber revolver, the British Army officer was permitted to purchase any pistol he liked as long as it accepted the issue 455-caliber service cartridge. On active service in 1914-15 the Webley-Fosbery was tried and found wanting, the recoil action being easily clogged and deranged by mud and dirt.

A very few were made in 38 ACP caliber, and a similar pattern (in 32 S&W caliber) was made in the United States by the Union Arms Company.

Length: 11.00in (280mm). **Weight unloaded:** 2lb 12oz (1247g). **Barrel:** 6.00in (152mm), 7 grooves, right-hand twist. **Magazine:** 6-round cylinder. **Muzzle velocity:** c.600 ft/sec (183 m/sec).

• The Webley & Scott Automatic Pistol

Webley & Scott Limited, Birmingham
455 Webley & Scott Auto

This pistol was introduced into the Royal Navy in 1915 as the Pistol, Self-

loading, Webley & Scott. 0.455in Mark 1. It is a solid and reliable weapon with an ungainly appearance owing to the square angle of the butt, which makes instinctive shooting difficult although deliberate shooting can be quite accurate. The cartridge is a semi-rimmed round of considerable power, which will—unfortunately—chamber in a service 455-caliber revolver. This caused the sudden destruction of a number of revolvers in World War I before the difference was appreciated. The diameter of the jacketed bullet is 0.456-inch (11.6mm), rather more than that of the lead revolver bullet as the revolvers' actual caliber was 0.441-inch (11.2mm) instead of the nominal 0.455-inch. This slight enlargement of the pistol bullet, together with its increased hardness and coupled with a fast-burning 7 grain (0.45gm) charge, was sufficient to build up excessive pressures and blow out the revolvers' cylinders.

The Webley pistol was also produced commercially in 9mm Browning Long and 38 Super Auto calibers. There were also blowback versions of similar appearance in 25 and 32 calibers.

The standard pattern of the Webley, the Mark 1, was fitted with a grip safety but in April 1915 a modified version was approved for issue to personnel of the Royal Horse Artillery. This differed from the Mark 1 in having the grip safety replaced by a mechanical catch on the hammer, a special rotating-drum rear sight (graduated to 200yd and with windage adjustment) instead of the fixed notch of the Navy weapon, and the butt was grooved for a shoulder stock. This model was known as the Number 2 Mark 1, and with its adoption the original pistol became the Pistol Number I Mark 1. Although a small quantity of No. 2 Mark 1 pistols were issued to Royal Horse Artillery units in France, they appear not to have been well received and it did not become a general army issue, and the balance of those produced were reallocated to the Royal Flying Corps.

The Webley is a locked-breech design, locked by oblique machined ribs on the square rear of the barrel which engage in recessed sections of the body. In the firing position the barrel and the slide are locked together by a lug on the barrel engaging with a shoulder in the slide. As barrel and slide recoil so the oblique ribs slide down the recesses in the body and draw the barrel out of engagement with the slide, allowing the slide to recoil. The mainspring is an unusual V-spring concealed under the left grip. Another unusual feature was the facility to partly withdraw the magazine and lock it in place so that the top round was not loaded by the slide; in this position the gun could be fired as a single-shot, handloading each round, with the magazine held in reserve.

Length: 8.50in (216mm). **Weight:** unloaded: 2lb 8oz (1134g). **Barrel:** 5.00in (127mm), 6 grooves, right-hand twist. **Magazine:** 7-round detachable box. **Muzzle velocity:** c.750 ft/sec (228 m/sec).

Pistol, Revolver, No 2 ('Enfield')

Royal Small Arms Factory, Enfield Lock; Albion Motor Company, Glasgow; Singer Sewing Machine Company, Clydebank

380-inch British Service

After World War I the British Army decided that the 455-caliber bullet

The Enfield Mark 1 resembled the Webley Mark 6 but was in 38-caliber.

demanded too heavy a weapon and too great a degree of skill from the firer. Investigating possible replacements, they found that Webley & Scott were testing a 38-caliber revolver for possible sale as a police weapon; with a 200-grain (12.97gm) bullet, this caliber gave the required stopping power for a combat weapon and was yet sufficiently docile to be passably accurate in the hands of hastily-trained wartime recruits. The design project was taken over in 1926-7 by the Royal Small Arms Factory at Enfield Lock and changes were made in the lockwork and trigger mechanism, largely in the provision of a hammer safety lock and a separate cylinder lock. With this modification the pistol, no longer a Webley pattern, was designated the 'Enfield' revolver or, in accordance with the system of nomenclature then used in British Service, the Pistol, Revolver, Number 2 Mark 1. Eventually there were three models.

Pistol, Revolver, Number 2 Mark I (June 1932)

This was similar in appearance to the 455-caliber Webley Mark 6 which it replaced but physically smaller. It was provided with a hammer mechanism which could be operated as single or double action. These pistols were declared obsolescent in June 1938 and all existing specimens were to be converted to Mark I* when passing through Ordnance Factories for repair. In consequence, original Mark 1 pistols are exceptionally rare.

Length: 10.25in (260mm). **Weight unloaded:** 1lb 11oz (765g). **Barrel:** 5.00in (127mm), 7 grooves, right-hand twist. **Magazine:** 6-round cylinder. **Muzzle velocity:** c.650 ft/sec (198 m/sec).

Pistol, Revolver, Number 2 Mark 1* (June 1938)

This differed from Mark I in that the hammer-comb and bent were removed to allow double-action firing only. The mainspring was lightened to reduce the trigger pull (when new) from the 13lb to 15lb (5.85kg to 6.75kg) of the Mark I to 11lb to 13lb (4.95kg to 5.85kg); the grip sideplates were reshaped to give a better grip, and a marking disc was recessed into the right butt sideplate. The date of introduction is of interest here, for it disproves the widely-held opinion that these double-action weapons were a wartime innovation for 'quick-draw' work by Commandos and other special forces. These pistols were introduced because their principal destination was the Tank Corps, and the earlier model had the habit of snagging the hammer on various internal tank fittings.

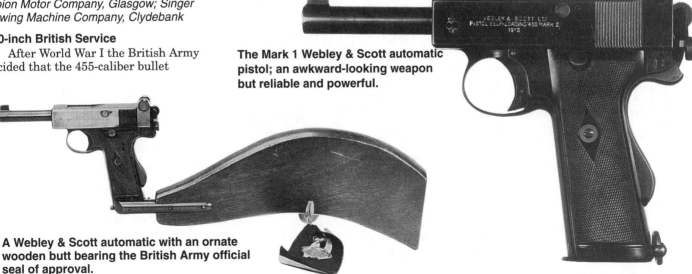

The Mark 1 Webley & Scott automatic pistol; an awkward-looking weapon but reliable and powerful.

A Webley & Scott automatic with an ornate wooden butt bearing the British Army official seal of approval.

The Enfield Mark 1* did away with the hammer spur and cut down on the number of accidents inside tanks.

The Webley 38 Mark 4 was the source of inspiration for the Enfield Mark 1, but came into its own during World War II.

The Smith & Wesson 38/200 was the Military & Police specially chambered for the British 38-caliber cartridge.

Pistol, Revolver, Number 2 Mark 1** (July 1942)

This was a wartime dispensation, introduced to hasten production; it is the same as the Mark I* but with the hammer safety stop removed and one or two minor manufacturing concessions granted. These weapons were all recalled after the war and, by the addition of the hammer safety stop, converted back into Mark 1* models since without the stop they were notoriously unsafe if dropped.

• Pistol, Revolver, Webley, 0.38in Mark 4

Webley & Scott Limited, Birmingham
38 Smith & Wesson

In addition to the 455-caliber pistols, a 38-caliber model was brought into service during World War II to augment supplies of Enfield pistols. This Webley-designed 38-caliber weapon was the final version of the design which had originated in 1923 as a potential police weapon and which, when modified by the Royal Small Arms Factory at Enfield Lock, eventually became the Enfield pistol. Externally the Webley shows differences in the design of the hammer and in cylinder details, and it has, of course. the Webley name impressed into the grips. The only internal difference lies in the

lock mechanism, which is of original Webley design unmodified by Enfield. The official title is Pistol, Revolver, Webley 0.38in Mark 4, and, although officially introduced into service—for record only—in September 1945 the pistols were actually in use early in 1942. They were declared obsolete in June 1963.

Length: 10.50in (266mm). **Weight unloaded:** 1lb 11oz (765g). **Barrel:** 5.00in (127mm), 7 grooves, right-hand twist. **Magazine:** 6-round cylinder. **Muzzle velocity:** c.600 ft/sec (183 m/sec).

• Pistol, Revolver, 0.38in, Smith & Wesson, Number 2 (38-200)

Smith & Wesson Arms Company, Springfield, Massachusetts
38 Smith & Wesson

This is virtually the regulation Smith & Wesson Police Model fitted with a six-chambered cylinder. The term '38/200' stems from the chambering, intended to fit the British Army 200 grain 38-caliber cartridge, as the design was first produced to meet British military contracts in 1940. Approximately 900,000 of these revolvers were eventually issued to Allied troops of many nations. A most accurate and handy weapon, the sole defect was a tendency of the mainspring to age during prolonged

storage, which eventually led to a light striker blow. This is only noticeable when using British Service ammunition since this demands a heavier cap blow than the commercial product. The finish on these weapons is a guide to their age. The first production—from April 1940 until April 1942—were polished and blued, and had barrels of 4-inch, 5-inch, or 6-inch (102mm, 127mm or 152mm). Until January 1942 the grips were checkered walnut with a silver S & W monogram medallion let into the top. After January 1942 the grips were of smooth walnut without the medallion and, after May 1942, the finish was that of sandblasting and only 5-inch (127mm) barrels were fitted.

Length: 10.13in (258mm). **Weight unloaded:** 1lb 8oz (680g). **Barrel:** 4in, 5in or 6in (102mm, 127mm or 152mm), 5 grooves, right-hand twist. **Magazine:** 6-round cylinder. **Muzzle velocity:** c.650 ft/sec (199 m/sec).

HUNGARY

• Pistol 12M, 19M, 39M (Frommer 'Stop')

Fémáru Fegyver és Gépgyár, Budapest
7.65x17SR Browning (32 ACP); 9x17mm Short (380 ACP)

These pistols represent a successful class of long-recoil operated automatics, a system of operation which demands that the barrel and bolt recoil locked together for a distance greater than the length of a cartridge. The bolt is then unlocked and held fast while the barrel is allowed to return to the forward position, during which movement the empty case is extracted and ejected. As the barrel reaches its firing position, the bolt is released and runs forward to chamber a new round and lock to the barrel. This system appears to have had a mesmeric attraction for the designers Rudolf Frommer, Georg Roth and Karel Krnka, who were, between them, responsible for a wide range of weapons employing this system. The Frommer Stop pistol is one of the few long recoil designs to ever prosper. It is open to question exactly why Frommer went to such lengths to lock the breech of a weapon firing the 7.65mm cartridge; a number were also made in 9mm Short caliber, but even this does not warrant the complexity of the design.

The pistol 12M was adopted by the Honved—the Hungarian element of the Austro-Hungarian reserve army—in 1912, chambered for the 7.65mm cartridge. In 1919 it was officially adopted as the pistol of the newly formed Hungarian Army as the 19M, though it was

The Walam was one of several copies of the Walther PP which appeared in the post-war years in Eastern Europe.

The Frommer 'Stop' in 7.65mm caliber, with the Hungarian Budapest proof mark on the triggerguard.

precisely the same weapon. A third version, the 39M, was to be made in 9mm Short caliber in 1939 but this project appears to have foundered on the outbreak of war, The 19M remained in production until about 1930 and the pistol is relatively common; it was well-made from excellent materials, somewhat ugly, but not as awkward as it looks and, for all its complexity, had a good reputation for reliability.

Length: 6.50in (165mm). **Weight unloaded:** 1lb 6oz (625g). **Barrel:** 3.80in (95mm), 4 grooves, right-hand twist. **Magazine:** 7-round detachable box. **Muzzle velocity:** c.920 ft/sec (280 m/sec).

• Pistol 29M, Pistol 37M
Fémáru Fegyver és Gépgyár, Budapest
9x17mm Short (380 ACP) (29M)
7.65x17SR Browning (32 ACP) or
9x17mm Short (380 ACP) (37M)

In the late 1920s the Hungarian Army decided to adopt a simpler design than the Frommer Stop, and Frommer responded with the Model 29M. This was a simple and robust blowback weapon, somewhat angular, but serviceable and reliable and it went into service in 1930. The pistol used an external hammer, the barrel was retained in the frame by four lugs and a grip safety was fitted into the rear edge of the butt. In the middle 1930s the Army required more pistols and again Frommer came to the rescue with the 37M design. This was simply an improved 29M, the changes being largely cosmetic and resulting in a somewhat better-looking weapon. During World War II a large number of 37M were made in 7.65mm caliber for the German Army, who adopted it as the Pistole 37(ü). These can be distinguished by the German marking 'P MOD 37 KAL 7.65' on the slide and they were also provided with a thumb-operated safety catch on the rear of the frame in addition to the grip safety. (Data table refers to 37M).

Length: 7.17in (182mm). **Weight unloaded:** 1lb 11oz (765g). **Barrel:** 4.33in (110mm), 6 grooves, right-hand twist. **Magazine:** 7-round detachable box. **Muzzle velocity:** 920 ft/sec (290 m/sec).

• Pistol 48M (Walam)
Fémáru Szerszamgépgyár, Budapest
9x17mm Short (380 ACP)

This pistol was manufactured in Hungary to meet an order from the Egyptian police in the early 1950s. For some reason the Egyptians abruptly terminated the contract and the balance of the order was completed and disposed of in the commercial market. The pistol is simply a copy of the Walther PP, though with a very slight difference in the chamber-loaded indicator. Early models have the name 'WALAM 48' on the slide; commercial models will have the company name and

The Frommer 38 improved on the 29 in appearance but was still a simple blowback design. This one was made during WWII for the German Army.

The Frommer Model 29 was a much simpler weapon than the 'Stop'.

The PA-63 was more or less the Walam for military consumption. There are a few minor changes but the parentage remains obvious.

an ornate star and wreath badge on the grips. Later production was disposed of through a number of West German dealers and may be found with their trade names stamped on the frame.

Length: 6.89in (175mm). **Weight unloaded:** 1lb 8.5oz (700g). **Barrel:** 3.90in (100mm), 6 grooves, right-hand twist. **Magazine:** 8-round detachable box. **Muzzle velocity:** c.965 ft/sec (295 m/sec).

• Pistol PA-63
State Arsenals
9x18mm Makarov

This is another copy of the Walther PP, developed for the Hungarian Army in the late 1950s. The dimensions differ slightly, and the weapon is lighter than the Walther due to extensive use of light alloy in the construction. It is also manufactured in 7.65mm caliber, probably for police use.

Length: 6.89in (175mm). **Weight unloaded:** 1lb 5oz (595g). **Barrel:** 3.94in (100mm), 6 grooves, right-hand twist. **Magazine:** 7-round detachable box. **Muzzle velocity:** c.965 ft/sec (295 m/sec).

• Pistol Model 48
State Arsenals
7.62x25mm Soviet M30

This is simply the standard Soviet TT33 Tokarev pistol made under license in Hungary. The Hungarian version can be distinguished by the crest on the grip (a star, wheatsheaf and hammer surrounded by a wreath) and by the vertical finger-grip cuts on the slide which are narrower and more uniform than those on Soviet weapons. Dimensions, etc., are exactly as for the Tokarev.

ISRAEL

• Uzi Pistol
Israel Military Industries, Ramat Hasharon
9x19mm Parabellum

The Uzi pistol is simply a shortened, lightened and simplified version of the Uzi submachine gun. It has the same general outline, with the magazine housing in the pistol grip at the center of bal-

ance and with the cocking handle on top of the receiver, but it has no automatic fire capability and is so designed that attempting to convert it to automatic fire would be virtually impossible. It may look cumbersome, but the weight sits well in the hand and makes the weapon very stable when fired. It is, of course, a blowback weapon, firing from a closed breech, and was originally proposed commercially as a weapon for home defense use, but it has obvious military and security applications and has been seen in the hands of such forces and also fitted with silencers and laser sights.

Length: 9.45in (240mm). **Weight unloaded:** 3lb 12oz (1700g). **Barrel:** 4.53in (115mm), 4 grooves, right-hand twist. **Magazine:** 20-, 25- or 30-round detachable box. **Muzzle velocity:** c.1132 ft/sec (345 m/sec).

• Jericho 941
Israel Military Industries, Ramat Hasharon
9x19mm Parabellum and others

The Jericho is a conventional locked-breech pistol using a dropping barrel which locks into the ejection opening in the slide. Hammer-fired and double action, the slide runs on internal frame rails, improving the accuracy. The pistol is normally in 9mm caliber but by replacing the barrel, return spring and magazine it can be made to fire 40 Smith & Wesson or 41 Action Express cartridges. It is also available with various options such as single-action only or double-action only, ambidextrous safety catch, and a butt-mounted safety lock. A compact model is also made. It has been adopted by various Israeli police and security agencies.

Length: 8.14in (207mm). **Weight unloaded:** 2lb 6oz (1090g). **Barrel:** 4.72in (120mm), 6 grooves, polygonal, right-hand twist. **Magazine:** 16-round detachable box. **Muzzle velocity:** c.1132 ft/sec (360 m/sec).

The Uzi pistol is simply the Uzi submachine gun reduced in size and restricted to single shot firing.

The Jericho, a simple and elegant design currently in use by the Israeli Defense Force.

ITALY

• Bodeo Revolver M1889
Various manufacturers
10.4x22R Italian Ordnance

The 'Pistola a Rotazione, Systema Bodeo, Modello 1889' became the Italian service revolver in 1891; it remained the principal sidearm until supplanted by the Glisenti pistol after 1910, but it was never declared obsolete and it remained as a reserve weapon until the end of World War II. The Model 1889 was a six shot solid frame double action 10.4mm center-fire revolver, with a loading gate and a rod ejector. The gate was connected to the hammer on the Abadie system, and little in the design was original; Bodeo was honored by virtue of heading the commission that recommended the design. The only unusual mechanical feature (for the period) was a hammer block to prevent the hammer falling far enough to fire the cartridge unless the trigger was pulled fully back.

One version of the Model 1889 had an octagonal barrel and a folding trigger without a guard; another had a cylindrical barrel and a conventionally guarded trigger. The former was for the rank and file, the latter for officers and NCOs. Both types went into production in 1889 and, as might be expected, the folding trigger type was made in greater numbers prior to 1914. Production continued sporadically until c. 1931 .

Bodeo revolvers were made by, among others, Castelli of Brescia, Metallurgica Bresciana; Siderurgica Glisenti of Turin, Real Fabricca d'Armi of Brescia and Vincenzo Bernardelli of Gardone Val Trompia. Errasti and Arrostegui of Eibar, Spain, also made guns on contract during the First World War.

Length: 9.25in (232mm). **Weight unloaded:** 2lb 2oz (950g). **Barrel:** 4.53in (115mm), 6 grooves, right-hand twist. **Magazine:** 6-round cylinder. **Muzzle velocity:** c.837 ft/sec (255m/sec).

• Glisenti Model 1910

• Brixia Model 1912
Societa Siderurgica Glisenti, Turin
Metallurgica Bresciana gia Tempini, Brescia
9x19mm Glisenti

The Glisenti pistol was designed by Captain A. B. Revelli of the Italian army (whose name also attaches to a machine gun) who spent several years working his way through a series of prototypes before assigning his patents, in 1902, to the Glisenti company.

Rumors concerning the existence of a new Italian service pistol began to circu-

late in 1903, and in 1906, the Glisenti factory obtained machine tools from Britain to begin production. Within a year, however, Glisenti opted out of the firearms business and sold the manufacturing rights to Metallurgica Bresciana gia Tempini (MBT or Brixia). MBT, already making components for the pistol, now took over the entire project.

Great difficulty was experienced in setting up production, but manufacture of a Glisenti pistol chambered for an odd 7.65x22mm bottle-necked cartridge began late in 1908. This **Model 1906** failed to satisfy the Italian army, so the pistol was redesigned to take a 9mm cartridge of the same dimensions as the German 9mm Parabellum, but loaded to a lower velocity in order to reduce the recoil. This was formally adopted by the Italian army and became the **Model 1910**.

The reduced charge was also dictated by the construction of the Glisenti. The breech lock was a wedge pivoting in the frame, which engaged in a recess beneath the bolt. The bolt moved in the barrel extension, which could slide along the top of the frame. On firing, barrel, extension and bolt recoiled together for about 7mm, whereupon the wedge had been turned far enough to disengage it from the bolt; the barrel unit stopped, held by the depressed locking wedge, and the bolt continued to recoil. When the bolt returned, chambering a fresh round, the wedge rose, freed the barrel and re-engaged the bolt. A barrel return spring then pushed the entire unit back into the firing position. The whole

One of the few military revolvers to have a folding trigger, the 10.6mm Italian Bodeo of 1889.

The Brixia was put forward as a possible replacement for the Glisenti, but the amount of improvement was scarcely detectable and the Italian Army refused it.

The Glisenti fired a 9mm cartridge of the same dimensions as the 9mm Parabellum, but of lesser power.

system operated so rapidly that it was more a delayed blowback than a fully locked breech.

The other feature demanding a reduced charge was the frame construction; in the front of the frame was a screw, held by a spring catch, which unscrewed to allow the entire left side of the frame to be removed. This reveals that the frame has no left side at all, resulting in a lack of stiffness and no support for much of the left side of the barrel extension. Prolonged use loosened the side plate and introduced a degree of play into the entire action.

The firing mechanism was also odd, as it did not cock when the slide ran back. Instead, pulling the trigger released the sear only after pushing it back against its spring, this gave a long and creepy trigger pull. A grip safety was provided in the form of a lever let into the front edge of the grip.

The Glisenti remained in production until the early 1920s, although from 1916 onward it was supplemented by increasing numbers of Beretta pistols. The Beretta became the official issue pistol in 1934, but numbers of Glisenti survived in service until 1945.

In 1912 MBT produced an 'improved' model, generally called the 'Brixia'; this slightly strengthened the frame and omitted the grip safety, and a number were submitted to the Italian Army for approval. It showed insufficient improvement over the M1909 model to warrant making a change, and MBT then placed it on the commercial market. The outbreak of war in 1914 put an end to that project, and the design was never revived. The Brixia is almost identical to the Glisenti, but has a flat (rather than stepped) left side and the grips are embossed with the 'MBT' monogram.

Length: 8.22in (207mm). **Weight unloaded:** 1lb 13oz (820g). **Barrel:** 3.91in (100mm), 6 grooves, right-hand twist. **Magazine:** 7-round detachable box. **Muzzle velocity:** c.855 ft/sec (280m/sec).

• Beretta Model 1915

Pietro Beretta SpA, Brescia
7.65x17SR Browning; 9x19mm Glisenti; 9mm Short

This pistol was produced by the Beretta company for military use in World War I. It is a simple blowback and was normally supplied either in 7.65 Browning or 9mm Short calibers. A small number were, however, provided with a stronger recoil spring and an added buffer spring, and chambered for the Italian service 9mm M10 (Glisenti) cartridge—with which cartridge they are as safe as with the other loadings. Since the Glisenti round is dimensionally similar to 9mm Parabellum but weaker in loading, it follows that using Parabellum

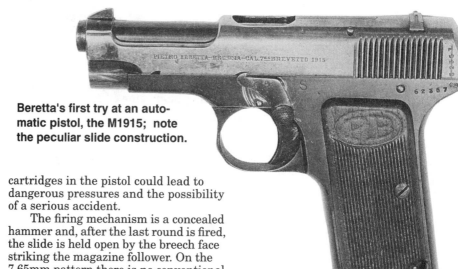

Beretta's first try at an automatic pistol, the M1915; note the peculiar slide construction.

cartridges in the pistol could lead to dangerous pressures and the possibility of a serious accident.

The firing mechanism is a concealed hammer and, after the last round is fired, the slide is held open by the breech face striking the magazine follower. On the 7.65mm pattern there is no conventional fixed ejector; the extracted case is ejected by the firing pin protruding from the breechblock at a position of full recoil. The 9mm weapons, on the other hand, use normal fixed ejectors. The interesting feature of this pistol, in relation to the designs which followed it, is the provision of a separate ejection port in the slide top in addition to the short cutaway section behind the front sight.

Length: 5.85in (149mm). **Weight unloaded:** 1lb 4oz (570g). **Barrel:** 3.32in (84mm), 6 grooves, right-hand twist. **Magazine:** 8-round detachable box. **Muzzle velocity:** c.875 ft/sec (266 m/sec) (9mm Short).

• Beretta Model 1922 (or 1915/19)

Pietro Beretta SpA, Brescia
7.65x17SR Browning, 9mm Short

At the end of World War I the Model 1915 was redesigned and produced as a commercial venture in the 9mm Short caliber which was then becoming very popular. The general appearance was slightly changed, principally in the design of the slide, which is built up so as to surround the muzzle and support the frontsight. These various changes were patented, with the result that the pistols are marked 'BREV. 1915-1919'.

The principal change in the pistol's action was a complete redesign of the lockwork, giving a much improved trigger pull. The system of holding the slide open on the magazine follower was retained, and thus demanded a hard pull to remove the empty magazine and the operation of the slide to reload when a full magazine was inserted.

This pistol, made to the 1915/19 system, was officially known as the 'Modello 1922' and served as a form of prototype for the succeeding 9mm design of 1923. It also marks the change of slide construction, from the separate ejection port of the M1915 to a long cutaway portion from the rear sight back almost to the mouth of the chamber, a characteristic of Beretta pistols ever since.

Length: 5.75in (146mm). **Weight unloaded:** 1lb 7oz (670g). **Barrel:** 3.50in (87mm), 4 grooves, right-hand twist. **Magazine:** 7-round detachable box. **Muzzle velocity:** c.975 ft/sec (297 m/sec).

The Beretta 1915/19 rationalized the slide by making one long cutaway portion, and they have preserved this system ever since.

The Beretta 1934 was the perfected design and armed the Italian forces throughout WWII.

The Beretta Model 1923 showed a few refinements on the basic design.

• Beretta Modello 1923
Pietro Beretta SpA, Gardone Val Trompia, Brescia
9x19mm Glisenti

The Beretta Model 1915 and Model 1922 (1915/19) in 7.65mm were made and issued in vast numbers, but since the official Italian automatic pistol round of the time was still the 9mm Glisenti, it was decided to produce an enlarged Beretta to accept that cartridge. The Model 1923 was otherwise similar in design to the preceding 1915 and 1922 designs, but with an external ring hammer. It was still a blowback, as the Glisenti's cartridge was of relatively low power, but since the 9mm Parabellum round of much greater power will also chamber in the pistol, there is an element of hazard if the wrong ammunition is used. It may be that this was the reason for the pistol being discontinued fairly quickly, few being made after 1925. Total production was small, and the gun is today uncommon. The slide is marked 'PISTOLA-BERETTA - 9M BREV. 1915-1919-mo 1923'.

Length: 7.00in (177mm). **Weight unloaded:** 1lb l0oz (800g). **Barrel:** 3.50in (87mm), 4 grooves, right-hand twist. **Magazine:** 7-round detachable box. **Muzzle velocity:** c.1000 ft/sec (305 m/sec).

• Beretta Model 1931
Pietro Beretta SpA, Gardone Val Trompia
7.65x17SR Browning

The Model 1931 was a direct derivation of the preceding patterns of 1922 and 1923, but in 7.65mm caliber only.

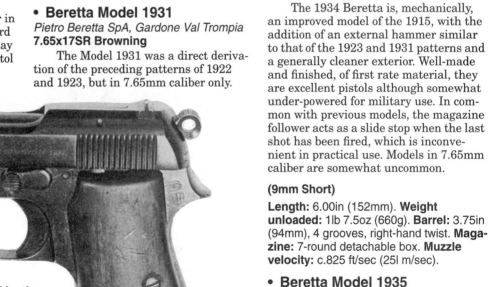

The Beretta M1931 was adopted by the Italian navy and bears their medallion.

Although used in small numbers by the Italian Army, the Model 31 was more widely issued to the Navy, and is most frequently seen with a medallion on the wooden grips bearing an 'R/anchor/ M' device, the property mark of the Regia Marina d'Italia (Italian Navy). The slide is marked 'PISTOLA BERETTA 7.65 BREV. 1915-1919-mo 1931', and the characteristics are essentially similar to those of the later Modello 1934, for which the 1931 design served as a basis.

• Beretta Model 1934
Pietro Beretta SpA, Gardone Val Trompia
7.65x17SR Browning, 9mm Short

The 1934 Beretta is, mechanically, an improved model of the 1915, with the addition of an external hammer similar to that of the 1923 and 1931 patterns and a generally cleaner exterior. Well-made and finished, of first rate material, they are excellent pistols although somewhat under-powered for military use. In common with previous models, the magazine follower acts as a slide stop when the last shot has been fired, which is inconvenient in practical use. Models in 7.65mm caliber are somewhat uncommon.

(9mm Short)

Length: 6.00in (152mm). **Weight unloaded:** 1lb 7.5oz (660g). **Barrel:** 3.75in (94mm), 4 grooves, right-hand twist. **Magazine:** 7-round detachable box. **Muzzle velocity:** c.825 ft/sec (25l m/sec).

• Beretta Model 1935
Pietro Beretta SpA, Gardone Val Trompia
7.65x7SR Browning

The Model 1935 pistol, issued to officers and aircrew of the Italian Air Force, was a lightened-slide version of the standard Model 1934.

The Beretta M951 was their first locked-breech pistol, using a wedge lock similar to the Walther P38.

• Beretta Model 1951

Pietro Beretta SpA, Gardone Val Trompia
7.65mm Parabellum, 9mm Parabellum

After World War II, the Beretta company decided to align themselves with the rest of the world and produce a military pistol in 9mm Parabellum caliber. The design of the Modello 1951 (or M951) appears to have been begun c.1950, but the weapon was not placed on the market until c.1957. One of the reasons for this delay may have been the original intention to make the pistol with a light alloy frame, keeping the weight down to about 24oz (0.70kg); this appears, however, to have produced a weapon which was neither accurate nor pleasant to shoot, and production models were entirely of steel. The result was a heavier and better-shooting weapon.

This is a locked-breech pistol utilizing a locking wedge swinging in the vertical plane, a similar system to that seen in the Walther P38. Locking of barrel and breech is achieved by a pair of lugs engaging in recesses in the breech slide; unlocking is done by a floating plunger carried on the rear barrel lug which releases the locking wedge to disengage the lugs from the slide on meeting a shoulder in the frame. Relocking is achieved automatically on the return stroke of the slide and the breech and slide are positively locked together at the moment of firing.

An improvement on previous models of Beretta's manufacture was the adoption of a slide stop which, under pressure from the magazine follower, held the slide open after the last round in the magazine had been fired and kept it open until a fresh magazine was inserted. Releasing the slide stop then allowed the slide to go forward and chamber the first round.

The M1951 was also adopted by Egypt and Israel. Some Egyptian models are marked 'UAR HELWAN' on the slide, and a special version, the Model 51/ 57EM or 'Berhama' was made as a target pistol with a 148mm barrel, ramp front sight, micrometer rear sight and target-style grips.
Length: 8.00in (203mm). **Weight unloaded:** 1lb 15oz ((890g). **Barrel:** 4.50in (114mm), 6 grooves, right-hand twist. **Magazine:** 8-round detachable box. **Muzzle velocity:** c.1300 ft/sec (396 m/sec).

• Beretta Model 951R

Pietro Beretta SpA, Gardone Val Trompia
9mm Parabellum

The 951R was a specialist machine pistol version of the 951 produced for the Carabinieri and differed in having a selector switch to permit single shots or full-automatic fire. It also had a wooden fore-grip attached to the front end of the frame, and an extended magazine, though the original 951 magazine would also fit. The nominal cyclic rate of fire was 1200 rounds per minute, but this could vary considerably according to the brand of ammunition used.
Length: 8.46in (215mm). **Weight unloaded:** 2lb 15oz (1350g). **Barrel:** 4.92in (125mm). **Magazine:** 10-round detachable box. **Muzzle velocity:** 1280 ft/sec (390m/sec).

• Beretta Models 92, 92S

Pietro Beretta SpA, Gardone Val Trompia
9mm Parabellum

Introduced in 1976, this is really the Model 951 brought up to date and in line with contemporary thinking. The magazine capacity is increased and the trigger mechanism is double-action, but the locking system and general appearance is still that of the Model 951.

Model 92S resembles the Model 92 but has an improved safety system. The safety catch is now on the slide (instead of the frame) and functions also as a decocking lever. When applied it deflects the firing pin away from the path of the hammer, releases the hammer, and breaks the connection between the trigger bar and the sear. Both models were adopted by the Italian and other armies and police forces in some considerable numbers. Production ceased in the middle 1980s.

The Beretta 951R was a selective fire machine pistol with a front grip to improve control.

and lanyard ring were fitted. The barrel is chromed internally and the external finish is 'Bruniton', a Teflon-type material. After adoption by the US Army the Model 92F was taken into use by many military and police forces throughout the world. The dimensions, etc., are as for the Model 92SB.

• Beretta Model 93R
Pietro Beretta SpA, Gardone Val Trompia
9mm Parabellum

This is really the 951R brought up-to-date, a selective-fire pistol with a three-round burst facility and several other refinements aimed at turning it into a passable machine pistol. The basic weapon is almost identical to the Model 92. There is a front grip which can be folded down to be grasped by the firer's free hand, giving better support than the fashionable two-handed grip usually used. For more deliberate work a folding stock can be attached to the butt. A fire selector lever on the left side of the frame allows selection of single shots or three-round bursts, and this facility is best used with the stock in place. Another accessory is an extended 20-shot magazine, useful when the burst-fire facility is used. A muzzle brake adds to

Beretta jumped ahead of the competition in the late 1970s when they introduced the double-action Model 92 with a high-capacity magazine.

Length: 8.54in (217mm). **Weight unloaded:** 2lb 2oz (950g). **Barrel:** 4.92in (125mm), 6 grooves, right-hand twist. **Magazine:** 15-round detachable box. **Muzzle velocity:** c.1280 ft/sec (390 m/sec).

• Beretta Model 92SB
Pietro Beretta SpA, Gardone Val Trompia
9mm Parabellum

In 1980 the US Army began trials to find a pistol to replace the Colt M1911A1, and Beretta modified their Model 92 to suit the US specification, resulting in the Model 92SB. It differed from the 92 in having a safety catch on both sides of the slide, a magazine catch behind the triggerguard, where it can be moved to either side as desired, and a new system of safeties including an automatic firing pin lock. The hammer was given a half-cock notch, and the butt is grooved at the rear to improve grip. The dimensions, etc., are exactly as for the Model 92, except that the weight is now 2lb 3oz (980g).

• Beretta Model 92F
Pietro Beretta SpA, Gardone Val Trompia
9mm Parabellum

The Model 92SB walked away with the US trials, but the Army required some minor changes before accepting it as the Pistol M9. The triggerguard was reshaped to suit the two-handed grip, the magazine had its base extended to improve the grip and the butt front edge was curved at the toe, new grip plates

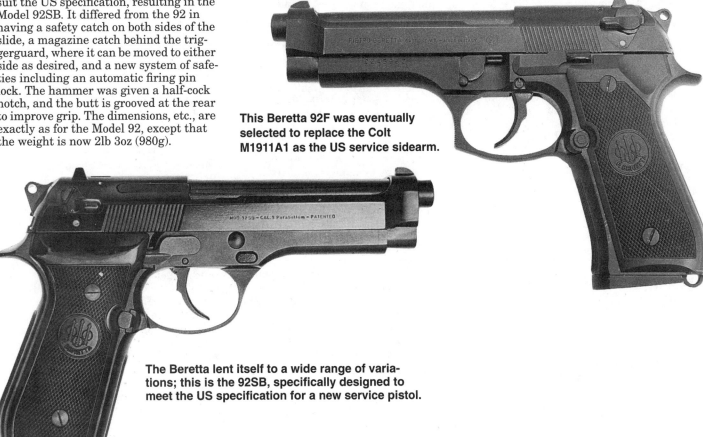

This Beretta 92F was eventually selected to replace the Colt M1911A1 as the US service sidearm.

The Beretta lent itself to a wide range of variations; this is the 92SB, specifically designed to meet the US specification for a new service pistol.

The Beretta 92's equivalent to the 951R was this 93R, another selective fire weapon but with a folding front grip, muzzle compensator, longer magazine and an optional metal buttstock.

the controllability of the weapon. The 93R has been adopted by Italian and other special forces.

Length: 9.45in (240mm). **Weight unloaded:** 2lb 7.5oz (1120g). **Barrel:** 6.14in (156mm), 6 grooves, right-hand twist. **Magazine:** 15- or 20-round detachable box. **Muzzle velocity:** c.1230 ft/sec (375 m/sec).

• Beretta 92 Variations

There are many variations upon the basic Beretta 92 pistol which deserve recording, since they may turn up in military or police service, but are not sufficiently different to deserve full entries.

9mm Model 92D. This is a self-cocking model, similar to the DS described below, but has no manual safety devices whatever and no levers on the slide.

9mm Model 92DS. This is a self-cocking (or 'double-action only') version of the Model 92F in which the hammer always follows the slide home after each shot and comes to rest in the double-action position. The hammer spur has been removed and the hammer is flush with the rear end of the slide.

9mm Model 92FC. This is a smaller version of the 92F and has a 13-round magazine. It was originally called the **Model 92F Compact**.

9mm Model 92FCM. Also a smaller version of the 92F but with a thinner butt grip and a single-column 8-round magazine.

9mm Model 92FS. This is dimensionally and mechanically the same as the Model 92SB but has the triggerguard shaped for a two-handed grip, the magazine base extended, new grip plates, a lanyard ring, a chromed barrel and a Bruniton finish.

9mm Model 92FS Compact. This is the Model 92SB-C modified in the same way as the 92FS above. The dimensions are the same as the Model 92 SB-C.

9mm Model 92 FS Compact, Type M. As for the FS Compact but with a thinner butt and an eight-round magazine.

9mm Models 92FS Inox and 98FS Inox. These are the Models 92FS and 98FS manufactured in stainless steel.

9mm Model 92G. 'G' is for 'Gendarmerie', this being the model adopted by the French Gendarmerie National. It generally resembles the 92F but has a de-cocking lever only instead of the combined safety catch and de-cocking lever of the 92F. When the lever is released, after the hammer has been lowered, it springs back up to the ready position. There is no manual safety device. It was subsequently adopted by the French Army and is manufactured in France as the PA-MAS-G1.

9mm Model 92SB-C. A smaller and handier version of the Model 92SB, with a 135mm barrel and 13-shot magazine.

9mm Model 92SB-C Type M. This is the Model SB-C but with an 8-shot single-column magazine with a shaped base providing a rest for the little finger.

9mm Models 98 and 98FS. are the same as the Model 92 and Model 92FS but chambered for the 9x21mm IMI cartridge.

9mm Model 98FS Target. This is generally the same as the 92F but is a target pistol chambered for the 9x21mm cartridge, thus permitting it to be sold to countries in which 9mm Parabellum is legally a 'military' caliber and thus prohibited for commercial sale. It is also fitted with anatomical grips, target sights and a muzzle counterweight.

7.65mm Model 98. The original Model 98 was the 92SB-C chambered for the 7.65mm Parabellum cartridge, and was primarily intended for police use. Production ceased in 1993, after which the term

'Model 98' became applied to an entirely different series of pistols.

7.65mm Model 98F. This was the same as the 92F but chambered for the 7.65mm Parabellum cartridge. Production ceased in 1993.

7.65/9mm Model 98FS. This was the same as the Model 92FS but could be chambered for the 7.65mm Parabellum or 9mm IMI cartridges. Production ceased in 1993.

7.65mm Model 99. This was the same as the SB-C Type M but chambered for the 7.65mm Parabellum cartridge. Production ceased in 1993.

• Model 96 Series pistols

Introduced in 1993, this series consists of the 96, 96 Compact, 96DS, 96G, 96 Target and 96 Centurion. They are the same in all respects to the similarly lettered 92 models except that they are chambered for the 40 Smith & Wesson cartridge and have a 10-round magazine capacity (9 for the Target model).

• Centurion Models

These have the frame and magazine capacity of the standard Model 92FS with the reduced length of barrel and slide of the Compact versions. Special D Centurion, G Centurion and DS Centurion were marketed in some countries; these applied the same construction system but with the particular features of the D, G and DS models described above. Data is given here for the 92FS Centurion model.

Length: 7.75in (197mm). **Weight unloaded:** 2lb 1oz (940g). **Barrel:** 4.29in (109mm), 6 grooves, right-hand twist. **Magazine:** 15-round detachable box. **Muzzle velocity:** c.1260 ft/sec (382 m/sec).

• Benelli Model B-76
Benelli Armi SpA, Urbino, Italy
9mm Parabellum

This pistol appeared in 1977 and was the first military-style weapon from this manufacturer. Although apparently conventional, it uses a most unusual form of toggle lock to retain the breech closed during firing. The breechblock is a separate component, fitted in the slide. Behind the block is a small toggle lying between block and slide, and the block is capable of downward movement so that a shaped lug can interlock with a recess in the pistol frame. As the slide runs forward on loading, the block chambers a cartridge and stops; the slide continues for a short distance, moving the toggle over-center and thus forcing the rear end of the breechblock into the locking recess. On firing, the recoil pressure against the

The Benelli B-76 used an unusual form of toggle lock but failed to gain much success in the market place.

block forces it harder into the recess. At the same time, pressure is placed on the toggle, and due to its mechanical disadvantage this takes some time to move and lift the rear of the block, by which time the bullet has left the muzzle and the chamber pressure has dropped to a safe level. The block is then lifted and the slide recoils in the usual way, taking the block with it.

The Benelli was well made of good materials; it used a double-action lock, and the grip was set at an angle which gave a good shooting grip. It was assessed by a number of military forces but although it enjoyed reasonable commercial sales for a while, military adop-

tion eluded it and production ceased in the mid-1980s.

Length: 8.07in (205mm). **Weight unloaded:** 2lb 2oz (970g). **Barrel:** 4.25in (108mm), 6 grooves, right-hand twist. **Magazine:** 8-round detachable box. **Muzzle velocity:** c.1150 ft/sec (350 m/sec).

• Bernardelli Model P-018
Vincenzo Bernardelli SpA, Gardone Val Trompia
7.65mm or 9mm Parabellum

The Bernardelli company has produced firearms for many years, notably a long series of commercial pocket auto-

matic pistols, but this model was their first major-caliber venture into the military and police field, which appeared in the late 1970s. It is a double-action pistol, recoil operated and using a locking block system of breech locking. Somewhat square in outline, it balances well and is said to have a relatively soft recoil. The 7.65mm model (P-018) was for commercial sale and police use, while the 9mm model (P-018-9) was for military use. A compact version, with shorter barrel and the magazine capacity reduced to 14 rounds, appeared in the early 1980s.

(P-018-9)

Length: 8.4in (213mm). **Weight unloaded:** 2lb 3oz (998g). **Barrel:** 4.8in (122mm), 6 grooves, right-hand twist. **Magazine:** 15-round detachable box. **Muzzle velocity:** c.1150 ft/sec (350 m/sec).

• Tanfoglio TA-90
Fratelli Tanfoglio SpA, Gardone Val Trompia
9mm Parabellum

The TA-90 is a conventional double-action pistol which owes a good deal of its inspiration to the Czech CZ-75. However, the quality is exceptionally good, as is the accuracy, and it has been widely sold to police and security forces. There were a number of variant models chambered for 7.65mm Parabellum, 9x18mm Police and 9x21mm IMI cartridges, and also a compact version.

Length: 7.95in (202mm). **Weight unloaded:** 2 lb 3.8oz (1012g). **Barrel:** 4.7in (120mm), 6 grooves, right-hand twist. **Magazine:** 15-round detachable box. **Muzzle velocity:** c.1150 ft/sec (350 m/sec).

The Bernardelli P-019. a no-frills service pistol widely used by Italian police.

Tanfoglio's TA-90 owes quite a lot to the Czech CZ75; it is popular with police forces in Europe.

JAPAN

• 26th Year Revolver
Koishikawa Arsenal, Tokyo (1893-1923)
9mm Meiji 26 Japanese revolver

Adopted in 1893, this is known as the Meiji 26 Nen Ken Ju (Pistol, Pattern of the 26th year of the Meiji era). It is of native Japanese design and manufacture insofar as it is an amalgam of features of various Western revolvers; one can but suppose that, as in the case of their self-loading pistols, patriotism held a greater attraction than efficiency. The mechanical details of the barrel latch and cylinder mechanism are copied from Smith & Wesson designs, the lock and trigger mechanism from various European weapons, and the general construction leans heavily on Nagant principles. Early models were to a high standard of finish, but this appears to have deteriorated in later production.

It can charitably be described as serviceable, but little more. It is double-action only, uses a top-break hinged frame and has a hinged cover-plate which can be opened to expose the lockwork for cleaning in much the same way as the French Modéle 1892 revolver. The ammunition is unique to the weapon and although Western ammunition of some makes of 38-caliber revolver might be persuaded to fit, such a practice cannot be recommended.

Length: 8.50in (216mm). **Weight unloaded:** 1lb 15oz (880g). **Barrel:** 4.70in (120mm), 6 grooves, left-hand twist. **Magazine:** 6-round cylinder. **Muzzle velocity:** c.750 ft/sec (229 m/sec).

• Pistol Type Nambu 'A'
Koishikawa Arsenal, Tokyo (1906-1927)
Tokyo Gas & Electric Co., Tokyo (1915-1932)
8mm Nambu

This pistol, designed by Kijiro Nambu, was apparently never accepted as an issue weapon although many were undoubtedly purchased by officers of the Imperial Army and Navy, which must have led to quasi-official recognition. The exact date of these weapons' appearance has long been a subject for debate and was often said to have been 1904 (based on a wrong assessment of the Japanese system of chronology); the pistol seems to have been first publicly exhibited in 1909 at the Toyama Military Academy, although specimens bearing 1906 and 1907 dates have been seen, suggesting that production was begun well before the official unveiling. The army encouraged the design but had no funds to adopt the pistol; they therefore permitted officers to purchase them and also allowed them to be sold commercially so as to keep production afloat.

The pistol was formally adopted by the Japanese Navy in 1909, and shortly thereafter some changes were made in the design. The wooden bottom of the magazine was replaced by aluminum, with two finger grips; the triggerguard was enlarged; the trigger itself was squared-edged rather than chamfered; and the buttstock slot in the butt was removed. The completion of these changes appears to have taken some time, since they tend to appear erratically in the serial number range 2100-2600, but in 1915 (the 4th Year of the Taisho era) the modified pistol became officially known as the 4th year Type. Japan was now at war, and the arsenal was unable to supply both the army and the navy, so production was extended to the Tokyo Gas and Electric Company.

The Nambu breech-lock, achieved by a floating locking block working on the 'prop-up' system, is rather better than the similar type used by the Glisenti. A grip safety was fitted into the forward edge of the butt, and there was no manual safety device. Quality was generally good, though the striker spring was poorly made to the extent of ultimately giving weak strikes. The action remained open after the last shot had been fired, the slide being held by the magazine follower.

Length: 9.00in (228mm). **Weight unloaded:** 1lb 10oz (738g). **Barrel:** 4.70in (120mm), 6 grooves, right-hand twist. **Magazine:** 8-round detachable box. **Muzzle velocity:** c.1100 ft/sec (335 m/sec).

• Nambu 14th Year
Nagoya Arsenal (1927-33, 1941-45).
Koishikawa Arsenal (1928-34). Kokura Arsenal (1934-1936). Nambu Rifle Mfg Co (1936-1944)
8mm Nambu

The 14th Year Nambu is virtually an improved 4th Year and was introduced in 1925-6, the object of the improvements being to simplify manufacture and reduce the cost to a level at which the Japanese Army would be prepared formally to adopt the pistol. There are minor changes in the design to this end, but the basic weapon is the same. A safety catch was added, which can only be operated by the firer's free hand, to replace the grip safety, and the

The Nambu '4th Year' pistol with grip safety and an optimistic tangent sight.

The Japanese Type 26 revolver, a top-break self-cocking design firing a unique 9mm rimmed cartridge.

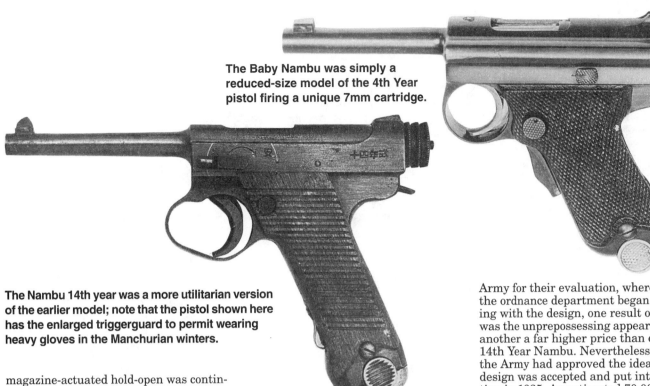

The Baby Nambu was simply a reduced-size model of the 4th Year pistol firing a unique 7mm cartridge.

The Nambu 14th year was a more utilitarian version of the earlier model; note that the pistol shown here has the enlarged triggerguard to permit wearing heavy gloves in the Manchurian winters.

magazine-actuated hold-open was continued. Dual recoil springs and a magazine retaining spring (on later models) ensured that the chances of removing the magazine were only good when the weapon was well-maintained and the user's hands were dry. The 14th Year was officially adopted by the Army in 1927 as an issue pistol for NCOs and was available for purchase by officers. In the last quarter of 1939 the triggerguard was enlarged, as a result of experience in Manchuria, to allow the pistol to be used in a gloved hand. This version also has a magazine retaining spring let into the front edge of the grip. The model is sometimes referred to as the 'Kiska' model, since the first to be seen outside Japan were captured in the Aleutian Islands.

Length: 8.93in (227mm). **Weight unloaded:** 1lb 15oz (900g). **Barrel:** 4.76in (121mm), 6 grooves, right-hand twist. **Magazine:** 8-round detachable box. **Muzzle velocity:** c.1100 ft/sec (335 m/sec).

• Small (Baby) Nambu
Koishikawa Arsenal (1911-1927)
Tokyo Gas & Electric Co (1927-1933)
7mm Nambu

The Type 04 Nambu had disappointing sales, because most officers thought it too cumbersome, so in about 1910 Nambu developed this weapon, a three-quarters size version chambered for a new 7mm cartridge. Even so, it was still not widely liked since it cost about twice as much as contemporary Western designs. It remained in production until 1927 at Koishikawa Arsenal, and until the early

1930s at Tokyo Gas & Electric, but it is doubtful if more than 6,000 or so were made.

Length: 6.75in (171mm). **Weight unloaded:** 1lb 7oz (650g). **Barrel:** 3.25in (83mm) 6 grooves, right-hand twist. **Magazine:** 7-round detachable box. **Muzzle velocity:** c.950 ft/sec (290 m/sec).

• 94 Shiki Kenju
Nambu Rifle Mfg Co, Kokubunji
8mm Taisho 14

Confronted by sales resistance to his designs, due principally to their bulk and price, Nambu set about designing a smaller and cheaper pistol in 1929. The first prototypes were submitted to the

Army for their evaluation, whereupon the ordnance department began tinkering with the design, one result of which was the unprepossessing appearance and another a far higher price than even the 14th Year Nambu. Nevertheless, since the Army had approved the idea, the design was accepted and put into production in 1935. An estimated 70,000 or so were made before production ceased in 1945. Although pre-war guns were well made and finished, the Type 94 rates as one of the world's worst automatic pistols. The design allows it to be fired before the breech is locked, and an exposed sear bar can be released to fire the pistol if clumsily handled. Breech locking is done by a very simple vertical sliding block which is cammed out of engagement during recoil. Guns manufactured in 1944-5 are generally crudely put together and finished.

Length: 7.2in (183mm). **Weight unloaded:** 1lb 11oz (765g). **Barrel:** 3.77in (96mm) 6 grooves, right-hand twist. **Magazine:** 6-round detachable box. **Muzzle velocity:** c.1000 ft/sec (305 m/sec).

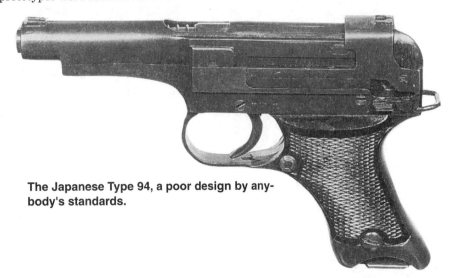

The Japanese Type 94, a poor design by anybody's standards.

The New Nambu, used extensively by Japanese police, is a conventional double-action revolver.

The first model Hamada bears obvious affinities with the Browning 1910 design.

• New Nambu Model 60
Shin Chuo Kogyo, Tokyo
38 Special

The New Nambu revolver is a conventional solid-frame side-opening type. The grip is rather small by Western standards but the pistol is well made and robust, and is accurate. It has been the official Japanese police revolver since the early 1960s, being adopted in deference to American influence at that time. Since then two designs of automatic pistol, in 9mm and 7.65mm calibers, have been put forward but have not been accepted. The Model 60 is also used by the Japanese Maritime Safety Guard.

Length: 7.75in (197mm). **Weight unloaded:** 1lb 8oz (680g). **Barrel:** 3.03in (77mm), 6 grooves, right-hand twist. **Magazine:** 5-round cylinder. **Muzzle velocity:** c.725 ft/sec (220 m/sec).

• Pistol, Hamada, Type 1
Japan Firearms Manufacturing Co., Tokyo
7.65mm Browning

The Japan Firearms Mfg. Co. was a maker of sporting weapons but was ordered, in 1941, to apply itself to military production, and the owner, Mr. Hamada, designed a 7.65mm blowback pistol which in most respects was a copy of the Browning 1910. The only significant design difference was that the barrel was fitted into the frame by a dovetail joint rather than by the interrupted lugs of the Browning design. Manufacture began in late 1941 and continued until February 1944, about 5000 pistols being made.

Length: 6.50in (165mm). **Weight unloaded:** 1lb 7oz (650g). **Barrel:** 3.55in (90mm), 6 grooves, right-hand twist. **Magazine:** 9-round detachable box. **Muzzle velocity:** c.984 ft/sec (300 m/sec).

• Pistol, Hamada, Type 2
Nagoya Arsenal, Notobe Factory
8mm Nambu

In 1941 the Japanese Army demanded a new pistol in 8mm caliber to supplement the Type 14 and Type 94 pistols for issue to officers. Hamada was asked to develop a design and more or less scaled-up his Type 1 pistol. The army, however, appeared to have felt that while adoption of a 7.65mm pistol from outside the military sphere was acceptable, once the caliber was raised to the service 8mm, the design had to come from a military agency. Not having a suitable design, the military therefore took Hamada's pistol, made some cosmetic changes, and approved it as the Type 2 in June 1943. Production began in early 1944 as the manufacture of the Type 1 was ended.

The Type 2 is a blowback pistol, essentially the same mechanism as the Type 1 but in a rather more angular shape. Reports indicate that it was a well-made and serviceable weapon, but relatively few were made. The production system was for them to be made 'in the white' at Notobe, and then sent to Torii-matsu arsenal for bluing and final

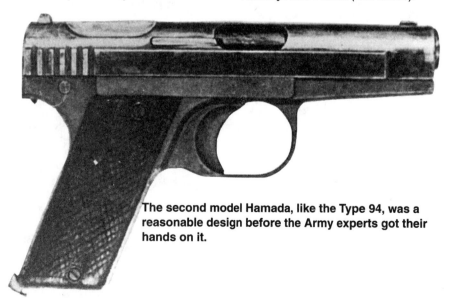

The second model Hamada, like the Type 94, was a reasonable design before the Army experts got their hands on it.

assembly; unfortunately Toriimatsu was severely damaged by bombing early in 1945 and no more than about 50 pistols were ever completed.

Length: 6.97in (177mm). **Weight unloaded:** 1lb 10oz (738g). **Barrel:** 3.72in (94.5mm), 6 grooves, right-hand twist. **Magazine:** 6-round detachable box. **Muzzle velocity:** c.1066 ft/sec (325 m/sec).

• Pistol, Type Inagaki

Naguchi Inagaki, Tokyo
7.65mm Browning

Inagaki was a Tokyo gunsmith who had been trained in Koishikawa arsenal and who had set up his own business in the late 1920s. In 1938 he set about designing a military pistol and produced this blowback model. It is of conventional appearance, except perhaps for the protruding barrel, but internally is unusual in using two leaf springs, set vertically in the butt, one as the return spring and the other as the hammer. The design was approved for production, which probably began early in 1942, and a small number, probably less than 400, were produced. They appear to have been principally issued to naval officers.

Length: 6.25in (158mm). **Weight unloaded:** ca.1lb 8oz (680g). **Barrel:** 2.99in (76mm), 6 grooves, right-hand twist. **Magazine:** 6-round detachable box. **Muzzle velocity:** c.984 ft/sec (300 m/sec).

KOREA, NORTH

• Type 68

State arsenals
7.62x25mm Soviet

This is a much-modified Tokarev TT-33, shorter and more bulky than the original weapon or any other copies. It can be easily distinguished by the narrow oblique serrations at the rear of the slide. Internally the link system which pulls the barrel in and out of engagement with the slide has been replaced by a Browning cam cut into the lug beneath the chamber; the magazine catch has been relocated to the heel of the butt; the slide stop pin has been strengthened, and the firing pin is retained by a plate instead of a cross-pin. The Tokarev magazine will work in this pistol, but the North Korean magazine has no cut-out for the magazine catch in the Tokarev pistol and is thus unusable in that weapon.

Length: 7.28in (185mm). **Weight unloaded:** 1lb 12oz (795g). **Barrel:** 4.25in (108mm), 4 grooves, right-hand twist. **Magazine:** 8-round detachable box. **Muzzle velocity:** c.1296 ft/sec (395 m/sec).

The Daewoo DP51, an unremarkable 9mm double-action design.

KOREA, SOUTH

• Daewoo DP51

Daewoo Precision Industries Ltd., Kumjung, Pusan
9mm Parabellum

This is the standard sidearm of the South Korean military forces and is a delayed blowback double-action design of conventional form. The delay is obtained by using a radially grooved chamber into which the cartridge case extends under chamber pressure, thus resisting opening of the breech, but contracts after the bullet has left the barrel so as to permit the operating cycle to begin.

The **DH40** is the same pistol in 40 S&W caliber, and the **DH45** the same in 45 ACP caliber. These are offered commercially.

Length: 7.48in (190mm). **Weight unloaded:** 1lb 12oz (800g). **Barrel:** 4.13in (105mm), 6 grooves, right-hand twist. **Magazine:** 13-round detachable box. **Muzzle velocity:** c.1150 ft/sec (351 m/sec).

MEXICO

• Pistola Automatica Sistema Obregon (1934-38)

Fabrica de Armas, Mexico City
45 ACP

Outwardly, this weapon resembles a Colt 45-caliber M1911A1, with slight contour changes in the slide and a peculiar safety-catch/slide lock. Inwardly, it is based on the Austro-Hungarian 'Steyr-Hahn' system, using a helical cam on the barrel engaging with a locking lug on the frame to rotate the barrel out of engagement with the slide on recoil. It is

The Mexican Obregon, one of the few rotating-barrel designs to achieve military service.

unusual in that the pistol has followed the Colt design closely enough to have the barrel rifled with a left-hand twist, making it the only pistol in the world ever to operate on a right-hand barrel unlocking system, since the motion of unlocking is resisted by the torque generated by the bullet in its travel up the rifling.

Chambered for the 45 ACP round, this is a well-designed weapon which, owing to the axial movement of the barrel on unlocking, is theoretically more accurate than the Colt or Browning designs of swinging barrel; there appears to be no record of comparative tests by which this contention could be proved or disproved.

Length: 8.25in (210mm). **Weight unloaded:** 2lb 5oz (1020g). **Barrel:** 4.88in (124mm), 6 grooves, left-hand twist. **Magazine:** 7-round detachable box. **Muzzle velocity:** c.850 ft/sec (260 m/sec).

POLAND

• Pistol wz/35 (VIS)
Fabryka Broni, Radom
9mm Parabellum

The Polish Model 35 is variously known as the Radom, from the arsenal at which it was made, or as the VIS (from the initials of the designers, Wilneiwczyc and Skrzypinski). The locking of breech and slide is controlled by a cam on the barrel, as in the FN-Browning GP35. On the side of the slide is a catch which drops the hammer under control onto a loaded chamber after first blocking the hammer's path to the firing pin, allowing subsequent thumb-cocking. On the frame, the device which appears to be a safety catch is in fact no more than a slide lock to facilitate stripping; the only

The wz/64, the Polish equivalent of the Russian Makarov.

true safety device is a grip safety, although the hammer drop lever could also be considered as an additional type.

During the German occupation of Poland, these weapons were made for the German Army (as the Pistole 35[p]) and may be found very roughly finished and without the hammer release catch or the slide lock; the original Polish pistols are easily identified by the prominent Polish eagle engraved on the slide, and by their outstanding finish and fit. Production for Germany is marked simply with 'Pistole 35(p)' and the usual Wehrmacht acceptance stamps. Unusually, the Radom factory did not have the normal German three-letter code but marked the pistol in exactly the same way as the original Polish production, except omitting the year and the Polish eagle.

Heavier and larger than the general run of pistols chambered for 9mm Parabellum, the wz/35 is among the best—

and is certainly among the more comfortable— to shoot.

In 1992 the Zaklady Metalowe Lucznik of Radom—the commercialized arm of the Radom arsenal—put the Radom pistol back into production, principally for collectors but also as a service pistol for anyone so inclined. The original engineering drawings of 1937 were used as the basis, and the pistol is virtually identical though with very slight differences in weight and overall length. It is, of course, to an exceptionally high quality of manufacture and finish.

Length: 8.31 in (211 mm). **Weight unloaded:** 2lb 5oz (1050g). **Barrel:** 4.53in (115mm), 6 grooves, right-hand twist. **Magazine:** 8-round detachable box. **Muzzle velocity:** c.1150 ft/sec (350 m/sec).

• Pistol wz/64
State Arsenals
9mm Soviet Makarov

The wz/64 was the replacement in the Polish Army for the obsolete Pistolet TT. It bears a strong resemblance to the Soviet Makarov, and fires the same ammunition, but it also has some features copied from the German Walther PP models. Like the Makarov, the operation is by blowback without any form of breech locking and while this probably makes the pistol a little less pleasant to fire than one with a locked breech, it is apparently perfectly reliable. Like the Walther, the trigger has a double action and the hammer can be cocked by a straight pull through for the first round. The mechanism is relatively simple and quite robust and is a fairly close copy of the Makarov design. The whole thing was neat and serviceable, which is about all that is required in this class of pistol.

The Polish Radom, a heavy 9mm pistol and one of the first to use a decocking lever.

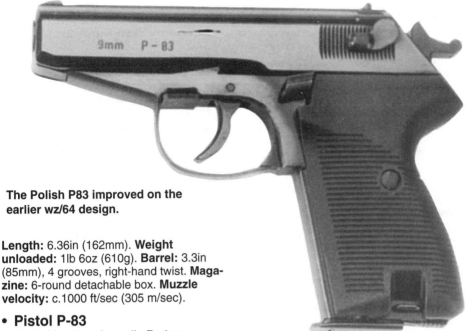

The Polish P83 improved on the earlier wz/64 design.

Length: 6.36in (162mm). **Weight unloaded:** 1lb 6oz (610g). **Barrel:** 3.3in (85mm), 4 grooves, right-hand twist. **Magazine:** 6-round detachable box. **Muzzle velocity:** c.1000 ft/sec (305 m/sec).

• Pistol P-83
Zaklady Metalowe Lucznik, Radom
9mm Makarov; 9mm Short

This was developed in the late 1970s as a cheaper and easier to manufacture replacement for the wz/64. Its general appearance and operation are similar to the wz/64, a fixed-barrel blowback, but there is more use of stampings and forging in the design and less machining work required. The lockwork is double action, and a slide-mounted lever drops the hammer safely onto the loaded chamber, lowering the end of the firing pin out of the hammer path as it does so. It also has a loaded chamber indicator.

Length: 6.49in (165 mm). **Weight unloaded:** 1lb 10oz (730g). **Barrel:** 3.54in (90mm), 4 grooves, right-hand twist. **Magazine:** 8-round detachable box. **Muzzle velocity:** c.1023 ft/sec (312 m/sec) (9mm Makarov).

• Pistol P-93
Zaklady Metalowe Lucznik, Radom
9mm Makarov

The P-93 is a further development of the P-83, which it generally resembles. The principal difference is the placement of the de-cocking lever on the frame, above the left side grip, instead of on the slide. The hammer is a ring type, rather than a spur, and the rear sight is adjustable.

Length: 7.00in (178mm). **Weight unloaded:** 1lb 10oz (750g). **Barrel:** 3.93in (100mm), 6 grooves, right-hand twist. **Magazine:** 8-round detachable box. **Muzzle velocity:** c.1036 ft/sec (316 m/sec).

• MAG-95
Zaklady Metalowe Lucznik, Radom
9mm Parabellum

The MAG-95 is a conventional double-action locked-breech military pistol with overtones of Browning and SIG. The tapering frame resembles the Browning GP35, while the barrel locks into the central ejection port in a similar manner to the SIG 220 series. There is a frame-mounted de-cocking lever, a slide

The most recent Polish design is this MAG-95 which appears to have borrowed a few ideas from SIG.

The P93 is a further improvement and is also offered for export sale.

stop lever and also a stripping catch on the left side, and an automatic firing pin safety system is incorporated. The barrel is chromed internally, and a laser target indicator can be fitted to the front of the frame. A lengthened 20-round magazine is available as an extra. There is a variant model, the **MAG-98**, which has an alloy slide and a recoil buffer, reducing the weight to 875g.

Length: 7.87in (200mm). **Weight unloaded:** 2lb 5oz (1050g). **Barrel:** 4.53in (115mm), 6 grooves, right-hand twist. **Magazine:** 15- or 20-round detachable box. **Muzzle velocity:** c.1247 ft/sec (380 m/sec).

PORTUGAL

• Savage M/908 and M/915

Savage Arms Corporation, Chicopee Falls, Mass., U.S.A.

7.65mm Browning (32 ACP)

Portugal was the only country ever to adopt the Savage pistol as service issue, although the design was unofficially used elsewhere. The M/908 was the same weapon as Savage's 1907 commercial model, with a rounded cocking piece, made to the 1904 patents of E. H. Searle and the result of an experimental 45-caliber pistol submitted to the US Army pistol trials of 1907. The standard pistol of the Portuguese army was either the 7.65mm Parabellum M/909 or the 9mm Parabellum M/910, and after they entered World War I on the Allied side there was no way that they were going to augment their stocks of those. Since every other army in the world was also clamoring for pistols, the Portuguese had to take what they could find, though since their army was small, so was their requirement for pistols, and they were able to solve their problem on the American commercial market. A small quantity

of the later M/915 design, which differed principally in the provision of a large spur-type cocking piece, were also procured.

The operation of the Savage pistols lies in that twilight class known as delayed or retarded blowback: the barrel and slide are unlocked by the rotational movement of the barrel, resisted by the torque of the bullet taking the rifling. Since the unlocking movement is only 5° of rotation—compared, for example, with the 90° of the Austro-Hungarian M07 Roth-Steyr—the effectiveness of the breech-lock has been the subject of much debate. Spark photographs, taken in Germany in the 1920s, appear to have shown that the breech of the Savage opens rather faster than that of the 25 ACP Colt pocket pistol, which is a pure blowback design. Though, given the relative strengths of the 7.65 and 6.35mm cartridges and the relative weights of the Colt and Savage slides, this should not come as much of a surprise. Nevertheless, it throws some doubt upon the inventor's claim that it was actually a locked breech, and even calling it delayed blowback is being generous.

Length: 6.60in (167mm). **Weight unloaded:** 1lb 5oz (570g). **Barrel:** 3.50in (87mm), 4 grooves, right-hand twist. **Magazine:** 10-round detachable box. **Muzzle velocity:** c.950 ft/sec (289 m/sec).

RUSSIA

• Nagant Model of 1895

Manufacture d'Armes Nagant Fréres, Liege, Belgium
Tul'skiy Oruzheynyi Zavod, Tula
7.62x38R Nagant

The Nagant revolver, adopted by the Tsarist Army in 1895, is of much the same general appearance as other military revolvers of the period, but incorporates an unusual feature into the mechanism. In an endeavor to extract the maximum performance from the weapon, an attempt has been made to overcome one of the theoretical drawbacks of a revolver, the leak of propelling gas between the front face of the cylinder and the rear face of the barrel. In theory at least, this reduces the efficiency of the weapon, although in the best revolver designs emanating from highly regarded manufacturers, the tolerances are such that this objection becomes negligible until the weapon becomes worn.

The Russian M95, produced to the 1894 patent of Léon Nagant (although largely based on an earlier Pieper design), incorporates a cam mechanism which, on cocking, causes the cylinder to be moved forward so that the rear of the barrel is enclosed within the mouth of the aligned chamber. The cartridge

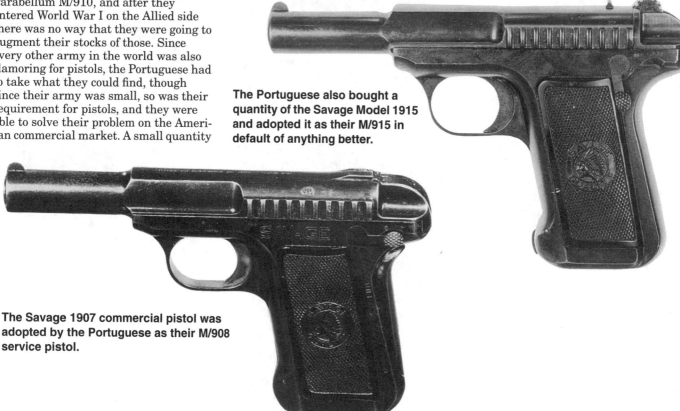

The Portuguese also bought a quantity of the Savage Model 1915 and adopted it as their M/915 in default of anything better.

The Savage 1907 commercial pistol was adopted by the Portuguese as their M/908 service pistol.

The Tokarev TT-33; note the absence of any form of safety catch.

Nagant M1895 revolver, cocked, showing the long firing pin necessary to reach the cartridge when the cylinder is fully forward to effect the gas seal between barrel and chamber.

is also unusual in that the bullet is totally contained within the case, and the mouth is slightly reduced in diameter; thus, when the cylinder is pressed forward, the case mouth actually enters the barrel. On firing, the expansion of the case mouth and the enclosure by the chamber effectively combine to provide a sealed joint and to prevent the leakage of gas. As the action is operated for the next shot to be fired, so the cylinder is withdrawn, rotated, and returned once more to seal.

The Nagant design, produced both in Belgium and in Russia, in single-action (trooper's) and double-action (officer's) patterns, was the only 'gas-seal' mechanism to achieve total success: various other manufacturers produced weapons of this form but none became widespread. The value of such a seal is in any case questionable, particularly as it is achieved at the expense of needless mechanical complication; since the gun barrel is short, the bullet is within the barrel for less than one millisecond and in this time there is little chance for much gas to escape.

Length: 9.06in (229mm). **Weight unloaded:** 1lb 12oz (790g). **Barrel:** 4.35in (110mm), 4 grooves, right-hand twist. **Magazine:** 7-round cylinder. **Muzzle velocity:** c.1000 ft/sec (305 m/sec).

• Tokarev TT-30 and TT-33
Tul'skiy Oruzheynyi Zavod, Tula
7.62x25mm Soviet M30

The Tokarev pistols, formerly the standard weapons of the Soviet Army, were based upon the Colt-Browning design and used a swinging link beneath the barrel to unlock the barrel from the slide on recoil. Some minor modifications

were made with the intention of simplifying manufacture and maintenance: a notable feature was that the lockwork could be removed *en bloc* for cleaning purposes. A further and very useful modification was the machining of the magazine guide lips into the pistol itself, which meant that damage to the mouth of the magazine was less likely to result in a malfunction than in most other designs of pistol.

Two versions of the pistol were made, normally called the TT-30 and the TT-33 (TT representing Tula-Tokarev). On the TT-30 the locking lugs were machined on to the top surfaces of the barrel as in the Colt M1911A1, but on the TT-33 they were machined entirely around the barrel in an endeavor to quicken manufacture; there are also other smaller differences, notably in the design of the frame and the sub-assembly carrying the lockwork.

As with most Soviet equipment, the standard of finish of the TT pistols was a long way below Western standards, but there was nothing wrong with the mechanism, and where precision was necessary it was provided. Chambered for the 7.62mm M30 Soviet automatic pistol cartridge, the Tokarev will in most cases fire the 7.63mm Mauser (depending on the tolerance allowed by the ammunition manufacturers): because of these high-powered rounds, however, the muzzle velocity is rather higher than that generally expected in a pistol and, owing to the violent recoil, the pistols are difficult to fire with accuracy.

The pistol was manufactured in several of the Eastern bloc countries, where

it was known by different titles and incorporated minor modifications. In Poland and Yugoslavia it was known as the M48, though the 9mm Yugoslav version was the M65. In Hungary it was the M48, in China the M51 and M54, and in North Korea as the M68.

Length: 7.68in (193mm). **Weight unloaded:** 1lb 13oz (830g). **Barrel:** 4.57in (116mm), 4 grooves, right-hand twist. **Magazine:** 8-round detachable box. **Muzzle velocity:** c.1375 ft/sec (418 m/sec).

• Stechkin (APS)
State factories
9mm Makarov

As we have seen, many designers have been tempted to try their hand at converting a pistol to a submachine-gun. In the 1960s the game seems to have affected the Soviets, whose entry was the Stechkin.

It is a blowback pistol loosely based on the Walther PP, but rather larger and without the double-action lock. The safety catch, on the slide, has three positions: down for safe, horizontal for single shot, and up for fully automatic fire. Hand-held automatic fire is, of course, simply a waste of time and ammunition, and the Stechkin is supplied with a wooden holster-stock almost identical with that used with the Mauser c/96 Military model. With this attached, it becomes more manageable. Chambered for the 9mm Makarov cartridge, the Stechkin was rarely seen outside the Soviet bloc, and had been removed from service by the late 1970s.

Length: 8.85in (225mm). **Weight unloaded:** 1lb 10oz (760g). **Barrel:** 5.00in

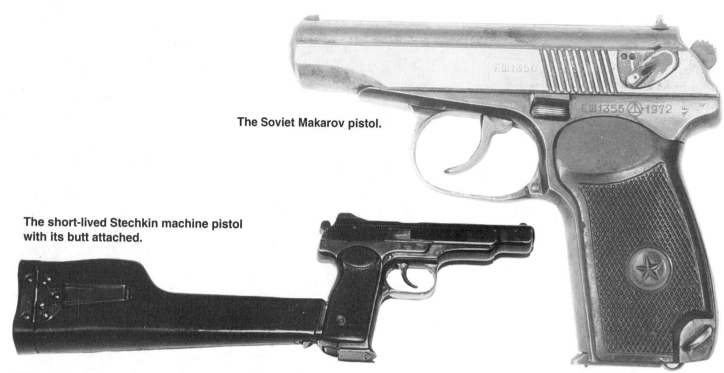

The Soviet Makarov pistol.

The short-lived Stechkin machine pistol with its butt attached.

(127mm), 4 grooves, right-hand twist. **Magazine:** 20-round detachable box. **Cyclic rate:** 725rpm. **Muzzle velocity:** c.1115 ft/sec (340 m/sec).

• Makarov (PM)
State factories
9mm Makarov

The Walther PP impressed most people who came into contact with it for the first time during the war; so much so, that many nations later produced copies, with or without benefit of license. The Soviets were among the latter number, as the Makarov is simply an enlarged Model PP chambered for the peculiar 9mm Makarov pistol round. This has a blunt bullet like a 9mm Short, but the case,

slightly longer than a 9mm Short, is shorter than a 9mm Parabellum and thus effectively clings to the Soviet tradition of chambering their weapons for their own ammunition and also preventing the use of their ammunition in anyone else's equipment. The 9mm Soviet round makes some sort of sense in being about the heaviest round that can safely be used in a blowback pistol, but it still seems to be an expensive and complicated way of achieving the end result.

Length: 6.35in (160mm). **Weight unloaded:** 1lb 9oz (720g). **Barrel:** 3.85in (98mm), 4 grooves, right-hand twist. **Magazine:** 8-round detachable box. **Muzzle velocity:** c.1070 ft/sec (325 m/sec).

• Pistolet Samozaryadniy Malogabaritniy (PSM)
State Arsenals
5.45x18mm

This pistol was first known in the West in 1983 and is understood to be issued to security police and troops in the Soviet Union. It resembles the Walther PP, being a fixed-barrel blowback weapon with double-action lock, but there are some small differences in the lock mechanism and the safety catch has been moved from its place on the side of the slide to a position alongside the hammer in an attempt to make the pistol as thin as possible for concealed carrying. It fires a unique 5.45mm bottle-necked cartridge of low power.

Length: 6.3in (160mm). **Weight unloaded:** 16.2oz (460g). **Barrel:** 3.34in (85mm), 6 grooves, right-hand twist. **Magazine:** 8-round detachable box. **Muzzle velocity:** 960 ft/sec (293 m/sec).

• SPP-1 Underwater Pistol
Tznitochmash, Moscow
4.5mm SPS Special

Of the several underwater weapons known or rumored to be in existence, this, together with its companion rifle, was the first to be publicly revealed in the early 1990s. Its general resemblance to the Heckler & Koch design may be coincidence; on the other hand, there may be a limited choice of design options is this somewhat restricted field of endeavor.

The pistol consists of a frame with four barrels in a square formation, with a large breechblock at the rear which con-

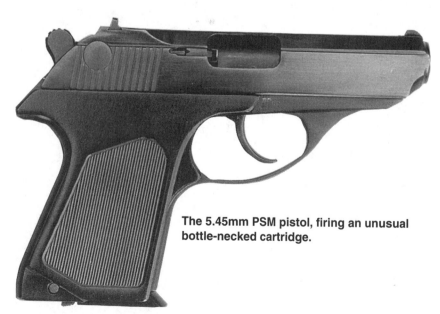

The 5.45mm PSM pistol, firing an unusual bottle-necked cartridge.

The Soviet underwater pistol, with its clip of four darts.

tains the firing mechanism. This breech unit is unlocked and the barrel unit tipped down in shotgun fashion, allowing a clip containing four cartridges to be loaded into the barrels. The barrel unit is then moved back into place and locked and the weapon is ready to fire. Pressure on the trigger will drive a self-cocking mechanism to fire one barrel at a time. The muzzle velocity and range vary according to the depth of water and the consequent water pressure; the effective range varies from 17 meters at 5 meters depth, to 6 meters at 40 meters depth. In air, it is effective to 50 meters range.

The cartridge consists of a rimless bottle-necked case which appears to be the 7.62x39mm case modified, carrying a 115mm long drag-stabilized dart.

Length: 9.60in (244mm). **Weight unloaded:** 2lb 2oz (950g). **Barrels:** not known. **Magazine:** 4-round clip. **Muzzle velocity:** 820 ft/sec (250 m/sec) in air.

• Gyurza P-9
Tznitochmash, Moscow
9x21mm Gyurza

This locked-breech pistol appeared in about 1995; chambered for a special cartridge firing a cored bullet which, it is claimed, is able to penetrate 30 layers of Kevlar fabric and two 1.4mm sheets of titanium at 100 meters range or 4mm of steel armor at 60 meters. It is also claimed that groups of 32cm (12.6 inches) can be achieved at 100 meters range.

The pistol is double-action, and appears to have a form of grip safety. At present, we have no information on how the breech is locked. The magazine is double-column, the frame is of polymer with steel inserts, and the slide and barrel are of steel. It is said to be in use by Russian military units and special forces.

Length: 7.68in (195mm). **Weight unloaded:** 2lb 3oz (995g). **Barrel:** not known. **Maga-**

zine: 18-round detachable box. **Muzzle velocity:** 1362 ft/sec (415 m/sec).

• PSS Silent
Tznitochmash, Moscow
7.62x42mm SP-4

This is a fairly simple and conventional, blowback, double-action, semi-automatic pistol which achieves silence by firing a special cartridge. The only unusual thing about the pistol is the length of the slide movement, due to the abnormal proportions of the cartridge.

The SP-4 cartridge uses a necked case, inside which is a piston. Beneath the piston is the propelling charge, and above it is a stem which is pressed against the base of the bullet. On firing, the propelling charge explodes, driving the piston forward. This movement is transmitted to the bullet, with sufficient force to propel it through the barrel and to an effective range of 50 meters or more. The piston, reaching the bottle-neck of the cartridge, jams there and thus seals the propellant gases—and hence the noise, smoke and flash—inside the case, so that there is no firing signature worth speaking of. The blowback action of the pistol then ejects the spent case and reloads, though in this case 'blowback' is something of a misnomer—'reaction' might be a better word.

Length: 6.50in (165mm). **Weight unloaded:** 1lb 9oz (700g). **Barrel:** not known. **Magazine:** 6-round detachable box. **Muzzle velocity:** 655 ft/sec (200 m/sec).

SOUTH AFRICA

• Vektor Z-88
LIW Division of Denel, Pretoria
9mm Parabellum

This pistol was developed in 1986 against a demand from the South African Defense Force and went into production in 1989. It takes its title from the late T.D. Zeederberg, former general manager of LIW and from its year of approval. The design is that of the Beretta 92, although the precise connection is not known and it is unlikely that Beretta would have flouted the UN embargo on weapons technology which existed at that time. Nevertheless, the appearance, functioning and dimensions are exactly the same as the Beretta 92. Perhaps 'imitation is the sincerest form of flattery'.

• Vektor SP
Vektor Division of Denel Ltd, Lyttleton.
9mm Parabellum; 40 S&W

There are two pistols in this group, the **SP1**, chambered for the 9mm Parabellum cartridge, and the **SP2** cham-

The Russian PSS silent pistol which fired an unusual piston-type cartridge.

The South African Z-88 pistol has more than a passing resemblance to the Beretta 92.

The Vektor SP2 is an original South African design.

bered for the 40 Smith & Wesson cartridge. Both are to the same design, which is a development of the Z-88 insofar as it uses the same dropping wedge system of breech locking, though the open-topped Beretta style of slide has been abandoned for the more usual type. The slide of steel, the frame of alloy; an automatic firing pin safety system is used, plus a manual safety catch. The safety catch is duplicated on both sides of the pistol, and the magazine release can be fitted to either side as the user prefers. The SP2 has an accessory conversion kit, consisting of a barrel, return spring and magazine, allowing it to be reconfigured in 9mm Parabellum caliber. The SP1 is in use by South African defense forces and

is also manufactured under license by the Arms Corporation of the Philippines.

Two compact versions, known as the **SP-1 and SP-2 General Officer's Pistols,** are also produced. These are 20mm shorter in overall length, with 103mm barrels and weigh 850g, but are otherwise identical with the full-sized weapons.

(SP-1)

Length: 8.27in (210mm). **Weight, unloaded:** 2lb 3oz (995g). **Barrel:** 4.65in (118mm); 4 grooves, polygonal, right-hand twist. **Magazine:** 15 round detachable box; (11 round in .40 caliber). **Muzzle velocity:** 1180 ft/sec (360m/sec) (9mm).

• Campo-Giro Models 1913, and 1913-16

Unceta y Compania, Guernica
9x23mm Largo (Bergmann-Bayard)

The Campo-Giro pistol, designed by Don Venancio Lopez de Ceballos y Aguirre, Count of Camp-Giro, was Unceta y Cia's first successful self-loading pistol, the origins of which stretched back to 1904. The first model of the Campo-Giro to be adopted by the Spanish government was that of 1913, rapidly replaced by the slightly modified pattern of 1916 which paved the way for the highly successful line of Astra pistols.

Like their successors, the Campo-Giro pistols were blowback weapons firing the 9mm Bergmann-Bayard cartridge, the standard Spanish service cartridge since their adoption in 1905 of the Bergmann 'Mars' pistol. It must be noted, however, that the original model of the Campo-Giro—the Modelo 1904—was designed around a special 9mm cartridge, after which the design was modified to cater to the regulation ammunition. This powerful cartridge demanded a powerful return spring in the pistol and thus an iron grip in order to pull the slide back and load it.

Although of awkward appearance, it was well made, and incorporated a shock absorber in the frame to withstand the hammering of the slide moving back and forth. About 1000 Model 1913 pistols were made, and then in 1916 a change was made in the magazine release, resulting in the 'Model 1913/16' of which about 13,000 were made.

(Model 13/16)

Length: 8.03in (204mm). **Weight unloaded:** 2lb 2oz (960g). **Barrel:** 6.49in (16mm), 6 grooves, right-hand twist. **Magazine:** 8-round detachable box. **Muz-**

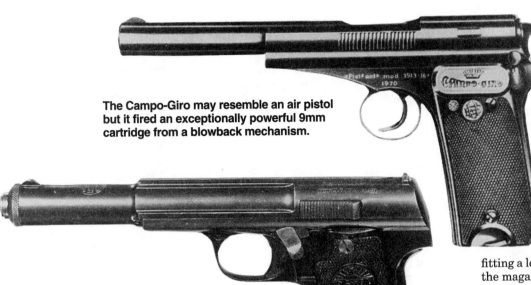

The Campo-Giro may resemble an air pistol but it fired an exceptionally powerful 9mm cartridge from a blowback mechanism.

The Astra 400 improved on and replaced the Campo-Giro as the official Spanish service pistol.

zle velocity: c.1165 ft/sec (355 m/sec).

• Astra Model 1921 and Model 400

Unceta y Compania, Guernica
9x23mm Largo

The Astra 400 is an unusual weapon in two particular respects: first, it is a blowback pistol using heavy and powerful cartridges and, second, the chamber dimensions are such that it will work—with varying degrees of success—with a number of different cartridges. Although primarily chambered for the 9mm Bergmann-Bayard cartridge, most will also accept 9mm Steyr, 9mm Parabellum, 9mm Browning Long, 9mm Glisenti and 380 ACP cartridges. The pistol was designed and manufactured by Unceta of Guernica, first appearing in commercial guise in 1921 as the Astra 400 and later adopted by the Spanish Army in 1922 as the Model 1921. The reliability of the blowback action is obtained by using a powerful recoil spring and relatively heavy recoiling parts, and pulling back the slide of an Astra in order to load requires a vise-like grip. The catholicity of ammunition is achieved not only by suitable selection of measurements and tolerances in the breech and extractor, but also by making the striker rather longer than usual in order that it can reach out to strike the primer of the shorter cartridges with sufficient force of blow. It has to be said, though, that the Astra is not at its best with some of the rounds—especially the 9mm Parabellum—since it does not always feed cleanly with the shorter cartridges.
Length: 9.25in (235mm). **Weight unloaded:** 2lb 6.5oz (1080g). **Barrel:** 5.50in. (140mm), 6 grooves, right-hand twist. **Magazine:** 8-round detachable box. **Muzzle velocity:** c.1125 ft/sec (343 m/sec).

• Astra Model 900

Unceta y Compania, Guernica
7.63mm Mauser

This is outwardly a copy of Mauser's C/96 Military pistol, but internally it is somewhat changed from the original design. The left side of the body is formed into a sliding plate which can be removed to give access to the lockwork, which is built into the frame and not—as in the Mauser—mounted in a separate detachable unit. The barrel is screwed and shrunk into the barrel extension and not, as in the Mauser, an integral forging. The general design of the frame is much different and the weapon is heavier and more solid, but all this modification (particularly that of the lockwork) has led to an unfortunately heavy trigger pull, since the mechanism has been designed more with an eye to cost than to efficiency. While the weapon is an avowed copy of Mauser's design and basic system, the recoil of the bolt and barrel while locked together is almost twice the distance covered by the Mauser—a fact which defies rational explanation.

The Model 900 began production in 1928, aimed largely at the Chinese and South American markets where the Mauser was a prestige weapon, but where the genuine article was too expensive; like the Mauser, it too was supplied with a wooden stock-holster. Production

ceased in 1934 in favor of the selective-fire Model 902.
Length: 12.50in (317mm). **Weight unloaded:** 2lb 14oz (1300g). **Barrel:** 5.50in (140mm), 6 grooves, right-hand twist. **Magazine:** 10-round integral box. **Muzzle velocity:** c.1450 ft/sec (442 m/sec).

• Astra Model 902

Unceta y Compania, Guernica
7.63mm Mauser

The Astra Model 902 was an improved version of the Model 900, made by fitting a longer barrel, adding a section to the magazine to raise its capacity to 20 rounds and arranging a switch whereby full automatic fire could be made available. This, with the shoulder stock fitted, turned the pistol into a rudimentary form of submachine gun.

The automatic fire selector is a short lever on the right side of the frame behind the triggerguard: set vertically to the figure 'I', it gives single shot self-loading action but, turned through about 45° to the rear to the figure '20', it gives automatic fire—on pressing the trigger the gun continues to fire until pressure is released or the magazine is empty, whichever happens first. A cam on the lever engages the trigger bar and causes it to move an additional distance when the trigger is pressed; this causes the bar to engage a second notch on the firing sear to prevent it from re-engaging with the hammer so long as the trigger is pressed. In this situation, a secondary sear, operated automatically by a recess machined in the barrel extension, delays the hammer fall until the breech is closed and thus ensures a fair blow on the striker. With the selector lever in its vertical position, the additional movement of the trigger bar is not applied and the automatic sear is overridden.

The material used in the firing mechanism is generally not of the best and, after firing a few hundred rounds under conditions of continuous operation, the amount of wear reaches the point where automatic action completely fails to take place. The weapon was manufactured for only two years—from 1934 to 1936—and specimens are rarely met today.
Length: 14.25in (362mm). **Weight unloaded:** 2lb 15oz (1360g). **Barrel:** 7.25in (183mm), 6 grooves, right-hand twist. **Magazine:** 20-round integral box. **Muzzle velocity:** c.1500 ft/sec (456 m/sec).

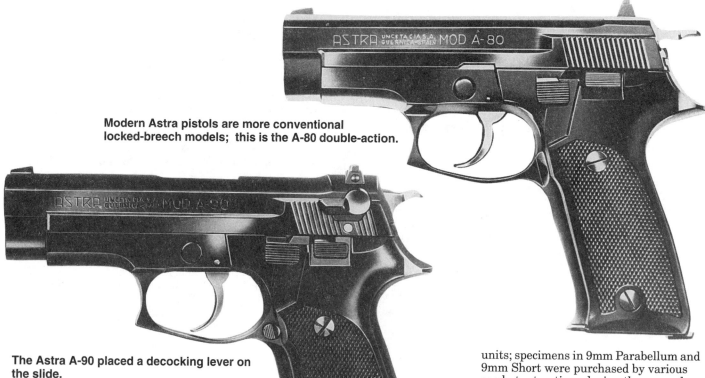

Modern Astra pistols are more conventional locked-breech models; this is the A-80 double-action.

The Astra A-90 placed a decocking lever on the slide.

• Astra Models A-80, A-90
Astra-Unceta y Cia SA, Guernica
9mm Parabellum

This pistol appears to have been influenced by the SIG P-220, having similar angular contours and a de-cocking lever which can lower the hammer safely. The firing pin is locked by a spring-loaded plunger which is engaged at all times except when the trigger is fully pulled back and is about to release the hammer. The breech is locked by a cam beneath the chamber which pulls the barrel from engagement with the slide. A safety catch is fitted on both sides of the pistol and the de-cocking lever can be removed from the left side, its normal place, and a special left-handed version fitted on the right side of the frame. The extractor functions as a loaded chamber indicator, and the sights have white inlays for use in poor light. The A-80 was introduced in 1980 and has been purchased by a number of military and security forces. In 1985 an improved design, the **A-90,** was introduced. This has an improved trigger mechanism and adjustable sights but is otherwise the same as the A-80.

Length: 7.09in (180mm). **Weight unloaded:** 2lb 3oz (980g). **Barrel:** 3.8in (96.5mm). **Magazine:** 15-round detachable box. **Muzzle velocity:** c.1150 ft/sec (350 m/sec).

• Llama Model IX
Gabilondo y Compania, Elgoibar
9mm - various chamberings.

The Llama series of pistols, produced in a variety of calibers to suit all comers, are simply copies of the Colt 45-caliber M1911A1 pistol differing only in dimensions. The model chambered for the 9mm Bergmann-Bayard cartridge was used in limited numbers by the Spanish Army for some years and also by Spanish police units; specimens in 9mm Parabellum and 9mm Short were purchased by various combatant nations during the general pistol shortage in World War II. A few pistols were also chambered for the 45 ACP cartridge.

Length: 6.25in (158mm). **Weight unloaded:** 1lb 5oz (600g). **Barrel:** 3.50in (87mm), 6 grooves, right-hand twist. **Magazine:** 7-round detachable box. **Muzzle velocity:** c.850 ft/sec (260 m/sec).

• Llama M-82
Llama Gabilondo y Cia SA, Vitoria
9mm Parabellum

This is a modern double-action pistol introduced in 1988 and adopted by the Spanish Army. Breech locking is performed by a dropping wedge, similar to the system used on the Walther P38. There is a slide-mounted safety catch which, when operated, conceals and locks the firing pin and disconnects the trigger bar. With the safety

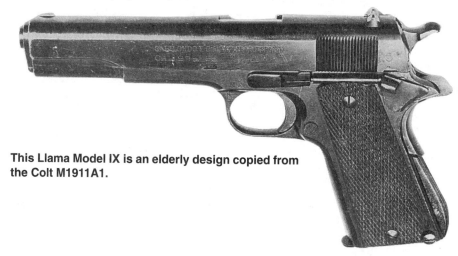

This Llama Model IX is an elderly design copied from the Colt M1911A1.

Llama's M82 design is a modern double-action pistol.

catch applied, loading the pistol will cause the hammer to fall safely, after which removing the safety and pulling the trigger fires the first shot.

Length: 8.23in (209mm). **Weight unloaded:** 2lb 7oz (1110g). **Barrel:** 4.48in (114mm), 6 grooves, right-hand twist. **Magazine:** 15-round detachable box. **Muzzle velocity:** c.1132 ft/sec (345 m/sec).

• Star Model A and Model M
Star Bonifacio Echeverria SA, Eibar, Guipuzcoa
9x23mm Largo

The Star series of pistols were well distributed throughout the world in a wide variety of calibers and styles. The military models were generally based on the outline of the 45-caliber Colt M1911, though the smaller calibers were plain blowback types and the larger ones, while adhering to the Browning system of breech locking, show one or two simplifications—such as the absence of a grip safety—intended to make their manufacture easier and cheaper. In addition to the Spanish service caliber, the Model A could be supplied in 9mm Short and 7.63mm Mauser chambering, the latter being the more common.

A minor aberration of the 1930s was the attempt to turn a reasonable pistol into a submachine gun, generally one of questionable efficiency. Star made their attempt at this by modifying the 9mm Model A to achieve fully automatic fire. Some were provided with the usual type of detachable stock/holster and optimistic rear sight and with lengthened magazines holding 16 or 32 rounds, although many were without these additions. Like all other single-hand fully automatic weapons, these machine pistols were of little practical value, particularly with such a powerful chambering. Apart from problems of ammunition wastage, the guns climbed excessively in automatic fire.

The automatic versions were manufactured just prior to the Spanish Civil War (1936-39) and were known as Model M. A quantity were supplied to the Nica-

raguan government, but beyond that, their military employment was rare.

Length: 7.95in (202mm). **Weight unloaded:** 2lb 2oz (960g). **Barrel:** 5.00in (127mm), 4 grooves, right-hand twist. **Magazine:** 8-round detachable box (16-or 32-round units were available for Model M). **Cyclic rate:** 800rpm (Model M). **Muzzle velocity:** c.1200 ft/sec (365 m/sec) (9mm Largo).

• Star Super
Star Bonifacio Echeverria SA, Eibar
9x23mm Largo

The Super Star was little different from the Star Model A, its predecessor. There were slight changes in the butt contours, a two-piece slide stop appeared instead of a one-piece type, and it was generally of a better finish. The Spanish issue models were, of course, chambered for the 9mm Largo cartridge, but the pistol was commercially available in 9mm

Parabellum, 45 ACP and 38 Super Auto chambering.

Length: 8.03in (204mm). **Weight unloaded:** 2lb 4oz (1020g). **Barrel:** 5.25in (134mm), 4 grooves, right-hand twist. **Magazine:** 9-round detachable box. **Muzzle velocity:** c.1200 ft/sec (365 m/sec).

• Star Model BM
Star Bonifacio Echeverria SA, Eibar
9mm (Parabellum)

Echeverria have produced a large number of pistols under their 'Star' name; this one is included here since it was the official sidearm of all Spanish military and paramilitary forces, including the Guardia Civil, in the late 1970s.

Like most Star designs, it was based on the well-known Browning swinging link method of breech locking. An improved thumb safety locked both slide and hammer, whether the action was cocked or uncocked, and a magazine safety rendered the weapon safe when the magazine was removed.

Length: 7.17in (182mm). **Weight unloaded:** 2lb 2oz (965g). **Barrel:** 3.90in (99mm), 6 grooves, right-hand twist. **Magazine:** 8-round detachable box. **Muzzle velocity:** c.1280 ft/sec (390 m/sec).

• Star Model 28DA
Star Bonifacio Echeverria SA, Eibar
9mm Parabellum

Introduced in the late 1970s for police and military use, this is a conventional double-action recoil-operated pistol using the familiar Colt-Browning link method of breech locking. The slide runs inside the frame, which gives excellent support and contributes to accuracy; there is an ambidextrous safety catch

The Star Super B, another Colt look-alike, was the Spanish service pistol for several years.

The Star 28DA is one of the few designs other than SIG to run the slide on internal frame rails.

which retracts the firing pin, but does not lock the trigger or hammer, so that it is possible to 'dry-fire' the weapon while loaded. There is a loaded chamber indicator and a magazine safety which prevents firing if the magazine has been removed; in recognition of the fact that some users do not like this feature, it can be removed at will. The Star 28DA is currently in service with the Spanish Army. **Length:** 8.0in (205mm). **Weight unloaded:** 2lb 8oz (1140g). **Barrel:** 4.33in (110mm). **Magazine:** 15-round detachable box. **Muzzle velocity:** 1150 ft/sec (350 m/sec).

• Star 30M/30PK
Star-Bonifacio Echeverria y Cia, Eibar
9mm Parabellum

A modern design introduced in 1988, the Model 30 uses the cam method of locking the breech and is somewhat unusual in having the slide running in internal frame rails, this gives excellent support throughout the slide movement and adds to accuracy. The trigger is double-action, and there is an automatic firing pin lock which only frees the firing pin during the last movement of the trigger. There is an ambidextrous safety catch on the slide which retracts the firing pin into its tunnel, out of reach of the hammer. The trigger and hammer action are not controlled by the safety catch and it is possible, after applying the safety, to pull the trigger and drop the hammer quite safely.

The Model 30M is made entirely of forged steel, while the Model 30PK has a light alloy frame. Both have been adopted by Spanish military and police forces and by police and security forces of Peru.

(30M)
Length: 8.07in (205mm). **Weight unloaded:** 2lb 8oz (1140g). **Barrel:** 4.69in (119mm), 6 grooves, right-hand twist. **Magazine:**

15-round detachable box. **Muzzle velocity:** c.1250 ft/sec (380 m/sec).

(30PK)
Length: 7.60in (193mm). **Weight unloaded:** 1lb 14oz (860g). **Barrel:** 3.86in (98mm), 6 grooves, right-hand twist. **Magazine:** 15-round detachable box. **Muzzle velocity:** c.1200 ft/sec (365 m/sec).

SWEDEN

• Pistol, Browning m/07
Husqvarna Vapenfabrik, Huskvarna
9x20mm Browning Long

The Swedish Pistol m/07 is actually the Browning Model 1903 in 9mm Long Browning caliber. This was originally bought from Fabrique Nationale Herstal, but in 1908 Husqvarna Vapenfabrik began manufacture in Sweden, which continued until 1943, when the Pistol m/40 largely replaced it. In the middle 1980s the m/40 ran into trouble (see below) and the old m/07 models which had been put into reserve store were brought out and reissued for some years until a replacement for the Lahti was selected.

Dimensions, etc., are exactly as for the Model 1903 listed under Belgium.

• Pistol Model 40
Husqvarna Vapenfabrik AB, Husqvarna
9mm Parabellum

The Pistol m/40 is the Swedish-made version of the Finnish Lahti pistol (qv). In 1939 the Swedes had decided to adopt the Walther P38 but the outbreak of war stopped that; they therefore turned to Finland and obtained a license for the Lahti. Production was to be done by Svenska Automatvapen AB but they went bankrupt before they

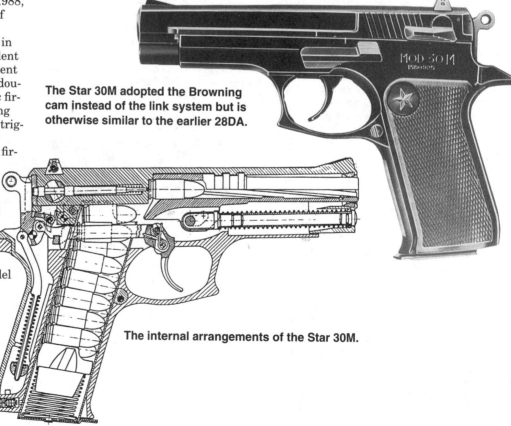

The Star 30M adopted the Browning cam instead of the link system but is otherwise similar to the earlier 28DA.

The internal arrangements of the Star 30M.

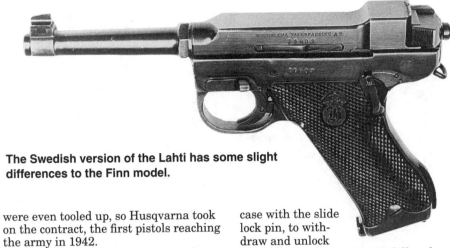

The Swedish version of the Lahti has some slight differences to the Finn model.

were even tooled up, so Husqvarna took on the contract, the first pistols reaching the army in 1942.

There are some differences in the Swedish version; it has a slightly longer barrel with a hexagonal at the breech reinforce, and the triggerguard is thicker and more oval. It does not have the Finnish loaded-chamber indicator and the front sight is higher, with a vertical rear edge. Some 83,950 pistols were made, the odd 950 being for the Danish Free Corps in Sweden, before production stopped in 1946. In general, the Swedish weapon was never as good as the original Finnish product, due to changes in the specification of the steels required in order to suit the wartime availability of steel in Sweden. This chicken came home to roost in the early 1980s when it was found that using the standard Swedish 9mm Parabellum round, which is hotted up for use in submachine-guns, in the m/40 pistols was leading to cracked frames; it was this which led to the resurrection of the m/07 pistol and the withdrawal of almost all the remaining m/40 weapons. The Lahti was eventually replaced, in the early 1990s, by the Glock 17.

Length: 10.70in (272mm). **Weight unloaded:** 2lb 7oz (1100g). **Barrel:** 5.50in (140mm), 4 grooves. **Magazine:** 8-round detachable box. **Muzzle velocity:** c.1275 ft/sec (389 m/sec).

SWITZERLAND

• Pistol Model 49 (SIG P210 or SP47/8)

Schweizerische Industrie-Gesellschaft, Neuhausen-am-Rheinfalls

7.65mm Parabellum, 9mm Parabellum

In 1937, the SIG company obtained a number of French patents held by Charles Petter, and began to develop a modern automatic pistol. After a number of prototypes and trial models the P210 appeared. It is basically of the standard Browning locked-breech pattern and, like the FN-Browning GP35, it uses a fixed cam beneath the barrel, engaging in this

case with the slide lock pin, to withdraw and unlock the barrel from the slide. It differs from the Browning cam in not being open-ended, but is a slot cut into a solid block beneath the chamber. Thus the pin upon which it bears must be withdrawn (like that of the Colt swinging link) before the barrel can be removed.

A notable feature of the SIG design is that the slide is carried inside the frame of the weapon rather than moving on the more common external milled surfaces. Furthermore, the workmanship and finish of SIG pistols, as is to be expected of the Swiss, is outstanding. In view of their accuracy and high quality they are rarely found in military inventories—being far too expensive to be issued in great numbers—although they were adopted in Switzerland and in Denmark (as the 9mm pistol m/49).

An interesting feature is that the pistol could be readily adapted to fire either 7.65mm or 9mm Parabellum cartridges by simply interchanging the barrel and recoil springs. A conversion kit to

permit use of the 22LR rimfire cartridge for practice was also available.

There are five versions of the P-210 pistol. The P-210-1 is the standard production model, with blued finish and wooden butt grips; the P-210-2 has a matte, sand-blasted finish and wooden butt grips; the P-210-4 was a special production model for the West German Border Police; the P-210-5 has a matte finish, a longer barrel and micrometer sights and is intended purely for competition shooting; and the P-210-6 is similar to the -5 but with a standard-length barrel.

Length: 8.50in (215mm). **Weight unloaded:** 2 lb 3oz (990g). **Barrel:** 4.75in (120mm), 6 grooves, right-hand twist. **Magazine:** 8-round detachable box. **Muzzle velocity:** c.1150 ft/sec (350 m/sec).

• SIG-Sauer P-220

SIG, Neuhausen-am-Rheinfalls; J.P. Sauer & Sohn, Eckernförde, Germany

9mm Parabellum

SIG are in an invidious position; they produce some of the world's best firearms but, due to the Swiss government's political stance, find it difficult to export; as somebody said, they are only allowed to sell guns to people who don't want them. By associating with J. P. Sauer & Sohn of Germany, their pistols can be made in Germany, where export regulations are rather less restrictive, opening up a wider market. The designs are almost entirely SIG, though there are one or two features which may have been influenced by Sauer.

The P-220 is really the result of re-engineering the P-210 to make it easier and less expensive to produce. It retains the dropping barrel, but the method of locking into the slide is much simpler; a squared block around the chamber fits into the enlarged ejection

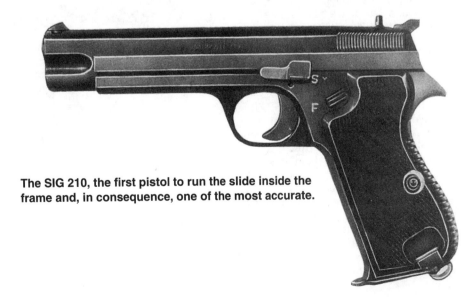

The SIG 210, the first pistol to run the slide inside the frame and, in consequence, one of the most accurate.

port in the slide and does the locking. Instead of machining from slabs of steel, the new design makes use of investment castings which are then machined on computer-controlled tools. The trigger is double action and there is a de-cocking lever on the left side of the frame to permit the hammer to be lowered safely and then, if desired, cocked for single-action firing. There is an automatic firing pin lock which only allows the pin to move when the trigger is correctly pulled. In view of these features SIG sees no reason to have a manual safety catch on the pistol.

The P-220 was adopted by the Swiss Army as their Pistol 75; it is also used by the Japanese Self-Defense Force, Chile, Iran, Nigeria, Uruguay and by a number of Special Forces.

Length: 7.79in (198mm). **Weight unloaded:** 1lb 13oz (830g). **Barrel:** 4.40in (112mm), 6 grooves, right-hand twist. **Magazine:** 9-round detachable box. **Muzzle velocity:** c.1132 ft/sec (345 m/sec).

The P220 was the first of the new generation of SIG-Sauer pistols; this is the 220-1 in 45 ACP caliber.

• SIG-Sauer P-225
SIG, Neuhausen-am-Rheinfalls; J.P. Sauer & Sohn, Eckernförde, Germany
9mm Parabellum

This is little more than a smaller and lighter version of the P-220 with an improved automatic firing pin locking system which quite positively prevents the pistol accidentally firing if dropped, even if the hammer is driven forward. The P-225 has been adopted by several Swiss and West German police forces (as the Pistole 6) and in other countries. It is believed that the US Secret Service have adopted it, and certainly a number of Special Forces use it.

Length: 7.08in (180mm). **Weight unloaded:** 1lb 10oz (740g). **Barrel:** 3.85in (98mm), 6 grooves, right-hand twist. **Magazine:** 8-round detachable box. **Muzzle velocity:** c.1115 ft/sec (340 m/sec).

• SIG-Sauer P-226
SIG, Neuhausen-am-Rheinfalls; J.P. Sauer & Sohn, Eckernförde, Germany
9mm Parabellum

This pistol was developed by SIG in response to specifications laid down by the US Army for their new 9mm pistol in 1980. Most of the parts are from the P-220 and P-225 and like them, it is a double-action locked breech weapon with automatic firing pin safety and a de-cocking lever. It differs principally in having a larger capacity magazine and an ambidextrous magazine catch. It failed to gain acceptance by the US Army on price grounds, it having performed exceptionally in all their tests. This proved no

The SIG-Sauer P-225.

The SIG-Sauer P-226.

The SIG-Sauer P-228.

drawback, however, and it has since sold widely to security forces.

Length: 7.72in (196mm). **Weight unloaded:** 1lb 10oz (750g). **Barrel:** 4.41in (112mm), 6 grooves, right-hand twist. **Magazine:** 15-round detachable box. **Muzzle velocity:** c.1150 ft/sec (350 m/sec).

• SIG-Sauer P-228
SIG, Neuhausen-am-Rheinfalls; J.P. Sauer & Sohn, Eckernförde, Germany
9mm Parabellum

The P-228 appeared in 1988 and was intended to round off the SIG line with a compact pistol having a large magazine capacity. The majority of the parts are from the P-225 and P-226 pistols and it uses the same automatic firing pin safety and decocking double-action system. The magazine catch can be mounted on either side of the frame to suit the user's preference.

Length: 7.08in (180mm). **Weight unloaded:** 1lb 13oz (830g). **Barrel:** 3.86in (98mm), 6 grooves, right-hand twist. **Magazine:** 13-round detachable box. **Muzzle velocity:** c.1115 ft/sec (340 m/sec).

• SIG-Sauer P-229
SIG, Neuhausen-am-Rheinfalls; J.P. Sauer & Sohn, Eckernförde, Germany
40 Smith & Wesson

The P-229 is, except for slight changes in the contours of the slide, the P228 chambered for the 40 Smith & Wesson cartridge. The standard model uses a steel slide and alloy frame; a variant is the P-229SL with stainless steel slide. Dimensions as for the P-228 except weight is 1lb 14oz (865g), magazine capacity 12 rounds, and muzzle velocity c.950 ft/sec (290m/sec).

• SIG-Sauer P-230
SIG, Neuhausen-am-Rheinfalls; J.P. Sauer & Sohn, Eckernförde, Germany
9mm Short

The P-230 is the baby of the SIG family, a blowback pocket or small holster pistol widely used by police and security forces. It was originally produced in 7.65mm Browning caliber, but the 9mm Short version proved more popular and production of the smaller caliber ceased in the 1980s. The pistol is double action, with a de-cocking lever on the left grip, and is fitted with the usual SIG automatic firing pin safety system. Production of the 9mm model ended in 1996.

Length: 6.61in (168mm). **Weight unloaded:** 1lb 0oz (460g). **Barrel:** 3.62in (92mm), 6 grooves, right-hand twist. **Magazine:** 7-round detachable box. **Muzzle velocity:** c.902 ft/sec (275 m/sec).

The SIG-Sauer P-229.

The SIG-Sauer P230.

The SIG-Sauer P239 shows some changes in styling from the previous models.

• SIG-Sauer P-232
SIG, Neuhausen-am-Rheinfalls; J.P. Sauer & Sohn, Eckernförde, Germany
7.65mm Browning; 9mm Short

The design was introduced in 1997 as the replacement for the P-230 and is really little more than a re-design of the 230 to take advantage of modern manufacturing techniques. The general shape is the same, with very slight changes in the slide contours. Variant models include one with a stainless steel slide, one with black slide and blued steel frame, and one which is self-cocking ('double action only'). The 7.65mm caliber has also been re-introduced.

Length: 6.61in (168mm). **Weight unloaded:** 1lb 2oz (500g). **Barrel:** 3.62in (92mm), 6 grooves, right-hand twist. **Magazine:** 7-round detachable box (8 rounds in 7.65mm caliber). **Muzzle velocity:** c.902 ft/sec (275 m/sec) 9mm; 1000 ft/sec (305m/sec) 7.65mm.

• SIG-Sauer P-239

SIG, Neuhausen-am-Rheinfalls; J.P. Sauer & Sohn, Eckernförde, Germany
357 SIG; 9mm Parabellum; 40 S&W

The P-239 was originally introduced in 1995 with the 357 SIG cartridge and was simply the P229 in the new chambering and with the magazine capacity slightly reduced so as to make the grip slimmer and better suited to concealed carrying. Since then it has been made available in 9mm and 40 S&W chambering.

(.357 SIG version)
Length: 6.77in (172mm). **Weight unloaded:** 1lb 13oz (820g). **Barrel:** 3.62in (92mm), 6 grooves, right-hand twist. **Magazine:** 7-round detachable box. **Muzzle velocity:** c.1352 ft/sec (412m/sec).

The Turkish Kirrikale, another design owing much to the Walther PP.

Colt's 38 New Army revolver of 1892.

Colt's 38 New Army revolver of 1894.

TURKEY

• Pistol, 9mm, Kirrikale

Makina ve Kimya Endustrisi Kurumu, Kirikale, Ankara; Kirikkale Tufek Fb, Istambul.
7.65x17SR Browning; 9mm Short (380 ACP)

The Kirrikale is yet another copy of the Walther Model PP. The only changes from the original design are relatively small modifications in machining to simplify production, and a finger-rest on the magazine platform (although this was sometimes seen on original Walther weapons). Stripping, functioning and operating are exactly as for the Walther (see Germany).

Length: 6.65in (168mm). **Weight unloaded:** 1lb 8oz (680g). **Barrel:** 3.83in (97mm), 6 grooves, right-hand twist. **Magazine:** 7-round detachable box. **Muzzle velocity:** c.950 ft/sec (289 m/sec) (9mm Short).

U.S.A.

• US Revolvers, 1889-1911

Colt's Patent Firearms Manufacturing Company, Hartford, Conn., Smith & Wesson Arms Company, Springfield, Mass.
38 Long Colt, 38 Special, 45 Colt

This heading covers a number of revolver designs manufactured either by Colt or by Smith & Wesson for issue to the forces of the United States prior to the issue of the M1911 pistol. Although some are of 19th century origin, they remained in service well into the 20th, since production of the M1911 was slow to catch up.

• US Revolver, Colt New Navy M1889
38 Long Colt

This was the parent of the subsequent small-caliber revolvers which followed into US military service. It lacked a separate cylinder bolt and was replaced on Colt's production line by the New Army revolver in 1892, but 5000 of this 1889 design were purchased for the US Navy.

• US Revolver, Colt New Army, M1892
38 Long Colt

In 1890, the United States Army decided that it must replace the revolvers then on its inventory with something a little more modern: after trials with the M1889 Navy revolver, it was decided to adopt this weapon provided that a separate cylinder bolt could be incorporated

into the design. This component was duly provided for the weapon, which was then adopted by the army in 1892. Although basically a sound design, the New Army revolver—like its New Navy predecessor—was handicapped by the anti-clockwise rotation of the cylinder (apparently insisted upon by the navy experts) which tended to push the cylinder out of the frame and, when worn to a sufficient degree, meant that the cylinder and barrel were not properly aligned.

• US Revolver, Colt New Army, M1894
38 Long Colt

Externally indistinguishable from the M1892, this weapon incorporated an additional safety feature in the form of Felton's trigger lock—a device which prevented operation of the trigger until the cylinder was fully closed. Most of the 1892 weapons were converted to this pattern.

• US Revolver, Colt New Navy, M1895
38 Long Colt

The navy's version of the army's M1894, this weapon incorporates Felton's lock and has a five-groove barrel whereas the army guns had six grooves.

• US Revolver, Colt New Army M1896
38 Long Colt

A minor variation of the M1894.

• US Revolver, Smith & Wesson Hand Ejector, M1899
38 Long Colt

A weapon of similar design to the various Colts, this weapon was also provided with a cylinder of counter-clockwise rotation. The M1899 is easily recognizable by the Smith & Wesson monogram on the grips and by the typically Smith & Wesson cylinder release-catch. Purchases of this design were relatively small: 1,000 in 1900 for the navy and 1,000 for the army in the following year.

• US Revolver, Colt New Army, M1901
38 Long Colt

Another variation of the M1894, provided with a lanyard swivel on the butt and with sideplates of a slimmer form.

• US Revolver, Smith & Wesson Hand Ejector, M1902
38 Long Colt

An improved version of the M1899, 1,000 of these weapons were purchased in 1902 by the United States Navy to the only contract let.

• US Revolver, Colt New Army, M1903
38 Long Colt

The last of the line of official army issue of this type, the M1903 is of the same pattern as the M1901 but with a slightly reduced bore diameter.

• US Revolver, Colt Marine Corps, M1905
38 Special

Identical with the M1903 army weapon but in a different caliber and with a slightly different butt shape, limited numbers of these were procured on behalf of the US Marine Corps.

Colt Army Special 38 or 1908.

Colt New Service model in 455 Webley caliber and with a 7.5 inch barrel.

• US Revolver, Colt Army Special, M1908
38 Special

This was the last of the 38-caliber revolvers adopted by the services and had a service life of just one year; a reversion to clockwise cylinder rotation was made in this weapon, which was an improvement over most of the earlier guns. The frame of the M1908 was more robust than that of the New Army patterns, and the cylinder latch was of a more rounded design. The reputation of the 38-caliber revolvers had suffered greatly in the Philippines campaigns of 1899-1900, where they had generally failed to stop the fanatics against whom they were used. One result of this was that quantities of 45-caliber revolvers (modified Colt Double Action Army Revolvers of 1878 pattern) were hastily procured, and another was that the 38-caliber sidearm was replaced in the American services by one of 45-caliber.
Length: 11.25in (285mm). **Weight unloaded:** 2lb 4oz (1020g). **Barrel:** 6.00in (152mm), 6 grooves, left-hand twist. **Magazine:** 6-round cylinder. **Muzzle velocity:** c.865 ft/sec (263 m/sec).

• US Revolver, Colt New Service, M1909
45 Colt

The last revolver to be adopted by the U.S. Army as its standard service sidearm, slightly over 21,000 of this New Service type were supplied to the Army, Navy and Marine Corps between February 1909 and April 1911. It was then replaced by the M1911 automatic pistol. The revolvers incorporated Colt's positive lock safety of 1905, which they inherited from the Army Special model.

• US Pistol, Automatic, Caliber 45, M1911 and M1911A
Colt's Patent Firearms Manufacturing Company, Hartford, Conn.
Ithaca Gun Company, Ithaca, NY.
Remington Rand Incorporated, Syracuse, NY.
Remington Arms-Union Metallic Cartridge Company, Bridgeport, Conn.
Springfield Armory, Springfield, Mass.
Union Switch & Signal Company, Swissvale, Pa.
North American Arms Company, Ltd, Quebec, Canada
45 ACP

Nothing succeeds like success, and the Colt M1911 pistols are without doubt among the most successful combat pistols ever invented. Incredibly robust, with more than enough lethality and stopping power from the 230gr (14.92gm) bullet—which delivers 380ft/lb (474J) of energy at the muzzle—the Colt armed the US Army and Navy from 1911 to 1992 and has been used by many other forces. Numbers were also made in 455 Webley & Scott chambering during World War I for the British Royal Navy and Royal Flying Corps, many of which were still serving in 1945.

The original M1911 model was developed from a series of improvements on Browning's 1900 design, and the first 45-caliber model of 1905 competed in the United States Government Trial of 1907. During the early years of the century, many inventors were pestering the world's war departments trying to secure contracts for automatic pistols and the

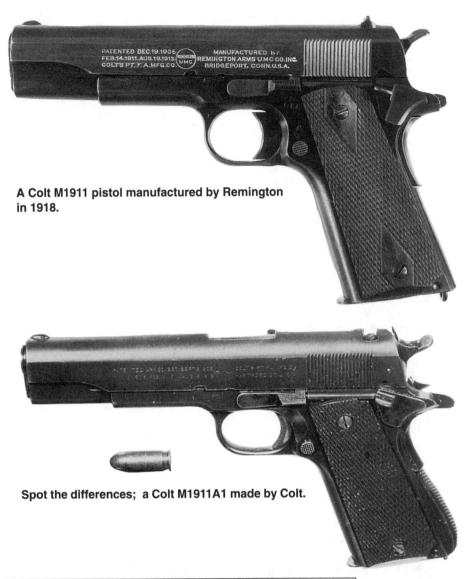

A Colt M1911 pistol manufactured by Remington in 1918.

Spot the differences; a Colt M1911A1 made by Colt.

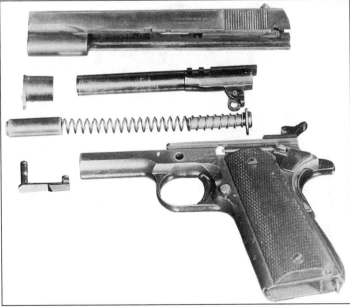

The Colt M1911A1 field-stripped.

United States Army decided to hold a contest to discover which, if any, of the designs held promise. The Chief of Ordnance, having had some sharp things said to him about the lack of effect of the recently-introduced 38-caliber revolver cartridge, laid down that all competing weapons must fire a 230gr 45-caliber bullet—a round which had been developed in 1906 for a commercial Colt pistol. The Board of Enquiry met in January 1907, tested nine pistols, and reported back in April 1907—an example of alacrity which is virtually unbelievable by modern standards. As a result, 200 Colt and 200 Savage pistols were bought for extended troop trials and, after some user experience, the Colt was selected, provided that Browning attended to one or two small points. This was done and, late in 1911, the pistol was adopted.

During World War I, the hammer was made longer and in the 1920s and as a result of war experience, further changes were made: the spur of the grip safety was lengthened, the shape of the grip was altered, the trigger was shortened and chamfered and the frame at the rear of the trigger was also chamfered to give a better grip. With these changes the pistol was standardized in June 1926 as the M1911A1 and has remained unchanged ever since.

While the gun is always known by the Colt name, other manufacturers' names will be found on the pistols. The M1911 was made by Colt, by the government arsenal at Springfield, and also by the Remington Arms-Union Metallic Cartridge Company of Bridgeport, Conn., during World War I. Arrangements were also made for the manufacture of the design in Canada, but the war ended before production got into its stride and only a few were made. During World War II, M1911A1 pistols were made by Colt, Remington Rand, the Union Switch & Signal Company, the Singer Sewing Machine Company, and the Ithaca Gun Company. In addition to the military issue, the pistols have been continuously manufactured by Colt for the commercial market, and such models can be distinguished by the more elegant finish and C-prefix serial numbers. Manufacture under Colt license has also taken place in Norway (m/1914) and Argentina (Model 1927).

Locking of breech and barrel on the Colt is achieved by having the top of the barrel ribbed and engaging in grooves on the underside of the slide top; the barrel has a link pinned beneath it and the lower end of this link pivots about the slide stop pin. Thus, as the slide recoils, it takes the barrel with it, but—as the link is held at its foot—it describes a semi-circular path with its upper end and so draws the breech down and free of the slide. The slide is thus allowed to recoil and, on the return stroke, it chambers a fresh round and pushes the barrel forward. The link now causes the breech to swing up and into engagement with the slide once more.

Length: 8.50in (216mm). **Weight unloaded:** 2lb 7.5oz (1120g). **Barrel:** 5.00in (127mm), 6 grooves, left-hand twist. **Magazine:** 7-round detachable box. **Muzzle velocity:** c.860 ft/sec (262 m/sec).

• General Officers Pistol M15, 45-caliber

Rock Island Arsenal, Rock Island, Ill.
45 ACP

The M15 was introduced in 1972 to replace the 380 ACP Colt Pocket Automatic as the issue pistol for General officers. Designed by Rock Island Arsenal, it is a cut-down and rebuilt M1911A1 Colt pistol. Its operation is precisely the same as that of the M1911A1; it is merely smaller in all dimensions. Due to the short barrel it develops more flash and blast than the issue pistol, but this is considered acceptable since it is only likely to be used in emergencies. It is finished in dark blue, with 'General Officer Model RIA' engraved on the slide; inset in the left grip is a brass plate which, on issue, has the individual officer's name engraved.

Length: 7.9in (200mm). **Weight:** 2lb 4oz (1030g). **Barrel:** 4.17in (106mm), 6 grooves, left-hand twist. **Magazine:** 7-round detachable box. **Muzzle velocity:** 800 ft/sec (245 m/sec).

• US Pistol, Automatic, 9mm, M9

Armi Beretta, Gardone VT, Italy; Beretta Inc, Accokeek, Md.
9mm Parabellum

Adopted in January 1985, the M9 is the Beretta Model 92F, which is described in the Italian section. The initial contract was for 315,390 pistols, the initial supply to be manufactured in Italy, with the Beretta USA factory taking over full production in 1988. As might be imagined, the provision of the standard US sidearm by a foreign manufacturer raised a political storm, but a second series of comparative tests confirmed Beretta as the weapon of choice, and the company was awarded the contract for the subsequent supplies. This choice, by an extremely searching comparative trial, was sufficient recommendation to lead several other military and police forces to adopt the Model 92 in one of its many variant forms.

• US Pistol, Automatic, Compact, M11

SIG, Neuhausen-am-Rheinfalls, Switzerland; J.P.Sauer & Sohn, Eckernförde, Germany
9mm Parabellum

The US Pistol M11 is the SIG P228, which is described under 'Switzerland'. In addition to being adopted by the US Army it is also widely used by various agencies including the FBI, DEA and BATF.

• US Revolver, Caliber 45, Smith & Wesson, M1917

Smith & Wesson Arms Company, Springfield, Mass.
45 ACP

When the United States entered the war in 1917, the standard pistol was the Colt M1911 automatic of 45-caliber; supplies of this weapon were short and it would obviously take time to provide the quantities needed to supply the vastly increased army. In view of this, numbers of Colt and Smith & Wesson revolvers were purchased, more than 150,000 of the former and more than 153,300 of the latter. Since the standard round in supply was the rimless 45 ACP, it meant that the revolver cylinders had to be shortened slightly and the rounds loaded in clips of three in order to prevent them sliding into the cylinder, and to give the extractor something to push against when unloading. As the Smith & Wesson has a stepped cylinder chamber, it is unnecessary to use the clips to ensure correct functioning, but without it, the ejector will not operate.

These pistols remained in service until well after World War II, although large numbers were released to the civilian market after World War I. In order to simplify matters, the Peters Cartridge Company developed a special thick-rimmed 45-caliber cartridge known as the '45 Auto-Rim'; this had a sufficiently thick rim to take up space behind the cylinder and present the primer to

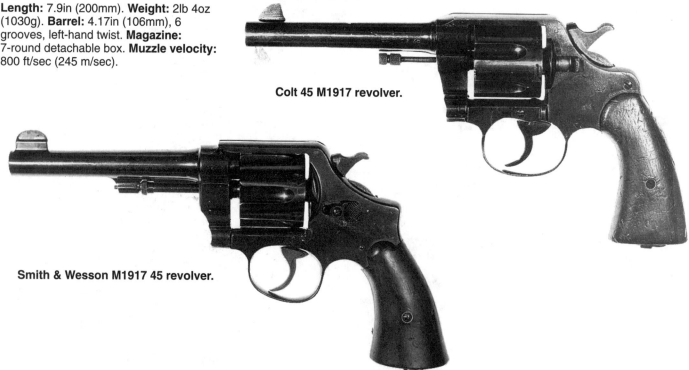

Colt 45 M1917 revolver.

Smith & Wesson M1917 45 revolver.

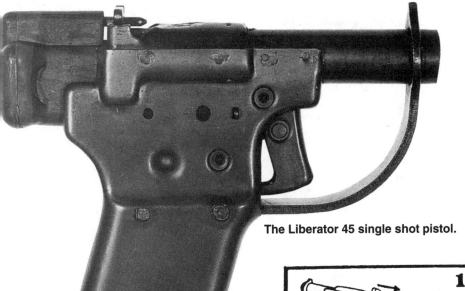

The Liberator 45 single shot pistol.

clips ('half-moon clips') so that rimless rounds could be located for the firing pin's strike, and to allow the extractors to have something to work against.

At the same time, Smith & Wesson produced a number of similar weapons, but their cylinder chambers were stepped so that the front edge of the cartridge case was thereby located—allowing them to be loaded and fired without clips—and this feature was adopted on later production of the Colt.

In addition to the service models, numbers of these revolvers chambered for 455-caliber were supplied to the British Army in 1915-16.

the firing pin, and also to give sufficient rim diameter for the extractor to work against. At the same time, the Smith & Wesson company produced replacement cylinders so that civilian owners could convert the guns to fire standard 45 Colt revolver ammunition.

Length: 10.80in (274mm). **Weight unloaded:** 2lb 4oz (1020g). **Barrel:** 5.50in (140mm), 6 grooves, right-hand twist. **Magazine:** 6-round cylinder. **Muzzle velocity:** c.860 ft/sec (262 m/sec).

• US Revolver, Caliber 45, Colt New Service, M1917

Colt's Patent Firearms Manufacturing Company, Hartford, Conn.
45 ACP

This pistol was commercially produced as the 'New Service' Model in 1897. It is a double-action revolver with swing-out cylinder and hand ejection, and it was made in a variety of calibers from 38-caliber to 476-caliber. It was first supplied to the United States Army in 1909 in 45-caliber rimmed chambering, but was superseded by the M1911 automatic. When the United States entered the war in 1917, over 150,000 of these pistols were taken into service between October 1917 and December 1918 to supplement the M1911 pistol. In order to achieve uniformity of ammunition supply, the revolvers were made with a special cylinder to take the 45 ACP M1911 pistol cartridge, which had to be loaded by using two three-shot semi-circular

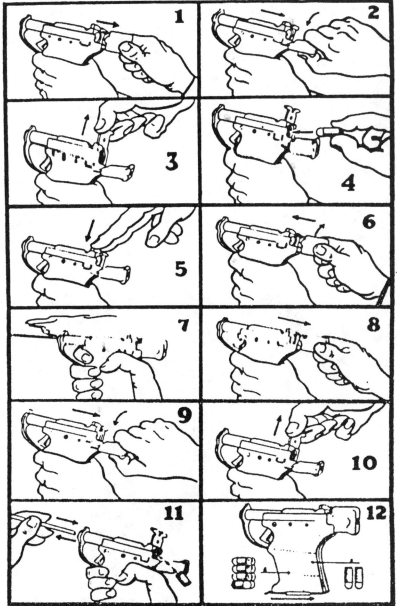

The set of instructions which accompanied each Liberator pistol.

Length: 10.15in (272mm). **Weight unloaded:** 2lb 8oz (1135g). **Barrel:** 5.50in (140mm), 6 grooves, left-hand twist. **Magazine:** 6-round cylinder. **Muzzle velocity:** c.866 ft/sec (262 m/sec).

• OSS' or 'Liberator' M1942 Pistol

Guide Lamp Corporation Division of GMC, Detroit, Michigan
45 ACP

This peculiar weapon was mass-produced during World War II for distribution by the Office of Strategic Services to clandestine forces in occupied countries. Designed to be made as cheaply as possible by the use of stamped metal parts, it was chambered for the United States Army's 45 ACP pistol cartridge and about 1,000,000 were produced between June and August 1942 by the Guide Lamp Division of General Motors. A simple twist-and-pull breechblock was opened, a round placed in the chamber and the breech closed. After firing, the breech was opened and the empty case ejected by pushing some suitable implement down the barrel. Five extra cartridges were carried in a trap in the butt.

The accuracy of the short smooth-bore barrel was sufficient for short-range work, and the pistol is reputed to have been put to good use as an assassination weapon. The short range probably helped in this as it would be politic to get as close as possible before opening fire in order not to miss, otherwise the chance of a second shot would be somewhat problematic. It was supplied with a comic-strip set of graphic instructions so that language barriers—or even illiteracy—were no bar to understanding how the thing worked or what to do with it.

Length: 5.55in (141mm). **Weight unloaded:** 1lb 0oz (455g). **Barrel:** 3.97in (101mm), smoothbore. **Magazine:** none, single-shot. **Muzzle velocity:** c.820 ft/sec (250 m/sec).

• Deer Gun

American Machine & Foundry Co., Alexandria, Va.
9mm Parabellum

The Deer Gun was a further extension of the 'Liberator' idea and was made under similar conditions of secrecy. It was the product of an idea by the CIA and was intended for distribution in Southeast Asia during the early days of the Vietnam war.

The design bore little resemblance to the 'Liberator', but the general principle was similar. The butt was an aluminum casting with the top formed into a cylindrical receiver carrying a simple striker. The steel barrel screwed into the front of this receiver portion. The butt was hollow, and had space for three loose rounds of ammunition, together with a rod for ejecting the spent case from the barrel.

To use the Deer Gun, the barrel was removed and a 9mm cartridge loaded into the chamber. The striker was pulled back and cocked, and a plastic clip snapped over the striker so as to impede its forward travel should the trigger be accidentally pressed. The loaded barrel was then screwed back into the receiver. To fire, the safety clip was removed from the striker and snapped on to the muzzle, where it now became the front sight. The gun was fired, the firer made his exit, and when opportunity offered the barrel was unscrewed, the empty case pushed out using the ejector rod kept in the butt, a fresh round loaded, the striker cocked and made safe, and the gun was ready for use once more. Each gun was totally devoid of any form of identification marking and was packed in an anonymous polystyrene box together with three unmarked 9mm cartridges and, like the Liberator, there was a highly colored and dramatic picture strip showing how to use the weapon.

A single lot of 1,000 pistols was made in 1964; larger production was planned, and the final cost was to have been $3.95 per pistol. But the scenario envisaged in 1962, of South Vietnamese guerrillas using the Deer Gun against Communist North Vietnamese invaders so as to obtain their weapons and equipment, looked outdated by 1964 when it was becoming obvious that a full-scale war was pending rather than a clandestine operation. A handful of Deer Guns went to Vietnam for evaluation, but the fate of the remainder is not entirely clear; some sources claim that they were entirely destroyed, but they do tend to turn up, from time to time, and sometimes in the most peculiar circumstances.

Length: 5.0in (127mm). **Weight unloaded:** 12oz (340g). **Barrel:** 2.60in (66mm); barrel may have 4 grooves or may be smooth-bored. **Magazine:** none; single shot, but 3 rounds held in butt. **Muzzle velocity:** c.1050 ft/sec (320 m/sec).

• Ruger P89

Sturm, Ruger & Co., Southport, Conn.
9mm Parabellum

This first appeared, as the P85, in 1987; slight modifications were made as a result of experience, and the perfected model is known as the P89. It is a conventional double-action semi-automatic pistol using the Browning link to lock the breech, but locking it into the ejection port rather than using multiple lugs as in the Colt M1911. The frame is of alloy, the slide of CrMb steel, and the barrel, hammer and sundry other components of stainless steel. The safety catch is fitted on both sides of the slide and locks the firing pin, disconnects the trigger and blocks the fall of the hammer when applied. The magazine release is in the

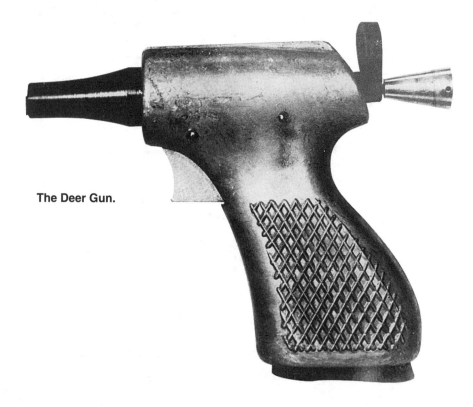

The Deer Gun.

The Ruger P85, basic model of the subsequent series.

forward edge of the butt and can be operated by either hand.

The **P89DC** is a variant model which has a decocking lever on the slide in place of the safety catch. Pressing the lever locks the firing pin and then drops the hammer. Upon releasing the lever it springs back into its normal position, and thereafter the pistol can be carried in safety and fired simply by pulling the trigger or by thumbing back the hammer to full-cock.

The **P89DAO** is another variant, in which the hammer follows the slide down after each shot and cannot be manually cocked.

There are a number of other Ruger models which are variants of the P89 in 45 ACP and 40 S&W calibers with normal, decocking or double-action-only options.

(P89)

Length: 7.87in (200mm). **Weight unloaded:** 2lb 0oz (907g). **Barrel:** 3.97in (114mm), 6 grooves, right-hand twist. **Magazine:** 15-round detachable box. **Muzzle velocity:** c.1180 ft/sec (360 m/sec).

• US Pistol 45-caliber, Mark 23 Mod 0 (SOCOM)

Heckler & Koch GmbH, Oberndorf-a-Neckar, Germany.
45 ACP

In 1990 the US Special Operations Command (SOCOM) requested proposals for an automatic pistol in 45-caliber which was to be of superior accuracy to the M1911A1 and be provided with an accessory silencer and a laser sight. Colt and H&K both produced designs, the latter was selected for development in 1991, prototypes were tested in 1992/3, and a production contract was awarded in 1994. A total of 1380 pistols were purchased at a unit price of $1186; a similar number of silencers was purchased from Knight's Armament Company, and 650 laser sights were also ordered.

The SOCOM pistol is generally similar to the Heckler & Koch USP (see entry under Germany), which formed the basis of the design. It is a double-action design, hammer fired, with the breech locked by the Browning dropping barrel system. An additional recoil buffer is incorporated into the buffer spring assembly to reduce the felt recoil and thus improve the accuracy. The muzzle protrudes from the slide and is threaded to accept the silencer (or sound suppresser), which is said to give a reduction of 25dB in noise. A slide lock is provided so that the pistol can be fired without the slide recoiling when the silencer is fitted, so that the noise of the slide and the ejected cartridge do not negate the silencing of the shot. The front of the frame is grooved to accept the laser sight which can project either visible or infra-red light. The normal iron sights are also fitted with three tritium markers for firing in poor light.

Length: 9.65in (245mm); with suppressor 16.57in (421mm). **Weight unloaded:** 2lb 10oz (1210g); with suppressor and full magazine: 4lb 4oz (1920g). **Barrel:** 5.87in (149mm), 4 grooves, polygonal, right-hand twist. **Magazine:** 12-round detachable box. **Muzzle velocity:** c.886 ft/sec (270 m/sec) (using M1911 ball).

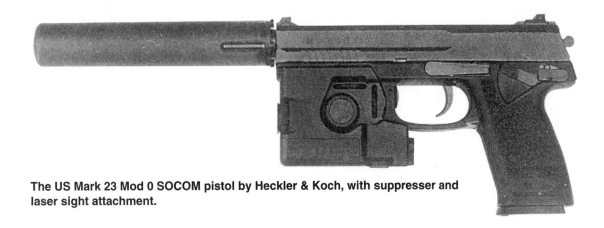

The US Mark 23 Mod 0 SOCOM pistol by Heckler & Koch, with suppresser and laser sight attachment.

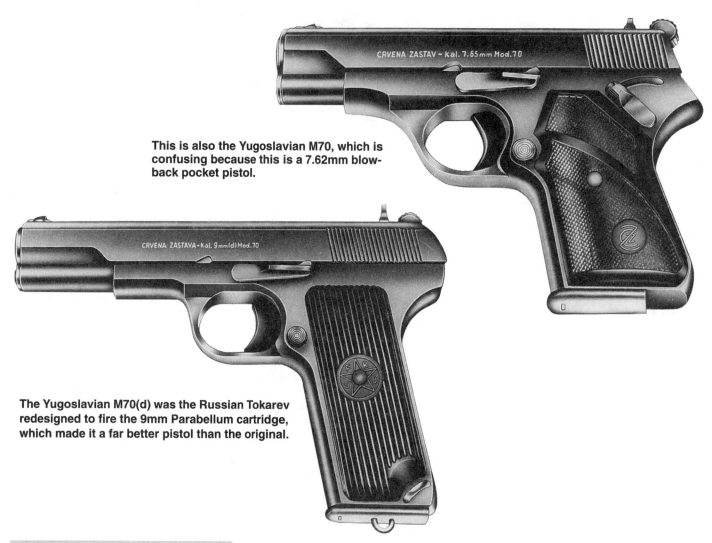

This is also the Yugoslavian M70, which is confusing because this is a 7.62mm blowback pocket pistol.

The Yugoslavian M70(d) was the Russian Tokarev redesigned to fire the 9mm Parabellum cartridge, which made it a far better pistol than the original.

YUGOSLAVIA

• Crvena Zastava Mod 70
Zavodi Crvena Zastava, Beograd
Various calibers - see text

The basic Yugoslavian Model 70 pistol is based on their earlier Model 57, which was a locally-made version of the Soviet Tokarev using the Soviet 7.62mm cartridge. Wisely, the Yugoslavs decided that 9mm Parabellum was a better combat round, and the Model 70 is simply a Tokarev redesigned to take the 9mm cartridge. In this respect, it resembles the Tokagypt.

In recent years, two blowback pistols have been produced, probably to arm police, under the Model 70 designation. The M70 is chambered for the 7.65x17mm (32 ACP) cartridge, while the M70(k) uses the 9x17mm Short (380 ACP) cartridge. Both are external-hammer designs, with magazine safety incorporated.

(M70(d))

Length: 7.88in (200mm). **Weight unloaded:** 1lb 15oz (900g). **Barrel:** 4.50in (116mm), 6 grooves, right-hand twist. **Magazine:** 9-round detachable box. **Muzzle velocity:** 1250 ft/sec (380 m/sec).

(M70 and M70(k))

Length: 7.8in (200mm). **Weight unloaded:** 1lb 8oz (700g). **Barrel:** 3.70in (94mm), 6 grooves, right-hand twist. **Magazine:** 8-round detachable box. **Muzzle velocity:** 7.65mm: 985 ft/sec (300 m/sec). 9mm Short: 900 ft/sec (275 m/sec).

SUBMACHINE GUNS

THE SUBMACHINE GUN, machine carbine or machine pistol—call it what you will, though the former is the more accurate of the three—was a child of World War I and in spite of being produced in prodigious numbers, and in a vast range of different designs, it has almost died out as a purely military weapon and lives on due to being in demand by police and para-military forces as a means of combating terrorism. If and when terrorists (who, of course, also use submachine guns) ever die out, the submachine gun will go.

The Vilar Perosa has often been cited as the first submachine gun, but in my opinion the Bergmann MP18 is the ancestor; there is more to a submachine gun than small size and a pistol caliber. The tactical use and practical utility counts as well, and on this score the Bergmann (which, on the evidence of prisoner interrogations, was in the German trenches in the latter half of 1916), is a clear leader. It first appeared as a trench weapon but failed to find a place; it was then appropriated for the 'Storm Troops' who formed the spearhead of the new German tactics, generally ascribed to Von Hutier, in which the Storm Troops probed in small parties, protected by their own agility and firepower aided by smoke and the fog of war, until they found a weak spot which they could force open and then hold to allow the main body of the assault to pass through.

For some years after the war the submachine gun was a curiosity looking for a tactical role, for it was not entirely clear where it would fit into the scheme of things if trench warfare was not employed in the future. Moreover, thanks largely to Thompson's somewhat careless sales policy, the weapon had attracted to itself the title of 'gangster gun' and this, of course, would never do.

Many writers, myself included, have reported that the submachine gun was widely used during the Spanish Civil War and that this persuaded the Germans and Russians to develop suitable weapons. The more I have considered this theory, the less I like it, and considerable study of Civil War memoirs and reports have failed to produce any evidence of the widespread use of submachine guns. A small number were made in Spain, small numbers were procured from Russia and from Germany, but compared to the total numbers of weapons involved, they were a drop in the ocean, and it is very doubtful any useful lessons were ever to be gleaned from their use in Spain.

It seems that what propelled the submachine gun into a major role in 1939-45 was firstly the formation of the German Panzer divisions, the troops of which demanded a compact short-range weapon which could be carried easily and safely inside an armored vehicle. And secondly the Winter War of 1940 in which the Finns used the Suomi submachine gun to very good effect against the Soviets in the arctic forests, where fifty meters was a long range. The cheapness and simplicity attracted the Russians, who were faced with the prospect of raising, training and equipping a vast conscript army; moreover it lent itself to the Soviet philosophy of war—get up and go for the enemy, rather than sit in a trench and snipe at long range. A third factor might also be adduced—the innovation of airborne forces who demanded high firepower in a compact package.

So the submachine gun finished World War II in a dominant position, and the immediate post-war years saw new designs appearing almost every week to replace the admittedly rough and ready designs which had appeared during the war. Some—the better ones—survived, most rarely got past the prototype and glossy brochure stage.

What finally put the submachine gun out of business in the military world was the arrival of the small-caliber assault rifle. Not satisfied with configuring them as rifles, the manufacturers configured them as carbines, with short barrels, for use by mechanized troops needing a compact weapon. Since this was the same clientele which had helped to foster the submachine gun in the first place, they needed no instructing as to the utility of such a weapon, and now it was available in the standard rifle caliber, so making a logistic saving. So the short assault rifle took over from the submachine gun; by the mid-1950s the submachine gun had vanished from the Soviet army. It took longer for the others to follow this lead, but by the 1980s the changeover was more or less universal.

This, of course, means that as the century closes, the demand for the submachine gun is at a very low level, and it can be met very easily by existing makers with existing designs. And yet even in the face of this economic picture, which is obvious to anyone who cares to study the matter even briefly, designs for new submachine guns come along with monotonous regularity. Some twenty years ago I was visiting with a major arms dealer and mentioned that a correspondent had approached me with a new submachine gun design. He opened his safe and showed me design proposals for three weapons and said "Come downstairs and I'll show you 25,000 submachine guns in my inventory. When anyone offers me a new design I only ask one question: "Who's going to buy it?" And that really sums the matter up.

There *is* a military market opening, even though it took some powerful thinking to see it. Towards the end of the 1980s Fabrique Nationale of Herstal asked the basic question 'What weapon does the soldier *need*?' The answer was that about one-third of an army—the front-line infantry and a few others—actually need an assault rifle. The remaining two-thirds—cooks, bakers, engineers, truck-drivers, signalmen—need a personal defense weapon but they do not need anything so involved and expensive as the assault rifle. A submachine gun would perhaps fill the bill, but it does not have the range to deal with, say, an ambush, and it does not have the ability to cope with the increasing use of body armor. So FN came up with the idea of the 'Personal Defense Weapon' (PDW); this is light, compact, easily carried, easily operated, but uses a modern cartridge with a useful range and an impressive penetrative ability: like 200 meters and 38 layers of Kevlar. The result of this thinking, the FN P90 may look peculiar but once you pick it up it makes good sense. It has taken the idea some time to soak into the layers of military thought, but it is beginning to make an impression, and sales of the P90 are healthy.

The other recent tendency in the submachine gun world has been the adoption of new calibers. For most of its life the submachine gun had a limited range of calibers, dominated by the 9x19mm Parabellum, with the 45 ACP and 7.62 Soviet pistol as runners-up and the 7.65 Parabellum and 9mm Mauser Export registering a few clients. But with the increasing adoption of the 40 Smith & Wesson and 10mm Auto cartridges in pistols, these two have also appeared in submachine guns. This, of course, makes perfectly good sense where police forces are concerned; if they have settled on 40 S&W for their pistols, then submachine guns in the same caliber become even more attractive. Armies are less fashion-conscious when it comes to changing caliber; while the soldier might urge the adoption of a new cartridge in order to obtain a few more feet per second, the purse-holders point to the stock of exist-ing ammunition and the manufacturing plant prepared to turn out even more whenever needed. It takes a powerful ballistic argument to overturn that sort of resistance, as history has frequently shown. So for those whose avocation is the submachine gun, my advice for the coming century is 'Watch the police.'

The Argentine Halcon of 1943 showed a few original features.

But the 1963 Halcon was an unashamed copy of the US M3.

ARGENTINA

• Pistola Ametralladora PAM1 and PAM2

Fabrica Militar de Armas Portatiles 'Domingo Matheu', Rosario, Santa Fe
9mm Parabellum

The PAM1 and PAM2 are almost identical to the US M3A1 from which they were derived; the only major differences are that the Argentine weapons are slightly shorter and lighter and chambers the 9mm cartridge. The guns were issued to Argentine military and police forces in the 1950-66 period and numbers may still be in use and in reserve stocks. The PAM2 differs in having an additional left-hand grip safety, intended to reduce the number of accidents due to inertial firing, ie: dropping a weapon hard enough to cause the bolt to fly back and chamber and fire a round. This safety locks the bolt in the forward position except when released by the firer gripping it, together with the magazine, when in the firing position.
Length: 28.54in (725mm). **Weight unloaded:** 6lb 9oz (2.97kg). **Barrel:** 7.87in (200mm), 6 grooves, right-hand twist. **Magazine:** 30-round detachable box. **Cyclic rate:** 450 rds/min. **Muzzle velocity:** c.1200 ft/sec (365 m/sec).

• Pistola Ametralladora Halcon Modelo 1943 and Modelo 1946

Metalurgica Centro SCPA (Armas 'Halcon'), Benfica, Buenos Aires
9mm Parabellum, 45 ACP

The Halcon M1943 was developed in the early 1940s and issued to the Argentine Gendarmerie Nacional. It was in 45-caliber, and the curious shape and considerable weight are evidence of pre-war design concepts. Nevertheless the design was ingeniously simple, and the weapon could be made in two hours by a skilled workman using simple machine tools. It was a blowback weapon, and the muzzle compensator and weight helped to make it quite steady in automatic fire. The M1946 was also made in 45 ACP and had a folding stock; it was issued to the Air Force and was known as the 'Modelo Aeronautica'. Like the M1943 it used 17- or 30-shot straight magazines.

Imrproved models appeared in 1949 (in 9mm caliber) and in 1957 (a lightweight version) but the most significant change was the 9mm M1963 which completely abadnoned the earlier design and, instead, produced a weapon closely resembling the US M3 but with a conventional external cocking handle and twin triggers for single or automatic fire.

(Modelo 1943)

Length: 33.38in (848mm). **Weight unloaded:** 10lb 8oz (4.76kg). **Barrel:** 11.50in (292mm), 6 grooves, right-hand twist. **Magazine:** 17- or 30-round detachable box. **Cyclic rate:** 700 rds/min. **Muzzle velocity:** c.910 ft/sec (277 m/sec) (.45in); c.1200 ft/sec (365 m/sec) (9mm).

(Model 1963)

Length, butt extended: 27.17in (690mm); butt folded 19.6in (500mm). **Weight unloaded:** 8lb 1oz (3,65kg). **Barrel:** 6.79in

The MEMS M52/58, a typical example of the MEMS design.

(170mm), 6 grooves, right hand twist. **Magazne:** 42-round detachable box. **Cyclic rate:** 600 rds/min. **Muzzle velocity:** 1148ft/sec (350 m/sec).

• Pistola Ametralladora 'MEMS'
Armas y Equipos SRL, Cordoba
9mm Parabellum

This weapon derives its name from Professor Miguel E. Manzo Sal, its designer, and in its final form (M75) was the perfection of several years of development and numerous prototypes (M52, M52/58, M52/60, M67, M69, etc.). The fundamental reasoning behind the design was to produce an integrated weapon system capable of production by any light engineering plant, without recourse to scarce raw materials or difficult manufacturing processes; much of the fabrication of the 'MEMS' is of steel stampings.

The mechanism is of the conventional blowback type, using advanced primer ignition, the design of the receiver and barrel being broadly based on that of the MP40. The barrel used a patented "Micro-Relieve" rifling system, while the trigger and selective fire mechanism were also of fresh and patented design. The magazine housing, beneath the receiver, was considerably larger than normal, affording rapid location of the magazine (which was of the Carl Gustav type) and also functioned as a forward hand grip. The M75/I (Infantry) model used a wooden stock, while the M75/II (Parachutist) model had a wooden receiver support and pistol grip with a wire butt which folded across the top of the receiver. Both models had a simple but effective compensator built onto the muzzle, and a bayonet or grenade launcher could be attached to the barrel.

The MEMS was extensively tested by the Argentine Army and police forces, but although highly commended, it was never formally adopted. Development continued for some time after this testing but eventually ceased by 1980.

Length, butt extended: 31.50in (800mm); butt folded: 25.20in (640mm). **Weight unloaded:** 7lb 4oz (3.30kg). **Barrel:** 7.09in (180mm), 24 grooves, right-hand twist. **Magazine**: 40-round detachable box. **Cyclic rate:** 850 rds/min. **Muzzle velocity:** c.1200 ft/sec (365 m/sec).

• Pistols Ametralladoras PA3DM
Fabrica Militar de Armas Portatiles 'Domingo Matheu', Rosario, Santa Fé
9mm Parabellum

This is a complete redesign of the PAM1, developed in the late 1960s and put into production in 1970. It was heavily influenced by the Uzi, adopting the use of the grip as the magazine housing and a wrap-around bolt used in the Israeli weapon, but the body and sliding wire butt are much the same as those of the PAM1. Some models were produced with a fixed wood or plastic butt, and all have a plastic forend. Manufacture ceased in 1978 after about 15,000 weapons had been made.

Length, butt extended: 27.30in (693mm); butt folded: 20.60in (523mm). **Length,** fixed

The PA3DM.

The Austen Mark 1.

stock: 27.56in (700mm). **Weight unloaded**: 7lb 10oz (3.45kg) **Barrel:** 11.42in (290mm), 6 grooves, right-hand twist **Magazine:** 25-round detachable box. **Cyclic rate:** c.650 rds/min. **Muzzle velocity:** c.1300 ft/sec (396 m/sec)

• FMK-3 Mod 2

Fabrica Militar de Armas Portatiles 'Domingo Matheu', Rosario, Santa Fé
9mm Parabellum

The FMK3 Mod 2 is little more than the PA3DM folding-butt model put back into production and given a new name in accordance with certain changes in Argentine military terminology. There are very slight dimensional differences, perhaps due to new machinery or techniques, but the weapon is essentially the same.

Length, butt extended: 27.16in (690mm); butt folded: 20.47in (520mm). **Weight unloaded:** 7lb 15oz (3.60kg). **Barrel:** 11.42in (290mm), 6 grooves, right-hand twist. **Magazine:** 25-round detachable box. **Cyclic rate:** c.600 rds/min. **Muzzle velocity:** c.1312 ft/sec (400 m/sec).

AUSTRALIA

• Machine Carbines, 9mm Austen, Marks 1 and 2

Diecasters Limited, Melbourne, Victoria; W. J. Carmichael & Company, Melbourne, Victoria
9mm Parabellum

When the Pacific War started in 1941, Australia was desperately short of modern weapons; Britain was in no position to supply any—being in dire straits herself—and so the Australians set about producing their own, with only a limited amount of machinery and plant. Designs therefore had to be both straightforward and easy to manufacture. Submachineguns were urgently needed for the jungle campaigns, and this version of the Sten combined many features of the Sten and the German MP40. The receiver, barrel, trigger mechanism and bolt were of Sten design, but the MP 40 was the basis for the main spring, folding butt and sloping pistol grip. The resulting weapon had few vices except for the inherited Sten difficulty over feed and a combined trigger and sear spring which had a tendency to break. The Austen went into production in mid-1942, some months after the Owen gun (below) had gone into service, and by April 1943 only 4000 or so had been made, the rate of production being about one-third that of the Owen. As a result the Owen was officially declared to be the Australian service weapon, and the Austen, although apparently allowed to continue in production until the war ended, was never used in any numbers.

Length, butt extended: 33.25in (845mm); butt folded: 21.75in (552mm). **Weight unloaded:** 8lb 12oz (3.97kg). **Barrel:** 7.72in (196mm), 6 grooves, right-hand twist. **Magazine:** 28-round detachable box. **Cyclic rate:** 500 rds/min. **Muzzle velocity:** c.1250 ft/sec (380 m/sec).

• Machine Carbines, 9mm Owen, Marks 1and 2

Lysaghts Newcastle Works, Newcastle, New South Wales
9mm Parabellum

This weapon was developed by Evelyn Owen in 22-caliber in June 1939, and he offered it to the Australian army without raising much interest. On the outbreak of war he was called up into the army and left the gun and details with a friend, who managed to spur the Army Inventions Board into asking Lysaghts, in January 1941, to manufacture a prototype in 32 ACP caliber. The Australian Army was then awaiting supplies of the Sten, but after some delay decided to purchase 100 Owen guns in 38-caliber, the necessary design work being done by G. S. Wardell, chief engineer of Lysaghts. The first of these were made in August 1941 but merely proved that the 38-caliber revolver round was useless as a submachine-gun cartridge, and Lysaghts, on their own responsibility, changed the design to 9mm Parabellum. The prototype was tested against the Thompson and Sten and proved superior to both, and went into production. Due to a shortage of machine tools it was not until mid-1942 that full production of 2,000 per month was achieved, and thereafter production was held at this rate solely by the availability of tooling. Although the US Army in Australia wanted to purchase 60,000 Owen guns, the proposal was refused by the Australian authorities since they could not find the necessary materials and machine tools.

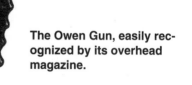

The Owen Gun, easily recognized by its overhead magazine.

The Owen was a simple blowback weapon with two odd features: the overhead feeding magazine, and a separate bolt compartment inside the receiver, so that the bolt was isolated from its cocking handle by a small bulkhead. This ensured that the bolt could not be jammed by dirt or mud, though it was expensive in terms of space. Two other unusual features were that the ejector was built into the magazine, rather than into the gun, and the barrel could be removed quickly by pulling up on a spring-loaded plunger, necessary because the gun could only be stripped by removing the barrel and then taking the bolt out forwards.

Three models of Owen were made; the Mark 1 (or 1/42), which went through several minor modifications; the Mark 1 Wood Butt (or 1/43), and the Mark 2 which was a simplified model and only produced in prototype. Total production amounted to about 45,000 before Lysaghts ended manufacture in September 1945. The Owen remained in use until the 1960s and numbers are still held in reserve stores.

Length: 32.00in (813mm). **Weight unloaded:** 9lb 5oz (4.22kg). **Barrel:** 9.75in (247mm), 7 grooves, right-hand twist. **Magazine:** 33-round detachable box. **Cyclic rate:** 700 rds/min. **Muzzle velocity:** c.1250 ft/sec (380 m/sec).

• 9mm Submachine gun F1
Small Arms Factory, Lithgow, New South Wales
9mm Parabellum

The Owen became somewhat out of date by the early 1960s and, although

extremely popular with the troops, it had features which could be eliminated in a more modern design. Another gun—the X3—was therefore designed and the first models were produced in 1962: the X3 could perhaps be described as an Australian version of the Sterling type, but this might be carrying the similarity too far. It has many features of the Sterling, particularly internally, though there are obvious differences in the trigger housing, and the bolt handle is on the left side. The rear sight is a special design and the top-mounted magazine of the Owen has been retained in response to the user's demands; the bolt handle has a separate cover to keep out mud and dirt (neither component moves as the gun fires). An interesting feature is the way in which the small of the butt fits into the rear of the receiver, which is possible with the straight-line layout of the X3. It is a simple and effective gun which performed well in the jungle war in Vietnam; so effective, indeed, that it was later adopted but with minor modifications, as the 9mm submachine-gun F1.

Length: 28.15in (715mm). **Weight unloaded:** 7lb 3oz (3.26kg). **Barrel:** 8.00in (203mm), 6 grooves, right-hand twist. **Magazine:** 34-round detachable box. **Cyclic rate:** 600 rds/min. **Muzzle velocity:** c.1250 ft/sec (380 m/sec).

AUSTRIA

• Steyr Maschinenpistole MPi 69
Steyr-Mannlicher AG, Steyr, Austria
9mm Parabellum

The MPi 69 was developed by Steyr, having been designed by Herr Stowasser, with the objectives of reliability and cheap manufacture firmly in view. The receiver is a steel stamping with a molded nylon cover, and much of the assembly of components is by welding and brazing. The barrel is cold-hammered by a Steyr-developed process which produces a cleaner rifling contour and tougher barrel at less expense than the usual system of boring and rifling. The machined bolt is 'overhung' or 'wrap-round' in form, in which the actual bolt face is about half-way along the length of the bolt body, allowing a large mass to lie around the barrel and also permitting the use of a barrel somewhat longer than normal while keeping the overall length of the weapon within reasonable bounds. The selection of single shot or automatic fire is achieved by pressure on the trigger; a light pressure produces single shots, while heavier pressure brings in a locking device which holds down the sear and permits automatic fire. An additional control is provided in the safety catch; this is a cross-bolt type, pushed to the right with the thumb to make the weapon safe, and pushed to the left with the fore-finger to ready the weapon for firing. If the bolt is pushed only half-way through its travel, the mechanism is locked so that only single shots can be fired. The gun is

The Australian F-1 owed a lot to the Sterling, but it kept the overhead magazine from the Owen.

cocked by pulling on the carrying sling—the front end of the sling is attached to the cocking lever. A telescoping wire butt is fitted.

Length, butt extended: 26.37in (670mm); butt folded: 18.30 in (465mm). **Weight unloaded:** 6lb 14oz (3.13kg). **Barrel:** 10.24 in (260mm), 6 grooves, right-hand twist. **Magazine:** 25- or 32-round detachable box. **Rate of fire:** 550 rds/min. **Muzzle velocity:** c.1250 ft/sec (380 m/sec).

• Steyr Maschinenpistole MPi 81
Steyr-Mannlicher AG, Steyr, Austria
9mm Parabellum

The MPi 69 has a unique cocking system whereby the sling is connected to the bolt and used to cock the weapon. Some purchasers did not like this system, so Steyr modified the design to use a conventional cocking handle. This version is known as the MPi 81. In all other respects it is identical with the MPi 69.

A special version of the MPi 81 was developed as a firing-port weapon for use in infantry fighting vehicles and similar

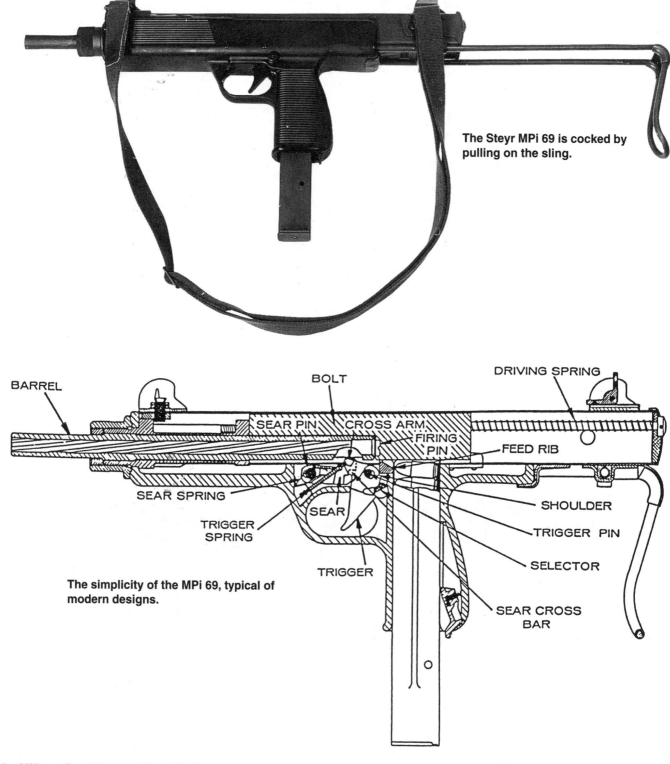

The Steyr MPi 69 is cocked by pulling on the sling.

The simplicity of the MPi 69, typical of modern designs.

BARREL

BOLT

DRIVING SPRING

SEAR PIN

CROSS ARM

FIRING PIN

FEED RIB

SEAR SPRING

SHOULDER

TRIGGER SPRING

SEAR

TRIGGER PIN

SELECTOR

TRIGGER

SEAR CROSS BAR

The Steyr MPi 81 had a conventional cocking handle.

vehicles fitted with firing ports for the occupants. The receiver is fitted with the optical sight of the AUG rifle, and the barrel is extended and fitted with a special collar which locks into the standard pattern of firing port. The sight is positioned, by a special bracket, so that it can be used with the vision blocks fitted above the firing ports.

• Steyr AUG 9mm Para

Steyr-Mannlicher AG, Steyr, Austria
9mm Parabellum

This is a submachine gun version of the standard AUG assault rifle. It uses the existing butt and receiver units of the rifle, with carrying handle and optical sight, but is fitted with a 9mm caliber barrel, a special blowback bolt group, a magazine adapter and a magazine. The adapter fits into the normal 5.56mm magazine housing in the stock, and the 9mm magazine then fits into the adapter.
Length: 26.18in (665mm). **Weight unloaded**: 7lb 11oz (3.5kg). **Barrel:** 16.54in (420mm), 6 grooves, right-hand twist. **Magazine:** 25- or 32-round box magazine. **Rate of fire:** 670-770 rds/min. **Muzzle velocity:** c.1312 ft/sec (400 m/sec).

• Steyr Tactical Machine Pistol (TMP)

Steyr-Mannlicher AG, Steyr
9mm Parabellum

This weapon, introduced in 1989, consists of a synthetic butt and frame, synthetic receiver top, and a steel barrel and breechblock combination. It is hammer-fired, the firing mechanism being modified from that of the AUG rifle. The weapon works on the delayed blowback principle, the delay being performed by a rotating barrel which owes a good deal to the Steyr 1912 pistol. The barrel lies inside a casing which fits into the top cover and acts as a guide for the bolt. On firing, bolt and barrel recoil 10-12mm or so and then a lug on the barrel, having moved down a slot, hits a cam surface and rotates the barrel about 45° clockwise. This unlocks the bolt, the barrel stops and the bolt goes rearwards. A spring drives the bolt back to collect a fresh round and chamber it and then drives the bolt into the barrel and the barrel forward again, rotating it so as to lock the bolt before it goes into battery. Semiauto or auto fire can be selected by a cross-bolt safety/selector or by trigger pressure, as in the MPi 69. There are 41 parts, and only one screw, the lateral adjustment for the rear sight. There is no stock, but a grip in front of the trigger-guard can be folded down to give a two-handed hold.
Length: 11.10in (282mm). **Weight unloaded:** 2lb 14oz (1.30kg). **Barrel:** 5.12in (130mm), 6 grooves, right-hand twist. **Magazine:** 15- or 30-round box magazine. **Rate of fire:** 900 rds/min. **Muzzle velocity:** c.1247 ft/sec (380 m/sec).

BELGIUM

• Mitraillette RAN

Société Anonyme Belge Répousemetal, Brussels
9mm Parabellum

The RAN was never taken into military service in any country, although it was offered to any interested buyer in the early and middle 1950s. It had, however, several unusual features and illustrates a line of thought which although not suc-

The Steyr Tactical Machine Pistol.

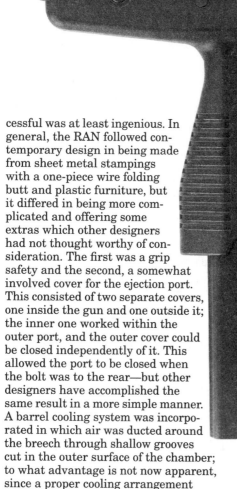

The Steyr Tactical Machine Pistol.

cessful was at least ingenious. In general, the RAN followed contemporary design in being made from sheet metal stampings with a one-piece wire folding butt and plastic furniture, but it differed in being more complicated and offering some extras which other designers had not thought worthy of consideration. The first was a grip safety and the second, a somewhat involved cover for the ejection port. This consisted of two separate covers, one inside the gun and one outside it; the inner one worked within the outer port, and the outer cover could be closed independently of it. This allowed the port to be closed when the bolt was to the rear—but other designers have accomplished the same result in a more simple manner. A barrel cooling system was incorporated in which air was ducted around the breech through shallow grooves cut in the outer surface of the chamber; to what advantage is not now apparent, since a proper cooling arrangement requires much more coolant volume than that offered by the RAN.

There were also a number of optional extras, including a folding bayonet, a bipod, a muzzle brake, and a grenade launcher for anti-tank grenades. Quite obviously the idea was to produce a one-man weapons system: needless complication, the fact that the gun was no great improvement over existing designs, and (presumably) the resultant high price, all combined to kill it within a short time.

Length, butt extended: 31.26in (794mm); butt folded: 23.00in (584mm). **Weight unloaded:** 6lb 8oz (2.95kg). **Barrel:** 11.81in (300mm), 6 grooves, right-hand twist. **Magazine:** 32-round detachable box. **Cyclic rate:** 650 rds/min. **Muzzle velocity:** c.1400 ft/sec (426 m/sec).

• Mitraillette Vigneron M2
Societé Anonyme Precision Liégeoise, Herstal-lez-Liege
9mm Parabellum

The Vigneron was a light and practical submachine gun designed in the early 1950s by a retired Belgian army officer and accepted for service in the Belgian forces in 1953. It was similar to many other designs of the period and was made from the usual steel stampings and uncomplicated components. The barrel was longer than normal for a submachine gun, but it also incorporated a compensator and partial muzzle-brake. The pistol grip had an integral grip safety which locked the bolt to the rear. The change lever also had a safety position and, when the lever was set for automatic fire, a light squeeze on the trigger would produce a single shot; further pressure produced automatic fire. A wire butt telescoped into tubes alongside the receiver and the butt length could be adjusted to suit the individual firer. When the Belgian Army retired from the Congo, a number of Vignerons were left with the Congolese troops and as a result they are now likely to be found in any part of central Africa. A number were also used by the Portuguese Army as the 'Pistola Metralhadora Vigneron M/961'.

Length, butt extended: 35.03in (890mm); butt folded: 27.75in (705mm). **Weight unloaded:** 7lb 4oz (3.29kg). **Barrel:** 12.00in (305mm) including compensator, 6 grooves, right-hand twist. **Magazine:**

The Belgian Vigneron M2.

The FN P90 showing the position of the magazine above the receiver.

The P90 field-stripped.

32-round detachable box. **Cyclic rate:** 625 rds/min. **Muzzle velocity:** c.1200 ft/sec (365 m/sec).

• FN P90 Personal Defense Weapon
FN Herstal SA, Herstal
5.7x28mm

This unusual weapon was introduced in 1988 by FN Herstal and is intended to arm that two-thirds of an army whose principle activity is something other than firing a weapon—cooks, drivers, clerks, storemen and similar personnel. In addition, FN felt that the 9mm Parabellum cartridge is outmoded and so developed a new cartridge with powerful ballistic capabilities.

The P90 is a blowback weapon firing from a closed bolt. The pistol grip is well forward so that when held at the hip most of the weight lies on the forearm giving good balance and support. When fired from the shoulder the rear of the receiver acts as the butt and the curved front of the triggerguard acts as a fore grip. The receiver is largely plastic, and the magazine lies on top, above the barrel, with the cartridges at 90° to the axis of the bore. A turntable device in the magazine aligns the cartridges with the bore as it feeds them down in front of the bolt. The magazine is translucent so that

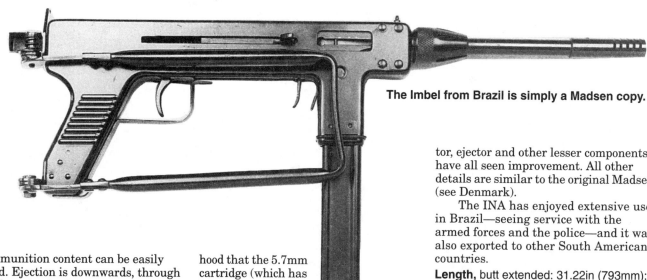

The Imbel from Brazil is simply a Madsen copy.

the ammunition content can be easily checked. Ejection is downwards, through the hollow pistol grip.

All controls are fully ambidextrous; a cocking handle is fitted on both sides and the selector/safety catch is a rotary switch beneath the trigger. There are open sights on both sides of the main collimating optical sight, so that should the optical sight be damaged one set of sights can be used by either left- or right-handed firers.

The ballistic performance is impressive; the standard ball bullet will defeat more than 48 layers of Kevlar body armor at 150 meters range, yet the recoil force is about one-third of that produced by a 9mm Parabellum cartridge. An experimental armor-piercing discarding sabot bullet has defeated the NATO standard steel target.

The P90 was greeted with some suspicion, and its initial acceptance was not helped by corporate upheavals as FN Herstal was purchased by Giat and subsequently regained its independence. It survived this period and by the latter 1990s had begun to gain acceptance in several countries in the Middle and Far East, though FN are reluctant to confirm which. There appears to be every likeli-

hood that the 5.7mm cartridge (which has been slightly shortened from its initial design so as to suit the Five-SeveN pistol) may be confirmed as a NATO-standard cartridge.

Length: 19.69in (500mm). **Weight unloaded:** 5lb 10oz (2.54kg). **Barrel:** 10.35in (263mm), 6 grooves, right-hand twist. **Magazine:** 50-round detachable box. **Cyclic rate:** 900 rds/min. **Muzzle velocity:** c.2346 ft/sec (715 m/sec).

BRAZIL

• Metralhadora de Mao 45-caliber, INA 953

Industrias Nacional de Armas, São Paulo
45 ACP

The INA is a modified version of the Danish Madsen made under license in Brazil in 45-caliber, although improvements and modifications have caused a gradual divergence between the INA and the Madsen, especially in the removal of the bolt retracting handle from the top of the receiver to the right side; the extrac-

tor, ejector and other lesser components have all seen improvement. All other details are similar to the original Madsen (see Denmark).

The INA has enjoyed extensive use in Brazil—seeing service with the armed forces and the police—and it was also exported to other South American countries.

Length, butt extended: 31.22in (793mm); butt folded: 21.46in (545mm). **Weight unloaded:** 7lb 8oz (3.40kg). **Barrel:** 8.46in (215mm), 4 grooves, right-hand twist. **Magazine:** 30-round detachable box. **Cyclic rate:** 650 rds/min. **Muzzle velocity:** c.750 ft/sec (228 m/sec).

• Metralhadora de Mao IMBEL MD1

Industria de Material Belico de Brasil, Itajuba
9mm Parabellum

This submachine gun was developed by the Brazilian Army's Fabrica de Itajuba, which was absorbed in the late 1970s and became IMBEL (Industria de Material Belico). Development was then stepped up, using as many components as possible of the FN FAL rifle, since this was already being manufactured in Brazil and thus would speed up production by commonality of parts. The MD1 has a fixed plastic butt and the MD1A1 has a folding stock. The weapons are of conventional blowback type, firing from the open bolt position and with a large aluminum cocking handle on top of the receiver. The barrel has a perforated jacket and there

The Imbel MD-A1, however, was a completely original design, though it never gained acceptance.

is a small wooden forward handguard. The design was adopted in the early 1950s by the Brazilian army and police and remained in service for about ten years.

Length, butt extended: 29.92in (760mm); butt folded; 22.83in (580mm). **Weight unloaded:** 7lb 10oz (3.45kg. **Barrel:** 8.31in (211mm), 4 grooves, right-hand twist. **Magazine:** 30-round detachable box. **Cyclic rate:** 550 rds/min. **Muzzle velocity:** c.1200 ft/sec (365 m/sec).

The Canadian C-1 is obviously derived from the British Sterling.

• Metralhadora de Mao Mekanika Uru

Mekanika Industria e Comercio Lda., Rio de Janiero
9mm Parabellum

This was designed in 1974 and first produced in 1975. After military testing and approval, production for the Brazilian police began in 1981. However, production lagged behind schedule, due to various financial and technical difficulties, and in 1988 the design was taken over by Bilbao SA, Division FAU Group, who improved production facilities. Guns were subsequently adopted by various Brazilian police forces and exported to various South American, African and Middle Eastern countries.

The Uru is of conventional design, using the blowback system of operation. It is largely made from tubular elements and stampings, spot-welded together; no pins or screws are used and there are only 33 component parts. The final production version was the Mark 2 model which showed several improvements over the original pattern. A grip safety prevents movement of the bolt should the weapon be jarred. A silencer can be fitted onto the muzzle, and with this in place the gun can still be used with full-power ammunition and at automatic fire.

A semi-automatic only version in 9mm Short (380 ACP) caliber and with an extended (406mm or 482mm) barrel was mar-

keted as the FAU Carbine, and a conversion kit was also made which permitted changing the Uru submachine gun to 9mm Short caliber in either full or semi-automatic versions.

Length: 26.42in (671mm). **Weight unloaded:** 6lb 10oz (3.0 kg). **Barrel:** 6.89in (175mm), 6 grooves, right-hand twist. **Magazine:** 30-round detachable box. **Cyclic rate:** 750 rds/min. **Muzzle velocity:** 1275 ft/sec (389 m/sec).

CANADA

• 9mm Submachine-gun C1 (Sterling)

Canadian Arsenals Limited, Long Branch, Ontario
9mm Parabellum

The C1 submachine gun is the Canadian version of the British Sterling, manufactured by Canadian Arsenals Limited of Ontario; all of the weapons are marked with 'CAL' and the date of manufacture on the magazine housing.

A few modifications have been made to the original British design, particularly in the magazine and the trigger mechanism. The magazine capacity has been reduced from 34 to 30 and an alternative magazine holding 10 rounds can be supplied for special operations. The other obvious difference lies in the bayonet, which is that of the Canadian version of the FN rifle. Apart from these external

changes, there are some internal modifications which are concerned solely with the method of manufacture and do not alter the dimensions. These changes are said to make it cheaper to build. Apart from this, the C1 is identical with the Sterling and its performance is similar.

Length: 27.00in (686mm). **Weight unloaded:** 6lb 8oz (2.95kg). **Barrel:** 7.80in (198mm), 6 grooves, right-hand twist. **Magazine:** 10- or 30-round detachable box. **Cyclic rate:** 550 rds/min. **Muzzle Velocity:** c.1200 ft/sec (365 m/sec).

CHILE

• SAF

FAMAE (Fabrica y Maestranzas del Ejercito) Santiago
9mm Parabellum

The SAF submachine gun fires from a closed bolt, and is largely based upon components of the SIG 540 rifle, which is manufactured in Chile under license. The principal change from the original SIG design is the adoption of the blowback system of operation and an unlocked bolt, but the same floating firing pin and hammer firing mechanism are used and a three-round burst device has been added.

Three models of the SAF are produced; the standard model with fixed butt, standard with side-folding butt, and a silenced version, also with side-folding butt. 20-and 30-round magazines are produced; the 30-round are translucent so

The SAF, from Chile, was designed to use as many parts of the SIG 540 rifle as possible, to economize on manufacture.

The Mekanika Uru is a simple and robust weapon.

The Uru Mark 2: not just field-stripped but completely stripped.

Variations on the SAF: Top, the silenced SAF, bottom the Mini-SAF, with the standard SAF in the center.

• (Silenced)

Length, butt extended: 31.89in (810mm); butt folded: 22.44in (570mm). **Weight unloaded:** 6lb 10oz (3.0kg). **Barrel:** 8.66in (220mm), 6 grooves, right-hand twist. **Magazine:** 20- or 30-round detachable box. **Cyclic rate:** 980 rds/min. **Muzzle velocity:** c.985 ft/sec (300 m/sec).

• Mini-SAF
FAMAE (Fabrica y Maestranzas del Ejercito) Santiago
9mm Parabellum

This uses the same SIG-based construction and the same mechanism as the SAF described above but is much shorter, has no butt, and has a forward hand-grip which also has a guard to prevent the fingers from straying in front of the muzzle. The 20-round magazine is the normal, to maintain compactness, but the 30 round magazine can be used if desired. There is a sling swivel at the rear of the receiver to which a special harness can be fitted for concealed carrying.

Length: 12.20in (310mm). **Weight unloaded:** 5lb 1oz (2.3kg). **Barrel:** 4.52in (115mm), 6 grooves, right-hand twist. **Magazine:** 20- or 30-round detachable box. **Cyclic rate:** 1,200 rds/min. **Muzzle velocity:** c.985 ft/sec (370 m/sec).

CHINA (PEOPLE'S REPUBLIC)

• Type 64 Silenced Submachine Gun
State arsenals
7.62x25mm Type 64 special cartridge

This is a selective-fire weapon, operated by the usual blowback system and looking very much as if the inspiration for the mechanism was the Soviet PPS43. The trigger mechanism may have been taken from the ZB 26 LMG, though it has been simplified and is produced from steel stampings. Unlike all Western silent submachine guns, the Type 64 is not a standard design with a silencer added; it was intended for one purpose from the outset, and the silencer is an

that the contents can be visually checked at any time, and like the SIG rifle magazines, they are provided with studs and slots on the side so that two or three magazines may be clipped together. One is then inserted into the magazine housing and fired, and changing magazines merely means releasing the empty magazine and shifting to the next one.

• (Standard)

Length, butt fixed or extended: 25.20in (640mm); butt folded: 16.14in (410mm). **Weight unloaded,** fixed butt: 5lb 15oz (2.70kg); folding butt: 6lb 6oz (2.90kg). **Barrel:** 7.87in (200mm), 6 grooves, right-hand twist. **Magazine:** 20- or 30-round detachable box. **Cyclic rate:** 1,200 rds/min. **Muzzle velocity:** c.1280 ft/sec (390 m/sec).

The Chinese Type 64 silenced gun.

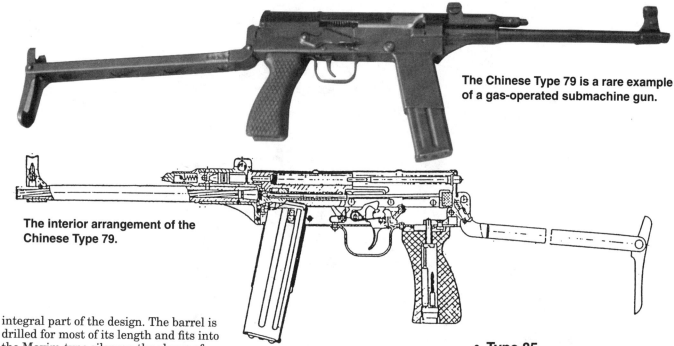

The Chinese Type 79 is a rare example of a gas-operated submachine gun.

The interior arrangement of the Chinese Type 79.

integral part of the design. The barrel is drilled for most of its length and fits into the Maxim-type silencer, the sleeve of which locks to the receiver by means of a threaded ring.

The top of the sheet steel body is an unstressed light cover which lifts off to disclose the bolt and return spring and a synthetic material buffer block. There are two manual safeties, the first is a pivoting plate on the right side which swings up to close part of the ejection opening and to hold the bolt forward, much like the AK47; and the second is a more usual button, which locks the trigger when the bolt is cocked. A change lever allows single shots or automatic fire—an unusual feature in a silenced weapon where automatic shots usually wear the silencer very quickly. The butt folds underneath the body, and the sights have two settings marked '10' and '20'. which mean 100 and 200 meters.

Length, butt extended: 33in (840mm); butt folded: 25.0in (635mm). **Weight unloaded:** 6lb 10oz (3.00kg). **Barrel:** 9.5in (242mm), 4 grooves, right-hand twist. **Magazine:** 30-round detachable box. **Cyclic rate:** 1000 rds/min. **Muzzle velocity:** c.1080 ft/sec (330 m/sec).

• Type 79
State arsenals
7.62x25mm Soviet

This is an extremely lightweight weapon made from steel stampings and firing the standard 7.62mm pistol cartridge. The receiver is rectangular and has a safety lever and fire selector on the right side which is modeled after that on the Kalashnikov rifles. Operation is by gas, using a short stroke tappet above the barrel which impels a short piston rod attached to the bolt carrier, operating a rotating bolt. This is a complex method of working a submachine gun, but it has the advantage of resembling the contemporary rifle, so making training easier, and it also does away with the need for a heavy bolt, and thus, makes the weapon lighter and probably rather easier to control.

Length, butt extended: 27.00in (740mm); butt folded: 17.50in (470mm). **Weight unloaded:** 7lb 4oz (1.90kg). **Barrel:** not known. **Magazine:** 20-round detachable box. **Cyclic rate:** 650 rds/min. **Muzzle velocity:** c.1800 ft/sec (500 m/sec).

• Type 85
State arsenals
7.62x25mm Soviet

This is a modified and simplified version of the Type 79, a blowback instead of gas operated. The receiver is cylindrical, with the barrel screwed on at the front end, and it contains a heavy bolt and return spring. The butt folds to the right side, and the magazine is the same as that of the Type 79.

Length, butt extended: 24.72in (628mm); butt folded: 17.48in (444mm). **Weight unloaded:** 4lb 3oz (1.90kg). **Barrel:** 8.27in (210mm), 4 grooves, right-hand twist. **Magazine:** 30-round detachable box. **Cyclic rate:** 780 rds/min. **Muzzle velocity:** c.1800 ft/sec (500 m/sec).

• Type 85 Silenced
State arsenals
7.62x25mm Type 64 sub-sonic

This is a simplified and lightened version of the Type 64 silenced weapon, using the Type 85 as the basis. It appears to have been developed primarily for export sales. The silencing system is the same as that of the Type 64, and

The Chinese Type 85 reverted to the simple blowback system.

The Type 85 Silenced replaced the Type 64 in Chinese service.

although the weapon is regulated for the subsonic cartridge it is still possible to fire the standard pistol round from it, though in such cases the silencer will have less effect and, of course, will only affect the report of the gun and not the noise of the bullet.

Length, butt extended: 34.21in. (869mm); butt folded: 24.84in (631mm). **Weight unloaded:** 5lb 8oz (2.50kg). **Barrel:** 9.45in (240mm), 4 grooves, right-hand twist. **Magazine:** 30-round detachable box. **Cyclic rate:** 800 rds/min. **Muzzle velocity:** c.985 ft/sec (300 m/sec).

CROATIA

• ERO
RH-ALAN, Zagreb
9mm Parabellum

This is a copy of the Uzi submachine gun—whether licensed or not is unknown—and appears to have no obvious differences, even the dimensions being identical. It appeared in 1994 and is in use by Croatian armed forces.

• Mini-ERO
RH-ALAN, Zagreb
9mm Parabellum

This, again, is a copy of the Mini-Uzi, but in this case some original changes

have been made, notably in providing it with a telescoping wire butt rather than a side-swinging type, and with some differences in the sights and their protective wings.

Length, butt extended: 21.46in (545mm); butt folded: 12.60in (320mm). **Weight unloaded:** 4lb 14oz (2.20kg). **Barrel:** 5.90in (150mm), 4 grooves, right-hand twist. **Magazine:** 20- or 30-round detachable box. **Cyclic rate:** 1100 rds/min. **Muzzle velocity:** c.1155 ft/sec (352 m/sec).

CZECHOSLOVAKIA/ CZECH REPUBLIC

• Machine Pistol ZK/383, ZK/383H, ZK/383P
Ceskoslovenska Zbrojovka, Brno
9mm Parabellum

The ZK/383 is one of the oldest Czech submachine guns; it was designed by the Koucky brothers, first produced in the middle 1930s and was still in use in the Balkan areas as late as the early 1960s. A large and heavy weapon, typical of its time, the ZK/383 was endowed with considerable reserves of strength. During World War II it was issued to troops of the Bulgarian Army and to some German units, but manufacture ceased in about

1948. It is similar to all the submachine guns of its time except for a few features which are peculiar to it; the first was a bipod which appeared with the earlier versions and obviously helped accurate shooting, the second was a quick-change barrel, and the third was a removable weight in the bolt. This latter arrangement allowed the gun to fire either at 500 or at 700 rounds per minute, although it is now hard to see why this was thought necessary as the gun weighed over 10lbs (4.5kg) loaded and could use the bipod to further steady it. Early versions had a rigid fixed barrel, a bayonet lug on the barrel jacket and a front pistol grip. One variation, the ZK/383H, had a folding magazine which stowed under the barrel by pivoting on a pin, and there were police versions (the ZK/383P series) in which the bipod was discarded and a simpler rear-sight installed. Despite this variety and apparent complication, the ZK383 sold in small quantities to the Bulgarian Army, and to Bolivia, Venezuela and other South American states.

Length: 35.51in (902mm). **Weight unloaded:** 9lb 6oz (4.25kg). **Barrel:** 12.75in (324mm), 6 grooves, right-hand twist. **Magazine:** 30-round detachable box. **Cyclic rate:** 500 or 700 rds/min. **Muzzle velocity:** c.1250 ft/sec (380 m/sec).

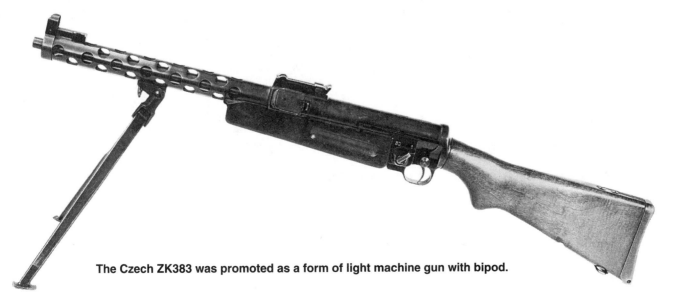

The Czech ZK383 was promoted as a form of light machine gun with bipod.

The Czech CZ23 pioneered the magazine in the hand-grip and the use of the 'overhung' or tele-scoped bolt.

The CZ25 was the CZ23 with a folding steel butt.

The CZ26 was the same as the 25 but fired the Russian 7.62mm pistol cartridge.

The Czech Skorpion was the only service submachine gun ever to fire the 7.62 Browning cartridge.

• Samopal CZ 48a (Samopal 23), Samopal CZ 48b (Samopal 25)
Ceskoslovenska Zbrojovka NP, Brno
9mm Parabellum

The CZ23 was designed in the late 1940s and was placed in production shortly afterwards. The weapon was present in substantial numbers in the Czech Army in 1951 and 1952, but manufacture stopped soon afterwards, perhaps because of the Soviet patronage which supplied arms to the Czech Army in enormous quantities. About 100,000 of these neat and handy little weapons were produced, and many found their way to the Middle East and Cuba. Another model, the CZ25, was made with a folding metal strip stock. Both featured a bolt which had a deep recess in its forward face to allow the breech to slide inside; thus the main part of the bolt was in front of the breech when the bolt was forward. The bolt was about 8inch (203mm) long, 6inch (152mm) of which telescoped over the barrel, permitting a much shorter weapon; this is now quite common, but in 1950 it was novel in the extreme and made the CZ23 a definite trend-setter. Another innovation was the placing of the magazine inside the pistol grip, which can only be done when the bolt travels as far forward as it does in the 'wrap around' method; this also represents another sensible and satisfactory

advance. The magazine was also a step forward, since it was of the semi-triangular pattern extensively marketed by the Carl Gustav factory in Sweden, and was probably the best type of magazine ever made for pistol ammunition. Two sizes were made, one holding 24 rounds and the other holding 40 rounds.

The CZ23 and 25 were the first post-war submachine guns to show any significant advance in design; since then, there has been a steady improvement in the directions so clearly shown by them, ultimately leading to the short, handy and simple weapons of the present day.

Length: 27.0in (686mm). **Weight unloaded:** 6lb 12oz (3.06kg). **Barrel:** 11.26in (286mm), 6 grooves, right-hand twist. **Magazine:** 24- or 40-round detachable box. **Cyclic rate:** 600 rds/min. **Muzzle velocity:** c.1250 ft/sec (381 m/sec).

• Samopal 24, Samopal 26
Ceskoslovenska Zbrojovka NP, Brno
7.62x23mm Type 48

The CZ24 and 26 replaced the earlier CZ23 and 25 as the standard weapons of the Czech Army—but it is an indication of the Soviet influence that this change should have been made at all, since the only real alteration between the two designs lies in the caliber. The later guns fire the 7.62mm Soviet pistol cartridge

but, in the case of these submachine guns, it is ammunition made in Czechoslovakia and loaded to give a higher velocity than the original Russian form. Apart from some obvious differences such as a new barrel, bolt and magazine, the weapon is virtually unchanged from the 9mm version. One small difference lies in the pistol grip/magazine housing which in the 7.62mm model has a noticeable forward lean, and there are some minor alterations to such items as the rear sight and sling swivels. Both the 24 and the 26 served the Czech Army from c.1952 until the 1960s.

Length, butt extended: 27.00in (686mm); butt folded: 17.50in (445mm). **Weight unloaded:** 7lb 4oz (3.29kg). **Barrel:** 11.20in (284mm), 4 grooves, right-hand twist. **Magazine:** 32-round detachable box. **Cyclic rate:** 600 rds/min. **Muzzle velocity:** c.1800 ft/sec (548 m/sec).

• Samopal 61 'Skorpion'
Ceska Zbrojovka as, Brno
7.65x17 SR Browning (32 ACP) and others

This weapon belongs in the class of true machine pistols rather than subma-

The Skorpion with its wire stock unfolded.

chine guns; it fires a bullet of no more than marginal combat effectiveness and the whole weapon is small enough to be fired comfortably from one hand in single-shot fire. The 61 appears to have been designed to provide a holster weapon for armored vehicle crews which is normally used as a pistol but which can, in emergency, provide automatic fire.

The Skorpion is a blowback weapon, and with its light reciprocating parts a high rate of fire might be expected; the designer has, however, ingeniously countered this by putting an inertia mechanism in the pistol grip. As the bolt recoils, it drives a weight down into the grip, against the pressure of a spring, and at the same time the bolt is held by a trip-catch in the rear position. The weight rebounds from the spring and, on rising, releases the trip to allow the bolt to go forward. The duration of this action is very brief, but it is sufficient to delay the bolt and thus reduce the rate of fire to manageable proportions. It might be expected that this action would make itself felt to the firer, but it is in fact masked by the general recoil and climb.

Since its original introduction, some variant models have appeared, the differences lying principally in the chambering. The 64 was chambered for 9mm Short and the 65 for 9mm Makarov (9x18mm), but were otherwise identical with the 61. The 68 was chambered for the 9mm Parabellum cartridge and was therefore somewhat larger and more robust. These models were primarily produced for export, but were made only in limited numbers before production ceased some time in the latter 1970s. They were replaced by a fresh series which had some small variations: the Model 82 chambered the 9x18mm Makarov cartridge, had a 115mm barrel and used a straight box magazine instead of the original curved model. It was not made in quantity but is still available to special order. The Model 83 is chambered for the 9mm Short cartridge and also uses a straight magazine; it, too, has not been made in any great numbers. Finally, in the late 1980s, the Model 91S appeared, which is

engineered so as to fire in the semi-automatic mode only. It is available in 7.65mm Browning, 9mm Short or 9mm Makarov chambering, and a silencer is available.

Various models of the Skorpion went into service with Czech and Slovak army units and have been observed in military use in Afghanistan, Angola, Egypt, Libya, Mozambique and Uganda. It has also been manufactured under license in Yugoslavia.

(vz/61) (7.65mm Browning)

Length, butt extended; 20.55in (522mm); butt folded: 10.65in (271mm). **Weight unloaded:** 2lb 14oz (1.31 kg). **Barrel:** 4.50in (114mm), 6 grooves, right-hand twist. **Magazine:** 10- or 20-round detachable box. **Cyclic rate:** 850 rds/min. **Muzzle velocity:** c.975 ft/sec (296 m/sec).

(vz/68) (9mm Parabellum)

Length, butt extended: 23.42in (595mm); butt folded: 12.00in (305mm). **Weight unloaded:** 4lb 7oz (2.03kg). **Barrel:** 5.00in (127mm). **Magazine:** 10-, 20- or 30-round detachable box. **Cyclic rate:** 750 rds/min. **Muzzle velocity:** c.1310 ft/sec (400 m/sec).

DENMARK

• Madsen m/45

Dansk Industri Syndikat AS 'Madsen', Copenhagen
9mm Parabellum

One of the last wooden-stocked submachine guns to be developed, this Madsen design had some unusual features. The breechblock is attached to a slide cover (instead of a cocking handle) which extends forward over the barrel and is formed at its front into a serrated grip. The recoil spring is wrapped around the barrel and contained within this slide.

In order to cock the weapon, the slide is grasped and the entire slide and breech unit pulled to the rear—like the

cocking of a giant automatic pistol. An advantage of the design is that the mass of the slide unit helps to resist the breech opening force and keep down the rate of fire, but the disadvantages are that the cover oscillates during firing and the spring, wrapped around the barrel and confined within the slide, soon overheats and weakens in use.

A version of the basic weapon with a folding butt was also manufactured.
Length: 31.50in (800mm). **Weight unloaded:** 7lb 2oz (3.22kg). **Barrel:** 12.40in (315mm), 4 grooves, right-hand twist. **Magazine:** 50-round detachable box. **Cyclic rate:** 850 rds/min. **Muzzle velocity:** c.1312 ft/sec (400 m/sec).

• Madsen m/46

Dansk Industri Syndikat AS 'Madsen', Copenhagen
9mm Parabellum

The name of Madsen had been associated with the manufacture of arms for many years and, as soon as World War II ended, the company started to produce for the post-war market. The m/46 submachine gun was an attempt to overcome the drawbacks of the cheap and hastily-made wartime guns while using their manufacturing techniques to the full. The result was a weapon which was completely conventional in operation, apart from an unusual safety catch, but which offered remarkable accessibility and ease of manufacture. The gun fires from the normal open-bolt position and is capable only of automatic fire. A grip safety behind the magazine housing has to be grasped and pulled forward to allow the gun to fire and a second safety catch on the rear of the receiver locks the bolt in the open position. The main body of the gun is formed from two metal stampings which comprise the two halves of the entire receiver, pistol grip, magazine-housing and barrel bearing; a massive barrel nut then screws on and holds both halves together. The left-hand side can be removed, leaving all the working parts in place, and so internal inspection and cleaning are greatly

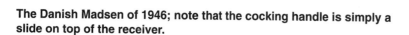

The Danish Madsen of 1946; note that the cocking handle is simply a slide on top of the receiver.

The 1953 Madsen had a more conventional cocking handle in the top of the receiver. It could also take a bayonet, a spectacularly useless fitting on a submachine gun.

simplified. The gun was well made and reliable, but it sold in only small numbers to a few South American countries and to Thailand. A modified pattern known as the Maskinpistol m/50 differed in the provision of an improved retracting handle, which no longer had to be removed before the weapon was stripped.

Length, butt extended: 31.50in (800mm); butt folded: 21.50in (546mm). **Weight unloaded:** 7lb 0oz (3.17kg). **Barrel:** 7.75in (196mm), 4 grooves, right-hand twist. **Magazine:** 32-round detachable box. **Cyclic rate:** 500 rds/min. **Muzzle velocity:** c.1250 ft/sec (381 m/sec).

• Maskinpistol m/49 ('Hovea')

Haerens Vabenarsenalet, Copenhagen
9mm Parabellum

Although bearing a considerable resemblance to the Swedish 'Carl Gustav' design, the m/49 owes its parentage to the Husqvarna company. It was originally manufactured in 1944 as a prototype for the Swedish Army, but was turned down in favor of the Carl Gustav. The gun was then offered to Denmark, who were in the market for a submachine gun after World War II, and the production models were all made under license in Denmark. There is little of note in the design; it is a simple blowback gun, designed with ease of production in mind and making use of the standard Carl Gustav magazine—an unusual example of standardization which could well be copied in other spheres. The m/49 was originally made to take the Suomi drum magazine, which accounts for the oddly-shaped magazine aperture.

Length, butt extended: 31.75in, (806mm); butt folded: 21.65in (550mm). **Weight unloaded:** 7lb 6oz (2.34kg). **Barrel:** 8.50in (216mm), 4 or 6 grooves, right-hand twist. **Magazine:** 36-round detachable box. **Cyclic rate:** 600 rds/min. **Muzzle velocity:** c.1300 ft/sec (396 m/sec).

• Maskinpistol m/53

Dansk Industri Syndikat AS 'Madsen', Copenhagen
9mm Parabellum

The m/53 is a development of the m/46 and the m/50, and differs from them mainly in the magazine which—on this model—is curved to improve the feeding and can also be used as a monopod when the gun is fired in the prone position. In common with the preceding models, the receiver, pistol grip and magazine housing form a novel two-piece frame hinging at the rear and locked at the front by the barrel locking nut. An optional barrel jacket carries a bayonet attachment, which is another noticeable departure from the previous versions. Some guns have wooden furniture on the pistol grip, and all have a distinctive leather sleeve on the tubular butt. Sales of this gun were fairly respectable and it was taken into service in some of the smaller countries of South America and Asia. The Madsen company left the arms manufacturing business in the 1970s, but the design has been perpetuated in Brazil.

Length, butt extended: 31.55in (800mm); butt folded: 20.75in (530mm). **Weight unloaded:** 7lb 0oz (3.17kg). **Barrel:** 7.80in (197mm), 4 grooves, right-hand twist. **Magazine:** 32-round detachable box. **Cyclic rate:** 550 rds/min. **Muzzle velocity:** c.1250 ft/sec (380 m/sec).

DOMINICAN REPUBLIC

• Cristobal Models 2 and 62

Armeria Fabricas de Armas, San Cristobal
30 MI US Carbine

The Cristobal Model 2 was produced in Dominica in a factory which was origi-

nally organized with the assistance of a number of experts who had previously worked with Beretta and with the Hungarian plant at Budapest. Although in shape the Cristobal is reminiscent of the early Berettas, it is rather different internally, using a lever system to delay the blowback opening of the bolt. The design is attributed to Kiraly, designer of the Hungarian 39M and 43M submachine guns. A pendant lever attached to the bolt engages with the gun body, and as the bolt is driven back by the exploding cartridge, it is forced to revolve the lever and disconnect it before being allowed to recoil freely. This produces sufficient delay to allow the bullet to leave the barrel before the case is extracted.

The Model 62 is a more modern version using the same mechanism, but with a perforated handguard instead of the three-quarter length wooden butt and forend of the earlier model; the M62 may also be found with a folding skeleton butt. Both models use double triggers, the front trigger for single shot operation and the rear one for automatic fire.

Probably the most unusual feature of the Cristobal is the use of the 30 M1 Carbine cartridge; the lightweight bullet with its inherent lack of stopping power—compared to such rounds as the 9mm Parabellum and the 45 ACP—is somewhat negated by the increased velocity, which is much higher than is common with this class of weapon.

(Model 2)

Length: 37.20in (945mm). **Weight unloaded:** 7lb 12oz (3.51kg). **Barrel:** 16.10in (409mm), 4 grooves, right-hand twist. **Magazine:** 25- or 30-round detachable box. **Cyclic rate:** 575 rds/min. **Muzzle velocity:** c.1850 ft/sec (563 m/sec).

The Cristobal M2 was unusual in adopting the US 30 Carbine cartridge.

The Egyptian Akaba, a simplified version of the Carl Gustav.

(Model 62)

Length, butt extended: 37.0in (940mm); butt folded: 25.60in (650mm). **Weight:** 8lb 3oz (3.72kg). **Barrel:** 12.20in (310mm), 4 grooves, right-hand twist. **Magazine:** 30-round box. **Cyclic rate:** 600 rds/min. **Muzzle velocity:** 1870 ft/sec (570 m/sec).

EGYPT

• Port Said

Maadi Engineering Co., Maadi, Cairo
9mm Parabellum

The Port Said is a licensed copy of the Swedish Carl Gustav m/45 which has been in more or less continuous production since the late 1950s. It is identical in appearance and operation, but differs somewhat in dimensions due to different manufacturing methods.

Length, butt extended: 31.81in (808mm); butt folded: 21.65in (550mm). **Weight unloaded:** 8lb 1oz (3.65kg). **Barrel:** 8.38in (213mm), 6 grooves, right-hand twist. **Magazine:** 36-round detachable box. **Cyclic rate:** 600 rds/min. **Muzzle velocity:** c.1312 ft/sec (400 m/sec).

• Akaba

Maadi Engineering Co., Maadi, Cairo
9mm Parabellum

The Akaba was manufactured for a short period in the 1970s as a cheaper and simpler version of the Port Said. There was no barrel jacket, and instead of the side-folding stock, a telescoping wire stock, similar to that on the US M3, was used. The rear sight was at the rear end of the receiver, and not in front of the safety slot.

Length, butt extended: 29.0in (737mm); butt folded: 19.0in (482mm). **Weight:** not known. **Barrel:** 5.9in (150mm), 6 grooves, right hand twist. **Magazine:** 36-round detachable box. **Cyclic rate:** c.700 rds/min. **Muzzle velocity:** c.1250 ft/sec (380 m/sec).

ESTONIA

• Tallinn M1923

Tallinn Arsenal, Tallinn
9mm Parabellum

An early and little known weapon, and probably the only weapon ever designed and manufactured in Estonia, the Tallinn was broadly compiled from the Bergmann MP18/1. It was a blow-back weapon with wooden butt and a slot-perforated jacket around the barrel. The magazine fit into the side, and there was the usual optimistic tangent sight of the period, marked up to 600m, on top of the receiver. The magazine was remarkably slender, and the bolt did not follow the massive Bergmann pattern but had a reduced-diameter front end similar to the Thompson. The barrel was unusual in having longitudinal cooling fins machined in its surface, concealed by the jacket except for the last few millimeters around the muzzle. The Tallinn was used by the Estonian Army and police, but appears to have been withdrawn some time in the early 1930s; a few turned up in Spain during the Civil War.

Length: 31.85in (809mm). **Weight unloaded:** 9lb 7oz (4.28kg). **Barrel:** 8.27in (210mm), 4 grooves, right-hand twist. **Magazine:** 40-round detachable box. **Cyclic rate:** 600 rds/min. **Muzzle velocity:** c.1280 ft/sec (390 m/sec).

FINLAND

• Suomi m/26 and m/31

Oy Tikkakoski Ab, Tikkakoski
7.63mm Mauser (m/26), 9mm Parabellum (m/31)

The Suomi (the Finnish word for Finland) submachineguns were manufactured to the designs of Aimo Lahti and produced by the state-owned Tikkakoski plant. The first model to be adopted by the Finnish Army was the m/26, itself preceded by a series of experimental weapons dating back to 1922; the m/26, chambered for the 7.63mm Mauser round, was distinguished by a large buffer housing extending from the rear of the receiver and by a severely-curved 36-round box magazine. Few of these weapons were produced, as the design was replaced within a few years by the improved m/31—an outstandingly successful weapon which is probably still to be found in the more remote parts of the world and which was actually produced in Sweden, Denmark and Switzerland. Although heavy by modern standards, the m/31 is capable of surprisingly good accuracy from the design's long barrel; it

The Finnish Suomi M1931, one of the classic designs which lasted for many years.

In postwar years the Finns adopted the Soviet PPS-43 but called it their Model 44/46.

is, of course, made in the 'old style' with all the components either machined from solid stock or forged from heavy gauge material. The bolt handle is at the rear of the receiver and works in much the same way as a bolt-action rifle in that it is lifted and pulled to the rear to retract the bolt and then pushed forward and turned down, remaining stationary while the bolt moves within the receiver. The barrel dismounts from the jacket reasonably easy and the bolt has a fixed firing pin, but the most significant feature of the Suomi design lies in the magazine. Box magazines of 20 rounds and 50 rounds were provided and so, too, was a large drum holding 71 rounds, which was later copied by the Soviets for the PPSh41. If, as had been suggested, Lahti drew on the drum magazine of the Thompson submachine gun for his inspiration, then he made a very good job of copying it for despite the loaded weight of 5lb 8oz (2.49kg), the magazine unit is remarkably robust. A smaller drum containing 40 rounds was also developed but, c.1955, all the m/31 guns were converted to take

the Swedish 36-round box magazine used on the m/45.

(m/3)
Length: 34.50in (875mm).
Weight unloaded: 10lb 12oz (4.87kg). **Barrel:** 12.50in (318mm), 6 grooves, right-hand twist. **Magazine:** 20-, 36-, 40-, or 50-round detachable boxes, or 71-round drum. **Cyclic rate:** 900 rds/min. **Muzzle velocity:** c.1300 ft/sec (396 m/sec).

• Konepistooli m/44
Oy Tikkakoski Ab, Sakara
9mm Parabellum

The m/44 is a copy of the Soviet PPS43 design, with suitable modifications made to the magazine and feed to enable the 9mm Parabellum cartridge to be used. The weapon is a simple blowback type, capable only of automatic fire and welded together from as many simple stampings and pressings as possible: the modified feed unit, however, permits the use of the 71-round drum of the earlier m/31 submachine gun as well as the other box magazines. In common with

the m/31, the m/44 was modified in the mid-1950s to take the 36-round Swedish box magazine design. The m/44 was the standard submachine gun of the Finnish Army from 1945 until replaced in service by the assault rifle m/62 in the mid-1960s.

It is interesting to note that the manager of Oy Tikkakoski at the time when the m/44 was produced, Willi Daugs, fled to Spain via Sweden and Holland at the close of World War II. He took with him copies of the manufacturing drawings of the m/44, which later appeared in Spain as the DUX 53 (see Germany).

Length, butt extended: 32.50in (825mm); butt folded: 24.50in (623mm). **Weight unloaded:** 6lb 3oz (2.80kg). **Barrel:** 9.75in (247mm), 4 or 6 grooves, right-hand twist. **Magazine:** 71-round drum, or 36- or 50-round detachable box. **Cyclic rate:** 650 rds/min. **Muzzle velocity:** c.1250 ft/sec (381 m/sec).

• Suomi m/44-46
Oy Tikkakoski Ab, Sakara
9mm Parabellum

The m/44-46 was derived from the earlier m/44, itself a copy of the Russian PPS43. Production of the m/44 carried on into the post-war years; the slight post-war modification which led to the m/44-46 concerned the standardization for the gun of the 36-round box magazine used on the m/45 ('Carl Gustav') submachine gun of the Swedish armed forces. Apart from this, the Finnish m/44-46 differed from its predecessor only in the standard of finish, as more care could be spared in time of peace. Unlike the m/44, the 1946 pattern would not accept the standard Suomi 71-round drum magazine.

The m/44-46 served in the Finnish forces until the mid 1960s, after which it was replaced in service by the m/62 and later assault rifles.

Length: 32.50in (826mm). **Weight unloaded:** 6lb 3oz (2.81 kg). **Barrel:** 9.80in (248mm), 4 grooves, right-hand twist. **Magazine:** 36-round detachable box. **Cyclic rate:** 650 rds/min. **Muzzle velocity:** c.1320 ft/sec (402 m/sec).

The Jati-Matic with 40-round magazine.

The French Mas 38, with the barrel and bolt at an angle to each other.

• Jati-Matic/GG-95 PDW

Tampeeren Asepaja Oy, Tampere (ca. 1980-87)
Oy Golden Gun Ltd, Turku (ca. 1995-
9mm Parabellum

The Jati-Matic was designed to be as small and light as possible, consistent with accuracy and control. The weapon uses a patented design in which the bolt recoils up an inclined plane at an angle to the barrel. This causes the bolt to press against the bottom of the receiver, adding an element of braking to its movement. This upward movement of the bolt allows the pistol grip to be set higher than normal so that the firer's hand lies almost on the axis of the barrel. This, it is claimed, reduces the usual lifting effect of the muzzle, allowing the firer to keep the weapon aligned on the target more easily. There is, moreover, no buttstock to assist in controlling the weapon.

The weapon consists of a pressed-steel receiver with hinged top cover. A forward folding grip beneath the barrel also acts as the cocking lever and, when closed, as a positive bolt lock. The trigger is pulled against a stop for single shots; pulling it past the stop gives automatic fire. The magazine is a double-column design and the Carl Gustav magazine will also fit. Various accessories were offered, such as silencer, different sizes of magazine and a laser pointing device.

The Jati-Matic appeared in the early 1980s, but in spite of assessment by various countries, found no takers. In the early 1990s it appeared again, offered by a Chinese company, but it rapidly disappeared again and re-appeared in Finland in the mid-1990s as the GG-95 Personal Defense Weapon, made by the Golden Gun Company.

Length: 14.75in (375mm).
Weight unloaded: 3lb 10oz (1.65kg). **Barrel:** 8.0in (203mm), 6 grooves, right-hand twist. **Magazine:** 20- or 40-round detachable box. **Cyclic rate:** 600 rds/min. **Muzzle velocity:** c.1247 ft/sec (380 m/sec).

FRANCE

• Pistolet Mitrailleur MAS Modéle 38

Manufacture'Armes de Saint-Etienne, Saint-Etienne
7.65mm Long Auto Pistol

Derived from the SE-MAS of 1935, the MAS38 submachine gun was first made in 1938 and continued in production until 1949, a limited number being manufactured for the German occupation forces during the war years. The MAS38 was a good and workman-like design, well-made and somewhat in advance of contemporary thinking. It was reasonably light, and diverged from the general contemporary pattern of one-piece wooden stocks extending well up the barrel and of relatively complicated mechanisms. Although primarily made from machined steel stock, the MAS contained nothing that was not strictly necessary and so managed to avoid the weight penalty.

A slide on the right-hand side of the receiver engages with the bolt and, on being pulled to the rear, cocks the weapon and opens the ejection port at the same time; it then stays to the rear. A sprung plate covers the magazine housing when the weapon is not loaded. The bolt moves in a tube which contains a long recoil spring and which is not in line with the barrel. The bolt therefore reaches the breech at an angle and the bolt face is machined to allow for this. The butt is almost in a straight line with the barrel and this, combined with the comparatively low-powered round which it fires, endows the gun with good accuracy and low recoil.

The MAS38 was never produced in any caliber other than 7.65mm Long and was consequently of no interest to other European nations. A 9mm version might well have enjoyed commercial success.

Length: 25.00in (635mm). **Weight unloaded:** 6lb 4oz (2.83kg). **Barrel:** 8.75in (222mm), 4 grooves, right-hand twist. **Magazine:** 32-round detachable box. **Cyclic rate:** 600 rds/min. **Muzzle velocity:** c.1150 ft/sec (350 m/sec).

• Pistolet Mitrailleur Hotchkiss 'Type Universel', 1949

Société de Fabrication des Armes A Feu Portatives Hotchkiss et Cie, Saint-Denis
9mm Parabellum

The Hotchkiss 'Universal' was introduced shortly after World War II and appears to have been designed with the intention of overcoming all the disadvan-

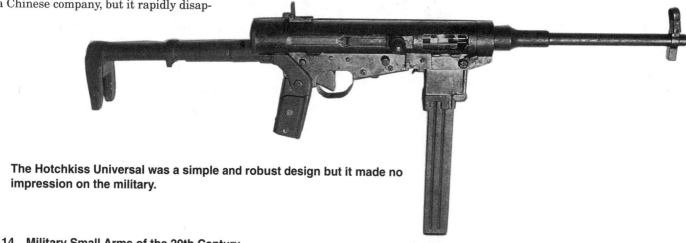

The Hotchkiss Universal was a simple and robust design but it made no impression on the military.

The French MAT 49 is still widely used by police forces.

tages shown by the wartime guns. It was originally produced as a self-loading police weapon but was soon marketed in a selective-fire version, and small numbers were taken into the French Army for extended trials. The many ingenious features of the design led to over-complication, manufacturing difficulties and even more difficult maintenance problems in the field, and the 'Universal' was out of production by the early 1950s, bringing to an end the long history of Hotchkiss automatic weapons.

The most notable feature of the design was its ability to be folded into a surprisingly small unit; the butt and pistol-grip could fold beneath the body, the magazine and its housing folded forward beneath the barrel, and even the barrel could be telescoped into the receiver to produce a package no more than 17.25in (438mm) long.

Length, butt extended: 30.60in (776mm); butt folded: 21.25in (540mm). **Weight unloaded:** 7lb 8oz

(3.41kg). **Barrel:** 10.75in (273mm). **Magazine:** 32-round detachable box. **Cyclic rate:** 650 rds/min. **Muzzle velocity:** c.1300 ft/sec (396 m/sec).

• Pistolet Mitrailleur MAT Modéle 49
Manufacture d'Armes de Tulle, Tulle
9mm Parabellum

The MAT was adopted by the French Army in 1949 and was their standard submachine gun throughout the fighting in Algeria and Indo-China. Like its predecessor the MAS38, it is a simple and effective design with few frills. It is mainly made from heavy gauge steel stampings and has a minimum of machined parts, and the effort to reduce manufacturing costs has given it a very 'square' look. The folding wire butt is similar to that of the United States' M3 submachine gun, and the pistol grip has

plastic furniture and a grip safety. The magazine housing is unusual in that it pivots forward to lie under the barrel when it is necessary to carry the gun in the smallest possible package, and the housing also serves as the forward hand grip. The magazine is a single-feed box very similar to that of the Sten, which was not noted for its reliability or freedom from stoppages, and it is probable that the MAT inherited this failing.

In all other respects, the gun is entirely conventional and its strength and robustness survived considerable active service. The North Vietnamese captured numbers of MAT 49 and converted them to fire the Tokarev 7.62mm pistol round. The MAT 49 has been superseded in the French Army by the FA-MAS assault rifle, but is still widely used by police forces.

Length, butt extended: 26.00in (661mm); butt folded: 16.00in

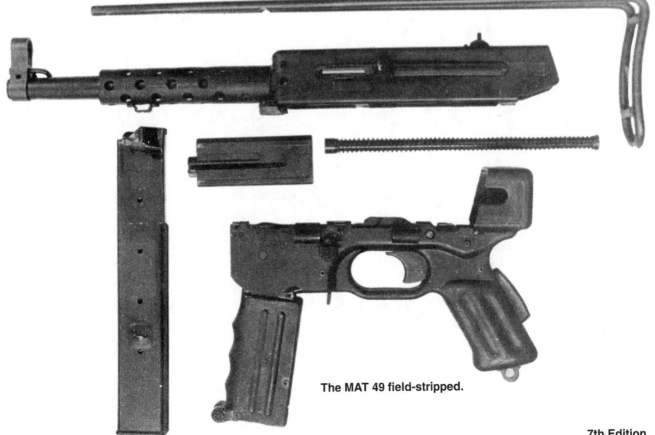

The MAT 49 field-stripped.

The Bergmann MP18 with its 'snail' magazine.

(406mm). **Weight unloaded:** 8lb 0oz (3.63kg). **Barrel:** 9.00in (228mm), 4 grooves, left-hand twist. **Magazine:** 32-round detachable box. **Cyclic rate:** 600 rds/min. **Muzzle velocity:** c.1200 ft/sec (365 m/sec).

• Gevarm
Société Anonyme Gevelot, Paris
9mm (Parabellum)

The Gevarm submachine gun was a simple, robust and conventional design-capable of being easily manufactured. Its simplicity also meant that the Gevarm-would give little trouble in service. It was a blowback weapon with a sliding wire stock, cocking lever on the left side, and a large fire-selector lever; the size of this, plus the size of the triggerguard, made it a particularly easy weapon to use with gloved hands in a cold climate. The Gevarm was offered for some years in the 1960s and early 70s, but it appeared to have aroused no interest and the design was abandoned.

Length, butt folded: 19.70in (500mm). **Weight unloaded:** 7lb 0.5oz (3.20kg). **Barrel:** 8.66in (220mm). **Magazine:** 32-round detachable box. **Cyclic rate:** c.600 rds/min. **Muzzle velocity:** c.1250 ft/sec (380 m/sec).

GERMANY (PRE-1945)

• Maschinenpistole 18/I (MP18/I)
Theodor Bergmann Waffenbau AG, Suhl
9mm Parabellum

The MP18/I is an historic weapon and the beginning of the story of the submachine gun. Development of the weapon started in early 1916 and over 30,000 had been made by November 1918. It was designed by Hugo Schmeis-ser, whose name is well known in the small arms field, and it was the first true blowback submachine gun. The MP18/I set the fashion for the pattern of submachine guns until c. 1936, and its influence can clearly be seen on all the designs of the 1920s and early 1930s. Its military use was proscribed by the conditions of the Versailles Treaty though, oddly, it was permitted as a police weapon.

Schmeisser had pioneered the blowback automatic principle in the series of pistols he designed for Bergmann in the late 1890s, and he simply extended that principle to a shoulder weapon firing a more powerful cartridge. The MP18 consists simply of a barrel inside a perforated jacket, a heavy bolt, a floating firing pin, a return spring and a trigger mechanism, all carried in a traditionally-shaped wooden stock. The gun was originally made to use the 'snail' magazine produced for the Parabellum pistol, with which an adapter had to be used to prevent the magazine fouling the bolt; this proved unsatisfactory and was corrected after two or three years of use by the police forces. A straight box magazine was substituted in the early 1920s and came in two sizes, of 20 or 32 rounds.

The MP18/I was simple, very strong, not too difficult to manufacture and—except for the initial feed troubles—very reliable. It was a success from the very beginning, and later designers who abandoned its principles frequently found themselves in difficulties.

Length: 32.00in (812mm). **Weight unloaded:** 9lb 4oz (4.19kg). **Barrel:** 7.75in (196mm), 6 grooves, right-hand twist. **Magazine:** 32-round helical drum; 20- or 32-round detachable box. **Cyclic rate:** 400 rds/min. **Muzzle velocity:** c.1250 ft/sec (380 m/sec).

• Maschinenpistole 28/II (MP28/II)
C. G. Haenel Waffen-und Fahrradfabrik AG, Suhl
7.63mm Mauser, 7.65mm Parabellum, 9mm Parabellum, 45 ACP

The MP28/II was a direct descendant of the MP18 and is substantially similar, apart from modifications and improvements; the main difference is that a selector mechanism is incorporated so that single shots may be fired. A separate firing pin and an improved mainspring are the chief internal changes and, apart from a new rear sight, the external appearance is hardly changed. The gun was intended purely as a commercial proposition and in this it was entirely successful, for large numbers were made both in Germany and under license by Pieper of Belgium in the early 1930s, and was adopted as a military or police weapon in Portugal and a number of South American countries. The customer could virtually state his preferred caliber and the gun would be modified to suit. In 45 ACP, it is perhaps noteworthy that the magazine capacity was reduced to 25 although there was no standardization in capacity and there were a few 20-round magazines made for 9mm Parabellum. Like its predecessor the MP18, the MP28/II was strong and could survive considerable ill treatment.

Lenght: 32.0in (812mm). **Weight unloaded:** 8lb 12oz (3.97kg). **Barrel:** 7.75in (196mm), 6 grooves, right-hand twist. **Magazine:** 20-, 32- or 50-round detachable box. **Cyclic rate:** 500 rds/min. **Muzzle velocity:** c.1250 ft/sec (381 m/sec).

The adoption of a straight side-feeding magazine turned the MP18 into the MP28; it was also able to fire single shots.

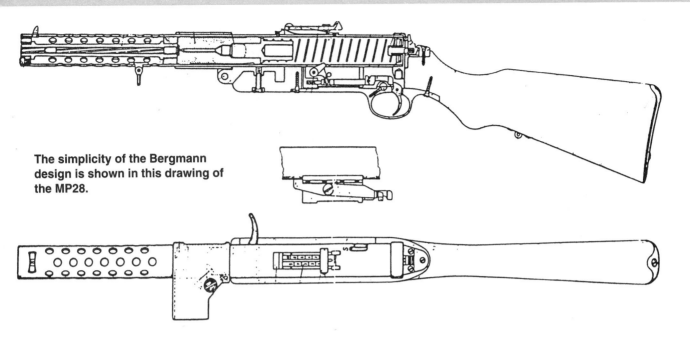

The simplicity of the Bergmann design is shown in this drawing of the MP28.

• Bergmann MP34/I and 35/I

Manufactured for Theodor Bergmann Co. GmbH, by Carl Walther Waffenfabrik AG, Zella-Mehlis (MP34), and by Junker & Ruh AG, Karlsruhe (MP35)
7.63mm Mauser, 9mm Parabellum, 45 ACP

This is the only submachine gun to be actually designed by a Bergmann brother, other so-called Bergmanns being actually due to Schmeisser. The prototypes were made in Denmark by Schutz & Larsen in 1932, due to the restrictions of the Versailles Treaty, after which Bergmann licensed production to Carl Walther. About 2,000 MP34/I were made for the German police and for export to Bolivia. The Bergmann was very well made and finished and had few unusual features, the most obvious of which was the right-hand side-feeding magazine.

The bolt handle was similar to that used on the Suomi M26, resembling a rifle bolt at the rear of the receiver, it had to be rotated and pulled back to retract the bolt. The advantage claimed for this was a stationary handle when firing and no bolt slot through which dirt could enter the mechanism. Another feature was the 'double-acting' trigger; the gun

fired semi-automatically when the trigger was pulled half-way back, and full automatic when pulled further back.

The MP34/I was offered in various calibers and with long and short barrels, but so far as is known only 9mm versions were ever produced. In 1935 some modifications were applied; these were almost entirely internal and designed to simplify production and improve reliability, and the resulting design became the MP35/I, quantities being sold to Ethiopia, Denmark and Sweden. In 1940 the Waffen SS arranged licensed production by Junker & Ruh AG, and this company produced some 40,000 weapons before 1945, entirely for the Waffen SS.

Length: 33.00in (840mm). **Weight unloaded:** 8lb 15oz (4.05kg). **Barrel:** 7.75in (196mm), 6 grooves, right-hand twist. **Magazine:** 24- or 32-round detachable box. **Cyclic rate:** 650 rds/min. **Muzzle velocity:** c.1250 ft/sec (380 m/sec).

• Maschinenpistole Erma, System Vollmer (MPE)

Erfurter Maschinenfabrik B. Geipel GmbH (Erma-Werke), Erfurt
9mm Parabellum

The Erma-Werke began as a general engineering works in the early 1920s and, among other things, manufactured components for Vollmer, who was a gunsmith making small quantities of submachine guns for sale to police forces. In 1931 Erma licensed the production rights for Vollmer's submachine gun; shortly afterwards Vollmer, who had run his business on the proverbial shoestring, sold out completely and went to work for Erma as their chief designer, and the Vollmer submachine gun became the Erma MPE. It was manufactured as commercial venture from 1930 until 1938, when mass-production of the MP38 swept all else aside in the Erma factory.

During the early 1930s numbers were sold to France, Mexico and South American countries, and it appeared in the Gran Chaco War of 1932-35. It also saw a little use in the Spanish Civil War. The German Army began taking deliveries in about 1933 and it remained in use

S43 The Erma EMP with its characteristic front grip.

The MP38 pioneered all-metal construction and the folding butt.

until about 1942, when it was eventually withdrawn and replaced by the MP40.

The design was a simple tubular receiver with a jacketed barrel and a side-feeding magazine; the most obvious recognition feature is the vertical wooden fore-grip located just behind the magazine area. Internally, the MPE used Vollmer's telescoping mainspring casing which later appeared on the MP38, and the bolt handle locked into a safety slot in the receiver. Minor variants include one with a conventional wooden forend, and one which has a bayonet attachment, though these are rare.

Length: 35.51in (902mm). **Weight unloaded:** 9lb 2oz (4.14kg). **Barrel:** 10.00in (254mm), 6 grooves, right-hand twist. **Magazine:** 25- or 32-round detachable box. **Cyclic rate:** 500 rds/min. **Muzzle velocity:** c.1250 ft/sec (380 m/sec).

• Maschinenpistole 38 (MP38), Maschinenpistole 38/40 (MP38/40)

Erfurter Maschinenfabrik B. Geipel GmbH (Erma-Werke), Erfurt
9mm Parabellum

This was probably the most famous military submachine gun of all time and it has gone down into history under a quite incorrect general name—the Schmeisser. In fact, Hugo Schmeisser had nothing to do with its design or early manufacture; it was first produced in the Erma factory and bears many innovations of that firm, although Schmeisser later took a hand in the manufacture of the MP40. The MP38 was made to specifications drawn up by the Oberkommando der Wehrmacht (OKW) and from the first, it was a leader in its field. It was the first submachine gun to have a successful folding butt, the first to be made entirely without any wood in its butt or furniture, and the first to be specifically intended for use by a fast moving mechanized army. Like its predecessor the MP18/I, it set a fashion which was followed by practically every other gun and even today its influence is still apparent. The MP38 suffered, however, from two drawbacks. The first—shared with the MP40—was the single-column feed system, which was inefficient and led to jams, and secondly the gun was expensive and time-consuming to make owing to the large number of machining processes and the use of high-quality steel. Not long after the war

started, the German authorities found that they could not afford the time and expense involved in making the MP38 and asked for a fresh design. This became the MP40.

Length, butt extended: 32.75in (832mm); butt folded: 24.76in (629mm). **Weight unloaded:** 9lb 2oz (4.14kg). **Barrel:** 9.72in (247mm), 6 grooves, right-hand twist. **Magazine:** 32-round detachable box. **Cyclic rate:** 500 rds/min. **Muzzle velocity:** c.1250 ft/sec (380 m/sec).

• Maschinenpistole 40, Maschinenpistole 40/II, Maschinenpistole 41. (MP40, MP40/II, MP41)

Erfurter Maschinenfabrik B. Geipel GmbH, Erfurt; C. G. Haencl Waffen-und Fahrradfabrik AG, Suhl; Osterreichische Waffenfabrik-Gesellschaft, Steyr
9mm Parabellum

The MP38 proved to be too slow and expensive to manufacture in wartime and the MP40 was introduced as a simplified version. It was substantially the same weapon, differing only in such matters as the ejector, the magazine catch and the receiver; the major and most important difference was that it had been

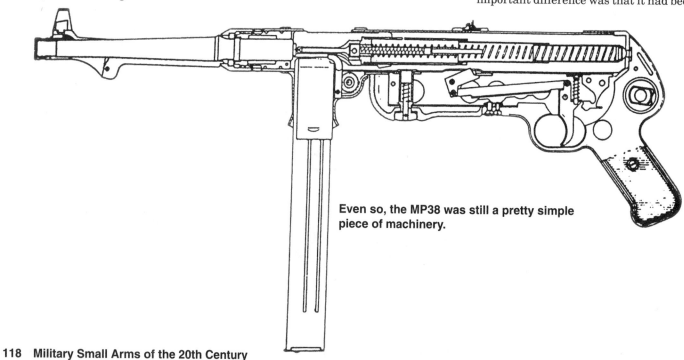

Even so, the MP38 was still a pretty simple piece of machinery.

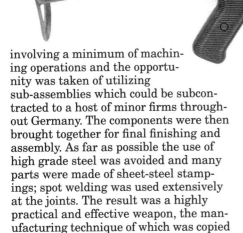

The MP40 introduced more stamped and pressed components, welded construction, and reduced price.

involving a minimum of machining operations and the opportunity was taken of utilizing sub-assemblies which could be subcontracted to a host of minor firms throughout Germany. The components were then brought together for final finishing and assembly. As far as possible the use of high grade steel was avoided and many parts were made of sheet-steel stampings; spot welding was used extensively at the joints. The result was a highly practical and effective weapon, the manufacturing technique of which was copied by almost every other nation, and the basic idea of building in sub-assemblies

was adopted by many gunmaking companies. The MP40 went through several variants and there were minor differences between the models made in different factories, but the external changes were few. The most interesting version was the MP40/II, produced in late 1943; this was a dual magazine gun made in an effort to match the capacity of the 71-round drum of the Soviet PPSh4l. It allowed two magazines of 32 rounds to be held in the housing and slid across one after the other. It was not a success, largely owing to the increased weight of

the unit. A wooden-butt weapon based on the MP40, usually known as the MP41 or the MP41/I, was also produced. This was Schmeisser's only contribution to this group of weapons, and it was unsuccessful largely because the concept strayed from that pioneered by the MP38 and reverted instead to the old style of manufacture and stocking.

The MP38 and MP40 had a long military life; they were well made and robust, and there are a good number of them still around in the hands of irregular forces.

Length, butt extended: 32.75in (832mm); butt folded: 24.75in (629mm). **Weight unloaded:** 8lb 12oz (3.97kg). **Barrel:** 9.75in (248mm), 6 grooves, right-hand

The MP 40 field-stripped.

The Schmeisser MP-41 was a curious reversion to traditional style, marrying the pressed-metal receiver of the MP40 to a wooden stock.

An example of the MP3008 made by the Blohm & Voss Shipyard; quite simply, a Sten gun but with a vertical magazine and a pistol grip.

twist. **Magazine:** 32-round detachable box. **Cyclic rate:** 500 rds/min. **Muzzle velocity:** c.1250 ft/sec (381 m/sec).

• Maschinenpistole 'Gerät Potsdam'
Mauser-Werke, AG, Oberndorf-am-Neckar
9mm Parabellum

Although by no means an outstanding weapon, the 'Gerät Potsdam' was one of the most interesting and unusual submachine guns produced during World War II and perhaps at any time. It was a careful and deliberate attempt to produce an identical copy of another design, in this case the British Sten Mark 2, and much effort went into ensuring that the resulting copy was indistinguishable from the original. Even the English factory markings were reproduced. Although it is possible to find differences, at the time these guns were made few people would have known what to look for, and the copies would have been accepted as being the genuine article. They were intended to be used by German guerrilla units in Allied-occupied territory, but the German guerrilla movement never started. Between 25,000 and 30,000 of these weapons were made and the making of them involved the Mauser-Werke plant in a prodigious effort under conditions of great secrecy. Few appear to exist today, principally because in the immediate aftermath of war they were not recognized as being a German product and were simply treated as weapons which had been captured from the British and were now returning to their original owners; it is an interesting speculation to wonder how many of these weapons actually found their way back into the British supply system and were reissued as Sten guns.

Length: 30.00in (762mm). **Weight unloaded:** 6lb 9oz (2.98kg). **Barrel:** 7.75in (196mm), 2 or 6 grooves, right-hand twist. **Magazine:** 32-round detachable box. **Cyclic rate:** 550 rds/min. **Muzzle velocity:** c.1250 ft/sec (381 m/sec).

• Maschinenpistole 3008 (MP3008)
Mauser-Werke AG, Oberndorf-am-Neckar; C. G. Haenel Waffen und Fahrradfabrik AG, Suhl; Erfurter Maschinenfabrik B. Geipel GmbH, Erfurt, and others
9mm Parabellum

The MP 3008 is another example of a weapon deliberately copied from the Sten, but in this case the motives were different. In the last few months of 1944, the German High Command was desperate for cheap and simple weapons with which to replace the staggering losses in Russia, and to arm the raw battalions of young men who were to make the last stand against the Allies. At the same time, the Volkssturm and various guerrilla bands were forming, all demanding arms. The British Sten had been one of the outstandingly successful designs of the war, despite its drawbacks, and it was noted for its economy of material and uncomplicated design. Accordingly, it was copied in an even cruder and simpler form, and several firms manufactured as many as the circumstances allowed. The resulting guns differed widely in finish and some were among the worst finished weapons ever made, but they worked, which was all that was required of them. The most obvious difference from the Sten was in the vertical magazine which fed upwards into the receiver. There were other minor changes, particularly in the design of the butt and in the joining and pinning of the components. Approximately 10,000 of these weapons were made and, although few saw action, it was remarkable enough that these guns had been manufactured in the chaotic conditions then prevailing in a Germany where raw materials and machining facilities were in equally short supply.

Length: 31.50in (800mm). **Weight unloaded:** 6lb 8oz (2.95kg). **Barrel:** 7.75in (196mm), 6 or 8 grooves, right-hand twist. **Magazine:** 32-round detachable box. **Cyclic rate:** 500 rds/min. **Muzzle velocity:** c.1250 ft/sec (381 m/sec).

• Maschinenpistole Erma 44 (MPE44 or EMP44)
Erfurter Maschinenfabrik B. Geipel GmbH, Erfurt
9mm Parabellum

This extraordinary weapon does not seem to have been produced in any numbers and it may never have proceeded beyond the prototype stage. The design was made either in 1942 or in 1943 at the Erma factory and few have survived. It is a submachine gun with the manufacturing processes reduced to the absolute minimum with the result that the finished gun is crude almost beyond belief. Barrel, body, butt and pistol grip are all made from steel tube of the same diameter and wall thickness; in fact the barrel, body and butt are all one tube.

The shoulder piece is also tubular. The magazine housing and muzzle brake are welded onto the body and other attachments are riveted. The magazine housing accepts the dual magazines in the same way as the MP40 variant and, similarly, MP40 magazines are used. The bolt and spring are of the same type as Erma-Werke patented and used in their more conventional designs, and the trigger mechanism is extremely simple. The sights are set well above the barrel line in robust protectors. Behind the rear sight a strengthening web is welded to form a bridge over the weak point of the magazine housing while, at the same time, forming part of the rear sight protector. The EMP44 is an object lesson in simple design and it obviously worked, although how well is not known. It was never adopted for service.

Length: 28.4in (722mm). **Weight unloaded:** 8lb 0oz (3.62kg). **Barrel:** 9.90in (250mm), 6 grooves, right-hand twist. **Magazine:** 32-round detachable box. **Cyclic rate:** 500 rds/min. **Muzzle velocity:** c.1250 ft/sec (380 m/sec).

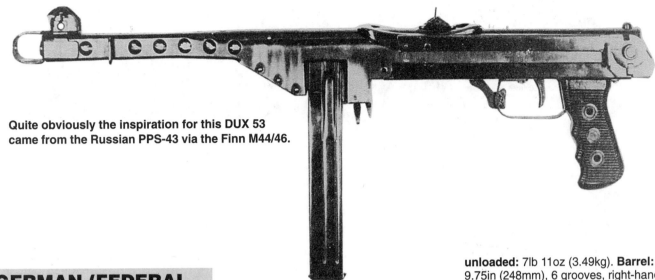

Quite obviously the inspiration for this DUX 53
came from the Russian PPS-43 via the Finn M44/46.

GERMAN (FEDERAL REPUBLIC)

• Maschinenpistole DUX Model 53

Fabrica de Armas de Oviedo, Oviedo, Spain.

9mm Parabellum

The DUX53 was a hybrid weapon designed by the Germans Daugs and Vorgrimmler, produced in Spain and used in Germany. The design was originally that of the Finnish m/44 (see Finland) which was in turn based on the Soviet PPS43: the drawings of the m/44 had been taken from Finland at the end of World War II and ultimately arrived in Spain, where they were used as the basis for the prototype of the DUX series, the DUX51. One thousand of the DUX53 were purchased by the Bundes-Grenz-Schiitz, the West German border guard, and were used by them for several years. The West German Army also spent some years testing the weapon and, indeed, some were modified by J.G. Anschütz GmbH of Ulm-a-d-Donau, some by Mauser-Werke

of Oberndorf-am-Neckar, and some by J. P. Sauer & Sohn of Cologne: none was accepted by the army. Eventually, Anschütz produced a modified weapon called the DUX59, a much-streamlined version of the DUX53, but Anschütz and Daugs then had a falling-out, and Daugs canceled the license agreement and vanished, putting an end to further development of the design.

The family resemblance between the DUX53, the Finnish m/44 and the Soviet PPS43 is very, close indeed—none too surprising considering the design lineage—but the DUX uses a 50-round box magazine of 'Suomi' design and purchased it from Switzerland where it had been made under license. The DUX was largely made from sheet-steel stampings and was angular and unattractive in appearance; capable only of automatic fire, it was, by the standards of the day, a little heavy although otherwise reasonably efficient.

Length, butt extended: 32.50in (825mm); butt folded: 24.25in (615mm). **Weight**

unloaded: 7lb 11oz (3.49kg). **Barrel:** 9.75in (248mm), 6 grooves, right-hand twist. **Magazine:** 50-round detachable box. **Cyclic rate:** 500 rds/min. **Muzzle velocity:** c.1200 ft/sec (365 m/sec).

• Walther Maschinenpistolen Lang (MP-L) and Kurz (MP-X)

Carl Walther Waffenfabrik, Ulm-a.d-Donau

9mm Parabellum

The Walther MP was a blowback weapon utilizing steel pressings for most of its basic structure. The bolt was overhung, the bulk of it being above the axis of the barrel and overlapping the breech in the closed position, and it was located on a guide rod which also carried the return spring. The sights were an ingenious combination of open sights for snap shooting and an aperture and barleycorn for more accurate aim when time allows.

Two models were produced, long and short, the sole difference lying in the length of the barrel and its associated handguard. These weapons were developed in 1963 and, although evaluated by several military authorities, were only ever adopted by the Mexican Navy and some police forces. Manufacture ceased in 1987.

This was the Dux 59, a rather tidier design but still
the same old PPS-43 under the skin.

The two types of Walther, the MPK and MPL, differed only in barrel length.

(MPL)

Length, butt extended: 29.40in (746mm); butt folded: 18.20in (462mm). **Weight unloaded:** 6lb 10oz (3.00kg). **Barrel:** 10.25in (260mm), 6 grooves, right-hand twist. **Magazine:** 32-round detachable box. **Cyclic rate:** 550 rds/min. **Muzzle velocity:** c.1150 ft/sec (350 m/sec).

(MP-K)

Length, butt extended: 25.98in (659mm); butt folded: 15.0in (381mm). **Weight unloaded:** 6lb 4oz (2.83kg). **Barrel:** 6.78in (173mm), 6 grooves, right-hand twist. **Magazine:** 32-round detachable box. **Cyclic rate:** 550 rds/min. **Muzzle velocity:** c.1100 ft/sec (335 m/sec).

• Maschinenpistole 5 (MP5), MP5A2 and MP5A3

Heckler & Koch GmbH, Oberndorf-am-Neckar
9mm Parabellum

This is derived from the highly successful H&K series of rifles insofar as it uses the same roller-locked delayed blowback system of operation and shares a number of components—such as the pistol grip and trigger unit with the rifles. Because of its system of operation it fires from a closed bolt and is thus a good deal more accurate than the average submachine gun. Constructed largely of stampings, with plastic furniture, the MP5 is a well-built and reliable weapon which is in service with numerous military and security forces around the world, including Special Forces such as the British Special Air Service and the German GSG9. There are two variant models of the MP5; the MP5A2 with rigid plastic butt and the MP5A3 with a telescoping metal stock. The stocks can be exchanged by removing a single locking pin in the rear of the receiver. The standard weapons are provided with single shot or automatic fire, but a three-round burst facility is available as an optional addi-

If you want to design a submachine gun, this is the one you have to beat: the Walther MP5, first choice for almost all the European anti-terrorist forces.

tion and most production weapons now incorporate it.

(MP5A2)

Length: 26.77in (680mm). **Weight unloaded:** 5lb 6oz (2.45kg). **Barrel:** 8.85in (225mm), 4 grooves, right-hand twist. **Magazine:** 10-, 15- or 30-round detachable box. **Cyclic rate:** 650 rds/min. **Muzzle velocity:** c.1312 ft/sec (400 m/sec).

(MP5A3)

Length, butt extended: 26.00in (660mm); butt folded: 19.29in (490mm). **Weight unloaded:** 5lb 10oz (2.55kg). **Barrel:** 8.85in (225mm), 4 grooves, right-hand twist. **Magazine:** 10-, 15-, or 30-round

detachable box. **Cyclic rate:** 650 rds/min. **Muzzle velocity:** c.1312 ft/sec (400 m/sec).

• Maschinenpistole 5 Kurz (MP5K)

Heckler & Koch GmbH, Oberndorf-am-Neckar
9mm Parabellum

This is a special short version of the MP5 intended for use by police and anti-terrorist squads who require very compact firepower. The weapon can be carried concealed under clothing or in the glove compartment of a car, and it can also be concealed in, and fired from, a specially fitted briefcase. Mechanically it is the same as the MP5 but with a shorter barrel and smaller magazines. Four versions are made; the MP5K is fit-

ted with adjustable iron sights or a telescope if desired; the MP5KA1 has a smooth upper surface with very small iron sights so that there is little to catch in clothing or a holster in a quick draw; the MP5KA4 is similar to the MP5K but has an additional three-round burst facility; and the MP5KA5 is similar to the A1 with the addition of the three-round burst facility. No butt is fitted, but there is a robust front grip which gives good control when firing.

Length: 12.67in (325mm). **Weight unloaded:** 4lb 6oz (1.99kg). **Barrel:** 4.5in (115mm), 6 grooves, right-hand twist. **Magazine:** 15- or 30-round detachable box. **Cyclic rate:** 900 rds/min. **Muzzle velocity:** c.375 m/sec.

The MP5K, short enough to hide under a jacket.

The Silenced MP5SD.

• Maschinen Pistole 5 Schall-Dampfer (MP5SD)

Heckler & Koch GmbH, Oberndorf-am-Neckar
9mm Parabellum

This is the silenced member of the MP5 family; the mechanism is exactly the same as the standard MP5 but the short barrel is drilled with 30 holes and surrounded by a large silencer casing. This casing is divided into two chambers; the first surrounds the barrel and receives the propellant gas via the 30 holes, which serve also to reduce the bullet's velocity to a value somewhat below the speed of sound. The gases swirl around in this chamber and lose some of their velocity and heat, and then pass to the second chamber where they expand and are again swirled around before being released to the atmosphere at a velocity and temperature unlikely to cause a loud report.

There are six versions of this weapon; the **MP5SD1** has the end of the receiver closed by a cap and has no buttstock; the **SD2** has a fixed plastic butt; the **SD3** has a sliding retractable butt; all three can fire either single shots or automatic. The **SD4** is as for the SD1 but with the addition of a three-round burst facility; the **SD5** is the SD2 with

three-round burst; and the **SD6** is the SD3 with three-round burst.
Length: SD1: 21.65in (550mm); SD2: 30.70in (780mm); SD3, butt extended 30.70in (780mm), butt retracted: 24.0in (610mm). **Weight unloaded:** SD1: 6lb 6oz (2.9kg); SD2: 7lb 1oz (3.2kg); SD3: 7lb 11oz (3.5kg). **Barrel:** 5.75in (146mm). 6 grooves, right-hand twist. **Magazine:** 15- or 30-round detachable box. **Cyclic rate:** 800 rds/min. **Muzzle velocity:** c.935 ft/sec (285 m/sec).

• MP5K-PDW Personal Defense Weapon

Heckler & Koch Inc., Sterling, Va. USA
9mm Parabellum

This was designed by the Heckler & Koch subsidiary in the USA as a weapon for aircrew or vehicle-borne troops who need something extremely compact. It is, in effect, the MP5K fitted with a folding butt and with the muzzle modified to accept a silencer. There is also provision for fitting a laser sight. Should the butt not be needed, it can be easily removed and a butt cap fitted on the end of the receiver. Selective fire is standard, but a two or three-round burst unit can be fit-

ted to the trigger mechanism if required.
Length with butt-cap: 13.75in (349mm); with butt extended: 23.75in (603mm); butt folded: 14.50in (368mm). **Weight unloaded,** with butt: 6lb 2oz (2.79kg); with butt-cap: 4lb 10oz (2.09kg). **Barrel:** 5.0in (127mm), 6 grooves, right-hand twist. **Magazine:** 30-round detachable box. **Cyclic rate:** 900 rds/min. **Muzzle velocity:** c.1230 ft/sec (375 m/sec).

• Maschinenpistole MP5/10 and 5/40

Heckler & Koch GmbH, Oberndorf-am-Neckar
10mm Auto; 40 Smith & Wesson

Subsequent to the adoption of the 10mm Auto cartridge by the FBI, Heckler & Koch saw that a submachine gun using the same cartridge made good sense and produced this model in the early 1990s. It is to the same basic design as the earlier MP5 weapons, but chambered for the 10mm Auto cartridge; this leads to an unusual forward rake to the straight magazine, in order to avoid feed problems, but there is no other visible difference to catch the eye. The magazine is actually of carbon fiber rather than steel, and there is a two-magazine clamp provided which allows two maga-

The American-developed MP5-PDW, with silencer attached.

The MP5/10 fired the 10mm Auto; identification point is the sloping magazine, shared also by the MP5/40 which fires the 40 S&W cartridge.

zines to be fixed together, one in the magazine housing, allowing a very fast change.

The standard firing arrangement is the usual single shot, three-round burst and automatic selection, but any preferred combination can be provided. This weapon also marked the introduction of the two-round burst, the submachine gun's equivalent of the pistol shooter's 'double tap', and which does away with the useless third round of the three-round burst, which generally went over the top of the target.

The MP5/40 is exactly the same weapon in every respect except that it is chambered for the 40 Smith & Wesson cartridge, for those who prefer it to the 10mm.

Length, fixed butt: 26.77in (680mm); butt extended: 25.98in (660mm); butt folded: 19.29in (490mm). **Weight unloaded**, fixed butt: 5lb 14oz (2.67kg); folding butt: 6lb 5oz (2.85kg). **Barrel:** 8.85in (225mm), 6 grooves, right-hand twist. **Magazine:** 30-round detachable box. **Cyclic rate:** 700 rds/min. **Muzzle velocity:** c.1473 ft/sec (449 m/sec) (10mm); 1205 ft/sec (367 m/sec) (40 S&W).

• MP5 SF
Heckler & Koch Inc., Sterling, Va, USA
9mm Parabellum

This is another product of the US subsidiary of Heckler & Koch, developed to meet a specific demand for an MP5 capable of only firing single shots. It is simply the standard MP5A2 or A3 with the mechanism modified to remove the full-automatic facility. Introduced in 1989, it was adopted by the FBI, BATF and several other law enforcement agencies.

Length, fixed butt: 28.03in (712mm); butt extended: 28.03in (712mm); butt folded: 20.55in (522mm). **Weight unloaded**, fixed butt: 5lb 10oz (2.54kg); folding butt: 6lb 6oz (2.88kg). **Barrel:** 8.85in (225mm), 6 grooves, right-hand twist. **Magazine:** 15- or 30-round detachable box. **Muzzle velocity:** c.1312 ft/sec (400 m/sec).

• Maschinenpistole HK53
Heckler & Koch GmbH, Oberndorf-am-Neckar
5.56x45mm

The HK53 is virtually the same weapon as the MP5, but chambered for the 5.56mm cartridge. The idea of a submachine gun in this caliber may at first seem strange, as until now, pistol ammunition has been almost exclusively used in this class of weapon. The 5.56mm bullet has, however, a

The HK53 is a submachine gun but fires the 5.56mm rifle cartridge.

The British Lanchester was simply a Bergmann MP28 but with fittings for the British Lee-Enfield bayonet.

lethality and stopping power disproportionate to its size, and the round might well prove successful in this role—and, of course, if the rifles, machine guns and submachine guns of an army are all chambered for the same round, logistics are greatly simplified.

The HK53 has yet to be adopted by any military force, but time will tell. The sights are graduated to 400m and are fully adjustable for windage and elevation, and there is a distinct possibility that the HK53 (though classified by its makers as a submachine gun) could become a very useful assault rifle.

Length, butt extended: 30.11in (765mm); butt folded: 22.00in (560mm). **Weight unloaded:** 7lb 6oz (3.35kg). **Barrel:** 8.85in (225mm), 4 grooves, right-hand twist. **Magazine:** 40-round detachable box. **Cyclic rate:** 600 rds/min. **Muzzle velocity:** c.2460 ft/sec (750 m/sec).

GREAT BRITAIN

• Machine Carbine, 9mm Lanchester Mark 1 and Mark 1*

Sterling Armament Company, Dagenham, Essex
9mm Parabellum

The Lanchester was made in 1941, and is memorable not for any oddity in its design, nor feature in its manufacture, but for the fact that it was ever made in the form that it was. It was nothing more than a direct copy of the German MP28/II designed by Hugo Schmeisser and the only visible differences were minor and not readily distinguishable.

The gun was conceived in haste and whatever may be said against the principle of copying one's adversaries' weapons

the MP28 was a proven design of known reliability. So too was the Lanchester. It took its name from its designer and was made by the Sterling Armament Company exclusively—somewhat unusually—for the Royal Navy. But 1941 was not a normal time in the United Kingdom and expediency was the order of the day: the Lanchester did all that was required of it until it was ultimately replaced in the early 1960s by the Sterling, emanating from the same factory. One change from the MP28/II was that the butt of the Lanchester was of similar pattern to that of the Rifle Number I (SMLE), and it had a bayonet lug to take the long bayonet (Pattern 1907 or Bayonet Number 1). Other differences lay in the design of the receiver lock catch and the magazine housing: the latter component was of solid brass, fully in the naval tradition but hardly appropriate in time of war.

The magazine (again a derivation from the MP28/II) held 50 rounds, although the 32-round Sten magazine could be inserted in some weapons. There were two versions of the Lanchester carbine; the original had a large Rifle Number 1 type of rear sight, and a selector switch on the front portion of the triggerguard. The later Mark 1*, which was capable of automatic fire only, had a much simplified rear sight and, of course, lacked a selector switch. Most Mark 1 guns were later converted to Mark 1* standards.

Length: 33.50in (851mm). **Weight unloaded:** 9lb 9oz (4.34kg). **Barrel:** 8.00in (203mm), 6 grooves, right-hand twist. **Magazine:** 50-round detachable box. **Cyclic rate:** 600 rds/min. **Muzzle velocity:** c.1250 ft/sec (381 m/sec).

• Machine

Carbine, 9mm Sten, Mark 1

Birmingham Small Arms Company Limited, Birmingham; Royal Small Arms Factory, Fazakerly, Liverpool (chief contractors)
9mm Parabellum

The Sten took its name from the initials of its designers (**S**hepherd and **T**urpin) and the Royal Small Arms Factory at **En**field, although much of the wartime production was subcontracted to other manufacturers, particularly the Birmingham Small Arms Company Limited (BSA) and other Royal Ordnance factories. It was a weapon conceived in a time of haste and extreme emergency. The United Kingdom entered World War II without a submachine gun of any kind, and the Blitzkrieg not only caught the British Army unawares, but also seriously ill-equipped. The threat of invasion by air and sea in the summer of 1940 led to a panic expansion of the arms industry and a frantic search for a submachine gun. The first Sten appeared in the summer of 1941, and by 1945, nearly four million had been made, in several different marks and variants. The basic Sten was very simple and was designed so that it could be assembled from components made by small subcontractors. Cheapness and simplicity were paramount in the design and, despite some shortcomings, the Sten was one of the outstanding war-winning weapons in the Allied armory; early versions cost about £2.50 to make (about $10 at 1941 rates), later ones slightly more. The Sten was never entirely popular with British troops, largely because its single feed magazine jammed frequently, though it was soon found that loading only 30 rounds reduced the problem. Another cause of jamming was holding the magazine as a

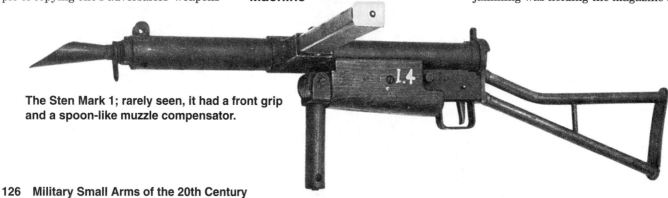

The Sten Mark 1; rarely seen, it had a front grip and a spoon-like muzzle compensator.

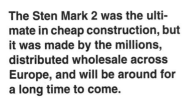

The Sten Mark 2 was the ultimate in cheap construction, but it was made by the millions, distributed wholesale across Europe, and will be around for a long time to come.

front hand grip; since it was a relatively loose fit in its housing, gripping it could easily pull it to the wrong angle and cause misfeeding. Great pains were taken to train soldiers to hold the barrel jacket in front of the magazine, allowing the magazine to rest on the left forearm. When held like this jams became much less frequent. The Sten survived, however, to equip many thousands of Allied soldiers, guerrillas and partisans in Occupied Europe. The gun illustrated is one of the very first of the Mark 1 guns. About 100,000 Mark 1 Stens were made in all.

The Sten Mark 1 consisted of a tubular receiver containing a bolt and return spring. At the front end of the receiver was a side-feeding magazine housing, a barrel surrounded by a perforated jacket, and a spoon-like muzzle compensator which resisted the usual tendency to climb on automatic firing. There was a metal skeleton butt and a small folding wooden foregrip. About 100,000 Mark 1 weapons were made.

Length: 35.25in (895mm). **Weight unloaded:** 7lb 3oz (3.26kg). **Barrel:** 7.75in (196mm), 6 grooves, right-hand twist. **Magazine:** 32-round detachable box. **Cyclic rate:** 550 rds/min. **Muzzle velocity:** c.1250 ft/sec (381 m/sec).

• Machine Carbine, 9mm Sten,

Mark 2
See Sten, Mark 1
9mm Parabellum

The Sten Mark 2 was the workhorse of the type, and over two million were made in three years. Even within the Mark classification there were variations and not all were officially noted with a separate variation number, although most of the divergences concerned the butt and forward handgrip and were not changes to the basic layout. In general, the Mark 2 was smaller, neater and handier than the Mark 1; the barrel was a drawn steel tube held on by a threaded perforated jacket, the butt was skeletal in the extreme—generally a single strut—and the magazine housing rotated to close the opening when it was not in use. The gun easily dismantled into its component parts and so was ideal for the clandestine operations of the underground forces in Europe and elsewhere. The mechanism was simplicity itself, being little more than a bolt and spring with the most basic trigger and fire selector equipment. Sights were fixed for 100yards and they could not be adjusted for zero. The magazine held 32 rounds, but was generally loaded with 30 to minimize strain on the magazine spring and hence reduce jams, and had to be filled with a special filler.

Length: 30.00in (762mm). **Weight unloaded:** 6lb 8oz (2.95kg). **Barrel:** 7.75in (196mm), 2 or 6 grooves, right-hand twist. **Magazine:** 32-round detachable box.

Cyclic rate: 550 rds/min. **Muzzle velocity:** c.1250 ft/sec (381 m/sec).

• Machine Carbine, 9mm Sten, Mark 2 (Silencer)
See Sten, Mark 1
9mm Parabellum

The Mark 2(S) was one of the few submachine guns to be produced as a separate variant with an integral silencer at a time when it was uncommon to find silencers on submachine guns at all. The Mark 2(S) differed from the standard Mark 2 first in respect of the silencer itself, which was a long cylinder of the same diameter as the receiver and contained baffles to trap the gas. The silencer threaded onto the receiver in the same way as the normal barrel, but the actual barrel inside it was very short and the bullet emerged at a speed below that of sound. It was almost inaudible at a few yards, although its effective range was reduced considerably. The greatest noise came from the mechanical movement of the bolt which, in this version, was reduced in weight and fitted with a weaker return spring to compensate the lower breech pressure resulting from the shortened barrel. The gun was intended to be fired in single shots only, as automatic fire quickly wore out the baffles and was also inclined to detach the end cap of the silencer. The Mark 2(S) was made for special forces and continued in service until after the Korean War. Several thousands were made, although none remain in service use. The life of the

The Sten Mark 2(S) was the silenced version of the Mark 2, used by Commandos and other surreptitious ruffians.

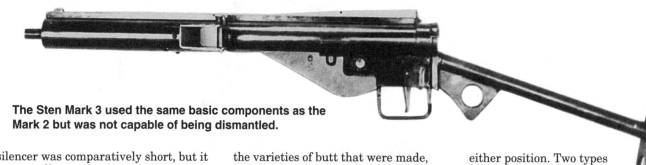

The Sten Mark 3 used the same basic components as the Mark 2 but was not capable of being dismantled.

silencer was comparatively short, but it was an effective device and quite widely used.

Length: 35.75in (908mm). **Weight unloaded:** 7lb 12oz (3.52kg). **Barrel:** 3.50in (89mm), 6 grooves, right-hand twist. **Magazine:** 32-round detachable box. **Cyclic rate:** 450 rds/min. **Muzzle velocity:** c.1000 ft/sec (305 m/sec).

• Machine Carbine, 9mm Sten, Mark 3

See Sten, Mark 1
9mm Parabellum

The Sten Mark 3 was the second of the series to be made in large numbers and, together with the Mark 2, is the one which was most frequently found in service with the British forces. It is really a variation of the basic Mark 1 for manufacture by alternative methods; the receiver and barrel jacket are in one piece, made from a formed sheet-steel tube which extends almost to the muzzle. The barrel is a fixture inside this jacket and so the easy dismantling of the Mark 2 is not repeated in the Mark 3. The magazine housing is also fixed. One small feature of the Mark 3 which does not appear on any others is the finger guard in front of the ejection opening—a projecting lug riveted to the receiver which prevents the firer's finger from straying into the opening. Internally, the Mark 3 was identical with the Mark 1 and it would accept all

the varieties of butt that were made, although it was usually supplied with the simple tubular butt similar to the Mark 2. The Mark 3 first appeared in 1943 and was made until 1944, both in the United Kingdom and Canada.

Length: 30.00in (762mm). **Weight unloaded:** 7lb 0oz (3.18kg). **Barrel:** 7.75in (196mm), 6 grooves, right-hand twist. **Magazine:** 32-round detachable box. **Cyclic rate:** 550 rds/min. **Muzzle velocity:** c.1250 ft/sec (381 m/sec).

• Machine Carbines, 9mm Sten, Mark 4A and Mark 4B

See Sten, Mark 1
9mm Parabellum

The Mark 4 Sten was an interesting gun which was made only in prototype in 1943 and never saw service. It was an attempt to produce a smaller and more compact submachine-gun for use by paratroops. The Mark 2 Sten was used as the basis, and the barrel was cut until it was roughly half the original length, but it was mounted in a jacket similar to the Mark 2 and retained the same magazine housing. A flash-hider was fitted to the muzzle and a curious folding butt swiveled on the rear of the receiver so that it stowed forward under the gun. A catch on the butt engaged in a recess on the bottom of the pistol grip and locked it in

either position. Two types were made, the differences lying in the pistol grip and trigger mechanism. Neither represented a really worthwhile submachine gun and it was probably a wise decision not to pursue the design. The additional manufacturing effort required to produce such a major alteration to the original would certainly not have been balanced by any increase in performance or utility, and the Mark 5 was introduced instead.

Length, butt extended: 27.50in (698mm); butt folded: 17.50in (445mm). **Weight unloaded:** 7lb 8oz (3.45kg). **Barrel:** 3.75in (95mm), 6 grooves, right-hand twist. **Magazine:** 32-round detachable box. **Cyclic rate:** 570 rds/min. **Muzzle velocity:** c.1250 ft/sec (381 m/sec).

• Machine Carbine, 9mm Sten, Marks 5 and 6

See Sten, Mark 1
9mm Parabellum

The Sten was never really popular with British troops, not so much because of its tendency to jam, but principally because it looked cheap and nasty. Whenever possible some other gun was acquired and used. The Thompson M1928 was a particular favorite of the paratroops, for whom submachine guns were a vital weapon. In

Two types of Sten Mark 4 were designed; this was probably the better of the two, and is shown here with its steel butt folded forward. But it showed no appreciable advantages over the Mark 2 and was not adopted.

The Mark 5 Sten was an attempt to persuade the British soldier to take the thing seriously; it had wooden furniture, decent sights and took a bayonet. But it was still the same old Sten gun.

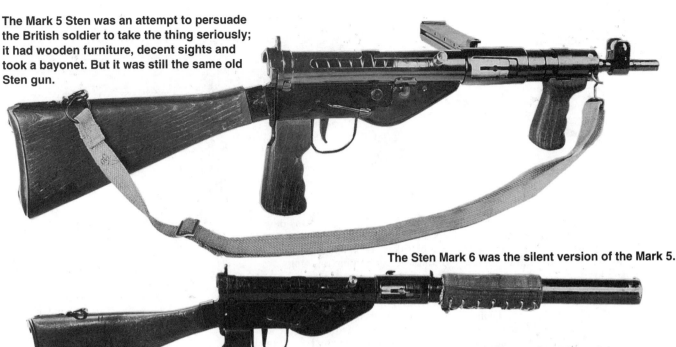

The Sten Mark 6 was the silent version of the Mark 5.

1944, an attempt was made to overcome the opposition to the Sten by producing a better version with a more robust and expensive appearance. Rather more care was taken in machining and assembly and the finish was improved, a wooden butt and pistol grip were fitted (which required the trigger mechanism to be moved forward along the receiver) and the front sight from the No. 4 rifle was adopted. This allowed the rifle bayonet to be fitted to the muzzle, and the buttplate trap provided a space for cleaning materials. The first Mark 5 weapons had a front handgrip, but this broke easily and was soon abandoned. In all other respects the model was similar to the Mark 2 and, in fact, showed very little actual improvement over it; the magazine still jammed occasionally and the wooden furniture merely added weight. It survived until the early 1960s, although replacement by the Sterling began in 1953.

The Mark 6 Sten was simply the Mark 5 with the addition of a silencer of the same type as that of the Mark 2(S), although the internal arrangements were slightly different. Or, if you prefer, it was a modified Mark 2(S) with the additional furniture of the Mark 5. It saw very little use before being replaced by the Sterling L34.

(Mark 5)

Length: 30.00in (762mm). **Weight unloaded:** 8lb 9oz (3.86kg). **Barrel:** 7.75in (196mm), 6 grooves, right-hand twist. **Magazine:** 32-round detachable box. **Cyclic rate:** 600 rds/min. **Muzzle velocity:** c.1250 ft/sec (381 m/sec).

(Mark 6)

Length: 33.74in (857mm). **Weight unloaded:** 9lb 8oz (4.32kg). **Barrel:** 3.74in (95mm), 6 grooves, right-hand twist. **Magazine:** 32-round detachable box. **Cyclic rate:** 550 rds/min. **Muzzle velocity:** c.1000 ft/sec (305 m/sec).

• Machine Carbine, 9mm, Vesely V42

Birmingham Small Arms Co., Birmingham
9mm Parabellum

The V42 was one of a number of designs developed by Josef Veseley, a Czech engineer who came to Britain in 1938 to help BSA get the Besa machine gun into production and who stayed with BSA when the Germans occupied Czechoslovakia. The submachine gun was made in prototype form by the BSA Company (at Veseley's personal expense) during World War II for submission to the British Army. This particular model, which more or less represents the ultimate Vesely design, was put forward in 1942, but by that time production of the Sten was in full swing and while the army were quite willing to try the weapon and evaluate it for future consideration, they made it quite plain that, irrespective of the results of any trials, there was no hope of official adoption at that time.

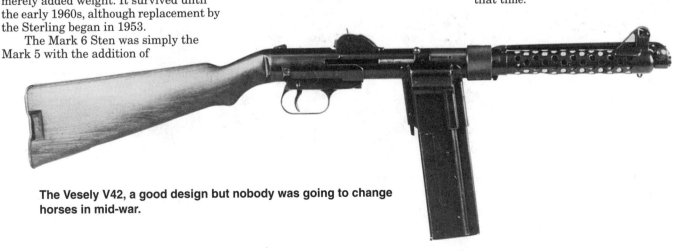

The Vesely V42, a good design but nobody was going to change horses in mid-war.

The Welgun; another attempt at a compact weapon for airborne troops.

The V42 was designed with production in mind, and used a large amount of stamped components in its assembly. It was rather unusual in that it did not rely on differential locking, as the bolt was seated and stopped at the moment of firing. To compensate for this, the recoil spring was larger than normal and concealed in the wooden butt. The magazine was also of an unusual type, having two columns of rounds in tandem. The front column was fired first, and when this was empty the rear column automatically came into use. In trials, this refinement proved to be a source of trouble at first, but it was eventually perfected—although it has never been used since.

Regardless of the performance of the gun - which was quite impressive—the V42 appeared at an inopportune moment and was never likely to have been successful.

Length: 32.00in (813mm). **Weight unloaded:** 9lb 3oz (4.17kg). **Barrel:** 10.00in (254mm), 6 grooves, right-hand twist. **Magazine:** 60-round detachable box. **Cyclic rate:** c.750 rds/min. **Muzzle velocity:** c.1350 ft/sec (412 m/sec).

• Machine Carbine, 9mm Welgun, Mark 1
Birmingham Small Arms Company Limited, Birmingham
9mm Parabellum

The Welgun was another example of an attempt to make a smaller type of submachine gun for parachutists. Although never put into production, it is included because it shows a sensible and original approach to the problem of

reducing size. The design was developed during World War II, and 1943 can be taken as a good representative date for it. A Sten barrel, magazine and operating spring were used, but the spring was wrapped around the barrel and pulled the bolt forward instead of pushing it, and the magazine fed vertically upwards. The bolt was exposed on both sides by two wide slots in the receiver and was cocked by being grasped by the fingers and pulled back; there was no other cocking handle and it is arguable that such large openings would allow mud and dirt to jam the mechanism. The firing pin was not fixed as in the Sten, but was forced forward by a rocking bar pivoted inside the bolt, which was in turn tripped back by a plunger engaging on the breechface as the bolt closed. This afforded a mechanical safety ignored in other designs of the time. A folding butt hinged over the top of the receiver. A possible weakness of the Welgun lay in the position of the spring, since it rapidly absorbed heat from the barrel, which might ultimately have led to spring failures. However, the Welgun was a well-made weapon typical of the advanced thinking of the firm which introduced it, and it might easily have been a great success.

Length, butt extended: 27.50in (700mm); butt folded: 17.00in (432mm). **Weight unloaded:** 6lb 13oz (3.09kg). **Barrel:** 7.75in (196mm), 6 grooves, right-hand twist. **Magazine:** 32-round detachable box. **Cyclic rate:** 650 rds/min. **Muzzle velocity:** c.1250 ft/sec (38 m/sec).

• Machine Carbine, BSA Experimental, 1949
Birmingham Small Arms Company Limited, Birmingham
9mm Parabellum

The 1949 design of BSA was produced in prototype form as one of the contenders for the replacement for the Sten submachine gun in the British services. It was an interesting and novel design which followed the general trend set by its predecessor the Welgun. The mainspring was returned to its more usual place behind the bolt and the large openings in the receiver were abandoned but, once again, there was no retracting handle and the bolt was pulled to the rear by the forward handgrip. This item was initially pushed forward and then pulled back: the latter movement engaged a bar with the bolt and conveyed the push. Slight rotation of the handgrip freed the bar and the bolt could then move freely on firing. The only openings to the receiver were the ejection port and the magazine housing and, when the bolt was forward, these were also covered. The magazine housing swung to the rear on a hinge to allow a jam to be cleared without removing the magazine, and also facilitated cleaning. The furniture was plastic, and the butt folded forwards under the receiver. Although quite successful, the BSA was thought to be unduly complicated for a submachine gun and was not adopted.

Length, butt extended: 28.0in (711mm); butt folded: 19.00in (481mm). **Weight unloaded:** 6lb 9oz (2.98kg). **Barrel:** 8.00in (203mm), 6 grooves, right-hand twist. **Mag-**

The BSA, shown here with the front grip extended in the act of cocking the bolt.

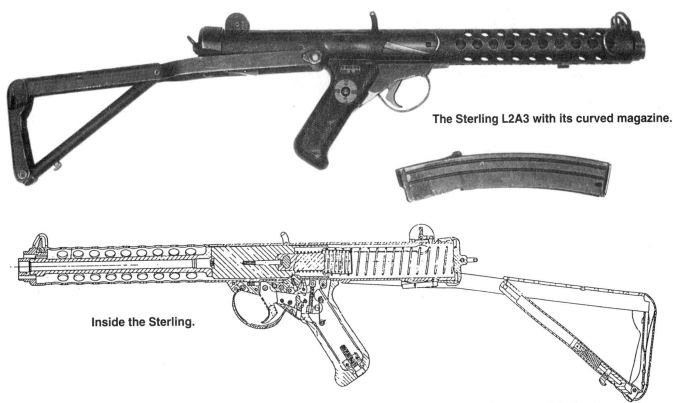

The Sterling L2A3 with its curved magazine.

Inside the Sterling.

azine: 32-round detachable box. **Cyclic rate:** 600 rds/min. **Muzzle velocity:** c.1250 ft/sec (381 m/sec).

• Machine Carbine, 9mm Sterling, L2A1, L2A2, L2A3, and L34A1

Sterling Armament Company, Dagenham, Essex
9mm Parabellum

The L2A3 was the militarized service version of the original Patchett machine carbine produced in the 1940s by the Sterling Armament Company. It was in service with British forces from 1953 until the early 1990s, being replaced by the L85A1 assault rifle. There were some minor alterations to the L2A1 during that time, but it was still substantially the same weapon. In outline, it is a conventionally modern submachine gun,

made entirely from steel and plastic with a side-feeding box magazine and a folding butt. There is rather more machining in the design than appears in other submachine guns and this led to a higher cost than many contemporaries. It is, however, extremely reliable and performs outstandingly well in adverse conditions. The bolt has four special clearance ribs machined on its body, and these push any dirt or fouling into special vent holes. There is an integral firing pin and a means of ensuring that it lines up with the primer only at the moment of firing, which is a useful safety measure. The curved magazine holds 34 rounds and has rollers instead of the more usual platform follower. A bayonet can be attached, the front sight can be adjusted for zero, and the rear sight has a 'flip' setting for 100 and 200 meters.

A version of the basic design but with an integral silencer, replacing the Mark 6 Sten, was known to the British Army as the L34A1.

(L2A3)

Length, butt extended: 27.0in (686mm); butt folded: 19.00in (481mm). **Weight unloaded:** 6lb 0oz (2.70kg). **Barrel:** 7.75in (196mm), 6 grooves, right-hand twist. **Magazine:** 34-round detachable box. **Cyclic rate:** 550 rds/min. **Muzzle velocity:** c.1250 ft/sec (380 m/sec).

(L34A1)

Length, butt extended: 34.0in (864mm); butt folded: 26.00in (660mm). **Weight unloaded:** 7lb 15oz (3.60kg). **Barrel:** 7.80in (198mm), 6 grooves, right-hand twist. **Magazine:** 34-round detachable box. **Cyclic rate:** 550 rds/min. **Muzzle velocity:** c.968 ft/sec (295 m/sec).

The Sterling L34 silenced.

The Kiraly-designed Model 39M from Hungary; the magazine folds forward into a slot in the underside of the forend.

GREECE

• Sumak-9
Hellenic Arms Industry SA, Athens
9mm Parabellum

This weapon appeared in the latter 1980s and appears to have been designed with a view to replacing the Heckler & Koch MP5, built under license in Greece for issue to the Greek armed forces. It is a neat and simple blowback gun using advanced primer ignition. The receiver is cylindrical, with a wrap-around bolt and a good length of the barrel concealed inside it. The cocking handle is to the left side and forward, similar to the H&K weapons, but the magazine housing is inside the pistol grip after the manner of the Uzi, giving the weapon excellent balance. There is a cross-bolt safety catch but fire selection is by a two-stage trigger. The sales literature speaks of a folding butt, but the only specimens seen had no butt whatever. It is presumed that the butt would be a sliding wire pattern.

In the event, the Sumak-9 appears to have made no impression on the Greek army; they continued using the MP5 and the Sumak-9 disappeared by the mid-1990s.

Length, butt extended: 25.98in (660mm); butt folded: 17.32in (440mm). **Weight unloaded:** 5lb 8oz (2.50kg). **Barrel:** 7.75in (260mm), 6 grooves, right-hand twist. **Magazine:** 25- or 24-round detachable box. **Cyclic rate:** 650 rds/min. **Muzzle velocity:** c.1312 ft/sec (400 m/sec).

HUNGARY

• Models 39M, and 43M
Danuvia Arms Company, Budapest
9mm cartridge M39

The Model 39M was designed by Pal Kiraly of Danuvia, and was the perfection of a design he had offered, through BSA Ltd., to the British Army early in 1939. They turned it down, and he then returned to Hungary and produced this model later in the same year. He had taken note of comments made by the British and simplified the design, doing away with a highly complicated and fragile rate reducer. The result was an excellent weapon, resembling a short rifle, and chambered the powerful 9x23mm Mauser 'Export' cartridge. This necessitated a delayed blowback breech, which was achieved by a two-part bolt, a design feature which Kiraly had patented in 1912 and which more or less became his trade-mark, appearing on several weapons of his design, notably the Neuhausen submachine gun made by SIG in the early 1930s. The light bolt head was propelled backwards by the chamber pressure on firing, but had to overcome a mechanical leverage before it could transfer its momentum to the heavier rear portion and thus start the entire bolt unit moving backwards. (A similar system is currently used on the French FA-MAS rifle.) Another Kiraly feature

was the magazine, which folded up and forward to lie in a slot under the forend when not in use. The muzzle accepted the standard Hungarian rifle bayonet. About 8000 of these weapons were made, most of which were lost on the Eastern Front.

The **Model 43M** was developed from the 39M and was simply the same basic weapon but with a pistol grip and a steel folding butt resembling that used on the German MP38, which folds under the receiver. The barrel was slightly shorter, and the magazine is at a noticeable forward angle, probably to improve the reliability of feeding. It served the Hungarian Army through the latter stages of World War II and afterwards until replaced in the post-war era by Soviet weapons.

(39M)

Length: 41.00in (1041mm). **Weight unloaded:** 9lb 0oz (4.08kg). **Barrel:** 17.75in (450mm), 6 grooves, right-hand twist. **Magazine:** 20- or 40-round detachable box. **Cyclic rate:** 730 rds/min. **Muzzle velocity:** c.1480 ft/sec (450 m/sec).

(43M)

Length, butt extended: 37.50in (953mm); butt folded. 29.50in (749mm). **Weight unloaded:** 8lb 0oz (3.64kg). **Barrel:** 16.75in (425mm), 6 grooves, right-hand twist. **Magazine:** 40-round detachable box. **Cyclic rate:** 750 rds/min. **Muzzle velocity:** c.1475 ft/sec (450 m/sec).

The Hungarian 43M was the 38M but with a folding stock.

The Hungarian KGP-9 is a much more basic weapon than Kiraly's designs.

• KGP-9

Fegyver és Gáz-
készülékgyär, Budapest
9mm Parabellum

This was first revealed in the latter 1980s and is the standard submachine gun of the Hungarian military and police forces. It is a conventional blowback weapon, principally assembled from pressed steel components stiffened with castings. It fires from an open bolt, but the bolt carries a floating firing pin and the firing is done by a hammer mechanism. An unusual feature is that the standard barrel can be removed and replaced by a longer one, presumably to convert the weapon into a form of carbine with a longer range.

Length, butt extended: 24.21in (615mm). **Length,** butt folded: 13.97in (355mm). **Weight unloaded:** 6lb 1oz (2.75kg). **Barrel:** 7.48in (190mm), 6 grooves, right-hand twist (250mm optional). **Magazine:** 25-round detachable box. **Cyclic rate:** 900 rds/min. **Muzzle velocity:** c.1280 ft/sec (390 m/sec).

ISRAEL

• Submachine Gun 9mm Uzi

Israel Military Industries, Ramat Ha Sharon, and Fabrique Nationale d'Armes de Guerre, Herstal-lez-Liége, Belgium
9mm Parabellum

First designed in the early 1950s and based on the Czech 23 series, the Uzi is one of the best and most satisfactory submachine guns in service today. As soon as Israel became independent in 1948 urgent steps were taken to develop a national arms industry and the Uzi was one of the first products. It has been extensively used in the border clashes between Israel and her neighbors, as well as in the various desert wars. It is an extremely compact weapon, achieving its short length by having the bolt recessed to take the face of the breech and so having the main mass of the bolt forward of the breech; the idea was not entirely novel when the Uzi was designed, but it was among the first guns to use the principle so successfully. The magazine housing forms the pistol grip and the whole gun balances so well that single-handed firing is perfectly possible. There is a fire selector switch and safety catch above the pistol grip, and a grip safety let into its rear edge. Early models had a wooden butt, but all of current production are fitted with a neat and strong folding butt which enables the gun to be carried by vehicle crews. West Germany adopted the Uzi (as did the Netherlands) and it was made in Belgium under license by Fabrique Nationale d'Armes de Guerre of Herstal, who supplied them to many South American armies. The weapon is also in wide use by police and security forces throughout the world.

The original Uzi, with wooden butt.

The Uzi with folding butt.

Length, butt extended: 25.00in (635mm); butt folded: 17.00in (432mm). **Weight unloaded:** 7lb 10oz (3.46kg). **Barrel:** 10.25in (260mm), 4 grooves, right-hand twist. **Magazine:** 25-, 32- or 40-round detachable box. **Cyclic rate:** 600 rds/min. **Muzzle velocity:** c.1250 ft/sec (381 m/sec).

• Submachine Gun 9mm Mini-Uzi

Israel Military Industries, Ramat Ha Sharon
9mm Parabellum

This was developed in response to a request for a smaller weapon. In all respects it is identical with the Uzi except that it is smaller and, due to this, has different ballistic characteristics. The muzzle has compensating ports cut into its upper surface in order to assist control of the weapon. A special 20-round magazine is provided, but it will also accept the normal 25- and 32-round Uzi magazines.

Length, butt extended: 23.6in (600mm); butt folded: 14.2in (360mm). **Weight unloaded:** 5lb 15oz (2.70kg). **Barrel:** 7.75in (197mm), 4 grooves, right-hand twist. **Magazine:** 20-, 25- or 32-round detachable box. **Cyclic rate:** 950 rds/min. **Muzzle velocity:** c.1150 ft/sec (350 m/sec).

• Micro-Uzi

Israel Military Industries, Ramat Ha Sharon
9mm Parabellum

This is an even smaller version of the Uzi, the design reduced to its absolute minimum. It is marginally larger than a heavy pistol, and in an attempt to keep the rate of fire down to a practical figure, the bolt has been given a tungsten insert in order to increase the mass. The folding stock is a much simpler pattern than that of the larger weapons, and folds sideways so that the shoulder piece can act as a front grip when firing from the hip. This model is also available in 45 ACP caliber, with a special 16-shot magazine.

Length, butt extended: 18.11in (460mm); butt folded: 9.84in (250mm). **Weight unloaded:** 4lb 5oz (1.95kg). **Barrel:** 4.61in (117mm), 4 grooves, right-hand twist. **Magazine:** 20-round detachable box. **Cyclic rate:** 1250 rds/min. **Muzzle velocity:** c.1150 ft/sec (350 m/sec).

ITALY

• Villar Perosa M915

Officine Villar Perosa, Villar Perosa; FIAT SpA, Turin; Canadian General Electric Company Limited, Toronto
9mm Glisenti

This venerable gun is frequently quoted as being the first submachine gun ever made; technically this has some substance, since while not appearing in the form in which subsequent guns were made, it nevertheless incorporated most, if not all, of the features apparent in more modern weapons. Tactically, however, it was designed and origi-

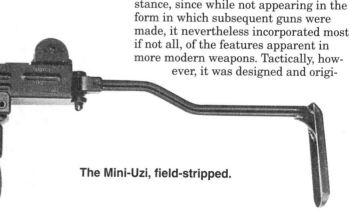

The Mini-Uzi, field-stripped.

The Micro-Uzi.

The Villar Perosa, two guns side-by-side on a bipod.

The OVP was half a Villar Perosa mounted onto a wooden butt.

nally deployed as a normal light machine gun for the support of Alpine troops and was always made as a double gun. The first models appeared in 1915 and went into service in the Italian Army as a light machine gun, but after two years of war, its proper potential was appreciated and it was then used very much as all submachine guns have been since: as highly mobile, short-range fire-power for foot infantry. The gun was made by a variety of Italian factories and also in Canada, and is often called either by the name of the designer (Revelli) or by the name of FIAT (one of the manufacturers) thus adding a certain amount of confusion.

A form of retarded blowback was used, involving the rotation of the bolt by cams, and a light bolt and strong return spring gave the combination a high rate of fire. The Villar Perosa appeared on a number of mountings, including tripods, fixed shields, on bicycles, and occasionally in armored vehicles (all of which added further date designations), and the gunner was provided with a large number of spare magazines. Although the weapon did not itself have a particularly long or distinguished life, it clearly pointed the way for those that followed, and it was a notable milestone.

Most of the original Villar Perosa weapons which survived combat were later converted by splitting the twin guns

and mounting each half into a wooden stock to produce the OVP and the Beretta M1918, described below.

Length: 21.00in (533mm). **Weight unloaded:** 14lb 6oz (6.52kg). **Barrel:** 12.50in (318mm), 6 grooves, right-hand twist. **Magazine:** 25-round detachable box. **Cyclic rate:** 1200 rds/min (each barrel). **Muzzle velocity:** c.1200 ft/sec (365 m/sec).

• Moschetto Automatico OVP
Officine Villar Perosa, Villar Perosa
9mm Glisenti

The OVP was derived from the Villar Perosa of 1915 and was produced in small numbers—in the 1920s—for the Italian Army. It uses exactly the same method of operation as the Villar Perosa and the same magazine and feed mechanism. It is, indeed, the half of an original VP twin gun with a longer barrel and traditional furniture. Selective fire is possible using the two triggers; the front one gives automatic fire and the rear one gives semi-automatic fire. The bolt handle is an oddity, taking the form of a cylinder over the receiver with a slot to clear the trigger mechanism. To cock, the cylinder is pulled back and then returned forward. An aperture rear sight is fitted, but it is rather too far forward, lying just in front of the magazine housing. The OVP was still in use to a small extent at the beginning of World War II.

Length: 35.50in (900mm). **Weight unloaded:** 8lb 1oz (3.67kg). **Barrel:** 11.00in (279mm), 6 grooves, right-hand twist. **Magazine:** 25-round detachable box. **Cyclic rate:** 900 rds/min. **Muzzle velocity:** c.1250 ft/sec (381 m/sec).

• Beretta Model 1918
Pietro Beretta SpA, Gardone Val Trompia
9mm Glisenti

The Beretta of 1918 is another of the modified versions of the original Villar Perosa similar to the OVP. The action, receiver, feed and barrel of the Villar Perosa were united with a new trigger mechanism and a wooden one-piece butt; a folding bayonet was also provided. The resulting gun was a great success, and so many Villar Perosa submachine guns were converted to Berettas that the original is now scarce.

Two versions of the Beretta gun are known, one with *'due grilletti'* (two triggers) and one with a single trigger. The double-trigger version was capable of

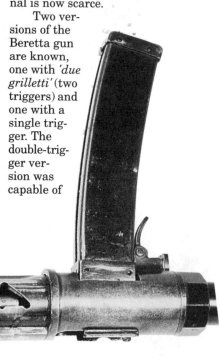

Cocking the OVP was done by drawing back the knurled sleeve; note the cam slot inside the receiver which rotates the bolt as it closes, so clearing the path of the firing pin.

The Beretta M1918 was also half a Villar Perosa mounted onto a wooden stock, but with a more conventional cocking handle and with the addition of a bayonet.

both semi-automatic and full-automatic fire, the triggers acting as the selector device, but the single-trigger gun was really a semi-automatic carbine in which the full-automatic mechanism was removed. Both worked by a system of retarded blowback utilizing two inclined planes machined in the receiver walls, whose resistance had to be overcome before the bolt unit could rotate and move backwards to open. This slowed the rate of fire compared to the Villa Perosa, which had used a similar type of retarding mechanism, but the automatic Beretta must have been difficult to hold. Guns of this pattern were still in use in World War II.

Length: 33.50in (850mm). **Weight unloaded:** 7lb 3oz (3.26kg). **Barrel:** 12.00in (305mm), 6 grooves, right-hand twist. **Magazine:** 25-round top-mounted detachable box. **Cyclic rate:** 900 rds/min. **Muzzle velocity:** c.1250 ft/sec (381 m/sec).

• Beretta Model 1918/30
Pietro Beretta SpA, Gardone Val Trompia
9mm Parabellum

The Beretta semi-automatic carbine of 1930 was based closely on the previous models of 1918, which themselves owed much to the old Villar Perosa. The principal differences were the caliber, 9mm Parabellum instead of the 9mm Model 10 Glisenti round (which of course necessitated stronger recoil springs owing to the more powerful round), and the substitution of a 25-round under-action box magazine instead of the former top-feeding pattern.

The Model 1918/30 was issued to the Italian Milizia Forestale and also saw sales to South America. The appearance and dimensions are the same as those of the M1918 weapon, but the 1918/30 can be distinguished by the magazine and by the cocking ring at the rear end of the receiver.

• Beretta Model 38A
Pietro Beretta SpA, Gardone Val Trompia
9mm Parabellum

The Model 38A Beretta design was derived from a series of submachine guns dating back to the 1918 type. It was an excellent design, very well made, and long lasting: it went into mass production from the start and continued to be made in quite large numbers until 1950. The Model 38A equipped the Italian Army throughout World War II and was also supplied to the German and Romanian armies. Although fairly large and

heavy—a legacy of its ancestry—the gun was popular with those who used it and has survived in many parts of the world. Early models were expensively made from machined steel, and carried both a bayonet and a muzzle compensator. These refinements were dropped in later wartime versions and, by 1941, a certain amount of sheet-steel had found its way into the construction and the bolt had been modified slightly. Apart from these, the gun remained the same to the end of its life. A special high-velocity 9mm cartridge was developed for this gun, called the 9mm *cartuccia pallottola Modello 38A*, and this round gave some credence to the rear sight adjustment which went up to 500 meters. This ammunition was separately and distinctly packed from the other 9mm varieties used in the Italian services. A distinctive feature of this Beretta lies in the provision of twin triggers, the forward one giving semi-automatic fire and the rear one providing fully automatic operation.

Length: 37.50in (953mm). **Weight unloaded:** 9lb 4oz (4.19kg). **Barrel:** 12.50in (318mm), 6 grooves, right-hand twist. **Magazine:** 10-, 20-, 30- or 40-round detachable box. **Cyclic rate:** 600 rds/min. **Muzzle velocity:** c.1370 ft/sec (417 m/sec).

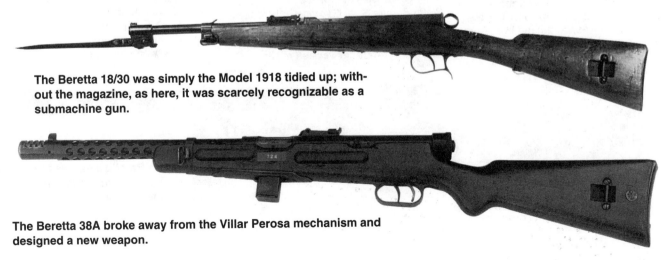

The Beretta 18/30 was simply the Model 1918 tidied up; without the magazine, as here, it was scarcely recognizable as a submachine gun.

The Beretta 38A broke away from the Villar Perosa mechanism and designed a new weapon.

The Beretta 38/42 went even further; note the double trigger, for single shots or automatic fire.

• Beretta Model 38/42

Pietro Beretta SpA, Gardone Val Trompia
9mm Parabellum

Beretta's Model 38A proved to be too expensive and too difficult to produce in the quantities necessary in wartime, and it soon became necessary to look for a simpler model. The Model 38/42 is a modified version incorporating a number of changes, the most noticeable of which are the shortening of the barrel and the removal of the barrel jacket. The receiver is made from sheet steel, and so are several of the other parts; the wooden butt is cut square at the front and the sights, triggerguard, and other minor parts are much simplified. A new bolt handle was designed with a form of dust cover incorporated, which undoubtedly stemmed from the experiences of the Italian Army in the North African Desert.

However, the 38/42 is still the same weapon as the Model 38A and, despite the simplifications, was still made to high standards. The rate of fire was slightly reduced and only 9mm Parabellum ammunition was used, as it was found to be impracticable in wartime to issue a separate round for submachine guns. The German and Romanian armies also took delivery of this model, and it may still be found either in service or in reserve stocks elsewhere.

Length: 31.50in (800mm). **Weight unloaded:** 7lb 3oz (3.26kg). **Barrel:** 8.50in (216mm), 6 grooves, right-hand twist. **Magazine:** 20- or 40-round detachable box.

Cyclic rate: 550 rds/min. **Muzzle velocity:** c.1250 ft/sec (381 m/sec).

• Beretta, Model 38/43 and Model 38/44

Pietro Beretta SpA, Gardone Val Trompia
9mm Parabellum

The 38/43 and 38/44 were minor variations of the earlier 38/42, and hence of the original Beretta Model 1938A. The 38/43 was an intermediate production stage between the 1942 and 1944 patterns, making use of a stamped receiver which was married to the bolt components of the 38/42. The external surface of the barrels of these weapons were of indifferent execution; like the 38/42, the external surface was longitudinally grooved.

The Model 38/44, production of which began at the beginning of the year, was a simplified version of the 1943 type making use of a stamped receiver and some redesigned internal components—which resulted in a lower cyclic rate of approximately 600 rds/min.

Length: 31.50in (800mm). **Weight unloaded:** 7lb 3oz (3.26kg). **Barrel:** 8.50in (216mm), 6 grooves, right-hand twist. **Magazine:** 20- or 40-round detachable box. **Cyclic rate:** 550 rds/min. **Muzzle velocity:** c.1250 ft/sec (381 m/sec).

• Beretta Model 38/49

Pietro Beretta SpA, Gardone Val Trompia
9mm Parabellum

The Model 38/49, as its name suggests, is yet another version of the

remarkably successful 38A and differs little from the Model 38/42, simply being a post-war version of the latter intended for sale to any country that would buy it. Minor modifications such as bayonet fittings were added at the whim of the customer, and the resultant sales were considerable. The countries that bought the weapon were mostly those too small to have arms industries of their own, which means that this weapon is to be found in Asia, North Africa and South America.

At least two versions were made with folding stocks; one in which the butt folded forward on a swivel behind the triggers and another in which a wire butt telescoped. Both these models had wooden pistol grips for the trigger hand. All were similar in operation and although one model had only a grip safety it does not appear to have been produced in very large numbers. These guns were the last to be produced with the well-known double trigger, and with the end of the series in about 1961 it went out altogether. All these versions of the 1938A had been the work of one brilliant designer, Tullio Marengoni, and this line of development ended on his death.

• Beretta Modello 12

Pietro Beretta SpA, Gardone Val Trompia, and Fabrique Nationale, Herstal, Belgium
9mm Parabellum

The Modello 12 is another of Beretta's post-war designs, produced in the late 1950s and offered for sale in the

The Beretta 38/49 was the 38/42 but with a new push-through safety catch in the forend.

Another version of the 38/49 was this simplified one made for the Italian Navy in 1956.

early 1960s. It is a modern design and owes little to the previous varieties from the same factory, having been developed by Domenico Salza, the successor to Tullio Marengoni. It is small, compact, very well made, and among the first to use the idea of recessing the barrel into the bolt head. This system allows the overall length of the weapon to be much reduced without sacrificing barrel length or bolt weight. The principle has become a general practice in recent designs and it is claimed, with some justice, that it greatly reduces the tendency of the muzzle to climb in fully-automatic fire. The Model 12 was designed for rapid and simple manufacture and is largely constructed of steel

stampings and pressings welded together. It can be fitted with either a folding metal butt or a removable wooden one, the latter being slightly heavier.

Length, butt extended: 25.40in (645mm); butt folded: 16.40in (416mm). **Weight unloaded:** 6lb 8oz (2.95kg). **Barrel:** 8.00in (203mm), 6 grooves, right-hand twist. **Magazine:** 20-, 30- or 40-round detachable box. **Cyclic rate:** 550 rds/min. **Muzzle velocity:** c.1250 ft/sec (381 m/sec).

• Beretta Model 12S
Armi Beretta SpA, Gardone Val Trompia
9mm Parabellum
The is an improved Model 12S, the principal changes being a new design of

manual safety and fire selector and modification to the sights. In addition, the rear cap retaining catch was strengthened and improved, a new buttplate was fitted, and the weapon was given a coating of epoxy resin-based anti-corrosion finish. The Model 12S replaced the Model 12 in production in the early 1980s and became the standard for Italian forces, was sold to other armies, and was also made under license by Taurus SA in Brazil. Dimensions, etc., are exactly as for the Model 12.

• FNAB Modello 1943
Fabbrica Nazionale d'Armi, Brescia
9mm Parabellum
The FNAB was manufactured in small numbers during World War II and

A complete break with the past and a new designer, and the Beretta Model 12 was a totally different weapon.

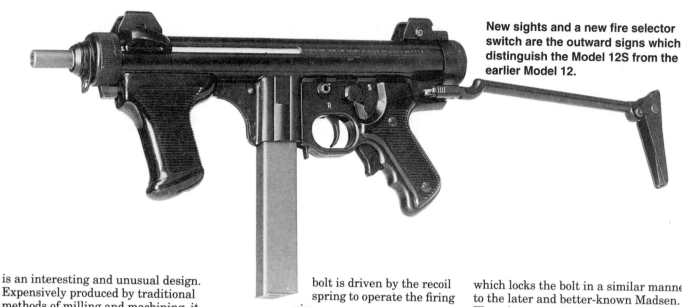

New sights and a new fire selector switch are the outward signs which distinguish the Model 12S from the earlier Model 12.

is an interesting and unusual design. Expensively produced by traditional methods of milling and machining, it would today be an economic impossibility. The butt and magazine housing fold to make an extremely compact unit and the barrel jacket incorporates a compensator.

The operation of the gun is also unusual, for it is a delayed blowback using a two-piece bolt unit with a combined accelerator/retarder lever separating the units. When fired, this lever first retards the opening of the breech by engaging with the receiver, then—after unlocking—it pivots to act as an accelerator and force the bolt body rearwards. On the return stroke, the front section of the bolt chambers the round, the lever rotates to lock, and the rear section of the bolt is driven by the recoil spring to operate the firing pin.

Length, butt extended: 31.15in (790mm); butt folded: 20.75in (527mm). **Weight unloaded:** 7lb 2oz (3.25kg). **Barrel:** 7.80in (198mm), 6 grooves, right-hand twist. **Magazine:** 20- or 40-round detachable box. **Cyclic rate:** 400 rds/min. **Muzzle velocity:** c.1250 ft/sec (381 m/sec).

• TZ45

Manufacturer unknown
9mm Parabellum

This weapon was developed in Italy in 1944, and 600 were produced during the last months of World War II. It is a conventional blowback weapon, typical of its era, with the addition of a simple safety on the magazine housing, a grip which locks the bolt in a similar manner to the later and better-known Madsen. The telescoping butt is held in the closed position by an index plate beneath the barrel casing.

The weapon was briefly evaluated by various Allied agencies after the war, but the general opinion seems to have been unfavorable. Most reports speak of the TZ45's unreliability in prolonged use and its poor standard of manufacture. In spite of this, the designers managed to sell it to the Burmese Army c.1956 and—as the BA52—it was produced in Burma for some years.

Length, butt extended: 33.50in (851mm); butt folded: 21.50in (546mm). **Weight unloaded:** 7lb 3oz (3.26kg). **Barrel:** 9.00in (229mm), 6 grooves, right-hand twist.

The FNAB of 1943 was a neat design of which very few were made.

The TZ45, another Italian wartime design which appeared at the wrong time, just as the Italians decided to surrender, and was therefore never produced in quantity.

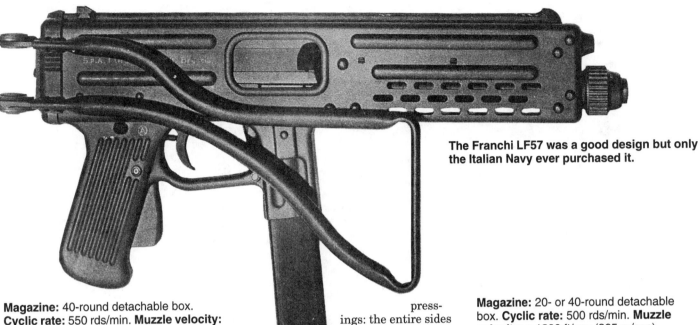

The Franchi LF57 was a good design but only the Italian Navy ever purchased it.

Magazine: 40-round detachable box.
Cyclic rate: 550 rds/min. **Muzzle velocity:** c.1250 ft/sec (381 m/sec).

• Franchi Model LF-57
Luigi Franchi SpA, Brescia
9mm Parabellum

The Franchi was first produced in 1956 and, when modified in the following year, became the Model 57. It was the first military weapon produced by the firm of Luigi Franchi of Brescia and although interesting and well made it was not a commercial success. Small numbers were ordered for the Italian Navy in the early 1960s. The LF-57 uses the principle of the recessed bolt head to reduce the length of the weapon, in much the same way as the Beretta Model 12. The difference lies in the fact that the Franchi carries the mass of the bolt above the barrel rather than around it as in the Beretta, thus simplifying manufacture to some extent. In fact, the Franchi is well designed and the great majority of the parts are made from stampings and pressings: the entire sides of the gun are made in one piece and the two are joined by one long seam. The weapon dismantles very easily as the barrel, for instance, is held by a single barrel nut. There is no furniture in the accepted sense, the pistol grip being entirely of steel, and the sights are rather crude fixtures. The tubular butt folds sideways onto the right side of the receiver. The Franchi was a neat weapon, but it was not significantly better than any of the many others being produced at the same time, and it failed to make an impact.

Length, butt extended: 27.00in (686mm); butt folded: 16.50in (419mm). **Weight unloaded:** 7lb 0oz (3.17kg). **Barrel:** 8.00in (203mm), 6 grooves, right-hand twist.

Magazine: 20- or 40-round detachable box. **Cyclic rate:** 500 rds/min. **Muzzle velocity:** c.1200 ft/sec (365 m/sec).

• Spectre M-4
SITES SpA, Turin
9mm Parabellum

Introduced in 1984, this unusual weapon is the only 'double-action' submachine gun in existence. It was designed primarily for security arid anti-terrorist forces, to provide them with a weapon which can be carried safely and brought into action instantly without requiring any safeties to be released or cocking handles to be pulled.

The weapon is loaded and prepared in the usual way by inserting a magazine, pulling back the cocking lever an releasing it This loads a cartridge and closes the bolt, but leaves the separate hammer unit cocked. Pressing a release lever now allows the hammer to run forward and be held a short distance behind the bolt. The weapon can now be carried in perfect safety; when required, a pull

The Spectre, the only double-action submachine gun, has been adopted by a number of police and anti-terrorist forces in Europe.

The Spectre with stock folded.

on the trigger will cock the hammer and release it to fire the round in the chamber, after which the weapon acts in the normal blowback manner. Firing from a closed bolt suggests a hot barrel, and a forced draft system controlled by the bolt ensures that cooling air is pumped through and around the barrel during firing. The magazines are an ingenious four-column design which enables a 50-round capacity in the length normally associated with 30 rounds. The Spectre has been well received and is in use by numerous security agencies.

Length, butt extended: 22.83in (580mm); butt folded: 13.78in (350mm). **Weight unloaded:** 6lb 6oz (2.90kg). **Barrel:** 5.12in (130mm), 6 grooves, right-hand twist. **Magazine:** 32- or 50-round detachable box. **Cyclic rate:** 850 rds/min. **Muzzle velocity:** 1312 ft/sec (400 m/sec).

• Socimi Type 8215
Societa Costruzioni Industriali Milano, Milan
9mm Parabellum

This was announced in 1983 and was apparently based on the Uzi design. It used the same type of telescoping bolt, had a similar safety mechanism and accepted the magazine in the hand grip. There are significant differences in construction, however, notably that the Socimi has a solid rectangular receiver

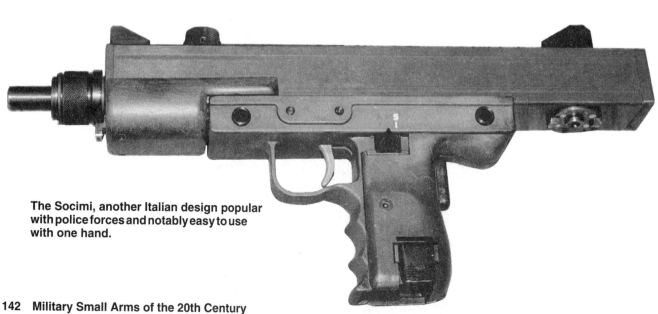

The Socimi, another Italian design popular with police forces and notably easy to use with one hand.

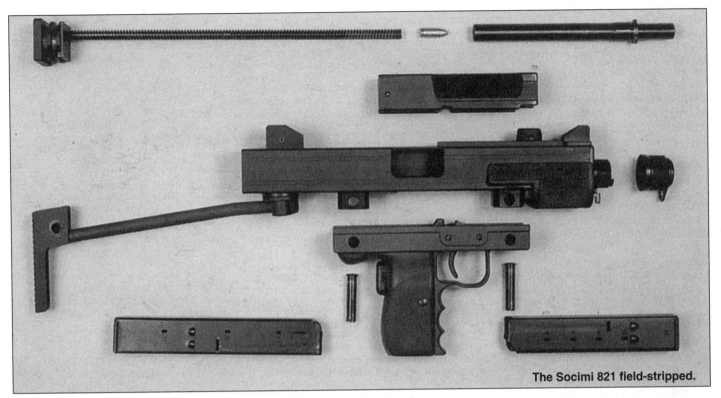

The Socimi 821 field-stripped.

into which the bolt is inserted from the rear end, and the barrel from the front, secured by a nut. The receiver, barrel housing and pistol grip are all of light alloy, and the stock folds forward by pivoting underneath the rear of the receiver and lying alongside the weapon. Accessories included a laser aiming device and a silencer.

The Type 821 went into series production, but there is no information as to its purchasers.

Length, butt extended: 23.6in (600mm); butt folded: 15.7in (400mm). **Weight unloaded:** 5lb 6oz (2.45kg). **Barrel:** 7.87in (200mm), 6 grooves, right-hand twist. **Magazine:** 32-round detachable box. **Cyclic rate:** 550-600 rds/min. **Muzzle velocity:** 1245 ft/sec (380 m/sec).

• Submachine-gun Benelli CB-M2

Benelli Armi SpA, Urbino
9mm AUPO

This was an interesting attempt to develop a half-way house between cased and caseless ammunition. The weapon was on generally conventional lines, a blowback feeding from a box magazine, but the special ammunition demanded some internal changes.

The AUPO cartridge resembled a 9mm Parabellum in outline, but did not consist of separate bullet and case; the entire round was in one piece, of a brass compound, and the 'case' section contained propellant and was open at the base. There was rimfire ignition filling around the inside of the round, about half-way along. The bolt had an extended nose which drove the round from the magazine in the usual way, but which then entered the open base of the round. The base was rolled, and a groove on the bolt nose engaged with this interior 'rim' to hold the round so that it could be unloaded if necessary. Once the bolt nose had thrust the round into the chamber, a side-mounted hammer was tripped by the forward movement of the bolt; this struck the outside of the round over the rimfire composition and thus fired the propellant. The round was then blown off the end of the bolt nose and traveled down the barrel in the usual way. Once the round had left the muzzle the usual blowback action forced the bolt back and operated the loading cycle. The point of the whole exercise was that as the bolt went back there was no empty case to extract and eject, since the complete round had left via the muzzle.

The CB-M2 was evaluated by various military agencies. It was found to be accurate and comfortable to fire but the prospect of adding an extra and unique round of ammunition to the supply line was probably enough to turn military eyes against it. In any event, no worthwhile sales were made and the design was quietly dropped in the latter 1980s.

Length, butt extended: 26.0in (660mm); butt folded: 17.7in (450mm). **Weight unloaded:** 6lb 15oz (3.15kg). **Barrel:** 7.87in (200mm), 6 grooves, right-hand twist. **Magazine:** 20-, 30- or 40-round detachable box.

The Benelli CB-M2 used an unusual cartridge.

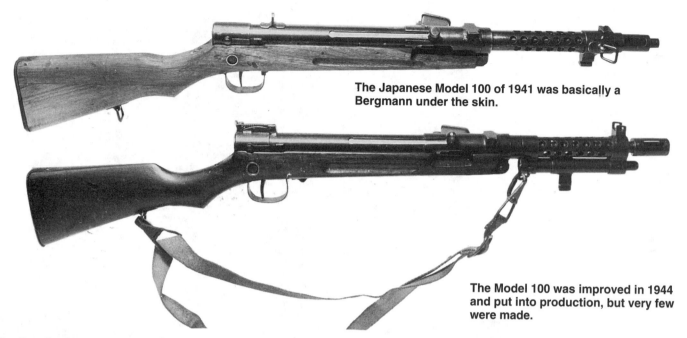

The Japanese Model 100 of 1941 was basically a Bergmann under the skin.

The Model 100 was improved in 1944 and put into production, but very few were made.

Cyclic rate: 800-1000 rds/min. **Muzzle velocity:** 1280 ft/sec (390 m/sec).

JAPAN

• Type 100 submachine-gun8
Kokura Army Arsenal; Nagoya Army Arsenal
8mm Nambu

Japan was surprisingly slow to adopt submachine guns, although they are the ideal jungle weapon, and their intention of dominating the Pacific had been germinating for several years. Sensible weapon development was not, however, a feature of the pre-World War II Japanese High Command and, apart from a few Bergmann and MP28/II guns bought in the 1930s, it was 1940 before a native design appeared. The Type 100, which used the weak 8mm Japanese automatic pistol cartridge, was well-made and of reasonably conventional design. About 10,000 of the original Type 100, with per-

haps another 7,500 of the folding-butt parachutist's model were made in the years before 1943. The former were manufactured by Kokura Army Arsenal and the latter at Nagoya. The guns were not really successful, largely because little factory space could be spared for a continuous development program and hence little effort was given to improving the weapons; another drawback lay in the poor quality of the ammunition which gave frequent jams.

In 1944, the Japanese introduced an improved model, which differed only in minor respects, but again, only about 8,000 were produced at one of Nagoya Arsenal's sub-plants before the end of the war. The manufacture of the Type 100 1944 version was much simplified to eliminate as far as possible the valuable machine time which otherwise would be wasted on non-essentials: consequently this meant the appearance of much rough welding, the sights were fixed, and

the firing pin could be replaced if it fractured. The rate of fire of the 1944 variety was considerably greater than that of the original 1940 version.

Length: 35.00in (889mm). **Weight unloaded:** 8lb 8oz (3.83kg) **Barrel:** 9.00in (228mm), 6 grooves, right-hand twist. **Magazine:** 30-round detachable box. **Cyclic rate:** 450 rds/min (1940), 800 rds/min (1944). **Muzzle velocity:** c.1100 ft/sec (335 m/sec)

• SCK Model 65 and 66
Shin Chuo Kogyo, Tokyo
9mm Parabellum

This design is an amalgam of several features found in other submachine-guns, and represents a sound attempt to produce a reliable but inexpensive weapon. In general form it resembles the Carl Gustav; the grip safety is of the Madsen type; there is an ejection port cover which acts as a safety catch, as in the American M3Al; and the

The only postwar Japanese submachine gun was this SCK Type 76.

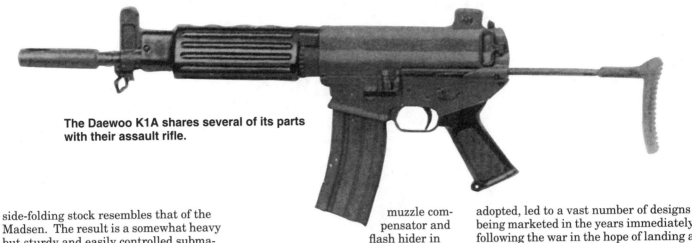

The Daewoo K1A shares several of its parts with their assault rifle.

side-folding stock resembles that of the Madsen. The result is a somewhat heavy but sturdy and easily controlled submachine-gun which uses the normal blow-back system of operation. Its use has been confined to the Japanese Self-Defense Force.

The Type 66 resembles the Type 65 but the bolt and return spring were modified slightly to lower the rate of fire.

Length, butt extended: 30.0in (762mm); butt folded: 19.70in (500mm). **Weight unloaded:** 9.00lb (4.08kg). **Barrel:** 5.50in (140mm). **Magazine:** 30-round detachable box. **Cyclic rate:** c.550 rds/min (Model 65) 465 rds/min (Model 66). **Muzzle velocity:** c.1180 ft/sec.

KOREA, SOUTH

• Daewoo K1A

Daewoo Precision Industries Ltd, Kumjeong, Pusan,
5.56x45mm M193

This is one of the growing number of submachine guns actually chambered for a rifle cartridge, being based on components of the Daewoo company's assault rifle but using a blowback bolt assembly. It has been given a large and efficient muzzle compensator and flash hider in order to reduce the effects of firing a rifle cartridge from a short barrel, and it is claimed that this reduces muzzle climb and flash by a considerable amount. The sights are provided with Tritium inserts for night shooting, and the weapon has an extremely simple sliding wire butt-stock. A selector on the left side permits a choice of single shots, automatic fire or three-round bursts.

Length: butt extended: 33.0in (838mm); butt folded: 25.71in (653mm). **Weight, unloaded:** 6lb 5oz (2.87kg). **Barrel:** 10.35in (263mm), 6 grooves, right-hand twist. **Magazine:** 20- or 30-round detachable box. **Cyclic rate:** 850 rds/min. **Muzzle velocity:** c.2690 ft/sec (820 m/sec)

LUXEMBOURG

• Sola-Super and Sola-Leger

Société Luxembourgeoise d'Armes SA, Ettelbruck
9mm Parabellum

The rise of the submachine-gun during World War II, together witn the inferior character of many of the weapons adopted, led to a vast number of designs being marketed in the years immediately following the war in the hope of landing a military contract to replace the war-time weapons. The 'Sola-Super' was manufactured in small quantities in 1954-7 and marketed with some success in North Africa and South America. It was evaluated by several other countries but was never adopted by any major power.

The Sola is a conventional blowback weapon capable either of firing single shots or fully automatic operation. The gun was obviously designed with an eye to cheapness and simplicity of production, for there is considerable use of stamped components and the design is pared to the point of having no more than thirty-eight components. It is, for its class, a long and cumbersome weapon, though the long barrel with an integral compensator gives a reasonable degree of accuracy and an above-average velocity. There is, however, nothing in the design which has not been done as well (if not better) elsewhere, and this was probably why the Sola failed to gain wide acceptance.

In an attempt to make it a commercial success, the makers redesigned the weapon, doing away with the bulky trig-

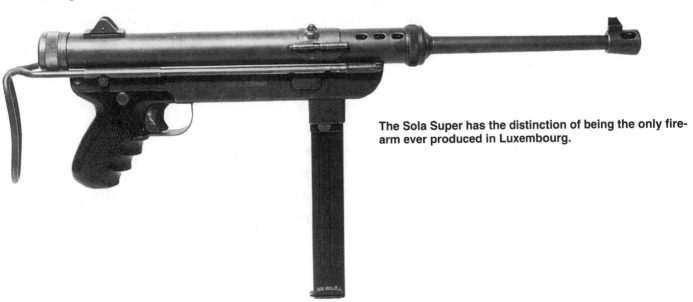

The Sola Super has the distinction of being the only firearm ever produced in Luxembourg.

The Mendoza HM-3 from Mexico.

ger mechanism housing and shortening the barrel. The resulting 'Light Model' was put on the market in 1957, but met with even less success than the original 'Super'; with this, the company decided to quit the armaments field.

• (Sola-Super)

Length, butt extended: 35.00in (889mm); butt folded: 24.00in (610mm). **Weight unloaded:** 6lb 6oz (2.90kg). **Barrel:** 12.00in (305mm), 6 grooves, right-hand twist. **Magazine:** 32-round detachable box. **Cyclic rate:** 550 rds/min. **Muzzle velocity:** c.1400 ft/sec (425 m/sec)

MEXICO

• Pistola Ametrallador HM-3
Produtos Mendoza SA, Mexico City
9mm (Parabellum)

The Mendoza company have been known for their machine-guns for several years. In the late 1950s they developed a submachine gun which was basically a machine pistol, but this met with small success. In 1973 they re-entered this field with a much more practical weapon, the HM-3.

The HM-3 was a lightweight weapon which used a wrap-around bolt to reduce its length and, as usual with this feature, the magazine was inserted through the pistol grip. A fixed tubular steel stock was used, together with a plastic forend grip. An alternative design,

announced as an 'improved HM-3', featured a sideways-folding stock which, when folded, acted as a forward hand grip; one unusual feature of this was that it became possible to fold or unfold the stock while still gripping the weapon with both hands.

A small number of HM-3 weapons were acquired by the Mexican Army, but it never became a general issue and was later replaced by the Heckler & Koch MP-5.

Length, butt extended: 25.00in (635mm); butt folded: 15.55in (395mm). **Weight unloaded:** 5lb 15oz (2.69kg). **Barrel:** 10.04in (255mm). **Magazine:** 32-round detachable box. **Cyclic rate:** c.600 rds/min. **Muzzle velocity:** 1300 ft/sec (396 m/sec).

PERU

• MGP-79A
Sima-Cefar, Callao
9mm Parabellum

This weapon was developed by Sima-Cefar, the manufacturing arm of the Peruvian Naval Base at Callao, and is a conventional blowback weapon. The barrel is enclosed in a perforated jacket, and both barrel and jacket can be easily

removed and replaced with a barrel/silencer assembly. The shoulder stock folds round the right side of the receiver and the butt pad then lies alongside the magazine housing where it helps to form a forward hand grip.

The safety catch is above the pistol grip, while the fire selector is positioned close to the magazine housing, so that the two controls can be operated by different hands. The MGP-79A was the standard submachine gun of the Peruvian armed forces until replaced by the MGP-87 in the late 1980s.

Length, butt folded: 21.42in (544mm); butt extended: 31.85in (809mm). **Weight unloaded:** 6lb 13oz (3.09kg). **Barrel:** 9.33in (237mm), 12 grooves, right-hand twist. **Magazine:** 20- or 32-round detachable box. **Cyclic rate:** c.600-850 rds/min. **Muzzle velocity:** 1345 ft/sec (410 m/sec).

• MGP-87
Sima-Cifar, Callao
9mm Parabellum

The MGP-87 is to the same basic design as the MGP-79A described above, but is a simplified design. There is no barrel jacket and the barrel and the folding stock are both shorter. The cocking handle is turned up into the vertical position and made larger so that it can be readily grasped and operated. The weapon was designed for use by

The MGP-7/A, a workman-like weapon made by the Peruvian Navy.

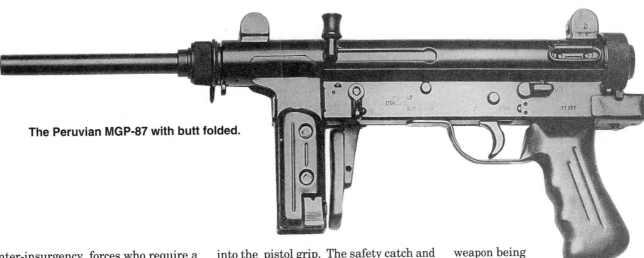

The Peruvian MGP-87 with butt folded.

counter-insurgency forces who require a more compact gun and one which can be brought into action quickly. The barrel can be quickly removed by unscrewing the securing nut and replaced by a combined barrel/suppressor unit. It will eventually completely replace the MGP-79A as the standard Peruvian weapon.

Length, butt folded: 19.69in (500mm); butt extended: 30.16in (766mm). **Weight unloaded:** 6lb 6oz (2.90kg). **Barrel:** 7.64in (194mm), 12 grooves, right-hand twist. **Magazine:** 20- or 32-round detachable box. **Cyclic rate:** c.600-850 rds/min. **Muzzle velocity:** 1187 ft/sec (362 m/sec).

• MGP-84
Sima-Cifar, Callao
9xmm Parabellum

This is a very small weapon designed for use by special forces and security guards. It is a blowback weapon, the basic mechanism of which is based on that of the MGP-79A described above. In this case, though, the barrel is considerably shortened and set back in the receiver, and the bolt is of the telescoping type, allowing the magazine to be placed into the pistol grip. The safety catch and fire selector switch is a single unit, placed ahead of the trigger-guard where it can be conveniently operated by the forward hand. The stock folds sideways and the buttplate acts as a forward grip. As with all Sima-Cefar weapons, the magazine uses the Uzi interface so that Uzi magazines can be used in an emergency.

Length, butt folded: 10.67in (271mm); butt extended: 19.29in (490mm). **Weight unloaded:** 5lb 1oz (2.31kg). **Barrel:** 6.0in (152mm), 12 grooves, right-hand twist. **Magazine:** 20- or 32-round detachable box. **Cyclic rate:** c.650 rds/min. **Muzzle velocity:** 1122 ft/sec (342 m/sec).

POLAND

• Pistolet Maszynowy wz 43/52
Fabryka Broni, Warsaw
7.62mm Soviet M30

The Polish Army was supplied with the usual armory of Soviet weapons afterWorld War II, and among them were some submachine-guns of the PPS43 type. In this, the Poles were fortunate since there are few instances of this weapon being sent anywhere else in the Communist bloc, and a variant of the PPS43 was developed and made in Poland under the designation wz/43-52.

Basically, it is the same gun fitted with a wooden stock and a few small production alterations to suit the Warsaw Arsenal machinery. It has been reported in the past that this weapon had a selector switch for single shots or automatic fire, but examination of a number of actual weapons has proved this to be wrong; like the Soviet original, it fires only at automatic, though single shots can be 'touched off' by skillful pressure on the trigger.

• Pistolet Maszynowy wz 63 'RAK' or PM-63
Fabryka Broni, Warsaw
9mm Makarov

This is really an enlarged automatic pistol in its construction. It was designed as a light and handy weapon for self-defense use by drivers and vehicle crews and similar groups whose primary job is not operating small arms. The

The Peruvian MGP-84 is their mini-submachine gun for security forces.

The Polish vz/43/54 is a copy of the Soviet PPS-453 but can be distinguished by the wooden butt.

weapon is built up from a frame, a slide and a barrel, just like a pistol, and even the barrel fits into the frame by interrupted lugs in the same way as the Browning 1903 and similar pistols. The magazine fits into the butt, and there is a small front grip which folds down. The butt is formed from two metal strips which slide alongside the frame so that the shoulder pad lies under the rear end; when extended it drops slightly and locks so as to position the weapon in front of the eye. The PM-63 is cocked by pulling back the slide until it locks; pulling the trigger then releases it to fly forward and chamber and fire a round. The slide is then blown back and is again held, ready for the next round. Pulling the trigger harder withdraws the sear and allows automatic fire. In this case, the lightness of the slide would result in a very high rate of fire, and therefore a rate reducer is used. This is a loose inertia pellet in the rear of the slide. When the slide runs back it is held, not by the sear but by a special catch; the slide stops moving but the inertia pellet continues backward, compressing a spring, and then rebounds forward. As it comes back, it trips the catch and releases the slide to fire the next shot. This device reduces the rate of fire to manageable proportions. The

weapon can be fired single-handed, like a pistol, or two-handed, but in either case accuracy is doubtful since the slide is moving backwards and forwards, and since it carries the sights it is impossible to aim once fire has been opened. Nevertheless, the PM-63 is a practical weapon for the purpose for which it was designed.

Length, butt extended: 22.95in (583mm); butt folded; 13.20in (333mm). **Weight:** 3lb 15oz (1.80kg). **Barrel:** 6.50in (165mm); 4 grooves, right-hand twist. **Magazine:** 15- or 25-round detachable box. **Cyclic rate:** 650 rds/min. **Muzzle velocity (special 9mm):** 1025 ft/sec (320 m/sec).

• PM-84 and 84P
Zaklady Metalowe Lucznik, Radom
9mm Parabellum; 9mm Makarov

Although claimed to be a development of the PM-63, there is little likeness between these two weapons. The PM-84 is far more conventional, using a bolt reciprocating inside a rectangular receiver and with the pistol grip/magazine housing located at the center of balance. There is a sliding wire butt, with a butt-plate which folds forward beneath the rear of the receiver, and a folding forward handgrip under the front end. An unusually useful touch is the provision of

two cocking handles, one on each side of the receiver.

The PM-84 fires the 9mm Makarov cartridge; a variant model is the **PM-84P** which is chambered for the 9mm Parabellum cartridge, presumably for export.

• (PM-84)

Length, butt extended: 22.64in (575mm); butt folded: 14.76in (375mm). **Weight:** 4lb 9oz (2.07kg). **Barrel:** 7.28in (185mm); 4 grooves, right-hand twist. **Magazine:** 15- or 20-round detachable box. **Cyclic rate:** 600 rds/min. **Muzzle velocity:** 1082 ft/sec (330 m/sec).

PORTUGAL

• Pistols Metralhadora FBP M/9489
Fabrica de Braco de Prata, Lisbon
9mm Parabellum

The FBP was a combination of features of the German MP40 and the American M3 guns, the design being the work of Major Gonçalves Cardoso of the Portuguese Army. The receiver section, with telescoping bolt and barrel attached by a screwed collar, was taken from the MP40, while the pistol grip, trigger

The Polish wz/63 is cocked by pulling back the slide like an automatic pistol.

The Polish PM84 is one of the few submachine guns to have the cocking handle duplicated on both sides of the receiver.

mechanism and retracting wire stock were of M3 parentage. Extensive use was made of steel pressings, and the result was a reliable and inexpensive weapon, though according to report, its accuracy left something to be desired.

Length, butt folded: 25.00in (635mm); butt extended: 32.00in (812mm). **Weight unloaded:** 8lb 4oz (3.74kg). **Barrel:** 9.80in (250mm), 6 grooves, right-hand twist. **Magazine:** 32-round detachable box. **Cyclic rate:** 500 rds/min. **Muzzle velocity:** c.1250 ft/sec (38l m/sec).

• Pistola Metalhadora FBP M/976
Fabrica Militar de Braco de Prata, Lisbon
9mm Parabellum

The M976 was an improved version of the M948 (above) and used the same mechanical components, though with some modifications to improve reliability and simplify production. Two versions have been seen, one with a plain barrel and one with a perforated barrel jacket; it is probable that the jacketed model gave rather better accuracy, due to fuller support for the barrel, thus removing one of the principal complaints about the M948. Metal pressings and stampings were used for much of the construction, though the barrel was cold-swaged from high-quality steel, another factor in the improved accuracy.

Length, butt extended: 33.50in (850mm); butt folded: 25.90in (657mm); **Weight unloaded:** 6lb 14oz (3.12kg). **Barrel:** 9.84in (250mm), 6 grooves, right-hand twist. **Magazine:** 32- or 36-round detachable box. **Cyclic rate:** c.650 rds/min. **Muzzle velocity:** 1300 ft/sec (396 m/sec).

• Indep Lusa A1
Indep SA, Lisbon
9mm Parabellum

This weapon appeared in 1987, replacing all previous submachine guns in Portuguese service, and is a compact and robust design which owes nothing to the previous models. The receiver is in the form of a double cylinder, with the barrel and bolt in the lower section, and the overhung mass of the bolt in the upper section, very similar to the Italian Franchi design. The sliding stock, of steel rod, retracts into the 'waist' between the two sections of the receiver. The pistol grip and trigger unit attach below the receiver and there is a prominent safety/selector switch convenient to the firer's thumb. Two versions are made, one with a detachable barrel secured by a nut, the other with a fixed barrel surrounded by a perforated jacket.

Length, butt extended: 23.62in (600mm); butt folded: 17.52in (445mm). **Weight unloaded:** 5lb 8oz (2.50kg). **Barrel:** 6.30in (160mm), 6 grooves, right-hand twist. **Magazine:** 30-round detachable box. **Cyclic rate:** c.900 rds/min. **Muzzle velocity:** 1280 ft/sec (390 m/sec).

The Portuguese FBP M/948 is an ingenious mixture of MP48 and M3 design features.

The FBP M/976 was an improved design based on the M/948.

• Indep Lusa A2
Indep SA, Lisbon
9mm Parabellum

The Lusa A2, which appeared in 1991, is an improved model of the Lusa A1. The mechanism is exactly the same, a blowback weapon with overhung bolt, and the changes are mainly in the construction of the receiver. The whole weapon is shorter and lighter, the sliding butt is stronger and slides into recesses alongside the receiver, and the fore-grip is removed and the magazine now performs that function. The barrel is retained by a screwed nut and can be removed and replaced by a combined barrel/suppresser unit, and there is provision for attaching a laser sight. The A2 will gradually replace the A1 as the standard issue for Portuguese troops.

Length, butt extended: 23.03in (585mm); butt folded: 18.03in (458mm). **Weight unloaded:** 6lb 5oz (2.85kg). **Barrel:** 6.30in (160mm), 6 grooves, right-hand twist. **Magazine:** 30-round detachable box. **Cyclic rate:** c.900 rds/min. **Muzzle velocity:** 1280 ft/sec (390 m/sec).

ROMANIA

• Orita Model 1941
Cugir Arsenal, Cugir
9mm Parabellum

This was the first locally designed submachine gun to be made in Romania, and though very few have ever been seen in the West the production was fairly extensive and was certainly sufficient to arm the Romanian Army by 1941. The designer was Leopold Jasek who probably chose the German MP 38 as a source of inspiration since there are several similarities, though the Orita was better finished and consequently would have been expensive to manufacture.

A firing pin was incorporated, in which a hammer inside the bolt was cammed forward as the bolt closed so as to strike the pin. Most of the production was fitted to a one-piece wooden stock, though a folding metal tubular stock has also been seen, making the weapon very like the MP 38. An unusual rear sight was mounted well forward on the body, elevating by means of a leaf and ramp and offering ranges up to 500 meters. A substantial change lever on the right-hand side of the body allowed single-shot or automatic fire, and the safety was a button in the front of the trigger guard which moved from side to side. In general terms the Orita was a good weapon for its time and it probably gave good service to its users. It could still be seen in the hands of factory guards and reservists until the late 1970s.

Length: 35.20in (894mm). **Weight unloaded:** 7lb 10oz (3.45kg). **Barrel:** 11.30in (278mm), 6 grooves, right-hand twist. **Magazine:** 25-round box. **Cyclic rate:** 600 rds/min. **Muzzle velocity:** 1280 ft/sec 399 m/sec).

In the 1980s the Portuguese broke with the past and deveoloped a completely new weapon, the LUSA-A1.

In 1991 the LUSA-A2 appeared, an improvement on the A1 model.

• Ratmil
Romtehnica, Bucharest
9mm Parabellum

This appeared in about 1994 and was first seen in the hands of Chechen irregulars during the civil unrest there. It is a conventional blowback weapon, firing from an open bolt, and is built almost entirely of steel stampings riveted together. Two unusual features are, firstly, the provision of a three-round burst facility in addition to single shots, with no provision for automatic fire, and secondly the use of a finned barrel, for cooling, surrounded by a perforated jacket to act as a fore-grip. The folding wire stock is of flimsy appearance, being a single strut heavy wire rod hinged to swing to the left side of the receiver. Much of the barrel is inside the receiver and the bolt is of the wrap-around type, enveloping the rear end of the barrel when closed. It is uncertain whether the weapon has been formally adopted by the Romanian army.

Length, butt extended: 25.60in (650mm); butt folded: 16.73in (425mm). **Weight unloaded:** 6lb 5oz (2.70kg). **Barrel:** not known. **Magazine:** 30-round detachable box. **Cyclic rate:** c.650 rds/min (in bursts). **Muzzle velocity:** 1213 ft/sec (370 m/sec).

RUSSIA

• Degtyarev PPD34/38
State factories
7.62mm Soviet Pistol

The PPD is really a series of several similar weapons produced in the Soviet Union during the period 1934-40. The Model 34/38 was a standard issue (in small numbers only) to the army until 1940, when it was supplemented by the PPD40 and then replaced by the PPSh4l. It is a fairly conventional gun for its time, although it looks as if it drew much inspiration from the German MP28/II and the Finnish Suomi. The mechanism is quite straightforward, but must have been somewhat expensive to manufacture as the components are machined from high-quality steel; there are no stampings. The 25-round box magazine feeds from the underside, and there was also an unusual pattern of drum magazine which had a peculiar extended lip which fitted into a magazine housing in a similar fashion to a box magazine. This was the first Soviet weapon to utilize a drum magazine which later (though in a different pattern) became a regular feature of all but two of the entire series of Soviet submachine guns. The 7.62mm round was, of course, the standard Soviet pistol round, firing a comparatively light bullet at a high muzzle velocity: this increased velocity, however, did not give it any greater effectiveness than that of the 9mm Parabellum, nor any more range. One feature

The Romanian Orita of 1941 resembled a lot of contemporaries with its wooden butt, but the large rear sight distinguishes it.

The Soviet PPD with its original drum magazine.

of this gun, and all the remainder of the series, was that the barrel was chromed: an expensive process but popular with the Soviet designers as it considerably extended barrel life.

Length: 30. 50in (775mm). **Weight unloaded:** 8lb 4oz (3.76kg). **Barrel:** 10.75in (272mm), 4 grooves, right-hand twist. **Magazine:** 25-round detachable box or 71-round drum. **Cyclic rate:** 800 rds/min. **Muzzle velocity:** c.1640 ft/sec (500 m/sec).

• Degtyarev PPD40
State factories
7.62mm Soviet Pistol

The Red Army began experimenting with submachine guns as early as 1926 but early designs of Tokarev and Korovin were manufactured in token numbers only, and it was not until the middle 1930s that Degtyarev produced a service-able weapon, the PPD34/38 described above. This was replaced in 1940 by the PPD40 - a better weapon in most respects; since it was designed with more of an eye to manufacturing processes, and the peculiar drum magazine was replaced by a model based on the Finn's Suomi drum - an open-topped pattern which slid into a recess in the forend of the gun.

The PPD40 was well made of good material and was obviously a peacetime product; when the war ensnared the Russians, the PPD was abandoned for weapons of even simpler make.

Length: 30.60in (777mm). **Weight unloaded:** 8lb 2oz (3.70kg).

Barrel: 10.60in (269mm), 4 grooves, right-hand twist.
Magazine: 71-round drum. **Cyclic rate:** 800 rds/min. **Muzzle velocity:** c.1640 ft/sec (500 m/sec).

• PPSh4l
State factories
7.62mm Soviet Pistol

Two national catastrophes contributed to the Soviet enthusiasm for submachine guns. The first was the Winter War with Finland in 1939-40 when the Finns used submachine guns with devastating effect during close combat in the forests, and the second was the German invasion of 1941 when the Russians lost in the retreats both huge quantities of small arms and much of their engineering capability. There then arose an urgent demand for a light and simple weapon capable of a high volume of fire, and the answer to this was the PPSh4l, designed by Georgii Shpagin. It was much cheaper and quicker to make than the preceding Degtyarev models and was finished roughly; the barrel was still chromed, however, and there was never any doubt about the weapon's effectiveness. Stripping was simplicity itself, as the receiver hinged open to reveal the bolt and spring. There was no selector lever on some of the late models, when the gun was capable only of automatic fire, and the magazine was the proved and tried 71-round Suomi drum. The rate of fire was high, but a rudimentary compensator helped to steady the climb of the muzzle. About five million PPSh guns had been made by

1945, and the Soviets adapted their infantry tactics to take full advantage of such huge numbers: often complete units were armed with nothing else. In Russia, the PPSh went out of service in the late 1950s, but it was supplied in enormous quantities to the satellite and pro-Communist countries. It was made in various Communist countries, and in Iran, and there were a multitude of variants. However, its place was gradually taken by the ubiquitous Kalashnikov rifle, and by the 1980s the PPSh was a rarity.

Length: 33.00in (838mm). **Weight unloaded:** 8lb 0oz (3.64kg). **Barrel:** 10.50in (266mm), 4 grooves, right-hand twist. **Magazine:** 35-round detachable box or 71-round drum. **Cyclic rate:** 900 rds/min. Muzzle velocity: c. 1600 ft/sec (488 m/sec).

• PPS42, PPS43
State factories
7.62mm Soviet Pistol

The PPS guns are, to some extent, an oddity in the Soviet armory since their policy during World War II was one of rigid concentration upon one model for each type of weapon. During the siege of Leningrad, however, the supply of guns ran very low, and the prototypes of the PPS42 were hurriedly manufactured in a local factory to a design best suited to the equipment available. Quite naturally it was simple in the extreme, but it proved surprisingly effective and continued to be made after the siege was raised; it was then improved to the PPS43, which differed only in the design of the folding

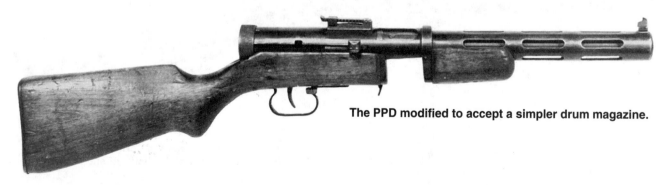

The PPD modified to accept a simpler drum magazine.

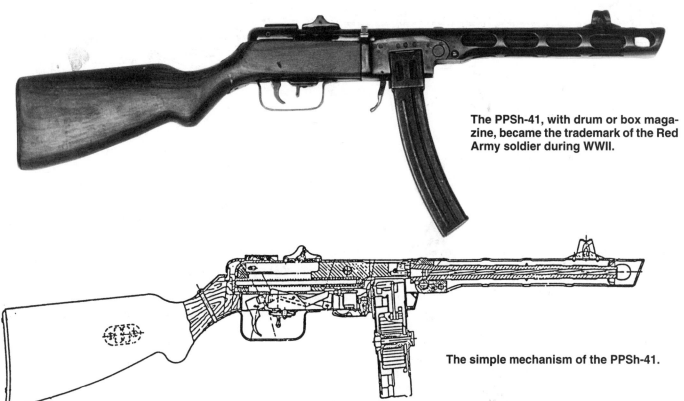

The PPSh-41, with drum or box magazine, became the trademark of the Red Army soldier during WWII.

The simple mechanism of the PPSh-41.

stock, the form of the safety catch and in the barrel jacket (which, in the first model, had a vertical joint in front of the magazine housing). In all, about one million of the PPS were made, and they continued in service for a few years after the war.

Unusually for a Soviet gun, the PPS used a box magazine holding 35 rounds and it was never adapted to take the more popular drum, Despite its extreme simplicity bordering on crudity, the PPS was highly effective. It has now disappeared, having been rarely offered to other Communist countries, though it was widely used by the Chinese forces in Korea in 1951-52. The Finnish m/44 and m/44-46 series, and the Spanish/German DUX guns, were derived from the PPS design. It is generally believed that the virtual suppression of the PPS in post-war years was due to a political deci-

sion by Stalin; the siege of Leningrad became something of a national legend of heroism and the leaders of that siege appeared to be gaining too much political influence in post-war years; they were all replaced, and the gun that reminded everyone of the siege was removed from public view.

(PPS42)

Length, butt extended: 35.31in (897mm); butt folded: 24.88in (632mm). **Weigh unloaded:** 6lb 7oz (2.93kg). **Barrel:** 10.75in (273mm), 4 grooves, right-hand twist. **Magazine:** 35-round detachable box. **Cyclic rate:** 700 rds/min. **Muzzle velocity:** c.1600 ft/sec (488 m/sec).

(PPS43)

Length: butt extended 31.81in (808mm); butt folded: 23.85in (606mm). **Weight**

unloaded: 7lb 5oz (3.33kg). **Barrel:** 10.00in (254mm), 4 grooves, right-hand twist. **Magazine:** 35-round detachable box. **Cyclic rate:** 700 rds/min. **Muzzle velocity:** c.1600 ft/sec (488 m/sec).

• AKS-74U
State Arsenals
5.45x39.5mm Soviet M1974

This weapon was first reported from Afghanistan late in 1983 and is a shortened version of the AKS 5.45mm assault rifle. The barrel and gas tube are much shorter and in order to reduce the violence of the gas action there is a cylindrical expansion chamber attached to the muzzle and fitted with a bell-shaped flash hider. The receiver top is slightly different from that of the normal AK series in that it is hinged at the front end and lifts forward on opening. There is a steel butt-stock which folds sideways and

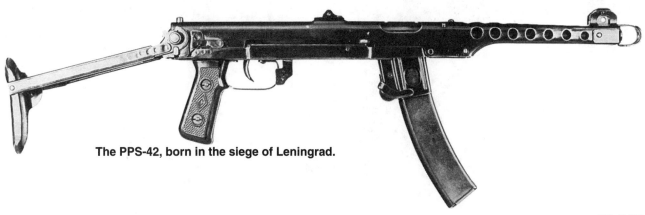

The PPS-42, born in the siege of Leningrad.

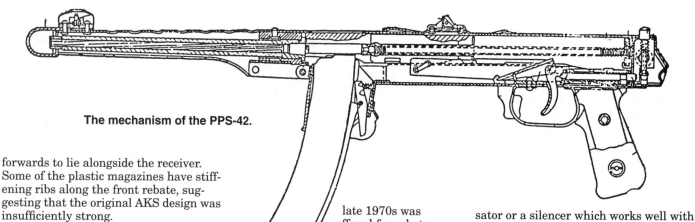

The mechanism of the PPS-42.

forwards to lie alongside the receiver. Some of the plastic magazines have stiffening ribs along the front rebate, suggesting that the original AKS design was insufficiently strong.

Length, butt extended: 28.74in (730mm); butt folded: 19.29in (490mm). **Weight unloaded:** 5lbs 14oz (2.70kg). **Barrel:** 8.15in (207mm). **Magazine:** 30-round detachable box. **Cyclic rate:** 700 rds/min. **Muzzle velocity:** 2410 ft/sec (735 m/sec)

SOUTH AFRICA

• Sanna 77

Dan Pienaar Enterprise (Pty) Ltd, Johannesburg.
9mm Parabellum

This was actually the Czech vz/25 (qv) sold in South Africa as the 'Sanna'. It is not entirely clear whether this weapon was bought in from Czechoslovakia, assembled in South Africa from Czech-supplied parts, or completely made in South Africa. It had the automatic fire capability removed, so that it could only fire single shots, and in the late 1970s was offered for sale to farmers, police and similar security organizations. For data, see Czech section under Samopal CZ 48 but note that only the 40-round box magazine was offered.

• BXP

Mechem, Silverton
9mm Parabellum

Developed in the early 1980s, this is a simple but effective weapon, built from stainless steel stampings and precision castings. It is very compact and with the butt folded can be fired one-handed like a pistol. The bolt is of the telescoped type, surrounding the rear end of the barrel when closed, and when forward it effectively seals all the apertures in the body, so preventing ingress of dirt and dust. The perforated barrel nut carries a screw-thread which will accept a compensator or a silencer which works well with standard or subsonic ammunition. There is a change-lever/safety catch on both sides of the receiver, and there is an extra notch on the bolt which will engage the sear should the weapon be dropped, so preventing accidental firing. The metal stock folds beneath the body with the shoulder pad acting as a forward hand grip and heat deflector. The exterior surfaces are coated with a rust-resistant finish which also acts as a life-long dry lubricant. The rate of fire is high, but the weapon is well-balanced and can be controlled quite easily.

Length, butt extended: 23.90in (607mm); butt folded: 15.24in (387mm). **Weight unloaded:** 5lb 11oz (2.60kg). **Barrel:** 8.19in (208mm), 6 grooves, right-hand twist. **Magazine:** 32-round detachable box. **Cyclic rate:** c.800 rds/min. **Muzzle velocity:** 1250 ft/sec (380 m/sec) (9mm Parabellum).

The 5.45mm AKSU-74; one of the first photographs to reach the West, this was taken by Afghan guerrillas who had taken the weapon from a Soviet soldier.

The South African BXP with its 'occluded eye sight'.

The BXP field-stripped.

SPAIN

• Star SI35

Bonifacio Echeverria SA, Eibar
9mm Largo

The Echeverria company of Eibar undertook a great deal of experimentation with submachine gun designs during the 1930s, and the SI35 is representative of their efforts - perhaps the most involved of the models. Stemming from a self-loader, the series stayed much the same in appearance and mechanism until c. 1942, when the company changed to more simple designs, broadly copying contemporary German models.

The SI35 incorporated delayed blowback operation performed by a locking block being driven up by the hammer (inside the bolt) to engage in the receiver body; after firing, the rearward movement of the bolt was delayed by the need to force the locking block down, out of engagement, against the pressure of the hammer and mainspring. A hold-open device indicated when the magazine was empty, and most unusual of all, a switch was provided to adjust the rate of fire to 300 or 700 rds/min.

While the weapon functioned reasonably well, it was unnecessarily complicated in design, and difficult and expensive to mass-produce. A small number appear to have been made and put into service in the closing months of the Spanish Civil War. A slightly altered version was offered to the United States Army in 1940 as the 'Atlantic', and the S135 was itself tested by the British Army at about the same time. Neither country considered the design suited to wartime production and the gun was rejected.

Length. 35.45in (900mm). **Weight unloaded:** 8lb 4oz (3.74kg). **Barrel:** 10.60in (269mm), 6 grooves, right-hand twist. **Magazine:** 10-, 30- or 40-round detachable box. **Cyclic rate:** 300 rds/min or 700 rds/min. **Muzzle velocity:** c.1350 ft/sec (412 m/sec).

• Labora

Industrio de Guerra do Cataluña, Cataluña
9mm Largo

This weapon was manufactured in the last few months of the Spanish Civil War in 1939 and, in view of this, is remarkable in being a most expensively machined design rather than the inferior weapon one might expect in such circumstances. This was probably due to the availability of skilled gunsmiths and

The Spanish Star SI-36, without magazine.

traditional machinery and the general absence of facilities for mass-production.

Of uncomplicated blowback design, the Labora is of interest because it is not a direct copy of any existing weapon, though the bolt has obvious affinities with early Schmeisser designs. The recoil spring is much stronger than average, which was probably necessitated by the combination of a powerful cartridge and an unusually light bolt.

Few examples of the Labora remain; with the end of the Spanish Civil War, production ceased, and it is unlikely that such a costly weapon will ever again be put into production.

Length: 31.75in (806mm). **Weight unloaded.** 9lb 6oz (4.25kg). **Barrel:** 10.25in (260mm), 4 grooves, right-hand twist. **Magazine:** 36-round detachable box. **Cyclic rate:** 750 rds/min. **Muzzle velocity:** c.1300 ft/sec (397 m/sec).

• Star Model Z45
Star, Bonifacio Echeverria y Compania SA, Guernica
9mm Largo, 9mm Parabellum

The Z45 was a Spanish adaptation of the German MP40 with the addition of some minor modifications. It was manufactured in Spain for several years from 1944 onwards and was adopted in the late 1940s by the Spanish police and armed forces. Star acquired the original German drawings in 1942 and used these for their basic design, but added some extra safety features such as a bolt lock to prevent accidental discharges. Selective fire was introduced, controlled by means of a two-position trigger, the initial movement of which gave semi-automatic fire and further pressure gave full automatic fire. The barrel was concealed inside a perforated jacket and retained in place by the muzzle compensator; by twisting the compensator it was possible to remove the barrel quite quickly. While interesting, this feature is not particularly necessary on a submachine-gun

although it was claimed by the manufacturers that simply by changing the barrel another caliber could be used. The Z45 was the first submachine-gun to use a fluted chamber, a refinement which was probably found necessary due to the higher pressures developed by the 9mm Largo cartridge.

The military version of the Z45 was fitted with the same type of folding stock as the original MP40, but another version was made with a full length wooden stock. This permitted more accuracy, and to some extent prevented the gun from climbing in automatic fire. Several South American and a few Middle Eastern countries are said to have bought the Z45, but precise numbers are not known.

Length, butt extended: 33.10in (841mm); butt folded: 22.85in (580mm). **Weight unloaded:** 8lb 8oz (3.87kg). **Barrel:** 7.75in (192mm), 6 grooves, right-hand twist. **Magazine:** 10- or 30-round detachable box. **Cyclic rate:** 450 rds/min. **Muzzle velocity:** c.1250 ft/sec (381 m/sec).

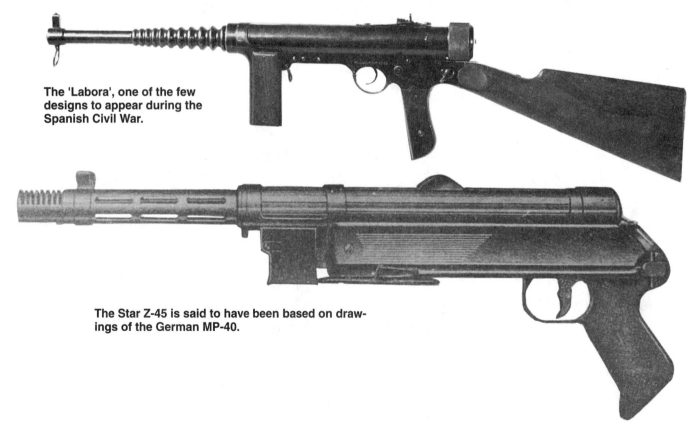

The 'Labora', one of the few designs to appear during the Spanish Civil War.

The Star Z-45 is said to have been based on drawings of the German MP-40.

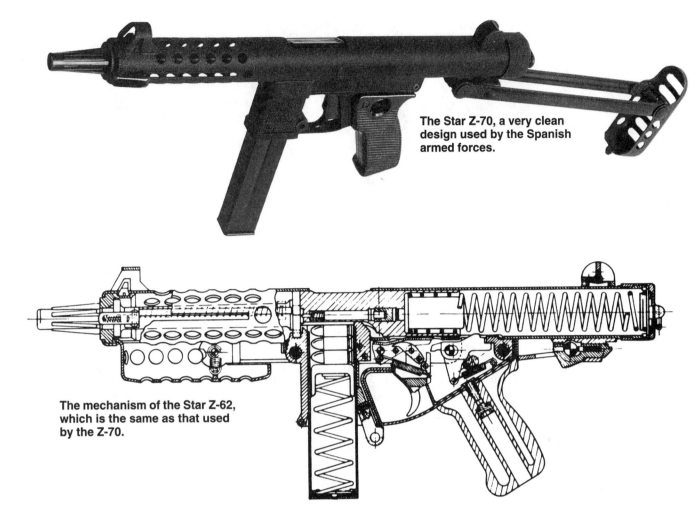

The Star Z-70, a very clean design used by the Spanish armed forces.

The mechanism of the Star Z-62, which is the same as that used by the Z-70.

• Pistola Ametralladora Star Model Z70/B

Star-Bonifacio Echeverria, Eibar
9mm Parabellum or 9mm Largo

The Star Z45 (above) was replaced in the mid-1960s by a new model, the Z62, which incorporated two unusual features: a hammer firing system, which was locked by the bolt except when the bolt was forward and the trigger pressed, and a double trigger which gave automatic fire when the upper portion was pressed and single shots when the lower portion was pressed. In service, it was found that this trigger mechanism gave trouble, and in 1971 the Z70/B appeared as a replacement. This, in 9mm Parabellum chambering, uses a conventional type of trigger and a separate selector lever above the grip. The lateral push-through safety catch of the Z62 was also discarded and replaced by a simple lever catch below the trigger guard. The rest of the design is conventional, a blowback weapon with ventilated barrel guard and folding steel stock. It went into service with the Spanish military and para-military forces in the early 1970s and remained until replaced by the Z/84 (below).

Rather confusingly, the 9mm Largo Z62 design threw off a variant model chambered for the 9mm Parabellum round which was called the Z/63. After the introduction of the Z70/B this Z63 model was continued in production, for export sale, but was re-named the Z/70.

Length, butt extended: 27.60in (701mm); butt folded: 18.90in (480mm). **Weight unloaded:** 6lb 5oz (2.87kg). **Barrel:** 7.91in (201mm). **Magazine:** 20-, 30- or 40-round detachable box. **Cyclic rate:** 550 rds/min. **Muzzle velocity:** 1248 ft/sec (380 m/sec).

• Pistola Ametralladora Star Model Z84

Star-Bonifacio Echeverria, Eibar
9mm Parabellum

With this design Star abandoned all that had gone before and started afresh. The result is a light, compact and efficient weapon which entered Spanish service in 1985 and has since been sold to several other countries. The design uses steel stampings and precision castings, and special attention has been paid to the feed system which will feed soft-point and semi-jacketed bullets as well as normal full-jacketed military ammunition. The Z84 fires from an open bolt, using the blowback system of operation, and the bolt is telescoped around the rear end of the barrel. The center of gravity is above the pistol grip, which contains the magazine, so allowing the gun to be fired single-handed with remarkable accuracy.

The bolt travels on two rails and there is ample clearance all round so that any dirt is unlikely to interfere with the action. There is a sliding fire selector on the left side and the safety is a sliding button inside the trigger guard. The bolt has three bents which hold it securely in any position, and there is also an automatic inertia safety unit which locks the bolt in the closed position. This is overridden by the cocking handle and is disconnected while the weapon is being fired.

Length, butt extended: 24.21in (615mm); butt folded: 16.14in (410mm). **Weight unloaded:** 6lb 10oz (3.0kg). **Barrel:** 8.46in (215mm). **Magazine:** 25- or 30-round detachable box. **Cyclic rate:** 600 rds/min. **Muzzle velocity:** 1312 ft/sec (400 m/sec).

The current Spanish service weapon is this Star Z-84.

SWEDEN

• Carl Gustav m/45

Carl Gustavs Stads Gevärfaktori, Eskilstuna
9mm Parabellum

World War II awakened Sweden to the realization that her own weapons were somewhat lacking, and the state arms factory 'Carl Gustav' set about remedying this as quickly as possible. As a stop-gap some Finnish Suomi submachine guns were made under license by Husqvarna Våpenfabrik, but by 1945 the Carl Gustav team had produced a design which was cheap and simple to manufacture. The m/45, as it became, is still used by the Swedish and other armies, and although it has passed through several minor variations in its long life, it retains its essential original characteristics.

The m/45 is a well-made gun of conventional blowback type, capable of automatic fire only. The tubular receiver resembles that of the Stan, but the barrel is concealed in a perforated jacket, and the stock hinges forward to fold along the right side of the weapon. The design was originally intended to use the 50-round Suomi magazine, but an excellent two-column 36-round magazine was also developed and the magazine housing was made detachable so that the correct housing could be quickly fitted. In due course the 36-round magazine became standard and, indeed, proved so reliable that it has been widely adopted for other designs in other countries, and the magazine housing became a fixed pattern changing the nomenclature to m/45/B. The m/45/C has a bayonet lug, and the

m/45/E has the option of single-shot fire. The m/45 is currently built under license in Egypt as the 'Port Said' and was also license-built in Indonesia.
Length, butt extended: 31.75in (806mm); butt folded: 21.75in (552mm). **Weight unloaded:** 7lb 9oz (3.43kg). **Barrel:** 8.00in (203mm), 6 grooves, right-hand twist. **Magazine:** 36- or 50-round detachable box. **Cyclic rate:** 600 rds/min. **Muzzle velocity:** c.1250 ft/sec (38l m/sec).

SWITZERLAND

• Solothurn SI-100 ('Steyr-Solothurn')

Waffenfabrik Solothurn AG, Solothurn
7.63mm Mauser, 7.65mm Parabellum, 9mm Parabellum, 9mm Steyr, 9mm Mauser Export

The history of this weapon shows the shifts to which German companies went to in order to get round the restrictions of

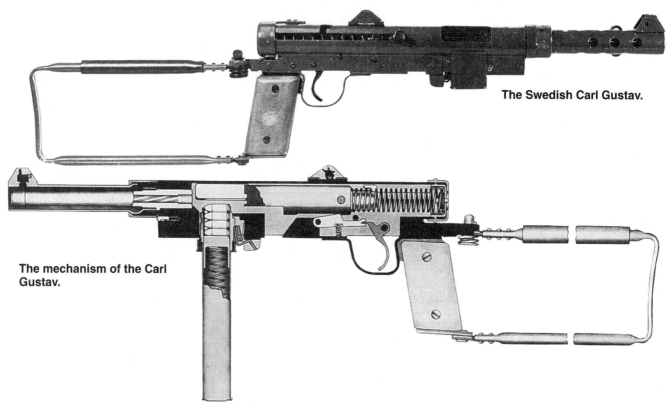

The Swedish Carl Gustav.

The mechanism of the Carl Gustav.

The Steyr-Solothurn SI-100.

the Versailles Treaty in the 1920-34 period. Manufacture of submachine-guns was forbidden to several German firms; design, however, was not. Rheinmetall designed this weapon, then passed the designs to a Swiss subsidiary, the Waffenfabrik Solothurn AG who made the prototypes, carried out the testing and made whatever modifications were necessary. But they were not equipped for mass production and Switzerland, even then, had restrictions on weapon export. So the prototype and manufacturing drawings now went to the Waffenfabrik Steyr in Austria where the actual manufacture was done. The weapon was adopted by the Austrian and Hungarian armies and sold widely in South America and the Far East. It was also bought by Portugal in 1935, and the Portuguese Guarda Fiscal were still using them into the mid-1970s. Manufacture ceased in 1940. Although the official submachine gun of the German Army was the MP40, the Solothurn was issued in quite large numbers as the Maschinenpistole 34(ö) and remained in service until 1945.

The Steyr-Solothurn is, without doubt, the Rolls-Royce of submachine-guns; machined from solid steel throughout, the quality and finish is perhaps the highest ever seen in this class of weapon.

Its design is quite conventional, a blowback firing from an open bolt, with a jacketed barrel, and it closely resembles the Bergmann MP28. One unique feature was the placing of the return spring in a tube inside the butt, connecting it to the bolt by means of a steel strut. Another was the formation of a quick-loading device for the magazine in the magazine housing. The ammunition was supplied in chargers, and a suitable charger slot is cut in the upper surface of the side magazine housing. The empty magazine slides into a secondary housing beneath this slot, the charger is placed in the top, and a sweep of the thumb loads the rounds into the magazine. Once loaded, the magazine can be quickly removed from its bottom position and replaced in to firing position.

Length: 33.50in (851mm). **Weight unloaded:** 8lb 8oz (3.87kg). **Barrel:** 7.75in (196mm), 6 grooves, right-hand twist. **Magazine:** 32-round detachable box. **Cyclic rate:** 500 rds/min. **Muzzle velocity:** c.1250 ft/sec (380 m/sec).

• MP41/44
Waffenfabrik Bern, Bern
9mm Parabellum

The MP41/44 was probably the most complicated and over-designed submachine-gun ever made, undoubtedly the most expensive, and should never have been allowed into military service. The design was by

Colonel Fürrer, Superintendent of the Federal Arms Factory; the factory had machinery for making Parabellum pistols, and Furrer became obsessed with the toggle action, designing an enormous variety of impractical ways of using this action on weapons of every sort, including heavy anti-aircraft and anti-tank guns. In 1940, when invasion by the German Amy seemed highly probable, the Swiss Army was panicked into making the decision to adopt this design; this was doubtless a political decision, since better designs were available within Switzerland. Indeed, a promising SIG design was turned down in favor of the Fürrer model.

It took almost three years to get the MP41/44 into production and in the following two years only about 4,000 were made, manufacture being slow and difficult. The principal difficulty lay in the mechanism. The weapon used a Parabellum-style toggle lock, but laid on its side, and with an addition link to the toggle to act as a form of accelerator to the bolt. This, of course, all had to be concealed within a casing, which made the weapon extremely clumsy to handle. The design was so complex that soldiers were forbidden to field strip them, and only armorers were allowed that luxury.

Length: 30.50in (775mm). **Weight unloaded:** 11lb 7oz (5.19kg). **Barrel:** 9.75in (247mm), 6 grooves, right-hand

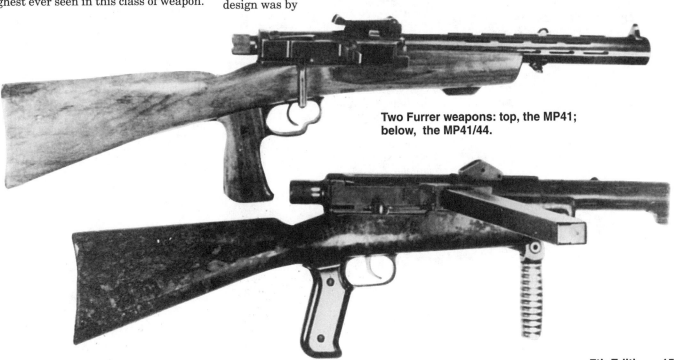

Two Furrer weapons: top, the MP41; below, the MP41/44.

The SIG MKMO with magazine folded and unfolded; the resemblance to the Hungarian 39M is plain.

twist. **Magazine:** 40-round detachable box. **Cyclic rate:** 900 rds/min. **Muzzle velocity:** c.1300 ft/sec (396 m/sec).

• MP43/44

Société Anonyme Suisse Hispano-Suiza, Geneva
9mm Parabellum

As might be expected, the Swiss Army was soon disillusioned with the MP41/44, particularly with its slow supply, and in 1943 they began looking about for something 'off the shelf'. The Finnish Suomi design appeared practical, and they therefore obtained a license from the Finns and set the Hispano-Suiza factory to make it. The weapon was scarcely changed other than to fit Swiss sling swivels and simplify the sights. The drum magazine was not adopted, a 50-round double-row box being used instead. With this the Swiss finally had a serviceable and inexpensive submachine gun which remained in service until the 1960s and is still held in reserve stocks.

Length: 34.00in (863mm). **Weight unloaded:** 10lb 8oz (4.76kg). **Barrel:** 12.50in (318mm), 6 grooves, right-hand twist. **Magazine:** 50-round detachable box. **Cyclic rate:** 800 rds/min. **Muzzle velocity:** c.1300 ft/sec (396 m/sec).

• Machine Pistol MKMO (or 'Neuhausen')

Schweizerische Industrie-Gesellschaft (SIG), Neuhausen-am-Rheinfalls
7.65mm Parabellum, 9mm Parabellum, 7.63mm Mauser, 9mm Mauser Export

This design appeared in 1933 from SIG, having been developed by the Ende brothers and Pal Kiraly, then employees of SIG. Like Kiraly's later efforts (e.g. the Hungarian M39) it was a full-stocked weapon resembling a rifle, used a two-part bolt to give delayed blowback operation of the breech (since the original was chambered for the 9mm Mauser Export round), and had a magazine which folded forward and up into a slot in the forend. It fired only in the full-automatic mode, and the whole weapon was luxuriously manufactured from solid steel to a very high standard. As a result, it did not sell in very large numbers, though it was manufactured from 1935 until early in 1938. Most weapons were in 7.63mm or 9mm Mauser, though the two Parabellum calibers were also made in small numbers.

A variant model was the MKPO, made for sale to police forces. This was to the same general design but had a shorter barrel and was perhaps more convenient

to handle. It also had a smaller magazine and a knob-type cocking handle rather than the hook type of the MKMO.

In 1937 SIG saw that there was little future in this expensive weapon and redesigned it, doing away with Kiraly's bolt and turning the weapon into a simple blowback. The result was known as the MKMS, and there was also a short-barreled version, the MKPS. Neither of these produced many sales before war broke out in 1939 and shut off Switzerland from its export markets.

(MKMO)

Length: 40.35in (1025mm). **Weight unloaded:** 9lb 4oz (4.19kg). **Barrel:** 19.69in (500mm), 6 grooves, right-hand twist. **Magazine:** 40-round detachable box. **Cyclic rate:** 900 rds/min. **Muzzle velocity:** c.1640 ft/sec (500 m/sec) (9mm Mauser).

(MKPO)

Length: 32.28in (820mm). **Weight unloaded:** 8lb 6oz (3.80kg). **Barrel:** 11.81in (300mm), 6 grooves, right-hand twist. **Magazine:** 30-round detachable box. **Cyclic rate:** 900 rds/min. **Muzzle velocity:** c.1312 ft/sec (400 m/sec) (9mm Parabellum).

• Machine pistol 48 (MP48)

Schweizerische Industrie-Gesellschaft (SIG), Neuhausen-am-Rheinfalls
9mm Parabellum

The MP48 was among the first submachine guns to be completely designed in-house by Schweizerische Industrie

The SIG MKPS was a shorter version of the MKMO for police use.

The SIG MP310 was their final attempt to interest armies in submachine guns.

Gesellschaft (SIG), although they had been famous international arms manufacturers for many years. Their previous weapons of this type had been noted for excellent finish and careful machining, but they were often relatively heavy. The MP48 was unusual for its day in using precision castings for many parts instead of the more normal stampings or pressings. If properly made, precision castings do not require machining, and this was what SIG was anxious to avoid in order to keep the price down. The MP48 followed two other models, the MP44 and the MP46, both of which generally resembled the MP48 and shared the folding magazine. This was a SIG innovation in the early 1930s and was continued for some years despite little success in the sales field. No mechanical safety was provided on the MP48, and it was taken that this would be applied by folding the magazine forwards under the barrel, so cutting off the ammunition supply. A spring-loaded shutter closed the feed opening when the magazine was folded and, of course, the weapon was easier to carry. A tubular steel stock could be retracted to reduce the overall length.

Despite its novelties, the MP48 offered very little that other cheaper guns did not also offer and only a few sales were made, mostly outside Europe.

Length, butt extended: 28.00in (711mm); butt folded: 22.50in (570mm). **Weight unloaded:** 6lb 7oz (2.92kg). **Barrel:** 7.75in (196mm), 6 grooves, right-hand twist. **Magazine:** 40-round detachable box. **Cyclic rate:** 700 rds/min. **Muzzle velocity:** c.1250 ft/sec (381 m/sec).

• Machine pistol 310 (MP310)

Schweizerische Industrie-Gesellschaft, Neuhausen-am-Rheinfalls
9mm Parabellum

Developed by SIG in the early 1950s (from the MP48), the MP310 was a standard pattern of blowback-operated submachine gun, although several unusual features were incorporated in the design. The magazine was a folding pattern, released by a spring-catch on the left side of the magazine housing to fold forward underneath the barrel. The trigger mechanism was constructed to give a two-stage pull, the first of which was used to fire single shots and the latter full automatic fire and a drum-type rear sight was used with settings for 50, 100, 200 and 300m. Despite the attractive features of the MP310, and the substitution by SIG of plastics and precision castings for some of their earlier weapons' expensive machined components, the gun failed to sell in large numbers; it is probably true to say that there were war-surplus guns to be had at far cheaper prices, and that this militated against the SIG weapon. It was adopted by Swiss police, and a few were sold overseas, but the lack of success seems to have decided SIG to abandon this class of weapon and they have, wisely, stayed out of the submachine gun field ever since.

Length, butt extended: 28.95in (735mm); butt folded: 24.00in (610mm). **Weight unloaded:** 7lb 0oz (3.15kg). **Barrel:** 7.83in (200mm), 6 grooves, right-hand twist. **Magazine:** 40-round detachable box. **Cyclic rate:** 900 rds/min. **Muzzle velocity:** c.1200 ft/sec (365 m/sec).

• Machine pistol 'Rexim-Favor'

Société Anonyme Suisse Rexim, Geneva
9mm Parabellum

The Rexim Company entered the arms business in the 1950s with a design which some aver was stolen from the French, though whether or not there is anything in that tale is of little consequence; the subsequent development of the weapon, however, was just as involved. Although the Rexim company was set up in Switzerland, the weapons were made for them in Spain, and samples were hawked round the world with little success until the company failed in 1957. After this, the Spanish manufacturers marketed the gun under their own name, La Coruña, with equally little success.

Strictly speaking, only the prototype, distinguishable by a smooth exposed barrel, was called the 'Favor', the production models, with perforated barrel jackets, being the 'FV Mark 4'. A variety of butt patterns and barrel lengths were produced as alternative models during prototype development, and offered in the company's somewhat optimistic brochures, but the basic configuration of the weapon remained the same.

The operation of the Rexim was unnecessarily complicated, firing as it did from a closed bolt by allowing an independent annular hammer to be released by the trigger to operate the firing pin. So far as can be ascertained the only service use of the Rexim was in Turkey where a number (without barrel jackets but with bayonet fittings) were issued as

The Rexim-Favor M4.

The well-known shape of the Thompson M1928A1, with a box magazine in place.

the 'Model 68' and remained in use until the mid-1970s.

Length, butt extended: 34.35in (873mm); butt folded: 24.35in (617mm). **Weight unloaded:** 10lb 5oz (4.67kg). **Barrel:** 13.35in (339mm), 6 grooves, right-hand twist. **Magazine:** 32-round detachable box (German MP40 magazine). **Cyclic rate:** 600 rds/min. **Muzzle velocity:** c.1400 ft/sec (427 m/sec).

U.S.A.

• US Submachine Gun, Caliber 45 M1928A1 ('Thompson')

Manufactured by Colt's Patent Firearms Manufacturing Corporation, Hartford, Connecticut, and Savage Arms Company Corporation, Utica, New York, for Auto-Ordnance Corporation, Bridgeport, Connecticut
45 ACP

This was the first model of the Thompson submachine gun to be definitely used by the military, although several models were offered in the 1920s as 'Military Models'. The 1928 version was undoubtedly used by the United States Marine Corps in Nicaragua and also by the United States Coast Guard. It was directly derived from the 1921 model, which it closely resembled, and some 1928 models appear to be 1921 models modified and overstamped with the new date. The so-called 'Navy' model has the horizontal foregrip, sling swivels and muzzle compensator, whereas the civilian model of the same year has the more familiar vertical foregrip with the finger

notches. Less than 400 were taken into service between 1928 and 1934, and serious manufacture did not start until 1939. Some of these pre-war Thompsons still survive in the hands of American police forces.

The early Thompson submachine guns made use of the much-disputed Blish principle, a method of slowing down the opening of the breech by the frictional forces created by the action of two blocks of metal sliding over each other at an oblique angle. Under high pressure the two surfaces freeze, but move when the pressure falls. The efficiency of this locking mechanism remains questionable, but if it did nothing else it at least helped to slow the cyclic rate of fire to a controllable level.

Length: 33.75in (857mm). **Weight unloaded:** 10lb 12oz (4.88kg). **Barrel:** 10.50in (266mm), 6 grooves, right-hand twist. **Magazine:** 18-, 20- or 30-round detachable box or 50- or 100-round drum. **Cyclic rate:** 800 rds/min. **Muzzle velocity:** c.910 ft/sec (277 m/sec).

• U.S. Submachine Guns, Caliber 45 M1 and M1A1 ('Thompson')

Savage Arms Corporation, Utica, NY for Auto-Ordnance Corporation, Bridgeport, Conn.
45 ACP

When the Thompson gun was required in large numbers during the early years of World War II, it was soon found that the manufacturing processes were not well suited to mass-production.

By 1942, when Lend-Lease was getting into full swing, it became imperative to simplify the weapon in order to keep up the supplies. The Savage Arms Corporation, who were manufacturing the M1928 gun, undertook to modify the design and the result was the M1, which functioned by simple blowback principles rather than by the delayed blowback of the previous models, and the bolt was slightly heavier as a result. The bolt handle was moved to the right-hand side, and the sights were considerably simplified. The drum magazine was dropped in favor of the 20- and 30-round boxes, and the muzzle compensator disappeared. The M1A1 further simplified the design by introducing a fixed firing pin in place of the previous hammer.

The Thompson in all its various forms was a popular gun, and it frequently found favor in place of the Sten and M3 which replaced it. It continued in production until 1945, reappeared in the Korean War and was still being offered to Asian countries under the Off-shore Program as late as 1960. It is no longer in service with any major military force, but the guns were so well made that they will last for a good many years yet, and will be seen periodically for many years to come.

Length: 32.00in (813mm). **Weight unloaded:** 10lb 9oz (4.82kg). **Barrel:** 10.50in (266mm), 6 grooves, right-hand twist. **Magazine:** 20- or 30-round detachable box. **Cyclic rate:** 700 rds/min. **Muzzle velocity:** c.910 ft/sec (277 m/sec).

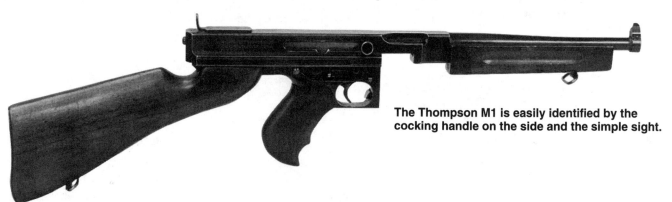

The Thompson M1 is easily identified by the cocking handle on the side and the simple sight.

The Hyde of 1935.

• Hyde Submachine Gun Model 35

Marlin Firearms Corporation, New Haven, Connecticut
45 ACP

George J. Hyde developed a number of submachine gun designs during the period 1935-43 and the Model 35 was one of the best. Although bearing obvious affinities in shape with the Thompson, it differed mechanically in that it was a plain blowback firing from an open bolt. The principal fault was purely psychological—the cocking handle protruded from the rear of the receiver and oscillated in front of the firer's eye as the gun fired.

Tested by the United States Army late in 1939, the Hyde was found to be a reliable and effective weapon in most respects, but there were a number of design deficiencies in the firing mechanism and magazine which caused it to be rejected. The British Army tested the Model 35 shortly afterwards, and the same defects were noted. Hyde was by this time working on newer designs and the Model 35 was abandoned.

Length: 35.00in (888mm). **Weight unloaded:** 9lb 9oz (4.34kg). **Barrel:** 11.25in (286mm), 7 grooves, right-hand twist. **Magazine:** 20-round detachable box. **Cyclic rate:** c.750 rds/min. **Muzzle velocity:** c.900 ft/sec (275 m/sec).

• Reising Submachine Gun Model 50

Harrington & Richardson Arms Company, Worcester, Massachusetts
45 ACP

This weapon was designed just before World War II and about 100,000 of this and the later Model 55 were made between 1941 and 1945. Most of those produced went to the US Marine Corps, though a few were sold to Allied countries and some were given to the Soviet Army.

The Reising was an ingenious design which fired from a closed bolt. The internal mechanism was complicated and the pressing of the trigger set off a series of inter-related movements which culminated in the striking of the primer, a far remove from the simplicity of most open-bolt blowback mechanisms. Automatic fire was really a series of semi-automatic shots in sequence, since the mechanism always operates in the same way. Another unusual feature was the 'semi-locking' of the bolt on firing, by being cammed upwards into a recess in the receiver. Cocking was performed by pulling back a lever concealed inside a slot under the fore-end.

The Reising proved entirely unsuitable for combat use; the complicated mechanism made no allowance for the presence of dirt or grit, which promptly jammed it, and the breech-locking recess soon attracted fouling or dirt which prevented the block rising and thus prevented the weapon firing at all. These shortcomings were discovered in the Guadalcanal operation, where most Marines jettisoned their Reisings in favor of anything else they could find. The weapons which remained were withdrawn and issued to police and security forces in the USA where, in the absence of combat conditions, they performed quite adequately.

Length: 35.75in (907mm). **Weight unloaded:** 6lb 12oz (3.10kg). **Barrel:** 11.00in (279mm), 6 grooves, right-hand twist. **Magazine:** 12- or 20-round detachable box. **Cyclic rate:** 550 rds/min. **Muzzle velocity:** c.920 ft/sec (280 m/sec).

• Reising Submachine Gun Model 55

Harrington & Richardson Arms Company, Worcester, Massachusetts
45 ACP

The Model 55 was an attempt to produce a slightly lighter version of the Model 50 and was a more militarized-looking weapon. Unfortunately it retained the same mechanism of the Model 50 and thus inherited all its many faults. The changes were: to cut down the wooden stock and substitute a folding wire butt, to add a wooden pistol grip, and to eliminate the muzzle compensator. It was no more successful than its predecessor.

Length, butt extended: 31.00in (787mm); butt folded: 22.50in (570mm). **Weight unloaded:** 6lb 4oz (2.89kg). **Barrel:** 10.50in (266mm), 6 grooves, right-hand twist. **Magazine:** 12- or 20-round detachable box. **Cyclic rate:** 500 rds/min. **Muzzle velocity:** c.920 ft/sec (280 m/sec).

• Submachine Gun UD M42 ('United Defense')

High Standard Manufacturing Company, Hamden, Conn.; Marlin Firearms Company, New Haven, Conn.
9mm Parabellum; 45 ACP

The UD M42 was designed prior to American involvement in World War II, by Carl Swebilius of High Standard, but was not made until late 1941 or early 1942, and so became the Model 42. The prototypes and early models were made by High Standard and the production run of about 15,000 in 9mm caliber by the Marlin Firearms Company to meet a Dutch order; most were shipped to the Dutch East Indies, but when the Japanese invasion of the Indies stopped that,

The Reising M50.

The UD M42. Note the double magazine formed by welding together two magazines back-to-back.

the balance was taken by the United States government. Most were used by the Office of Strategic Services (OSS), though a small number appear to have been sent to various allied countries.

The UD M42 was rather more complicated than the normal submachine gun, but it was very well made from expensive machined parts and it performed well in mud and dirt. A 45-caliber version was made, but it was unfortunate in appearing just after the Thompson had got into full production, thus never gaining a military contract. The gun fired from an open bolt and the firing pin was operated by a hammer as the bolt closed. The bolt handle was unusual in that it was a slide which did not move with the bolt and kept the bolt-way clear of dirt.

Length: 32.25in (820mm). **Weight unloaded:** 9lb 1oz (4.11kg). **Barrel:** 11.00in (279mm), 6 grooves, right-hand twist. **Magazine:** 20-round detachable box. **Cyclic rate:** 700 rds/min. **Muzzle velocity:** c.1310 ft/sec (399 m/sec).

• US Submachine Gun, Caliber 45 M2 ('Hyde')

Marlin Firearms Company, New Haven, Conn.
45 ACP

Often called the 'Hyde' after its designer, this was another of the many weapons tested in the USA in the early years of World War II when there was an urgent need for submachine guns and no fixed notions of how best to make them. Although the M2 was a relatively simple

and straightforward design, it was not easy to make, and when the Marlin company received a contract in mid-1942, the first production models did not appear until May 1943. By that time the M3 (below) had been approved for service and was in production, and manufacture of the M2 was stopped after no more than 400 had been made. The M2 performed well on test and appears to have been reliable and accurate. It was a simple blowback design, though the bolt was of peculiar shape with the rear end being quite large in diameter and the front half long and slender. The receiver was built up from a seamless tubular section and a steel forging, and it appears that the machining and finishing of this element was the Achilles heel of the design. It was a pity, because the M2 shoots quite well, feels good, and would probably have been a good deal more popular than was the M3.

Length: 32.00in (813mm). **Weight unloaded:** 9lb 4oz (4.19kg). **Barrel:** 12.0in (305mm), 6 grooves, right-hand twist. **Magazine:** 20- or 30-round detachable box. **Cyclic rate:** 500 rds/min. **Muzzle velocity:** c.960 ft/sec (292 m/sec).

• US Submachine Gun, Caliber 45 M3

Guide Lamp Division of General Motors, Detroit, Mich.
45 ACP, 9mm Parabellum.

In the early years of World War II, the United States government

was engaged in testing a large number of privately produced submachine guns, few of which showed any sign of fulfilling the army's specification. Eventually, a design team was formed at the Aberdeen Proving Ground, given a Sten gun, and told to produce a similar weapon and within two years a new design was in production.

This was the M3—a simple, robust, cheap and entirely adequate gun which fulfilled the specification in every way, although it was later found to have some defects, particularly in the magazine. As a first try at designing a submachine gun it was, nevertheless, a remarkable effort. It was approved for service in December 1942 and remained in first line service until 1960. It was designed for mass-production and the construction is mainly of stampings and pressings; there are few machining operations, and the barrel was swaged in a single process. The rate of fire was unusually low, but this allowed single shots to be fired by snatching the trigger (as no change lever was incorporated), and it also made for steadiness when firing bursts as the gun recoil was controllable. The bolt was cocked by means of a crank handle on the right side of the receiver, and safety was provided by a hinged flap on the ejection port; this had a metal stud on its inner surface which, when the flap was closed, engaged on a safety recess in the bolt if the bolt was closed, or into a notch on the face of the bolt if it was cocked.

Inevitably, some minor mistakes were made. One was in the magazine,

The M2 or Hyde-Inland almost got into production but was overtaken by the M3.

The M3, showing the retracting crank on the side of the receiver.

which gave constant feed troubles throughout the gun's life. Another was in the choice of materials for some of the earlier models, whose components broke too easily. But for all this, the M3 was practical and cheap, which was all that was asked of it. It had one interesting feature in that it could be converted to fire 9mm Parabellum merely by changing the bolt and the barrel, and by inserting a magazine adapter, thus allowing the Sten magazine to be used. All this could be done without tools. Very few were so modified and almost all of M3 type fired the 45 ACP cartridge.

Length, butt extended: 30.0in (762mm).
Length, stock retracted: 22.75in (577mm).
Weight unloaded: 8lb 2oz (3.70kg). **Barrel:** 8.0in (203mm), 4 grooves, right-hand twist. **Magazine:** 30-round detachable box.
Cyclic rate: 450 rds/min. **Muzzle velocity:** c.900 ft/sec (274 m/sec).

• US Submachine Gun, Caliber 45 M3A1

Guide Lamp Division of General Motors, Detroit, Mich.; Ithaca Gun Company, Ithaca, NY.
45 ACP

Although the M3 appeared to be simple to produce, it was found that still further improvement could be made and, at the same time, some of the deficiencies and faults of the original design could be corrected. In December 1944, the M3A1 was accepted for service. It differed from the M3 by eliminating the bolt retracting mechanism altogether, and the firer cocked the bolt by the unusual method of inserting his finger into a recess in the

bolt and simply pulling it back. For this to happen the ejection opening was enlarged and so was the hinged cover which now had the metal stud positioned so as to engage in the safety recess when the bolt was forward or into the finger-hole when it was cocked.

An oil reservoir was placed in the pistol grip and a variety of minor improvements were incorporated, as well as some ingenious ways of using various parts as tools to strip other parts. The troublesome magazine remained, but the frequency of jamming was reduced to some extent by fitting it with a plastic dust cap. Even so, the weapon never achieved any great popularity and it was usually referred to in rather disparaging terms; 'Grease Gun' was among the more polite. The 30-caliber M1 carbine was more sought after, and so the M3 played only a minor role in World War II and in Korea. About 700,000 were made in the United States, and many more have been produced in other countries who either made it under license or simply copied it.

Length, butt extended: 29.75in (756mm); butt folded: 22.75in (577mm). **Weight unloaded:** 8lb 3oz (3.71kg). **Barrel:** 8.00in (203mm), 4 grooves, right-hand twist. **Magazine:** 30-round detachable box. **Cyclic rate:** 400 rds/min. **Muzzle velocity:** c.910 ft/sec (277 m/sec).

• Ingram Submachine Gun Model 6

Police Ordnance Company, Los Angeles, Calif.
9mm Parabellum, 38 Super and 45 ACP

The Ingram is not a particularly inspired design, but it is one of the very few which have reached any sort of quantity production in the United States since the end of World War II. The Model 6 appeared in the early 1950s and was sold in limited numbers to various police forces, the Cuban Navy, the Peruvian Army and the Thailand forces. It was a simple design, and its main feature was that it had no selector lever. Semi-automatic fire was produced by pulling the trigger back to an intermediate position. Fully automatic fire occurred when the trigger was pulled fully back. The system was reliable and straightforward. Much trouble was taken to ensure that the Ingram could be made with the minimum of special tools, and the receiver, barrel and magazine were all made from steel tubing. There was little machining and no need for expensive stamping machinery.

The Ingram failed because no real market existed for it on the American continent at the time, and in Europe the market was flooded with cheap weapons from the war. Ingram was probably lucky to sell as many as he did.

Length: 30.00in (762mm). **Weight unloaded:** 7lb 4oz (3.29kg). **Barrel:** 9.00in (228mm), 6 grooves, right-hand twist. **Magazine:** 30-round detachable box. **Cyclic rate:** 600 rds/min. **Muzzle velocity:** c.900 ft/sec (274 m/sec).

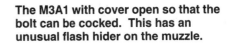

The M3A1 with cover open so that the bolt can be cocked. This has an unusual flash hider on the muzzle.

The Ingram Model 6 clung to the Thompson shape.

• Ingram Model 10
Military Armament Corporation,
Powder Springs, Ga.
45 ACP, 9mm Parabellum

Gordon Ingram left the Police Ordnance Corporation and in 1970 developed this submachine gun for the Military Armament Corporation. The Model 10 was extremely compact and built of steel stampings. The bolt was of the 'over-hung' or 'wrap-round' type, and the magazine was fed through the pistol grip; these two features ensured that the center of balance is over the grip, which gave a very steady weapon and even allowed it to be fired with one hand quite successfully. A cocking handle protruded through the top of the receiver and was notched to allow the line of sight to pass; to lock the bolt, this handle could be rotated through 90°, and this, of course obstructed the sight line and acted as an indication that the weapon was locked in a safe condition.

The barrel of the Ingram was threaded to accept a 'sound suppressor'; this was similar to a silencer but only muffled the sound of discharge and made no attempt to reduce the velocity of the bullet. As a result, the crack of a supersonic bullet could still be heard, but the suppression of the gun sound made it difficult for the target to discover the location of the gun firing at him.

A Model 11 submachine gun was also made; this was of the same shape and appearance as the Model 10, but smaller in all dimensions, since it was chambered for the 9mm Short cartridge. One of the very few submachine guns ever chambered for this round, it was suggested as a possible police weapon.

Small quantities of the Model 10 were sold to several countries, but the company was undercapitalized and went into liquidation. The design then passed through the hands of several other firms who attempted to promote the weapon with little success until production finally ceased some time in the mid-1980s. The Ingram received enormous publicity and was prominently seen in several films

and TV series, but in real life it failed to achieve the success it was thought to deserve.

Length: 10.5in (267mm). **Weight unloaded:** 6lb 4oz (2.84kg). **Barrel:** 5.75in (146mm), 5 grooves, right-hand twist. **Magazine:** 30-round detachable box. **Cyclic rate:** 1145 rds/min. **Muzzle velocity:** c.900 ft/sec (275 m/sec).

• Commando (XM177E2)
Colt Industries, Hartford, Conn.
5.56x45mm M193

After the success of the AR-15 as a rifle in the hands of the US Army in Vietnam, it occurred to someone that a shorter and handier version might be a useful weapon, particularly for jungle and close-quarter combat. As a result of this suggestion, the Colt designers produced the 'Commando', which, as the XM177E2, was adopted by the US Army's Special Forces.

Mechanically, the Commando is identical with the AR-15, but the barrel length was halved and the butt mounted on a telescoping tube. The shortening of the barrel, combined with the use of a cartridge originally designed for a full-length rifle, led to considerable muzzle flash and blast, so that a large flash suppressor had to be fitted. The short barrel also upset the ballistics, since the propelling charge is only just consumed by the time the bullet leaves the muzzle and the accuracy of the Commando does not compare to that of the AR15. Nevertheless, as a short-range weapon it is quite adequate and thus, in spite of its caliber, it is classed as a submachine gun.

Length, butt extended: 31.0in (787mm); butt folded: 28.00in (711 mm). **Weight unloaded:** 6lb 9oz (2.97kg). **Barrel:** 10.0in (254mm), 6 grooves, right-hand twist. **Magazine:** 20- or 30-round detachable box. **Cyclic rate:** 750 rds/min. **Muzzle velocity:** c.3000 ft/sec (915 m/sec).

But the Ingram Model 10 was completely different.

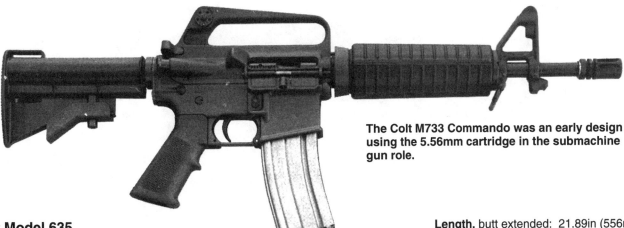

The Colt M733 Commando was an early design using the 5.56mm cartridge in the submachine gun role.

• Colt Model 635

Colt's Manufacturing Co, Hartford, Conn.
9x19mm Parabellum

This weapon, introduced in 1987, might be considered as the Commando redesigned to use a more suitable cartridge. It uses the basic body and configuration of the M16 rifle but with a short telescoping butt which is exceptionally rigid when extended, and with a blowback bolt assembly. As with the rifle, the submachine gun fires from a closed bolt, and the action remains open after the last shot. The original magazine housing of the M16 remains, modified internally to take a narrower 9mm magazine. Operation and controls are the same as the M16 rifle, so that troops trained on the rifle can easily adapt to the submachine gun. It was adopted by the US Drug Enforcement Agency and law enforcement agencies and by the US Marine Corps.

Length, butt extended: 28.74in (730mm). **Length,** butt folded: 25.59in (650mm). **Weight unloaded:** 5lb 11oz (2.59kg). **Barrel:** 10.50in (267mm), 6 grooves, right-hand twist. **Magazine:** 20- or 32-round detachable box. **Cyclic rate:** 900 rds/min. **Muzzle velocity:** c.1300 ft/sec (396 m/sec).

• Ruger MP-9

Sturm, Ruger & Co., Southport, Conn.
9x19mm Parabellum

This weapon was designed by Uzi Gal, designer of the Uzi submachine gun, in the early 1980s. It was originally to be manufactured in Canada, but this fell through and the design was eventually sold to Sturm, Ruger who made some minor changes and put the weapon into production in 1994.

The frame and lower receiver are of Zytel synthetic material, the upper portion of the receiver being of steel. Internally the operation is similar to that of the Uzi, using a telescoping bolt, but firing from a closed bolt. The pistol grip is at the center of balance and acts as the magazine housing, and behind the grip is an openwork frame which runs back and up to the rear of the receiver. The folding butt is hinged and jointed so as to fold down and lie alongside this fixed openwork frame when not required.

Length, butt extended: 21.89in (556mm); butt folded: 14.80in (376mm). **Weight unloaded:** 6lb 10oz (3.0kg). **Barrel:** 6.81in (173mm), 6 grooves, right-hand twist. **Magazine:** 34-round detachable box. **Cyclic rate:** 600 rds/min. **Muzzle velocity:** c.1148 ft/sec (350 m/sec).

• La France M16K

La France Specialties, San Diego, Calif.
45 ACP

Designed for use by special forces and similar units, the M16K utilizes the butt and other parts of the M16 rifle, and allies them to a blowback system of operation, firing from a closed bolt. This, combined with the straight-line layout, means that there is a better chance of a first-round hit with this weapon than with most submachine guns firing from open bolts. The forend and handguard are cylindrical, surrounding the barrel, and there is a short pronged flash-hider on the muzzle.

Length: 26.61in (676mm). **Weight unloaded:** 8lb 8oz (3.86kg). **Barrel:** 7.24in (184mm). **Magazine:** 30-round detachable box. **Cyclic rate:** 625 rds/min. **Muzzle velocity:** c.853 ft/sec (260 m/sec).

The Colt Model 635 resembled the Commando but fires the 9mm Parabellum cartridge.

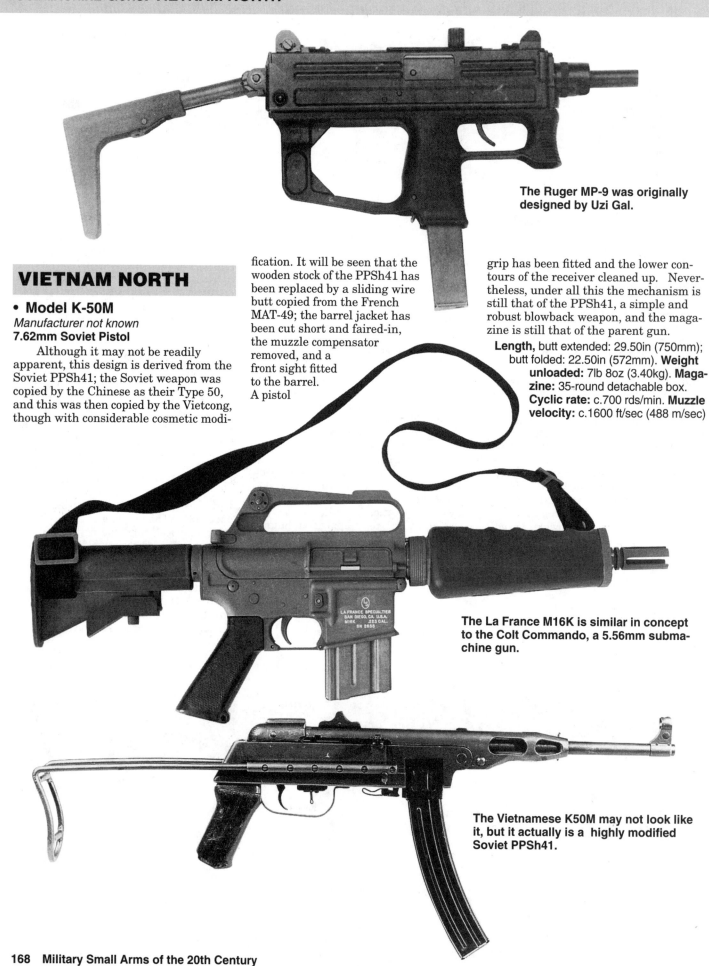

The Ruger MP-9 was originally designed by Uzi Gal.

VIETNAM NORTH

• Model K-50M
Manufacturer not known
7.62mm Soviet Pistol

Although it may not be readily apparent, this design is derived from the Soviet PPSh41; the Soviet weapon was copied by the Chinese as their Type 50, and this was then copied by the Vietcong, though with considerable cosmetic modi-fication. It will be seen that the wooden stock of the PPSh41 has been replaced by a sliding wire butt copied from the French MAT-49; the barrel jacket has been cut short and faired-in, the muzzle compensator removed, and a front sight fitted to the barrel. A pistol grip has been fitted and the lower contours of the receiver cleaned up. Nevertheless, under all this the mechanism is still that of the PPSh41, a simple and robust blowback weapon, and the magazine is still that of the parent gun.

Length, butt extended: 29.50in (750mm); butt folded: 22.50in (572mm). **Weight unloaded:** 7lb 8oz (3.40kg). **Magazine:** 35-round detachable box. **Cyclic rate:** c.700 rds/min. **Muzzle velocity:** c.1600 ft/sec (488 m/sec)

The La France M16K is similar in concept to the Colt Commando, a 5.56mm submachine gun.

The Vietnamese K50M may not look like it, but it actually is a highly modified Soviet PPSh41.

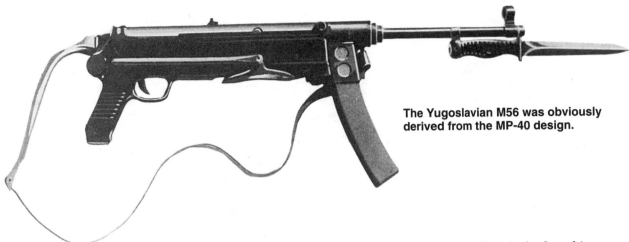

The Yugoslavian M56 was obviously derived from the MP-40 design.

YUGOSLAVIA

• Machine Carbines Model 49
Zavodi Crvena Zastava, Kragujevac
7.62mm Soviet Pistol

As with all the Communist-inclined countries of Eastern Europe, Yugoslavia was equipped with generous quantities of Soviet weapons when World War II ended, but in keeping with their intransigent attitude to the political parent, the Yugoslavs elected to make indigenous versions of some of them. The PPSh41 was modified for Yugoslav manufacture and was adopted as the M49 in the early months of 1949. The PPSh41 ancestry was quite clear, except for the box magazine: the Yugoslavs chose to discard the 71-round drum. The 35-round box was almost the same as the one made for the PPSh41, and was said to be interchangeable with it. The general outline of the M49 is very similar to the PPSh and it appeared to be little more than a neater version of the Soviet weapon; it is in fact more than that, as it has an improved bolt and spring apparently borrowed from the Beretta Model 38A and there is also a better buffer. The furniture is well-finished, in common with most of the construction. The gun was still made primarily from steel stampings, but more care appears to have been taken in the final assembly.

Length: 34.40in (847mm). **Weight unloaded:** 8lb 9oz (3.80kg). **Barrel:** 10.50in (267mm), 4 grooves, right-hand twist. **Magazine:** 35-round detachable box. **Cyclic rate:** 750 rds/min. **Muzzle velocity:** c.1700 ft/sec (518 m/sec).

• Machine Carbine Model 56
Zavodi Crvena Zastava, Kragujevac
7.62mm Soviet Pistol

The Model 56 was a replacement for the elderly Model 49 and was a simpler design to manufacture. It was basically similar in outline to the German MP40 and follows some of the internal design layout. The folding butt was a direct copy of the MP40, as was the pistol grip. The bolt was simplified and the return spring was a single large coil. A bayonet was fitted, and overall effect was of a modern well designed weapon. In fact, it suffered from using the 7.62mm Soviet pistol round, and something with more stopping power would have made it a more effective weapon.

Length: 34.25in (870mm). **Weight unloaded:** 6lb 9oz (2.98kg). **Barrel:** 9.84in (250mm), 4 grooves, right-hand twist. **Magazine:** 32-round box, staggered row. **Cyclic rate:** 600 rds/min. **Muzzle velocity:** 1700 ft/sec (518 m/sec).

• Submachine Gun M84
Zavodi Crvena Zastava, Kragujevac
7.62x17SR (32 ACP)

In the early 1980s the Yugoslavs obtained a license to manufacture the Czech 'Skorpion' submachine gun, and began advertising it as the M84. Whether many, or even any, were made remains in doubt. It seems probable that a few prototypes were made but that series production was deferred until somebody placed a worth-while order. This does not appear to have happened, and we can only assume that the project fell to pieces when the country split into is constituent parts in the late 1980s. The dimensions and performance are exactly the same as for the original Czech weapon, described on page 109.

• Submachine Gun M85
Zastava Arms, Belgrade
5.56x45mm

The M85 is the Yugoslavian equivalent of the Soviet AKS-74U described above, but chambered for the western 5.56mm rifle cartridge in a bid to attract export sales. It is somewhat longer than the Russian weapon and is distinguish-

The Yugoslavian M84 was a license-produced version of the Czech Skorpion.

The inside the M84; note the rate reducer in the butt.

able by the longer forend with three cooling slots and by the stock, which folds underneath the receiver and around the magazine. The magazine is shorter and somewhat deeper (front to back) than that of the AKS-74U. By most people's reckoning this would be considered a short assault rifle, but the manufacturers class it as a submachine gun.

Length, butt extended: 31.30in (790mm); butt folded: 22.44in (570mm). **Weight unloaded:** 7lb 1oz (3.20kg). **Barrel:** 9.84in (250mm), 6 grooves, right-hand twist. **Magazine:** 20- or 30-round detachable box. **Cyclic rate:** 700 rds/min. **Muzzle velocity:** c.2592 ft/sec (790 m/sec).

The Zastava M85 is similar to the Russian AKS-74U but fires the 5.56mm rifle cartridge instead of the 5.45mm, thus making it more attractive on the export market.

BOLT ACTION RIFLES

IN 1900 THE standard infantryman's weapon was a magazine rifle, using a bolt action—either a turnbolt or a straight-pull bolt—weighing 8 to 10 pounds, about five feet long and generally surmounted by 20 inches or so of bayonet. It fired a powerful cartridge of between 6.5 and 8mm caliber, and was usually sighted up to 2000 yards or meters. And, most important of all, the rifleman had been slowly and painstakingly trained to use this rifle effectively to at least 1000 yards range. (Such painstaking training was possible because apart from the use of the rifle and the spade, there was little else to train him on.)

But the infantryman was to be the recipient of the first major development in military firearms of the new century. Both the American and British design authorities appear to have realized that the practice of providing a long rifle for infantry and a carbine for the rest had become far too complicated, with every individual arm of 'the rest' demanding their own variation of the carbine, with or without bayonet, with or without stacking swivel, with this or that type of sight...there was no end to their idiosyncrasies. It played the devil with the designers, worse with the storekeepers, and cost far too much money, producing small runs of minor variations. So the answer that both countries arrived at, almost simultaneously, was to produce one rifle for everybody, shorter than the old infantry rifle, longer than a carbine, long enough to deliver the accuracy demanded, short enough to be convenient to carry. The British produced the Short Lee-Enfield and the Americans produced the Springfield. The rest of the world scratched their heads and sat back. It was to be another forty years or more before some of them gave up their carbines.

Apart from improving the ammunition by introducing the pointed bullet, there was little change in the bolt-action rifle for the remainder of the century; the design had reached its technical zenith by 1900, and subsequent designs were simply dedicated to producing the same thing but easier and cheaper to manufacture. Essentially there is no difference between the Lee-Enfield of 1900 and the Lee-Enfield of the 1970s, the Springfield of 1903 and 1943, the Mosin-Nagant of 1900 and 1944. A soldier trained on the early one would be perfectly at home with the later model.

And thus, without significant change from 1900, the bolt-action magazine rifle eventually reached the end of its first-line military career in the 1950s, with its general replacement with a semi-automatic weapon. The semi-automatic had been knocking on the door since the 1890s, but it was too unreliable and delicate to be invited inside. Not until Garand produced the immortal M1 did any major armed force put its money solely upon a semi-automatic rifle, and when it did so there was no great rush to follow suit. 'Wait and See' had always been a prime motto in military establishments.

World War II speeded up the transition process, and the adoption of bloc-standard calibers—7.62x51mm for NATO, 7.62x39mm for the Soviets—gave the armies the clean break which they needed to make an effective switch over to the semi-automatic.

But the bolt action repeater didn't die. Effective and combat-worthy as the early semiautomatic rifles were, even their best friends would scarcely call them precision target weapons, and snipers were not their best friends. Accuracy mean bolt action; the US Army hung on to its Springfield and the 30-06 cartridge, the British to their Lee-Enfield, though they at least had the grace to rebarrel them into 7.62mm. This has gradually changed; the Soviets introduced the Dragunov semi-automatic sniper, which led a number of other manufacturers to develop more carefully-assembled versions of their standard semi-auto rifle and then fine-tune them up to sniping standards, but even so, there are a number of armies, the British, American and French among them, who will start the 21st century as they started the 20th, with a supply of bolt-action magazine rifles in their racks. But instead of 20-inch bayonets they will have 8-12x zoom telescopes attached to them.

ARGENTINA

• Mauser Model 1891
Waffenfabrik Mauser AG, Oberndorf-am-Neckar
7.65x53mm Argentine Mauser

The Model 1891 was no more than the Turkish Model of 1890 with some very slight modifications. There were minor changes to the bolt, and the extractor was strengthened. Apart from these, it was virtually identical, and the reader should refer to the Turkish model for further information.

• Cavalry Carbine Model 1891
A short derivative of the rifle of the same year, the carbine could not be fitted with a bayonet.

• Mauser Model 1891/1909
This was a version of the original 1891 rifle with a regraduated sight to handle the improved pointed-bullet ammunition issued in 1908.

AUSTRIA-HUNGARY/ AUSTRIA

• 8mm Mannlicher Model 1895
Osterreichische Waffenfabrik-Gesellschaft, Steyr.
8x50R Austrian Mannlicher

This became the official Austro-Hungarian service rifle to the exclusion of the various earlier rifle patterns, most of which were quickly relegated to the Landwehr. The M95 was used throughout the Habsburg empire and was adopted c.1897 by Bulgaria; many survived until World War II, including many in the hands of the Italian Army who had received them in 1919-20 as war reparations. The 1895 rifle was mechanically the same as the 1890 carbine, using a straight-pull bolt with rotary locking and a clip-loaded magazine. The rifle was of conventional appearance, recognizable by the prominent spur of the cocking piece and the side-mounted stacking hook alongside the exposed muzzle.

Length: 50.00in (1270mm). **Weight unloaded:** 8lb 5oz (3.78kg). **Barrel:** 30.12in (765mm), 4 grooves, right-hand twist. **Magazine:** 5-round integral box. **Muzzle velocity:** c.2000 ft/sec (610 m/sec)

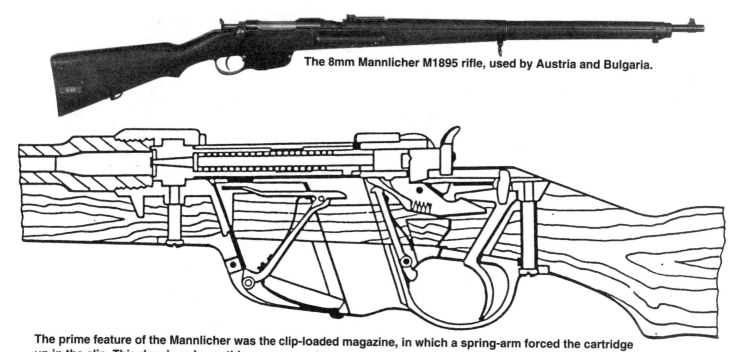

The 8mm Mannlicher M1895 rifle, used by Austria and Bulgaria.

The prime feature of the Mannlicher was the clip-loaded magazine, in which a spring-arm forced the cartridge up in the clip. This drawing shows this arrangement.

• 8mm Mannlicher Carbine Model 1895

This was the cavalry carbine derivation of the basic rifle designs and exists in two forms, varying only in minor respects. The same rotary-locking straight-pull action and clip-loaded magazine were used, and the carbine was fitted with sling swivels. One version was fitted for a bayonet and the other was not.

• 8mm Mannlicher Short Rifle Model 1895

This was a short version of the 1895 rifle, very similar in design to the cavalry carbine of the same year. The 'Stutzengewehr', issued to artillerymen, engineers and others to whom its handiness was an advantage, was fitted with a special knife bayonet with a front sight atop the muzzle ring. This was intended to compensate the altered impact of the bullets when the rifle was fired with a fixed bayonet.

Length: 39.37in (1000mm). **Weight unloaded:** 7lb 14oz (3.57kg). **Barrel:** 19.00in (482mm), 4 grooves, right-hand twist. **Magazine:** 5-round integral box. **Muzzle velocity:** c.1750 ft/sec (533 m/sec).

• SSG69 Sniping Rifle (1969)
Steyr-Daimler-Puch AG, Steyr
7.62x51mm NATO

The SSG69 was among the earliest of the many modern sniping rifles that have appeared from European manufacturers in recent years. The Steyr is very strongly made and has an exceptionally long barrel seating into the receiver, which makes for greater rigidity. The barrel is made by cold hammering, which gives greater accuracy, and the bolt is rigidly locked by six symmetrical lugs.

The military stock is entirely plastic, to eliminate warping, and is colored dark green; stocks for rifles purchased by police units can be provided in black. The magazine is the rotary-drum type which originated with the Mannlicher-Schoenauer rifles in the 1890s, though with modern overtones. It is made of very light metal and has a clear plastic window in the back face so that the remaining

The Steyr SSG in various forms, from top to bottom: the SSG Police, SSG 69 military, SSG-Police Suppressed and SSG-Police Special with heavy barrel.

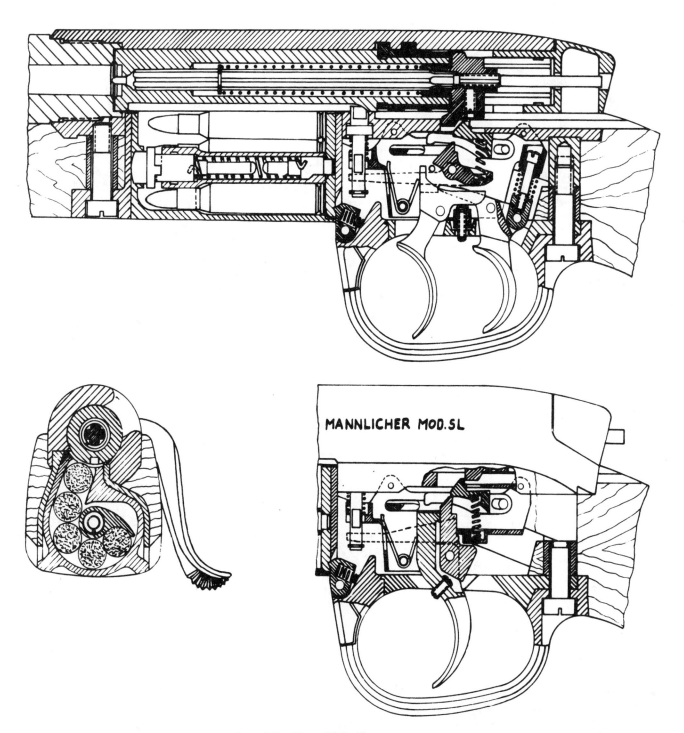

The trigger mechanism and rotary magazine of the Steyr SSG rifle.

ammunition can be easily seen when the magazine is removed. It fits snugly into the stock and does not protrude at all. Early production rifles could be furnished with a 10-round box magazine, but there was so little demand for this version that the option was eventually dropped. No iron sights are provided, since the rifle is intended to be used with a telescope sight. With selected ammunition, the SSG is extremely accurate, and it has been used to win competitions of international importance. The SSG is used by the Austrian Army and other armed forces and security forces.

Length: 44.88in (1140mm). **Weight unloaded:** 8lb 9oz (3.9kg). **Barrel:** 25.6in (650mm), 4 grooves, right-hand twist. **Magazine:** 5-round rotary drum. **Muzzle velocity:** 2820 ft/sec (860 m/sec).

BELGIUM

• Infantry Rifle Model 1889
Fabrique Nationale d'Armes de Guerre, Herstal
7.65x53mm Belgian Mauser

This was the first Belgian bolt-action rifle, and instead of designing a national weapon, it was decided to take the exist-

The Belgian Mauser of 1889; particular features are the shape of the magazine and the thick barrel jacket.

ing German Mauser and make whatever modifications were necessary for Belgian service. FN was specifically formed to manufacture the Mauser rifle, though the government plant also made them. The Belgian Mauser differed from any of the others by having a barrel jacket. The barrel is encased in a tube of thin sheet steel which isolates it from the furniture, the declared intention being to prevent warping woodwork from affecting the straightness of the barrel, and to minimize the effects of shocks, blows and bends. The sights are brazed to the tube so that the upsetting effect of local heat does not cause a change in the properties of the barrel steel. Such care of the barrel is commendable, but brings in its train other compensating disadvantages. One is the liability of rust to accumulate between the tube and the outer walls of the barrel, and most Belgian Mausers examined today are suffering from that defect.

The breech area of the Belgian Mauser; note the two typical Mauser features - the 90° bolt handle and the 'flag' safety catch on the end of the bolt.

Other effects of this protecting tube are that the rifle is more expensive to make and is more liable to heat up, since cooling air cannot get to it. Apart from the barrel tube, the Belgian Mauser is more or less standard, though there are minor differences between it and other models. It remained in service for a long time, and was still in use during World War II.

Length: 50.5in (1295mm). **Weight unloaded:** 8lb 13oz (4.01kg). **Barrel:** 30.6in (780mm), 4 grooves, right-hand twist. **Magazine:** 5-round integral box. **Muzzle velocity:** c.2000 ft/sec (610 m/sec).

• Civil Guard Rifle Model 1889

This was no more than a slight modification to the basic rifle pattern, in which the bolt handle was turned down. A different type of knife bayonet was used, with a different blade length, but the nosecap and bayonet bar were unchanged.

• Gendarmerie, Foot Artillery & Fortress Troops Carbine Model 1889

The carbine was a shortened version of the rifle with a turned-down bolt handle, and issued with a long-bladed sword bayonet (which used the same hilt as the infantry and Garde Civique rifle types).

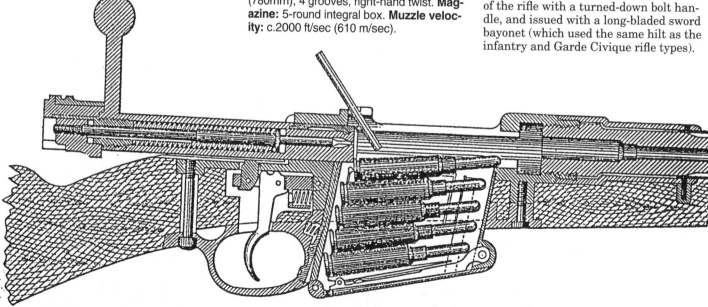

A further novelty on the Belgian Mauser was the introduction of charger loading, and this drawing shows how the charger was ejected by the forward movement of the bolt when loading the first round.

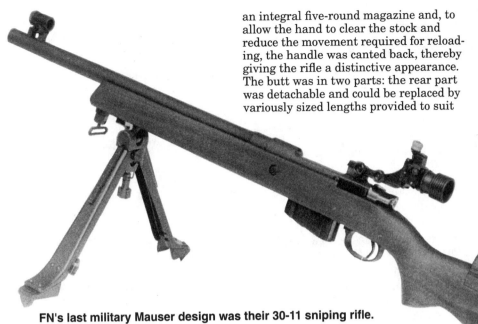

FN's last military Mauser design was their 30-11 sniping rifle.

an integral five-round magazine and, to allow the hand to clear the stock and reduce the movement required for reloading, the handle was canted back, thereby giving the rifle a distinctive appearance. The butt was in two parts: the rear part was detachable and could be replaced by variously sized lengths provided to suit

• Cavalry Carbine Model 1889

This was a lightened carbine which could be recognized by the almost half-stocked appearance; a long section of the barrel jacket protruded beyond the stock and there was no provision for a bayonet.

• Mounted Gendarmerie Carbine Model 1899

Intended for the use of the horsed police units, this was similar to the cavalry carbine, although the stock was continued nearer to the muzzle and an extra barrel band was used. A knife or saber bayonet could be attached.

• Infantry Rifle Model 1936

This was a modified version of the 1889 rifles incorporating some of the features of the 1898 system. It was issued in only small quantities.

• FN Model 30-11 Sniping Rifle (c.1972)

Fabrique Nationale Herstal SA, Herstal
7.62x51mm NATO

Developed from the FN big-game rifles, the Sniper was primarily intended for police and military engaged in anti-terrorist operations, though it was well suited to military field use. The aim was to make a rifle with precise shooting characteristics out to 600 meters and from the outset the sighting equipment was a paramount consideration.

The action was a high-precision Mauser bolt working to a heavy hammered barrel mounted in a one-piece stock made of wood. The barrel was fitted with a flash-hider and normally carried Anschütz iron sights. The bolt fed from

the requirements of different firers. The height of the cheek rest could be altered by inserts and, as a final adjustment, additional inserts could be put into the shoulder pad. A shooting sling was a standard accessory and the rifle was not meant to be fired without it, except when the FN MAG bipod was fitted.

The 30-11 was adopted by several European police and security forces, but demand fell during the 1980s and production ended in 1986.

Length: 43.97in (1117mm). **Weight unloaded:** 10lb 11oz (4.85kg). **Barrel:** 19.76in (502mm), 4 grooves, right-hand twist. **Magazine:** 9-round detachable box. **Muzzle velocity:** 2788 ft/sec (850 m/sec).

CANADA

• Ross Rifle Mark 1

Ross Rifle Company, Quebec
303 British

Sir Charles Ross designed his straight-pull bolt-action rifle in 1896 and first patented it in the following year. After several sporting and target models had been produced between 1897 and 1902, the Ross rifle was adopted in April 1902 by the Department of Militia and Defense, as an official weapon of the Royal Northwest Mounted Police. Manufacture began in 1903 though the first deliveries of the rifle did not take place until 1905.

Ross's original design made use of an unusual bolt locking system based on the Austro-Hungarian Mannlicher rifles, although undeniably using features of Ross's conception; the straight-pull bolt

locked into the chamber by means of an interrupted-thread in the original 1897 designs, although in 1900, Ross changed the pattern to a rotating lug system. A cam track was used to unlock the bolt when the handle was pulled to the rear, but Ross reverted to the interrupted-thread system on his 'perfected' 1910 design with inconspicuous results.

The Ross was extensively tested in Britain between 1900 and 1912, but on each occasion it was rejected as a possible service weapon. The Commandant of the Small Arms School, at Hythe, summed up military opinion in his 1910 report on the Ross Mark 2**: 'It seems clear that this rifle is designed as a target rifle pure and simple, without regard to the requirements of active service or of the training of large bodies of men of average attainment'.

In spite of this opinion, the Canadian Army of 1914 went to war armed with the Ross, but, by 1915, it was found that the troops had lost confidence in the weapon, and were discarding it in favor of Lee-Enfield rifles gleaned from the battlefields. Official investigations revealed that the muddy conditions of trench warfare were ill-suited to the bolt design, and that there was insufficient primary extraction, which caused difficulties with cartridges of indifferent wartime manufacture. It was also found that much of the trouble arose because of the position of the bolt-stop, which bore against the rearmost of the three locking lugs: the result was that the lug battered against the massive steel stop every time the breech was opened, damaging it to the extent that it became all but impossible to force the bolt into a locked position. The Ross was consequently withdrawn from combat and relegated to a training role, but it was revived for a short time during World War II when numbers were shipped to Britain to arm the Home Guard.

There were innumerable minor variants of the Ross rifles, mainly because Ross was constantly attending to minor difficulties in the design (it is said that one authority recognizes no fewer than 85 distinct models) and the picture is further confused by the periodic changes both in the rear sight and magazine design and by the changes in nomenclature; it is hoped that the following list will clarify the more important variants.

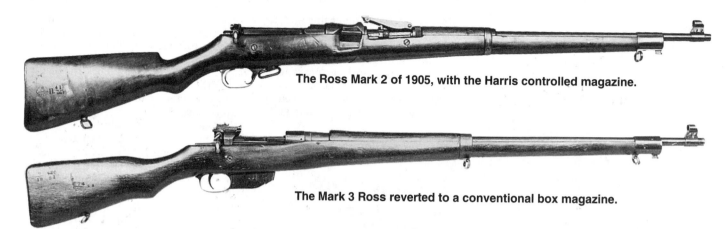

The Ross Mark 2 of 1905, with the Harris controlled magazine.

The Mark 3 Ross reverted to a conventional box magazine.

• Rifle, Ross, Mark 1

This was the first of the service weapons, fitted with an unusual pattern of magazine known as the 'Harris Controlled Platform Magazine', in which the platform could be depressed by hand through an external thumb-lever. This allowed five loose rounds to be quickly loaded, after which release of the lever then placed the cartridges under compression. Various sights were used, leading to the appearance of a confusing number of sub-varieties. It had originally been intended to make use of the Sight, Ross Mark I—a large leaf sight—but this proved too fragile for service use and was replaced before the rifles and carbines were actually issued by the Sight, Ross, Mark 2, a tangent sight based upon that of the Mauser Gew 98 type. A modified version of the Mark 2 sight, known as the Sight, Ross, Mark 3, was later found necessary.

• Carbine, Ross, Mark 1

A short version of the basic Mark 1 rifle, the carbine could be recognized by the forestock extending to the muzzle. Unlike the rifle, the carbine could not be fitted with a bayonet.

• Rifle, Ross, Mark 2

As a result of the trials and tribulations of the Mark 1, it was found necessary for Ross to devise an improved model in an attempt to stem the criticism. The Mark 2 had a slightly modified bolt mechanism which compressed the striker spring during the opening of the bolt, rather than the closing-stroke compression of the Mark 1. The chamber dimensions of the Mark 2 were also changed to accept standard British service ammunition.

• Rifle, Short, Ross, Mark 1

In April 1912, it was found necessary to change the nomenclature of the Ross rifles in an attempt to camouflage the number of modifications that had been made to the basic design. The Short Mark 1 was the new name for the Rifle, Ross, Mark 2.

• Rifle, Ross, Mark 2*

The Mark 2* was the same rifle as the Mark 2, with the substitution of the Mark 3 sight for the Mark 2 of the earlier rifle. Some modifications were also made to internal components both to rectify deficiencies and to simplify manufacture.

• Rifle, Ross, Mark 2**

The Mark 2**, similar to its predecessors, was fitted with a Sutherland rear sight in place of the various Ross types.

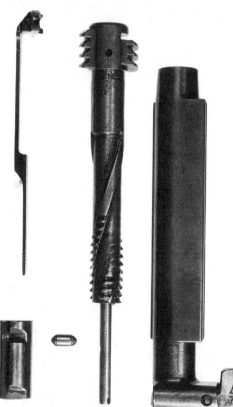

• Rifle, Ross, Mark 2***, and Rifle, Ross, Mark 2****

These were minor variations of the Mark 2*, using the Sutherland rear sight and incorporating minor manufacturing modifications. Neither saw much service. The barrels of the Mark 2*** and 2**** were 28in (711mm) long.

• Rifle, Ross, Mark 2*****

By the time five major modifications—discounting the innumerable minor ones—had been made to the Ross design, the Canadian authorities realized that something had to be done to further camouflage the amount of modifications, and so in April 1912, they renamed the rifles 'Short Mark 2' (although they were still no more than variants of the basic Ross Mark 2 pattern). The Mark 2***** was otherwise similar to its predecessors, with a Sutherland rear sight, although a change was made to the shape of the wooden handguard over the chamber. The extractor was also modified and a 28-inch (711mm) barrel was used.

• Rifle, Short, Ross, Mark 2

The Short Mark 2 was the result of the revised 1912 naming system; it was originally the Mark 2*****.

• Rifle, Ross, Mark 2

This designation arose as the result of the 1912 Programs, and was not the same thing as the earlier Mark 2 rifle of c.1906. The '1912' Mark 2 was the new name for the old Rifle, Ross, Mark 2**.

• Rifle, Ross, Mark 3

The Mark 3 was the first of the rifles manufactured to Ross's improved 1910 design, in which the solid locking lugs of the earlier service weapons were replaced by a form of triple-thread inter-

The bolt of the Ross Mark 3, showing the triple interrupted thread which locked into the chamber and the spiral grooves and multiple lugs which control the rotation of the bolt and lock it to the sleeve for withdrawal.

rupted-screw system. A double-pressure trigger unit was fitted, and charger guides were added to the action body so that the guns could be loaded from the standard British 303 charger. The standard model weighed 9lb 12oz (4.32kg), but a lighter version weighing 9lb 1oz (4.11kg) was made for trials in 1911.

• Rifle, Ross, Mark 3*

This is thought to have been a modification of the Mark 3, in which alterations were made to the action body and the bolt head improve the efficiency of the lock. This designation is uncertain. A different front sight and muzzle-band were also apparently fitted.

• Rifle, Magazine, Ross, .303in Mark 3B

This was the only rifle in the Ross series to have been adopted by the British Army, in October 1915. It was the same as the standard Mark 3 with the addition to the action of a Lee-Enfield type cut-off, added above the magazine so that the rifle could be used as a single-loader while keeping a full magazine in reserve. The Mark 3B was declared obsolete in November 1921.

Length: 50.56in (1284mm). **Weight unloaded:** 9lb 14oz (4.48kg). **Barrel:** 30.15in (765mm), 4 grooves, left-hand twist. **Magazine:** 5-round detachable box. **Muzzle velocity:** c.2600 ft/sec (790 m/sec).

• Rifle, Ross, Mark 3 (Sniper's)

A standard Ross rifle fitted with a telescope sight manufactured by the Warner and Swasey Company of Cleveland, Ohio. The telescope sight, which was offset to the left side so that the action could still be loaded from a charger, was a 5.2x type similar to the US Army's Telescopic Musket Sight M1913. The Ross snipers' rifles were much loved by those to whom they were issued on account of their undoubted accuracy, helped by the 30.53in (775mm) barrel, and many were retained after the standard service rifles had been recalled. The snipers' weapons were not subject to the severe conditions suffered by the line weapons.

Approximately 419,130 Ross military rifles were manufactured between 1903 and 1915, 342,040 of which were delivered to the Canadian military authorities and 67,090 to Britain. In 1940 a number were supplied to the Soviet Army; enough of these survived the war to be rebarreled to 7.62x54R chambering and used by the Soviet 'Running Boar' shooting team to win a gold medal in the 1954 World Shooting Championships.

CHINA

• Mauser M1895 Rifle
Waffenfabrik Mauser AG, Oberndorf-am-Neckar
7x57mm Spanish Mauser

This was the same rifle as the Chilean M1895, which in turn was derived from the Spanish M1893. Full-stocked, half-length handguard, exposed muzzle, cleaning rod, bayonet bar. The bolt had a flush face, locked by two lugs, but had no hold-open on the magazine follower. Charger-loaded, there being a charger guide cut in the receiver bridge.

Length: 48.56in (1232mm). **Weight unloaded:** 8lb 10oz (3.92kg). **Barrel:** 29.05in (738mm), 4 grooves, right-hand twist. **Magazine:** 5-round integral box. **Muzzle velocity:** c.2230 ft/sec (680 m/sec).

• Mannlicher M1904 Rifle
Oesterreichische Waffenfabrik Gesellschaft, Steyr, Austria
7.92x57mm Mauser

This rifle, a standard turnbolt clip-loading Mannlicher design almost identical to the Dutch M1895 except for the caliber, was originally produced as a potential export military design and offered in a variety of calibers. Stiff competition from Mauser meant few sales, and the only substantial order came from China for a version in 7.92mm Mauser caliber. An unknown quantity—but certainly several thousand—were delivered, but the Revolution of 1911 put an end to the contract. The balance of those manufactured—about 11,000—were sold to the Ulster Volunteer Force in Ireland in 1913-14.

Length: 48.23in (1225mm). **Weight unloaded:** 8lb 13oz (4.0kg). **Barrel:** 28.54in (725mm), 4 grooves, right-hand twist. **Magazine:** 5-round box. **Muzzle velocity:** c.2247 ft/sec (685 m/sec).

• 'Hanyang' Rifle
Hanyang Arsenal
7.92x57mm Mauser

The history of this weapon is far from clear, but it appears to have been based upon the Mannlicher 1904 design and was probably put into manufacture during World War I when supplies from other countries dried up. It has the Mannlicher magazine and clip loading system, allied to a bolt which had a separate head and locks into the receiver. Manufacture continued until the late 1920s.

Length: 49.25in (1251mm). **Weight unloaded:** 8lb 8oz (3.87kg). **Barrel:** 29.25in (743mm), 4 grooves, right hand twist. **Magazine:** 5-round box. **Muzzle velocity:** c.2870 ft/sec (875 m/sec).

• Model 21 Short Rifle
Kwangtung Arsenal
7.92x57mm Mauser

The Chinese purchased several thousand FN-made Mauser M1924 rifles, and in 1932 they began making their own copy in Kwangtung. (It was called the Model 21 because 1932 was the 21st year after the revolution.) The bolt was standard Mauser 1898 pattern and the rifle was a short type with half-length handguard.

Length: 42.91in (1090mm). **Weight unloaded:** 8lb 6oz (3.81kg). **Barrel:** 23.26in (591mm), 4 grooves, right hand twist. **Magazine:** 5-round integral box. **Muzzle velocity:** c.2755 ft/sec (840 m/sec).

• 'Generalissimo' or 'Chiang-Kai-Shek' Rifle
State arsenals
7.92x57mm Mauser.

Manufactured 1936-49, and based on the Mauser Kar98a. Full-stocked, exposed muzzle, bayonet bar, finger groove in forend, one barrel band.

Length: 43.75in (1111mm). **Weight:** 9lb 0oz (4.08kg). **Barrel:** 23.62in (600mm), 4 grooves, right-hand twist. **Magazine:** 5-round integral box. **Muzzle velocity:** c.2755 ft/sec (840 m/sec).

DENMARK

• Krag-Jorgensen Gevaer M1889
State arsenals
8x58R Danish Krag

The Krag-Jorgensen system was developed in the late 1880s by Captain Ole Krag of the Royal Norwegian Artillery and Erik Jorgensen, an engineer at the Norwegian State Arsenal, of which Ole Krag later became Superintendent. The rifles were first adopted in 1889 by Denmark and in 1892, in a modified version, by the United States of America. After various improvements had been carried out to the desires of the Board of Officers supervising the United States Army trials, Krag and Jorgensen patented an improved version of the rifle in 1893; this was later adopted by the Norwegian Army, whose first rifle pattern appeared in the following year.

The turnbolt action makes use of a single locking lug at the front of the bolt unit, although the bolt handle turns down into a recess in the receiver body to act as an auxiliary lock; this locking system has in the past been the subject of much criticism but, with the relatively low-powered cartridges for which it was originally conceived, the action is unquestionably safe. The most remarkable feature of the design lies, however, in the pattern of the magazine, which loads laterally under the

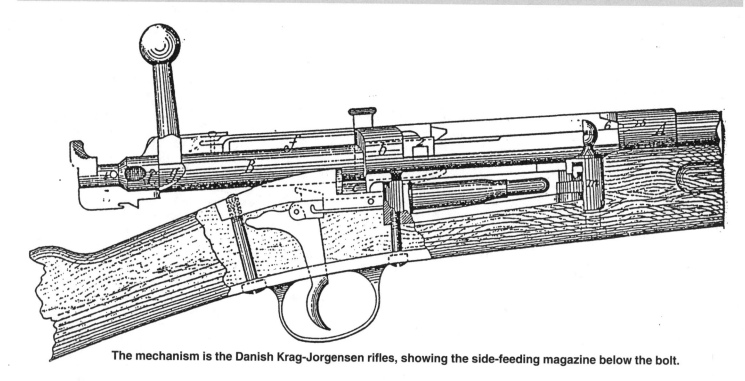

The mechanism is the Danish Krag-Jorgensen rifles, showing the side-feeding magazine below the bolt.

bolt through a hinged trapdoor. On the door's inner face is a leaf spring and the magazine follower, and with the trap open, loose cartridges can be dropped into the loading slot. Closing the trap brings the spring and follower to bear upon the last cartridge, pushing the rounds across the magazine, under the bolt and up to the left side of the action where the round rests against the bolt. When the bolt is operated, the closing stroke pushes against the rim of the first cartridge, easing it forward to an enlargement of the feed slot, at which point the rim can pass through; the round can then enter the feedway and into the chamber. The original Danish Krag-Jorgensen was given a loading trap vertically hinged at the front, which meant that it swung forward for loading: it also meant that the rifle had to be canted towards the left when loading, as the cartridges would otherwise fall to the ground. The 1892 American design, and the later Norwegian pattern, replaced the Danish gate with a type having a horizontal hinge at the bottom of the gate, which meant that the open trap also served as a loading platform.

The pattern of 1889 was the first of a series of similar weapons; a long, somewhat clumsy rifle instantly recognizable by the barrel jacket—a feature possessed by few other guns—and the side-loading gate was hinged at the front of the receiver.

Length: 52.28in (1328mm). **Weight unloaded:** 10lb 1oz (4.58kg). **Barrel:** 37.40in (950mm), 6 grooves, right-hand twist. **Magazine:** 5-round internal 'tray'. **Muzzle velocity:** c.1969 ft/sec (600 m/sec).

• 8mm Rifle m/89-08

In 1908, it was decided to modify the rifle design to incorporate a new type of safety catch fitted on the cocking piece.

• 8mm Rifle m/89-10

In 1910, a second set of minor modifications were made, the most important being the regraduation of the rear sight from 2000m to 2100m. Most of the earlier rifles then in service were altered to the new system, just as they had been in 1908, which means that original 1889-type rifles are now very scarce indeed.

• 8mm Cavalry Carbine m/89

This was the cavalry carbine version of the 1889 rifle, a shortened and lightened rifle with a wooden handguard and sling swivels on the left side of the stock and on the left side of the top band. The original leaf sight was replaced by one of tangent pattern. The carbine was adopted in 1912, which leads to an alternative designation, 'Rytterkarabin m/89-12'.

Length: 43.31in (1100mm). **Weight unloaded:** 8lb 14oz (4.04kg). **Barrel:** 23.62in (600mm), 6 grooves, right-hand twist. **Magazine:** 5-round internal 'tray'. **Muzzle velocity:** c.2034 ft/sec (620 m/sec).

• 8mm Cavalry Carbine m/89-23

The basic cavalry carbine was modified in 1923 to accept the light sword bayonet of 1915, which necessitated the addition of a suitable bayonet bar to the muzzle. All carbines of the type then in service were so altered.

• 8mm Engineer Carbine m/89-24

This variation of the carbine was fitted with sling swivels under the butt, the barrel band and the nosecap. A bayonet bar was fitted to the underside of the muzzle, and a wooden handguard appeared over the barrel.

• 8mm Carbine m/89-24

The infantry's carbine, this was basically a short version of the rifle m/89, even to the fitting of a steel barrel-jacket. There was no handguard and the stock was fitted with grasping grooves—one to each side—below the rear sight. A bayonet bar was fitted to the barrel jacket at the muzzle.

Length: 43.50in (1105mm). **Weight unloaded:** 8lb 12oz (3.96kg). **Barrel:** 24.0in (610mm), 6 grooves, right-hand twist. **Magazine:** 5-round internal 'tray'. **Muzzle velocity:** c.2034 ft/sec (620 m/sec).

• 8mm Artillery Carbine m/89-24

This was essentially similar to the infantry carbine of the same year, except that the bolt handle was turned downwards towards the stock.

FINLAND

• Sako TRG-21 Sniper's Rifle (1985)

Sako Ltd., Riihiimaki.
7.62x51mm NATO

This is a conventional bolt-action magazine rifle, since Sako is convinced that for first-shot accuracy the bolt action

The Sako TRG-21 sniping rifle.

cannot be beaten. The barrel is fitted with a muzzle brake/flash hider which can be removed and replaced by a silencer. The bolt and receiver are rather larger than usual for the 7.62mm caliber so that the rifle can be upgraded to heavier ammunition in the future. The bolt has three forward locking lugs and an indicator at the rear end showing whether the action is cocked. The safety catch, on the right side, is silent in operation.

The trigger is a two-stage type which can be adjusted for position and pressure without dismantling the rifle, and the trigger mechanism and triggerguard can be removed as a unit.

The stock is of wood or glass-fiber, and the action is bedded in special epoxy resin. The stock can be adjusted for height and length, and a sling can be fitted. The steel bipod is articulated so that the rifle has some degree of movement without requiring the bipod to be shifted. Folding iron sights are provided, but the receiver is shaped into a mount for optical or electro-optical sights which are normally used.

Length: 47.25in (1200mm). **Weight unloaded:** 11lb 11oz (5.308kg). **Barrel:** 25.98in (660mm), 4 grooves, right-hand twist. **Magazine:** 10-round box. **Muzzle velocity:** c.2756 ft/sec (840 m/sec).

FRANCE

• Infantry Rifle Model 1886 (Lebel)

Various state arsenals, including those at Chatellerault, Saint-Etienne and Tulle
8x50R Lebel Mle 86

In 1886, the French Army replaced their single-shot M1875 Gras rifles with a weapon which, for a short time, put them ahead of the world. The new weapon, ultimately known as the Fusil d'Infanterie Modéle 1886—or the Lebel, after the senior officer on the design committee—was notable in that it introduced a smokeless cartridge firing a small-caliber jacketed bullet. The rifle itself was a strange combination of ideas and, in view of contemporary advances elsewhere, it could well be described as mechanically backward (indeed, better weapons became wide-spread within a couple of years) utilizing as a tube magazine system dating back to the 1870s. The bolt was a variation of that found on the Gras of 1874, incorporating modifications made when the French adopted the Kropatschek rifle in 1878.

The turnbolt action of the Mle 86 employed a magazine tube running forward beneath the barrel, and as the bolt was withdrawn so a lifting mechanism brought a fresh round in line with the chamber. When the bolt was closed, this round was swept into the chamber and the lifter moved down to be supplied with

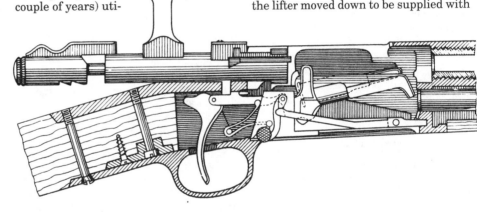

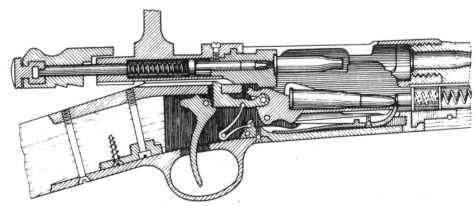

The breech mechanism of the Lebel, showing the action of the tubular magazine and cartridge lifter.

The French M1886 Lebel infantry rifle.

a new cartridge pushed backwards by the pressure of the magazine spring. The result was a long and heavy weapon which retained its superiority for a very short time before being overtaken by the mechanically more perfect patterns of Mauser and Mannlicher. The Mle 86, however, continued in service until the end of World War II; many had been greatly shortened in 1935, but others survived unmodified in the reserve.

From time to time, various minor improvements were effected: in 1898, the French authorities replaced the round-nosed Balle M with the boat-tailed spitzer Balle D, but the days of the tubular-magazine rifles, in which there was always a danger of jarring two cartridges together tip-to-base with attendant chances of an explosion, were numbered by the advent of the clip-loaded Berthier weapons.

The original production variant of the basic pattern could be easily recognized by the unusual receiver and the two-piece stock. The under-barrel tubular magazine held eight rounds, and a long cruciform bayonet could be fixed underneath the protruding muzzle.

Length: 51.00in (1295mm). **Weight unloaded:** 9lb 5oz (4.28kg). **Barrel:** 31.50in (800mm), 4 grooves, left-hand twist. **Magazine:** 8-round under-barrel tube. **Muzzle velocity:** c.2350 ft/sec (716 m/sec).

• Infantry Rifle Model 1886/93

After the original rifles had seen service several deficiencies were discovered; the entire machining of the receiver was revised to eliminate weakness caused by insufficient torsional rigidity, a hole was bored in the bolt-head to enable gas to escape from a ruptured cartridge, the rear sight underwent minor modifications, and a stacking hook was added to the muzzle cap.

• Infantry Rifle Model 1886R35

A much-shortened version of either the Mle 86 or the Mle 86/93 intended to make a much more handy weapon, the conversion was executed by reducing the barrel and the forestock, fitting a middle band similar to that of the Mousqueton Mle 16, and replacing the original rear sight with the pattern of the Mousqueton

Mle 16, which had to be suitably modified to enable it to fit the contours of the Lebel barrel.

Length: 37.20in (944mm). **Weight unloaded:** 6lb 12oz (3.10kg). **Barrel:** 17.75in (451mm), 4 grooves, left-hand twist. **Magazine:** 3-round under-barrel tube. **Muzzle velocity:** c.2000 ft/sec (609 m/sec).

• Berthier Rifles
Various state arsenals, including those of Chatellerault, Saint-Etienne and Tulle
8x50R Lebel Mle 86; 7.5x54mm French Mle 29

With the adoption by Germany of the Gewehr 88, and the issue in Austria-Hungary of the various Mannlicher weapons, the French quickly realized that the Lebel was inferior to the rifles of their neighbors and likely enemies. As a result of deliberations, therefore, they sanctioned the issue of small quantities of a cavalry carbine designed by a committee headed by André Berthier, one of the most competent of the designers to come from France. The carbine continued to use the well-tried (but somewhat complicated) bolt-action used on the Mle 86 and its derivatives, but it allied the action to a magazine very similar to that of Mannlicher. The Carbine Mle 90 was loaded through the open action with a clip containing three cartridges, which were then forced up and into the loading position by a spring-loaded follower, and after the last round had been chambered, the clip fell through a slot in the magazine floor-plate.

A modified pattern of the carbine followed in 1892, in which a slight modification was made to the design of the clip, and the shape of the rifle stock was considerably altered; apart from detail difference in the action components, the carbines manufactured to the system of 1892 were otherwise identical with that of 1890. Various rifles followed, similar in action to the carbines and differing only in dimensions, including the patterns of 1902 and 1907.

Experience in World War I convinced the French authorities that the three-round clip of their rifles and carbines placed the French troops at a disadvantage, as the German Gewehr 98 magazine held 5 rounds and that of the British Lee-Enfield rifles held 10, so in

1915 it was decided to introduce a five-round clip. A modified rifle pattern, that of 1916, was introduced to make use of the increased magazine capacity, although it was structurally little different from the model of 1907. At a later date many of the 1892 carbines were altered to take the five-round clip, and in 1916 the opportunity was also taken to produce new carbines to the modified system.

Little changed until 1934 when, as a result of trials involving modified ammunition, the French introduced a new rifle firing the 7.5mm cartridge Mle 29, although the rifle was still in reality a Berthier. The chance was also taken to replace the Mannlicher magazine, in which the clip was an integral part, with a staggered-row Mauser magazine into which five rounds were stripped from a charger.

• Cavalry Carbine Model 1890

A distinctive pattern of carbine with a combless stock, the Mle 90 cavalry type had a turned-down bolt handle and a sling ring attached to the left side of the stock. There was neither handguard nor bayonet, although a cleaning rod was contained within the stock.

Length: 3.20in (945mm). **Weight unloaded:** 6lb 11oz (3.02kg). **Barrel:** 17.85in (453mm), 4 grooves, left-hand twist. **Magazine:** 3-round integral clip-loaded box. **Muzzle velocity:** c.2000 ft/sec (609 m/sec).

• Cuirassiers Carbine Model 1890

Essentially similar to the cavalry carbine, the pattern intended for the Cuirassiers had a leather butt-plate fixed to the butt by means of two screws.

• Gendarmerie Carbine Model 1890

Similar to the other two guns on the 1890 system the Gendarmerie design was adapted for a rod bayonet - similar to that of the Rifle Mle 86 - which required a special nosecap.

• Artillery Short Rifle Model 1892

The 1892 system was very similar to that of 1890, although the weapons are readily recognizable by the combed stock which gives them an altogether conventional appearance. The Artillery

The M1886/93 Lebel was an improvement on the M1886 design and was the result of a few years of practical experience.

The bolt action of the Berthier M1892 rifle was still basically a Lebel, even though the bolt handle was now turned down.

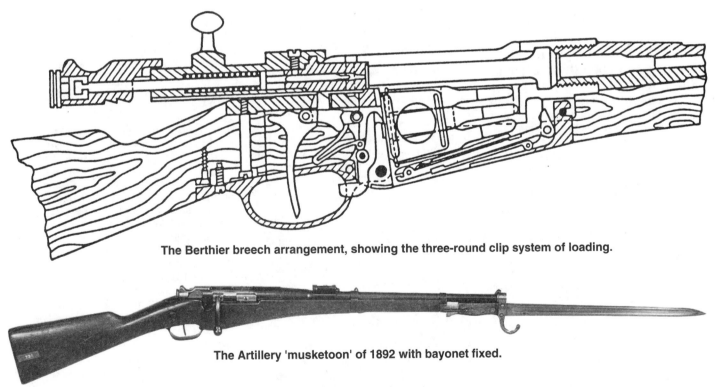

The Berthier breech arrangement, showing the three-round clip system of loading.

The Artillery 'musketoon' of 1892 with bayonet fixed.

'mousqueton'—in reality a short rifle—carried a cleaning rod in a channel hollowed out in the left side of the forend. A knife bayonet was supplied with the gun, whose three-round magazine was entirely contained within the stock.

Length: 36.90in (937mm). **Weight unloaded:** 6lb 12oz (3.06kg). **Barrel:** 17.50in (444mm), 4 grooves, left-hand twist. **Magazine:** 3-round integral clip-loaded box. **Muzzle velocity:** c.2000 ft/sec (609 m/sec).

• **Gendarmerie Short Rifle Model 1892.**

Identical with the artillery model of the same year.

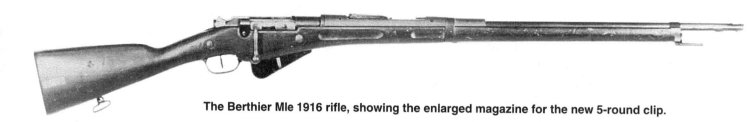

The Berthier Mle 1916 rifle, showing the enlarged magazine for the new 5-round clip.

• Short Rifle Model 1892/27

A conversion of the 1892 system guns—applied to either Artillery or Gendarmerie weapons—in which the action was suitably modified to use the five-round clip. Apart from various detail alterations mainly concerning the removal of the cleaning rod and the filling-in of the stock channel, the Mle 92/27 was recognizable from the Mle 16 or the Mle 16/27 by the absence of an over-barrel handguard.

• Rifle, Indo-China, Model 1902

The first rifle to be manufactured on the Berthier system, the Mle 02 was no more than a rifle-length version of the Mle 92 carbines. The rifle was not issued on a large scale, except to native levies in French Indo-China, and served essentially as a prototype for the succeeding designs of 1907 and 1915.

• Rifle, Sénégal, Model 1907 (sometimes called the 'Colonial Rifle')

As a result of the trials of the Mle 02 in Indo-China, a modified rifle was issued to colonial troops in 1907, although the two patterns only differed in minor respects. The three-round clip of the Mousqueton Mle 92 was used, and the rifle had a one-piece stock without a handguard. The caliber of the Mle 07, like all the rifles and carbines before it of similar system, was 8mm.

• Infantry Rifle Model 1907/15

After the start of World War I, the French authorities soon realized that the Berthier rifles were much superior to the Lebel patterns then in the hands of the line infantry; the 'colonial' Mle 07 rifle was seized upon as a replacement and entered into production—with only minor variations to the sights and action - as the Fusil Mle 07/15. As well as the French production, some of the rifles were manufactured in the United States of America by the Remington Arms-Union Metallic Cartridge Company of Ilion, NY.

Length: 51.24in (1303mm).
Weight unloaded: 8lb 6oz (3.79kg).

Barrel: 31.40in (798mm), 4 grooves, left-hand twist. **Magazine:** 3-round integral clip-loaded box. **Muzzle velocity:** c.2350 ft/sec (716 m/sec).

• Infantry Rifle Model 1916

It was soon realized that the three-round Chargeur Mle 92 had insufficient capacity for the trenches, and so a modified pattern—the Chargeur Mle 15—was issued in 1916 to hold five rounds; as a result, the Fusil Mle 07/15 was redesigned to use the enlarged clip and became the Mle 16. The weapon is easily recognized by the full-length one-piece stock—with a handguard—and the protruding magazine box. The caliber was still 8mm.

Length: 51.24in (1303mm). **Weight unloaded:** 9lb 3oz (4.15kg). **Barrel:** 31.40in (798mm), 4 grooves, left-hand twist. **Magazine:** 5-round clip-loaded box. **Muzzle velocity:** c.2350 ft/sec (716 m/sec).

• Short Rifle Model 1916

A carbine version of the Fusil Mle 16 built around the five-shot clip, the Mousqueton Mle 16 could again be distinguished from the earlier 1892 system by the presence of a handguard and the protruding magazine. A cleaning rod was carried in a channel in the left side of the stock, and the butt had a sling bar.

• Short Rifle Modéle 1916/27

A conversion of the basic five-shot Mle 16 to approximate to the Mle 92/27 conversion, executed by the removal of the cleaning rod (and the filling of the stock channel) and the addition to the nosecap of a piling hook

• Infantry Rifle Model 1907/15 M34 (or Mle 1934)

A much-modified and shortened form of the basic rifle Mle 07/15, in which the Mannlicher pattern magazine was discarded in favor of a staggered-row box of Mauser type. The old 8mm Lebel cartridge had been replaced in the French service the rimless 7.5mm Mle 24—an experimental issue—and its successor the 7.5x54mm Mle 29. The Fusil Mle 07/15 M34 was chambered for the latter round.

Length: 42.70in (1084mm). **Weight unloaded:** 7lb 13oz (3.53kg). **Barrel:** 22.62in (575mm), 4 grooves, left-hand twist. **Magazine:** 5-round integral box. **Muzzle velocity:** c.2600 ft/sec (792 m/sec).

• Cavalry Carbine Model 1907/15 M34

Identical with the infantry rifle of the same pattern, but with the bolt handle turned down so that it lay along the stock.

• Fusil MAS 36, Fusil MAS 36-CR39 (1936)

Manufacture d'Armes de Saint-Etienne, Saint-Etienne
7.5x54mm Mle 29

French experience in World War I convinced them that the 8mm Mle 86 cartridge had outlived its usefulness; an awkward shape, with a wide rim and a sharp taper to the bottleneck, it was particularly inconvenient for automatic weapons and could not stand comparison with the better-proportioned cartridges used elsewhere. Since one of the prime French needs in the post-war years was a good light machine gun, the logical place to start was by designing a new cartridge. After much trial, in 1924 a new 7.5mm rimless round, more or less based on the 7.92mm Mauser, appeared but it turned out to be less than successful and after more development a slightly shorter round appeared in 1929. The desired machine gun followed, and after that thoughts turned to a new magazine rifle.

The result was known as the MAS 36, in general design a modified Mauser, but with the bolt altered so as to lock into the receiver of the weapon behind the magazine rather than into the breech aperture. This allows a shorter bolt stroke, but is, of course, less strong than the original Mauser design, and owing to this design it proved necessary to bend the bolt handle forward (in a very awkward fashion) to bring it into a convenient position for the firer's hand. Like its predecessors in French service, the MAS 36 had no safety catch. It was the last bolt-action general-service rifle ever

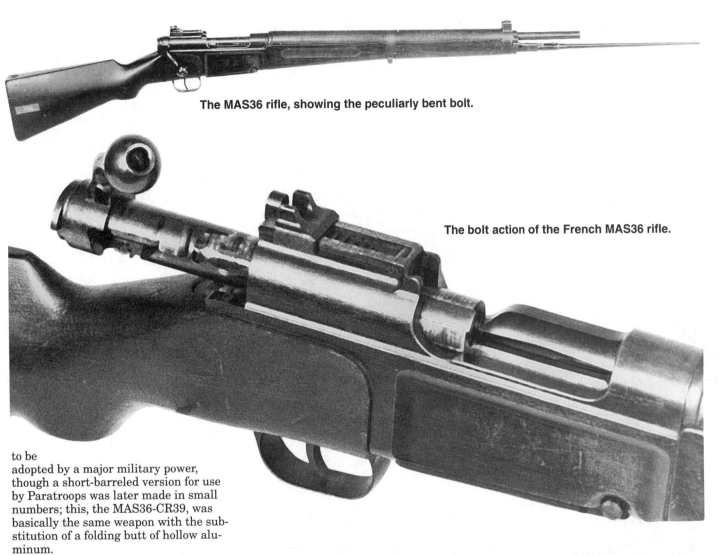

The MAS36 rifle, showing the peculiarly bent bolt.

The bolt action of the French MAS36 rifle.

to be adopted by a major military power, though a short-barreled version for use by Paratroops was later made in small numbers; this, the MAS36-CR39, was basically the same weapon with the substitution of a folding butt of hollow aluminum.

Length: 40.15in (1020mm). **Weight unloaded:** 8lb 5oz (3.78kg). **Barrel:** 22.60in (573mm), 4 grooves, left-hand twist. **Magazine:** 5-round integral box. **Muzzle velocity:** c.2700 ft/sec (823 m/sec).

• Fusil 1, o Fusil Modéle F1 (1979)

Manufacture Nationale d'Armes de Saint-Etienne, Saint-Etienne
7.5x54mm Mle 29; 7.62x51mm NATO

The Model F1 was a bolt-action magazine rifle of modern design and considerable precision. It was offered in three versions: Modéle A for sniping, Modéle B for competition shooting and Modéle C for big-game hunting. The Modéle A is in service with the French Army and so, too, was the Modéle B, as it was used by the victorious French Army team in the 1966 Prix Leclerc NATO shooting competition. In design, the rifle is of no great novelty, since it is little more than the action of the MAS-36, but it is

The French FR-F1 sniping rifle.

undoubtedly carefully constructed, and much effort went into the machining of the components and the setting up of the whole weapon; it was not cheap. Butt length could be adjusted by a series of extension pieces and the sniping version had a folding bipod which made for steadier aiming. A night sight to aid shooting in poor light was available, and the rifle was normally fitted with a telescope sight for daylight use. The trigger pull could be adjusted by a micrometer screw and a number of different front sight fittings were supplied. The weapon was really a specialized competition rifle which had been militarized for the sniping role, and this might be a better approach than the more usual one of attempting to improve the accuracy of a standard military rifle which was never meant to shoot to such fine limits.

Length: 44.70in (1138mm). **Weight unloaded:** 11lb 7oz (5.20kg). **Barrel:** 21.70in (552mm), 4 grooves, right-hand twist. **Magazine:** 10-round detachable box. **Muzzle velocity:** c.2800 ft/sec (853 m/sec).

• Fusil FR-F2 (1990)
Giat Industries, Versailles-Satory
7.62x51mm NATO

After some years of experience with the F1 sniping rifle, the French Army suggested some improvements, which were incorporated into a fresh design, the FR-F2. The basic action remains the same repeating bolt action. The bipod is stronger and has been moved back to a position at the front of the receiver where it can be more readily adjusted by the firer without unnecessary movement, and it is suspended by a yoke around the rear end of the barrel. The forend is of steel, covering a black plastic. The most obvious change is the enclosure of the barrel inside a thermal sleeve which

The French FR-F2 with thermal sleeve around the barrel.

reduces disturbance of the sight line by heat haze and also reduces the infrared signature of the rifle.

Length: 44.80in (1138mm). **Weight unloaded:** 11lb 7oz (5.20kg). **Barrel:** 21.73in (552mm), 4 grooves, right-hand twist. **Magazine:** 10-round detachable box. **Muzzle velocity:** c.2690 ft/sec (820 m/sec).

GERMANY (PRE-1945)

• Commission Rifle Model 1888
Various manufacturers
7.92x57mm Gew Patr 88 (originally)

The Commission rifle was adopted by the German Army in 1888. Committees in general design poor weapons, as they tend to try to add too many desirable features, resulting in an over-complicated or inefficient weapon; in the case of this rifle, however, the result was a strong and workable design in no way inferior to the weapons of other contemporary armies (although the rifle became obsolescent within a few years). Probably the best and longest-lasting result of the 1888 committee's work was the adoption of the 7.92mm cartridge which has continued, with periodic improvements, to the present day, and which has become so inseparably linked with the Mauser rifle that it has become popularly known as the '7.92mm Mauser'.

The Reichs-Commissions-Gewehr had a short life. While mechanically sound (many thousands survive to this day, converted to fire various commercial

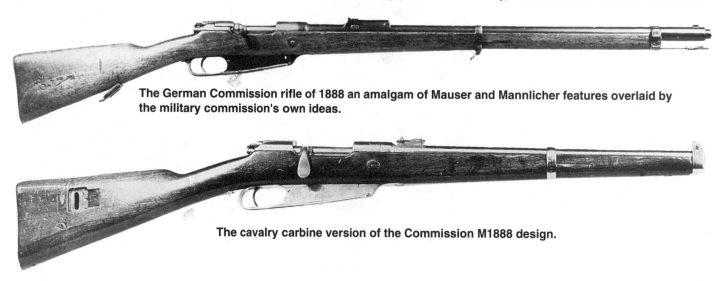

The German Commission rifle of 1888 an amalgam of Mauser and Mannlicher features overlaid by the military commission's own ideas.

The cavalry carbine version of the Commission M1888 design.

cartridges), its downfall was caused by the limitation imposed by the clip-loading system which prevented the rifle being use as a single-loader and also prevented the firer topping-up the magazine with loose rounds. Other nations were content with the Mannlicher system, but the Germans demanded something better and evolved the Mauser Gew. 98.

This original rifle had a barrel jacket in the manner of the later Belgian Mauser of 1889, a straight or 'English' style stock, a protruding box magazine formed as a continuation of the triggerguard, and a split-bridge receiver in front of which the bolt handle locked down. A bar for the sword or knife bayonet appeared on the right side of the nosecap. The various versions of the Gewehr 88 saw wide service in World War I, particularly in the hands of the German Army's second-line, garrison and line of communication troops.

Length: 48.80in (1240mm). **Weight unloaded:** 8lb 7oz (3.82kg). **Barrel:** 29.15in (740mm), 4 grooves, right-hand twist.

Magazine: 5-round clip-loaded box. **Muzzle velocity:** c.2100 ft/sec (640 m/sec).

• Infantry Rifle Model 1898 (Gewehr 98)

Waffenfabrik Mauser AG, Oberndorf-am-Neckar
7.92x57mm Gewehr Patrone 1898

This version of the Mauser rifle was one of the most widely adopted. It shared the distinction of being the most extensively distributed Mauser rifle with the Spanish model, which also spread far and wide across the world. The Gew. 98 introduced an improved bolt with a third locking lug behind the bolt handle engaging in a recess in the body. Although not a particularly valuable item in itself, it formed a useful and perhaps necessary safety factor. Other recognition features were the stock with its pistol-grip swelling on the underside, its horizontal bolt-handle, rather an ugly and clumsy arrangement; and the tangent rear sight. The rear sight was a most elaborate affair of substantial ramps and slides.

The magazine was wholly contained within the body, and the lower plate of the magazine was a continuation of the triggerguard. Loading was by means of a five-round charger inserted into the open action, from which the rounds were pressed down into the magazine. Mauser 98 bolt actions are still being manufactured, by a number of firms, and form the basis of more than half the world's sporting rifles.

The Gew 98 was among the most successful military rifles ever produced, and it has only been rivaled in recent years by the phenomenal numbers of Soviet AK47 and derivatives which are now in circulation. Literally millions of rifles based on the Gew 98 have been made, and many of them still survive. The German Army was still carrying substantial numbers of them in 1939, as were many other countries. They were reliable, robust and accurate. Their detractors always pointed to the forward locking lugs and claimed that they were difficult to keep clean and free from

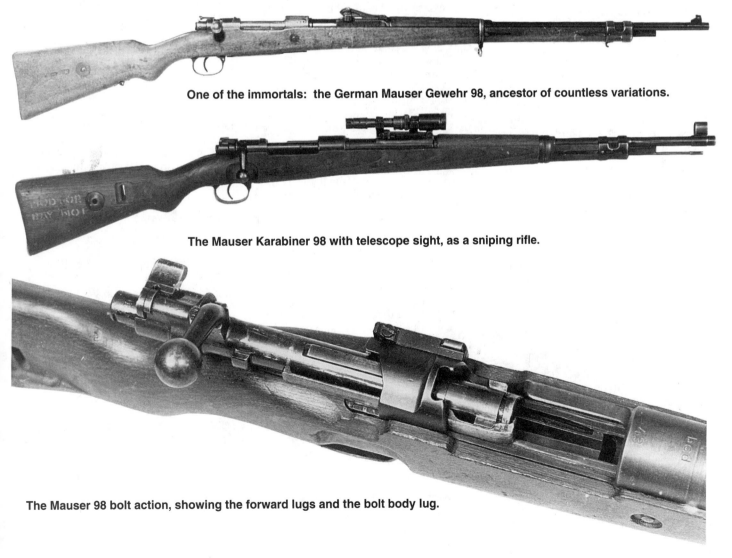

One of the immortals: the German Mauser Gewehr 98, ancestor of countless variations.

The Mauser Karabiner 98 with telescope sight, as a sniping rifle.

The Mauser 98 bolt action, showing the forward lugs and the bolt body lug.

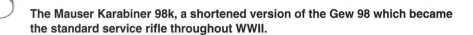

The Mauser Karabiner 98k, a shortened version of the Gew 98 which became the standard service rifle throughout WWII.

fouling, but this was never entirely borne out in practice, and those who carried the Mauser were content with its excellent performance. Only in one respect could it be faulted: the straight bolt did not lend itself to rapid fire, and the arm motion necessary to work it was both awkward and slow.

Length: 49.40in (1255mm.). **Weight unloaded:** 9lb 0oz (4.14kg). **Barrel:** 29.15in (740mm), 4 grooves, right-hand twist. **Magazine:** 5-round internal box. **Muzzle velocity:** c.2850 ft/sec (870 m/sec).

• Carbine Model 1898 (Kar 98), Model 1898a (Kar 98a), Model 1898k (Kar 98k)

Waffenfabrik Mauser AG, Oberndorf-am-Neckar
7.92x57mm Mauser

The Kar 98 was no more than a short-stocked version of the original Mauser Gew 98 rifle. It was a rather clumsy little carbine and was only manufactured from 1899 to 1903. After this, there was a break in the issue of carbines while other designs were considered. In 1904, Mauser had startled the military world with his 'spitzer' pointed nose bullets, and there was some consideration at Oberndorf as to the best pattern of carbine to fire it. Another factor was the adoption by the British and US armies of 'universal' rifles which could serve as both infantry rifles and cavalry carbines, and which were manifestly as successful in both roles as had been their specialist predecessors.

The 1904 pattern of the Kar 98 differed from the previous one in that the handguard was removed on the upper surface of the barrel forward of the first band. The bolt was turned down not only to make it easier to grasp, but also to prevent it catching in clothing and equipment. At the same time,

a recess was cut into the wood of the stock to allow an easier grip. There was a prominent stacking hook under the muzzle. The 1904 carbine was not issued until 1908, but it steadily replaced the rifle in general service, and was the standard weapon of World War I.

After 1920, the 1904 pattern was regularized by being renamed the Kar 98a, but no changes were made to the weapon itself. The 98b was an aberration; it was the Gew 98 rifle given a turn down bolt, and simplified sights. It was not a carbine at all.

The Kar 98k was the standard rifle of World War II. The 'k' stands for '*kurz*' (short) and distinguishes it from the 98a, which was a bit longer. The 98k appeared in 1935 and was little different from the 98a, except that it was of new manufacture. No real attempt was made to bring the model up to date, largely because at that time, German industry was overloaded with other projects, particularly tanks and aircraft. Infantry weapons received scant attention in the excitement of re-arming, and it was easy to take the existing drawings and simply make the same design. Manufacture continued throughout the war, not necessarily in the Mauser factory, but later models showed the shortages in Germany towards the end, particularly in the inferior wood used in the stocks. The 98k was the last Mauser bolt-action military rifle. It was in the best traditions of the Mauser design, and was both reliable and strong. Argument will always flourish as to whether it was better or worse than other designs, particularly the British Lee derivatives, but whatever the failings of the 98k, it served the German infantryman well.

Length: 43.60in (1110mm). **Weight unloaded:** 8lb 9oz (3.90kg). **Barrel:** 23.60in (600mm), 4 grooves, right-hand twist.

Magazine: 5-round internal box. **Muzzle velocity:** c.2450 ft/sec (745 m/sec).

The success of the 1904 pattern carbine inspired a number of nations to copy it, or make it under license, and both Czechoslovakia and Poland built versions of it. Subsequently, the German Army was able to take these into service as part of the spoils of war. The two most notable and widely used were:

• Gewehr Model 29/40(ö)

This was the German service version of the Austrian-manufactured Model 31 commercial rifle, made at Steyr by Osterreichische Waffenfabrik; most were delivered to the Luftwaffe.

• Gewehr Model 33/40

Sometimes known as 'Gew 33/40(t)', this was a German-adopted variation of the Czech Carbine 33, with modifications made to shorten and lighten it. The result was a short lightweight carbine issued to mountain troops; like all such guns firing a full-powered cartridge, the Gew 33/40 had a violent recoil and excessive muzzle blast.

Length: 39.37in (1000mm). **Weight unloaded:** 7lb 15oz (3.65kg). **Barrel:** 19.30in (490mm), 4 grooves, right-hand twist. **Magazine:** 5-round internal box. **Muzzle velocity:** c.2350 ft/sec (715 m/sec).

GERMANY (FEDERAL REPUBLIC)

• Mauser SP66 Sniping Rifle (1976)

Mauser-Werke Oberndorf Waffensysteme GmbH, Oberndorf-am-Neckar
7.62x51mm NATO

Introduced in 1976, this was offered as a military sniping rifle, but was actually Mauser's commercial 'Model 66S Super Match', the 'S' indicating the use of the Gehmann-designed 'short action' bolt and receiver. The barrel is heavy gauge

The Mauser SP66 sniping rifle with an image-intensifying night vision sight by the Dutch company Oldelft.

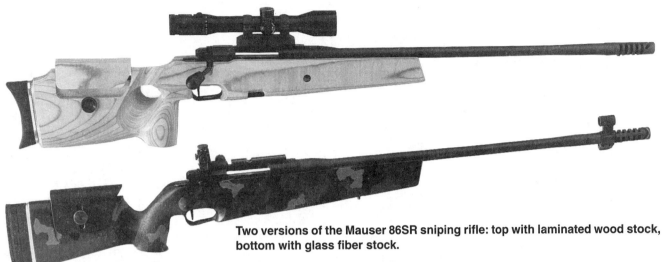

Two versions of the Mauser 86SR sniping rifle: top with laminated wood stock, bottom with glass fiber stock.

and made of special rust-inhibiting steel, fitted with a combined muzzle brake and flash hider. The stock is fully adjustable and incorporates a thumb-hole to assist in maintaining a regular grip. Iron sights are available, but the rifle is normally fitted with a Zeiss 'Diavari ZA' zoom telescope giving 1.5 to 6x magnification. It can also be fitted with more or less any type of telescope or image-intensifying sight to order, and the rifle can also be supplied to special order in any chosen caliber.

Length: 44.09in (1120mm). **Weight:** 13lb 8oz (6.12kg) with Zeiss telescope. **Barrel:** 28.74in (730mm) with muzzle brake; 4 grooves, right-hand twist. **Magazine:** 3-round integral. **Muzzle velocity:** c.2850 ft/sec (869 m/sec).

• Mauser Model 86 Sniping Rifle (1985)
Mauser-Werke Oberndorf Waffensysteme GmbH, Oberndorf-am-Neckar
7.62x51mm NATO

This was introduced as an alternative to the SP66, using the same short-throw bolt but with a much larger capacity magazine. The forend is ventilated to dissipate heat, the trigger is fully adjustable and the barrel is fitted with a muzzle brake. The laminated stock has an adjustable recoil pad, and the forend carries a rail for fitting a sling, hand-stop or bipod. No iron sights are fitted, a telescope mount being provided instead.

Length: 47.63in (1210mm). **Weight:** 10lb 9oz (4.90kg). **Barrel:** 28.74in (730mm) with muzzle brake. 4 grooves, right-hand twist. **Magazine:** 9-round integral. **Muzzle velocity:** c.2850 ft/sec (869 m/sec).

• Mauser SR93 sniping rifle (1993)
Mauser-Werke Oberndorf Waffensysteme GmbH, Oberndorf-am-Neckar
300 Winchester Magnum or 338 Lapua Magnum

This rifle appeared in 1993, having been developed in answer to a German Army requirement for a sniping rifle capable of defeating body armor at 600 meters range. It uses a short-throw bolt action which is unusual in that it can be adapted very quickly and easily for right- or left-handed firers without the use of tools. The action is assembled on a light alloy frame which is then clad in a synthetic stock with fully adjustable butt and a pistol grip. A bipod is fitted into the forend, and a collapsible monopod is fitted into the pistol grip. The barrel is free-floating and fitted with a muzzle brake.

Length: 48.43in (1230mm). **Weight:** 13lb 0oz (5.90kg). **Barrel:** 27.17in (690mm) with muzzle brake; 4 grooves, right-hand twist. **Magazine:** 6-round integral (.300); or 5-round integral (.308). **Muzzle velocity:** c.3238 ft/sec (987 m/sec) (.300).

GREAT BRITAIN

• The Lee-Metford System
Royal Small Arms Factory, Enfield Lock
303 British

During the 1880s the British Army busied itself with the study of various rifle systems, in an endeavor to determine which might best suit their requirements, and their deliberations ended with the adoption in 1888 of the Lee-Metford rifle, under the official designation of 'Rifle, Magazine, Mark 1'. This utilized the turn-bolt action and magazine of James Paris Lee, the Scots-born American inventor, together with the rifling and barrel designed by William Metford specifically to combat the fouling inherent in the blackpowder propelling charges of the time.

• Rifle, Magazine, Mark 1 (1888)
A bolt-action rifle with dust-cover, and with a box magazine holding eight rounds of 303 British cartridges in a single column. The front sight was a square block with a vertical slot in it, and the rear sight was a square notch, fixed in its lowest place at 300yds and graduated to 1900yds. On the side of the stock were a set of 'Extreme Range Sights' graduated from 1800yds to 3500yds. In August 1891, the designation of this rifle was changed to 'Rifle, Magazine, Lee-Metford Mark 1'.

Length: 49.50in (1257mm). **Weight unloaded:** 9lb 8oz (4.37kg). **Barrel:** 30.20in (769mm), 7 grooves, left-hand twist. **Magazine:** 8-round detachable box. **Muzzle velocity:** c.2200 ft/sec (670 m/sec).

• Rifle, Magazine, Lee-Metford Mark 1* (1892).
The design was sealed to govern future manufacture and also to govern the conversion of stocks of the Mark 1 Rifle. The safety catch on the cocking

The Mark 1 or 'Long Lee-Metford' rifle.

piece was omitted, the handguard was modified and a brass disc for regimental numbering was let into the butt, the stacking swivel was strengthened, the bolt mainspring was of 32 coils of .049-inch wire instead of 39 coils of .040-inch wire (with a length of 3.25-inch instead of 5.00-inch), the magazine spring had four coils instead of three, a blade front sight was fitted—in converted rifles it was pinned into the original front sight block—and the sight graduations were altered to take account of new ammunition having a velocity of 2000 ft/sec (609 m/sec). The long-range sight was consequently regraduated from 1600 yards to 2900 yards.

• Rifle, Magazine, Lee-Metford Mark 2 (1892)

The principal difference between this and the previous models was that the magazine was changed to a pattern holding ten rounds in two columns, and as a result, the body was somewhat modified in contour. The magazine spring was of 'C' shape instead of a coil, the barrel was lighter, and there were minor variations in the construction of the bolt and magazine cut-off. The weight was now 9lb 4oz (4.25kg). A number were rebarreled with Enfield rifling in 1902, and had 'E' stamped on the Knox-form, though the nomenclature remained unchanged.

• Rifle, Magazine, Lee-Metford Mark 2* (1895)

This differed from the Mark 2 in that the bolt was lengthened by 1.00in

(25.40mm) and fitted with two grooves for a safety catch, and the cocking piece was also lengthened and fitted with the safety catch. In 1903, some rifles were rebarreled with Enfield rifling, and marked 'E' on the Knox-form, the designation being changed to 'Rifle, Magazine, Lee-Enfield Mark 1' if fitted with the original pattern of nose-cap, or 'Mark 1*' if fitted with the later pattern of solid forend and nose-cap,

• Rifle, Charger-Loading, Magazine, Lee-Metford Mark 2 (1907).

This is a conversion from the Mark 2, achieved by fitting a bridge charger guide across the bolt way, and a new magazine; the rifle also had an adjustable blade front sight with a fixed protector, and a new rear sight graduated for smokeless powder ammunition.

Length: 49.50in (1257mm). **Weight unloaded:** 9lb 8oz (4.31kg). **Barrel:** 30.18in (766mm), 7 grooves, left-hand twist. **Magazine:** 10-round detachable box. **Muzzle velocity:** 2060 ft/sec (642 m/sec).

• Carbine, Magazine, Lee-Metford Mark 1 (1894)

The carbine was based on the Rifle Mark 2, but differed in a number of small ways as well as in major dimensions; the total length was a mere 39.94in (1014mm), the barrel length was 20.75in (527mm), and the weight 7lb 7oz (3.42kg). The carbine's rifling was identical with that of the rifle.

• The Lee-Enfield System
Royal Small Arms Factory, Enfield Lock, Middlesex
303 British

With the adoption of cordite as the standard military propellant, a change in rifling was made. Because cordite left virtually no residue in the bore after firing, the principal advantage of Metford rifling no longer existed, and it was possible to adopt a more efficient pattern of rifling which was better suited to a high-velocity rifle. This was the Enfield rifling—named from its development at the Royal Small Arms Factory, Enfield Lock—and the marriage of this to the Lee action produced the Lee-Enfield rifle. A carbine model was also produced, and there were a number of earlier patterns which were modernized by rebarreling with Enfield barrels.

• Rifle, Magazine, Lee-Enfield Mark 1 (1895)

This was much the same as the Lee-Metford Mark 2*, differing only in the rifling which had 5 grooves, .005-inch deep, with a left-hand twist pitched to make one turn in 10 inches. The front sight was positioned .05-inch left of the bore axis to compensate for the drift of the bullet. The rifle's length was 49.50in (1257mm), the barrel length 30.22in (767mm) and the weight 9lb 4oz (4.19kg).

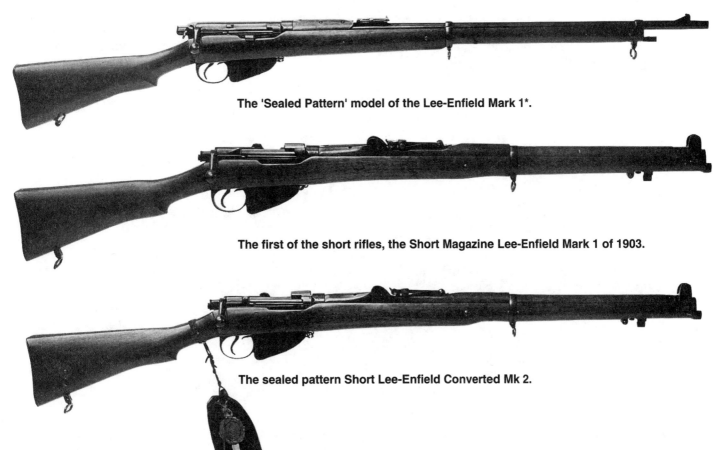

The 'Sealed Pattern' model of the Lee-Enfield Mark 1*.

The first of the short rifles, the Short Magazine Lee-Enfield Mark 1 of 1903.

The sealed pattern Short Lee-Enfield Converted Mk 2.

• Rifle, Magazine, Lee-Enfield Mark 1* (1899)

This is simply the Mark 1 without the attached cleaning rod and its fittings. The reduction in fouling due to the use of cordite propellant rendered the ramrod obsolete; it was replaced by the cord pull-through.

• Rifle, Short, Magazine, Lee-Enfield Mark 1 (1903)

With the intention of developing one rifle which would serve the infantryman as a rifle and everybody else as a carbine, the 'Short Lee-Enfield' was designed. Universally execrated by every self-styled expert in the Western world when it was introduced, the rifle was held to be too short to be a target-shooter's arm and too long to be a cavalryman's companion—and that, in fact, it was an abortionate device developed by unscrupulous government technicians, by robbing wherever possible every good feature from other rifles and then ruining them. In spite of this chorus of woe the 'SMLE' survived, to become in its later versions probably the finest combat bolt-action rifle ever developed. Its most obvious feature was the all-embracing furniture and the snub nose. The rear sight was half-way down the barrel, at a time when advanced thought was turn-ing to aperture rear sights under the shooter's eyelids, and the familiar Lee magazine protruded through the bottom. The original introduction was cancelled, and the design was slightly altered by the addition of a wind-gauge to the rear sight, and the substitution of screws for rivets in one or two minor places, after which it was reintroduced on 14 September 1903.

Length: 44.57in (1132mm). **Weight unloaded:** 8lb 2oz (3.71kg). **Barrel:** 25.19in (640mm), 5 grooves, left-hand twist. **Magazine:** 10-round detachable box. **Muzzle velocity:** c.2200 ft/sec (670 m/sec).

• Rifle, Short, Magazine, Lee-Enfield Mark 1* (1906)

This was a version of the Mark 1 incorporating several small improvements suggested after the originals had passed into the hands of the troops. The old butt plate was replaced by one of gun-metal and incorporated a butt-trap for cleaning materials and an oil-bottle, a Number 2 pattern magazine and spring were substituted (being slightly deeper at the front), the striker was retained by a keeper screw which had a slot big enough to be turned by a coin, and the sharp corners on various components were rounded.

• Rifle, Short, Magazine, Lee-Enfield Converted Mark 1 (1903)

A conversion of the Lee-Metford Mark 1* by fitting new sights, shorter and lighter barrels, and adapting them for charger loading. The original announcement stated that the design was 'sealed to govern such conversion as might be ordered,' but none except the sealed pattern was ever made and the design was declared obsolete in 1906.

• Rifle, Short, Magazine, Lee-Enfield Converted Mark 2 (1903)

A conversion of the Lee-Enfield Marks 1 and 1* and Lee-Metford Marks 2 and 2* achieved by fitting new sights, shorter and lighter barrels and modifying the action bodies to permit loading by charger.

• Rifle, Short, Magazine, Lee-Enfield Converted Mark 2* (1906)

A conversion similar to the Converted Mark 2, from which it differed in having the butt recessed for the sling swivel, provision for a butt trap, and a Number 2 magazine.

The perfected design, the SMLE Mark 3, was the rifle with which the British Army fought WWI.

The closed bolt of the SMLE Mark 3, showing the charger guide (in the receiver bridge), the cut-off (protruding between the bolt and magazine) and the safety catch just visible on the far side of the bolt handle. The safety was always applied with the forefinger, while the remaining fingers of the right hand pressed the bolt handle down. (There were no left-handed soldiers in the British Army—by order!).

Another SMLE bolt, this time of 1917 manufacture; as a concession to speed up wartime production the cocking-piece on the bolt has no knurled head, and there is no cut-off in the magazine.

• Rifle, Short, Magazine, Lee-Enfield Mark 3 (1907)

The principle change in the Mark 3 lay in the sights: it was otherwise the same as the Mark l or 1*. The front sight was a simple blade instead of a barley-corn (an inverted V) and was supplied in five heights. The rear sight bed was wider, and the sight leaf—graduated on the left and right sides to 2000yds—had a fine adjustment worm wheel. A 'U' notch replaced the former 'V' notch. The body was fitted with a bridge charger-guide shaped so that the closing movement of the bolt would automatically eject the

The SMLE Converted Mark 4 rifle.

charger; and the charger guide on the bolt head was omitted. The weight was 8lb 10.5oz (3.94kg).

In 1916, as a wartime concession to the manufacturers, it was agreed that rifles might embody any of the following modifications: omission of the long-range sights, replacement of the rear sight wind gauge by a fixed cap, alteration of the contours of the striker, and omission of the stacking swivel lugs.

• Rifle, Short, Magazine, Lee-Enfield Converted Mark 4 (1907)

This differed from the Converted Mark 2* in so far as it embodied the various special features of the SMLE Mark 3. Weight: 8lb 14.5oz (4.13kg).

• Rifle, Charger Loading, Magazine, Lee-Enfield Mark 1* (1907)

A conversion of Lee-Enfield Marks 1 and 1* or Lee-Metford Mark 2* by the addition of a bridge charger guide, a new magazine and a new rear sight.

• Rifle, Short, Magazine, Lee-Enfield Mark 1** (1909)

This weapon was issued only to the Royal Navy, and was a conversion from SMLE Mark 1 rifles carried out in naval ordnance depots at Chatham, Portsmouth and Plymouth. It consisted of fitting a SMLE Mark 3 front sight, and a rear sight wind-gauge with a 'U' notch to suit.

• Rifle, Short, Magazine, Lee-Enfield Converted Mark 2** (1909)

Another naval conversion, the same as the Mark 1** but performed on the SMLE Mark 2 rifle.

• Rifle, Short, Magazine, Lee-Enfield Converted Mark 2*** (1909)

The third naval conversion, as before, applied to the SMLE Converted Mark 2*.

• Rifle, Short, Magazine, Lee-Enfield Mark 1*** (1914)

A conversion from the SMLE Mark 1* achieved by fitting a wind-gauge with 'U' notch to the rear sight and a new blade front sight to suit Mark 7 ball ammunition. This marked the adoption of the Mark 7 pointed bullet, which superseded the Mark 6 blunt-nosed bullet.

• Rifle, Short, Magazine, Lee-Enfield Mark 3* (1916)

This was a wartime model differing from the Mark 3 in having the magazine cut-off omitted during manufacture.

• Carbine, Magazine, Lee-Enfield Mark 1 (1902)

To quote the official paragraph: 'When Carbines Magazine Lee-Metford Mark 1 are fitted with Lee-Enfield barrels and have the wings of the nosecaps drawn out to the same height as that on the Lee-Enfield Carbines, they will be described as above. The barrels will be marked by the manufacturer on the Knox-form with the letter "E".

• Carbine, Magazine, Lee-Enfield Cavalry Mark 1 (1907)

The first purpose-built Enfield-rifled carbine, it was basically the Lee-Metford carbine Mark 1 with Enfield rifling, improved sights, the sling fittings omitted, and an attached leather cover for the rear sight. The weight and dimensions remained the same as the earlier gun.

Between the wars, the British Army decided to change the system of nomenclature of its rifles. The foregoing examples have shown how cumbrous the titles had become, and in the interests of brevity and accuracy the rifles were now listed in a numbered series, so that the 'Rifle, Short, Magazine, Lee-Enfield Mark 3' now became the 'Rifle Number 1 Mark 3', although nobody but quartermasters and armorers ever called it that. Since the last mark issued under the old system was the Converted Mark 4, the first under the new system was the Rifle Number 1 Mk 5. This was made in limited numbers in the early 1920s, but was never accepted as a service weapon. The principle difference between it and the Mark 3 was the moving of the rear sight back to the receiver bridge in an endeavor to improve shooting by making a longer sight base. This model led to the Rifle Number 1 Mark 6, which was a

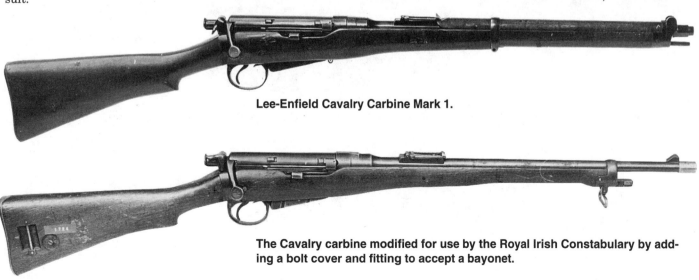

Lee-Enfield Cavalry Carbine Mark 1.

The Cavalry carbine modified for use by the Royal Irish Constabulary by adding a bolt cover and fitting to accept a bayonet.

The Rifle No 1 Mark 5 was a Short Lee-Enfield with a new aperture rear sight. It was never issued, being simply a step towards the Rifle No 4.

further simplification of the Mark 5 and a step on the way to the design of the Rifle Number 4. The Mark 6 was never issued.

The object of all this redesign was to produce a rifle which would retain the general characteristics of the Mark 3, but which would be easier to mass-produce in wartime. The result was the Rifle Number 4.

• Rifle, Number 4, Marks 1-2
Royal Small Arms Factory, Enfield Lock, Middlesex
303 British

The Number 4 was similar to the Short Magazine Lee-Enfield but with an aperture rear sight hinged at the rear of the body, the nosecap abolished and the muzzle exposed

for about three inches. All screw threads were to standard industry specifications instead of being 'gun-maker's specials'.

• Rifle Number 4 Mark 1(T) (1942)

This was the Mark 1 fitted with a tangent rear sight and prepared for a telescopic sight; the butt was fitted with a cheek rest.

• Rifle Number 4 Mark 1* (1941)

This was similar to the Mark 1 pattern, but with the following exceptions: the cutting of a slot and the omission of machining for the breech bolt-head catch, the omission of the breech bolt-head catch (with the

attendant spring and plate), and the addition of a new pattern bridge piece to permit more ready removal of the bolt. The magazine catch screw was replaced by a pin, and the sear pin was increased in length. In other words, a simpler method of bolt removal was devised and instituted. Most of these Mark 1* rifles were made in the United States of America or Canada.

• Rifle Number 4 Mark 2 (1949)

Similar to the Mark 1, the Mark 2 was provided with a new design of trigger mechanism in which the trigger was hinged about a pin located in a bracket forged integrally with the body, instead of being hinged to the trigger guard as hitherto.

The bolt area of the Rifle No 4, which was designed for speed of production and also adopted the aperture rear sight behind the receiver bridge.

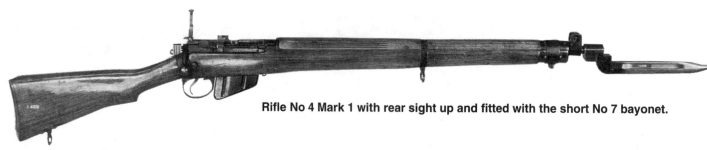

Rifle No 4 Mark 1 with rear sight up and fitted with the short No 7 bayonet.

Rifle No 4 Mark 1* had a two-aperture flip sight and wore the No 4 bayonet.

An experimental version of the Rifle No 4 Mark 2 made entirely of steel; the stock and hand-guard are steel pressings with a plastic coating.

The Rifle No 5 or 'Jungle Carbine'; a handsome weapon with a fatal flaw.

The Rifle No 6 (Australian) was to be the Australian version of the No 5. This is a development model which has the characteristic long handguard but has the rear-set aperture sight instead of the later for-ward-set U-notch sight.

• Rifle Number 4 Mark 1/2 (1949)

A Number 4 Mark 1 modified to approximate to Mark 2 by having the trigger rebuilt.

• Rifle Number 4 Mark 1/3 (1949)

A Number 4 Mark 1* with trigger modified to approximate to Mark 2.
Length: 44.43in (1128mm). **Weight unloaded:** 9lb 1oz (4.17kg). **Barrel:** 25.19in (640mm), 5 grooves, left-hand twist. **Magazine:** 10-round detachable box. **Muzzle velocity:** 2400 ft/sec (731 m/sec).

• Rifle, Number 5, Mark 1 (1945)

Royal Small Arms Factory, Enfield Lock, Middlesex
303 British

This was the famous 'Jungle Car-bine'—virtually a Rifle Number 4 Mark 1 shortened by about 5 inches (126mm). The other distinctive features were the belled-out flash-hider on the muzzle, a single handguard, a short forend stock and a rubber recoil pad on the butt. The rear sight was graduated to 800yds and set by a screw. While dashing in appear-ance and light and handy to carry, it suf-fered from an inbred 'wandering zero' which meant that its accuracy was not consistent. With that and the fact that the gun's recoil was excessive, few sol-diers were sorry to see it go.
Length: 39.37in (1000mm). **Weight unloaded**: 7lb 3oz (3.24kg). **Barrel:** 18.7in (478mm), 5 grooves, left-hand twist. **Maga-zine:** 10-round detachable box. **Muzzle velocity:** c.2000 ft/sec (609 m/sec).

• Rifle No 6 (Australian) Mark 1

Australian Ordnance Factory, Lithgow, NSW.
303 British

This was the Australian equivalent of the British Number 5 rifle, a short car-bine for use in the Far Eastern theater of war. It was almost identical to the Num-ber 5, differing principally in using the tangent U-notch sight of the Short Lee-Enfield rifle instead of the aperture sight of the No 4 and No 5 rifles. The flash hider was modified so that a full-sized bayonet could be fitted, and there were finger-grooves in the forend. It can be readily recognized by the hand-guard being the same length as the forend, rather than being shorter as in the No 5 rifle. It was formally approved for the Australian Army, but just as pro-duction was about to begin the war ended, and no more than a few dozen were made.
Length: 39.00in (991mm). **Weight unloaded:** 7lb 8oz (3.40kg). **Barrel:** 18.5in (470mm), 5 grooves, left-hand twist. **Maga-zine:** 10-round detachable box. **Muzzle velocity:** c.2000 ft/sec (609 m/sec).

The Enfield Pattern 1914 276-caliber rifle.

The open bolt of the P14 rifle, showing the Mauser-pattern locking lugs, aperture sight and right-hand safety catch.

• Rifle, Magazine, .303in Pattern 1914

Various manufacturers (see text)
303 British

When the Short Magazine Lee-Enfield was introduced into British service, it met with a storm of criticism—though little of it came from the soldiers. A typical example, from *Arms and Explosives* magazine for November 1908, states: 'The rifle was always bad, its defects always notorious, and the propagation of badness will doubtless continue for several more generations to come'. Whether or not this campaign of calumny had any effect, the War Office began developing a rifle more in keeping with the critics' ideas of what a military weapon ought to be. The result was based on the Mauser action and was of 0.276-inch (7mm) caliber; after extensive experimentation, both in theory and in practice, it was approved for issue on a trial basis in 1913. The cartridge was roughly based on the Ross 280 and was exceptionally powerful; loaded with cordite, the results included excessive muzzle flash and blast, barrel overheating, severe erosive wear, irregular chamber pressures and premature ignition owing to barrel heat. Before these problems could be

resolved, the outbreak of war caused the whole idea to be indefinitely shelved.

The demands of the war raised problems in mass-producing rifles, high-speed production of the Lee-Enfield was out of the question. The .276-inch rifle had, however, been designed with an eye to rapid production in wartime so the design was taken out and rapidly converted to the standard 303 British chambering; in 1915, manufacturing contracts were placed with Remington and Winchester in the USA and the rifles entered British service as the 'Pattern 1914'.

• Rifle, Magazine, .303in Pattern 1914 Mark 1E (1916)

These rifles can be recognized by the long exposed muzzle and 'wings' protecting the front sight, the prominent aperture rear sight, and also by the fact that the magazine is concealed within the body. Although they may have been designed to the specifications of the target shots, they were not liked by the brutal and licentious soldiery: the P14 was too long, badly balanced, and cumbersome to handle in combat—particularly when garnished by a long bayonet. The 'E' models were made by the Remington Arms-Union Metallic Cartridge Company at their plant at Eddystone Arsenal,

Pennsylvania, and were distinctively marked on the front top of the body appeared 'RE', on the right side of the stock 'IR', and on all the principle components 'E'. The guns survived to serve in World War II, when they were principally used for Home Guard issue, and were finally declared obsolete in July 1947.

Length: 46.30in (1176mm). **Weight unloaded:** 8lb 11oz (3.94kg). **Barrel:** 26.00in (661mm), 5 grooves, left-hand twist. **Magazine:** 5-round integral box. **Muzzle velocity:** 2785 ft/sec (943 m/sec).

• Rifle, Magazine, .303in Pattern 1914 Mark 1R (1916)

Identical with the 'E' model, these were made by the Remington Arms-Union Metallic Cartridge Company at their Bridgeport, Connecticut plant. They were marked 'ERA', '1E' and 'R' in the places noted above. This individual marking was necessary because the components made in the various factories were not completely interchangeable.

• Rifle, Magazine .303in Pattern 1914 Mark 1W (1916)

As for the previous models but made by the Winchester Repeating Arms Company plant in New Haven, Connecticut, and marked 'W', '1W' and 'Ww'.

• Rifle, Magazine, .303in Pattern 1914 Mark 1E', Mark 1R*, Mark 1W*

These three weapons were all introduced in February 1917. They were improved designs, in which the left locking lug on the bolt was lengthened and corresponding changes made to its seat on the rifle's receiver. These rifles were identified by a five-pointed star stamped on the bolt handle and chamber.

• Rifle, Magazine, .303in Pattern 1914 Mark 1*W(T) (1918)

The Mark 1W* with the addition of an Aldis sniping telescope and a cheekpiece on the butt.

The Pattern 1914 rifles were removed from service after World War I and were placed in store. In 1940, they were again issued, but in 1926 the system of rifle nomenclature had changed and hence they were reintroduced as 'Rifles Number 3 Mark 1 or 1* (the 'E', 'R' and 'W' suffixes being no longer distinguished). The sniping version became the Mark 1*(T)'A', the 'A' indicating the use of an Aldis telescope.

• De Lisle Silent Carbine (1943)
Sterling Armaments Co., Dagenham
45 ACP

The De Lisle carbine is an unusual weapon which was produced in England in small numbers during World War II for use by Commandos and other clandestine forces. It was based on a Lee-Enfield bolt action fitted to a 45-caliber barrel which then formed part of a large and highly efficient silencer.

It is, without doubt, one of the few really silent weapons ever developed. The bullet is subsonic, so there is no bullet crack, and the massive silencer muffles the noise of discharge so completely that the only audible noise is that of the firing pin striking the cap. Unfortunately, of course, all this is negated by the clatter of the opening bolt, but, provided the aim had been sure, this really didn't matter in most cases. It is also vastly superior to other silent weapons in the matter of accuracy and range, even though the 45-caliber bullet is not usually considered a long range projectile. The longer-than-usual barrel for this caliber allows the De Lisle to shoot very effectively out to three or four hundred yards, and it is recorded that during the acceptance trials of the weapon, a visiting VIP took the head off a wild duck at 200 yards with his first shot.

Although military use of the De Lisle ceased with the war's end, in the 1980s the weapon was revived by a private manufacturer in Britain and was offered for sale to police and security forces.

Length: 37.80in (960mm). **Weight unloaded:** 8lb 3oz (3.7kg). **Barrel:** 8.27in (210mm), 4 grooves, right hand twist. **Magazine:** 4-round detachable box. **Muzzle velocity:** 854 ft/sec (260 m/sec).

• Parker-Hale Model 82 (1982)
Parker-Hale Limited, Birmingham
7.62x51mm NATO

The Model 82 was a sniping rifle developed with all the expertise of Parker-Hale, who for decades dominated British target shooting with their products. It was a Mauser-type action, with all the components carefully selected and assembled. The one-piece body screwed onto a heavy hammered barrel and there were two bridge sections which carried for the sight mounts. The fully floating barrel

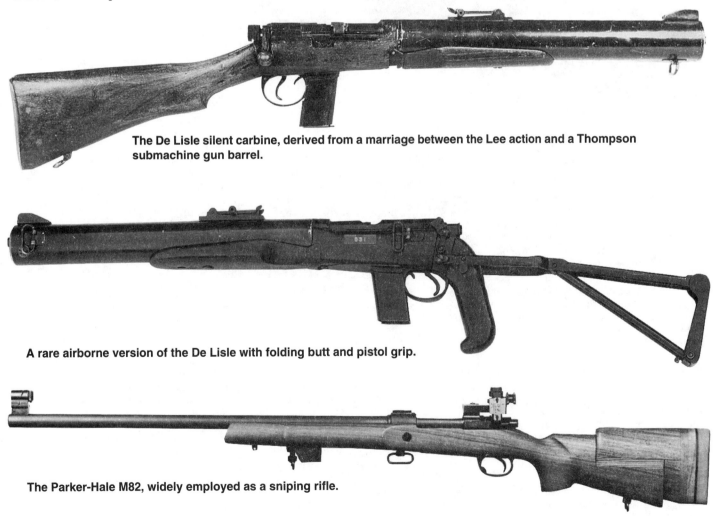

The De Lisle silent carbine, derived from a marriage between the Lee action and a Thompson submachine gun barrel.

A rare airborne version of the De Lisle with folding butt and pistol grip.

The Parker-Hale M82, widely employed as a sniping rifle.

The Parker-Hale M83, adopted as the Cadet Training Rifle L81A1.

Breech area of the Parker-Hale M83, showing the Mauser-style bolt.

The L42A1 sniping rifle was a Lee-Enfield action adapted to the 7.62x51mm cartridge.

was the heaviest target type available and was carefully bedded into the one-piece wooden stock with epoxy resin. The front sight fitted onto a dovetail base at the muzzle, and the actual bore at the muzzle was recessed to prevent damage to the rifling when cleaning. The bolt had the usual Mauser twin front-locking lugs and a smaller rear lug which rode in an inclined camway to give primary extraction. The trigger mechanism was a separate self-contained assembly located by axis pins in the body. The single-stage trigger was adjustable for pull, backlash and creep, but as set by the factory it gave a short pull with the minimum mechanical lock time. A useful military feature was that the safety was silent in operation and worked on trigger, bolt and sear at the same time, providing total safety against accidental firing. The butt was adjustable for different firers and the forward sling swivel and hand stop could be moved over a wide range along the forend.

The Parker-Hale was adopted by Australia and Canada as a sniping rifle

and may have been taken by other armies also, but precise information is not easy to obtain.

Length: 47.75in (1213mm). **Weight unloaded:** 10lb 9oz (4.80kg). **Barrel:** 25.98in (660mm), 4 grooves, right-hand twist. **Magazine:** 4-round, internal box. **Muzzle velocity:** 2821 ft/sec (860 m/sec).

• **Parker-Hale Model 83 (Cadet Training Rifle L81A1) (1983)**
Parker-Hale Limited, Birmingham
7.62x51mm NATO

This was developed from the Model 82 (above) and the P-H 1200TX target rifle, and its appearance is almost identical with that of the Model 82. It is a single-shot rifle, the absence of a magazine and feedway stiffening the action and so improving accuracy. The rifling was matched to the standard 144-grain 7.62mm NATO ball bullet, and the entire length of the action was bedded with Devcon F metal compound. Accuracy is within a half-minute of angle over ten rounds, depending upon the quality of the ammunition; which means all shots

within a 1.5-inch circle at 300 yards range. The target trigger is single-stage and fully adjustable for pull-off, creep and backlash. The length of stock is adjustable, the sights are fully adjustable, and a range of front sight inserts is provided to suit individuals.

This rifle was adopted in 1983 as the British Army's 'Cadet Training Rifle L81A1'. Parker-Hale subsequently developed a Model 85 sniping rifle, but in 1990 closed their rifle business and sold their designs to the Gibbs Rifle Co. in the USA. A description of the Model 85, as made by Gibbs, will be found in the USA section.

Length: 46.73in (1187mm). **Weight unloaded:** 10lb 15oz (4.98kg). **Barrel:** 25.98in (660mm), 4 grooves, right-hand twist. **Magazine:** Single-shot. **Muzzle velocity:** c.2820 ft/sec (860 m/sec).

• **Rifle, 7.62mm, L42A1 (1970)**
Royal Small Arms Factory, Enfield Lock
7.62x51mm NATO

This is a conversion of the .303in Rifle No. 4 Mark 1 or Mark 1*(T) sniping rifle to take the 7.62mm NATO cartridge.

The current sniping rifle in British service is the L96A1 by Accuracy International.

It has a shortened 'sporterized' forend and is fitted with the Telescope, Straight, Sighting, L1. Iron sights are also fitted, and modifications have been made to the extractor to accommodate the rimless cartridge. The same rifle, fitted with a commercial zoom telescope sight, was offered as a police sniping rifle under the name 'Enfield Enforcer'.

Length: 46.50in (1181mm). **Weight unloaded:** 9lb 12oz (4.43kg). **Barrel:** 27.50in (699mm), 4 grooves, right-hand twist. **Magazine:** 10-round detachable box. **Muzzle velocity:** 2750 ft/sec (838 m/sec).

• Rifle, 7.62mm, L39A1 (1970)
Royal Small Arms Factory, Enfield Lock.
7.62x51mm NATO

The L39 was introduced to give the British Forces a competitive target rifle for use by those units which were equipped with the L1A1. It was made by RSAF and was a modified 303 British No. 4. RSAF fitted a heavy barrel and modified the body, bolt and extractor to accept rimless 7.62mm ammunition. At the same time the forend was cut down as far as the lower band. The butt was also from the original No. 4 rifle, but the handguard was taken from a No. 8 22LR rifle, suitably altered. An unusual feature was that the 303 British magazine was retained, since it was assumed that for target shooting each round would be hand-loaded and the only purpose of the magazine was to provide a platform for the round to slide along. There was no positive ejector with this magazine and the fired case lay on the platform until removed by hand. However, a 10-round magazine for 7.62mm ammunition could be fitted and this did eject.

Although this rifle was normally fitted with Parker-Hale target sights, it would also accept the old No. 32 sniping telescope.

Length: 46.50in (1180mm). **Weight unloaded:** 9lb 11oz (4.42kg). **Barrel:** 27.55in (700mm), 4 grooves, right hand twist. **Magazine:** Single-round loading, or 10-round detachable box. **Muzzle velocity:** 2758 ft/sec (841 m/sec).

• Rifle L96A1 (1987)
Accuracy International, Portsmouth
7.62x51mm NATO

In 1985 the British Army began a series of trials to select a new sniping rifle; the final contestants were the Parker-Hale 85 and a design from a private company called the 'PM'. The latter was eventually selected and became the L96A1, and 1212 rifles were purchased.

The rifle broke new ground in design by assembling the various components around a light alloy skeleton frame which was then clad in a plastic stock of more or less conventional shape. As a result, casual damage to the stock makes no difference to the integrity of the weapon and it can actually be fired even if the stock is entirely removed. The stainless steel barrel is free-floating, and the bolt action is a turnbolt with three forward locking lugs and one rear safety lug provided by the handle turning down in front of the receiver bridge. A fully adjustable bipod is fitted to the forward end of the skeleton frame. The British army's specification called for a first-round hit at 600 meters range and accurate harassing fire at 1000 meters; both these requirements are easily met by the L96A1. Iron sights are fitted, but the normal sight is a 6x42 Schmidt & Bender telescope.

The basic design is manufactured for the commercial market in various models, including collapsible and silenced versions, and can be provided in several calibers.

Length: 44.25-47.04in (1124-1194mm) depending on butt adjustment. **Weight unloaded:** 14lb 5oz (6.50kg). **Barrel:** 25.79in (655mm), 4 grooves, right-hand twist. **Magazine:** 10-round detachable box. **Muzzle velocity:** 2790 ft/sec (850 m/sec).

GREECE

• The Mannlicher-Schoenauer

Towards the end of the nineteenth century, many inventors attempted to design and perfect rotary magazines, in an effort to eliminate some of the less desirable feeding characteristics of rimmed cartridges when in a box magazine. Among the Austrians and Hungarians who produced rifles were Antonin Spitalsky, Otto Schoenauer and Josef Schulhof; Mannlicher himself produced two rifles using rotary or 'spool' magazines, one in 1887 (which had been designed c.1885) and 'a straight-pull' rifle in 1888.

Few of these weapons had met with success, and it was not until Schoenauer perfected this design in the 1890s that a chance arose of military adoption of such a magazine. Schoenauer's magazine was allied to a bolt-action designed by Mannlicher, and in c.1900 the rifle was offered to the Austro-Hungarian authorities, who promptly rejected it on the grounds that full-scale production of the 1895 straight-pull design had begun and they did not wish to involve themselves in expensive retooling. But the Greek Army adopted the Mannlicher-Schoenauer rifle in 1903 and many were supplied for the Portuguese trials of 1901-4, where the Mauser-Vergueiro was eventually selected for adoption.

The Schoenauer magazine, also extensively employed in Steyr sporting rifles, used a spring-tensioned rotary spool into which five rounds were loaded from a Mauser-type charger. While ingenious and neat, the spool magazine conferred little advantage over the simpler and cheaper box magazine when rimless cartridges were used, though the design did permit surer feeding of rimmed rounds.

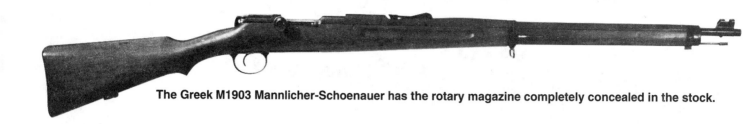

The Greek M1903 Mannlicher-Schoenauer has the rotary magazine completely concealed in the stock.

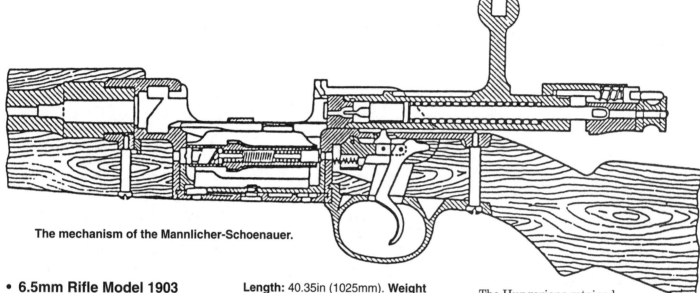

The mechanism of the Mannlicher-Schoenauer.

• 6.5mm Rifle Model 1903

Osterreichische Waffenfabrik-Gesellschaft, Steyr, Austria; Societa Industria Ernesto Breda, Brescia, Italy.
6.5x54mm Mannlicher-Schoenauer

The Greek rifle was the only rotary magazine rifle ever to achieve general service issue (the Johnson autoloading rifle of 1941 and the Steyr SSG69 also used rotary magazines but were restricted issue) and was easily recognized by the lack of a protruding magazine, unique amongst Mannlicher-type rifles. The gun was otherwise similar to the Romanian rifle of 1893, with a split-bridge receiver in which the bolt handle locked down in front of the bridge to supplement the dual locking lugs on the bolt head. Unlike many of the other Mannlichers, the Greek could be cocked simply by raising and lowering the bolt handle, an idea taken from the Mauser system used by the Gew 98.

Length: 48.25in (1225mm). **Weight unloaded:** 8lb 5oz (3.78kg). **Barrel:** 28.55in (725mm), 4 grooves, right-hand twist. **Magazine:** 5-round rotary box. **Muzzle velocity:** c.2230 ft/sec (680 m/sec).

• 6.5mm Carbine Model 1903

The 1903 carbine was simply a shortened full-stocked version of the rifle of the same year. Unlike the later carbine of 1914, the 1903 type was not fitted for a bayonet.

Length: 40.35in (1025mm). **Weight unloaded:** 7lb 12oz (3.53kg). **Barrel:** 20.66in (525mm), 4 grooves, right hand twist. **Magazine:** 5-round rotary box. **Muzzle velocity:** 2057 ft/sec (627 m/sec).

6.5mm Rifle and Carbine Model 1903/14.

The M1903/14 rifle was simply an improved model of the 1903 pattern. The action was the same, but the handguard now ran for the full length of the barrel, the finger groove differed and a piling hook was added to the muzzle cap. Production began at Steyr but the outbreak of World War I immediately stopped deliveries. The Greek Army soldiered on with its existing weapons until the middle 1920s when fresh supplies of 100,000 M1903/14 rifles and 10,000 carbines were ordered from the Italian Breda firm, deliveries of which commenced in 1927. The M1903/14 carbine was similar to the 1903 pattern but with fittings for a bayonet. Both weapons were similar in dimensions to the 1903 models, though about two ounces heavier.

HUNGARY

• Rifle Model 35M

Femaru Fegyver es Gepgyar, Budapest
8x56R Hungarian Mannlicher

After the dissolution of the Habsburg empire in 1918, the Austrian and Hungarian armies went their separate ways.

The Hungarians retained the M1895 straight-pull Mannlicher in 8mm Austrian chambering until they adopted an entirely new cartridge, the 8x56R Model 31M, in 1931. They then rebarreled a vast number of the M1895 rifles to take this new cartridge, but experience showed that they gave trouble with extraction, probably because of higher chamber pressure. The Hungarians therefore developed their own turn-bolt rifle based on the Mannlicher system. This was the last Mannlicher to be adopted as a service weapon, and was basically the Romanian 1893 rifle, redesigned in Hungary to fire their improved 31M rimmed cartridge, and shortened to more handy proportions. The result was a serviceable rifle using the protruding Mannlicher clip-loaded magazine, a two-piece stock, and a bolt handle which locked down ahead of the receiver bridge.

Length: 43.75in (1110mm). **Weight unloaded:** 8lb 14oz (4.04kg). **Barrel:** 23.62in (600mm), 4 grooves, right-hand twist. **Magazine:** 5-round integral box, clip loaded. **Muzzle velocity:** c.2400 ft/sec (730 m/sec).

• 7.92mm Gewehr 98/40

Femaru Fegyver es Gepgyar, Budapest
7.92x57mm Mauser

This was not really a Hungarian service rifle, for it was manufactured in the Hungarian factories under German

The Hungarian M98/40, a Mannlicher converted to Mauser charger-loading.

The Hungarian Model 48M was the 98/40 with Hungarian furniture and fittings.

supervision. The Germans decided that they were in need of rifles, and so in 1940, they redesigned the 35M rifle to accept the standard 7.92x57mm Mauser service cartridge. They also deleted the Mannlicher clip-loading feature in favor of the Mauser charger-loading system. The resulting Gew 98/40 was stocked in German fashion and used the German service bayonet.

Length: 43.19in (1097mm). **Weight unloaded:** 9lb 0oz (4.08kg). **Barrel:** 23.62in (600mm), 4 grooves, right-hand twist. **Magazine:** 5-round integral box, charger loaded. **Muzzle velocity:** c.2477 ft/sec (755 m/sec).

• 7.92mm Huzagol 43M

The Hungarians were so impressed by the German improvements to the 35M

rifle that they adopted the Gew 98/40 as the 43M rifle, although the stock and fittings reverted to standard Hungarian pattern. The Mannlicher bolt mechanism was all that remained of the original design of the 1890s.

ITALY

• The Mannlicher-Carcano
Real Fabricca d'Armi, Turin and others
6.5x52mm Mannlicher-Carcano

This Italian rifle design was developed at Turin Arsenal between 1890 and 1891 and was adopted by the authorities on 29 March 1892. Salvatore Carcano was the Chief Inspector of the Real Fabbrica d'Armi, Turin and collaborated with Colonel Paravi-

cino in the design; Carcano's contribution was principally the turning bolt, which was adapted from Mauser's 1889 Belgian design, with the addition of Carcano's bolt-sleeve safety mechanism, and had the handle rather further forward.

The only Mannlicher feature to be retained by the designing committee was the clip-loaded magazine. The rifle was never adopted by any other country, though some examples, chambered for the Japanese 6.5mm cartridge, were supplied to the Japanese government, c.1905.

• 6.5mm Fucile Modello 91

This was the original pattern of the rifle, adopted on 29 March 1892, and distinguishable by the full length stock, the box magazine, the split-bridge receiver and the tangent rear sight. A wooden

A cutaway specimen of the Italian Mannlicher-Carcano M1891 rifle.

Looking down on to the open action of the M1891 Mannlicher-Carcano, showing the aperture in the magazine through which the empty clip will fall and the tip of the lever which presses the cartridges up to the bolt.

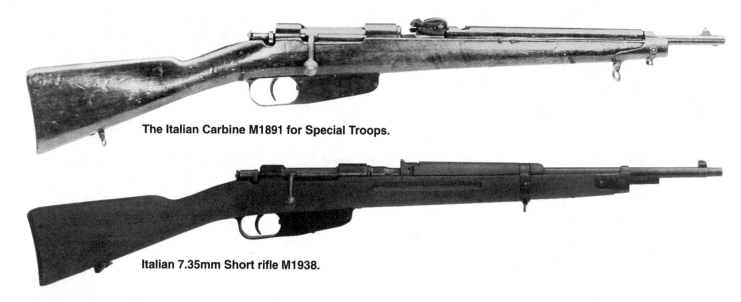

The Italian Carbine M1891 for Special Troops.

Italian 7.35mm Short rifle M1938.

handguard covered the barrel between the front of the rear sight and the first barrel band. The Italians also developed their own design of reversible clip, which allowed one more cartridge than usual to be loaded.

Length: 50.47in (1282mm). **Weight unloaded:** 8lb 5oz (3.78kg). **Barrel:** 30.71in (780mm), 4 grooves, right-hand twist. **Magazine:** 6-round integral box. **Muzzle velocity:** c.2300 ft/sec (700 m/sec).

• Cavalry Carbine Model 91

The cavalry carbine version of the basic rifle, adopted during the course of 1893, this was half-stocked with a folding bayonet under the exposed muzzle. The bolt handle was turned down and there was no handguard. In 1903 the design was slightly modified by adding a short handguard and changing the bayonet lock from a sliding catch to a push-button.

Length: 37.52in (953mm). **Weight unloaded:** 6lb 15oz (3.16kg). **Barrel:** 17.75in (451mm), 4 grooves, right-hand twist. **Magazine:** 6-round integral box. **Muzzle velocity:** c.2083 ft/sec (635 m/sec).

• Carbine Model 91, per truppe speciali (Mod 91 TS)

Another of the short derivations of the rifle design of 1891, the M91 TS existed in two forms, the first of which was provided with a peculiar bayonet with a transverse fixing slot across the back of the pommel. This mated with a transverse lug underneath the Moschetto's nosecap. It is thought that this feature was introduced by the Italians in an attempt to overcome the problem - which rarely arose anyway - of an opponent snatching the bayonet from the muzzle of the rifle during combat. The

later version of the Moschetto 91 TS reverted to a standard pattern of nosecap and utilized the normal ModelIo 94 bayonet. A third version of the Moschetto, the 'Moschetto Modello 91 per truppe speciali modificato', was an alteration of the first pattern to approximate to the second; it can be recognized by a barrel band behind the nosecap.

• 6.5mm Moschetto Modello 91/24

This was a shortened version of the original rifles, which were cut down after World War I. The gun, which was otherwise similar to the M91 TS, can be recognized by the large rifle-type rear sight in place of the smaller carbine type, though the graduations were different.

• 6.5mm Fucile Modello 91/38

This was a shortened and modified version of the 1891 rifle, intended to approximate in dimension the 7.35mm rifle of 1938. The object was to provide a similar rifle to use up the stocks of 6.5mm ammunition before changing over completely to the new 7.35mm caliber.

Length: 42.32in (1075mm). **Weight unloaded:** 7lb 10oz (3.46kg). **Barrel:** 22.13in (562mm), 4 grooves, right-hand twist. **Magazine:** 6-round integral box. **Muzzle velocity:** c.2150 ft/sec (655 m/sec).

• Short Rifle Model 38
Fabricca Nazionale d'Armi, Turin
7.35x52mm

As a result of their campaign in Abyssinia, the Italians found that their 6.5mm cartridge was insufficiently lethal, and so an enlarged 7.35mm round was introduced in 1938 along with a modified version of the 1891 rifle. Apart from the caliber, the Fucile Modello 38 had a

fixed 300m rear sight in place of the earlier weapons' tangent sight.

Length: 40.16in (1020mm). **Weight unloaded:** 8lb 2oz (3.68kg). **Barrel:** 22.12in (562mm), 4 grooves, right-hand twist. **Magazine:** 6-round integral box. **Muzzle velocity:** c.2510 ft/sec (765 m/sec).

• Cavalry Carbine Model 38 and Model 38TS

These were the cavalry and special troop carbine versions of the Model 38 rifle, with a fixed rear sight and a folding bayonet under the carbine's muzzle. Most were simply conversions of the Model 91 carbines with a new 7.35mm barrel and action, fixed 200-meters notch rear sights and a new nosecap for the M91 sword bayonet.

• Short Rifle Model 38/43

In 1944 an Italian military factory in Cremona modified quantities of the Italian Model 38 carbines by reboring them to 7.92mm caliber in order to equip the Italian 'Co-Belligerent' force fighting alongside the German army in Northern Italy. In order to accept the German cartridge a modified clip was welded into the magazine, and rounds had to be individually loaded, since there was no provision for a charger. The results were somewhat dangerous owing to the increased chamber pressures, and although some later appeared in Syria and Israel, few appear to have survived. They can be identified by a large 'S' stamped on the chamber top and '7, 92' stamped into the barrel in front of the rear sight.

• Beretta Sniper (1985)
Pietro Beretta SpA, Gardone Val Trompia
7.62x51mm NATO

This is a conventional bolt-action weapon with a heavy, free-floating barrel

The Beretta 7.62mm sniping rifle of 1985.

fitted with a muzzle brake. There is a tube in the forend which carries the bipod mounting and also contains a harmonic balancer to smooth out barrel vibrations. The rifle is fitted with target-type iron sights, and the receiver carries a NATO-standard sight mount which will accept any telescope or electro-optical sight. The thumb-hole stock is of wood, with an adjustable recoil pad and cheekpiece. An adjustable hand-stop is fitted on a rail in the forend, which also locates the firing sling when fitted.

Length: 45.87in (1165mm). **Weight unloaded:** 12lb 4oz (5.55kg). **Barrel:** 23.07in (586mm), 4 grooves, right-hand twist. **Magazine:** 5-round detachable box. **Muzzle velocity:** c.2755 ft/sec (840 m/sec).

JAPAN

• Arisaka Rifles

During the Sino-Japanese War of 1894 the Japanese Army was principally armed with the 8mm Murata rifle (Meiji 20) of 1887 - a turnbolt design with an under-barrel tube magazine. This was generally considered outdated and unsatisfactory, and since all Western nations were beginning to rearm with small-caliber magazine rifles, the Imperial authorities followed suit and appointed a commission, headed by Colonel Arisaka, to devise a suitable replacement for the Murata. The commission considered various designs and finally settled upon a 6.5mm rifle based, for the most part, on Mauser principles, which was adopted in 1897 as the Meiji 30th Year; a carbine

was introduced at the same time. Although the weapons made use of Mauser features, particularly noticeable in the design of the magazine, the bolt unit was an odd combination of Mauser and Mannlicher ideas in that it was fitted with a separate bolt head and a bolt-mounted ejector.

• Rifle Meiji 30th year type (1897)
Koishikawa Arsenal, Tokyo
6.5x51SR Arisaka

The 1897 rifle design was the original pattern, and was immediately recognizable by the unusual safety lever protruding from the cocking piece—which earned for the gun the sobriquet 'hook safety'. The Meiji 30 was fitted with a bolt-mounted ejector and extractor, and the internal box magazine was loaded through the action by means of a five-round charger of Mauser type.

Length: 50.04in (1271mm). **Weight unloaded:** 9lb 0oz (4.08kg). **Barrel:** 30.98in (787mm), 6 grooves, right-hand twist. **Magazine:** 5-round integral box. **Muzzle velocity:** 2493 ft/sec (760 m/sec).

• Carbine Meiji 30th year

The 1897 carbine, introduced at the same time as the rifle, shared the rifle action with the bolt-mounted ejector and extractor and the five-round magazine, but was otherwise much smaller.

Length: 37.87in (962mm). **Weight unloaded:** 7lb 7.5oz (3.39kg). **Barrel:** 18.90in (480mm), 6 grooves, right-hand twist. **Magazine:** 5-round integral box. **Muzzle velocity:** ca 2360 ft/sec (720 m/sec).

• Rifle, Meiji 35th year (1902)
Koishikawa Arsenal, Tokyo
6.5x51SR Arisaka

The 1897 rifle having failed to live up to its promise, this new design was prepared in 1902. There were improvements to the bolt, a better feedway, a sliding bolt cover, a tangent rear sight and a full-length handguard. Something over 30,000 were manufactured, but by that time their use in the Russo-Japanese War had shown that even more modifications were required, and manufacture ceased. It appears that the rifles were then withdrawn from the army and issued to the Imperial Navy.

Length: 50.19in (1275mm). **Weight unloaded:** 8lb 15oz (4.07kg). **Barrel:** 31.10in (790mm), 6 grooves, right-hand twist. **Magazine:** 5-round integral box. **Muzzle velocity:** c.2543 ft/sec (775 m/sec).

• Rifle, Meiji 38th year (1905)
Koishikawa Arsenal, Tokyo; Kokura, Nagoya, Jinsen, Mukden and Nanking arsenals at various times.
6.5x51SR Arisaka

This 1905 design was a considerable improvement on those of 1897 and 1902, with a different bolt more closely based on Mauser's work and a receiver-mounted ejector. The mushroom-head safety device replaced the earlier hook type and the bolt handle was

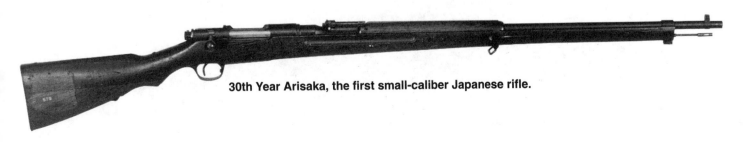

30th Year Arisaka, the first small-caliber Japanese rifle.

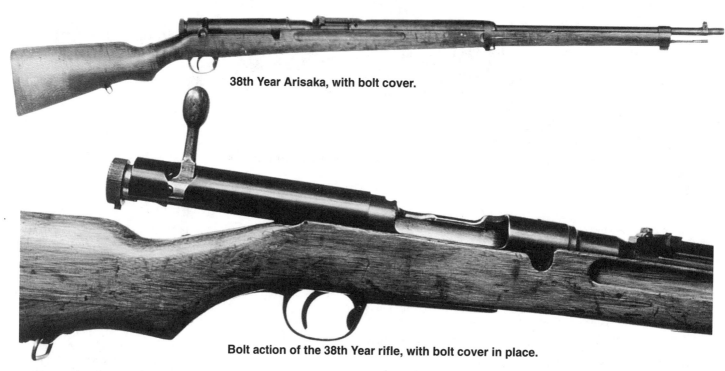

38th Year Arisaka, with bolt cover.

Bolt action of the 38th Year rifle, with bolt cover in place.

enlarged. It was accompanied by a new cartridge, the 38th year Type, using the same case as its predecessor but with a new pointed bullet.

Length: 50.25in (1275mm). **Weight unloaded:** 9lb 8oz (4.31kg). **Barrel:** 31.45in (798mm), 4 or 6 grooves, right-hand twist. **Magazine:** 5-round integral box. **Muzzle velocity:** c.2500 ft/sec (762 m/sec).

• Carbine, Meiji 38th year

This was the standard carbine version of the 1905 rifle, of which it was a much-shortened derivative. The Meiji 38 carbine could be fitted with the standard Meiji 30 infantry bayonet.

Length: 37.91in (963mm). **Weight unloaded:** 7lb 6oz (3.35kg). **Barrel:** 19.17in (487mm), 4 or 6 grooves, right-hand twist. **Magazine:** 5-round integral box. **Muzzle velocity:** 2250 ft/sec (685 m/sec).

• Carbine Meiji 44th year (1911)

The 1911 carbine pattern was intended as an arm for the cavalry, although otherwise essentially similar to the 1905 carbine; it was fitted with a folding bayonet attached under the muzzle.

Length: 38.50in (978mm). **Weight unloaded:** 8lb 13oz (4.0kg). **Barrel:** 18.50in (469mm), 6 grooves, right-hand twist. **Magazine:** 5-round integral box. **Muzzle velocity:** c.2250 ft/sec (685 m/sec).

• Sniper's rifle, Type 97 (1937).

This rifle fired the standard 6.5mm cartridge, and was given a bipod and a telescope sight offset to the left side of the gun so that it could still be loaded by a charger. The bolt handle was turned down to clear the scope when open, but in all other respects it was the same as the 38th Year rifle, though slightly heavier.

As with the Italians in Abyssinia, so the Japanese in the Sino-Japanese fighting in Manchuria in the 1930s discovered that the 6.5mm bullet was insufficiently lethal and that a heavier cartridge was therefore desirable. In 1932, a machine-gun was introduced firing a 7.7mm semi-rimmed round called the Type 92, and this cartridge was promptly

Arisaka 38th Year cavalry carbine.

Arisaka bolt on the 38th Year carbine, without bolt cover.

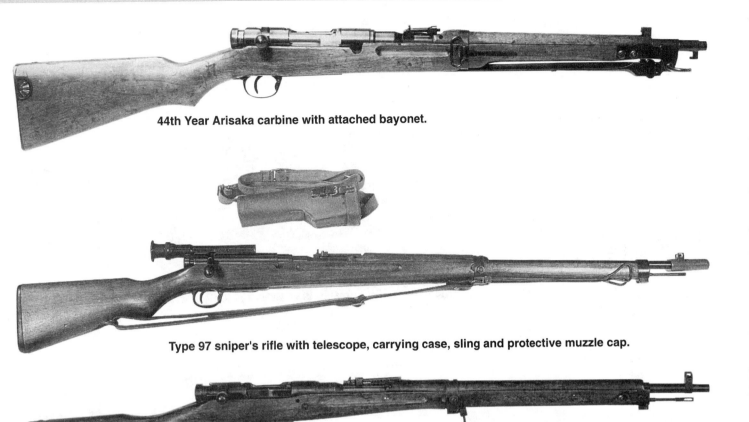

44th Year Arisaka carbine with attached bayonet.

Type 97 sniper's rifle with telescope, carrying case, sling and protective muzzle cap.

The Japanese Model 99 rifle with its flimsy wire monopod.

redesigned in a rimless form as the Type 99. A modified form of the Meiji 39 rifle was introduced to accompany it.

• Rifle, Type 99 (1939)
Toriimatsu Arsenal, Nagoya; Dai-Nippon Heiki Kogyo, Notobe; Kayaba Kogyo, Tokyo; Toyo Juki, Hiroshima; Tokyo Juki, Tokyo; Jinsen Arsenal, Korea.
7.7 x 58mm Arisaka

The 1939 rifle pattern was little more than a rechambered version of the earlier Meiji 38, although the opportunity was taken to produce a 'short rifle' in line with the weapons of contemporary armies abroad, and to redesign some of the components to make manufacture less exacting. The Type 99 rifle was remarkable for being fitted with a flimsy wire monopod and a most optimistic sighting device (consisting of folding lead bars on the rear sight) intended for use against aircraft. This reflects the concern for air attack at the time, but it was more in the nature of a psychological crutch for the soldiers than a serious anti-aircraft threat.

Length: 43.90in (1115mm). **Weight unloaded:** 9lb 2oz (4.19kg). **Barrel:** 25.75in (654mm), 4 grooves, right-hand twist. **Magazine:** 5-round integral box. **Muzzle velocity:** c.2400 ft/sec (730 m/sec).

• Parachutist's Rifle, Type 99 (c.1940-1)
The Type 99 rifle was modified for airborne use by the addition of a joint between the barrel and the action which, in this pattern, took the form of an interrupted-screw joint. The design of the joint distinguishes the design of the Type 99 from the later Type 2, and it was not a success.

• Parachutist's Rifle, Type 2 (1942-3)
The Type 2 was introduced as an attempt to improve upon the abortive Type 99; the screw joint was replaced by a sliding horizontal wedge which mated with a cut-out in the top surface of the barrel. The result was quite serviceable, but relatively few were ever made.

Length: 45.28in (1150mm). **Weight unloaded:** 8lb 15oz (4.05kg). **Barrel:** 25.39in (645mm), 4 grooves, right-hand twist. **Magazine:** 5-round integral box. **Muzzle velocity:** c.2370 ft/sec (722 m/sec).

It is as well to note that, towards the end of World War II, the quality of the Japanese rifles rapidly deteriorated owing to the universal shortage of raw materials and the lack of available machine time. Various production short-cuts were used. This resulted in rifles in which the leaf rear sights were eliminated in favor of 300m standing blocks and the finish was so generally ignored that the rifles were covered in machine marks. Inferior substitute steels were also used towards the end of the war, which made firing some of the rifles a distinctly hazardous business.

A little-known and unusual fact about the Arisaka rifle is that for a period of time it was an official British weapon. In 1914, the British Army needed vast numbers of rifles for training and arming its rapidly-expanding army, and so a quantity of Arisaka rifles were purchased from Japan and used for training purposes. They were given official British nomenclature as follows:

• Rifle, Magazine, 256-caliber Pattern 1900
(introduced on 24 February 1915). This was the 6.5mm Meiji 30 rifle, the model developed by the Imperial commission.

• Rifle, Magazine, 256-caliber Pattern 1907
(introduced on 24 February 1915). This was the same as the Japanese Meiji 38.

Open bolt of the Type 2 Parachutist's rifle, showing the area of the joint.

Parachutist's rifle Type 2, showing details of the joint and the ornate rear sight.

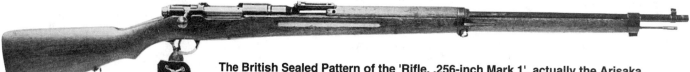

The British Sealed Pattern of the 'Rifle, .256-inch Mark 1'. actually the Arisaka 30th Year rifle adopted as a training weapon in 1915.

• Carbine, Magazine, 256-caliber Pattern 1907

(introduced on 24 February 1915. This was the Carbine Meiji 38.

The terminology '1907' is of interest; the *British Textbook of Small Arms, 1909* quotes the rifle Meiji 38 as having been introduced in 1907, and presumably this is from where it was derived. All three 256-caliber weapons were declared obsolete for British service on 25 October 1921.

NETHERLANDS

• Rifle Model 1895.

Osterreichische Waffenfabrik-Gesellschaft, Steyr, Austria; Dutch Royal Rifle Factory, Hembrug.

6.5x54R Dutch Mannlicher

The Dutch rifle was a slightly modified version of the Romanian 1893 design, firing the Dutch version of same 6.5mm rimmed cartridge. As a result, the rear sight on the Dutch weapons differed

from the Romanians; apart from the different graduations due to using a slightly different propellant charge, the Dutch authorities selected a tangent sight similar to the contemporary Italian pattern. The M1895 rifle could also be recognized by the positioning of the bayonet bar on the nosecap, for the Dutch used an unusual type of bayonet fitting adapted from the British type used on the Lee-Metford and Lee-Enfield rifles; this meant that the bayonet bar protruded from the lower part of the nosecap and slotted into the underside of the pommel,

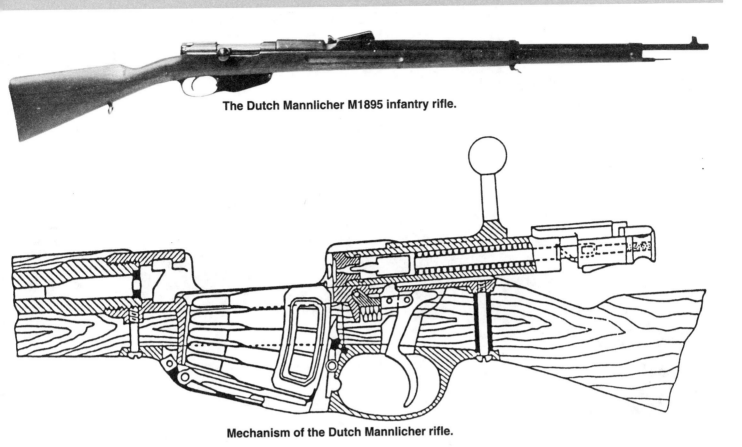

The Dutch Mannlicher M1895 infantry rifle.

Mechanism of the Dutch Mannlicher rifle.

and resulted in the bayonet lying directly underneath the barrel - although this was not immediately obvious.

Length: 51.00in (1295mm). **Weight unloaded:** 9lb 11oz (4.39kg). **Barrel:** 31.13in (790mm), 4 grooves, right-hand twist. **Magazine:** 5-round integral box. **Muzzle velocity:** c.2400 ft/sec (730 m/sec).

• Carbine Model 1895 No. 1, OM
Osterreichische Waffenfabrik-Gesellschaft, Steyr, Austria; Dutch Royal Rifle Factory, Hembrug.
6.5x54R Dutch Mannlicher

The Old Model Number 1 carbine was a short form of the rifle, with a short sporting-type stock, no handguard, a straight bolt handle, and sling swivels on the left side of the butt and the barrel band. A socket bayonet, taken from the old Beaumont rifle of 1871, was used with the carbine.

Length: 37.48in (952mm).
Weight unloaded: 6lb 13oz (3.10kg).

Barrel: 17.72in (450mm), 4 grooves, right-hand twist. **Magazine:** 5-round integral box. **Muzzle velocity:** c.2050 ft/sec (625 m/sec).

• Carbine Model 1895 No. 2, OM
The Old Model Number 2 carbine, issued to the Dutch Gendarmerie, was distinguished by the addition to the muzzle of a cruciform-bladed folding bayonet. The bolt handle was straight, and the sling swivels were fitted to the side of the forestock and the underside of the butt.

• Carbine Model 1895 No. 3, OM
The Old Model Number 3 carbine was distinguished by the unusual handguard which protruded forward of the nosecap and forestock. The carbine was otherwise fitted with swivels on the underside of the nosecap and the butt, and a straight bolt handle. It was issued to artillery and engineer troops.

• Carbine Model 1895 No. 4, OM
The Old Model Number 4 carbine, for cyclists and machine gunners, was recognizable by the standard handguard and forestock assembly, which distinguished it from the number 3 carbine's overhanging handguard. The sling swivels were on the side of the butt and forestock.

Most of the foregoing carbines were modified in 1915 to 'New Model' standard, which involved the addition of a wooden fairing to the left side of the magazine to prevent the metal wearing away the soldier's tunic when the carbine was slung across his back. This changed their terminology; the original weapons which remained unchanged were called 'No. X OM' while the modified weapons became 'No. X NM'.

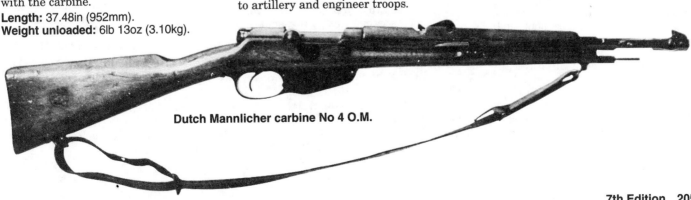

Dutch Mannlicher carbine No 4 O.M.

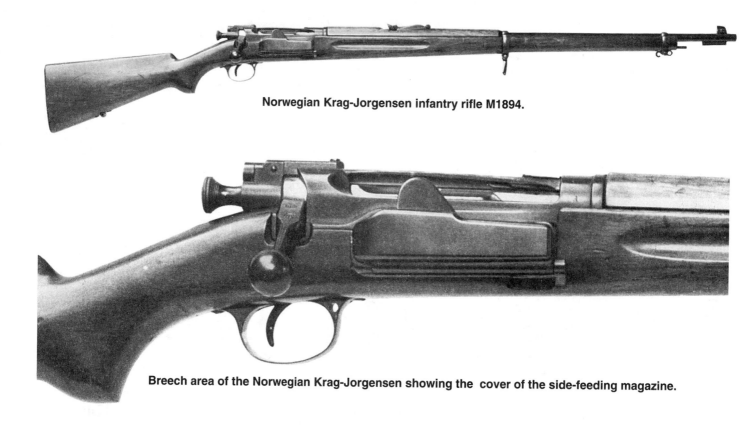

Norwegian Krag-Jorgensen infantry rifle M1894.

Breech area of the Norwegian Krag-Jorgensen showing the cover of the side-feeding magazine.

• Carbine, Colonial, Model 1895 No 1

This 'Colonial Model' carbine was essentially similar to the New Model Number 1, but with the handguard removed and a new turned-down bolt handle. The wooden magazine extension was also used on this gun.

• Carbine Model 1895 No. 5

Manufactured from shortened M1895 infantry rifles, this carbine was issued to personnel of the Dutch Air Force. The bolt handle was straight, the magazine unprotected, and the sling swivels were situated under the butt and on the left side of the forestock. The handguard and forend assembly resembled that of the Number 4 carbines, and the standard infantry bayonet was apparently used.

Length: 37.80in (960mm). **Weight unloaded:** 8lb 12oz (3.96kg). **Barrel:** 18.31in (455mm), 4 grooves, right-hand twist. **Magazine:** 5-round integral box. **Muzzle velocity:** c.2050 ft/sec (625 m/sec).

It is worth recording that recent research has shown, beyond any doubt, that the reputed 'Machine Gunners Rifle Model 1917', an M1895 chambered to fire the 7.92mm rimmed cartridge used with Dutch machine guns, never existed.

NORWAY

• Krag-Jorgensen Gevaer M/1894

Osterreichische Waffenfabrik-Gesellschaft, Steyr, Austria; Fabrique Nationale, Liege, Belgium; Kongsberg Våpenfabrik. Kongsberg.

6.5x55mm M94 Norwegian Krag

The original Norwegian Krag, the M/1894 rifle was quickly recognized by the semi-pistol grip stock and the wooden handguard which covered only the rear portion of the barrel between the breech and the rearmost barrel band. The loading gate, on the right side of the receiver below the bolt guideway, had a bottom-hinged trap and a rotary cut-off. The turn-bolt action used a single locking lug on the bolt head and relied upon the handle turning down in front of the receiver bridge for its second locking lug; additional security was provided by the bolt handle closing into a slot in the receiver body. A tangent-leaf rear sight was fitted and a bayonet bar appeared below the front sight.

Length: 50.00in (1270mm). **Weight unloaded:** 8lb 15oz (4.05kg). **Barrel:** 30.07in (763mm), 4 grooves, left-hand twist. **Magazine:** 5-round internal tray. **Muzzle velocity:** c.2400 ft/sec (731 m/sec).

• Cavalry Carbine M/1895

Kongsberg Våpenfabrik, Kongsberg
6.5x55mm Norwegian Krag

A short version of the rifle M/94 was introduced in 1895 for the cavalry, easily distinguishable by the half-stock which gave it the appearance of a sporting gun. A tangent sight was used with a very small wooden handguard between the receiver ring and the rear sight: no bayonet was provided for the carbine.

Length: 39.96in (1015mm). **Weight unloaded:** 7lb 8oz (3.40kg). **Barrel:** 20.47in (520mm), 4 grooves, left-hand twist. **Magazine:** 5-round internal tray. **Muzzle velocity:** c.2100 ft/sec (640 m/sec).

• Mountain Artillery and Pioneer Carbine M/1897

This was no more than the cavalry pattern of 1895 with a repositioned butt swivel, which was moved to a position 10cm from the heel of the butt. Unusually, for an artillery/engineer carbine, it was not provided with a bayonet.

• Engineer Carbine M/1904

A variation of the 1895 cavalry pattern with a full stock and a full-length handguard over the barrel. Again unusual for its day in not having a bayonet.

Norwegian Krag-Jorgensen cavalry carbine M1895.

Breech of the M1895 carbine, giving a different angle on the magazine system.

• Artillery Carbine M/1907

A version of the M/1904 engineers' carbine, from which it differed primarily in the positioning of the swivels (one on the top band and one on the underside of the butt).

• Short Rifle M/1912
Kongsberg Våpenfabrik, Kongsberg
6.5x55mm Norwegian Krag

By 1912 the authorities had obviously had enough of the various idiosyncrasies of carbine users and decreed a universal shoulder arm for all comers. This final version of the Norwegian rifle was originally fitted with a down-turned bolt handle although later examples reverted to straight ones. The barrel of the rifle was some 9cm longer than that of the preceding carbines, and the gun was full-stocked and with a full-length handguard. A bayonet bar was provided underneath the top-band/nosecap assembly.

Length: 43.54in (1106mm). **Weight unloaded:** 8lb 14oz (4.02kg). **Barrel:** 24.0in (610mm), 4 grooves, left-hand twist. **Magazine:** 5-round internal tray. **Muzzle velocity:** c.2330 ft/sec (710 m/sec).

• Carbine M/1912/16

A strengthening band was added to the forestock, immediately to the rear of the bayonet bar. The gun was otherwise the same as the original Karabin M/1912 and the modification was retrospectively applied to all service weapons of this pattern.

• Sniping Rifle M1894
Kongsberg Våpenfabrik, Kongsberg
6.5x55mm Norwegian Krag

The sniping rifle was a specially-built version of the M1894 rifle, using a heavier barrel. It was finished to a higher standard, with checkered pistol-grip, and provided with target-quality iron sights.

Length: 50.00in (1270mm). **Weight unloaded:** 9lb 14oz (4.50kg). **Barrel:** 29.90in (760mm), 4 grooves, left-hand twist. **Magazine:** 5-round internal tray. **Muzzle velocity:** c.2400 ft/sec (731 m/sec).

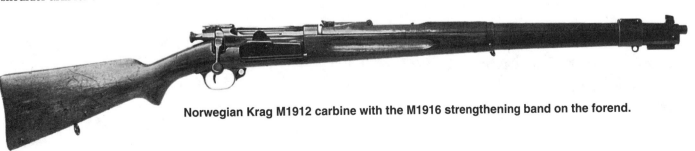

Norwegian Krag M1912 carbine with the M1916 strengthening band on the forend.

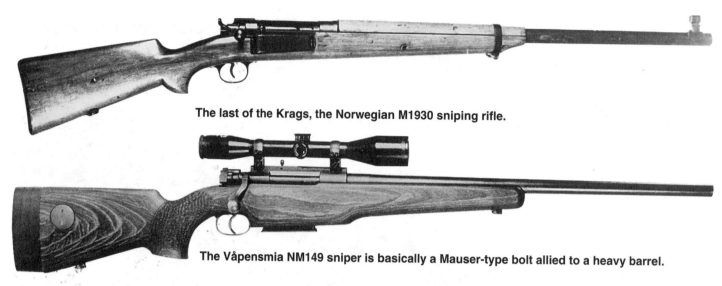

The last of the Krags, the Norwegian M1930 sniping rifle.

The Våpensmia NM149 sniper is basically a Mauser-type bolt allied to a heavy barrel.

• Sniping Rifle M/1923

An improved version of the M1894 sniping rifle, fitted with an aperture rear sight and a hooded front sight. The conversion was due to the adoption of the M23 spitzer-bullet cartridge.

• Sniping Rifle M/1925

The M/1923 appears not to have been entirely satisfactory and was replaced by this M/1925 model. A micrometer-adjustable aperture rear sight was fitted, but otherwise is was essentially similar to the M1894 version.

• Sniping Rifle M/1930

This rifle was fitted with a half-stock, which gave it the appearance of a sporting gun. The heavy barrel was provided with a hooded front sight and an aperture rear sight and, unlike the previous sniper's rifles, the M/1930 had no provision for a bayonet.

• Sniping Rifle NM 149
Våpensmia A/S, Dokka
7.62x51mm NATO

This rifle appeared in the late 1980s and was developed by Våpensmia, makers of sporting rifles, in collaboration with the Norwegian Army and police forces. It is half-stocked, with a Mauser bolt action and heavy barrel. The stock is made of resin-impregnated laminated beechwood and the butt can be adjusted for length by the use of spacers; the ver-

sion for police use is also provided with an adjustable cheekpiece. A match trigger is fitted, adjusted to give a 1.5kg (3.3lb) pull, and the rifle is normally fitted with a Schmidt & Bender 6x42 telescope sight, so mounted that it can be removed and replaced without affecting the rifle's zero.

Length: 44.10in (1120mm). **Weight unloaded:** 12lb 6oz (5.60kg) with telescope. **Barrel:** 23.62in (600mm), 4 grooves, left-hand twist. **Magazine:** 5-round detachable box. **Muzzle velocity:** c.2820 ft/sec (860 m/sec).

PORTUGAL

• Mauser-Vergueiro rifle M1904
D.W.M., Berlin, Germany
6.5x58mm Vergueiro

The Portuguese Army spent 1900-1901 conducting trials with a variety of rifles, eventually deciding that the Mannlicher-Schoenauer was what they wanted. The Ministry of Finance then told them it was too expensive, go and find something cheaper. Enter Major Vergueiro who put together a design using a generally Mauser-like outline, and with the Mauser charger-loaded integral magazine, but with a Mannlicher-like split-bridge receiver and a simplified Mannlicher bolt. The bolt locked by two lugs on the head engaging into the receiver wall, and the bolt handle, turned

down in front of the receiver bridge, acted as a third lug.

The design appears to have been serviceable enough, since the Portuguese carried it in France in the 1914-18 war without complaint, and retained it in service until 1937, when they adopted the 7.92mm Mauser Kar 98K as their service rifle. Some of the redundant Vergueiros were then re-barreled for the 7.92mm cartridge, with a few modifications to strengthen them.

About 5000 Mauser-Vergueiro rifles were built by DWM of Germany after the Portuguese contract had been completed (about 1912) and were supplied to the Brazilian Rural Police force.

Length: 48.15in (1223mm). **Weight unloaded:** 8lb 6oz (3.80kg). **Barrel:** 29.05in (738mm), 4 grooves, right-hand twist. **Magazine:** 5-round integral box. **Muzzle velocity:** 2345 ft/sec (715 m/sec).

ROMANIA

Mannlicher's perfected turning-bolt action was developed in 1890 after some years of experimental work, and was of the split-bridge receiver type in which the bolt handle locked down in front of the bridge to form an additional safety feature, acting as an auxiliary locking lug. Mannlicher also incorporated a removable bolt head which allowed the bolt to be hollowed from the front and left

This Mauser-Vergueiro M1904 was the Portuguese service rifle for several years.

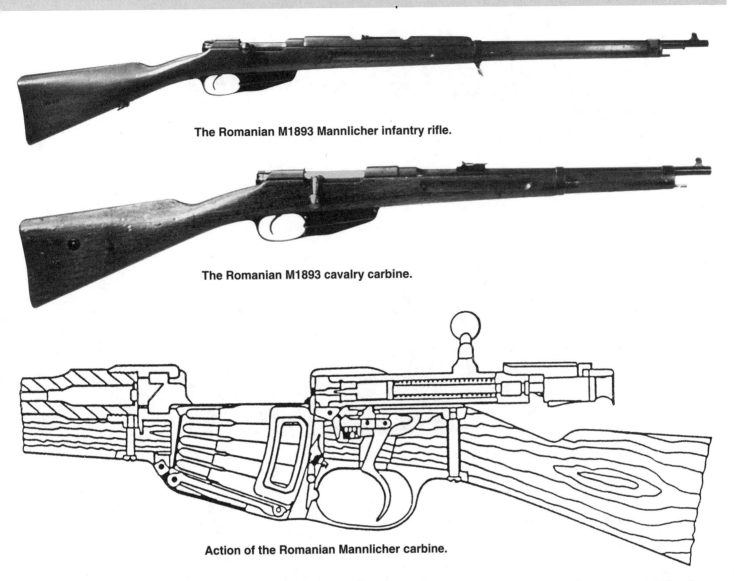

The Romanian M1893 Mannlicher infantry rifle.

The Romanian M1893 cavalry carbine.

Action of the Romanian Mannlicher carbine.

only the tiny firing-pin hole at the rear. The result was a strong and simple rifle adopted in 1893 by Romania, and in 1895 by The Netherlands; the Austro-Hungarians were, however, quite satisfied with the performance of their straight-pull rifles and so Mannlicher's turn-bolt designs met with little success in his native land.

• Rifle, Model 1892
Österreichische Waffenfabrik-Gesellschaft, Steyr, Austria
6.5x54R Romanian Mannlicher

This was the first of the Romanian rifles and served as a prototype for the definitive pattern of 1893 which followed. The ejector of the 1892 rifle was mounted on the bolt itself, and there was no stacking hook on the top band, features which distinguished the two weapons. The rifle was clip-loaded using a standard Mannlicher clip and the magazine held five 6.5mm rimmed rounds.

• 6.5mm Rifle Model 1893
Österreichische Waffenfab-rik-Gesekkschaft Steyr, Steyr, Austria
6.5x54R Romanian Mannlicher

The rifle of 1893 was officially adopted as the service weapon of the Romanian Army. In reality it was little different from the earlier 1892 semi-prototype; the ejector was moved from the bolt to a position at the left rear of the receiver, and an offset piling hook and a side-mounted bayonet bar appeared on the nosecap. The gun used a split receiver bridge giving a third locking surface when the bolt handle was turned down ahead of the bridge; the usual Mannlicher clip-loaded magazine was used and the rifle was chambered for the rimmed 6.5mm cartridge. In appearance, the gun differed from most contemporary Mannlicher designs in having a slimmer magazine, owing to the use of a smaller cartridge.

Length: 48.50in (1232mm). **Weight unloaded:** 8lb 13oz (4.00kg). **Barrel:** 28.56in (725mm), 4 grooves, right-hand twist. **Magazine:** 5-round integral box. **Muzzle velocity:** c.2400 ft/sec (730 m/sec).

• 6.5mm Carbine Model 1893

This was no more than a much-shortened version of the rifle of the same year, introduced for the use of mounted troops. The bolt handle was turned down closer to the stock and the bayonet bar and piling hook were eliminated.

Length: 37.52in (953mm). **Weight unloaded:** 7lb 4oz (3.29kg). **Barrel:** 17.71in (450mm), 4 grooves, right-hand twist. **Magazine:** 5-round integral box. **Muzzle velocity:** c.2295 ft/sec (700 m/sec).

RUSSIA

• The Mosin-Nagant System

The Mosin-Nagant was the first Russian rifle to incorporate the ideas of a small-caliber high-velocity magazine rifle, and it replaced the earlier single-shot Berdan rifle in the hands of the

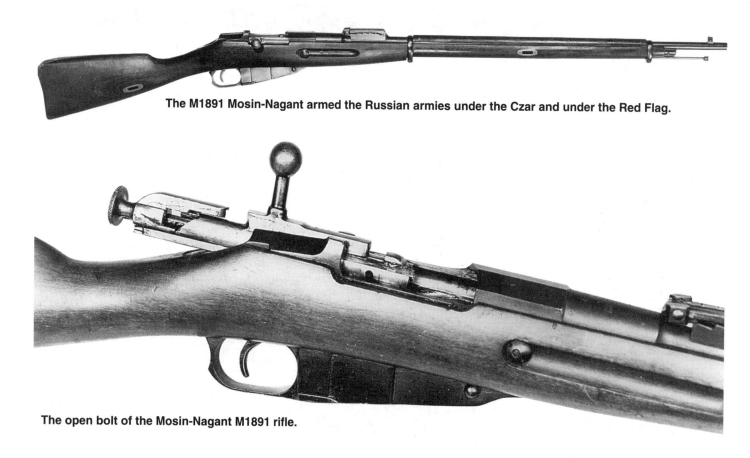

The M1891 Mosin-Nagant armed the Russian armies under the Czar and under the Red Flag.

The open bolt of the Mosin-Nagant M1891 rifle.

Tsar's troops. The first models were introduced in 1891, after a year of trials in which the Russians had sought to combine the features of a series of rifles designed by the Belgians Emile and Leon Nagant, with those of one designed by Sergey Ivanovich Mosin—a captain in the artillery. Upon their introduction, the rifles were known as the *'3-lineyaya vintovka obr 1891g'* ('3-line rifle, model of the year 1891'.)—the 'line' being a Russian unit of measure equivalent to one-tenth of an inch.

In general appearance, the rifles were of a straightforward turn-bolt magazine pattern, loaded through the open action by means of a five-round charger. It was usually conceded that the bolt bore a resemblance to contemporary French designs and was unnecessarily complicated, but this apart, the rifles were serviceable enough. The magazine was unusual in that it used a control latch which secured the second and lower rounds in the magazine and thus relieved the top round of pressure during the loading movement. Once the bolt was closed, the latch moved clear and allowed the magazine spring to force the next cartridge against the underside of the bolt ready for the next reloading stroke.

• Mosin-Nagant rifle M1891
National Factories at Tula, Sestrorets, Izhevsk and others
7.62x54R Russian

This was the basic model, fully stocked except for a few inches of the muzzle, to which a socket bayonet could be fitted. Although obsolete elsewhere, the Russians placed great reliance upon the socket bayonet, which was intended to be carried in a permanently-fixed attitude: indeed, alterations were incorporated in the sights to allow for the altered point of impact owing to the effect of the bayonet on the barrel vibrations. The bayonet blade ended in a screwdriver point with which the rifle could be dismantled, and the cleaning rod, which was carried in the forend, protruded beneath the muzzle where it acted as a stacking hook. A leaf sight was fitted, graduated to 2700 arshins (an arshin being a native measurement equivalent to approximately 28 inches (711mm)) although after 1908, most rifles' sights were re-graduated to allow for the then-new Type L cartridge, whose lighter bullet had a different trajectory.
Length: 51.25in (1304mm). **Weight unloaded:** 9lb 10oz (4.43kg). **Barrel:** 31.60in (802mm), 4 grooves, right-hand twist. **Magazine:** 5-round integral box. **Muzzle velocity:** c.2650 ft/sec (805 m/sec).

• Dragoon Rifle M1891
This, originally issued to the Russian cavalry, was identical with the rifle, with the exception of a shorter barrel (28.8 inches (732mm)). It was produced in place of a carbine, probably owing to a belief, prevalent at the time, that the new smokeless powders could not develop reasonable ballistics in a short barrel—a theory which was soon proved wrong.
Length: 48.75in (1240mm). **Weight unloaded:** 8lb 12oz (3.95kg). **Barrel:** 28.75in (730mm), 4 grooves, right-hand twist. **Magazine:** 5-round integral box. **Muzzle velocity:** c.2600 ft/sec (790 m/sec).

• Cossack Rifle M1891
A near-identical variant of the dragoon rifle, the Cossack rifle was also intended as a weapon for mounted troops; few of this pattern were ever manufactured. Unlike the dragoon rifle, they were issued without a bayonet.

• Carbine M1910
The Dragoon and Cossack rifles were neither true carbines nor true rifles, and

The Mosin-Nagant M1938 carbine.

The Russian M1891/30 Sniper rifle was a selected M1891 rifle with a telescope sight added.

Something of an anachronism for 1944 was this Mosin-Nagant carbine with permanently-attached bayonet.

so they fell between two requirements; it was therefore found necessary to introduce a genuine carbine, some 10 inches (254mm) shorter than the guns it replaced, and consequently much more handy. The carbine's action was identical with that of the rifles. After the October Revolution, the Russians adopted the metrics system and after c.1922 many of the infantry and dragoon rifles' sights were replaced by new patterns graduated in meters; none of the 1910 carbines were apparently so treated.

Length: 40.00in (1016mm). **Weight unloaded:** 7lb 8oz (3.40kg). **Barrel:** 20.00in (510mm), 4 grooves, right-hand twist. **Magazine:** 5-round integral box. **Muzzle velocity:** c.2500 ft/sec (760 m/sec).

• Short Rifle M1891/1930

This was the first of the Soviet developments, a modified version of the 1891 rifle pattern shortened to approximate to the dragoon rifle, and with the receiver body changed from hexagonal to cylindrical (a change which simplified manufacture). At the same time, an opportunity was taken to alter the archaic sights from the leaf pattern to a tangent-leaf type, and to change the front sight from an open barleycorn (an inverted V) to a tapered post hooded by a cylindrical guard.

Length: 48.43in (1230mm). **Weight unloaded:** 8lb 13oz (4.00kg). **Barrel:** 28.74in (730mm), 4 grooves, right-hand twist. **Magazine:** 5-round integral box. **Muzzle velocity:** 2838 ft/sec (865 m/sec).

• Carbine M1938

This resembled the preceding 1910 design, upon which it was based, although it incorporated the changes made on the 1930 rifle; the receiver was changed to a plain cylinder and the front sight was hooded.

Length: 40.00in (1016mm). **Weight unloaded:** 7lb 12oz (3.54kg). **Barrel:** 20.15in (512mm), 4 grooves, right-hand twist. **Magazine:** 5-round integral box. **Muzzle velocity:** c.2690ps (820 m/sec).

• Sniper's Rifle M1891/30

These were issued from about 1937 onwards. The original pattern was fitted with a telescope sight known as the PU, which was held to the rifle by a single block mount dovetailed into the left side of the receiver. Owing to the short length of the unit, which meant that the firer had to crane forward to adjust his sights each time he fired, the PU telescope was often replaced by the larger and heavier PE sight in two ring mounts, which meant that the windage and elevation adjustments were in a more convenient place. The rifles were still issued with conventional iron sights: indeed, apart from the special sight blocks, they were no different from the standard pattern.

• Carbine M1944

The 1944 carbine design was no more than the 1938 type, with the addition to the muzzle of a folding, cruciform-bladed bayonet. One is at a loss to explain the adoption of such an archaic design at such a late date. It was later copied and produced in China as the Type 53.

Length: 40.16in (1020mm). **Weight:** 8lb 9oz (3.90kg). **Barrel:** 20.35in (517mm), 4 grooves, right-hand twist. **Magazine:** 5-round integral box. **Muzzle velocity:** 2690 ft/sec (820 m/sec).

SPAIN

• Rifle Model 1893
Ludwig Loewe & Cie, Berlin, Germany;
Fabrica de Armas, Oviedo, Spain
7x57mm Spanish Mauser

The Spanish Mauser was one more example of the willingness of the manufacturers to produce whatever the customer required. The differences between this rifle and the German model are only minor in nature, but are an interesting example of the many approaches made by separate nations to the same subject.

The barrel was virtually the same as the German one, being stepped in section and browned, the portions between steps being slightly tapered. The rear sights were different on the Spanish models, being a simple leaf. The Spanish magazine was similar to the German, being flush with the stock and holding five rounds, but the small of the stock was straighter, not unlike an English pattern sporting gun. Finally there were changes in the forend, handguard and the stocking bands. The Spanish bayonet was smaller.

Apart from these national changes, and the fact that they stipulated a caliber of 7mm, the Spanish forces thus carried a Mauser rifle very similar to that of the German Army.

Length: 48.62in (1235mm). **Weight unloaded:** 8lb 11oz (3.95kg). **Barrel:** 29.03in (738mm), 4 grooves, right-hand twist. **Magazine:** 5-round internal box. **Muzzle velocity:** c.2300 ft/sec (700 m/sec).

• Cavalry Carbine Model 1895
Ludwig Loewe & Cie, Berlin, Germany;
Fabrica de Armas, Oviedo, Spain
7x57mm Spanish Mauser

The cavalry carbine version of the Model 93 rifle could be recognized by its short length; stocked to the muzzle, small rear sight and turned-down bolt handle.

As usual with cavalry weapons, no bayonet was used with the carbine.

Length: 37.00in (940mm). **Weight unloaded:** 7lb 7oz (3.27kg). **Barrel:** 17.60in (447mm), 4 grooves, right-hand twist. **Magazine:** 5-round internal box. **Muzzle velocity:** c.2182 ft/sec (665 m/sec).

• Artillery Carbine Model 1916
Fabrica de Armas, Oviedo; Industrias de Guerra de Cataluña, Tarassa.
7x57mm Spanish Mauser

The 1916 pattern of short rifle, issued to the Spanish artillery with a sword bayonet, was similar to the 1895 carbine, although longer because of the ballistics of an improved cartridge introduced in 1913. The barrel band and nose-cap were also more widely spaced, additional gas escape holes were provided in the bolt and chamber, and the left side of the receiver was cut away to facilitate charger-loading.

Length: 41.34in (1050mm). **Weight unloaded:** 8lb 4oz (3.75kg). **Barrel:** 21.70in (551mm), 4 grooves, right-hand twist. **Magazine:** 5-round integral box. **Muzzle velocity:** c.2705 ft/sec (825 m/sec).

• Rifle Model 1943
Fabrique Nacional de Armas, Oviedo; Fabrica de Armas, La Coruña
7.9x57mm Mauser

This was adopted due to the acquisition by the Spanish Army of large numbers of machine guns firing the standard German 7.92mm cartridge, and was more or less the same sort of weapon as the German Kar. 98k, a useful short rifle. It had, however, a straight bolt handle and a finger groove in the forend, a short handguard and a sling bar on the butt.

Length: 43.50in (1105mm). **Weight unloaded:** 8lb 10oz (3.91kg). **Barrel:** 23.62in (600mm), 4 grooves, right-hand twist. **Magazine:** 5-round integral box. **Muzzle velocity:** c.2460 ft/sec (750 m/sec).

SWEDEN

• Mauser Carbine m/1894
Waffenfabrik Mauser AG, Oberndorf-am-Neckar, Germany; Carl Gustavs Stads Gevärsfactori, Eskilstuna.
6.5x55mm Swedish Mauser

In 1894, Sweden bought a few Mauser rifles and carbines as an experiment to see if they were better than their existing Jarmann bolt-action rifles and carbines. Finding that the Mausers were a substantial improvement, the Swedish Army adopted the Mauser carbine in 1894, and stipulated a caliber of 6.5mm. The first issues were made by Mauser in Oberndorf, but manufacture was taken on in Sweden by the state-owned Carl Gustavs Stads Gevärsfactori.

Apart from the caliber, the Swedish carbines were very similar to the Spanish M1893 rifle in their mechanism, apart from a somewhat different safety catch. They were full-stocked to the muzzle, with a half-length handguard, and wings protected the front sight.

Length: 37.40in (950mm). **Weight unloaded:** 7lb 5oz (3.31kg). **Barrel:** 17.32in (440mm), 4 grooves, right-hand twist. **Magazine:** 5-round internal box. **Muzzle velocity:** c.2132 ft/sec (650 m/sec.).

• Mauser Rifle m/1896
Waffenfabrik Mauser AG, Oberndorf-am-Neckar, Germany; Carl Gustavs Stads Gevärsfactori, Eskilstuna; Husqvarna Våpenfabrik AB, Husqvarna
6.5x55mm Swedish Mauser

This closely resembles the Spanish Mauser of 1893 but has a few individual touches. The bolt is provided with a dismantling catch, there is a bolt guide rib and the receiver wall is cut away to facilitate loading from a charger. The stock is straight, without a pistol grip, and the barrel is rather heavier than usual, giving the weapon somewhat better accuracy.

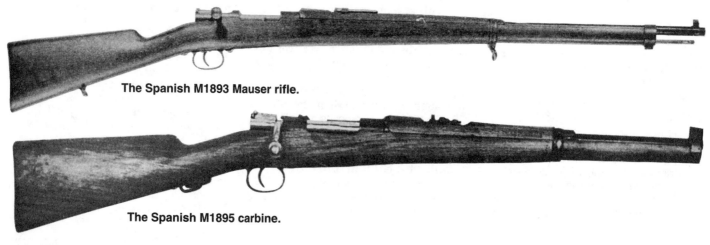

The Spanish M1893 Mauser rifle.

The Spanish M1895 carbine.

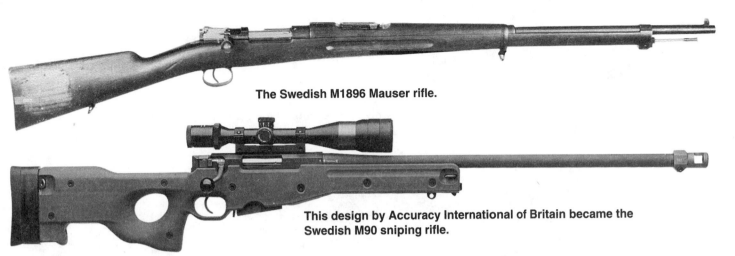

The Swedish M1896 Mauser rifle.

This design by Accuracy International of Britain became the Swedish M90 sniping rifle.

The bolt had only two front lugs, and it appears to have been so reliable that improvement to the three-lug standard was never contemplated.

Length: 49.60in (1260mm). **Weight unloaded:** 8lb 13oz (3.99kg). **Barrel:** 29.13in (740mm), 4 grooves, right-hand twist. **Magazine:** 5-round internal box. **Muzzle velocity:** c.2380 ft/sec (725 m/sec.).

• Mauser Rifle m/1938

The original m/96 rifle ultimately proved too clumsy, and so in 1938, the authorities shortened some of the rifles' barrels to approximately 24 inches (60mm), reducing the rifles' overall length to 44.10in (1120mm).

• Mauser Rifle m/1941

In 1941, it was found necessary to fit some of the m/96 rifles with telescope sights; special sights in two ring mounts were fitted to specially-selected rifles, and the result was an extremely accurate sniper's weapon.

• Rifle M/1939 and M/1940

In 1939, fearful of the imminence of a European War, the Swedish Army decided to convert a number of rifles to fire the same 8x63mm Browning cartridge which they had adopted for their machine guns. These rifles would be issued to machine-gunners and thus simplify ammunition supply. The M/1939 8mm rifle was merely a re-bored German Mauser Kar 98k, which soon proved that the 8mm cartridge was so powerful (it launched a 220 grain (14.2g) bullet at 2500 ft/sec (762 m/sec)) as to be uncontrollable in a short rifle. The M/1940 was then developed, with simply an added muzzle brake to try and reduce the recoil, and several thousand were apparently made. In the event, however, Swedish neutrality was universally respected, and once this was apparent the 8mm rifles were rapidly scrapped.

(M40)
Length: 49.20in (1250mm). **Weight unloaded:** 8lb 13oz (3.99kg). **Barrel:** 29.10in (739mm), 4 grooves, right-hand twist. **Magazine:** 4-round internal box. **Muzzle velocity:** c.2500 ft/sec (762 m/sec).

• Psg 90 Sniping Rifle
Accuracy International,
Portsmouth, England
7.62x51mm NATO

This is really an improved version of the PM sniping rifle which was adopted by the British Army as their L96A1 and is described under Britain. The Psg 90 was developed as Accuracy International's Model 'AW' and put forward when the Swedish Army decided to conducts comparative trials for a sniping rifle. The AW was carefully designed to cater for low temperatures and has various improvements to the bolt, trigger mechanism, stock, bipod, sling attachments and other components. In general it follows the same policy as the earlier rifle, using an alloy skeleton upon which the components are assembled, and a synthetic stock to enclose them. The makers have also developed a discarding-sabot ball cartridge which, together with the rifle, has been adopted by the Swedish Army.

Length: 47.24in (1200mm). **Weight unloaded:** 14lb 5oz (6.50kg). **Barrel:** 25.60in (650mm), 4 grooves, right-hand twist. **Magazine:** 9-round internal box. **Muzzle velocity:** c.2788 ft/sec (850 m/sec) service ball; 4256 ft/sec (1300 m/sec) saboted ball.

SWITZERLAND

• The Schmidt-Rubin System

This, the national rifle of Switzerland, is a straight-pull bolt-action rifle, one of the few such designs which ever prospered. The weapons are usually

known as 'Schmidt-Rubin', from the names of the two designers; Colonel Rudolf Schmidt was one of the foremost firearms experts of his day, and to him is due the design of the rifle. Colonel Rubin was responsible for the development of the jacketed small-caliber bullet and the general conception of the small-caliber high-velocity military rifle.

It is difficult to understand why a straight-pull mechanism was selected, especially as Schmidt could draw upon the ideas of many of Europe's top designers, but it may be that there was in the design more than a hint of national pride—with an attendant desire to produce something different. It could also have been a way of avoiding existing patents, which could sometimes be costly to license. The principal drawback of the 1889 system lay in its inordinate length, something which was to some extent solved by the later 1931 system, devised long after Schmidt's death, and it can be seen from the illustration that there is a considerable length of receiver behind the magazine.

The operation of the Schmidt action is relatively simple; what appears to be the bolt handle is actually attached to an operating rod sliding in its own groove alongside the bolt in the action body. This carries a lug which engages in a helical groove on the bolt carrier. When the rifle has been fired, a rearward pull on the handle causes the lug to travel along the helical groove, thus rotating the bolt assembly to unlock the lugs and then withdrawing the bolt to the rear. The return stroke moves the bolt forward to chamber the round, after which the final movement of the operating handle drives the lug through the helical groove and rotates the bolt lugs into the locked position. The ring which protrudes from the rear is a combination safety device and re-cocking handle.

The complication of the Schmidt action does not compare favorably to the

The M1889 Schmidt-Rubin Swiss Army rifle, recognizable by the oddly isolated and square magazine and the large rear sight protecting wings.

The breech area of the Schmidt-Rubin rifle.

more widespread turnbolt designs. Straight-pull systems are usually more difficult to manufacture, and there are more moving and bearing surfaces involved: the action, as a result, is usually more difficult to operate and it is often particularly difficult to unseat a tight-fitting cartridge case. There is of course no primary camming extraction in a straight-pull system. Most straight-pull enthusiasts claim that the action's speed is superior to that of any manual turnbolt type, but it is open to considerable doubt whether the Schmidt designs can be operated anymore quickly than a Lee-Enfield. It is interesting to note the fate of the only other straight-pull rifles adopted for military service: the Ross and the Lee were failures, and even Austria-Hungary—long the champion of straight-pull operation—had intended by 1914 that her Mannlicher rifles would be replaced by Mausers. It is also possible that the Schmidt would not have been retained for long by a combatant power, as it is likely that the deficiencies would have shown more clearly when subjected to the stress of war.

• Rifle Model 1889
Schweizerische Industrie-Gesellschaft, Neuhausen-am-Rheinfalls and others
7.5x53mm Schmidt-Rubin M1890

This was the first of the Schmidt weapons, making use of Rubin's first perfected cartridge with a rimless case. The

rifle used a bolt with rear locking lugs and an exceptionally long receiver to accommodate the bolt stroke. The box magazine was abruptly rectangular and especially prominent as it was designed to hold twelve rounds. Most of the original 1889 rifles were later converted to fire improved ammunition; 212,000 Model 1889 rifles were manufactured. It is also noteworthy for being one of the few rifles to have three-groove rifling.
Length: 51.26in (1302mm). **Weight unloaded:** 10lb 11oz (4.85kg). **Barrel:** 30.71in (780mm), 3 grooves, right-hand twist. **Magazine:** 12-round detachable box. **Muzzle velocity:** c.1936 ft/sec (590 m/sec).

• Rifle Model 1889/96
This was a modified version of the original 1889 type, in which the receiver and bolt mechanism were slightly shortened to provide a shorter action and the bolt locking lugs moved to the front of the bolt sleeve. The 1896 action was readily recognizable by the trigger being some 10mm closer to the magazine. 127,000 of the 1896-type rifles were manufactured.

• Cadet Rifle Model 1897
This single-shot cadet rifle was a much-lightened derivative of the M1889/96 rifle, intended for cadets whose stature was smaller than that of the regular infantry. The rifle introduced a peculiar spike bayonet to the Swiss service; 7,000 were manufactured.

Length: 43.50in (1105mm). **Weight unloaded:** 7lb 13oz (3.53kg). **Barrel:** 23.30in (592mm), 3 grooves, right-hand twist. **Magazine:** none; single shot. **Muzzle velocity:** c.1853 ft/sec (565 m/sec).

• Short Rifle Model 1889/00
The 1900 pattern of short rifle, intended to be issued to bicyclists and machine-gunners, was really a hybrid of the M1889/96 rifle and the 1897 Kadettengewehr, also for issue to fortress artillery and other ancillary troops, it had a 6-round box magazine and weighed about 7lb 15oz (3.60kg). Eidgenossische Waffenfabrik, of Bern, made 18,750 of these rifles from 1900 to 1904.

• Cavalry Carbine Model 1905
The 1905 cavalry carbine was immediately recognizable by the full-stock, the 6-round magazine and the action of the 1900 short rifle. No bayonet was used. The carbine, 7,900 of which were manufactured by Eidgenossische Waffenfabrik, weighed approximately 7lb 15oz (3.60kg) and was 42.10in (1070mm) long.

• Infantry Rifle Model 1911
Eidgenossische Waffenfabrik, Bern
7.5x55mm Schmidt Rubin M1911

In order to improve on the ballistics of the M1890 and M1890/03 cartridges, a new 7.5x55mm M1911 round was designed, using a streamlined and pointed bullet, a more powerful charge,

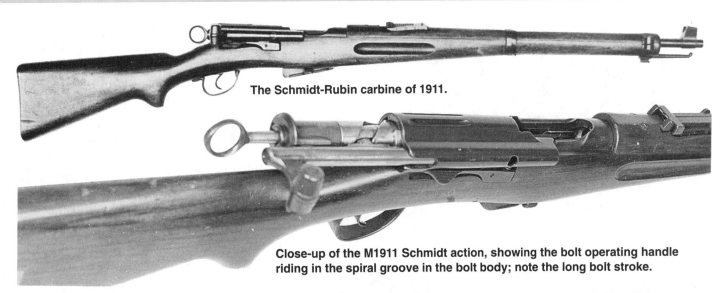

The Schmidt-Rubin carbine of 1911.

Close-up of the M1911 Schmidt action, showing the bolt operating handle riding in the spiral groove in the bolt body; note the long bolt stroke.

and a redesigned cartridge case. To accommodate the additional chamber pressures, and to lessen strain on the bolt, the 1896 modified action was redesigned and strengthened. The magazine capacity was reduced from 12 rounds to 6, a pistol grip pattern replaced the straight-line butt, and a new type of tangent-leaf rear sight replaced the old tangent type of the M1889 and M1889/96 rifles. The rifling was also changed to four grooves. 133,000 M1911 rifles were made.

Length: 51.65in (1312mm). **Weight unloaded:** 10lb 2oz (4.59kg). **Barrel:** 30.75in (780mm), 4 grooves, right-hand twist. **Magazine:** 6-round detachable box. **Muzzle velocity:** c.2640 ft/sec (805 m/sec).

• Carbine Model 1911

The carbine of 1911 was the short version of the 1911 rifle design, making use of the same modified action. It was issued to all for whom the short length was advantageous - cavalry, artillery, engineers, etc. Eidgenossische Waffenfabrik, of Bern, made 185,000 of the Model 1911.

Length: 43.43in (1103mm). **Weight unloaded:** 8lb 10oz (3.92kg). **Barrel:** 23.30in (592mm), 4 grooves, right-hand twist. **Magazine:** 6-round detachable box. **Muzzle velocity:** c.2477 ft/sec (755 m/sec).

• Infantry Rifle Model 1896/11

This was a conversion of the original 1889/96 rifle to make use of the 1911 cartridge. The original 12-round magazine was replaced by the 6-round pattern of the 1911 rifle, a pistol-grip stock was added, and the old barrel was replaced by a modified one with a new design of rear sight similar to that of the 1911 rifle.

• Carbine Model 1900/11

This was a modified version of the original Kurzgewehr Model 1889/00 to handle the modified cartridge: alterations included the provision of a new barrel with a modified design of chamber, and the magazine pattern of 1911.

• Carbine Model 1905/11

The opportunity was also taken to modify surviving cavalry carbines to handle the 1911 type of cartridge. The barrels were changed and the magazines modified.

• Carbine Model 1931 (Kar 31)

The carbine—or short rifle—of 1931 was the first radical change in the Schmidt action. The principal objection to the earlier models had been the excessive length of the action owing to the design of the bolt mechanism, and so the unit was redesigned to operate in half the length, although still clinging to the basic ideas. The 1931 gun, issued to replace all the previous rifles and carbines, was undoubtedly the best of the Schmidt types and remained in service until replaced after

Close-up of the M1931 Schmidt action, partially opened, showing the shorter stroke of the bolt.

The Schmidt-Rubin M1931 carbine incorporated a short action.

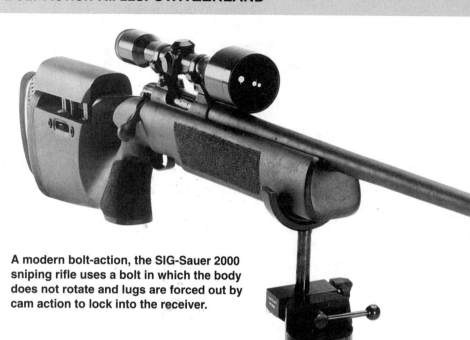

A modern bolt-action, the SIG-Sauer 2000 sniping rifle uses a bolt in which the body does not rotate and lugs are forced out by cam action to lock into the receiver.

1957 by the Stgw 57; quantities of the Kar 31, however, are still retained as reserve. 528,180 were manufactured.
Length: 43.50in (1105mm).
Weight unloaded: 8lb 13oz (4.0kg). **Barrel:** 25.70in (655mm), 4 grooves.
right-hand twist. **Magazine:** 6-round detachable box. **Muzzle velocity:** c.2550 ft/sec (775 m/sec).

• Carbine Model 1931/42 (Kar 31/42)

The M31/42 was a version of the basic 1931 carbine fitted with a peculiar form of telescope sight (1.8x) permanently fixed on the left side of the receiver. The head of the sight could be folded out of use, in which position it lay down alongside the stock.

• Carbine Model 1931/43 (Kar 31/43)

This was a second telescope-sighted rifle, of similar pattern to the preceding Kar 31/42, but with a 2.8x sight - the Swiss had found the lower-powered M42 scope insufficient.

• Sniping Rifle Model 1955 (S Gew 55)

This was the last of the Schmidt-Rubin designs to be introduced to the Swiss forces; based on the Kar 31,

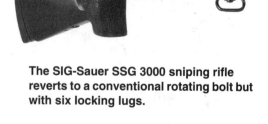

The SIG-Sauer SSG 3000 sniping rifle reverts to a conventional rotating bolt but with six locking lugs.

the M55 was fitted with a pistol-grip half-stock, a muzzle brake, a bipod, and a telescope sight mounted above the receiver.

• Sniping Rifle SSG2000 (1983)
Schweizerische Industrie-Gesellschaft, Neuhausen-am-Rheinfalls.
7.62x51mm NATO and others

This was designed to be usable either as a military and police sniping rifle or as a target rifle; in the former case it is chambered for the NATO cartridge, while in the target role it can be supplied in a number of commercial calibers to suit the particular competitor's requirements.

The bolt action is a turnbolt, but completely different from any previous type; rotation of the bolt handle turns a shaft inside the bolt which operates cam surfaces which thrust hinged lugs at the rear of the bolt outwards into recesses in the receiver walls. This gives a very much reduced arc of movement to the bolt handle—only 65° —and a bolt body which does not revolve, so giving very positive extraction and a fast and smooth action. The hammer-forged heavyweight barrel is fitted with a combination flash-hider and muzzle brake, which reduces recoil effects, and there is a double set trigger. The thumb-hole stock is fully adjustable, and right- or left-handed stocks can be supplied. No iron sights are fitted, the usual sight being a 1.5 - 6 x 42 Schmidt and Bender zoom sight or a Zeiss 8 x 56 Diatal ZA8, though others can be accommodated.

Length: 47.64in (1210mm). **Weight unloaded:** 14lb 8oz (6.60kg) with sight. **Barrel:** 24.0in (610mm), 4 grooves. right-hand twist. **Magazine:** 4-round detachable box. **Muzzle velocity:** c.2460 ft/sec (750 m/sec).

• Sniping Rifle SSG3000 (1992)
Schweizerische Industrie-Gesellschaft, Neuhausen-am-Rheinfalls.
7.62x51mm NATO

The SSG3000 is designed to produce the highest possible first-round hit probability figure. It is a turn-bolt, using a conventional bolt design, though with six frontal locking lugs locking directly into the barrel, so that none of the firing stresses are passed to the receiver. The barrel is hammer-forged and of heavy section, and fitted with a muzzle brake/ flash suppresser. The ergonomically-designed stock is adjustable for length and height, offset and drop, so that the firer can maintain his position for long periods without fatigue. A light firing pin with short travel ensures a very short lock time, and two different precision trigger actions are available, single-stage or double-stage. The cocking piece on the bolt has a signal pin to indicate whether the weapon is cocked.

As usual with this class of weapon, there are no iron sights; a Hensoldt 1.5—6 x 42 telescope has been specially designed for this rifle, but other optical sights can be provided or the rifle can be fitted with a NATO-STANAG sight mount.

Length: 46.46in (1180mm). **Weight unloaded:** 11lb 14oz (5.4kg). **Barrel:** 23.63in (600mm), 4 grooves. right-hand twist. **Magazine:** 5-round detachable box. **Muzzle velocity:** c.2625 ft/sec (800 m/sec).

TURKEY

• Rifle Model 1890
Waffenfabrik Mauser AG, Oberndorf-am-Neckar
7.65x53mm Turkish Mauser

The Turkish Model Mauser was one of a number of variants on the basic Belgian model. In fact, there are several minor differences between them, but the fundamental components of both are generally the same. The Turkish model does not employ the peculiar Belgian barrel jacket and the Turkish barrel is thicker and stronger. Another change is the provision of a hold-open device on the magazine platform, in which a rib on the platform meets the bolt when the last round has been fed. Finally, the Turks called for a cut-off, which is on the right-hand side and is operated by the firer's thumb. The bolt handle was turned down somewhat, but there were few other changes, and to all intents and purposes, the Turks carried a standard Mauser. It remained in service throughout World War II, until replaced by equipment of US origin in the 1950s.

Length: 48.62in (1235mm). **Weight unloaded:** 9lb 1oz (4.11kg). **Barrel:** 29.13in (740mm), 4 grooves, right-hand twist. **Magazine:** 5-round box. **Muzzle velocity:** c.2000 ft/sec (610 m/sec).

U.S.A

• The Navy Lee

James Paris Lee (1831-1904) was a talented inventor whose greatest triumph was the box magazine which subsequently appeared in different forms on practically every military rifle in the world, but he also designed and developed many other projects. In the early 1890s, he produced his design for a straight-pull bolt-action, thus circumventing the existing patents and offering what—so it was hoped—would be a better and faster action. The United States Navy adopted the idea in 1895, in the caliber of .236-inch (6mm), and the manufacturing contract was awarded to Winchester, who had to go to the Lee Arms Company for the patent rights.

• Rifle, Caliber 236-caliber M1895 (US Navy)
Winchester Repeating Arms Company, New Haven, Conn.
6mm US Navy M1895

The bolt on the 1895 Lee pattern does not rotate; it is locked by cam action into the receiver, and is operated by a small movement of the cam handle, which lies downward along the right-hand side and looks very much like a conventional bolt handle. By pulling the handle to the rear, the cams unlock from a recess in the receiver, permitting the bolt to move slightly uphill—it is not an altogether easy motion to work. No doubt the United States Navy found the same thing, for their original order for 10,000 rifles was not extended, and Winchester discovered that private sales (allowed by their contract with Lee) were sluggish. A sporting rifle was tried, but when the final clearance was made in 1916, only 1,700 sporters out of a total of 20,000 made had been sold. The best feature of the Lee was the magazine, which is said to have been the first made commercially in the United States of America with clip loading.

The Lee rifle is pleasant to handle and was probably good to shoot, except for the slightly awkward mechanism; but it failed to catch on as a rival to the almost universal turnbolt system, and it passed from sight very quickly.

Length: 47.60in (1210mm). **Weight unloaded:** 8lb 2oz (3.69kg). **Barrel:** 28.0in (711mm), 5 grooves, right-hand twist. **Magazine:** 5-round integral box. **Muzzle velocity:** c.2560 ft/sec (780 m/sec).

• The Springfield Rifle
Springfield Arsenal, Rock Island Arsenal, and private contractors
Cartridges 30-caliber, M1903 and M1906

For reasons which no doubt seemed good at the time, the US Army had adopted the Krag-Jorgensen rifle in 1892, at the beginning of the smokeless powder era, but within a very short space of time, the Krag's limitations were realized and the Ordnance Department were forced to look into the question of replacing the guns with something more advanced. It has to be admitted that this step must have taken a great deal of courage, considering the large sums of money which had been laid out for tooling up and producing the Krag. Be that as it may, after considerable investigation of contemporary rifle designs and the painful lessons of the Spanish-American War, the Ordnance Department decided the Mauser system had the most to offer and entered into arrangements with the Mauser company to build a modified Mauser under license in the United States.

Since it was first manufactured at the Springfield Arsenal, the rifle came to be widely known as the 'Springfield Rifle', although correctly titled the 'US Magazine Rifle, Caliber .30, Model of 1903'. As originally designed, it was built round a blunt-nosed bullet of 220 grains weight (Caliber .30in M1903), but while troop trials were in progress with this model, the German Army introduced its 'spitzer' (pointed) bullet, and the rest of the world hurried to follow suit. A 150-grain pointed bullet was adopted by the USA to replace the earlier model and the rifle was redesigned to suit it. The cartridge with this bullet entered service as the 'Cartridge, Ball, Caliber 30, Model of 1906', and inevitably both rifle and cartridge have come to be known as the '30-06 Springfield'. As has already been indicated, the rifle is basically a Mauser, but it is interesting to see that the American designers appreciated the waste of effort that went into the contemporary practice of designing a rifle for infantry and a carbine for the rest; in similar fashion to the designers of the Short Lee-Enfield in Britain, they produced a short rifle which successfully filled both roles, sufficiently long to be accurate as an infantry weapon and short enough to be carried in a saddle scabbard as a cavalry weapon.

The Springfield survives to this day in the hands of private owners, and survived for military use until the Korean War (1950-3), in which it was used as a sniping rifle, and during this long career there have been surprisingly few variations, and the following list summarizes the military or service models; it must be noted that a variety of match rifles also existed.

• US Magazine Rifle, Caliber 30, M1903
National Armory, Springfield, Mass.; Rock Island Arsenal, Rock Island, Ill.; Remington Arms Co., Ilion, NY.
30-03; 30-06 Springfield

This was the original version of the design, first supplied with a rod bayonet and chambered for the M1903 cartridge with a 220-grain round nose bullet; alterations were made to the barrel's chamber in 1905 and, with the introduction in 1906 of the 150-grain spitzer bullet, the rifles were fitted with re-graduated rear

The US Navy 6mm Lee straight-pull bolt rifle of 1895.

The Lee bolt open, showing the massive locking wedge underneath the front portion.

The Lee bolt closed, showing how it hooked unto the receiver and then swung so as to force the locking lug down in front of a recess in the receiver.

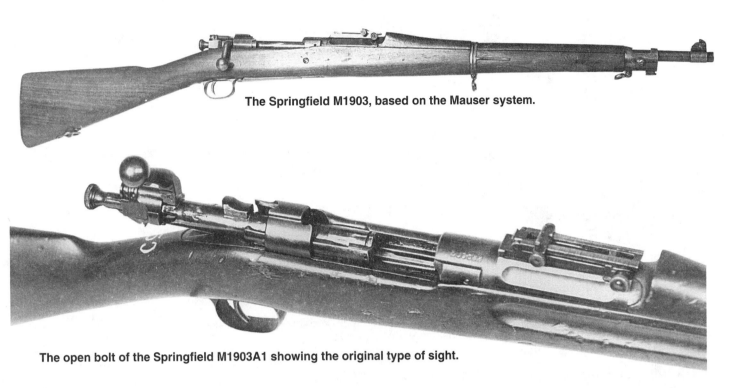

The Springfield M1903, based on the Mauser system.

The open bolt of the Springfield M1903A1 showing the original type of sight.

sight leaves. The M1903 was easily recognized by the straight or 'English' style-stock in which no pistol grip appears. The rod bayonet had disappeared abruptly when President Theodore Roosevelt personally had the system suppressed.

Length: 43.41ins (1103mm). **Weight unloaded:** 8lb 8oz (3.86kg). **Barrel:** 24.21in (615mm), 4 grooves, right-hand twist. **Magazine:** 5-round internal box. **Muzzle velocity:** c.2300 ft/sec (701 m/sec).

• US Rifle, Caliber 30, M1903, Mark 1

The Mark 1 was identical with the service M1903 with the exception of a few modifications made to accept the ill-fated Pedersen Device (see 'US Automatic Pistol, Caliber 30, M1918'). Changes were made to the sear mechanism, the cut-off was discarded, and an ejection port was cut through the left wall of the receiver—to the rear of the chamber—to permit the passage of spent cases. It is recorded that 101,775 of these rifles were produced between 1918 and 1920, after which, the devices were scrapped and the rifles reconverted to M1903 specifications; they can, of course, be recognized by the ejection port.

• US Rifle, Caliber 30, M1903, Special Target

This was a specially-assembled and finished version of the standard M1903 intended for use in the National Match shooting competitions. Competitors were given the option of purchasing their weapons, but those who did not, returned them to the military authorities by whom the guns were classified as 'Special target'. These rifles were renamed in 1928.

• US Rifle, Caliber 30, M1903A1, Special Target

This was the new name applied in 1928 to weapons of 'Special Target' class.

• US Rifle, Caliber 30, M1903A1
National Armory, Springfield, Mass.
30-06 Springfield

This, standardized in the US Army on 5 December 1929, was no more than a standard M1903 fitted with a Type C semi-pistol grip stock. Relatively few were made.

Length: 43.21in (1105mm). **Weight unloaded:** 8lb 0oz (3.64kg). **Barrel:** 24.01in (610mm), 4 grooves, right-hand twist. **Magazine:** 5-round internal box. **Muzzle velocity:** c.2800 ft/sec (853 m/sec).

• US Rifle, Caliber 30, M1903A2

This was not a personal weapon, but the barrel and action of an M1903 rifle carried in mounting blocks, which enabled it to be mounted in the breech of an artillery piece to allow the parent weapon to be used for training at restricted ranges and at low cost. Originally produced for the 3-inch Seacoast Gun, the M1903A2 was later supplied for a variety of other weapons.

• US Rifle Caliber 30, M1903A3

This, standardized on 21 May 1942, was a redesign of the M1903Al devised to facilitate mass-production. The principal and most obvious differences lay in the adoption of an aperture sight - adjustable for windage and elevation - mounted at the rear of the receiver, in which position it replaced the leaf sight of the earlier rifles placed on top of the barrel. Various minor components, including the triggerguard, were fabricated from sheet-steel stampings.

• US Rifle, Caliber 30, M1903A4 (Sniper's)

The standard sniper's rifle derivative of the M1903, the M1903A4 was fitted with permanently-mounted telescope sight blocks. The Telescope Sight M73Bl

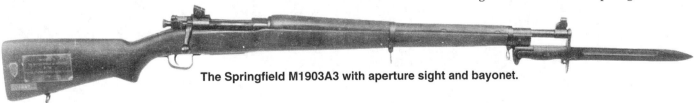

The Springfield M1903A3 with aperture sight and bayonet.

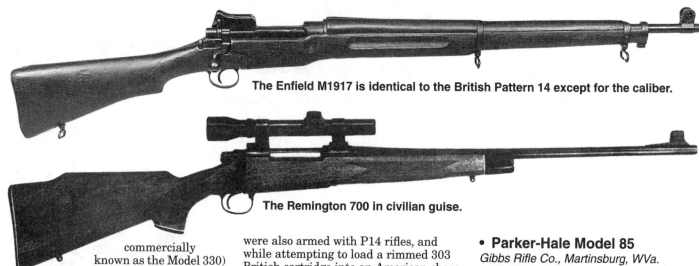

The Enfield M1917 is identical to the British Pattern 14 except for the caliber.

The Remington 700 in civilian guise.

commercially known as the Model 330) manufactured by the W. R. Weaver Company of El Paso, Texas, was chosen as the standard although various alternatives were accepted to offset supply difficulties. The M1903A4 weighed 9lb 6oz (4.34kg) with the optical sight. No conventional iron sights were used.

• US Rifle, Caliber 30in, M1917 (Enfield)
Various manufacturers
30-06 Springfield

When, in 1917, the United States entered World War I, it too had a rifle shortage and since production facilities for the British Pattern 1914 rifle existed in some quantity the Pattern 1914 was quickly redesigned to accept the standard American 30 caliber M1906 rimless cartridge. The gun entered American service as the US Rifle, Caliber 30 Model 1917 though commonly called the 'Enfield' as a tribute to its birthplace.

were also armed with P14 rifles, and while attempting to load a rimmed 303 British cartridge into an American chamber led to nothing more serious than a minor jam, the reverse usually demanded the services of an armorer to remove it.

Length: 46.25in (1175mm). **Weight unloaded:** 9lb 10oz (4.36kg). **Barrel:** 26.00in (661mm), 5 grooves, left-hand twist. **Magazine:** 5-round integral box. **Muzzle velocity:** c.2800 ft/sec (853 m/sec).

• Remington Model 700
Remington Arms Company, Ilion, NY.
7.62x51mm NATO

This rifle is a current military version of the Remington Model 700 'Varmint' rifle offered for commercial sale. The only real differences lie in the adoption of a military grade of finish rather than the more polished finish demanded in the civilian market, and the factory fitting of a Redfield variable power (3-9x) telescope sight. The caliber is commercially known as 308 Winchester, so there is no change in the actual chambering. These rifles have been supplied to the United States Marine Corps in small numbers for snipers' use.

• Parker-Hale Model 85
Gibbs Rifle Co., Martinsburg, WVa.
7.62x51mm NATO

As indicated elsewhere, this rifle was originally developed by Parker-Hale in Britain to compete for adoption by the British Army in their trials in the latter 1980s. The Army chose the rifle produced by Accuracy International, and, with no prospect of a military contract and a rapidly shrinking commercial market, Parker-Hale decided to find some other and more lucrative way of making a living. They therefore sold their rifle designs, patents and tooling to the Gibbs Rifle Company in the U.S.A, who now produce this rifle and several other commercial patterns previously made by Parker-Hale.

The Model 85 is a conventional Mauser-action turn-bolt rifle of high precision, with a guaranteed first-round hit capability out to 600 meters range. The heavy barrel is threaded at the muzzle to take the front sight, which can be removed and a suppresser fitted to the thread. The stock is fully adjustable, and there is a bipod and an adjustable hand rest in the forend. Aperture iron sights are fitted, but the receiver has an integral dovetail mounting for a variety of optical and electro-optical sights. A special bracket is also available for mounting the Simrad KN250 electronic converter which can be attached to any conventional optical day sight to turn it into an image-intensifying night sight.

The Parker-Hale M85 as made by the Gibbs Rifle Company in the USA and fitted with an image-intensifying sight.

The M1917 is identical in appearance with the British Pattern 1914 rifle, so much so that during World War II (when a million or so Model 1917 rifles were sold to Britain for the Home Guard) they were marked around the butt with a two-inch stripe of red paint to draw attention to their caliber. Many units

Length: 41.50in (1055mm). **Weight unloaded:** 6lb 12oz (3.06kg), without sights. **Barrel:** 22.60in (558mm), 4 grooves, right-hand twist. **Magazine:** 5-round integral box. **Muzzle velocity:** c.2800 ft/sec (853 m/sec).

Length: 47.64in (1210mm) at maximum adjustment. **Weight unloaded:** 12lb 9oz (5.70kg) with telescope. **Barrel:** 27.56in (700mm), 4 grooves. right-hand twist. **Magazine:** 10-round detachable box. **Muzzle velocity:** c.2723 ft/sec (830 m/sec).

AUTOMATIC RIFLES

THE AUTOMATIC, OR semiautomatic, or self-loading, rifle took sometime to gain acceptance. Regardless of claims forwarded by many, anxious to claim for themselves the honor of having produced the first semiautomatic rifle, the first service pattern was a Madsen recoil-operated gun issued in 1896 to the Royal Danish Navy and Coast Guard; in advance of its time, this rifle was not issued to the Danish Army and so its potential largely passed unnoticed. In the event, it proved to be a somewhat cumbersome and temperamental device, and it was soon withdrawn, to reappear a year or two later as the Madsen machine gun.

The turn of the century saw various inventors striving to make practical propositions of their brainchildren. Their principal hurdle was the formidable list of demands laid down by virtually all armies in their specification for an automatic rifle. That issued by the British War Office in 1909 included:

"Ballistics: Range for maximum height of trajectory of 5.5 feet must not be less than 800 yards... The rifle must be as light as possible and not exceed 9.5 pounds.. The rifle must be capable of being worked either as an automatic loading rifle or as a magazine rifle.. [in which case] the bolt or block must work freely by hand..." and so on. Added to that was a 'Memorandum for Inventors' which included such inviting statements as 'Should the Army Council consider it desirable to try an invention, the inventor will, as a general rule, be required to bear the expense of the provision of the article, its carriage, fitting up and removal.' and 'All claims for remuneration will be carefully considered; but any award which may be made will only be payable to the claimant when approved by the Treasury and money is available from funds voted by Parliament for such purposes.' It is remarkable that any inventions were submitted at all.

The first successful design of the century came from Mexico; the Mondragon rifle was built in Switzerland (since Mexico had no suitable factory at that time) and appears to have worked reasonably well. Unfortunately, shortly after the first issues began, Mexico went through a revolution, and the rifle, which had been named after the now ex-President, was rapidly dropped by the new government, leaving SIG in Switzerland with a few thousand rifles on their shelves. These

found their way to Germany in World War I and, thanks to their rather delicate mechanisms, failed to make much of an impression when exposed to the mud and filth of the Western Front. This, of course, did the future prospects for automatic rifles no good at all.

Even so, there were a few people prepared to persevere in the 1920s, among them Pedersen and Garand in Springfield Arsenal. The Pedersen, a delayed blowback rifle in 276-caliber, was on the point of gaining approval when General MacArthur, then Chief of Staff, refused to countenance the new caliber and demanded a redesign in 30-06 Springfield. Like all toggle actions, the Pedersen was designed around a particular cartridge and changing from 276 to 30-06 meant a major redesign, virtually starting again from scratch. The Garand, a gas-operated action, was more amenable to alteration and was successfully changed to the 30-06 Springfield cartridge, to become the standard US rifle. Which, in a nutshell, points up another of the problems faced by automatic rifles. Innumerable studies and analyses have shown that the ideal caliber for a combat rifle is 7mm (0.276-inch), and innumerable committees have recommended the adoption of a 7mm cartridge. But every time anyone approached with a 7mm rifle, they were instructed to go away and redesign it in some other caliber, generally because there were enormous stocks of ammunition on hand and vast sums of money invested in production machinery.

By 1939, then, one army—the US Army—had adopted an automatic rifle as its standard infantry arm, even though there was insufficient money to fully implement the change. Another army - the Soviet - had two designs on extensive trial. And in the rest of the world there were about half-a-dozen designs being tinkered with or tested or mulled over by various military authorities.

World War II concentrated minds wonderfully, and in Germany an idea which had been germinating since about 1936 suddenly began to take shape. A number of officers who had served in World War I had observed that rifle shooting at ranges over about 400-500 meters was rare; moreover, it was difficult for the soldier to even see a target at that range, now that soldiers were wearing drab clothing and employing camouflage. So why have rifles and cartridges capable of 2000 meters range? Why not have a shorter, less powerful, cartridge

capable of being effective up to about 600 meters? This meant a smaller and lighter rifle, since it would not be so highly stressed, less recoil on the man's shoulder, light ammunition so that he could carry more...there were more advantages every time you stopped to think about it. And, of course, it was proposed in 7mm caliber. And, of course, the German army threw it out straight away, pointing to all the millions of 7.92x57mm cartridges lying in their ammunition depots. So the designers compromised and designed a short cartridge in 7.92mm caliber, so that existing machinery could be used for manufacturing most of it.

The object in view was a selective fire automatic rifle, by which is meant one which could fire single shots as a self-loader or could fire automatic bursts as a species of light machine gun. The Germans were already trying to do this in 7.92mm caliber, and it was proving to be a difficult task (though one at which they eventually succeeded, against all the odds) and the light cartridge enabled them to succeed with this design very rapidly. The result became the 'Sturmgewehr', or Assault Rifle, and it was such a formidably effective weapon that it had every rifle designer in the world sharpening his pencil once the war was over.

Once more a 7mm design appeared; this time in Britain, accompanied by the first military application of the 'bullpup' design. This means a design in which the bolt and breech are brought to the rear of the rifle, under the firer's chin, so as to allow the greatest length of barrel within a moderate overall length. This time the caliber and the rifle were accepted and approved for service. But before it could go into production the infant NATO threw a wrench into the works. NATO had to have one standard small arms cartridge for its infantry. And the USA, who at that time practically owned NATO, refused to look at anything less than the 30-06 cartridge. They hadn't moved out of the World War I era as far as small arms cartridges went, and the idea of the assault rifle was totally incomprehensible. So NATO got the 7.62x51mm cartridge, which was simply the 30-06 with the case shortened in a lip-service gesture to the short cartridge fraternity. The British, finding it impossible to alter their bullpup for the new cartridge, bought the FN-FAL rifle from Belgium.

Some fifteen years later the US unilaterally decided that, NATO standardization be damned, they would adopt the

5.56x45mm cartridge for their new rifle, the M16. This eventually led to general down-sizing of cartridges, with the Soviets adopting a 5.45mm round. The arguments advanced were much the same as those advanced by the Germans for the 7mm Short round and by the British for their 7mm Medium round—lighter ammunition, less recoil, shorter combat ranges and so forth. But to a good number of soldiers, this was a step too far, it being generally considered that the 5.56mm bullet simply does not deliver the same effect on the target as did the 7.62mm bullet. But ballistics have very little to do with it. The simple fact is that today's soldier had rather more than a rifle and a spade to think about. He (or she) has to be trained in anti-tank rocket launchers, anti-aircraft missiles, rifle grenades, hand grenade, light and medium machine guns, mortars, driving tracked vehicles ..... not to mention attending racial discrimination lectures, AIDS symposiums, drugs discussions... there simply isn't time to waste on an old-fashioned thing like a rifle. Make it light to carry, make it simple to use, make it painless to shoot, give it an expensive optical sight so that he can't miss; but don't waste time on rifle ranges. Besides, the neighbors are complaining about the noise.

The final rifle achievement of the century was the successful production of a rifle to fire a caseless cartridge. A design of caseless cartridge was discovered in Germany after the war, but no information about a suitable weapon was ever discovered. But in about 1970 the German army, taking the long view, decided that they would require a rifle with an exceedingly high first round hit probability, and issued a broad specification. It was soon obvious that the only way to obtain the desired performance was to loose off a burst of three rounds at such a high rate of fire—around 2000 rds/minute—that one of the three was bound to hit the aiming point. But such a rate with conventional ammunition and rifle design was impossible. Heckler & Koch therefore developed a rifle firing a caseless cartridge; by removing two functions from the operating cycle—extracting and ejecting the empty case—it was possible to speed things up and achieve the desired three-round burst rate. The rifle was perfected after almost 20 years of work, but at the last moment the reunification of Germany took financial priority and the contract was canceled.

In the mid-1980s the US Army mounted an expensive project known as the Advanced Combat Rifle. This left the design of the rifle entirely open, stipulating only that it should not exceed a certain weight, but must improve upon the hit probability of the existing M16A1 rifle by a specified amount. Several gunmakers were circularized, a number made proposals, and four actually produced weapons for a most extensive (and expensive) series of trials. After the expenditure of something in the order of $350 million, the conclusion was that none of the competing designs offered sufficient improvement of performance over the M16A1 as to warrant their manufacture.

And there we rest at the century's end; on a plateau of excellence in rifle design which it is going to be very expensive to advance from and the returns, in improved performance, will not be worth the price paid. It is no longer a question of "Where do we go from here?" but of "Where can we go from here?"

ARGENTINA

• FARA 83

Fabrica Militar de Armas Portatiles
Domingo Matheu, Rosario
5.56x45mm

This was a fairly simple and uncomplicated gas-operated rifle using a gas cylinder above the barrel to contain a piston attached to a bolt carrier holding a two-lug rotating bolt. The cocking handle was forward and to the right, apparently influenced by the Heckler & Koch pattern, and the plastic butt was hinged to fold around to the right side of the receiver. On removing a lock pin at the bottom rear of the receiver, the pistol grip and butt could be hinged down, allowing the bolt and piston to be withdrawn from the rear of the receiver.

The rifle went into production late in 1983 but after about 1200 had been issued to the Argentine Army a financial crisis caused the issue to be stopped, and apart from a small batch made as demonstrators for sales purposes, no more have been made since about 1986.

Length, stock extended: 39.37in (1000mm); stock folded: 29.33in (745mm). **Weight unloaded:** 8lb 11oz (3.95kg). **Bar-rel:** 17.79in (452mm); 6 grooves, right-hand twist. **Magazine:** 30-round detachable box. **Cyclic rate:** c.750rpm. **Muzzle velocity:** 3166 ft/sec (965 m/sec).

AUSTRIA

• Steyr AUG (1978)

Steyr-Mannlicher AG, Steyr
5.5x45mm

The Steyr 'Armee Universal Gewehr' is so called since it can function as a submachine gun, a carbine, an assault rifle, or a heavy-barreled automatic rifle (HBAR) for use in the squad automatic role. The difference between these models is simply the length of the barrel and the addition of a bipod for the HBAR version. Further details of the HBAR model can be found in the Machine Gun section. All models are normally equipped with an optical sight in the carrying handle; but by substitution of the receiver casting this can be changed to a mounting rail capable of accepting any telescope or night vision sight. The AUG is in use in the Australian, Austrian, Irish, New Zealand, Tunisian and Omani Armies and innumerable security agencies.

The AUG is a 'bullpup' of somewhat futuristic appearance and its construction is unusual. A basic structure of high-quality plastic supports the receiver, which is an aluminum casting with steel inserts for the barrel lugs and bolt guides. The sight bracket-cum-carrying handle is an integral part of this casting. The steel barrel, with chromed chamber, locks into the receiver by means of an interrupted thread, and the barrel carries a short sleeve containing the gas port, and cylinder and the front hand grip. A flash suppresser is fitted to the muzzle, and this is internally threaded to take a blank-firing attachment. The hand grip folds, and is also used to rotate and remove the barrel when necessary. The magazine is transparent, allowing the firer an instant check of its contents, and slots into the butt behind the hand grip. There is a cross-bolt safety catch above the grip, which can be set to 'fire' by a quick movement of the thumb. No selector lever is fitted; selection of single shots or automatic is done by varying the pressure on the trigger: the first pressure on the trigger allows single shots, but pulling past this position allows automatic fire. The rifle can be adjusted for right-or left-handed firers by exchanging the bolt and blanking off one of the two ejection ports.

The Steyr AUG in standard form with unit-power optical sight.

The AUG field-stripped into its major components.

The weapon operates by gas tapped from the barrel driving back a piston, in the conventional manner, though the piston is slightly offset and acts on one of the bolt guide rods; this asymmetry does not appear to have any ill-effects and the weapon functions very reliably. The guide rods hold the bolt carrier, and the bolt is locked by rotating it so that forward lugs lock into the chamber recess. A grenade launcher and a bayonet are provided as accessories. The barrel is rifled one turn in 9 inches (228mm), which allows it to fire 5.56x45mm ammunition of any type, either the original American M193 or the NATO-standard SS109, with equal facility and accuracy.

Length: 24.64in (626mm) (SMG); 27.0in (690mm) (carbine); 31.0in (790mm) (rifle); 35.43in (900mm) (HBAR). **Weight unloaded (rifle):** 7lb 15oz (3.60kg). **Barrels:** 13.77in (350mm); 16.0in (407 mm); 20.0in (508mm); 24.45in (621mm), all 6 grooves, right-hand twist. **Magazine:** 30- or 40-round detachable box. **Muzzle velocities:** 3085 ft/sec (940 m/sec) (carbine; 3182 ft/sec (970 m/sec) (rifle); 3280 ft/sec (1000 m/sec) (HBAR).

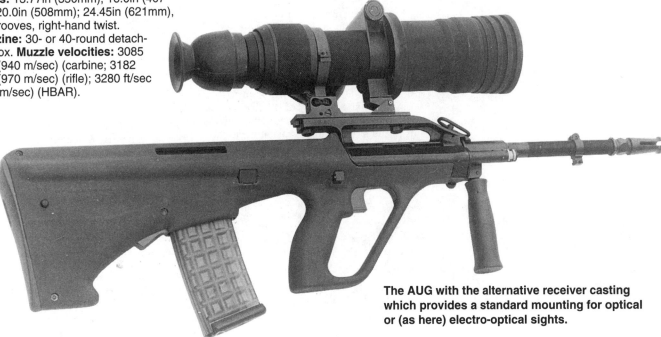

The AUG with the alternative receiver casting which provides a standard mounting for optical or (as here) electro-optical sights.

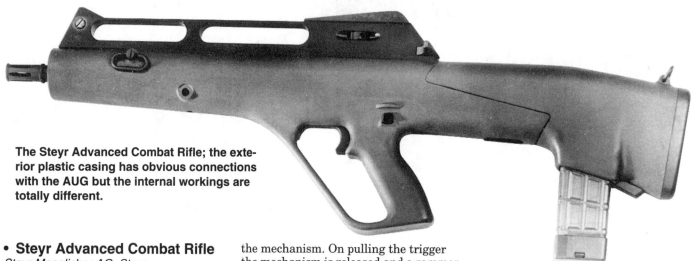

The Steyr Advanced Combat Rifle; the exterior plastic casing has obvious connections with the AUG but the internal workings are totally different.

• Steyr Advanced Combat Rifle
Steyr-Mannlicher AG, Steyr
5.56mm Flechette

This rifle was designed in 1987-9 as an entry for the US Army Advanced Combat Rifle (ACR) program, a project intended to determine the likely shape of the US Army's rifle in the 21st century. None of the competing rifles provided the desired 100 percent improvement on the first-round hit probability, and the program was closed down. But it is considered probable that this rifle will form the basis of Steyr's next generation of assault rifles and is therefore worth recording here. (The other three rifles will be found in the USA section).

There is a distinct family resemblance between this and the AUG rifle, both being bullpups and having similar plastic basic structures. There is a push-through firing selector giving single shots, three-round bursts or safe. A shotgun-style rib acts as a rough aiming guide and carrying handle, and mounts iron sights as well as providing a mount for an optical sight. The transparent magazine fits into the butt.

The weapon is gas operated, a sleeve around the barrel being driven backwards to actuate the mechanism. The breech unit is a vertically rising block with the chamber in it; to load, the cocking handle, beneath the rear sight block, is pulled back and returned. This cocks

the mechanism. On pulling the trigger the mechanism is released and a rammer drives a cartridge into the chamber; the chamber then rises into alignment with the barrel and the cartridge is fired by a fixed firing pin mounted vertically above the chamber. The gas action now lowers the chamber again, into alignment with the rammer, and when the next cycle of operation begins the new cartridge entering the chamber pushes the empty cartridge case out forward and ejects it below the rifle.

The action will be more easily understood when the ammunition is explained: the cartridge is a plastic cylinder containing a flechette, a fin-stabilized dart about 1.6mm diameter and 41mm long, held in a plastic sabot. The propellant is behind the sabot, and a circular primer runs around the case near its rear end, also acting as a locator for the fins of the flechette. As the chamber rises into alignment with the barrel, a fixed firing pin above the chamber passes through a hole and stabs the circular primer, so firing the propelling charge. The flechette is ejected into the barrel, where it is held stable by its sabot until it leaves the muzzle, whereupon the sabot falls away and the flechette is left flying to the target. The sights have no form of adjustment, since the velocity of the flechette is so high that the trajectory is virtually flat out to the maximum operational range.

The rifle functioned well during its trials in the USA, and after some initial teething troubles the ammunition proved to be accurate and consistent. Whether it will re-appear in some new guise remains to be seen.

Length: 30.11in (765mm). **Weight unloaded:** 7lb 2oz (3.23kg). **Barrel:** smoothbore; length not known. **Magazine:** 24-round detachable box. **Muzzle velocity:** c.4905 ft/sec (1495 m/sec).

BELGIUM

• Fusil Automatique Modéle 1930
Fabrique Nationale d'Armes de Guerre, Herstal
Various calibers

The Belgian Mle 1930 rifle is an FN-manufactured Browning Automatic Rifle, originally based on the United States Army's M1918 type. There are some small differences—notably in the design of the magazine, the ejection port covers, and the gas regulator—and the barrel is ribbed as a gesture towards solving the cooling problem.

In addition to being a standard Belgian army weapon (in 7.65mm), the Mle 1930 was offered commercially and can be met in a variety of calibers. Some were

The FN M1930 version of the Browning automatic rifle.

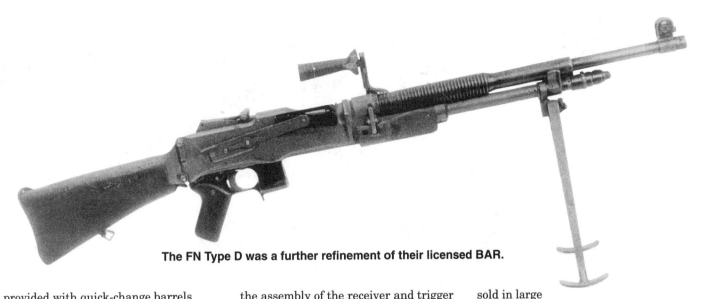

The FN Type D was a further refinement of their licensed BAR.

provided with quick-change barrels. Guns are known to have been supplied by FN to Chile, China, Poland and Sweden - all of whom received deliveries prior to 1939. Sweden also developed and manufactured indigenous guns, made by the state-owned Carl Gustavs Stads Gevärsfaktori at Eskilstuna.

• Fusil Automatique Browning Type D

Fabrique Nationale d'Armes de Guerre, Herstal

7.92x57mm Mauser; 30-06 Springfield

The Type D automatic rifle is a modernized version of the Browning Automatic Rifle (or BAR) first designed in 1917, and of Fabrique Nationale's Modéle 30. After World War II, Fabrique Nationale saw a market for an improved model of this gun, which would provide a light machine gun, lighter than those available at the time. It was bought in small numbers by the Belgian and Egyptian armies, by the latter after their defeat in the 1947 Israeli War when they set about rearming and replacing their rather antiquated equipment. Two significant improvements over the original Browning design are incorporated in the Type D. The first is the fact that the barrel can be easily and quickly changed, so allowing the gunner the capability of continuous fire provided that he has spare barrels. The second is a simplification of

the assembly of the receiver and trigger mechanism so that these components can be more easily removed, replaced, or cleaned. These changes made the Type D a much better light machine gun—but it came too late and could not compete with others that were appearing at the same time. One drawback was the 20-round magazine which, mounted below the gun, could not be enlarged. However, the Type D served the Egyptian Army well enough for several years until the Russians replaced it with their patterns.

Length: 45.00in (1143mm). **Weight unloaded:** 20lb 4oz (9.18kg). **Barrel:** 20.0in (508mm), 4 grooves, right-hand twist. **Magazine:** 20-round detachable box. **Muzzle velocity:** c.2400 ft/sec (730 m/sec).

• Fusil Automatique Modéle 49 (often known as the SAFN)

Fabrique Nationale d'Armes de Guerre, Herstal

7mm, 7.65mm, 7.92mm, 30-caliber

The Modéle 49—offered in standard (selective-fire), automatic only, and sniper versions—was designed before World War II and was shelved during the German occupation, appearing in time to catch the immediate post-war market for self-loading rifles which became surprisingly large and lucrative. As the range of calibers shows, every effort was made to please the customer and the rifle was

sold in large numbers in Egypt, Europe and South America. The bolt system is similar to the Russian Tokarev as the action is locked by the bolt tilting under the influence of cams in the receiver sides. The action is operated by gas, with a long cylinder and tappet above the barrel. The firing pin is struck by a hammer, and the 10-round magazine can be loaded either by chargers or with individual rounds. The whole construction of the rifle is of a very high standard, making it expensive to produce, and the Mle 49 was taken as a basis for the development of the later FAL—which is an undeniable improvement on it.

Amongst the users of the Mle 49 were Colombia (30-caliber), Venezuela (7mm), Egypt (7.92mm), and Indonesia (30-caliber).

Length: 44.00in (1116mm). **Weight unloaded:** 9lb 8oz (4.31kg). **Barrel:** 23.25in (590mm), 4 grooves, right-hand twist. **Magazine:** 10-round detachable box. **Muzzle velocity:** c.2400 ft/sec (730 m/sec).

• Fusil Automatique Légére (FAL)

Fabrique Nationale d'Armes de Guerre, Herstal

7.62x51mm NATO

Probably the most successful of the many designs produced by Fabrique Nationale, the FAL sold to over seventy

The FN Model 1949 or SAFN was one of the first successful post-war designs.

Used, in one form or another, by over 55 armies, the FN-FAL became one of the most widely-distributed rifles ever made.

The FN CAL was more or less a scaled-down FAL but with a rotating bolt; it was one of the first 5.56mm rifles to appear, well before there was any demand for them.

countries and was made under license in many countries all over the world. When 7.62mm was the NATO standard, the FAL was the equipment of most of the NATO partners, and its NATO acceptance acted as a powerful sales promotion factor. Such enormous success stems partly from political and economic factors, but these would be of little influence if the original weapon were not sound and practical. This it was in every way. Developed from the Modéle 49, the FAL first appeared in 1950, and large orders were first placed in 1953. Changes in the trigger mechanism made the rifle capable of automatic fire, but it was a little light and climbed excessively, even when fitted with a light bipod. A version with a heavier barrel and a robust bipod was intended to be a squad light automatic gun and was used by several armies for this purpose. All versions were outwardly similar, although there were some changes in furniture and such smaller items as flash-hiders and bayonet fixings. The cocking handle was on the left-hand side—so leaving the right-hand on the trigger when cocking - and there was a folding carrying handle. Robust, reliable, and simple to maintain and operate, the FAL set a new standard when it appeared and it continued as a leading design for over twenty years. Many countries adopted the FAL—Austria, Belgium, Canada, Chile, Ecuador, Ireland, Israel, Libya, Netherlands, Paraguay, Peru, Portugal, South Africa, the United

Kingdom, West Germany and Venezuela being merely the major ones.

Length: 41.50in (1053mm). **Weight unloaded:** 9lb 8oz (4.31kg). **Barrel:** 21.00in (533mm), 4 grooves, right-hand twist. **Magazine:** 20-round detachable box. **Muzzle velocity:** c.2800 ft/sec (853 m/sec).

• Carabine Automatique Légére (CAL) (1966)

Fabrique Nationale d'Armes de Guerre, Herstal
5.56x45mm

The Vietnam war brought about a new family of small arms, just as previous wars have done, and in this case it was the 5.56mm series. The success of this caliber prompted several manufacturers to make their own weapons in 5.56mm and the CAL (Carabine Automatique Légére) was the one first produced by Fabrique Nationale. It resembled a scaled-down version of the FAL although the system of operation used a rotating bolt. Early models had a 3-round selector system, an integral part of the trigger, which permitted three consecutive rounds to be fired with one trigger pull. There was also provision for fully automatic and semiautomatic fire.

The barrel was held to the receiver by a single large threaded nut and, once the handguard had been removed, dismounting the barrel was simple. The magazine held 20 rounds, and the entire weapon was neat and workmanlike. The gas system used a tappet piston rod to drive the bolt carrier by giving it an

impulsive blow, and the bolt had double interrupted lugs to lock into the chamber. Extensive trials and field experience in the early 1970s revealed that there were difficulties in field stripping and maintenance, and the rifle proved expensive to manufacture. It was therefore taken out of production and the engineers went back to their drawing boards to produce the FNC (below).

Length: 38.50in (978mm). **Weight unloaded:** 6lb 8oz (2.94kg). **Barrel:** 18.50in (469mm), 6 grooves, right-hand twist. **Magazine:** 20-round detachable box. **Cyclic rate:** 850rpm. **Muzzle velocity:** c.3200 ft/sec (975 m/sec).

• FN-FNC (1978)

Fabrique Nationale Herstal SA, Herstal
5.56x45mm

The FN CAL 5.56mm rifle attained some success but was withdrawn by its makers in 1975 since it was considered too expensive to be competitive, difficult to maintain in the field, and of questionable reliability. FN then set to work to produce an improved 5.56mm model to be entered in the NATO trials of 1977-80. The development time, however, was too short and the FNC, although entered, was soon withdrawn to undergo further work.

The FNC is a gas-operated automatic rifle of conventional form which can be considered as an improved and simplified CAL. The operating system is still a rotating bolt, but in this design the bolt carrier is attached to the gas piston

The CAL was not a success, but there was enough time for FN to correct the defects and produce this, the FNC, before the demand for a 5.56mm rifle grew.

rod and the bolt head has two heavy lugs which lock into the barrel extension. It is far easier to field-strip and replace a broken firing pin in the FNC than it was in the CAL. The upper receiver is of pressed steel, with hardened steel insert rails for the bolt carrier. The lower receiver and trigger unit are of light alloy, and the two parts are held together by a pin at the lower front of the receiver and a lock pin at the rear; by removing the lock pin the lower receiver can be hinged down and the bolt and carrier easily withdrawn. The muzzle is formed into the NATO-standard diameter for grenade launching, and the gas regulator can be closed so as to allow maximum gas for firing grenades. The tubular skeleton butt folds to the right side of the receiver; a version with a fixed synthetic butt is also available. The magazine housing is to the

standard M-16 interface, and the rifle can be supplied with the barrel rifles to suit either M193 or SS109 ammunition.

Length, stock extended: 39.25in (997mm).
Length, stock folded: 30.15in (766mm).
Weight unloaded: 1lb 6oz (3.80kg). **Barrel:** 17.71in (450mm); 6 grooves, right-hand twist. **Magazine:** 30-round detachable box.
Cyclic rate: c.700rpm. **Muzzle velocity:** 3166 ft/sec (965 m/sec).

BRAZIL

• LAPA Modele 03 Assault Rifle
Laboratorio de Pesquisa de Armamento Automatico, Rio de Janiero
5.56x45mm

This rifle began development in 1978, and testing of the prototypes commenced in 1983. It was hoped that, sub-

ject to official approval, production would commence early in 1985. Official approval never appeared, and the design was not heard of after 1988. Which was a pity, because it was a worthy attempt to produce a completely new rifle.

The LAPA 03 used a bull-pup configuration and was largely made of plastic material. The carrying handle housed a flip-type aperture sight giving 200m and 400m ranges and adjustable for windage. The cocking handle was inside the carrying handle. Operation was by a gas piston actuating a rotating bolt, and the firing mechanism was unique in that it included a 'double-action' position on the selector lever. This allowed the hammer to fall in safety and the rifle could then be carried with the selector set at 'fire', but requiring only a long pull of the trigger to cock and drop the hammer to fire a

The LAPA 03, a Brazilian bullpup, was a good design but it failed to gain acceptance.

Instead of the LAPA, the Brazilian army preferred these locally-manufactured versions of the FN FAL: the Imbel LAR.

round. If more precision was required the selector could be set to 'SA' (single action'), when the trigger mechanism operated in the conventional manner. Double or single action could be selected for either single shots or automatic fire. Prototype models used the M16 magazine, but it was intended that production models would use a plastic magazine.

Length: 29.65in (738mm). **Weight unloaded:** 7lb 10oz (3.48kg). **Barrel:** 19.25in (489mm), 6 grooves, right-hand twist. **Magazine:** 20-, 30- or 40-round detachable box. **Cyclic rate:** 650-700rpm. **Muzzle velocity:** 3280 ft/sec (1000 m/sec).

• Imbel LAR
Industria de Material Belico do Brasil, Vila Estrela
7.62x51mm NATO

The Light Automatic Rifle is simply the well-known FN-FAL manufactured in Brazil under license. It is produced in two forms, a standard model with a fixed butt and a Paratroop model with short barrel and a side-folding butt. Except for some very small dimensional changes it is exactly the same as the original Belgian weapon.

Length: 43.30in (1100mm); Para: 38.97in (990mm). **Weight unloaded:** 9lb 15oz (4.50kg); Para: 9lb 10oz (4.37kg). **Barrel:** 20.98in (533mm); Para: 17.20in (437mm); 4 grooves, right-hand twist. **Magazine:** 20-round detachable box. **Cyclic rate:** 650-750rpm. **Muzzle velocity:** 2805 ft/sec (855 m/sec).

• Imbel MD2 (1985)
Industria de Material Belico do Brasil, Vila Estrela
5.56x45mm

The MD2 is a 5.56mm version of the LAR (above), suitably scaled down. Development began in about 1982, with the intention of capitalizing on the experience gained in manufacturing the LAR and, wherever possible, using existing components of that weapon. The first prototype, the MD1, appeared in 1983 and after extensive troop trials, modifications were made which produced the MD2, which went into service with the Brazilian army and police forces in the late 1980s.

Although using a certain amount of common parts and having a similar general outline, there is little other relationship between the LAR and the MD2. The MD2 is gas operated, using the now-familiar bolt carrier and rotating bolt; you could almost say it is an M16 in FAL clothing. It uses a 20-round magazine but the interface will accept the standard 30-round M16 magazine if required. A light bipod is available and may be attached to the forend, and the standard construction used a folding tubular butt. The result is rather heavier than the average 5.56mm rifle but it produces a very accurate and steady weapon which is perhaps easier to control in automatic fire.

There are a number of variations on the basic model. The MD2 is the standard, with long barrel and folding butt and providing selective fire. The MD3 is the same weapon but with a fixed plastic butt. The MD2A1 and MD3A1 are the same as the MD2 and MD3 but are engineered so as to provide only single-shot fire, and they are principally intended for police use.

The Imbel MD2 is simply a scaled-down FN FAL firing the 5.56mm cartridge.

(MD2) (data for MD3 in [])
Length: 39.76in (1010mm); MD2, butt folded: 30.07in (764mm). **Weight unloaded:** 9lb 11oz (4.40kg); [10lb 1oz (4.56kg)]. **Barrel:** 17.83in (453mm), 6 grooves, right-hand twist. **Magazine:** 20- or 30-round detachable box. **Cyclic rate:** 700rpm. **Muzzle velocity:** 3083 ft/sec (940 m/sec).

CANADA

• C7/C7A1 rifle
Diemaco, Kitchener, Ontario.
5.56x45mm NATO

The Canadian forces moved to 5.56mm in 1984 and adopted the US M16 rifle; this they later changed for the C7, which is the US M16A2 design but with the full-automatic option rather than the three-round burst as favored by the US Army. The sight is also different, a simple two-position flip aperture allowing for short and long-range firing. The receiver has a spent case deflector, so permitting it to be used by left-handed men, and the rifling will permit firing of US M193 or SS109 NATO ammunition.

The C7A1 variation is basically the same rifle but with the carrying handle removed and a flat platform fitted so as to accept a variety of optical or electro-optical sights. A back-up iron sight is carried in the rifle butt and can be fitted should the optical sight be damaged.

Both weapons are in use by the Canadian and Netherlands armies, and the C7A1 has also been adopted by the Danish army.

Length: 40.16in (1020mm). **Weight unloaded:** 7lb 4oz (3.30kg). **Barrel:** 20.0in (510mm), 6 grooves, right-hand twist. **Magazine:** 30-round detachable box. **Cyclic rate:** 800 rds/min. **Muzzle velocity:** c.3018 ft/sec (920 m/sec).

• C8 Assault carbine
Diemaco, Kitchener, Ontario
5.56x45mm NATO

This is a smaller version of the C7 rifle, having a telescoping butt and short barrel, though the receiver and internals are exactly the same as those of the

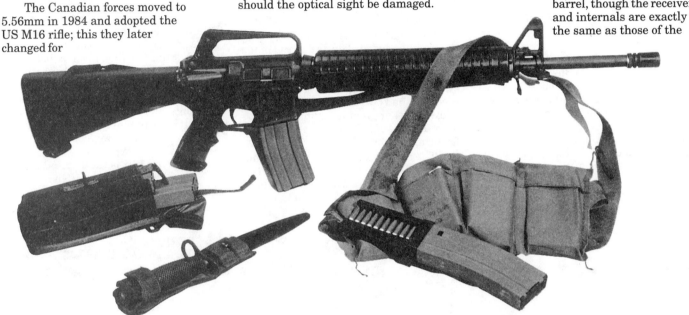

Canada's C7 is actually the Colt M16A2 but with automatic fire instead of a three-round burst.

The C8 carbine is simple a smaller rifle, with a telescoping butt.

C7. It was originally intended for the crews of armored vehicles, but its issue later extended to various specialist units and those who required a more compact weapon. It is also in use by the Netherlands special forces.

Length, butt extended: 33.07in (840mm); butt folded: 29.92in (760mm). **Weight unloaded:** 5lb 15oz (2.70kg). **Barrel:** 14.56in (370mm), 6 grooves, right-hand twist. **Magazine:** 30-round detachable box. **Cyclic rate:** 900 rds/min. **Muzzle velocity:** c.2953 ft/sec (900 m/sec).

CHINA (PEOPLE'S REPUBLIC)

• Type 56 Carbine
State arsenals
7.62x39mm Soviet

This was simply a direct copy of the Soviet Simonov SKS carbine, so much so that the early models could only be distinguished by the Chinese markings. They used the same type of folding knife bayonet as the Soviet model, but later production adopted a folding spike bayonet which makes identification rather easier.

Length: 40.35in (1025mm). **Weight unloaded:** 8lb 8oz (3.85kg). **Barrel:** 20.51in (521mm), 4 grooves, right-hand twist. **Magazine:** 10-round box. **Muzzle velocity:** 2411 ft/sec (735 m/sec).

• Type 68 Rifle
State arsenals
7.62x39mm Soviet M43

Although this rifle looks similar to the Simonov SKS it is quite different and is a native Chinese design. It incorporated features from more than one rifle, modified to suit Chinese requirements. The barrel was slightly longer than that of the SKS and the gas regulator was different, but the one-piece wooden stock and folding bayonet were retained. Bolt locking was by the same rotating bolt system used in the AK47, but the magazine could be loaded with chargers if needed. The size of the magazine was similar to that of the AK, though to use AK magazines it was necessary to grind off the bolt stop. The gas regulator had two settings, which allowed rather greater flexibility than with the AK, but there was no provision for firing grenades.

The rifle was a curious mixture and almost an anomaly in modern times, but it was obviously straightforward to make and reliable in use, and for China that was probably enough.

Length: 40.50in (1030mm). **Weight unloaded:** 7lb 11oz (3.49kg). **Barrel:** 20.50in (521mm), 4 grooves, right-hand twist. **Magazine:** 15-round detachable box; 30-round AK47 box can be used. **Cyclic rate:** 750rpm. **Muzzle velocity:** 2395 ft/sec (730 m/sec).

• Type 56 rifle family
State arsenals
7.62x39mm Soviet

The Type 56 rifle is simply a Chinese-manufactured copy of the Kalashnikov AK47; the only difference is the presence of a folding bayonet beneath the barrel and, on early models, Chinese markings on the receiver to indicate the positions of the safety/selector lever. Later models are marked 'L' for automatic and 'D' for the single shot position.

The rifle was then given a folding butt which folds under to lie beneath the receiver, as in the AKS. Again, the only visible differences are the bayonet, the markings, and the fact that the arms of the butt have prominent rivets which are not seen on Russian weapons. This version became the Type 56-1.

The Type 56-2 is the Type 56-1 but without the bayonet and with a new side-folding butt.

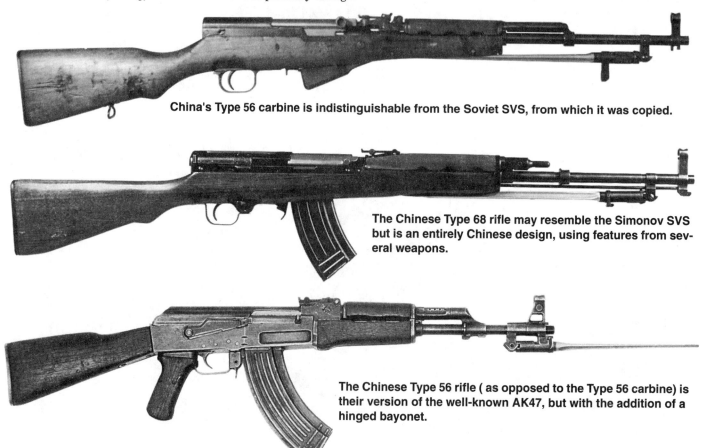

China's Type 56 carbine is indistinguishable from the Soviet SVS, from which it was copied.

The Chinese Type 68 rifle may resemble the Simonov SVS but is an entirely Chinese design, using features from several weapons.

The Chinese Type 56 rifle (as opposed to the Type 56 carbine) is their version of the well-known AK47, but with the addition of a hinged bayonet.

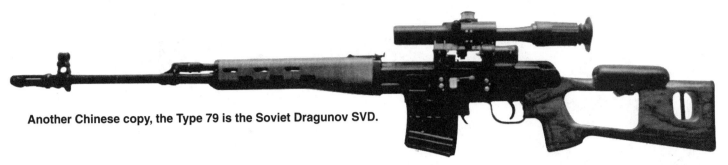

Another Chinese copy, the Type 79 is the Soviet Dragunov SVD.

The Type 56C, first seen in 1996, is a shorter pattern which appears to have been based upon some of the manufacturing improvements seen in later Kalashnikov designs such as the AK-47, though it still uses the 7.62x39mm cartridge. It has a new muzzle brake-cum-flash hider, plastic furniture instead of wood, and a new side-folding metal butt which carries a cheekpiece.

(Type 56)

Length: 34.41in (875mm). **Weight unloaded:** 8lb 6oz (3.80kg). **Barrel:** 16.30in (414mm), 4 grooves, right-hand twist. **Magazine:** 30-round detachable box. **Cyclic rate:** 600rpm. **Muzzle velocity:** 2330 ft/sec (710 m/sec).

(Type 56-1)

Length, butt extended : 34.40in (875mm); butt folded: 25.40in (645mm). **Weight unloaded:** 7lb 11oz (3.49kg). **Barrel:** 20.50in (521mm), 4 grooves, right-hand twist. **Magazine:** 30-round detachable box. **Cyclic rate:** 600rpm. **Muzzle velocity:** 2330 ft/sec (710 m/sec).

(Type 56C)

Length, butt extended : 30.10in (765mm); butt folded: 22.16in (563mm). **Weight unloaded:** 7lb 11oz (3.50kg). **Barrel:** 23.58in (345mm), 4 grooves, right-hand twist. **Magazine:** 30-round detachable box. **Cyclic rate:** 600rpm. **Muzzle velocity:** 2247 ft/sec (685 m/sec).

• Type 79 sniping rifle
State arsenals
7.62x54R Russian

The Type 79 is a copy of the Russian Dragunov SVD rifle, differing only in some dimensions, which is probably due to slight differences in manufacturing practices. It is fitted with a 4x telescope sight which is a copy of the Russian PSO model and has the same infra-red detecting capability.

Length: 48.23in (1225mm). **Weight unloaded:** 8lb 3oz (3.72kg). **Barrel:** 24.41in (620mm), 4 grooves, right-hand twist. **Magazine:** 10-round detachable box. **Muzzle velocity:** 2330 ft/sec (830 m/sec).

CZECHOSLOVAKIA

• Rifle ZH 29
Ceskoslovenska Zbrojovka, Brno
7.92x57mm Mauser

Designed by Emmanuel Holek of the Brno factory in the middle 1920s, the ZH 29 was widely tested by many countries in the 1930s but few ever found their way into military service. Operation was by a gas piston upon the principle later perfected in the various ZB machine guns, although the ZH 29 made use of a tilting bolt cammed into a recess in one side of the receiver.

Long and heavy, the ZH 29 was nevertheless reliable and was obviously

designed to provide a weapon capable of sustained fire, as shown by the unusual ribbed handguard of light alloy intended to prevent barrel heat from blistering the firer's fingers. The guns were made in single-shot or selective single-shot/automatic patterns, the customers' demands being as readily met in this respect as they were in the matter of caliber and barrel length.

Length: 45.50in (1155mm). **Weight unloaded:** 10lb 0oz (4.54kg). **Barrel:** 21.50in (545mm), 4 grooves, right-hand twist. **Magazine:** 10- or 25-round detachable box. **Muzzle velocity:** c.2700 ft/sec (823 m/sec).

• Rifle ZK 420
Ceskoslovenska Zbrojovka, Brno
7.92x57mm Mauser

The ZK 420 was one of several designs by the talented pair Josef and Franticek Koucky (hence the 'K' in ZK) and first appeared in 1942: there was progressive improvement on the original prototype until the final version of 1946. This had a short forestock and a prominent gas cylinder projecting from it. The one-piece bolt is inside a bolt carrier and is rotated into and out of lock by a stud and cam cut in the carrier; locking is achieved by rotating the forward-lugs into recesses immediately behind the breech. The construction relies heavily on milling and similar time-consuming and

Recognizable by the ribbed aluminum forend, the Czech ZH29 rifle.

The Czech ZK420 had too much exposed barrel to make it acceptable to Eastern European armies which still revered the bayonet.

The Czech vz/52/57.

It may look like a Kalashnikov but it is an entirely different weapon: the Czech vz/58V.

expensive processes, so that the rifle was too expensive and rather heavy to compete in the post-war markets. It was not adopted by the Czech Army, which did not help its potential sales, although it was offered in several calibers including 7mm, 7.5mm and 30-caliber.

The design was improved in certain respects and renamed the ZK 420S, but it met with no better success and passed out of production when the vz 52 was adopted by the Czech Army. There were no real faults in either the 420 or the 420S; their only trouble was that by the time they had been perfected, there were too many self-loading rifles from which to choose, and after World War II any new design had to contend with the huge numbers of surplus arms flooding the market.

(ZK 420)

Length: 41.25in (1047mm). **Weight unloaded:** 10lb 0oz (4.54kg). **Barrel:** 21.00in (533mm), 4 grooves, right-hand twist. **Magazine:** 10-round detachable box. **Muzzle velocity:** c.2700 ft/sec (822 m/sec).

• Rifle vz 52/57
Ceskoslovenska Zbrojovka, Brno
7.62x45mm vz 52 (vz 52), 7.62x39mm Soviet M43 (vz 52/57)

This rifle was originally chambered for the Czech 7.62x45mm round and known as the vz 52. It was an unremarkable weapon which relied heavily on other designs for its ideas; not long in

service in the Czech Army, it was not made in large numbers.

The system of operation was an adaptation of that found in the wartime German MKb42(W) and this was linked to a trigger mechanism which owed much to the M1 Garand. However, the locking of the bolt was probably original, as it was achieved by locking lugs at the front of the bolt engaged by tipping the unit. This is a most unusual way of doing it and makes the vz 52 interesting for that reason alone. It is not a satisfactory way of locking and has only ever been used in isolated instances. The magazine was loaded by chargers and another rather outdated idea was the attachment of a folding bayonet.

A later model, called the vz 52/57, was chambered for the Soviet 7.62x39mm short cartridge; it did not survive in service for very long either, and both models are long obsolete.

Length: 40.00in (1015mm). **Weight unloaded:** 9lb 0oz (4.08kg). **Barrel:** 20.50in (520mm), 4 grooves, right-hand twist. **Magazine:** 10-round detachable box. **Muzzle velocity:** c.2440 ft/sec (743 m/sec).

• Rifles vz 58P, vz 58V
Ceskoslovenska Zbrojovka, Uhersky Brod
7.62x39mm M43 Soviet, 7.62x45mm Czech

The vz 58 is a Czech-designed and produced assault rifle which became the standard service rifle of the Czech Army as well as being sold in other countries.

Two versions exist—the vz 58P, with a conventional wooden stock, and the vz 58V, fitted with a folding metal stock. The dimensions of both are the same. Early models had natural wood furniture, but this was replaced with a plastics-impregnated wood-fiber compound and some may even be found with all-plastic fittings. Superficially, the vz58 resembles the AK47, but internally, the two are quite different; the Czech weapon has a tilting bolt and an axial hammer, whereas the AK47 has a rotating bolt and a swinging hammer. The vz58 is very slightly shorter than the AK and uses a shorter barrel, but its overall weight is roughly the same as the AKM.

The vz 58 is well made and finished, and one interesting feature is the simplicity of the trigger mechanism, which is better than that of the AK series. There are several ancillary items that can be fitted to the weapon, including a light bipod which clamps to the barrel immediately behind the front sight, and in so doing, prevents a bayonet being fitted. Whether the changes in design have produced a better weapon than the original AK is difficult to say, since the vz 58 has not seen the same amount of use as the AK series.

Length: 33.20in (843mm). **Weight unloaded:** 6lb 14oz (3.11kg). **Barrel:** 15.80in (400mm), 4 grooves, right-hand twist. **Magazine:** 30-round detachable box. **Muzzle velocity:** c.2330 ft/sec (710 m/sec).

The Carbine (above) and Standard (below) versions of the CZ 2000 assault rifle.

• CZ 2000
Ceska Zbrojovka, Uhersky Brod
5.56x45mm NATO

This rifle first appeared in 1993, chambered for the Russian 5.45mm cartridge and called the 'Lada'. which was unfortunate. At that time there was a cheap and unreliable Russian automobile called the Lada which was the butt of innumerable jokes throughout Europe, and Ceska Zbrojovka wisely abandoned the name and in 1995 re-launched the rifle as the CZ2000. They also produced it in 5.56mm caliber, playing down the 5.45mm version, since by that time the Czechs were looking to align themselves with the NATO group, and a NATO caliber would, of course, be obligatory if they were accepted. Since then the Czech economic situation has taken precedence over questions of strategic policy, and their membership of NATO is still in abeyance. But there seems little doubt that the CZ2000 will be the next Czech service rifle.

The design is quite conventional, a gas-operated weapon using the usual bolt carrier and rotating bolt; the receiver is of stamped steel, the gas cylinder is above the barrel, there is a side-folding tubular butt and a curved plastic magazine. Two models have been developed; the standard rifle is long-barreled and with a bipod attached to the front sight base and a slotted muzzle compensator which doubles as a grenade-launcher, while the short rifle is short-barreled with a bell-mouthed flash hider. Both have the same butt and magazine; the magazine housing has been engineered so that it accepts any M16-type, and it will also accept the 75-round drum magazine which is the normal for the CZ2000 light machine gun, the third member of the family.

(Standard)
Length, butt extended: 33.46in (850mm); butt folded: 25.27in (642mm). **Weight unloaded:** 6lb 10oz (3.0kg). **Barrel:** 15.03in (382mm), 6 grooves, right-hand twist. **Magazine:** 30-round detachable box. **Cyclic rate:** 800rpm. **Muzzle velocity:** 2986 ft/sec (910 m/sec).

(Short)
Length, butt extended: 26.57in (675mm); butt folded: 18.0in (457mm). **Weight unloaded:** 5lb 12oz (2.60kg). **Barrel:** 7.28in (185mm), 4 grooves, right-hand twist. **Magazine:** 30-round detachable box. **Cyclic rate:** 800rpm. **Muzzle velocity:** 2410 ft/sec (735 m/sec).

DENMARK

• Bang-Gevaer
Manufactured by various companies
Supplied in various calibers

Soren H. Bang, an inventive Dane, was greatly taken with the prospects of putting a neglected Maxim idea to some practical use. This—an idea which Maxim had patented in the 1880s—concerned tapping the muzzle blast and making it actuate a loading mechanism. Bang developed a number of rifles and machine-guns which used muzzle-cones to trap the gas blast, which were consequently driven forward taking an operating rod with them. By various linkages this rod was made to unlock and retract the breechblock, the whole cycle then being completed by the usual type of return spring.

The weapons were extensively tested by several nations prior to World War II and again, in improved forms, in the 1920s; none was adopted. Their principal drawbacks were a lack of robustness in their construction (especially in the barrel, which readily overheated) and high manufacturing costs.

A version of the Danish Bang rifle in 303-caliber; it relied upon muzzle blast for its operation.

The Madsen Light Automatic Rifle, an excellent design which arrived on the market too late.

The principle was later revived by Walther and Mauser during the development of the Gew 41(W) and Gew 41(M) designs produced for the German Army.

No data is given since virtually every Bang weapon was unique; the dimensions and caliber were largely dependent upon Bang's contemporary ideas and the market for which he was designing the gun.

• Madsen Light Automatic Rifle m/62
Dansk Industri Syndikat AS 'Madsen', Copenhagen
7.62x51mm NATO

The much respected firm of Madsen has now ceased to make small arms, but for many years after World War II they adapted existing designs and manufactured a wide variety of infantry weapons which all displayed the same high standards maintained by the firm for over a century. In the early 1960s, a light automatic rifle was produced in NATO caliber and offered for sale to interested nations. Unfortunately, it came a little late into the arena and most countries had by that time already made their selections. The m/62 was extremely well made, and exhibited several good design features, the most notable of which was the extensive use of light alloys in the general construction. The return spring was above the barrel and around the piston rod, so that it pulled the bolt forward instead of the more usual push action. There were similarities, no doubt unintentional, to

the Soviet Kalashnikov—particularly in the action and design of the bolt, but in all other respects it appears to be quite original. It was intended to be remarkably versatile and could be fitted with a telescope and a bipod, the latter being of value when the gun was used in fully automatic fire. Two types of stock were offered: a fixed wooden one and a folding metal one which telescoped alongside the receiver. There is no doubt that it was an excellent design, and the remaining examples are beautifully made, but it was too expensive and too late. The weapon was the last big effort of the Madsen company and they then turned to more profitable products of a less warlike nature.

Length: 42.50in (1080mm). **Weight unloaded:** 10lb 9oz (4.80kg). **Barrel:** 21.00in (533mm), 4 grooves, right-hand twist. **Magazine:** 20-round detachable box. **Cyclic rate:** 600rpm. **Muzzle velocity:** c.2650 ft/sec (807 m/sec).

DOMINICAN REPUBLIC

• Cristobal M62 rifle (1962)
Armeria San Cristobal
7.62x51mm NATO

It would appear that this was intended to arm the Dominican armed forces with a full-caliber automatic weapon, but that financial considerations prevented the adoption of the perfected weapon. It was a gas-operated rifle with a short-stroke piston driving an operat-

ing rod in much the same manner as the US M14 rifle, but instead of a rotating bolt it had a tipping bolt based upon that of the FN-FAL. Half-stocked, with an exposed barrel having the gas cylinder below it, it was a competent piece of design but never got past the prototype stage.

Length: 42.50in (1080mm). **Weight:** 10lb 6oz (4.72kg). **Barrel:** 21.30in (540mm), 4 grooves, right-hand twist. **Magazine:** 20-round detachable box. **Cyclic rate:** 600 rds/min. **Muzzle velocity:** 2700 ft/sec (823 m/sec).

EGYPT

• Misr
State Factory 54
7.62x39mm Russian

The Misr is simply a direct copy of the Russian AKM, with the slight difference that while the butt and forend are of wood, the pistol grip and handguard are of plastic. There is also a version with a single-strut side-folding buttstock. A variant known as the 'ARM' is marketed as a police and sporting weapon and is simply a semiautomatic version of the Misr but with a rather more ambitious wooden thumb-hole butt.

Length: 30.10in (880mm). **Weight unloaded:** 6lb 15oz (3.15kg). **Barrel:** 16.34in (415mm), 4 grooves, right-hand twist. **Magazine:** 30-round detachable box. **Cyclic rate:** 700rpm. **Muzzle velocity:** 2625 ft/sec (800 m/sec).

The Egyptian Misr is obviously a clone of the Kalashnikov

The Egyptian ARM is another derivative of the Kalashnikov but at least the butt and grip show some originality.

FINLAND

• Assault Rifles m/60 and m/62
Valtion Kivaarithedas, Jyvaskyla, and others
7.62x39mm Soviet M43

The Finnish Army uses a variety of weapons of basically Soviet origin and the m/60 is one of them; it is no more than a copy of the AK47, modified in some minor respects. The fore handgrip is made of plastic instead of wood, the stock is of tubular steel and the rear sight is placed on the sliding cover of the receiver. The only other obvious differences are the triggerguard—which is virtually nonexistent—and the bayonet, which is more of a knife than a conventional bayonet. A later version, designated m/62, was also been produced, and the changes in design were little more than some slight changes in the handguard and the introduction of a triggerguard. Nevertheless, the Finnish version of the AK47 is fairly distinctive and, on the surface, looks to be an improvement.

Length: 36.00in (914mm). **Barrel:** 16.50in (419mm), 4 grooves, right-hand twist. **Magazine:** 30-round detachable box. **Cyclic rate:** 650rpm. **Muzzle velocity:** c.2400 ft/sec (730 m/sec).

• Assault Rifle M76
Valmet Oy, Helsinki
7.62x39mm or 5.56x45mm

This is an improved version of the earlier M62 which, in the process, has moved back much closer to the original AK47 from which the M60 series was copied. Much use has been made of

Another Kalashnikov relative, the Finnish Valmet M76.

The Valmet 82, however, was a much more original design, though it was not acceptable to the military.

The Valmet M78 in 5.56mm caliber is described as a 'long rifle' and can function equally well as a squad automatic.

stamping and formed metal (in order to reduce production costs), the forend and butt are of plastic, and the rear sight position on the receiver cover was retained. Both sights have tritium illumination for firing in poor light.

Various models of the M76 have been developed in 7.62x39mm or 5.56x45mm calibers: the M76T with folding tubular buttstock; the M76W with wooden buttstock; the M76F with folding plastic buttstock; and the M76P with a fixed plastic buttstock. The Finnish army adopted the weapon in 7.62mm caliber, and it was sold to the army of Qatar and to Indonesia in 5.56mm caliber.

(M76W)

Length, butt extended: 37.40in (950mm); butt folded: 23.95in (710mm). **Barrel:** 16.46in (418mm), 4 grooves, right-hand twist(7.62mm) or 6 grooves (5.56mm). **Magazine:** 15-, 20- or 30-round detachable box. **Cyclic rate:** 700rpm. **Muzzle velocity:** c.2358 ft/sec (719 m/sec) (7.62mm); 3150 ft/sec (960 m/sec) (5.56mm).

• Assault Rifle Model 82
Valmet Oy, Jyvaskyla
5.56x45mm

The M82 Short or Model 255-470 was a bullpup rifle developed as far as possible from the existing components of

the M76 series. The only changes to the M76 mechanism involved the sights and trigger unit, changes which were due to the adoption of the short layout. It was originally seen with wooden furniture, but a later version had a black plastic stock. The rifle was produced as a design exercise by Valmet and was tested by the Finnish army and sundry other forces, but no orders resulted and the design was dropped.

Length: 27.95in (710mm). **Weight unloaded:** 7lb 4oz (3.30kg). **Barrel:** 16.54in (420mm). **Magazine:** 20- or 30-round detachable box. **Cyclic rate:** 650rpm. **Muzzle velocity:** c.3150 ft/sec (960 m/sec).

• Long Barrel rifle M78
Sako Ltd, Riihimaki
7.62x39mm Soviet; 7.62x51mm NATO

This weapon was originally put on the market as a light machine gun, having the ability to fire from box or drum magazines, but found no customers. It was then modified to use box magazines only and reintroduced as a 'long barrel rifle'. It is more or less a derivative of the existing M76 rifle but with a heavier barrel and a bipod so that it can, in emergency, double as a light machine gun. The

standard model fired the 7.62x39mm Soviet cartridge and a variant, firing the 7.62mm NATO round but regulated to fire only in the semiautomatic mode, was also offered. Numerous armies tried the weapon but none bought it, and although still available if requested, it was taken out of production in the early 1990s.

Length: 41.73in (1060mm). **Weight unloaded:** 10lb 6oz (4.70kg). **Barrel:** 22.04 in (560mm), 4 grooves, right-hand twist. **Magazine:** 20- or 30-round detachable box. **Cyclic rate:** 650rpm. **Muzzle velocity:** c.2360 ft/sec (719 m/sec).

• Sako M90
Sako Ltd, Riihimäki
7.62x39mm Soviet M1943

The Sako M90 is an improved version of the earlier M62/M76 design, which in turn was based upon the Kalashnikov AK47. The M90 has been lightened and built to a very high standard; a new side-folding butt is used, new sights have an adjustable tangent aperture and a fixed aperture battle sight, and there is an entirely new design of flash eliminator which also functions as a grenade launcher. Tritium auxiliary

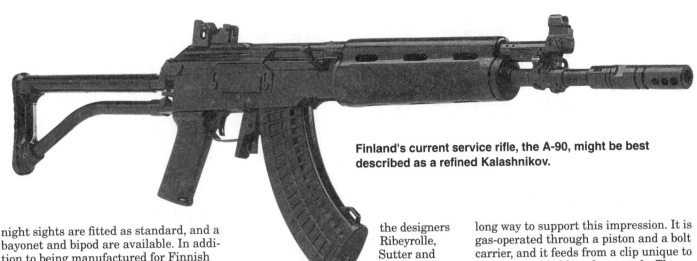

Finland's current service rifle, the A-90, might be best described as a refined Kalashnikov.

night sights are fitted as standard, and a bayonet and bipod are available. In addition to being manufactured for Finnish service in 7.62x39mm chambering, it is also available in 5.56x45mm NATO chambering for export.

Length, butt extended: 36.61in (930mm); butt folded: 26.57in (675mm). **Weight unloaded:** 8lb 8oz (3.85kg). **Barrel:** 16.38in (416mm), 4 grooves, right-hand twist. **Magazine:** 30-round detachable box. **Muzzle velocity:** 2625 ft/sec (800 m/sec).

FRANCE

• Fusil Mitrailleur RSC Modéle 1917, Fusil Mitrailleur RSC Modéle 1918
Manufacture d'Armes de Saint-Etienne
8x50R Lebel

This semiautomatic rifle, properly known as the Modéle 1917 or RSC (from the designers Ribeyrolle, Sutter and Chauchat) takes its common name 'St-Etienne' from the place of manufacture. It was the end product of a number of experimental weapons which had been developed in the early years of the century, and was issued in great haste during World War I. Better designs were available, but the Modéle 1917 was the only one which used the standard French 8mm rimmed Lebel cartridge, and it was thus selected in order not to disrupt ammunition production or complicate supply.

It seems to have been beyond the power of early French firearms designers to produce an aesthetically acceptable weapon and the RSC is no exception to this rule, an ugly and awkward-looking weapon whose length and weight go a long way to support this impression. It is gas-operated through a piston and a bolt carrier, and it feeds from a clip unique to this rifle and holding five rounds. The Modéle 1918 was an attempt to improve matters by shortening and tightening the weapon and altering the feed system to take the standard rifle cartridge clip, the Chargeur Mle 16. The Modéle 1917 rifle was used in limited numbers during World War I, but the 1918 design did not appear until after the Armistice. A transitional form of the Fusil Mitrailleur Mle 17 is known to exist; this is basically a Mle 17 shortened to approximately the length of the Mle 18, probably a retrospective alteration.

In 1935, the surviving rifles were altered to a type of manual straight-pull bolt action, achieved simply by blocking the gas port. It is believed that these were then issued to colonial troops in French Equatorial Africa.

The French St-Etienne M1917 automatic rifle, cumbersome and not very reliable.

The breech and magazine area of the St-Etienne rifle.

The MAS49 was the postwar French service rifle.

(Modéle 1917)

Length: 52.40in (1331mm). **Weight unloaded:** 11lb 9oz (5.25 kg). **Barrel:** 31.40in (798mm), 4 grooves, right-hand twist. **Magazine:** 5-round internal box. **Muzzle velocity:** c.2350 ft/sec (716 m/sec).

(Modéle 1918)

Length: 43.10in (1095mm). **Weight unloaded:** 10lb 9oz (4.79kg). **Barrel:** 23.10in (586mm), 4 grooves, right-hand twist. **Magazine:** 5-round internal box. **Muzzle velocity:** c.2200 ft/sec (670 m/sec).

• Fusil Mitrailleur Modéle 49 (MAS 49)
Manufacture d'Armes de Saint-Etienne
7.5x54mm French Mle 29

France was early in the field in Europe with a semiautomatic rifle for her infantry and the MAS 49 was first issued—as its title suggests—in 1949, at a time when most of the other European countries were still using pre-war bolt-action weapons. In many ways, the MAS 49 resembles the earlier bolt-action MAS 36, for it uses the same two-piece stock and sights and is generally similar in outline. In fact, it is not an auto-matic version of the MAS 36, but a new design which incorporated some of the earlier fittings to reduce costs. It is a rather heavy, very strong, and highly reliable gas-operated rifle.

The gas system uses no piston or cylinder: the gas is conducted through a pipe to blow directly on to the face of the bolt and force it backwards. This arrangement has not always proved popular with other designers, largely owing to rapid accumulation of fouling, but this is largely a question of the propellant, and the system seems to work well enough in this rifle. A grenade launcher is fitted as an integral part of the muzzle, and the MAS 49 was one of the first weapons to be produced with such a fitting: There are also permanent grenade-launching sights on the left side of the rifle and the front sight near the end of the stock moves the grenade stop up or down the barrel, according to the range set on the sight. This shift alters the muzzle velocity and, therefore, the range.

Unusually, the Modéle 49 was not intended for a bayonet, but a few were adapted for the small 'spike' of the Modéle 36. The breech was locked by tilting the breechblock in the same manner as the Tokarev designs and the SAFN produced by Fabrique Nationale, a simple and reliable arrangement. The MAS 49 and its derivatives were in service with the French army for over thirty years, being used in Indo-China, Algeria and Egypt with complete success.

Length: 42.36in (1076mm). **Weight unloaded:** 9lb 0oz (4.07kg). **Barrel:** 22.83in (580mm), 4 grooves, left-hand twist. **Magazine:** 10-round detachable box. **Muzzle velocity:** c.2788 ft/sec (850 m/sec).

• Fusil Mitrailleur Modéle 49/56 (MAS 49/56)
Manufacture d'Armes de Saint-Etienne
7.5x54mm French Mle 29

In 1956 NATO was taking its first steps towards standardization of equipment, and one of the first agreements was over the form of rifle muzzles to fire grenades. These would be 22mm in diameter, with machined rings to support the grenade and act as gas seals inside the tail tube of the grenade. So the Mle 49 rifle was redesigned to accommodate this new standard. This meant shortening the wooden forend and handguard, securing them with a single band, and leaving a length of exposed barrel upon which the front sight was mounted on a ramp. Then came a thick grenade stop ring and the remainder of the barrel was shaped to the NATO standard with a perforated muzzle compensator. Beyond giving the rifle a more sporting appearance, there was little difference to be seen, but there were small dimensional differences.

Length: 40.24in (1022mm). **Weight unloaded:** 8lb 6oz (3.88kg). **Barrel:** 22.83in (580mm), 4 grooves, left-hand twist. **Magazine:** 10-round detachable box. **Muzzle velocity:** c.2750 ft/sec (838 m/sec).

• Fusil Automatique MAS 5.56 (FA-MAS G1) (1980)
Groupement Industriel des Armes Terrestre/Manufacture d'Armes de St-Etienne
5.56x45mm French

The FAMAS 5.56 replaced the MAS Modéle 49. It incorporates a remarkable

"Le Clairon", the French FA-MAS G-1, the first bullpup to enter military service.

amount of modern technology and design thought. Small, rugged and amazingly versatile, it offers the firer several options in the mode of fire and method of use. Its short overall length makes it suitable for vehicle-borne troops, to achieve which, the designer had to go to a bullpup layout. There are objections to this in most designs, but in the MAS great care has been taken to overcome all but the most minor difficulties.

The barrel is only fractionally shorter than that of the M16, yet the whole weapon is nearly 10 inches shorter. It is operated by a system of delayed blowback. On firing, the breech forces the spent case against the face of the bolt. This action unlocks a pair of levers which then impart an accelerated motion to the bolt itself. During the rotation of the levers, the bolt is moved a very small distance backwards, thus giving the cartridge case a primary extraction movement. It is then thrown rapidly back, extracting the case completely. The usual danger of sticking bottle-necked cartridge cases in a delayed blowback weapon have been evaded by fluting the chamber, so allowing the case to 'float' on a layer of high pressure gas. There is the usual option for semi or full automatic fire and, in addition, there is a three-round-burst counter that is tucked away in the butt, just in front of the butt pad.

The sling is considered to be an integral part of the rifle and its use is recommended for all firing when a steady shot is required; in particular, it is used when firing grenades. For shooting from the ground, there is a folding bipod. The sights are contained within the long channel-section carrying handle, beneath which is the cocking handle. A plastic cheekpiece clips on to the stock, just in front of the butt, and covers one of two ejection openings. An interesting feature of this rifle is that it can very easily be converted for either left- or right-shoulder firing: the cheekpiece is taken off and turned round, exposing an ejection opening on the opposite side. The bolt is then taken out and the extractor claw and ejector are swapped from one side to the other (each fits into identical slots). The entire operation takes but a few minutes. There is a small knife-bayonet that clips onto the muzzle, and the mounting accepts the standard range of French grenades.

The FA-MAS G-2 has been improved in the light of experience. Its most obvious feature is the 'whole-hand' triggerguard.

Despite its unconventional design, the MAS 5.56 is an extremely effective weapon which was soon popular with its users; they call it *'le clairon'*—the bugle—due to its shape.

Length: 29.8in (757mm). **Weight unloaded:** 7lb 15oz (3.61kg). **Barrel:** 19.2in (488mm), 3 grooves, right-hand twist. **Magazine:** 25-round box. **Cyclic rate:** 900-1000rpm. **Muzzle velocity:** 3150 ft/sec (960 m/sec).

• FA-MAS G-2 (1994)
Giat Industries, Versailles-Satory
5.56x45mm French

This is a second-generation FA-MAS rifle which appeared in the early 1990s. The French navy adopted it in 1995, followed by the French army, and quantities have been sold to other countries.

The general shape of the weapon remains the same, as does the method of operation. The most visible change is that the pistol grip now has a 'whole hand' triggerguard, but internally the breechblock buffer has been reinforced in order to better withstand the hammering it gets when firing grenades, and the magazine interface is now to NATO STANAG 4179 and will accept any M16-type magazine. The rifling is one turn in 228mm (8.97 inches) which means it will happily fire any type of 5.56mm ammunition without loss of accuracy; the 5.56x45mm French cartridge differs slightly from the NATO specification.

Other changes include a new selector/safety catch inside the triggerguard,. and a lip on the forend which prevents the firer's hand straying in front of the muzzle.

Length: 29.92in (760mm). **Weight unloaded:** 8lb 6oz (3.80kg). **Barrel:** 19.2in (488mm), 3 grooves, right-hand twist. **Magazine:** 30-round box. **Cyclic rate:** 1100 rds/min. **Muzzle velocity:** 3035 ft/sec (925 m/sec).

GERMANY (PRE-1945)

• Mauser-Selbstladegewehre, 1898-1918
Waffenfabrik Mauser AG, Oberndorf-am-Neckar
7.92x57mm Mauser

The first self-loading rifle patents were granted to Peter-Paul Mauser in February 1898, although it is possible that some of his employees contributed to the developments: it was company policy that all patents should be granted in Mauser's name. This, of course, was normal commercial practice, the based upon the reasoning that what the company's employees developed in the company's workshops and in the company's time was therefore the company's property. Mauser seems to have been fascinated by recoil operation, as all of his rifle designs (and all his locked-breech pistols) utilized the recoil forces in some way.

• Gewehr Construction 98 (Gew c/98)
(Short recoil operation). This was the first of the rifles based on a block of five patents granted late in February of 1898. The barrel and bolt were securely locked together by two flaps—one on either side of the breech—which were positioned in a housing built around the chamber. When the rifle was fired, recoil of the barrel cammed the locking flaps out of engage-

ment with the bolt, which was then allowed to continue rearwards; it was then returned to battery by the recoil spring, and the return of the barrel once again forced the locking flaps into the recesses cut in the bolt. A drawback of the design was that the locking mechanism was not totally enclosed and the flaps protruded behind the flap housing during the unlocking and reloading cycle which, although providing a positive means by which the firer could tell whether or not the bolt was locked, also allowed the ingress of dirt and mud, with the resultant derangement of the somewhat delicate mechanism. Although an entire infantry regiment was armed in 1901 with the c/98, extensive field trials failed to impress the military authorities and the design was abandoned.

• Gewehr Construction 02 (Gew c/02)

(Long recoil operation). The patents for this design were granted to Mauser in November 1902 and covered another recoil-operated rifle in which locking was achieved by a two-piece rotating bolt. Barrel recoil was used to force the back part of the bolt unit towards the rear, which turned the two bolt-lugs from the barrel recesses by means of a screw joint between the two parts of the bolt. Production weapons of c/02 pattern also incorporated a separate cocking lever which could either be used to cock the mechanism for self-loading fire, when the handle was turned downwards to disengage it from the bolt, or for single-shot bolt-action operation, when the handle was left in a horizontal attitude. Although issued on a small scale for troop trials, the C02 was relatively heavy and rather too long; it was quickly abandoned in favor of the c/06/08.

• Gewehr Construction 06/08 (Gewehr c/06/08)

(Short recoil operation). The designation c/06/08 covered three rifles of basically similar operating cycles, but with different forms of locking mechanism. The most popular type used a form of locking flap similar to the Friberg-Kjellmann system, which had been revived in 1904 and was later successfully used in the gas-operated Russian Degtyarev light machine gun; two rear-pivoted locking flaps supported the rear of the bolt in the Mauser design, and barrel recoil cammed the flaps in and out of recesses cut in the receiver by means of two studs sliding in suitably cut channels. The bolt unit was then allowed to recoil along a guide rod, compressing the recoil spring as it did so. The return of the block to battery was then accomplished by the spring, and the return of the barrel once more cammed the flaps behind the breechblock. Two variants of this system, patents for which were granted in June and November 1906, discarded the locking flaps and substituted a block in the form of a saddle; the breechblock slid backwards within the 'saddle', which was cammed in and out of a recess cut in the top of the receiver by the recoil of the barrel unit.

The German Army tested the c/06/08 until the beginning of World War I, although they never sanctioned wide-spread issue of the rifles.

• Flieger-Selbstladekarabiner Modell 15.

The only use for the Mauser-designed self-loading rifles was in arming aircraft observers and balloon crews before the advent of sufficient flexible machine guns. When production of the latter weapons had become adequate the rifles were removed from service,

although a few later appeared on the Western Front as infantry weapons—by which time, they had been fitted with full-length stocks and bayonet attachments—where they had little success. The aircraft weapon was developed from the 'flap-locking' version of the c/06/08.

In retrospect, it is hard to say why the Mauser rifles were such dismal failures in view of the care with which they were made: perhaps, the single-mindedness with which Mauser pursued recoil operation blinded him to the possible use of gas, although it must be admitted that the recoil-operated rifles were no more successful than most of the contemporary gas-operated types. One important factor might well have been the standard of contemporary metallurgy, as the Mauser rifles were all relatively complex and relied heavily on the precise metal-to-metal fit of the cam surfaces and the various bearings: despite the care taken to ensure the smooth motion of the barrel (itself the subject of several patents), wear often rendered the too-delicate mechanism inoperative. It is interesting to note that some of the operating principles of these weapons later appeared in others, with degrees of success ranging from complete failure to considerable usefulness.

• Gewehr 41 (Walther) ('Gew 41[W]')
Carl Walther Waffenfabrik AG, Zella-Mehlis
7.92x57mm Mauser

As we have just seen, Germany had issued self-loading rifles of one sort or another in World War I, but only in small numbers and not all were of her own design or manufacture. An experimental program was started in 1940, as a matter of urgency, to produce a semi-automatic rifle, and the Gew 41 weapons were the ultimate result. Two designs

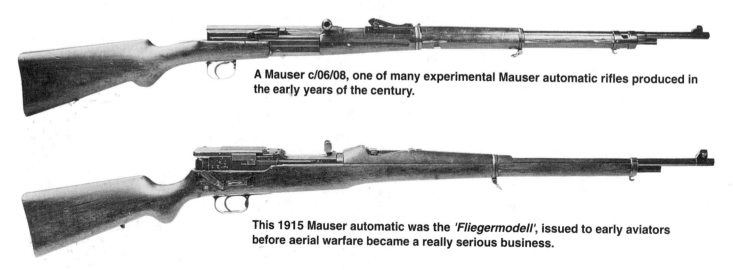

A Mauser c/06/08, one of many experimental Mauser automatic rifles produced in the early years of the century.

This 1915 Mauser automatic was the *'Fliegermodell'*, issued to early aviators before aerial warfare became a really serious business.

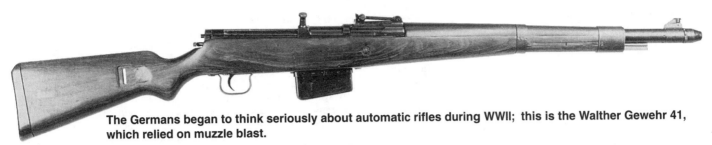

The Germans began to think seriously about automatic rifles during WWII; this is the Walther Gewehr 41, which relied on muzzle blast.

were made, a Mauser—the Gew 41(M)—and the Walther-designed Gew 41(W), but the Mauser type was soon dropped. The Walther Gew 41(W) was adopted, a gas-operated rifle using a variation of the rather crude Bang system in which gas was deflected by a muzzle cup to turn back and strike an annular piston around the barrel and so move a piston rod. Locking was by hinged flaps similar to the Russian Degtyarev machine gun design: The 10-shot magazine was integral with the action and was slow to load. Manufacture was expensive as much machining was involved and the gas system was particularly complicated. The rifle was not a great success as it was heavy and ill-balanced. It was noticeably muzzle-heavy to hold and, although about 8000 were made, it was only issued to special units principally stationed on the Russian Front. When the Gew 43 appeared, all production of the Gew 41 stopped, although it never completely passed from service: Germany was too short of equipment to allow that to happen.

Length: 44.50in (1130mm). **Weight unloaded:** 11lb 0oz (4.98kg). **Barrel:** 21.50in (545mm), 4 grooves, right-hand twist. **Magazine:** 10-round internal box. **Muzzle velocity:** c.2550 ft/sec (776 m/sec).

• Fallschirmjägergewehr 42 (FG42' or 'FjG42')

Rheinmetall-Borsig AG, Düsseldorf: Heinrich Krieghoff Waffenfabrik, Suhl
7.92x57mm Mauser

The *Fallschirmtjägergewehr* ('Paratroop rifle) 42 was one of the outstanding small arms designs of World War II, and it was very nearly a complete success. In the event, a combination of circumstances militated against it and probably no more than 7,000 were produced. This remarkable weapon nearly achieved the impossible feat of being a serviceable selective-fire design using old-style full power ammunition. It was one of the notable forerunners of the present-day assault rifles, all of which use ammunition of lower power and are thus more easily controlled. The FG42 was produced for the Luftwaffe paratroops, and was first used in the dramatic rescue of Mussolini; it later appeared in Italy and France. Many were captured by the Allies, which gave the impression that more were in service than was actually the case.

The FG42 is a gas-operated rifle with several novel features: it fires from an open breech when set at automatic fire, in order to avoid 'cook-offs' (premature discharges caused by heating the round

in the chamber), and from a closed breech, to improve accuracy, when set for semi-automatic operation. The FG42 was one of the first service rifles to be made in the now common 'straight line' configuration, and it had a light bipod and an integral bayonet: all of this in a weapon weighing less than ten pounds (4.54kg). The magazine, rather awkwardly, fed from the left side, and while most-of the ideas embodied in the FG42 have been subsequently copied, this has not, as it tends to unbalance the gun.

There were two distinct models of the FG42, sometimes referred to for convenience as the FG42-1 and FG42-2. Both use the same mechanism but they differ externally. The FG42-1 was designed for Rheinmetall by Louis Stange, and manufactured by Heinrich Krieghoff in Suhl, about 2000 being made. It is recognized by the almost-triangular shape of the metal butt - like a shark's tail—and the acute rearward rake of the pistol grip. The short wooden forend has ventilating slots in its upper portion and the muzzle brake is of the pepper-pot type, with holes.

The FG42-2, about 7000 of which were also made by Krieghoff was slightly redesigned to take cognizance of comments from the users. The bolt stroke

The parachutist's FG42 in its original form with a steel fish-tail butt and steeply-raked pistol grip.

The second version of the FG42 with a more conventional wooden butt and a less angular grip.

was increased and the muzzle brake improved, a measure which reduced the felt recoil and also reduced the breakage of internal parts. This increased the length and weight slightly. The butt was of a more conventional shape and made of wood, the forend was made of plastic, and the pistol grip was closer to the vertical. The muzzle brake is slotted and finned.

Unfortunately, in either form the FG42 was expensive and time-consuming to make, and as a result, it was not favored by the Oberkommando der Wehrmacht (armed forces high command). The parachute arm of the Luftwaffe had sponsored the design, supported by Hermann Goering, but after their disastrous losses in Crete they were rarely employed as parachute troops again, declined in importance as the war progressed and as a result the rifle was never completely developed.

(FG42-1)

Length: 36.90in (937mm). **Weight unloaded:** 9lb 10oz (4.38kg). **Barrel:** 20.00in (508mm), 4 grooves, right-hand twist. **Magazine:** 20-round detachable box. **Cyclic rate:** c.800rpm. **Muzzle velocity:** c.2395 ft/sec (730 m/sec).

(FG42-2)

Length: 41.73in (1060mm). **Weight unloaded:** 11lb 2oz (5.05kg). **Barrel:** 20.67in (525mm), 4 grooves, right-hand twist. **Magazine:** 20-round detachable box. **Cyclic rate:** c.750rpm. **Muzzle velocity:** c.2395 ft/sec (730 m/sec).

• Maschinenkarabiner 42(H) (MKb42(H)

C.G. Haenel Waffen- und Fahrradfabrik AG, Suhl

7.92x33mm Kurz

The MKb42(H) was produced by Haenel to the same specification that inspired the MKb42(W); the Haenel weapon was designed by Louis Schmeisser in the period 1940-1, and fifty specimens had been produced by mid 1942.

A gas-operated tipping-bolt type, the MKb42(H) was more conventional in design than its Walther competitor, with a standard form of gas tube and piston. When the tapped gas struck the piston—which was attached to the bolt carrier—it drove the carrier rearwards until the carrier unlocked the bolt by moving it back and down from the locking recesses; the bolt, the carrier and the piston continued to travel back until halted by the recoil spring, from which position the components were returned to battery. The MKb42(H) was externally similar to the later MP43 (for which it served as a prototype), except for the visible gas tube above the barrel, the attachment of a bayonet lug, and a different trigger and grip assembly.

Approximately 8,000 of the MKb42(H) wire produced from November 1942 to April 1943 and, after trials on the Russian Front, it was decided to place the weapon in production after Schmeisser had attended to a few minor details. It then became the MP43.

Length: 37.00in (940mm). **Weight unloaded:** 10lb 13oz (4.90kg). **Barrel:** 14.37in (364mm), 4 grooves, right-hand twist. **Magazine:** 30-round detachable box. **Cyclic rate:** 500rpm. **Muzzle velocity:** c.2100 ft/sec (640 m/sec).

• Maschinenkarabiner 42(W) (MKb42 [W])

Carl Walther Waffenfabrik AG, Zella-Mehlis

7.92x33mm Kurz

The MKb42(W) was produced by the Walther factory in response to a specification calling for an 'assault rifle' chambered for the 7.92mm 'intermediate' round, then being produced on an experimental basis by Polte-Werke of Magdeburg. Development was instigated in 1940 and the first prototype was produced in July 1942. Like the competing design emanating from Haenel, the MKb42(W) was designed for uncomplicated production in the simplest possible manner, and using as little as practicable of the more scarce and valuable raw

materials; much use was made of pressings and stampings which were riveted or welded together.

The MKb42(W) was a gas-operated locked-breech design with a tipping bolt locked by front lugs; an unusual gas assembly was used in the form of an annular piston which surrounded the barrel and which reciprocated within a cylindrical housing. Gas impinged upon the piston and pushed it back within the housing, and a sleeve attached to the piston unlocked the bolt. The gun was externally recognizable by the circular forestock, and by the lack of a separate gas tube; a bayonet lug was fitted and there was a larger gap between the magazine and trigger assembly than in the MKb42(H).

Approximately 3,000-5,000 guns were made for comparative trials on the Russian Front, after which it was decided to place the MKb42CH) in volume production and abandon the MKb42(W).

Length: 36.68in (931mm). **Weight unloaded:** 9lb 11oz (4.40kg). **Barrel:** 16.00in (406mm), 4 grooves, right-hand twist. **Magazine:** 30-round detachable box. **Cyclic rate:** 600rpm. **Muzzle velocity:** c.2125 ft/sec (646 m/sec).

• Gewehr 43, Karabiner 43 (Gew 43, Kar 43)

Carl Walther Waffenfabrik AG, Zella-Mehlis; Berliner-Lübecker Maschinenfabrik AG, Lübeck; Gustloff-Werk, Weimar

7.92x57mm Mauser

The Gew 43 was the logical development of the Gew 41(W), applying the lessons of combat to the design. It incorporated the same bolt locking system but radically altered the gas system. The gas cylinder was placed above the barrel with a simple gas nozzle and cupped piston, and the magazine was made detachable. More significantly, a dovetail was machined on the receiver to take a telescope sight, and the rifle was generally used for sniping. The Gew 43 was probably first used on the Eastern Front in late 1943, though it was encoun-

Walther's MKb42(W) was one of the first designs to rely upon stampings, pressings and welding rather than machining and turning.

Also by Walther, and a year later, the Gewehr 43 reverted to the traditional wooden furniture and rifle shape.

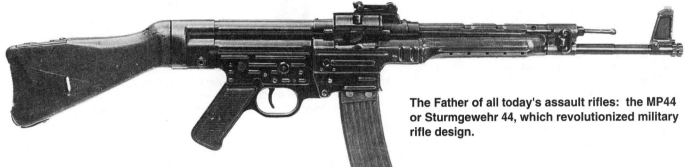

The Father of all today's assault rifles: the MP44 or Sturmgewehr 44, which revolutionized military rifle design.

tered fairly generally on all fronts—always in small numbers and always as a specialist's weapon. A definite improvement on the Gew 41(W), the Gew 43 was much easier to make; most were found with laminated wooden furniture, but towards the end of the war plastic was also used. Owing to the economic situation, there was ultimately a further simplification of manufacture which gives some of the remaining models a very rough external appearance.

The Gew 43 remained in production until the end of the war and, after 1945, was adopted in small numbers by the Czech Army as a sniper's rifle. The Karabiner 43 differed from the Gewehr 43 only in the substitution of a large trigger-guard, although it was also some 2 inches (51mm) shorter.

(Gew 43)
Length: 44.00in (1117mm). **Weight unloaded:** 9lb 9oz (4.33kg). **Barrel:** 22.00in (558mm), 4 grooves, right-hand twist. **Magazine:** 10-round detachable box. **Muzzle velocity:** c.2450 ft/sec (746 m/sec).

• Maschinenpistole 43, Maschinenpistole 43/1, Maschinenpistole 44, Sturmgewehr 44 (MP43, MP43/1, MP44, StG44)
C.G. Haenel Waffen- und Fahrradfabrik AG, Suhl; Erfurter Maschinenfabrik B Geipel GmbH, Erfurt; Mauser-Werke AG, Oberndorf-am-Neckar, and an unidentified company.
7.92x33mm Kurz

The MP43 was the developed version of the MKb42(H) with certain modifica-

tions made in the light of combat experience on the Russian Front; the first deliveries of the weapon were made in July 1943 and production continued until the first months of 1945. In late 1943, a variation of the basic MP43 was manufactured, under the designation MP43/1 in which the clamp-on grenade launcher was replaced by one of screw-on pattern: a short threaded section appeared at the muzzle of the MP43/1 to allow the grenade launcher to be attached. A mounting bracket for optical sights was also fitted, something which never appeared on the original MP43.

In April 1944, the nomenclature was advanced—for some undetermined reason—to MP44, which was otherwise identical with the MP43 although some weapons were fitted with the sight bracket. Towards the end of 1944, a further term was given to the weapon; this, StG44 (for *Stürmgewehr* -'assault rifle' -44), is said to have been bestowed upon the rifles by a well-satisfied Adolf Hitler. At any rate, it more adequately describes the rifles' role. The weapon was originally designated as a machine pistol—or submachine gun—in order to circumvent Hitler's directive that development of rifles was to cease and production of machine pistols stepped up; by calling the weapon an MP the production figures thus appeared in the 'MP' columns of the monthly production reports, boosting the figures, and disappeared from the rifle columns. Honor was satisfied, and the true situation was only revealed after the MP44 had proved its worth on the Eastern front. Nothing succeeds like success.

Versions of the StG44 were developed with curved barrels; they are described in the next entry.

Length: 37.00in (940mm). **Weight unloaded:** 11lb 4oz (5.10kg). **Barrel:** 16.50in (418mm), 4 grooves, right-hand twist. **Magazine:** 30-round detachable box. **Cyclic rate:** 500rpm. **Muzzle velocity:** c.2125 ft/sec (647 m/sec).

• Maschinenpistole mit Vorsatz J, P or V; (Maschinenpistole 44 mit Krummlauf)
C.G. Haenel Waffen- und Fahrradfabrik, Suhl; Rheinmetall-Borsig AG, Düsseldorf
7.92x33mm Kurz

The curved-barrel *Maschinenpistolen* were a remarkable wartime development and illustrate the gusto with which the German High Command entered into futile projects, which promised relatively little and diverted valuable production time from more conventional weapons.

The base for the Krummlauf device was an MP44 to which was fitted a curved-barrel unit with suitable mirror sights attached to the muzzle. The prime object was to have a weapon which the occupants of armored personnel carriers could poke through firing ports and deal with hostile infantry who were close to the vehicle and attempting to stick mines or grenades to it.

The idea originated in a system for testing aircraft machine guns, which have to be capable of functioning irrespective of the attitude of the aircraft. To test a gun at a high angle of elevation demands a very long impact area, not always conveniently found. Therefore a curved barrel attachment was devised, to be clamped to the

The StuG 44 lent itself to the fitting of the *Krummlauf*—the 'gun which shot round corners'.

machine gun barrel and divert the bullets into a sandpit some short distance away from the gun. From this arose the idea of applying it to a combat weapon for close protection of vehicles.

Three versions of the Krummlauf were envisaged: one which turned the bullet through 30°, (MP44 *mit Vorsatz J* or MP44 K/30); another which was intended to turn it through 90° , (MP44 *mit Vorsatz P* or MP44 K/90') and a final design, no more than a paper exercise, the MP44 *mit Vorsatz V* capable of a 40° deflection. Only the first type, 10,000 of which are said to have been ordered in 1944, was ever properly developed.

The principle of operation was to have the curved barrel pierced with a number of holes on the outside of the curve through which gas could be progressively expelled, thereby decreasing the pressure behind the bullet as each successive port was passed and ensuring that the barrel remained in one piece. The MP44 was chosen for this role because of the shorter bullet which could be persuaded more easily to go round a bent barrel than could a normal-length full-power bullet. This escape of gas, of course, reduced the velocity substantially and the bullet—initial muzzle velocity c.2100 ft/sec (640 m/sec) in an unmodified specimen—emerged from the curved barrel at a velocity of c.900-1000 ft/sec (275-305 m/sec). It is evident from this that the effectiveness of the rifle was

greatly diminished as a result of the much reduced exit velocity: but the Krummlauf-MP44 was intended solely as an ultra-short-range equipment and the low velocity was quite acceptable in that role.

• Versuchs-Gerät 1-5 or Volkssturm-Gewehr 1-5

Gustloff-Werke, Suhl
7.92x33mm Kurz

The VG 1-5 was a self-loading 'assault rifle' hurriedly developed by the Suhl-based Gustloff-Werke concern as part of the *Primitiv-Waffen-Programm* of l944; the weapons were intended for issue to the Volkssturm ('Home Guard') and sundry last-ditch organizations ('Werewolves') which ultimately came to nothing.

The rifle was designed by Barnitzke, Gustloff-Werke's chief designer, who had developed the operating principles in 1943, taking an MP43 as his base. The VG 1-5 is remarkable as the mechanism incorporates a textbook case of delayed-blowback operation; the barrel is surrounded by a hollow sleeve, which can reciprocate and carries with it the bolt which is attached to the rear of the sleeve. Some 2.5 inches (6.4mm) from the muzzle are four gas ports and, when the gun is fired, the gas passes through these ports and into the annular space between the barrel and the sleeve. The pressure thus generated is sufficient to hold the

breech closed until the bullet has passed from the muzzle, by which time the pressure has dropped sufficiently to allow the breechblock to move rearwards in normal blowback manner. The breechblock takes with it the gas sleeve and, in doing so, vents the gas into the atmosphere; the recoil spring then returns the breech mechanism to the forward position, loading a fresh cartridge as it does so.

One drawback of the design was that the bearing surfaces of the gas-sleeve, and the barrel surfaces on which they slid, had to be machined to relatively close tolerances; gas residue soon fouled the surfaces unless they were carefully greased, and barrel expansion sometimes jammed the weapon completely.

The VG 1-5 was designed to fire the 7.92x39mm Kurz cartridge, and in order to simplify production, used the 30-round magazine produced for the MP43. Small-scale production is said to have begun in January 1945, but none of the few weapons which were found after the war bear formal Wehrmacht acceptance stamps and it is presumed that whatever production did take place was entirely on the initiative of the factory staff, who, by that time, doubtless had one ear cocked for the approaching Red Army.

Length: 34 85in (885mm). **Weight:** 10lb 2oz (4.52kg). **Barrel:** 14.90in (378mm), 4 grooves, right-hand twist. **Magazine:** 30-round detachable box. **Muzzle velocity:** c.2150 ft/sec (655 m/sec).

The People's Rifle looks crude but used an unusual gas-delayed operating system.

The Mauser Sturmgewehr 45 never got into production, but nevertheless it was to form the basis the next German service rifle ten years later.

• Mauser StuG 45 assault rifle
Mauserwerke, Oberndorf-am-Neckar
7.92x33mm Kurz

This design was produced in prototypes only, to satisfy a demand for a lighter and simpler assault rifle than the StuG44. Although it never got even close to service adoption, it earns its place here for being the ancestor of the later CETME and Heckler & Koch rifles, since it was the roller-delayed blowback breech system developed for this rifle which was eventually perfected by those two companies and employed in their rifle designs.

The Mauser design began as a gas-operated weapon using a roller-locked breech, but the Army Weapons Office objected, considering it too complicated for rapid manufacture, and as a result the delayed blowback system was devised. The remainder of the weapon was built up from steel stampings, using welded joints wherever possible, and the final design was said to show a saving in material and manufacturing effort of some 50 percent over the StuG44. A pre-production order for troop trials was placed, but the war ended before even this could be completed.

After the war a Mauser engineer, Louis Vorgrimmler, left Germany and worked for some time for the French, where he is said to have developed a prototype rifle firing the 30 M1 carbine cartridge and using the roller-delayed breech. He then went to work for CETME in Spain, where he again pursued the same operating system, this time with greater success.

Length: 35.15in (893mm). **Weight:** 8lbs 3oz (3.71kg). **Barrel:** 15.75in (400mm), 4 grooves, right hand twist. **Magazine:** 30-round box. **Cyclic rate:** 400 rds/min. **Muzzle velocity:** 2100 ft/sec (640 m/sec).

GERMANY (FEDERAL REPUBLIC)

• Gewehr 3 (G3) (1961)
Heckler & Koch GmbH,
Oberndorf-am-Neckar
7.62x51mm NATO

Although classed as a State-produced rifle that has had more than one manufacturer in the past, in its country of origin the G3 is no longer made by Heckler & Koch. but it is still produced in other countries under license and has been bought direct from Heckler & Koch by more than forty-five countries in all parts of the world.

The rifle is a modification and development of the Spanish CETME, and since the CETME was itself founded on a wartime German rifle (the Mauser StuG 45), the wheel has turned full circle and the design has come home—though it would no longer be recognizable when compared with the original. Like the CETME, the G3 uses the principle of blowback with delay by rollers, in which the movement of the rollers is controlled by the large firing-pin, which forces them into engagement in the receiver sides. In the G3, the design has been refined to a most reliable and robust system. The rifle is made from sheet metal stampings with plastic furniture, the whole rifle requiring a minimum of expensive machining. The resulting weapon is not particularly pretty, but it is undeniably functional and effective. A grenade launcher is incorporated into the muzzle, and the standard magazine holds 20 rounds. The rear sight rotates to provide elevation and the front sight is a thick post. There are a number of variants to the design:

7.62mm Gewehr 3. This was the first G3 design. It had a 'flip over' rear sight and a wooden butt.

7.62mm Gewehr 3A1. A variant of the G3 in which the butt was retractable. The 'flip over' rear sight was retained.

7.62mm Gewehr 3A2. A variant of the basic G3 in which the rotary rear sight was introduced.

• 7.62mm Gewehr 3A3.
The final production variant of the G3, the G3A3 has the rear sight of the G3A2, but the front sight design has been modified and a prong-type flash-suppresser has been added to the muzzle.

(G3A3)
Length: 40.35in (1025mm). **Weight unloaded:** 9lb 11oz (4.40kg). **Barrel:** 17.72in (450mm), 4 grooves, right-hand twist. **Magazine:** 20-round detachable box. **Cyclic rate:** 550 rds/min. **Muzzle velocity:** c. 2625 ft/sec (800 m/sec).

7.62mm Gewehr 3A3Z. A version of the G3A3 fitted with a telescope sight on suitable mounts, the 'Z' in the designation representing *zielfernrohr*—'telescope'.

7.62mm Gewehr 3A4. Another folding stock variant, this time of the G3A3, and fitted with a retractable stock which slides in channels cut along the receiver sides.

7.62mm Gewehr 3A6. Company designation for the G3A3 made under license in Iran.

7.62mm Gewehr 3A7. Company designation for the G3A3 when made under license in Turkey. There are slight dimensional differences due to different manufacturing techniques.

7.62mm Gewehr 3A7A1. Turkish-manufactured version on the G3A4; slight dimensional differences.

7.62mm Gewehr 3SG/1. This is a specially-selected G3A3 rifle fitted with a set trigger, telescope sight, folding bipod and cheekrest on the butt. Dimensions are as for the G3A3 except that the weight is 12lb 3oz (5.54kg). It is issued as a sniping rifle to the German army.

• HK32A2 rifle
Heckler & Koch GmbH,
Oberndorf-am-Neckar
7.62x39mm M1943

In the early 1960s Heckler & Koch thought they saw a market in various countries which had adopted the Soviet AK47 rifle and its associated cartridge, and they therefore produced the HK32 series rifle, which was identical to the G3A2 but chambered for the Soviet M1943 short cartridge. Numbers of pilot models and demonstration weapons were produced, but since nobody seemed keen on the idea, the rifles never went into series production.

Length: 40.20in (1021mm). **Weight, unloaded:** 7lb 11oz (3.50kg). **Barrel:** 15.35in (390mm), 4 grooves, right-hand twist. **Magazine:** 20-, 30- or 40-round detachable box. **Cyclic rate:** 600 rds/min. **Muzzle velocity:** 2360 ft/sec (720 m/sec).

The Heckler & Koch G3A3 (top) and G3A4 (above) can trace the ancestry of their operating system back to the Mauser of 1945.

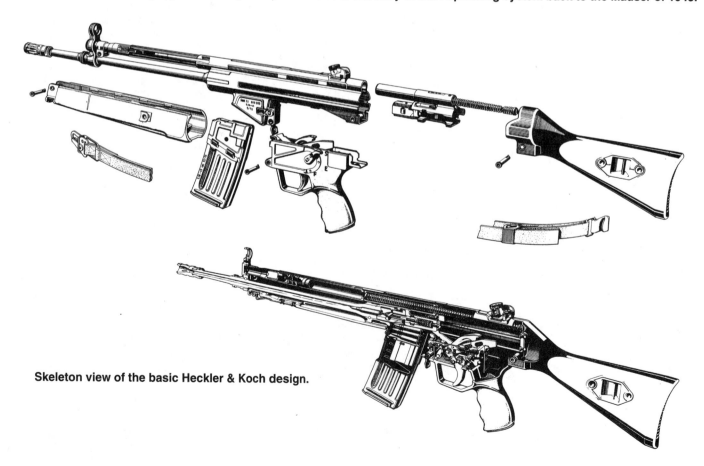

Skeleton view of the basic Heckler & Koch design.

The HK32 fired the Soviet 7.62x39mm cartridge, but there was no demand and it was withdrawn from production.

• HK32A3

Heckler & Koch GmbH,
Oberndorf-am-Neckar
7.62x39mm M1943

This was the folding butt version of the HK32 family. Dimensions were similar to the HK32A2 above except butt extended 37.0in (940mm), butt retracted 28.7in (729mm) and weight 8lb 8oz (3.49kg).

• HK32KA1

Heckler & Koch, Oberndorf-am-Neckar.
7.62x39mm M1943

This was a short-barreled carbine version of the HK32A3, with the same retracting butt. As with the others of the family it was quietly dropped in the early 1970s.

Length, butt extended: 34.0in (864mm); butt retracted: 26.40in (670mm). **Weight unloaded:** 8lb 6oz (3.80kg). **Barrel:** 12.67in (322mm), 4 grooves, right-hand twist. **Magazine:** 20-, 30-, or 40-round detachable box. **Cyclic rate:** 600 rds/min. **Muzzle velocity:** 2295 ft/sec (700 m/sec).

• HK33E (1985)

Heckler & Koch GmbH,
Oberndorf-am-Neckar
5.56x45mm

The HK33E (E for Export) replaces the earlier series of HK33 rifles; there are no mechanical differences, the change being one of rationalization. The rifle operates on the same roller-locked delayed blowback system as the G3, and can really be considered as a G3 in a smaller caliber. Selective fire is available, since the smaller cartridge permits better control at automatic fire, and there are five variant models: the standard rifle with fixed butt; rifle with retractable butt; rifle with bipod; sniping rifle with telescope sight; and the HK33KE carbine version. The longer-barreled models are capable of launching standard rifle grenades from their muzzles without requiring any special attachment.

Lengths Rifle: fixed butt 36.2in 910mm) extended butt 37.0in (940mm); telescoped butt 28.94in (735mm). Carbine: extended butt 34.0in (865mm); telescoped butt 26.57in (675mm). **Weight unloaded:** fixed butt rifle 8lb 0oz (3.65kg); folding butt rifle 8lb 12oz (3.98k); carbine 8lb 9oz (3.89kg). **Barrel:** Rifle 15.35in (390mm); carbine 12.67in (322mm); both 6 grooves, right-hand twist. **Cyclic rate:** rifle 750rpm; carbine 700rpm. **Muzzle velocity:** rifle c.3018 ft/sec (920 m/sec); carbine c.2887 ft/sec (880 m/sec).

• HK36 assault rifle

Heckler & Koch GmbH,
Oberndorf-am-Neckar
4.6x36mm Löffelspitz

This was developed c.1970 at the height of the reduced-caliber craze and was designed round an odd 4.6mm cartridge with a 'spoon-point' bullet designed to have superior stopping power. It has a slightly odd appearance, with an upswept butt, short foregrip, long exposed barrel with flash suppresser, carrying handle with collimating sight and a fixed magazine which was to be loaded by inserting a pre-packed box of cartridges into the rear of the magazine. It used the normal H&K roller-locked delayed blowback mechanism and gave selective fire with the addition of a selectable burst-fire mechanism which provided 2, 3, 4 or 5 shots for a single pull on the trigger. It was a very advanced and sophisticated weapon which worked very well, but once the G-11 project began to take shape and show results, the G36 was dropped.

Length, butt extended: 35.04in (890mm); butt folded: 31.38in (797mm). **Weight, unloaded:** 6lb 4oz (2.85kg). **Barrel:** 15.0in (381mm), 6 grooves, right-hand twist. **Magazine:** 30-round integral box. **Cyclic rate:** 1100 rds/min. **Muzzle velocity:** 2811 ft/sec (857 m/sec).

The odd-looking 4.6mm NK36 with butt-stock folded.

The HK33E is the 5.56mm equivalent of the G3 series.

HK33

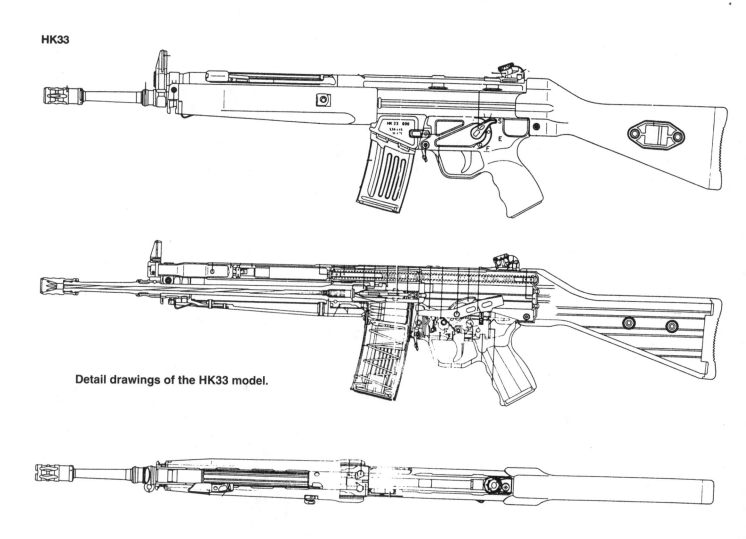

Detail drawings of the HK33 model.

• G11 Caseless Rifle

Heckler & Koch GmbH,
Oberndorf-am-Neckar
4.7x33mm DE11 caseless

Development of this rifle, in response to a German Army requirement, began in 1969; the principal demand was for a very high first-round hit probability, and Heckler & Koch soon concluded that the only solution was an exceptionally fast three-round burst, one round of which would almost certainly strike the aiming point. Conventional rifles are poor in three-round burst performance since the rifle begins climbing after the first shot and spreads the other two far from the point of aim. This led them to examine ways of speeding up the action, which in turn led to the concept of caseless ammunition, since this removes the extraction and ejection phase from the operating cycle.

The G11 rifle uses an all-enclosing casing made of composite material, shaped to form a butt, pistol grip, and carrying handle with optical sight. Within this casing the gas-actuated rifle mechanism is free to move in recoil. The cartridge is a rectangular block of propellant with the bullet buried inside it and with a combustible cap at the rear end. Fifty such cartridges are carried in the weapon's magazine, which slides in horizontally, above the barrel. The cartridge is fed down from the magazine, into a chamber formed in a rotating metal breech-piece, and as soon as the cartridge is chambered this rotates through 90° and the chamber is aligned with the barrel. A percussion firing pin then strikes the cap and the cartridge is fired, leaving no residue of any kind in the chamber. The mechanism—barrel and breech unit—then recoil inside the rifle's casing, during which movement the breech-piece is rotated back so that the chamber is vertical and ready to receive another round to recommence the operating cycle. In automatic fire this sequence is continued so long as the trigger remains pressed. In the three-round burst sequence, however, the operation is entirely different. The first shot is fired as described; but as the mechanism begins its recoil stroke the second round is chambered and fired; recoil continues and the third round is chambered and fired. Only after the third round has been fired is the recoil stroke completed, and thus the firer does not feel any recoil blow until after all three shots have gone, so that the rifle does not begin to rise away from the target until it is too late to affect the

The final service version of the G11 caseless rifle, with bayonet, twin magazines and electro-optical sight.

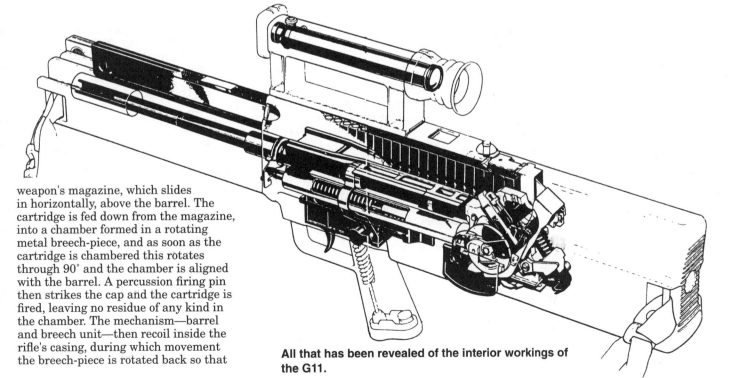

All that has been revealed of the interior workings of the G11.

The PSG-1 sniping rifle.

flight of the bullets. As a result the three shots fall quite close together, much closer than can be achieved with any other weapon. The rate of fire in the three-round burst mode is about 2,200rds/min, the three shots sounding like one continuous explosion.

The rifle was included in the NATO small arms trials of 1978-79 but was withdrawn after it displayed a tendency to cook off its cartridge when loaded into a hot barrel. At that time the cartridge was a block of nitro-cellulose propellant with a bullet in the front end and a combustible cap in the rear. Heckler & Koch then worked with Dynamit Nobel and developed an entirely new type of propellant, based upon a denatured Hexogen explosive, which raised the cook-off temperature by about 100° C and effectively cured the problem. The shape of the cartridge also changed, to a long rectangle with the bullet buried inside it.

By the mid-1980s the design was perfected and all that remained was to tidy it up so as to make mass-production easier. In 1987 the company announced that they have designed an experimental machine gun using caseless ammunition, and the rifle was scheduled to be generally adopted throughout the Federal German Army in 1990. However, the political events of Middle Europe, resulting in the integration of East and West Germany, placed an immense financial burden on the German government. By 1990 about 1000 G11 rifles had been issued to German Special Forces, but at that point the contract was canceled, the funds being taken for the rehabilitation of East Germany. Heckler & Koch went into receivership and were bought by British Aerospace, and the manufacture and further development of the G11 rifle came to an end. It is possible that the G11 design may be revived in the future, but it is highly improbable.

Length: 29.52in (750mm). **Weight unloaded:** 7lb 14oz (3.60kg). **Barrel:** 21.25in (540mm), polygonal rifling, right-hand twist. **Magazine:** 50-round disposable pack. **Cyclic rate:** 600rpm; 3-round burst at 2000rpm.

• HK PSG-1 Sniping Rifle (1985)
Heckler & Koch GmbH, Oberndorf-am-Neckar
7.62x51mm NATO

The PSG-1 (Präzisionsschützengewehr 1) rifle has been developed for precision sniping use by police and military forces. It is a semi-automatic, single-shot weapon using the H&K roller-locked bolt system and is mechanically the same as the G3 rifle. A 6x42 telescope sight with illuminated cross-hairs is an integral part of the weapon, and the bolt has been specially designed and engineered to permit silent closure. An adjustable trigger shoe provides a variable-width trigger with a proximately 1.5kg (3lb) pull. Length of stock, height of cheekpiece, and drop of butt are all adjustable, and a supporting tripod is available.
Length: 47.55in (1208mm). **Weight unloaded:** 17lb 13oz (8.10kg). **Barrel:** 25.59in (650mm), 4 grooves, right-hand twist. **Magazine:** 5- or 20-round detachable box. **Muzzle velocity:** c.2850 ft/sec (868 m/sec).

• G-41 (1985)
Heckler & Koch GmbH, Oberndorf-am-Neckar
7.62x51mm NATO

The G41 rifle was generally similar to the HK33E, the principal mechanical difference being the incorporation of a three-round burst facility in addition to normal automatic fire. However, in this design care was taken to adhere to several NATO standards; thus the magazine aperture was to STANAG 4179 which means that it will accept M16 magazines and others built to the same specification—e.g. the British L85Al rifle magazine. The chamber dimensions and contour conformed to STANAG 4172 for the 5.56x45mm NATO cartridge, and there was a STANAG 2324 sight mount. Other features included low-noise, positive-action bolt closure, a hold-open bolt catch and a dust-proof cover for the cartridge ejection port. It was available in fixed butt, retracting butt or carbine (G41K) form.

Introduced in 1987, by 1989 this rifle was undergoing evaluation in several countries and it was suggested that it would be adopted by the German Army to replace the G3 in second-line formations when first-line troops received the G11. But the collapse of the G11 program appears to have taken the G41 down with it; the rifle ceased production and by 1996 was no longer mentioned in Heckler & Koch sales brochures. Instead, the German army turned to the G36 (below).

(G41)

Length, fixed butt: 39.25in (997mm); butt extended: 39.21in (996mm); butt folded: 31.73in (806mm). **Weight unloaded,** fixed butt: 9lb 1oz (4.10kg); folding butt: 9lb 9oz (4.35kg). **Barrel:** 17.71in (450mm), 6 grooves, right-hand twist. **Magazine:** 30-round detachable box. **Muzzle velocity:** c.3067 ft/sec (935 m/sec).

(G41K)

Length, butt extended: 36.61in (930mm); butt folded: 29.13in (740mm). **Weight unloaded:** 9lb 6oz (4.25kg). **Barrel:** 14.96in (380mm), 6 grooves, right-hand twist. **Magazine:** 30-round detachable box. **Muzzle velocity:** c.2985 ft/sec (910 m/sec).

• G-8 (1985)
Heckler & Koch GmbH, Oberndorf-am-Neckar
7.62x51mm NATO

This is a revised version of a previous design, the HK11E, and has been specially designed as an exceptionally versatile arm for police and security forces. It uses the same roller-locked system as other H&K rifles and has the additional facility of a three-round burst. Feed is by a standard box magazine or from a special 50-shot drum, or, by means of a conversion kit, it can be belt fed. The barrel is heavier than normal, precisely rifled, and capable of being rapidly changed when the weapon is used in the machine-gun role. Iron sights are fitted, but the rifle is normally provided with a 4x telescope sight. The sight mount is

The Heckler & Koch G41 rifle with bipod.

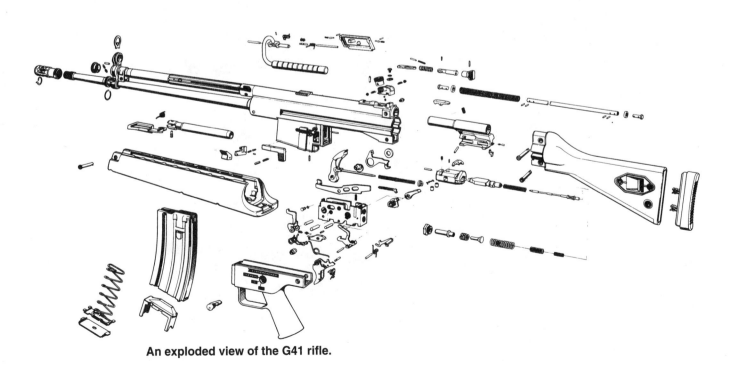

An exploded view of the G41 rifle.

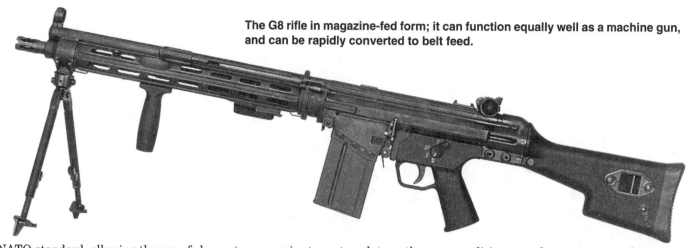

The G8 rifle in magazine-fed form; it can function equally well as a machine gun, and can be rapidly converted to belt feed.

NATO-standard, allowing the use of electro-optical sights.

Length: 40.55in (1030mm). **Weight unloaded:** 18lb 0oz (8.15kg). **Barrel:** 17.71in (450mm), 4 grooves, right-hand twist. **Magazine:** 20-round detachable box, 50-round drum, or metal belt. **Muzzle velocity:** c.2625 ft/sec (800 m/sec).

• G-36 (1995)
Heckler & Koch GmbH, Oberndorf-am-Neckar
5.56x45mm NATO

When the G11 program collapsed the German Army was left without a 5.56mm rifle to conform to NATO standard; the G41 had been suggested to accompany the G11, as described above, but it appears to have been too expensive to contemplate as the all-round standard rifle. The German army then conducted a rapid trial between a Heckler & Koch design and the Steyr AUG. The HK design was chosen, and became the G36. Note that this weapon bears no relationship to the earlier HK36 rifle described above, and the two should not be confused.

The G36 broke new ground so far as H&K were concerned; for the first time (apart from the G11) they abandoned their well-tried roller-locked delayed blowback system and, in the interests of cheapness and simplicity, went for a gas-operated rotating bolt solution. It also reduced the weight and catered for widely-differing ammunition characteristics. Apart from a slab-sided appearance, the layout was conventional, with the gas cylinder beneath the barrel, a pistol grip, box magazine, and folding tubular butt. A raised sight block at the rear of the receiver carried a 3x optical sight, and the integral carrying handle ran from this block to the front end of the receiver, with an aperture for the line of sight. The cocking handle is underneath the carrying handle and also acts as a bolt-closing assist if needed.

The G36 was adopted by the German army in 1996. An export version, the G36E is also avail-

The Heckler & Koch G36 as issued to the German Army, with 3x optical sight and above it, a red dot collimating sight for quick engagement of targets up to 120 meters distant.

The export model of the G36 rifle, which differs in having a 1.5x optical sight and no red dot sight.

Heckler & Koch MSG-90 sniping rifle.

able; this differs only in the optical sight, the G36E having a 1.5x telescope. A short-barreled version, the G36K, is issued to German special forces; it differs in having a prong-type flash hider.

(G36)

Length, butt extended: 39.29in (998mm); butt folded: 29.84in (758mm). **Weight unloaded:** 7lb 9oz (3.43kg). **Barrel:** 18.89in (480mm), 6 grooves, right-hand twist. **Magazine:** 30-round detachable box. **Cyclic rate:** 750 rds/min. **Muzzle velocity:** c.3018 ft/sec (920 m/sec).

G36K

Length, butt extended: 33.78in (858mm); butt folded: 24.13in (613mm). **Weight unloaded:** 6lb 14oz (3.13kg). **Barrel:** 12.60in (320mm), 6 grooves, right-hand twist. **Magazine:** 30-round detachable box. **Cyclic rate:** 750 rds/min. **Muzzle velocity:** c.2788 ft/sec (850 m/sec).

• MSG-90 sniping rifle
Heckler & Koch GmbH, Oberndorf-am-Neckar
7.62x51mm NATO

Introduced in 1987, this is based upon the standard H&K roller-locked delayed blowback breech system and uses a special cold-forged heavy barrel and a wider trigger with a light and crisp pull. The butt is adjustable for length and has an adjustable cheek-piece. No iron sights are fitted, the weapon being normally equipped with a 10x telescope sight carried on a NATO-standard mount which will, alternatively, accept various types of optical or electro-optical sight. A folding bipod is standard.

A variation of this weapon is the MSG3, which is essentially the same but with the addition of iron sights as well as the telescope mount. It has been developed solely for supply to the German army.

Length: 45.87in (1165mm). **Weight unloaded:** 14lb 2oz (6.40kg). **Barrel:** 23.62in (600mm), 4 grooves polygonal, right-hand twist. **Magazine:** 5- or 20-round detachable box. **Muzzle velocity:** c.2850 ft/sec (868 m/sec).

• MSG-90A1 sniping rifle
Heckler & Koch, Oberndorf-am-Neckar
7.62x51mm NATO

This is a variant of the MSG-90 (above) developed to meet a US Department of Defense specification. It is basically the same but with some additional features. Iron sights, adjustable to 1200 meters, have been added, a spent case deflector has been added to the right side of the receiver behind the ejection port,

and the muzzle is threaded to accept a silencer. Dimensions are as for the MSG-90 except that the weight is 14lb 11oz (6.67kg).

• WA2000 (1985)
Carl Walther Sportwaffenfabrik, Ulm-a-d-Donau
300 Winchester Magnum

This rifle was developed by Walther as a purpose-built sniping weapon, rather than a modified basic military rifle. In standard form it was chambered for the 300 Winchester Magnum cartridge, since tests had shown that this gave the minimum variation in point of impact, compared with standard military cartridges. It could also be supplied chambered for 7.62x51mm NATO cartridges.

The design was, for a rifle, unusual. Since the barrel is the most important component of a sniping rifle, the whole design was built around a barrel set into a rigid frame. The rear part of the frame formed the rear of the receiver and in front of the action, in the area of the sight mount, the frame was strengthened by attached side-plates. The barrel was supported by two brackets between the lower and upper arms of the frame. This construction created a supporting structure

The Walther WA2000, a most unusual construction but one which proved too expensive for the market.

in which the barrel was accurately placed and in which the recoil force was delivered to the firer's shoulder in a straight line. There was thus no torque effect lifting the barrel and the sights remained aligned on the target after firing.

The action was of the bull-pup type, with the breech and bolt under the firer's cheek. This allowed a full-length barrel to be used in a comparatively short rifle, another feature which assisted in making the rifle controllable and which was of value when operating the weapon in a confined space. The barrel was carefully manufactured, rifled and chambered to suit the ballistics of the specified bullet and cartridge and the exterior surface was longitudinally fluted to make it highly resistant to vibration and harmonic effects and also as an aid to cooling.

Breech closure was by a rotating bolt with seven locking lugs, actuated by a gas piston contained in one of the frame arms. The rifle fired from a closed bolt, though the bolt remained open after the last shot in the magazine had been fired. The double-pull trigger controlled a hammer unit which struck a firing pin in the bolt. The entire trigger unit, firing mechanism, disconnector, magazine feed and catch were built on to the lower rail as one unit but could be separately removed from the weapon for cleaning. The stock was attached to the frame; the rubber buttplate was adjustable for height, length and cast-off, while the pistol grip was of thumb-hole pattern. The magazine feed incorporated guide ramps which ensure that the bullet point is not deformed during loading and prevented any forward movement of the cartridge, due to inertia, during recoil. There was a muzzle brake, also designed to meet the ballistic requirements of the specified cartridge.

A grip-type sight mount was attached to the receiver and the rifle was supplied as standard with a Schmidt and Bender 2.5-10x56 mm variable power telescope sight, though any other make could be fitted. The telescope mount was a quick-detach type, allowing the telescope to be removed and replaced without affecting the point of impact.

Altogether, the WA2000 was perhaps the ultimate sniping tool; but such a specification does not come cheaply, and few armies were prepared to spend that sort of money on their snipers. The WA2000 was announced in 1985, but orders were few and far between, and production ended in 1989.

Length: 35.63in (905mm). **Weight:** 15lb 5oz (6.95kg). **Barrel:** 25.59in (650mm), 4 grooves, right-hand twist. **Magazine:** 6-round box. **Muzzle velocity:** 3238 ft/sec (987 m/sec).

GREAT BRITAIN

• Rifle, Automatic, 7mm Number 9 Mark 1 (EM2) (1950)

Royal Small Arms Factory, Enfield Lock
7mm (280-caliber) SAA Ball

Although it had been realized for many years that the old series of small arms ammunition based on various cartridges from 6.5mm to 8mm was too powerful, few countries had the resources or energy to change. In post-war Britain, the time seemed right, for the old 303 British bolt-action rifles were obsolete and, in the late 1940s, the EM2 appeared in small numbers. The rifle fired a 280-caliber bullet from a short case, and had been made on the premise that 1,000 yards was the maximum range at which any round would need to be effective. The rifle was a gas-operated selective-fire weapon of highly unconventional appearance for its day and short overall length. The mechanism was very neat (though complicated) and it fired from a closed bolt at all times. Locking was by front-pivoting flaps, and some trouble was taken to ensure that they ran freely and would not jam if dirt and mud entered the receiver; the balance of the weapon was extremely good owing to the breech lying behind the trigger. The sight was a simple optical tube mounted in the carrying handle: it had no provision for range alteration as this was incorporated in the sight picture on the reticule.

The performance of this unusual rifle was extremely good and it was found to be highly reliable and easily learned. Although formally approved for service it was never put into manufacture, mainly because NATO was not ready for it and political opposition was widespread, particularly in the USA where the concept of a short-case short-range cartridge appeared to be incomprehensible. After much argument NATO chose the 7.62x51mm cartridge and the EM2, which could not be converted to this caliber without a major re-design, was abandoned. It should be noted that the L85 rifle (below), although a bullpup, has no relationship whatever with the EM2.

Length: 35.0in (889mm). **Weight unloaded:** 7lb 8oz (3.41kg). **Barrel:** 24.50in (623mm), 4 grooves, right-hand twist. **Magazine:** 20-round detachable box. **Cyclic rate:** 600 rds/min. **Muzzle velocity:** c.2,530 ft/sec (771 m/sec).

• 7.62mm Rifle L1A1

Royal Small Arms Factory, Enfield Lock. Royal Ordnance Factory, Fazackerley.
7.62x51mm NATO

With the NATO acceptance of the 7.62x51mm cartridge and the abandonment of the EM2 rifle, Britain was faced with the problem of arming with an automatic rifle and with no native design available. The solution was simply to buy a design from abroad, and the FN-FAL (see Belgium) was selected. Early supplies were bought from FN but a license to manufacture was also obtained.

The L1A1 was the standard British service rifle from 1954 until its replacement by the L85A1 in the late 1980s. It was adapted from the FN-FAL but there were some minor differences. The dimensions were all changed to Imperial mea-

The British EM2 very nearly made it as the replacement for the Lee-Enfield.

Instead, the British got the FN FAL; this is an early trials model using a rather unusual cartridge charger.

sure to facilitate manufacture in Britain, and spring sizes and material specifications also had to be changed. The resulting rifle, though almost identical to the FAL, does not, therefore, have interchangeability of components. All dimensions and weights are the same as for the FAL.

• **5.56mm Individual Weapon L85A1 (SA80)**
Royal Small Arms Factory, Enfield Lock and Nottingham
5.56x45mm NATO

The Enfield Individual Weapon was first produced in 4.85mm caliber and submitted to the NATO trials in 1977-79. As a result of this trial the 5.56x45mm cartridge was selected as the future NATO standard, and therefore the 4.85mm cartridge became obsolete, The rifle, however, had been designed with this possibility in mind and conversion to 5.56mm caliber was not difficult. Other changes resulting from the extended and searching NATO trial were incorporated into the design and it was formally issued for service with the British Army in October 1985.

The L85A1 is a completely new departure for RSAF and is a weapon designed from the outset as a battle rifle. The bullpup layout results in a short and handy overall length without losing barrel length, and it is a handy weapon to carry and shoot. It operates by a conventional gas piston system, acting upon a bolt carrier and rotating bolt. The bolt carrier rides on two rods which also carry the return springs. The body and many other parts are steel stampings,

and welding and pinning is extensively employed for fastening. The cocking handle is on the right side and has a sliding cover to keep dirt from the interior.

There are three positions for the gas regulator, two for firing in normal and adverse conditions and one for grenade-launching. A special feature of the IW is that it was designed from the start to use an optical sight, the SUSAT (Sight Unit, Small Arm, Trilux) with which excellent accuracy is easily attained. For emergencies, when the SUSAT sight has suffered damage, there is a set of iron sights which fold down for carriage. Infantry units are issued with SUSAT-sighted weapons; support units are issued with

The Enfield L85A1 or SA80 'individual weapon'.

The L85A1 field-stripped. The latest production versions will accept the M16 magazine.

iron-sighted weapons. All furniture is of high-impact plastic and much attention was paid to ergonomics in positioning the grips and sights.

It must, however, be said that the first five years of this rifle's service were disastrous. A number of manufacturing defects showed up in service conditions, and it was not until the closure of the RSAF at Enfield and the setting-up of an entirely new production line, with new computer-controlled machine tools, at the new RSAF Nottingham, that the quality of the production weapons began to improve. It will take some time for the poor reputation gained by the initial issue weapons to be overcome; the only consolation is that the same sort of thing has happened to other military rifles in the past, and they have managed to live down their early reputation and prove their innate reliability. It is to be hoped that the L85A1 will do as well.

Length: 30.90in (785mm). **Weight, unloaded:** 10lb 15oz (4.98kg). **Barrel:** 20.39in (518mm), 6 grooves, right-hand twist. **Magazine:** 30-round detachable box (to NATO/M16 standard). **Cyclic rate:** 650-800 rds/min. **Muzzle velocity:** 3084 ft/sec (940 m/sec).

• 5.56mm SA80 Carbine
Royal Small Arms Factory, Nottingham
5.56x45mm NATO

The SA80 Carbine was probably the last design to come from RSAF Enfield prior to its dissolution, and it was subsequently neglected while the various production problems of the L85 rifle were sorted out It was then revived in about 1994 but there were some changes in the design, which means that there have actually been two Enfield SA80 carbines, differing in barrel and overall length; The first design had an overall length of 556mm and a barrel length of 290mm This proved to be rather too much of a condensation, and the second version is somewhat longer. It has not been adopted by the British Army in any great number, but is currently offered on the export market.

The carbine is simply a shortened version of the L85 rifle, for use by specialist troops, helicopter and vehicle crews and anyone requiring a short and light weapon. It is, in effect, a submachine gun version of the L85. The receiver, grip and

sight arrangements are exactly as for the rifle, the only changes being a shorter barrel and a short, fixed, handgrip instead of the more conventional rifle-type forend. About 80 percent of the parts are interchangeable with the rifle, and any M16 type magazine will fit. It is a good example of the advantages of the bullpup design; the weapon itself is 11 inches (281mm) shorter than the M16A2 rifle but the barrel is only 2.5 inches (66mm) shorter than the M16 barrel.

Length: 27.91in (709mm). **Weight, unloaded:** 8lb 3oz (3.71kg) with iron sight. **Barrel:** 17.40in (442mm), 6 grooves, right-hand twist. **Magazine:** 30-round detachable box (to NATO/M16 standard). **Cyclic rate:** 650-800 rds/min. **Muzzle velocity:** c.2690 ft/sec (820 m/sec).

• 5.56mm Cadet Rifle L86A1
Royal Small Arms Factory, Nottingham
5.56x45mm NATO

The Cadet Rifle is a modified version of the Enfield Individual Weapon, resembling the L85A1 but with the mechanism redesigned so as to act as a single-shot

The SA 80 carbine is simply a short rifle with iron sights.

The SA 80 Cadet Rifle has the gas system removed and functions as a bolt-action repeating rifle.

The Hungarian AMD65, a Kalashnikov with a difference.

repeating rifle. The gas system has been removed, and the weapon must be operated by manually pulling back the cocking handle so as to chamber a round for each shot. The SUSAT sight is not fitted, and a two-position aperture rear sight is set into the carrying handle, a blade front sight being fitted. It is normally used with a 10-round magazine, though the standard 30-round magazine can also be used. An adapter kit to convert the weapon to fire the 22 rimfire cartridge is available for marksmanship training at low cost.

Length: 29.72in (775mm). **Weight, unloaded:** 9lb 1oz (4.10kg). **Barrel:** 19.49in (495mm), 6 grooves, right-hand twist. **Magazine:** 10- or 30-round detachable box (to NATO/M16 standard). **Cyclic rate:** 650-800 rds/min. **Muzzle velocity:** 2952 ft/sec (900 m/sec).

HUNGARY

• 7.62mm AKM-63
State factories
7.62x39mm Soviet M43

In common with other Warsaw Pact armies, the Hungarian forces were equipped with the Soviet AK47 rifle in the 1950s. In the 1960s it was decided to replace the wooden furniture of these

rifles with new plastic stock and a plastic handgrip which is attached to a perforated sheet steel forend. The resultant weapon was called the AKM-63 and apart from weighing about 8oz (250g) less, the dimensions and performance are as for the standard AK47.

• 7.62mm AMD-65 assault rifle
State factories
7.62x39mm Soviet M43

The AMD-65 is a further development of the AKM-63, intended to be a more convenient weapon for use by infantry in armored personnel carriers. The barrel is shortened, a single-strut folding butt fitted. The receiver body is extended forward to form a slotted metal forend and a plastic handgrip is fitted to this. There is a prominent two-port muzzle brake.

Length: butt extended: 33.50in (851mm); butt folded: 25.51in (648mm). **Weight unloaded:** 7lb 3oz (3.27kg). **Barrel, with muzzle brake:** 14.88in (378mm), 4 grooves, right-hand twist. **Magazine:** 30-round detachable box. **Cyclic rate:** 600 rds/min. **Muzzle velocity:** 2296 ft/sec (700 m/sec).

• 5.56mm NGM assault rifle
State factories
5.56x45mm

The NGM is more or less the Hungarian equivalent of the Soviet AK-74 assault rifle, but it is chambered for the western 5.56x45mm cartridge and offered for export. The weapon is well-made of good quality materials and the barrel is cold forged and chromium-plated internally. The rifling is to a pitch of one turn in 200mm, a compromise which will deliver accurate shooting with either M193 or SS109 ammunition. The rifle is made only in standard form, with wooden butt and furniture and with selective-fire capability.

Length: 36.81in (935mm). **Weight unloaded:** 7lb 0oz (3.18kg). **Barrel:** 16.22in (412mm), 4 grooves, right-hand twist. **Magazine:** 30-round detachable box. **Cyclic rate:** 900 rds/min. **Muzzle velocity:** 2953 ft/sec (900 m/sec).

INDIA

• 5.56mm INSAS assault rifle
Ishapore Rifle Factory
5.56x45mm

(INSAS - Indian Small Arms System) Developed in the middle 1980s, this is a gas-operated selective-fire assault rifle which is

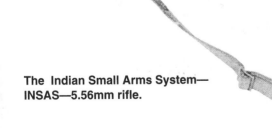

The Indian Small Arms System— INSAS—5.56mm rifle.

an interesting mixture of features taken from other designs. The receiver and pistol grip show Kalashnikov influence, the forend resembles that of the M16, and the forward cocking handle is based on the Heckler & Koch rifles. Nevertheless, these various features have been well combined to produce a well-balanced and attractive weapon. An unusual feature is the use of the old Lee-Enfield buttplate so as to provide a trap for the cleaning material and oil bottle. The rifle uses the well-tried operating system of a gas piston driving a bolt carrier and rotating bolt, and the magazine housing has been standardized on the M16 dimensions. The fire selector permits single shots or three-round bursts, but there is no provision for automatic fire. The assault rifle is made in fixed and folding butt versions, and there is also a heavy-barreled version for use in the squad automatic role.

It was intended to bring this rifle into service by 1994, but difficulties arose in the provision of 5.56mm ammunition which, though based on the FN SS109 design, is not NATO-standard, and the program has fallen several years behind schedule.

Length, fixed butt: 37.20in (945mm); butt folded: 29.52in (750mm); butt extended: 37.80in (960mm). **Weight, unloaded:** 7lb 1oz (3.20kg). **Barrel:** 18.27in (464mm), 6 grooves, right-hand twist. **Magazine:** 22-round detachable plastic box. **Cyclic rate:** 650 rds/min. **Muzzle velocity:** 3000 ft/sec (915 m/sec).

IRAQ

• Tabuk
State arsenals
7.62x39mm Soviet

The Tabuk, first revealed in the late 1980s, is a copy of the Russian AKM, though with some small differences. The forend is of a different shape, and an anti-aircraft sight is attached to the gas regulator block. The butt is different in shape and longer than that of the AKM. There is also a folding-butt short model which has a different pistol grip, a hooded front sight, and has the muzzle shaped to act as a grenade launcher.

Recent information indicates that a 5.56mm version of this rifle now exists, but no details are yet available.

Length, fixed butt: 35.43in (900mm); butt extended: 31.50in (800mm); butt folded: 21.85in (555mm). **Weight unloaded:** 8lb 4oz (3.75kg); short version : 7lb 1oz (3.21kg). **Barrel:** not known. **Magazine:** 20- or 30-round detachable box. **Cyclic rate:** 600 rds/min. **Muzzle velocity:** 2296 ft/sec (700 m/sec); short version 2198 ft/sec (670 m/sec).

• Tabuk Sniper
State arsenals
7.62x39mm Soviet

This is based generally on the Kalashnikov action but is fitted with a skeleton butt with cheekpiece, a long barrel with muzzle brake, and usually mounts an optical sight. The general effect resembles the Yugoslavian M76, but this fires the normal intermediate cartridge; the makers claim an effective range of 800 meters which, given the length of the barrel, may well be possible.

Length: 43.70in (1110mm). **Weight unloaded:** 9lb 15oz (4.50kg). **Barrel:** 23.62in (600mm), 4 grooves, right-hand twist. **Magazine:** 20-round detachable box. **Muzzle velocity:** 2428 ft/sec (740 m/sec).

• Al Kadisa
State arsenals
7.62x54R Russian

The Al Kadisa sniping rifle is simply the locally-manufactured version of the Russian Dragunov SVD. The only visible differences between this and the original are some slight changes in the contours of the butt and the presence of four long slots on each side of the handguard instead of six short ones. There are some small differences in dimensions which are probably due to manufacturing methods and the altered butt.

Length: 48.43in (1230mm). **Weight unloaded:** 9lb 7oz (4.30kg). **Barrel:** 24.40in (620mm), 4 grooves, right-hand twist. **Magazine:** 10-round detachable box. **Muzzle velocity:** 2723 ft/sec (830 m/sec).

ISRAEL

• 5.56mm Galil assault rifle
Israel Military Industries, Ramat Hasharon
5.56x45mm

The idea for this rifle was born after the 1967 war, when the Israeli Army decided that it needed a lighter and handier rifle than the FN-FAL. The Arab armies had used the AK47 with great success, and IMI decided that the action of that rifle was worth copying. The operating system of the Galil, therefore, owes a lot to its principal military rival, and the first production batch actually used bodies made by Valmet in Jyväskylä for the Finnish M62 assault rifle. They may also have used other parts, but the choice of the 5.56mm cartridge meant that most of the internal components had to be redesigned to suit the smaller dimensions.

The basic rifle can be fitted with a wide variety of accessories; a bipod allows steady and accurate shooting and permits automatic fire with reasonable consistency, and it also doubles as a wire-cutter. The flash-suppresser on the muzzle also acts as a grenade-launcher, and every rifle is fitted with luminous night sights. The Israeli Army uses a version with a folding metal butt; for other purchasers there are options of fixed wood or plastic butts. A shortened version of the ARM (the standard rifle) is the SAR (Short Assault Rifle) which differs only in the length of barrel. While the Israeli Galil is in 5.56mm caliber, a version in 7.62x51mm chambering is also made for export; this, too, comes in standard and carbine forms.

The Iraq 7.62mm Tabuk, another AK variant.

Even the Israeli Galil owes some of its features to the Kalashnikov.

Right-side view of the Galil with the butt folded, showing the prominent vertical cocking handle.

A Galil rifle mounting an Elbit 'Falcon' Galilean optical sight.

(5.56mm ARM)

Length: butt extended: 38.54in (979mm); butt folded: 29.21in (742mm). **Weight unloaded:** 9lb 9oz (4.35kg). **Barrel:** 18.11in (460mm), 6 grooves, right-hand twist. **Magazine:** 35- or 50-round detachable box. **Cyclic rate:** 650 rds/min. **Muzzle velocity:** 3117 ft/sec (950 m/sec).

(5.56mm SAR)

Length: butt extended: 33.07in (840mm); butt folded: 24.17in (614mm). **Weight unloaded:** 8lb 4oz (3.75kg). **Barrel:**

13.07in (332mm), 6 grooves, right-hand twist. **Magazine:** 35- or 50-round detachable box. **Cyclic rate:** 650 rds/min. **Muzzle velocity:** 2953 ft/sec (900 m/sec).

(7.62mm ARM)

Length, butt extended: 41.34in (1050mm); butt folded: 31.89in (810mm). **Weight unloaded:** 8lb 13oz (4.00kg). **Barrel:** 21.07in (535mm), 4 grooves, right-hand twist. **Magazine:** 25-round detachable box. **Cyclic rate:** 650 rds/min. **Muzzle velocity:** 2790 ft/sec (850 m/sec).

• 5.56mm Galil MAR

Israel Military Industries, Ramat Hasharon
5.56x45mm NATO

The MAR (Micro Assault Rifle) appeared in 1995 and might be considered the Israeli equivalent of the Russian AKS-74U short assault rifle. It is a much-shortened version of the 5.56mm Galil, and the internal mechanism is exactly the same, several of the component parts being interchangeable. The rest of the weapon is shortened and lightened as much as possible, to the point where the forend has been made with a distinct lip on it to prevent the firer's fingers straying in front of the muzzle. The tubular butt folds sideways to lie along the right side of the receiver.

Length: butt extended: 27.17in (690mm); butt folded: 17.52in (445mm). **Weight unloaded:** 6lb 8oz (2.95kg). **Barrel:** 7.68in (195mm), 6 grooves, right-hand twist. **Magazine:** 35-round detachable box. **Cyclic rate:** 650 rds/min. **Muzzle velocity:** 2329 ft/sec (710 m/sec).

• 5.56mm Marksman's Assault Rifle Mark 1 (1996)

Israel Military Industries, Ramat Hasharon
5.56x45mm NATO

This is an 'accurized' version of the standard Galil AR model. The barrel is specially selected, carefully lapped and chromed, and rifled one turn in 7 inches (178mm) so as to provide the optimum

stability for the NATO bullet. There is an adjustable bipod, and a telescope mount is attached to the left side of the receiver. An adjustable cheek pad is fitted to the folding butt. Dimensions are the same as for the AR rifle except that the weight is now 10lb 14oz (4.95 kg).

• 7.62mm Galil sniping rifle (1983)

Israel Military Industries, Ramat Hasharon
7.62x51mm NATO

This was developed in conjunction with the Israel Defense Forces to provide an extremely accurate sniping rifle. It begins with the basic Galil rifle mechanism in 7.62mm caliber but there are a number of special features. A bipod is mounted on the forend, close to the receiver where it can be easily adjusted by the firer; the barrel is heavier than standard; the telescope sight mount is on

the side of the receiver and is particularly robust, and the sight can be mounted and dismounted without disturbing the zero. A Nimrod 6x40 telescope sight is provided as standard. The butt folds for convenience in storage and transport, and the cheekpiece and recoil pad are both adjustable. The barrel is fitted with a combined compensator and muzzle brake; this can be removed and replaced by a silencer, for which subsonic ammunition is provided. There is a two-stage trigger, and the rifle's mechanism has been altered so that only semi-automatic fire is possible.

Length, butt extended: 43.89in (1115mm); butt folded: 33.0in (840mm). **Weight unloaded:** 14lb 2oz (6.40kg). **Barrel:** 20.0in (508mm), 4 grooves, right-hand twist. **Magazine:** 20-round detachable box. **Muzzle velocity:** 2674 ft/sec (815 m/sec).

The Galil Marksman's Assault Rifle.

The Galil Sniper, with stock folded.

Among the earliest automatic rifles, the Italian Cei-Rigotti of 1900.

BM59 Type Ital Para, one of the several variants of the Beretta BM59.

ITALY

• Fucile Mitragliatrice Cei-Rigotti
Officine Glisenti, Bettoni
6.5x52 Mannlicher-Carcano

In 1900 Captain Cei-Rigotti of the Bersagliere invented and constructed a gas-operated selective-fire carbine which attracted considerable interest in European military circles. Gas was led into a cylinder about half-way up the barrel and operated a short-stroke piston from which a tappet curved up to the right-hand side of the barrel. This tappet struck a long operating rod connected to the bolt, and a lug on the rod ran in a cam track cut in the bolt; the reciprocating movement of the rod rotated the bolt, drove it to the rear, pulled it forward again and locked it by final rotation. Locking was achieved by two lugs on the bolt head engaging in recesses in the barrel. The system is very similar to that later adopted by the US M1 carbine and many other designs. A simple change-lever gave single shots or automatic fire, and there were different sizes of magazine, up to 50 rounds. The few remaining examples show that the design had several failings, and contemporary reports speak of frequent jams and erratic shooting, although some of this may have been due to the ammunition. The Cei-Rigotti must be considered almost the earliest workable selective-fire rifle and it was unfortunate that no army could be found to take enough interest in it for, with a little development work, it would probably have been quite successful. Eventually, despite efforts by the Glisenti firm to find buyers, the rifle had to be abandoned without hope of revival.

Length: 39.37in (1000mm). **Weight unloaded:** 9lb 9oz (4.30kg). **Barrel:** 19.0in (483mm), 4 grooves, right-hand twist. **Magazine:** 10-, 20- or 50-round detachable box. **Cyclic rate:** not known. **Muzzle velocity:** 2400 ft/sec (730 m/sec).

• Beretta Model 59 (BM59)
Pietro Beretta SpA, Gardone Val Trompia
7.62x51mm NATO

After World War II the Italian Army adopted the US Garand rifle, which was made under license by Beretta (who also exported it to Indonesia and Morocco). When NATO adopted the 7.62mm cartridge it was decided to bring the Garand up to date rather than go to the expense of designing a new rifle, and Beretta took the basic Garand and from it developed a modern selective-fire rifle. The BM59 incorporated the basic mechanism of the Garand, a gas-operated weapon with rotating bolt, but did away with its greatest tactical defect, the eight-round clip loading system. A 20-round box magazine was fitted, which could be charger loaded through the open action. The firing mechanism was altered to permit automatic fire and a new trigger group installed. The barrel was already of 7.62mm caliber, but the gas operating system and return spring had to be 'tuned' to the new cartridge. The standard BM59 had a full-length wooden stock, a rubber recoil pad and an optional light bipod. The BM59 Ital TA version, for mountain troops, had a cut-down stock, a pistol grip, a bipod, and a folding skeleton butt. The BM59 Ital Para, for airborne troops, was very similar except that the flash-hider could be removed. A more elaborate version of the standard model, the BM59 Mark 4, had a heavier bipod, a pistol grip, a plastic butt, and a hinged shoulder-plate, all intended to steady the weapon in automatic fire.

(BM59.)

Length: 43.0in (1095mm). **Weight unloaded:** 9lb 10oz (4.40kg). **Barrel:** 19.30in (491mm), 4 grooves, right-hand twist. **Magazine:** 20-round detachable box. **Cyclic rate:** 800 rds/min. **Muzzle velocity:** 2700 ft/sec (823 m/sec).

(BM59 Ital TA)

Length: 43.70in (1110mm). **Weight unloaded:** 10lb 11oz (4.87kg). **Barrel:** 19.33in (491mm), 4 grooves, right-hand twist. **Magazine:** 20-round detachable box. **Cyclic rate:** not known. **Muzzle velocity:** 2664 ft/sec (812 m/sec).

The Beretta AR 70-223, the company's first attempt at a 5.56mm assault rifle.

• 5.56mm Assault Rifle Model 70/223 (1970)

Pietro Beretta SpA, Gardone Val Trompia
5.56x45mm

The Model 70/223 was a lightweight gas-operated magazine rifle for both full- and semi-automatic fire. It was offered in two forms, the assault rifle designated AR70 and the Special Troops Carbine SC70. The AR70 resembled many other similar rifles in this group and was made from steel stampings and pressings, with plastic furniture. Extensive use was made of spot welding for the main components, and the removable parts were held by pins and spring catches. An optional light bipod could be fitted, and the muzzle had a combination flash-hider and grenade launcher. A special flip-up grenade sight was fitted which not only raised the sight line but also closed the gas regulator to ensure that the full force of the cartridge was available to drive the grenade. The SC70 was very similar in all respects except that it had a folding metal butt-stock. A variant of this was the SC70 Short, which had a 320mm (12.60in) barrel instead of the standard 450mm length.

The AR70 system was adopted by Italian Special Forces, Jordan, Malaysia and some other countries. Experience showed that there were some minor defects in the design and Beretta therefore set about developing the 70/90 model (below).

(AR70)

Length: 37.60in (955mm). **Weight unloaded:** 7lb 10oz (3.50kg). **Barrel:** 17.80in (450mm), 6 grooves, right-hand twist. **Magazine:** 30-round detachable box. **Cyclic rate:** 700 rds/min. **Muzzle velocity:** 3150 ft/sec (960 m/sec).

(SC70)

Length, butt extended: 37.80in (960mm); butt folded: 28.98in (736mm). **Weight unloaded:** 8lb 8oz (3.85kg). **Barrel:** 17.80in (459mm), 6 grooves, right-hand twist. **Magazine:** 30-round detachable box. **Cyclic rate:** 650 rds/min. **Muzzle velocity:** 3150 ft/sec (950 m/sec).

(SC70 Short)

Length, butt extended: 32.28in (820mm); butt folded: 23.54in (598mm). **Weight unloaded:** 8lb 8oz (3.85kg). **Barrel:** 12.60in (320mm), 6 grooves, right-hand twist. **Magazine:** 30-round detachable box. **Cyclic rate:** 600 rds/min. **Muzzle velocity:** 2904 ft/sec (885 m/sec).

• 5.56mm Assault Rifle 70/90 (1985)

Armi Beretta SpA. Gardone Val Trompia
5.56x45mm NATO

The 70/90 system (rifle, carbine, short carbine and heavy-barrelled rifle) was developed primarily in response to an Italian Army demand for a new service rifle, but at the same time opportunity was taken to deal with the design defects which had shown up in the 70/223 rifle. In the earlier weapon, for example, the receiver was a pressed-steel rectangle in which the bolt moved on pressed-in rails; service use showed that under extreme conditions this could distort, jamming the bolt; in the 70/90 therefore, the receiver is of trapezoidal section and has steel bolt guide rails welded in place. Like the earlier weapon, the 70/90 uses a gas-operated rotating bolt system. The trigger mechanism allows single shots, three-round bursts or automatic fire, and the design is such that the mechanism can easily be adjusted to give any two of the three options. The receiver is topped by a carrying handle which can be removed to expose a NATO-standard sight mount; holes in the carrying handle

The Beretta AR70/90, the second attempt, which was adopted as the Italian service rifle in 1990.

The Beretta SC70/90 is the same as the AR model but with a folding butt.

The Beretta SCS70/90, with butt folded.

A specimen of the SC 70/90 with the carrying handle/sight mount removed.

allow for the sight line of the iron sights. One of the most unusual features is the retention of the barrel in the receiver by a barrel nut; this is not to facilitate changing the barrel so much as to allow for replacement of the barrel in forward echelons without the need to adjust bolt headspace.

The Carbine SC70/90 differs from the AR70/90 rifle only in having a folding tubular metal butt; the special carbine SCS70/90 has a folding butt and a shorter barrel and does not have any facility for grenade launching. The SCP70/90 is an SCS which is supplied with a grenade-launching attachment which can be screwed on to the muzzle in place of the standard flash hider. All weapons have an ambidextrous magazine catch which means that with the butts folded, changing magazines is still easily accomplished. The heavy-barrel weapon is intended for use as a squad machine gun and is dealt with in the machine guns section.

The Italian Army stated its intention to run competitive trials in 1984; Beretta produced the 70/90 system in 1985; in July 1990 the rifle was approved for service with the Italian forces.

(AR70/90)

Length: 39.29in (998mm). **Weight unloaded:** 8lb 12oz (3.99kg). **Barrel:** 17.71in (450mm), 6 grooves, right-hand twist. **Magazine:** 30-round detachable box. **Cyclic rate:** 625 rds/min. **Muzzle velocity:** 3050 ft/sec (930 m/sec).

(SCS70/90)

Length, butt extended: 34.49in (876mm); butt folded: 25.47in (647mm). **Weight unloaded:** 8lb 6oz (3.79kg). **Barrel:** 13.86in (352mm), 6 grooves, right-hand twist. **Magazine:** 30-round detachable box. **Cyclic rate:** 600 rds/min. **Muzzle velocity:** 2952 ft/sec (900 m/sec).

JAPAN

• Rifle Type 64 (1964)
Howa Machinery Company, Nagoya
7.62x51mm Type 64

Although this rifle is a purely governmental undertaking, the design and manufacture was done by the Howa Machinery Company. The Japanese Defense Force decided that the 7.62x51mm NATO cartridge was too

The Japanese 7.62mm Type 64 assault rifle.

powerful for their needs and the Type 64, resulting in a reduction in performance of about ten percent. It is a perfectly adequate round and gives a welcome reduction in recoil force on the firer's shoulder. The Type 64 rifle can also take the full-power round if necessary, the gas regulator being adjustable to allow for the greater gas pressure. The regulator can also be closed to permit the firing of rifle grenades, the muzzle being formed into a launcher spigot which is also designed to act as a muzzle brake. The rifle is fitted with a bipod which folds under the forend, and the Japanese soldier is taught to use it whenever possible; another aid to accurate shooting is a butt strap hinged to the top of the butt which lies on the shoulder and prevents the butt slipping down during firing. The bolt locking system uses a tipping bolt which rises to lock into the receiver and is lowered and driven back by a conventional gas piston.

Issued to the Japanese Self-Defense Force in the middle 1960s, production of the Type 64 ceased in 1990, after which it was replaced by the Type 89 (below)

Length: 38.98in (990mm). **Weight unloaded:** 9lb 11oz (4.40kg). **Barrel:** 17.71in (450mm), 4 grooves, right-hand twist. **Magazine:** 20-round detach-

able box. **Cyclic rate:** 500 rds/min. **Muzzle velocity:** 2297 ft/sec (700 m/sec).

• Rifle Type 89 (1989)
Howa Machinery Company, Nagoya
5.56x45mm NATO

The Type 89 rifle was developed by the Japanese Defense Agency in cooperation with the Howa Machinery Company in order to provide the Japanese Self-Defense Force with a modern small-caliber assault rifle. The Type 89 is gas-operated, using a rotating bolt, but the gas system is rather unusual; instead of the gas entering the gas cylinder and striking the piston, giving it a rapid and sudden movement, the piston is actually situated some distance down the cylinder and it is the expansion of the gas admitted to the cylinder which drives the piston back, giving it a more gradual acceleration and thus a less violent movement. This makes the rifle rather more pleasant to fire and, more important, it reduces the stresses on the moving parts and contributes to a long and trouble-free service life. The trigger assembly is also unusual, being set up to provide single shots and automatic fire; there is an entirely separate three-round burst

mechanism set into the rear of the trigger housing which is brought into operation by the change lever; this system is adopted so that should the three-round burst system fail, the normal firing ability of the weapon is not affected.

Two versions of the rifle are produced; one has a fixed plastic butt, the other a folding steel tubular butt with a plastic shoulder pad. All rifles are provided with a high efficiency muzzle brake and a bipod, though the latter can be easily removed if not required.

Length, fixed or extended butt: 36.07in (916mm); butt folded: 26.38in (670mm). **Weight unloaded:** 7lb 11oz (3.50kg). **Barrel:** 16.54in (420mm), 6 grooves, right-hand twist. **Magazine:** 20- or 30-round detachable box. **Cyclic rate:** 750 rds/min. **Muzzle velocity:** 3018 ft/sec (920 m/sec).

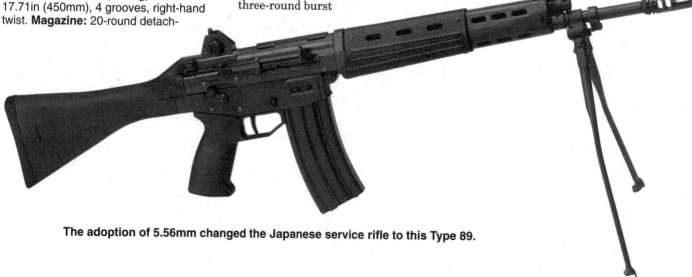

The adoption of 5.56mm changed the Japanese service rifle to this Type 89.

All Daewoo weapons have a distinctive family resemblance; this is the K2 rifle.

The Daewoo K1A1 carbine is a short version of the K2 rifle with a sliding wire butt.

KOREA, SOUTH

• Daewoo K2 assault rifle (1987)

Daewoo Precision Industries Ltd, Pusan
5.56x45mm NATO

This is a gas-operated, selective-fire rifle with a folding plastic butt. The gas system uses a long-stroke piston above the barrel, driving a bolt carrier with rotating bolt. The receiver is machined from aluminum alloy forgings, giving a very stiff and robust system. The weapon can fire single shots, three-round bursts or full automatic fire and the barrel is fitted with a muzzle brake and compensator dimensioned so as to function as a grenade-launcher. The three-round burst mechanism is unusual in that it does not re-set to zero if a part-burst is fired; thus if only two rounds of a burst are fired, the next trigger pressure will result in a single shot, the last of the three round burst. The sights are provided with luminous spots to aid in night shooting. The K2 is in use by the South Korean Army.

Length, butt extended: 38.98in (990mm); butt folded: 28.74in (730mm). **Weight unloaded:** 7lb 3oz (3.26kg). **Barrel:** 18.30in (465mm), 6 grooves, right-hand twist. **Magazine:** 30-round detachable box. **Cyclic rate:** 650 rds/min. **Muzzle velocity:** 3018 ft/sec (920 m/sec).

• Daewoo K1A1 Carbine (1987)

Daewoo Precision Industries Ltd, Pusan
5.56x45mm

This resembled the K2 assault rifle, though smaller and with a sliding wire stock, but used an entirely different method of operation. It had the usual bolt carrier and rotating bolt, but the gas was piped back from the barrel and struck the bolt carrier directly, not through the agency of a piston; it was the same system as used with the M16 rifle. The fire selector gave the same options as the K2 rifle, and the muzzle brake/compensator was much larger so as to reduce the muzzle flash and blast otherwise to be expected with the short barrel.

This carbine was developed in the early 1980s, alongside the K2 rifle, but appears not to have found any military buyers. A small number were sold in the USA in the late 1980s as the 'Max-1 Auto Carbine', but production ceased in the early 1990s.

Length, butt extended: 32.68in (830mm); butt folded: 25.40in (645mm). **Weight unloaded:** 6lb 6oz (2.88kg). **Barrel:** 10.35in (263mm), 6 grooves, right-hand twist. **Magazine:** 20- or 30-round detachable box. **Cyclic rate:** 800 rds/min. **Muzzle velocity:** 3018 ft/sec (820 m/sec).

MEXICO

• Mondragon Rifle

Schweizerische Industrie Gesellschaft, Neuhausen-am-Rheinfalls, Switzerland
7x57mm Spanish Mauser

The Mexican-designed Mondragon, conceived in the early 1890s, was one of the earliest semi-automatic rifles to be taken into military service. General Manuel Mondragon, granted a United States patent in 1907, was forced to seek a European manufacturer since there were no adequate facilities in Mexico and no US manufacturer was interested; as a result, the weapons were produced by SIG in Switzerland. The Mondragon used gas, tapped from the barrel, to drive an actuating piston to the rear and open the bolt, a now common-place method. Locking was achieved by lugs on the bolt, which was rotated by projections on the bolt operating handle engaging in cam tracks cut into the bolt body; there is some degree of resemblance between this and the Schmidt Rubin straight-pull bolt action. As with many automatic designs of the period, it was possible to disconnect the bolt from the gas mechanism and thus turn the rifle into a manually operated straight-pull bolt-action weapon, a proviso often insisted upon by military authorities with small faith in the reliability of any automatic mechanism.

As might be expected from SIG the rifles were beautifully made from the finest materials, and there are several separate models. Apart from the development models, which appear to have been made in a number of different calibers including 7mm Spanish and 7.5mm Swiss, the basic model, adopted by the Mexican Army in 1908 (as the 'Fusil Porfiro Diaz, Systema Mondragon, Modelo 1908') was in 7mm Spanish Mauser caliber and had

A Swiss-made Mondragon rifle, with the drum magazine adopted by the Germans when they used it as an aviators weapon.

a box magazine into which eight round were loaded by a charger. At the same time, however, SIG marketed a version with a 20-shot box magazine and a rather spindly bipod, which was intended to serve as a rudimentary light machine-gun, though it seems that sales did not justify very large production. The squad automatic weapon concept was unknown in 1908.

Some 400 rifles had been delivered to Mexico when the 1911 Revolution removed President Diaz, and the new government repudiated the contract with SIG, leaving the Swiss company with the balance of the 4000-rifle order on their hands. They attempted to sell them to whoever was interested, but at the outbreak of war in 1914 about 3000 of the rifles were still on SIG's shelves and these were bought by Germany for issue to aviators as the 'Fliegerselbstladekarabine Modell 1915'. Most of these were fitted with a 30-shot helical 'snail' magazine, similar in principle to that used on the Luger pistol and Bergmann submachine-gun. After being replaced on aircraft by machine guns, some of the rifles were sent for infantry use but the mud of the Western Front soon defeated them and the survivors were withdrawn. A large number were issued to the German Navy where most survived until the war's end.

Length: 43.50in (1105mm). **Weight unloaded:** 9lb 4oz (4.18kg). **Barrel:** 22.75in (577mm), 4 grooves, right-hand twist. **Magazine:** 8-round charger-loaded box. **Muzzle velocity:** 2495 ft/sec (760 m/sec).

POLAND

• wz/88 'Tantal'
Zaklady Metalowy Lucznik, Radom
5.45x39.5mm Soviet

This is little more than a Polish-manufactured copy of the Russian AK-74S rifle. There are small differences in dimensions, and the furniture is usually a black synthetic material. The principal mechanical differences are that the wz/88 has a three-round burst mechanism added and the muzzle brake/compensator is shaped so as to act also as a grenade launching spigot and a bayonet boss.

There is a variant mode, also called 'Tantal' but known as the wz/90; this is simply the wz/88 chambered and rifled for the NATO 5.56x45mm cartridge. This is currently offered for export but could well become the next Polish service rifle if their aim of joining

NATO is achieved.

Length, butt extended: 37.13in (943mm); butt folded: 29.21in (742mm). **Weight unloaded:** 7lb 8oz (3.40kg). **Barrel:** 16.65in (423mm), 6 grooves, right-hand twist. **Magazine:** 30-round detachable box. **Cyclic rate:** 600 rds/min. **Muzzle velocity:** 2887 ft/sec (880 m/sec).

• wz/89 'Onyx'
Zaklady Metalowy Lucznik, Radom
5.45x39.5mm Soviet

The 'Onyx' is another locally-brewed copy, this time of the Russian AKS-74U short assault rifle or submachine gun - the terms are almost synonymous east of the River Oder. The principal changes from the Russian design lie in the addition of a three-round burst mechanism and the provision of a single-strut side-folding butt. The rear sight has been enlarged, partly to give an increased range of 400 meters, and partly to provide a base to which electro-optical or collimating sights can be fitted. The muzzle expansion chamber and compensator has also been slightly changed in order that it

The Polish Tantal rifle.

The Polish Onyx is obviously based on the Soviet AKSU design.

can function as a grenade-launching spigot.

The wz/91 Onyx is the same weapon but chambered for the 5.56x45mm NATO cartridge. As with the wz/90 rifle, this is currently offered for export but could well be officially adopted if Poland joins NATO.

Length, butt extended: 28.35in (720mm); butt folded: 20.43in (519mm). **Weight unloaded:** 6lb 6oz (2.90kg). **Barrel:** 8.15in (207mm), 6 grooves, right-hand twist. **Magazine:** 30-round detachable box. **Cyclic rate:** 725 rds/min. **Muzzle velocity:** 3018 ft/sec (700 m/sec).

RUSSIA

• Federov Automat M1916
Sestrorets and elsewhere
6.5mm Meiji 30 (Japanese)

The Federov selective-fire rifle can probably lay claim to being the ancestor of the present generation of assault rifles, although it falls into that category perhaps more by chance than by design. Vladimir Federov was a prominent Tsarist arms designer who later continued in the service of the Soviets, to become the author of many official textbooks. Prior to World War I he had produced a number of experimental rifles with varying degrees of success, but one of his major problems lay in the ammunition with which he was forced to work; the standard 7.62x54R rifle cartridge of the

Russian Army was a fat, awkward, rimmed-case round which did not easily lend itself to automation and much of it was of inferior and inconsistent quality. Furthermore, it was typical of its period—a powerful round which demanded a heavy and robust weapon. After the Russo-Japanese War of 1904-5, for reasons concealed in history, the Russians produced a number of rifle designs chambered for the Japanese 6.5mm Arisaka rifle cartridge, most of which remained no more than paper exercises. In 1916, Federov developed a selective-fire rifle around the Japanese round, using short recoil of the

barrel to operate the mechanism; the rifle had a forward pistol-grip, a curved magazine, and weighed some 9lb 8oz (4.37kg).

Although the October Revolution stopped production of the 'Automat' before it had fairly begun, it was re-started in mid-1919 and continued until finally halted in 1924, some 9000 or so being manufactured. It was used by the Red Army during the Civil War and Federov continued development of this system and took part in numerous trials as late as 1928. Very few specimens are known to have survived.

Length: 41.15in (1045mm). **Weight unloaded:** 9lb 8oz (4.38kg). **Magazine:** 25-round detachable box. **Cyclic rate:** 600-650 rds/min. **Muzzle velocity:** c.24 m/sec (730 m/sec).

• Simonov 1936 (AVS36)
State factories
7.62x54R M91 Russian

The Simonov was the first automatic rifle to be adopted in quantity by the Red Army, who accepted it in 1936. It was a gas-operated weapon using a piston mounted above the barrel to unlock and retract the bolt; the locking system is itself rather unusual, relying on a vertically-moving block to lock the bolt and the carrier securely to the receiver before firing.

The standard weapon was provided with a selective fire device to permit its use as a light machine-gun. The AVS

The breech area of the AVS-36, showing the charger guide, magazine release and cocking handle.

The Simonov AVS-36, complete with a highly efficient muzzle brake.

The Tokarev SVT-38, like the AVS-36, fired the potent 7.2x54mm cartridge and thus, like the AVS, needed a muzzle brake.

Tokarev improved his design into this SVT-40 which differed very little but was a better weapon.

Rarely encountered, the Tokarev SKT-40 carbine was a shorter version of the SVT and a most unpleasant weapon to shoot.

The breech of the Tokarev SVT, generally similar to the Simonov layout.

suffered from excessive muzzle blast and recoil, and in an endeavor to reduce this, a two-port muzzle-brake was fitted. The receiver was cut open to allow movement of the cocking—handle and thus the interior of the weapon was exposed to mud and dirt. Whether it was this defect, or simply that the unusual locking system failed to live up to its promise, the fact remains that the AVS had a very short service life, being replaced in 1938 by the more simple Tokarev.

Length: 49.60in (1260mm). **Weight unloaded:** 9lb 13oz (4.40kg). **Barrel:** 24.69in (627mm), 4 grooves, right-hand twist. **Magazine:** 15-round detachable box. **Muzzle velocity:** c.2740 ft/sec (935 m/sec).

• Tokarev 1938 (SVT38)
State factories
7.62x54R Russian

The Tokarev-designed weapons relied on gas operation with a locking block cammed downwards at the rear into a recess in the receiver floor. The SVT38 had a two-piece wooden stock with a prominent magazine; there were two steel barrel bands and the forward portion of the wooden handguard was replaced by one of sheet steel, with circular cooling apertures drilled into each side; immediately behind these, rectangular cooling slots were cut into the wooden guard. An unusual feature was the positioning of the cleaning rod, inserted along the right side of the stock rather than underneath the barrel of the weapon. The rifle was originally fitted with a six-baffle muzzle brake, replaced in late 1940 or early 1941 by a two-baffle unit. Owing to its frail construction, manufacture of the l938 pattern was abandoned in 1940, but not before some selected weapons had been fitted with telescope sights.

Length: 48.10in (1222mm). **Weight unloaded:** 8lb 10oz (3.95kg). **Barrel:** 24.02in (610mm), 4 grooves, right-hand twist. **Magazine:** 10-round detachable box.

Muzzle velocity: c.2756 ft/sec (840 m/sec).

• Tokarev 1940 (SVT40)
State factories
7.62x54R Russian

A more robust version of the 1938 Tokarev design, the SVT40 was characterized by the removal of the earlier rifle's externally mounted cleaning rod, to the more conventional position beneath the barrel. There was only a single barrel band, beyond which a sheet metal handguard extended forward; on the SVT40 it was of wrap-around type as opposed to the metal-and-wood forward guard of the SVT38. Air circulation holes

You know you've got a good weapon when the enemy starts using it in preference to his own: a German patrol in the Don Basin, 1942, with the NCO carrying a Tokarev rifle.

were drilled into the guard, and four rect-angular slots appeared through the wooden continuation. Two variations in muzzle brake design existed: the first had six slim baffles, replaced in later production by a unit having only two large baffles.

These self-loading rifles were issued mainly to NCOs although, as with the SVT38 models, selected specimens were equipped with telescopic sights and issued to snipers. A fully automatic version, called the AVT40, was outwardly identical with the self-loading SVT40 from which it was converted, except for alteration to the surround of the safety catch to permit the addition of an automatic fire setting. Only very few rifles were thus converted. A carbine version, the SKT-40, some converted from rifles and some of new manufacture, also exist but are relatively uncommon.

(SVT-40)

Length: 48.27in (1226mm). **Weight unloaded:** 8lb 9oz (3.90kg). **Barrel:** 24.02in (610mm), 4 grooves, right-hand twist. **Magazine:** 10-round detachable box. **Muzzle velocity:** c.2756 ft/sec (840 m/sec).

(SKT-40)

Length: 41.93in (1065mm). **Weight, unloaded:** 8lb 1oz (3.65kg). **Barrel:** 18.50in (470mm), 4 grooves, right-hand twist. **Magazine:** 20-round detachable box. **Muzzle velocity:** 2445 ft/sec (745 m/sec).

• Simonov SKS

State factories
7.62x39mm M1943

The SKS carbine was the first Soviet weapon developed to make use of the M1943 'intermediate' cartridge. The history of this cartridge is in some doubt; it is known that the Soviets were experimenting with short cartridges in various calibers prior to the war, but it is generally accepted that it was the appearance of the German MP44 and its short 7.92mm round which led them to capitalize on their previous work and develop the 7.62x39mm round. Although the SKS is important for its introduction of this round, it is otherwise a fairly uninspired design. It was simple, easy to operate and robust, but a little heavy for the cartridge it fired; all of which is understandable, since it was developed under the stress of war.

The system of operation and locking appears to have been taken from the PTRS anti-tank rifle, locking being done by the same type of tipping bolt. Stripping and maintenance is easy, and the hinged bayonet and one-piece wooden stock are also prominent features of the weapon. Loading can be done by chargers or by pushing single rounds into the magazine. Unloading can be quickly done by releasing the pivoting magazine cover, swinging it away from the receiver and spilling out the rounds. Enormous numbers of this carbine have been made, and although it is no longer in use in the Russian forces it has appeared in almost every Communist country in the world. It has also been made, with slight variations, in several countries; in Yugoslavia it is known as the M59, while in China it is the Type 56. North Korea calls it the Type 63, and the East German version was the 'Karabiner-S'.

Length: 40.20in (1022mm). **Weight unloaded:** 8lb 8oz (3.86kg). **Barrel:** 20.50in (520mm), 4 grooves, right-hand twist. **Magazine:** 10-round box, fixed to receiver. **Muzzle velocity:** c.2410 ft/sec (735 m/sec).

When the Soviets adopted the 7.62x39mm cartridge, this Simonov SKS was the first weapon to fire it.

The original Kalashnikov, the AK47, which actually entered service in 1949.

The AKS of 1950 was simply the AK47 with a folding steel butt.

The AKM was the AK47 Modified, using steel stampings instead of a machined receiver, and with various other manufacturing economies.

And the AKMS was, of course, the AKM with a folding butt.

• Kalashnikov AK47, AKM, AKMS

State factories
7.62x39mm M1943

The Kalashnikov has been the standard Russian assault rifle since the early 1950s. After seeing the German MP44 and its intermediate cartridge the Soviets rapidly appreciated the logic behind it and set about developing their own version, which evolved into the Kalashnikov. It may not be the best automatic rifle in existence but it is certainly the most widely distributed, having been supplied to every satellite nation, many of which evolved their own variations. More than 35 million are reputed to have been produced and the design lives on the AK74 pattern. In addition to its service in regular forces, the Kalashnikov will always be found where Communist-inspired Nationalist movements are pressing their cause.

The AK is gas operated, and is rather unusual in having the gas piston rod permanently attached to the bolt carrier. A cam track in the carrier rotates the bolt to lock and unlock, and during the rearward stroke a hammer is cocked. The barrel, like that of many Soviet weapons, is chromium-plated internally. In spite of its popularity and efficiency the AK is not without its defects. There is, surprisingly, no hold-open device on the bolt to indicate an empty magazine nor, indeed, any method of retaining the bolt in the open position. Its accuracy over 300m is relatively poor.

After contemplating the inferior finish of Soviet wartime weapons, it is a pleasant surprise to find that the AK reverted to more traditional methods of construction and finish, the receiver being machined from solid steel. This state of affairs was not conducive to cheapness and mass production and the design which followed the AK47 in 1959, the AKM ('M' for 'modernized'), reverted to a stamped steel construction. The bolt is Parkerized instead of the polished steel of the AK47, and the bayonet is an ingenious design with a slot in the blade which, when engaged with a stud on the

scabbard, converts the assembly to a wire-cutter—an innovation widely copied since. The muzzle is formed into a spoon-like lower extension which acts as a simple compensator to reduce climb during automatic fire. There were other, minor modifications in the AKM but they were an entirely logical development from the AK47 with the intention of reducing manufacturing time and cost and improving combat efficiency. Variant models are the AKS-47 and AKMS, which have folding skeleton butts and were generally found in use by parachute troops and armored units.

(AK-47)

Length: 34.21in (869mm). **Weight unloaded:** 9lb 7oz (4.30kg). **Barrel:** 16.34in (415mm), 4 grooves, right-hand twist. **Magazine:** 30-round detachable box. **Cyclic rate:** 775 rds/min. **Muzzle velocity:** c.2330 ft/sec (710 m/sec).

(AK-M)

Length: 34.49in (876mm). **Weight unloaded:** 8lb 7oz (3.82kg). **Barrel:** 16.34in (415mm), 4 grooves, right-hand twist. **Magazine:** 30-round detachable box. **Cyclic rate:** 775 rds/min. **Muzzle velocity:** c.2330 ft/sec (710 m/sec).

(AKM-S)

Length, butt extended: 35.24in (895mm); butt folded: 25.87in (657mm). **Weight unloaded:** 7lb 13oz (3.55kg). **Barrel:** 16.34in (415mm), 4 grooves, right-hand twist. **Magazine:** 30-round detachable box. **Cyclic rate:** 775 rds/min. **Muzzle velocity:** c.2330 ft/sec (710 m/sec).

• Kalashnikov 1974 (AK-74)

State factories
5.45x39.5mm Soviet

The Soviet Army began experiments with small-caliber weapons in the 1970s and there had been persistent rumors of such weapons for several years before, in November 1977, the AK74 rifle was seen for the first time in the annual Red Square parade, carried by parachute troops. Within a short time it became the standard Soviet infantry rifle, replacing the 7.62mm AKs in

the hands of regular troops. It appeared in other Warsaw Pact armies and was manufactured in Poland and Bulgaria. The general design has also been copied in China and Yugoslavia but chambered the Western 5.56mm cartridge and intended for export. In general terms the AK74 is a small-caliber version of the AKM, and it uses the same receiver, furniture and system of operation. Indeed, it is quite likely that apart from a new barrel and bolt little else needed to be changed. The 5.45mm round is almost the same length as the 7.62x39mm round and the magazine thus fits into the same opening in the receiver. A noticeable feature of this rifle is the laminated plastic and steel magazine, the design of which has subtly changed since its introduction as stiffening fillets have been added. Another feature is the muzzle brake and compensator, designed to reduce the recoil and compensate for the upward climb always present in automatic weapons. It is highly efficient, reducing the felt recoil to a low level and keeping the weapon steady during automatic fire, though it is said to be somewhat harsh on bystanders since the muzzle gases are diverted sideways. The AKS74 version has a folding steel butt which swings to lie along the left side of the receiver.

Length: 36.53in (928mm); (AKS stock folded: 27.2in (690mm)). **Weight unloaded:** 8lb 8oz (3.86kg). **Barrel:** 15.75in (400mm) 4 grooves, right-hand twist. **Magazine:** 30-round detachable plastic box. **Cyclic rate:** 650 rds/min. **Muzzle velocity:** 2952 ft/sec (900 m/sec).

• AN-94

Izhmash Joint Stock Co., Izhevsk
5.45x39.5mm Russian

In the early 1990s the Russian military held a competitive trial of potential assault rifles in order to select their next generation infantry rifle; the trial is generally referred to as the 'Abakan Trial'. As a result of this a design by G.Nikonov known as the 'ASN' was selected, and this has now been formally approved as the AN (Automat Nikonov) 94. Whether it will enter service this century, or at all,

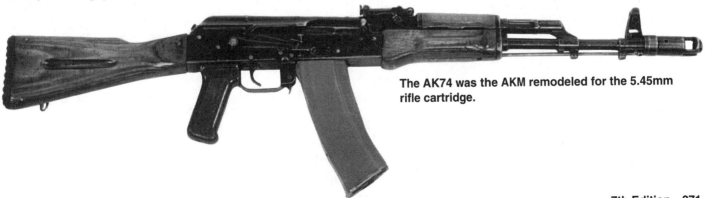

The AK74 was the AKM remodeled for the 5.45mm rifle cartridge.

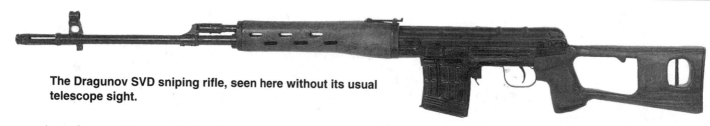

The Dragunov SVD sniping rifle, seen here without its usual telescope sight.

remains to be seen; the present chaotic state of Russia's economy has led to the rifle replacement program being shelved indefinitely.

Information of the weapon is, at present, sketchy and confusing. For example, one report says it is a blowback weapon but refers to a gas cylinder, while another refers to locking the bolt. Much play is made of the operating system, which is called the 'delayed blowback shifted pulse' system and, quite frankly, defies rational explanation. We are told that the barrel and barrel extension are free to move within the receiver, and that the bolt and bolt carrier can move independently within the barrel extension. At single shot this presumably works in a conventional manner, with the gas cylinder delivering some sort of impulse to the bolt carrier. When set for automatic fire, however, the first two rounds are fired at a cyclic rate of 1800 rds/min, after which the mechanism automatically shifts to continue firing at 600 rds/min.

This is achieved by having the first shot fired in the normal way. The barrel and extension then recoil, and the bolt and carrier also recoil within the barrel extension at a higher speed. Thus the case is ejected and a fresh round loaded while the barrel and extension are still moving backwards, and the second shot is fired. How the mechanism then sets itself back to normal operation is not explained. Nor is it at all obvious how the two rounds are loaded in succession when the barrel and bolt are in entirely different positions relative to the (presumably) fixed magazine. It would seem that this method of operation has been inspired by the mechanics of the Heckler & Koch G11 at burst-fire, though the mechanical problems are considerably different.

We shall doubtless have it all explained in due course. Meanwhile we can only repeat the specification, as divulged by the manufacturers.

Length: 36.6in (943mm). **Weight unloaded:** 7lb 14oz (3.86kg). **Barrel:** length not known; 4 grooves, right-hand twist. **Magazine:** 30-, 45- or 60-round detachable plastic box. **Cyclic rate:** 1800/600 rds/min. **Muzzle velocity:** not known.

• Dragunov SVD sniping rifle (1963)
State factories
7.62x54R Russian

The Dragunov is the standard sniper's rifle of the Russian and ex-Warsaw Pact armies, and although it uses the basic bolt mechanism of the Kalashnikov it is a completely fresh rifle, designed from the start with sniping in mind. It is an excellent and accurate weapon, firing the old, powerful, rimmed 7.62mm rifle cartridge, but the operation differs from that of the AK series. The AK rifles and light machine guns use a long-stroke gas piston system; this is not advisable for a sniping rifle, since the shifting mass of the piston tends to move the rifle and spoil the accuracy. The SVD, therefore, uses a light short-stroke piston which moves back rapidly to give the bolt carrier a quick impulsive blow, relying upon the momentum thus imparted to drive the carrier back. All parts are most carefully made and assembled, and a telescope sight known as the PSO-1 is part of the outfit of each rifle, though iron sights are also fitted. The PSO-1 is also capable of detecting infra-red emissions, though it has no pretensions to being a night sight. The rifle is easy and pleasant to fire, the trigger mechanism, although that of the AK series, having been carefully refined to give a smooth and consistent pull-off. It has been copied in several countries and a commercial version, known as the Medved

('Bear') is available chambered for the 9x54R sporting cartridge.

Length: 48.20in (1225mm). **Weight unloaded:** 9lb 8oz (4.31kg) with PSO sight. **Barrel:** 24.48in (622mm), 4 grooves, right-hand twist. **Magazine:** 10-round detachable box. **Muzzle velocity:** c.2723 ft/sec (830 m/sec).

• Dragunov Assault sniper rifle SVU
State factories
7.62x54R Russian

This odd weapon, first seen in 1996, is a bullpup version of the SVD rifle described above. The mechanism is the same but the layout is much different. There is no stock, merely a shaped shoulder rest at the rear end of the receiver, and the pistol grip is repositioned in front of the magazine and roughly at the rear end of the handguard. The barrel is fitted with a cylindrical appendage at the muzzle which may be a sound suppresser or an expansion chamber, or both, or neither, and which also incorporates a flash hider. If we assume that the barrel has remained the same length, it would seem that the only real advantage of this weapon is to cut 300mm or so from the overall length.

Length: 35.43in (900mm). **Weight unloaded:** 9lb 11oz (4.40kg) with PSO sight. **Barrel:** 24.48in (622mm), 4 grooves, right-hand twist. **Magazine:** 10-round detachable box. **Muzzle velocity:** c.2720 ft/sec (830 m/sec).

• AS Silent Assault rifle
Institute of Precise Mechanical Engineering, Izhevsk
9x39mm SP-6

This specialized weapon was revealed in the early 1990s, though it is believed that it had been in service for some years by that time. It is

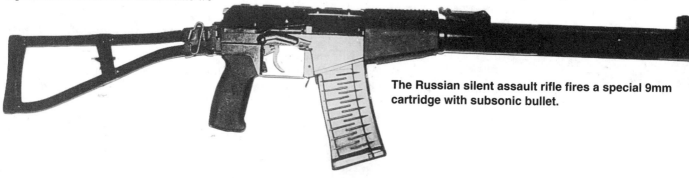

The Russian silent assault rifle fires a special 9mm cartridge with subsonic bullet.

The Silent Sniper Rifle is simply the silent assault rifle with the addition of a telescope sight and a fixed butt-stock.

This cumbersome device is the Russian underwater assault rifle, firing drag-stabilized darts.

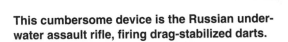

gas-operated, using a rotating bolt system broadly derived from the Kalashnikov weapons, and contains an integral silencer. It fires a special cartridge with a heavy sub-sonic bullet, and can fire single shots or automatic fire without damaging the silencer assembly. The cartridge case is that of the 7.62x39mm rifle round, with the neck expanded to take the 9mm bullet, and this accounts for the unusually deep magazine. The rifle has a lightweight tubular stock which folds to the left side of the receiver, and the most prominent feature is the cylindrical silencer.

Length, butt extended: 34.57in (878mm); butt folded: 24.21in (615mm). **Weight unloaded:** 5lb 8oz (2.50kg). **Barrel:** not known. **Magazine:** 20-round detachable box. **Muzzle velocity:** c.967 ft/sec (295 m/sec).

• VSS Silent Sniping rifle
Institute of Precise Mechanical Engineering, Izhevsk
9x39mm SP-5

The VSS silent rifle is more or less the same weapon as the AS rifle described above, except that it has a fixed stock, is provided with an optical or electro-optical sight, and is optimized for a slightly different 9x39mm cartridge, the SP5 which uses an armor-piercing bullet. Like the AS, the VSS was developed for and issued to the Spetznaz and other special Soviet Army forces.

Length: 35.19in (894mm). **Weight unloaded:** 5lb 12oz (2.60kg). **Barrel:** not

known. **Magazine:** 10- or 20-round detachable box. **Muzzle velocity:** c.950 ft/sec (290 m/sec).

• APS Underwater Assault rifle
Institute of Precise Mechanical Engineering, Izhevsk
5.66mm special

This weapon is designed for use by frogmen and other amphibian troops; it can be fired underwater with reasonable accuracy and it can also be fired on land, though only at short ranges and as a last resort. It is a gas-operated rifle, the mechanism of which appears to be more or less based on the usual rotating bolt and carrier, and which fires an unusual drag-stabilized dart. This is about 4.7 inches (120mm) long and seated in a cartridge case similar to that of the 5.56x45mm round. The size and shape of this cartridge dictates the unusual shape and depth (front to back) of the rifle magazine. The dart has a lethal range of about 100 meters in air, and the underwater range varies according to the depth and therefore the pressure, but is no more than about 36 feet (11 meters) at 130 feet (40 meters) depth.

Length, butt extended: 32.40in (823mm); butt folded: 24.17in (614mm). **Weight unloaded:** 5lb 7oz (2.46kg). **Barrel:** 11.81in (300mm) smoothbore. **Magazine:** 26-round detachable plastic box. **Muzzle velocity:** 1197 ft/sec (365 m/sec) in air.

SINGAPORE

• SAR 80 Assault Rifle
Chartered Industries of Singapore (CIS)
5.56x45mm

CIS was set up to manufacture the M16 rifle under license, and as a result of this experience decided to develop a local design which would be more cost-effective. The design was done by Sterling Armaments of England, and the prototypes were made in Singapore in 1978. After trials and modification, production began in 1980.

The SAR 80 was a conventional gas-operated, rotating-bolt weapon, firing automatic or single shots. The barrel had a flash suppresser which served as a grenade launcher. Barrel, bolt and butt were in a straight line, reducing jump and making the rifle very controllable in automatic fire. The rifle could be easily field stripped by simply hinging the lower part of the receiver downwards and extracting the bolt carrier, bolt, return springs and guide rod assembly. The magazine was of the M16 pattern.

The SAR-80, manufactured in Singapore.

The latest Singapore weapons are these SR88A rifle and carbine.

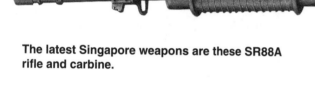

Barrel: 18.07in (459mm), 6 grooves, right-hand twist. **Magazine:** 20- or 30-round detachable box. **Cyclic rate:** c.700 rds/min. **Muzzle velocity:** c.3182 ft/sec (970 m/sec).

A folding butt model was also made and was recommended for paratroops and armored forces. Numbers of both were taken into service by the Singapore military forces.

Length, fixed butt: 38.19in (970mm); butt folded: 29.05in (738mm). **Weight unloaded:** 8lb 3oz (3.70kg). **Barrel:** 18.07in (459mm), 6 grooves, right-hand twist. **Magazine:** 20- or 30-round detachable box. **Cyclic rate:** c.700 rds/min. **Muzzle velocity:** c.3182 ft/sec (970 m/sec).

• SR-88A

Chartered Industries of Singapore
5.56x45mm

This is a lightweight gas-operated rifle which can be considered as an improved version of the SAR80. The same gas-operated rotating bolt system is used, housed in a cast aluminum alloy receiver. The gas system is chrome-plated throughout, giving high resistance to fouling and wear. The stock is of fiberglass reinforced nylon and the tubular skeleton butt is fixed, though there is an optional folding butt which folds to the right side of the receiver.

The butt can be adjusted for length by changing the butt pad, and it can be removed for greater compactness. The barrel is fitted to the receiver by a locknut system which simplified barrel replacement. Other features include luminous night sights, a carrying handle, an arctic trigger unit, and provision for mounting optical and electro-optical sights. A selector for full automatic or three-round bursts can be fitted, as desired, and the handguard is so designed that the US M203 grenade-launcher can be fitted without requiring any dismantling.

Length, fixed butt: 38.19in (970mm); butt folded: 29.37in (746mm).
Weight unloaded: 8lb 1oz (3.66kg).

SOUTH AFRICA

• Rifle R1

Lyttleton Engineering Works, Lyttleton
7.62x51mm NATO

In the early 1950s the South African government decided to have a modern facility for the production of small arms, and with the assistance of BSA Ltd of Britain, set up the Lyttleton Engineering Works. In 1960 it was decided to adopt an automatic rifle, and after negotiations with FN of Belgium, the FN-FAL was made by Lyttleton under license, and became the R1 rifle. Dimensions and performance were exactly the same as for the Belgian product.

• R4 Rifle (1975)

Lyttleton Engineering Works, Lyttleton
5.56x45mm

The R1 was supplemented by a relatively small number of German G3 rifles, which were given the nomenclature 'R2', but by the 1970s the various arms embargoes which has been decreed against South Africa meant that a fresh design had to be entirely developed and

The South African R4 rifle is based on the Israeli Galil

The South African R5 is a short carbine version of the R4.

built inside the country. After examining all the various rifles then in use by other countries, the Israeli Galil was chosen as the model, and a new design drawn up. Various aspects of the Galil were changed; for example the butt is stronger and longer, better suited to the stature of South African troops who are generally taller than Israelis, and better suited to the severe treatment that rifles receive in bush country. Mechanically the R4 is the same as the Galil, a gas-operated weapon using the Kalashnikov system of bolt carrier and rotating bolt. The bipod is strengthened and is also adapted for use as a wire-cutter. After its introduction into service in 1975 the R4 saw considerable combat use, as a result of which many improvements were incorporated. The original butt was of aluminum covered with nylon, and this was replaced by a glass-filled nylon butt with a strengthening web. The metal magazine was replaced by a glass-fiber/nylon pattern, the gas system was improved and the sights strengthened.

The R5 Rifle is a short-barreled model; it is identical to the R4 but has no bipod and a shorter handguard.

Length, R4, butt extended: 39.56in (1005mm); butt folded: 29.13in (740mm). **Length,** R5, butt extended: 34.53in (877mm); butt folded: 24.23in (615mm). **Weight unloaded,** R4: 9lb 8oz (4.30kg). R5: 8lb 2oz (3.70kg). **Barrel,** R4: 18.10in (460mm). R5: 13.07in (332mm); 6 grooves, right-hand twist. **Magazine:** 35- or 50-round detachable box. **Cyclic rate:** c.650 rds/min. **Muzzle velocity,** R4: c.3215 ft/sec (980 m/sec). R5: 3018 ft/sec (920 m/sec).

• Rifle R6
LIW Division of Denel Pty, Lyttleton
5.56x45mm

The R6 is a sub-compact version of the R4 rifle described above, intended for use by vehicle crews, airborne troops and others who require the most compact weapon available. It operates in precisely the same way as the R4, differing only in dimensions.

Length, butt extended: 31.69in (805mm); butt folded: 22.24in (565mm). **Weight unloaded:** 8lb 2oz (3.68kg). **Barrel:** 11.02in (280mm), 6 grooves, right-hand twist. **Magazine:** 35-round detachable box. **Cyclic rate:** c. 585 rds/min. **Muzzle velocity:** c.2706 ft/sec (825 m/sec).

SPAIN

• Cetme Assault Rifle Modelo 58
Centro de Estudios Tecnicos de Materiales Especiales (CETME), Madrid
7.62x51mm NATO special

This rifle design originated in Germany during World War II as the Mauser StuG 45, a weapon which never got past the prototype stage. The designers moved to Spain after the war, to work for CETME, the Spanish government design bureau, and continued to develop the unique roller-locked delayed blowback mechanism which they had devised for the Mauser, eventually producing a 7.92mm rifle firing a special short-case cartridge with lightweight bullet.

Through a Dutch licensee this rifle was offered to the German Army in the late 1950s, but they requested a 7.62mm caliber weapon. The development was passed to Heckler & Koch and resulted in the G3, but the design team in Spain also studied the 7.62mm conversion and eventually developed a rifle firing a reduced-charge 7.62x51mm round. This entered Spanish service in 1958 as the CETME Model 58. The Model 58 was made of stamped and formed metal in order to simplify manufacture, and used

The early CETME Model 58 was mechanically similar to the German G3, since both had their roots in the Mauser Stgw 45 design.

The CETME Model L uses the same delayed blowback two-part bolt as the German G3 but the weapon itself is of purely Spanish origin.

The CETME Model LC is the usual short carbine variation on the rifle.

A further variation on the CETME rifle is this stripped-down version for firing through side ports in armored vehicles.

the same delayed blowback system as the H&K rifles. In order to reduce problems due to cases sticking in the chamber, the walls of the chamber were fluted so as to float the case on a layer of gas and ease extraction. Automatic fire was from an open bolt, single shots from a closed bolt. A light bipod was permanently fitted and folded back to form a handguard on the early model. Later models had tubular bipods or wooden handguards without bipods.

In 1974 the Spanish Army decided to adopt the full-power 7.62x51mm NATO cartridge; this necessitated some modification to the Model 58, turning it into the Model C. In general the rifle was the same but certain components needed to be strengthened to cope with the heavier charge. (Data table refers to the Model C.)

Length: 40.00in (1015mm). **Weight unloaded:** 9lb 15oz (4.50kg). **Barrel:** 17.70in (450mm), 4 grooves, right-hand twist. **Magazine:** 20-round detachable box. **Cyclic rate:** 550-650r. **Muzzle velocity:** c.2580 ft/sec (786 m/sec).

• Cetme Assault Rifle Model L (1988)
Centro de Estudios Tecnicos de Materiales Especiales (CETME), Madrid; Empresa Nacional 'Santa Barbara', Oviedo.
5.56x45mm

This is a 5.56mm assault rifle which is basically a scaled-down CETME Model C, using the same roller-locked delayed blowback system. There are two versions, the Model L in standard length and the Model LC in carbine length. A 20-shot magazine was used at first but this was later changed and the magazine housing is now to NATO standard and will accept any 30-shot M16-type magazine. Similarly, the sights were originally a

four-position type but were soon changed to a simple flip-over graduated for 200m and 400m, which caters for most applications. First models had a three-round burst mechanism but this was soon removed, since it was found that it was easy to 'squeeze off' three rounds at automatic by trigger control instead of requiring an additional piece of mechanism. The Models L and LC entered service with selected Spanish Army units in 1988.

(Model L)
Length: 36.40in (925mm). **Weight unloaded:** 7lb 8oz (3.40kg). **Barrel:** 15.75in (400mm), 6 grooves, right-hand twist. **Magazine:** 30-round detachable box. **Cyclic rate:** c.750 rds/min. **Muzzle velocity:** 3018 ft/sec (920 m/sec).

(Model LC)
Length, stock extended: 33.80in (860mm); stock folded: 26.20in (665mm). **Weight, unloaded:** 7lb 2oz (3.22kg). **Barrel:** 12.60in (320mm), 6 grooves, right-hand twist. **Magazine:** 30-round detachable box. **Cyclic rate:** 750 rds/min. **Muzzle velocity:** 2730 ft/sec (832 m/sec).

• Firing Port Weapon Model R
Empresa Nacional 'Santa Barbara', Madrid
7.62x51mm NATO

The Model R is a highly modified variant of the earlier Model C rifle, designed to be fired from the interior of armored personnel carriers and similar vehicles equipped with a ball-mount firing port. The weapon uses the same roller-locked delayed blowback system of operation but has no butt, a short barrel with large flash hider, and a special locking collar at the front of the receiver which secures the weapon into the vehicle firing port. Due to the positioning of

the weapon in this mounting, the usual forward cocking handle cannot be used, and a modified MG42 handle is fitted to the side of the weapon. No sights are fitted, aiming taking place via the vision blocks above the firing ports, and tracer ammunition being used to give visual indication of the strike of shots. The weapon fires at full-automatic only.

Length: 26.18in (665mm). **Weight unloaded:** 14lb 1oz (6.40kg). **Barrel:** 12.0in (305mm), 4 grooves, right-hand twist. **Magazine:** 20-round detachable box. **Cyclic rate:** c.550 rds/min. **Muzzle velocity:** c.2264 f/sec (690 m/sec).

SWEDEN

• Automat Gevär Model 37 (Browning 'BAR')
Carl Gustavs Stads Gevärsfaktori, Eskilstuna
6.5x55 mm Swedish Mauser

The Automat Gevär m/37 is a modification of the Browning Automatic Rifle developed at the Carl Gustavs Stads Gevärsfaktori before World War II. The chief differences lie in the caliber, and in the fact that the barrel can be easily changed. The barrel is held by a simple latch on the front of the receiver and, when this is unlocked, the barrel can be lifted clear by a carrying handle. To allow for this, the usual large fore handgrip of the Browning has disappeared, and the gun has to be carried by grasping the folded bipod legs . The m/37 is far more of a light machine-gun than its parent Browning, although the 20-round magazine detracts from its tactical value as it does with all the Browning conversions. The m/37 has now been phased out of first line service with the Swedish Army,

This Swedish Model 37 variation of the Browning Automatic Rifle features a quick-change barrel.

but it is still held on the inventory of the reserve forces.

Length: 46.00in (1168mm). **Weight unloaded:** 21lb 0oz (9.53kg). **Barrel:** 24.00in (610mm), 6 grooves, right-hand twist. **Magazine:** 20-round detachable box. **Cyclic rate:** 500 rds/min. **Muzzle velocity:** c.2450 ft/sec (746 m/sec).

• Halvautomatisk Gevär 42, 42B (Eklund-Ljungmann system)
Carl Gustavs Stads Gevärsfaktori, Eskilstuna
6.5mm patron m/96

The AG42 was designed in Sweden by Erik Eklund, and was introduced to the Swedish Army less than one year after having left the drawing board, an extraordinary feat by any standards. The basic feature of the Eklund-Ljungmann system was unusual when first introduced, although it has since gained more widespread acceptance: the usual gas piston assembly was discarded in favor of a simple direct-gas system in which the gases impinge directly upon the bolt, thus doing away with the usual piston and rod devices used to convert the gas pressure into mechanical action. The gas strikes the face of the bolt carrier, which is then blown back and rotates the bolt by suitably-shaped cam tracks; the recoil spring then returns the carrier and bolt, which strips a cartridge from the magazine in the process. This direct gas system was later used with great success on the Stoner-designed AR10 and AR15 rifles.

After having adopted the AG42, the Swedes found deficiencies in their rifle—which is scarcely surprising in

view of the haste with which it was adopted—and so a modified pattern, the AG42B, was introduced in 1953. The trigger mechanism and the extractor were revised, the front sight strengthened, the magazine modified, and stainless steel was used in the manufacture of the gas tube.

Apart from the Swedish patterns, the rifle was also manufactured in Denmark by Dansk Industri Syndikat 'Madsen'. The Madsen version had a longer gas tube coiled around the barrel and, although thereby lessening the fouling generation rate, on the bolt and carrier, the tube was difficult to clean. Largely owing to the inability of Madsen to persuade the Danish Army to adopt the rifle, it quickly passed from production. The Egyptians have also manufactured the Ljungmann Rifle in 7.92mm Mauser caliber; it is known by them as the 'Hakim'.

Length: 47.80in (1215mm). **Weight unloaded:** 10lb 6oz (4.74kg). **Barrel:** 24.50in (623mm),

6 grooves, right-hand twist. **Magazine:** 10-round box. **Muzzle velocity:** c.2450 ft/sec (745 m/sec).

• FFV 890C
FFV Ordnance Division, Eskilstuna
5.56x45mm

In 1976 the Swedish General Staff decided that it was time to re-equip the Swedish forces with a modern rifle. After much debate and many trials they decided to adopt 5.56mm caliber but, in keeping with Sweden's humanitarian and safety-conscious image, one with a barrel having a reduced pitch of rifling. This served the dual purpose of rendering the standard 5.56mm bullet rather less destructive and enabling the 890C to

The cocking handle gives the clue to the ancestry of this FFV890C; it was a licensed copy of the Galil.

The Ljungmann AG42 was one of the first automatic weapons to use direct gas impingement as a method of moving the bolt.

The ancestry of the Swedish army's AK-5 is less obvious; it began life as the FN FNC and was then extensively modified to suit the Swedish taste.

accommodate more modern, heavier and longer bullets. Instead of the usual one turn in 54 calibers barrel, the Swedish design is for one turn in 41 calibers; the bullet is therefore more stable and less likely to topple on impact and cause excessively severe wounding. Apart from this twist of rifling, and the adoption of an FFV grenade launcher on the muzzle, the rifle was in other respects the Israeli 'Galil' with a few cosmetic changes—deeper grooving in the hand-guard, for example. The FFV890C was extensively tested by the Swedish Army, but was eventually rejected in favor of the FN FNC 5.56mm rifle.

Length, stock extended: 33.85in (860mm); stock folded: 24.80in (630mm). **Weight unloaded:** 7lb 11oz (3.5kg). **Barrel:** 13.46in (342mm), 6 grooves, right-hand twist. **Magazine:** 35-round detachable box. **Cyclic rate:** c.650 rds/min. **Muzzle velocity:** 2820 ft/sec (860 m/sec).

• Assault Rifle AK5 (1986)
Bofors Carl Gustav AB, Eskilstuna
5.56x45mm NATO

Having selected the FN-FNC as their preferred model, the Swedes then acquired a license to manufacture it and set about making changes to suit their own preferences. These included a new triggerguard for use with gloved hands, a deeply-incised forend for a better grip, changes to the bolt, extractor and gas block to improve operation in sub-zero temperatures, a new folding butt, cocking handle, selector lever and magazine housing. Virtually all that was left of the original FN rifle was the basic operating system. It was finished in a deep green baked enamel, after which some variant models were developed.

The AK5B has a cheekpiece fitted to the top rail of the butt and has the British 'SUSAT' (Sight Unit, Small Arms, Trilux) optical sight mounted on the receiver. The AK5D has an American Mil-Standard 'Picatinny Rail' sight mount built on to the receiver and thus will accept almost any optical or electro-optical sight in existence. The AK5 is the Swedish army standard weapon, and limited numbers of the 5B and 5D are also in service.

Length, stock extended: 39.57in (1005mm); stock folded: 29.53in (750mm). **Weight unloaded:** 8lb 10oz (3.90kg). **Barrel:** 17.72in (450mm), 6 grooves, right-hand twist. **Magazine:** 30-round detachable box. **Cyclic rate:** c.650 rds/min. **Muzzle velocity:** 3050 ft/sec (930 m/sec).

SWITZERLAND

• Selbstladekarabiner Modell 46 (SK46)
Schweizerische Industrie-Gesellschaft, Neuhausen-am-Rheinfalls
7.92x57mm Mauser and others

The SIG concern developed some self-loading rifles during World War II and, shortly after the war ended, the SK46 was produced and offered for sale in a variety of calibers. It was a simple weapon which showed marked Schmidt-Rubin influence both in outline and in the design of the receiver. Gas was tapped from a port on the right-hand side just forward of the breech and operated a fairly conventional tilting breechblock. The semiautomatic system could be disconnected by turning the cocking handle upright, and the rifle could then be fired as a conventional bolt-action weapon; by fitting a launcher, the rifle could be used for firing grenades. A telescopic sight of 2.2x magnification was fitted as standard, adding 13.5oz (.38kg) to an already heavy rifle. Placing the gas port close to the breech is not a popular method of tapping gas as the pressure is very high at that point in the barrel and also very hot; erosion of the gas port is far less if the port is farther from the point of ignition, and it also allows a longer delay before starting to operate the breech mechanism.

The SK46 did not sell, as too many war-surplus weapons were to be had cheaply to allow new designs much of a chance on the market.

Length: 44.25in (1125mm). **Weight unloaded:** 10lb 0oz (4.54kg). **Barrel:** 23.63in (600mm), 4 grooves, right-hand twist. **Magazine:** 5- or 10-round detachable box. **Muzzle velocity:** c.2700 ft/sec (823 m/sec).

• Automatische Karabiner Model 53 (AK53)
Schweizerische Industrie-Gesellschaft, Neuhausen-am-Rheinfalls
7.5x54mm Swiss M1911

Another post-war design from SIG was the AK53, an attempt to make an easily manufactured selective-fire weapon. The rifle worked on the entirely

The SIG AK53 was the only automatic rifle ever to operate on the blow-forward system.

The Swiss Sturmgewehr 57 used a variant of the Mauser Stgw 45 delayed blowback system; a heavy weapon, but accurate and reliable and a pleasure to shoot.

The SIG SG510 was the 7.62mm NATO version of the 7.5mm Stgw 57, and was somewhat lighter into the bargain, but it found few customers.

novel principle of moving the barrel forward and leaving a stationary bolt. This offers the advantages of a short overall length but compensates with some severe disadvantages, among them maintenance of accuracy from the moving barrel, and the difficulty of preventing jamming when the barrel heats and expands. The rate of fire is also very low. Another drawback is that the AK53 fired from a closed breech, and so there was always a danger, after several bursts, of heat igniting the round in the breech. No doubt these points presented themselves to potential buyers, because this interesting weapon never sold and it remains one of the more unusual rifles of the century.

Length: 39.37in (1000mm). **Weight unloaded:** 10lb 12oz (4.90kg). **Barrel:** 23.63in (600mm), 4 grooves, left-hand twist. **Magazine:** 30-round detachable box. **Cyclic rate:** 300 rds/min. **Muzzle velocity:** c.2450 ft/sec (750 m/sec).

• Sturmgewehr Stgw57

Schweizerische Industrie-Gesellschaft, Neuhausen-am-Rheinfalls
7.5x54mm Swiss M1911

The early history of the Stgw57 is not entirely clear, although it seems that SIG were aware of the development of the Mauser StuG45 very shortly after the war ended and set about making their own version of the two-part bolt and roller-locked delayed blowback system which was later perfected by CETME and Heckler & Koch.

As in the CETME and the G3, the locking rollers are in the head of the bolt, which is far lighter than the main portion, and on retracting, they force the heavier bolt to the rear with a mechanical disadvantage. In an attempt to prevent sticking cases, the M57 uses a fluted chamber—another feature of the CETME. A major difference between the two systems is that in the Stgw57 some

of the flutes stretch to the mouth of the chamber and direct a small amount of gas blast through holes in the bolt face, allowing the gas pressure to strike the bolt body and thereby assist the rearward thrust of the cartridge case in actuating the bolt mechanism.

A bipod is permanently fitted and it can be moved to any position along the barrel to suit the firer. There is an integral grenade launcher on the muzzle and a rubber butt pad to absorb recoil. By modern standards this is a heavy and powerful rifle, but the weight helps to absorb recoil and it is exceptionally accurate, a pleasure to shoot, and very reliable under extreme conditions. It has been replaced as the Swiss service rifle by the Stgw 90 (below) but numbers are held in reserve.

Length: 43.50in (1105mm). **Weight unloaded:** 12lb 4oz (5.55kg). **Barrel:** 23.00in (583mm), 4 grooves, right-hand twist. **Magazine:** 24-round detachable box. **Cyclic rate:** 450-500 rds/min. **Muzzle velocity:** c.2500 ft/sec (761 m/sec).

• Sturmgewehr Model 510 Series (SG510)

Schweizerische Industrie-Geseltschaft, Neuhausen-am-Rheinfalls
7.62x51mm NATO

The SIG 510 series of rifles was developed from the Stgw57 and can be considered as the commercial variant of the Swiss service weapon. The same system of delayed blowback action is used, the significant change being that of caliber, a change to 7.62mm NATO. With this change the opportunity was taken of improving the weapon in some minor aspects and the result was of a very high standard. From a technical standpoint the SG 510 was probably the best 7.62mm selective-fire rifle ever made, but such quality meant a high price. More-

over, it appeared on the market after other designs had made their mark, and thus its use has been limited to the Swiss Army and to a few African and South American states. There were a number of variant models; the 510-1 was almost identical to the Stgw57 except for the change of caliber; the 510-2 was to the same design but lighter; the 510-3 was among the first West European designs to be chambered for the 7.62x39mm Soviet round, in an attempt to attract sales from countries already committed to that cartridge; and the 510-4 was the final, perfected, design, using a wooden butt, a small wooden forend, and chambered for the 7.62mm NATO round. The 510-3 failed to attract many customers and few were made; the 510-4 was adopted by the Swiss Army and by Chile and Bolivia.

(SG510-3)

Length: 35.00in (889mm). **Weight unloaded:** 8lb 4oz (3.75kg). **Barrel:** 16.50in (419mm), 4 grooves, right-hand twist. **Magazine:** 30-round detachable box. **Cyclic rate:** 450-600 rds/min. **Muzzle velocity:** c.2300 ft/sec (700 m/sec).

(SG510-4)

Length: 40.00in (1015mm). **Weight unloaded:** 9lb 6oz (4.25kg). **Barrel:** 19.80in (505mm), 4 grooves, right-hand twist. **Magazine:** 20-round detachable box. **Cyclic rate:** 500-650 rds/min. **Muzzle velocity:** c.2635 (790 m/sec).

• Sturmgewehr Model 530-1 (SG530-1)

Schweitzerische Industrie-Gesellschaft, Neuhausen-am-Rheinfalls
5.56x45mm

The SG 530 started life as a scaled-down SG 510 chambered for the 5.56mm cartridge, but it was soon found that the 5.56 round was not happy with the SIG delayed blowback system and

The SIG 530 was, in effect, a 510 in 5.56mm caliber, but the 5.56mm cartridge wasn't happy with their delayed blow-back system.

the weapon was redesigned to use a gas piston action. The piston acted upon the two-part breech-block to withdraw the rollers and then open the breech, which was an unnecessary complication but saved a total redesign. The rifles were neat and well-made but they failed to attract any sales since they appeared in the late 1960s when most European armies were waiting to see which way the wind blew before they committed themselves to any new caliber.

Length: 37.00in (940mm). **Weight unloaded:** 7lb 8oz (3.45kg). **Barrel:** 15.50in (394mm), 4 grooves, right-hand twist. **Magazine:** 30-round detachable box. **Cyclic rate:** 600 rds/min. **Muzzle velocity:** c.3000 ft/sec (912 m/sec).

• Sturmgewehr Model 540 and 542 (SG540, SG542)
Schweizerische Industrie-Gesellschaft, Neuhausen-am-Rheinfalls; Manurhin, Mulhouse, France
5.56mm (SG540), 7.62mm NATO (SG542)

One of the faults of the SG 530 was its high price, and SIG set about designing a new 5.56mm rifle with a less complicated breech mechanism, adopting the familiar bolt carrier and rotating bolt system. Stampings and castings are used and the weapon is much easier and cheaper to make than its forerunners.

It is a selective-fire weapon, with a three-round burst facility which is a separate unit and can be installed or removed without tools and without affecting the basic operation of the firing mechanism. Various accessories are supplied, including bipods, telescope sights and bayonets of tubular or conventional type. The muzzle has a combined flash-suppressor/compensator which doubles as a grenade-launcher, and a gas regulator on the front of the gas cylinder allows for two degrees of opening and a closed position for grenade-launching. The SG 540 was manufactured in Switzerland, and was also licensed to

The 5.56mm SIG 540 was more successful, selling to France, Portugal and Chile, among others.

Scaling up the SIG 540 to take the 7.62x51mm NATO cartridge produced this SIG 542, but it was never as popular as its smaller companion.

The SIG 543 was the customary short carbine variant of the 540 rifle.

The SIG 550 was adopted by the Swiss Army as their Sturmgewehr 90. Note the triple magazines, done by having studs and slots on each magazine so that any number can be fitted together. They have sufficient separation to allow each one to be slotted into the magazine housing in turn.

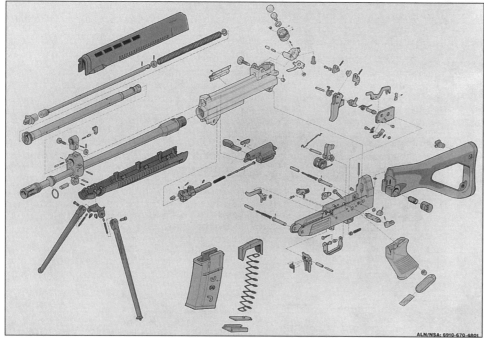

An exploded view of the SIG 550/Stgw 90 assault rifle.

The SIG 551 is also called the Stgw 90 Assault Carbine when used by the Swiss Army. This version, with special sight mount, is the 'SWAT' model for sale to police and anti-terrorist forces.

The final variation on the SIG 550 is this SSG550 sniping rifle with adjustable butt, heavy barrel and a variety of optical and electro-optical sight options.

Manurhin of France, who supplied large numbers to the French Army to familiarize them with the 5.56mm caliber prior to the development and issue of the FA-MAS rifle. It has been widely exported by both SIG and Manurhin and is in use in 17 countries in Africa, South America and the Middle East.

A variant model, the SG 542, was developed in 7.62x51mm caliber, but this appears never to have been produced in quantity, the 5.56mm weapon proving more attractive to purchasers. The SG 543 is a short, folding-butt version of the SG 540.

(SG540, fixed stock)

Length: 37.40in (950mm). **Weight unloaded:** 6lb 3oz (3.26kg). **Barrel:** 18.11in (460mm), 6 grooves, right-hand twist. **Magazine:** 20- or 30-round detachable box. **Cyclic rate:** 650-800 rds/min. **Muzzle velocity:** 3215 ft/sec (980 m/sec).

(SG542, fixed stock)

Length: 39.37in (1000mm). **Weight unloaded:** 7lb 13oz (3.55kg). **Barrel:** 18.30in (465mm), 4 grooves, right-hand twist. **Magazine:** 20- or 30-round detachable box. **Cyclic rate:** 650-800 rds/min. **Muzzle velocity:** 2690 ft/sec (820 m/sec).

(SG543, folding stock)

Length, butt extended: 31.70in (805mm); butt folded: 22.40in (569mm). **Weight unloaded:** 6lb 9oz (3.00kg). **Barrel:** 11.81in (300mm), 6 grooves, right-hand twist. **Magazine:** 20- or 30-round detachable box. **Cyclic rate:** 650-800 rds/min. **Muzzle velocity:** 2870 ft/sec (875 m/sec).

• Sturmgewehr Model 550/551 (Stgw 90)
Schweizerische Industrie-Gesellschaft, Neuhausen-am-Rheinfalls
5.56x45mm

This rifle was developed in response to a Swiss Army requirement for a 5.56mm rifle to replace the 7.5mm Stgw 57. Development took place in 1979-80 in competition with a design from the Swiss Federal Arms factory, and in 1983 the SG 550 was selected. Shortly afterwards it was announced that due to funds being required for the provision of tanks and other armored vehicles, the issue of the new rifle would be delayed. Production

eventually began in 1986 and it is now in service as the Stgw90. The design paid careful attention to weight-saving, using plastics for the butt, handguard and magazine; the latter is transparent, so that the ammunition can be easily checked, and is provided with studs and lugs so that two or more magazines can be clipped together for rapid changing. The butt can be folded to one side and even when this is done the weapon is still well-balanced. There is a three-round burst mechanism, and the sights are provided with luminous dots for use in poor light. There is an integral sight mount which accepts Swiss telescope and electro-optical sights, though this mount can be provided to NATO standard if required. The SG 551 is a short carbine version of the rifle; it is mechanically identical except for its size. The SG550SP and 551SP are semi-automatic versions available on the commercial market as sporting rifles, though they obviously have an application for military and security forces who do not require the automatic fire capability. Apart from their restriction to single shots, they are identical to the service weapons.

(SG 550)

Length, butt extended: 39.29in (998mm); butt folded: 30.39in (772mm). **Weight unloaded:** 9lb 1oz (4.10kg) with magazine and bipod. **Barrel:** 20.79in (528mm), 6 grooves, right-hand twist. **Magazine:** 20- or 30-round detachable box. **Cyclic rate:** 700 rds/min. **Muzzle velocity:** 3028 ft/sec (923 m/sec).

(SG 551)

Length, butt extended: 32.56in (827mm); butt folded: 23.66in (601mm). **Weight unloaded:** 7lb 11oz (3.50kg). **Barrel:** 14.64in (372mm), 6 grooves, right-hand twist. **Magazine:** 20- or 30-round detachable box. **Cyclic rate:** 700 rds/min. **Muzzle velocity:** 3000 ft/sec (915 m/sec).

• SSG550 Sniper
Schweizerische Industrie-Gesellschaft, Neuhausen-am-Rheinfalls
5.56x45mm

The SSG550 was developed from the standard SG550 rifle by fitting it with a

heavy hammer-forged barrel and altering the mechanism for semi-automatic fire only. The trigger is a two-stage type, adjustable to the firer's personal preference, and the butt is adjustable for length and has an adjustable cheekpiece. The pistol grip is also adjustable for rake and carries a handrest which can be positioned as required. A bipod is fitted, and the telescope can be varied in its position so as to fall naturally to the eye when the firer's face is against the cheekpiece. An anti-reflective screen can be drawn over the top of the rifle, which also prevents air disturbance due to barrel heat interfering with the sight line. Altogether, just about everything for the sniper's convenience has been considered and catered for in this rifle.

Length, butt extended: 44.49in (1130mm); butt folded 35.63in (905mm). **Weight unloaded:** 16lb 1oz (7.3kg). **Barrel:** 25.60in (650mm), 6 grooves, right-hand twist. **Magazine:** 20- or 30-round detachable box. **Muzzle velocity:** 3130 ft/sec (954 m/sec).

U.S.A.

• US Self-loading Pistol, Caliber 30, M1918
Remington Arms-Union Metallic Cartridge Company, Ilion, NY
30 Caliber, M1918

In the course of studying the actions in France during 1916 and 1917, the United States Army observed that the most dangerous time for the infantryman was during his advance across 'No Man's Land', when the covering fire had stopped and the enemy was alert. With encouragement from the French, the American authorities came to the conclusion that the best solution would be to equip every man with an automatic rifle and to have him fire it from the hip as he advanced, so covering the entire area with bullets and making it most hazardous for defenders to show themselves on the defense parapets.

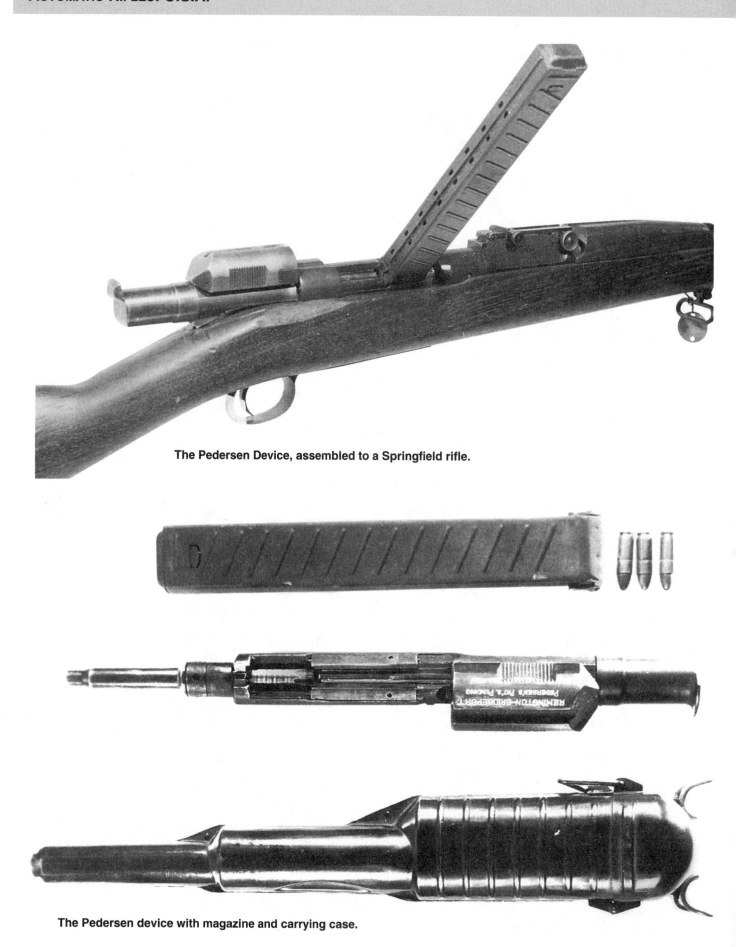

The Pedersen Device, assembled to a Springfield rifle.

The Pedersen device with magazine and carrying case.

The Browning Automatic Rifle M1918A1 with double butt plate.

The prospect of producing sufficient automatic rifles for every man was out of the question and, since the normal bolt-action rifle would be required on most other occasions, the problem seemed a little difficult until it was cleverly solved by John Pedersen, who was at the time working as a designer for Remington at their Ilion plant. It was found possible to remove the bolt from the standard M1903 rifle and replace it with a simple blowback device fitted with its own magazine and with a short barrel which outwardly resembled a standard 30-caliber M1906 cartridge case. This fitted into the chamber of the rifle after the original bolt had been removed, the magazine protruded obliquely to one side, and the soldier—in fifteen seconds—had converted his rifle to a form of submachine gun or automatic rifle. The cartridge was specially designed by Pedersen to suit the device and has never been used in any other weapon; it is rather like a much-lengthened 32 ACP round in appearance.

The M1903 rifle when altered to accept the device became the 'Rifle, Magazine, Caliber 30, M1903 Mark I' and some 65,000 of these devices (together with the special holster, two pouches of magazines sufficient to provide each man with 400 rounds, and the necessary converted rifles) were prepared by Remington in conditions of great secrecy during 1918, in order to prepare the United States Army for the 1919 spring offensive. The war then ended and a more leisurely evaluation of the Pedersen device concluded that it was not entirely desirable. Soldiers who used the device invariably lost their rifle bolt or, if using the rifle, misplaced or damaged the Pedersen device. Moreover, the claimed 15-second change-over only held good in ideal conditions, and the time increased in conditions of cold, wet or darkness. In the mid-1920s the device was sentenced obsolete, and almost the entire stock was broken up for scrap under military control.

Although the Pedersen device was originally intended for the M1903 American Springfield rifle, some were made for the M1917 Enfield rifle for trial purposes. There is also evidence that examples were also made for the French Fusil M07/15 and the Russian rifle M1891, both of which were being made by Remington at that time to foreign contracts.

• US Automatic Rifle, Caliber 30 M1918-M1922 (Browning)

Colt's Patent Firearms Manufacturing Company, Hartford, Conn.; Winchester Repeating Firearms Company, New Haven, Conn.; Marlin-Rockwell Corporation, New Haven, Conn.

30-06 Springfield

The Browning Automatic Rifle (BAR) was another weapon which arose from the concept of 'Walking Fire', an idea urged upon the Americans by the French Army. The weapon never entirely lived up to the designer's hopes; being neither a rifle nor a machine gun, it fell between the two. As a rifle it was too heavy and could not be fired from the shoulder with any accuracy as it vibrated from the forward movement of the bolt. Set for automatic fire it was too light and moved excessively, and the small magazine demanded frequent reloading. For its day, though, it was a brilliant design produced in record time by John Browning, and it was bought and used by many countries around the world. It was the standard squad light automatic of the US infantry during World War II and saw use in every theater of war. It was also supplied in considerable numbers to the British Home Guard.

The BAR is a gas-operated weapon, using a piston moving in a cylinder below the barrel. This is linked to the bolt, which has a separate bolt lock which is cammed upwards as the bolt closes and wedges in front of a recess in the roof of the receiver; this is why the BAR had a characteristic 'hump' on the top of the receiver just in front of the rear sight, to allow space for the bolt lock to move up. The weapon fires from an open bolt, and the mechanism is extremely complicated; this, combined with the machined steel receiver, made the Browning slow and expensive to build but also made it virtually unbreakable and incapable of wearing out.

The World War I version had a selector allowing single shots or automatic fire; this was later modified so that there was no provision for single shots but two rates of automatic fire, 350 or 550rds/min. The US Marine Corps preferred to have single shots available and therefore modified many of their weapons back to the old standard. As a result of this and also of slight modifications made by other countries which adopted the weapon, the varieties and sub-varieties of the BAR are legion. The US forces abandoned the BAR in the middle 1950s, though it was retained in reserve stocks for several years; it survived in smaller countries until the late 1970s.

• US Automatic Rifle, Caliber 30, M1918 (Browning)

The M1918 is fitted with a smooth tapered barrel, and the stock is provided with a swivel between the pistol-grip and the stock-toe. No bipod assembly is fitted.

Length: 48.00in (1219mm). **Weight unloaded:** 16lb 0oz (7.28kg). **Barrel:** 24.00in (610mm), 4 grooves, right-hand twist. **Magazine:** 20-round detachable box. **Cyclic rate:** 500 rds/min. **Muzzle velocity:** c.2650 ft/sec (807 m/sec).

• US Automatic Rifle, Caliber 30, M1918A1 (Browning)

The M1918A1 shares the barrel and stock design of the M1918, with a similar butt swivel: a 'double buttplate' is fitted, the outer part of which can be hinged upwards to provide a shoulder support, and a hinged bipod is attached to the gas cylinder just forward of the wooden forearm. The M1918A1 weighs approximately 18lb 4oz (8.30kg).

• US Automatic Rifle, Caliber 30, M1918A2 (Browning)

Similar to the preceding M1918 designs, the M1918A2 has a shortened forearm with an internal metal plate intended to protect the recoil spring from barrel heat, and a bipod with 'skid feet' rather than the 'spike feet' of the M1918A1. A butt monopod of questionable utility is sometimes fitted, and the firing mechanism incorporates provision for altering the cyclic rate; unlike the two earlier patterns, the M1918A2 is incapable of firing single shots. The first

The BAR M1918A2, an early model with the bipod at the muzzle.

M1918A2 production were originally issued with a bipod at the muzzle: later weapons returned it to a position around the gas cylinder.

• US Automatic Rifle, Caliber 30, M1922 (Browning)

A short-lived variation of the M1919 types, with a finned barrel to accelerate barrel cooling and a sling swivel on the left side of the stock. A bipod can be fitted, and a wide groove cut around the butt is intended to accommodate the butt monopod.

• Pedersen Self-loading Rifle, Caliber 276, T2E1

Springfield Armory, Springfield, Mass.
276 Pedersen

John Pedersen was a designer who, after working commercially for Remington, joined the government designers at Springfield Armory in the years between the wars, where he developed a 276-caliber cartridge and a rifle to go with it.

The Pedersen rifle used a toggle-joint very similar to that found on the Parabellum pistol, but designed to function as a delayed blowback device. The thrust axis through

the toggle is slightly below the pivot axis, and careful design of the toggle hinge - incorporating progressive cam surfaces rather than a simple pivot—makes the first movement of the opening so slow that the chamber pressure has time to drop before the full opening movement is developed and the empty case extracted. Unfortunately, it means that when the extraction movement begins, there is still sufficient pressure in the chamber to keep the cartridge case expanded against the chamber wall, and this friction leads to hard extraction, torn rims and separated cases. The only cure for this was to lubricate the cases, and so Pedersen developed a system of wax-coating the cases during manufacture, and with this special ammunition the rifle worked well. Had Pedersen thought to use a fluted chamber to solve his extraction problem, there is every likelihood that the weapon would have been accepted. The final blow was General MacArthur's decision to retain the 30-06 cartridge, to which the Pedersen could not be converted.

In addition to the T2E1 rifles made for the US trials, Pedersen-system rifles

were made for tests in Britain by Vickers-Armstrong Limited in 1930-32. A similar weapon was also made in Japan in 1934-35 for military trials.

Length: 45.00in (1143mm). **Weight unloaded:** 9lb 0oz (4.10kg). **Barrel:** 24.00in (610mm), 6 grooves, right-hand twist. **Magazine:** 10-round integral box. **Muzzle velocity:** 2500 ft/sec (762 m/sec).

• US Rifle, Caliber 30 M1 ('Garand')

Springfield Armory, Springfield, Mass.; Winchester Repeating Arms Company, New Haven, Conn.; Harrington & Richardson Arms Company, Worcester, Mass.; International Harvester Corporation.
30-06 Springfield

The M1 rifle has the distinction of being the first self-loading rifle to be adopted as a standard weapon; this took place in 1932 and the rifle actually began issue in 1936, and by 1941 the major proportion of the American regular army had it as their basic arm. Very large numbers had been made by 1945,

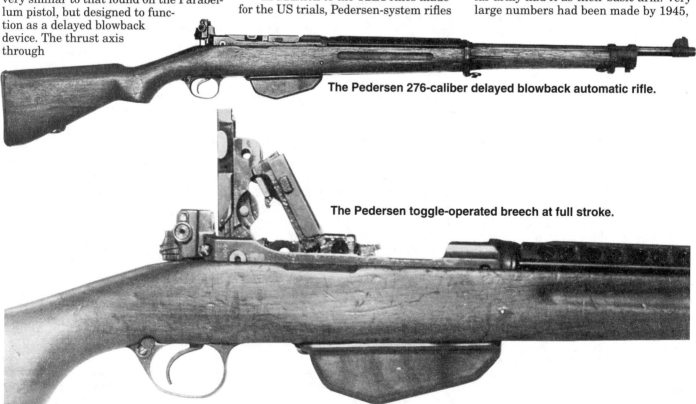

The Pedersen 276-caliber delayed blowback automatic rifle.

The Pedersen toggle-operated breech at full stroke.

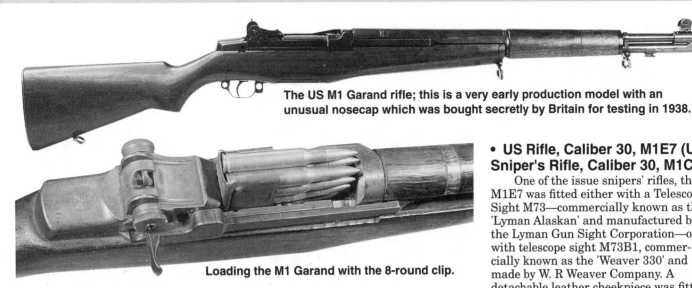

The US M1 Garand rifle; this is a very early production model with an unusual nosecap which was bought secretly by Britain for testing in 1938.

Loading the M1 Garand with the 8-round clip.

and by the time manufacture ended in the 1950s, some 5.5 million had been made. Garands were still in regular service in Vietnam in 1963, and many are still no doubt in use in various parts of Asia. They were made under license by Beretta for the Italian Army and also for Indonesia.

The rifle is simple and robust; it is not particularly light, and the forestock is somewhat bulky for a small hand, but by the standards of its day the weight was reasonable enough. It operates by gas action, using a piston beneath the barrel which terminates in an 'operating rod' with a cam groove interacting with a stud on the bolt. As the rod is driven back, so the groove rotates and then withdraws the bolt; a spring then returns the rod, drawing the bolt forward to chamber a fresh round and rotate to lock. Firing is performed by an ingenious and robust hammer mechanism which has been widely copied in subsequent years.

The magazine held only eight rounds and did not project beneath the stock; this had the advantage of smoothing the contours but restricted the magazine capacity. Another criticism of the Garand, the major one, was the loading system, by a clip of eight rounds. Single rounds could not be loaded, it was an eight-round clip or nothing. The spent clip was automatically ejected after the last round had been fired, making a distinctive sound which sometimes led to fatal results in close-quarter fighting. But these were small matters, and the main thing was that the US Army carried a self-loading rifle throughout World War II.

Length: 43.50in (1103mm). **Weight unloaded:** 9lb 8oz (4.37kg). **Barrel:** 24.00in (610mm), 4 grooves, right-hand twist. **Magazine:** 8-round internal box. **Muzzle velocity:** c.2800 ft/sec (853 m/sec).

• US Rifle, Caliber 30 M1E1.

A slight variation of the standard Rifle M1, with modifications made to the fit of the operating mechanism and with a more gradual cam-angle in the operating rod handle. Few were made in this pattern.

• US Rifle, Caliber 30, M1E2

The first version of the Rifle M1 adapted for optical sights, an International Industries telescope sight was fitted with suitable mounts; the M1E2 was strictly experimental issue and was quickly replaced by the Rifle M1E7.

• US Rifle, Caliber 30, M1E3

Another of the experimental weapons produced in an attempt to make the operation of the M1 more smooth. A roller bearing was attached to the bolt cam lug and the cam-angle of the operating rod was suitably altered.

• US Rifle, Caliber 30, M1E4

An experimental arm produced in an attempt to achieve a less violent operation, by increasing the time lag between the tapping of the gas and the opening of the bolt, and also by lessening the rearward velocity of the operating rod. An expansion chamber was introduced into the gas system.

• US Rifle, Caliber 30, M1E5

This was a shortened version of the Rifle M1 provided with a folding stock, and with the barrel shortened to 18 inches (457mm), but although the accuracy remained virtually unimpaired, muzzle blast and flash were excessive.

• US Rifle, Caliber 30, M1E6

An experimental project in which an offset telescope sight was to be fitted to a sniper rifle in order that the fixed open sights could still be used if necessary.

• US Rifle, Caliber 30, M1E7 (US Sniper's Rifle, Caliber 30, M1C)

One of the issue snipers' rifles, the M1E7 was fitted either with a Telescope Sight M73—commercially known as the 'Lyman Alaskan' and manufactured by the Lyman Gun Sight Corporation—or with telescope sight M73B1, commercially known as the 'Weaver 330' and made by W. R Weaver Company. A detachable leather cheekpiece was fitted to the stock, and a flash-suppresser was added in 1945. The M1E7 was renamed M1C in June 1944.

• US Rifle, Caliber 30, M1E8 (US Sniper's Rifle, Caliber 30, M1D)

The second issue version of the MI intended for snipers' use, the M1E8 was fitted with the Telescope Sight M73 in a block mount in which guise it was known as the Sight M81 (crosswire reticle) or the Sight M82 (tapered-post reticle). A Sight M84 was also issued. The M1E8 was renamed M1D in June 1944.

• US Rifle, Caliber 30, M1E9

An experimental variation of the M1E4, with an alteration made to the gas expansion system in which the gas piston served as a tappet for the operating rod. It was hoped by this to avoid the overheating troubles of the M1E4.

• US Rifle, Caliber 30, T26

A quantity of these rifles was ordered in 1945 for the Pacific Theatre, although the order was later rescinded; the title combined the action of the M1E5 with a shortened M1 stock.

• Johnson Self-loading Rifle Model 1941

Cranston Arms Company, Providence, R.I.
30-06 Springfield

The Johnson rifle was designed shortly before World War II as a light military weapon, and it was extensively tested by the American Army and Marine Corps. Neither accepted it—which is hardly surprising as the Garand had just been put into mass-production—but Johnson obtained an order to manufacture them for the Dutch forces in Sumatra and Java. With the Japanese occupation of the Dutch East Indies, this contract was abruptly terminated, but as the US forces were expanding rapidly

The M1941 Johnson rifle, recoil-operated and with a rotary magazine.

and Garand production barely getting into its stride, the US Marine Corps moved rapidly to take the balance of the order, issuing them to Raider Battalions and to their early paratroop force. They were also used to some extent by US Marines in the European Theater of Operations, but experience showed that they were less robust than the Garand, their mechanism jammed more easily and the long exposed barrel was vulnerable to damage. It has been estimated that about 70,000 Johnson rifles were made before production was ended early in 1944.

The Johnson was recoil-operated, one of the few rifles so designed to be accepted into service in any army. It also had several other unusual features including the rotary magazine with its lips machined into the receiver; this was less prone to damage than the removable magazine, and could be loaded or emptied with the bolt closed and the weapon safe. The barrel could be easily dismounted and was easier for a parachutist to carry.

Length: 45.50in (1156mm). **Weight unloaded:** 9lb 8oz (4.31kg). **Barrel:** 22.00in (558mm), 4 grooves, right-hand twist. **Magazine:** 10-round detachable rotary box (+1 round in magazine feedway). **Muzzle velocity:** c.2650 ft/sec (807 m/sec).

• Smith & Wesson 9mm Model 1940 Light Rifle
Smith & Wesson Arms Company, Springfield, Mass.
9mm Parabellum

Smith & Wesson's self-loading carbine has a very clouded history. The gun was developed in 1939 as a possible police arm and, in 1940, it was offered for trials to the British. The M1940 was a blowback gun of relatively simple construction and, although of superior finish, the only truly unusual feature lay in the magazine housing; this fixed component not only accepted the box magazine, but also acted as a forward handgrip, and the rear half contained a chute down which the spent cases were ejected.

The carbine was rejected by the British on the grounds of fragility and expense, especially as other weapons had become available which were cheaper and more reliable. The trouble with the original Smith & Wesson guns lay in the ammunition, for the British service 9mm Parabellum round was more powerful than that for which the Light Rifle had originally been chambered, and a series of component breakages ensued. A modified version of the gun was developed as the Mark 2, and it appears that small numbers were taken by the Royal Navy in 1941-2; there is no official record of the carbine's introduction

into British service, but it is recorded that in 1942, the Royal Small Arms Factory at Enfield Lock designed a 'Butt, Folding, Mark 2' for the 'Carbine, Self-loading, Smith & Wesson, 9mm'.

It seems that a version of the Light Rifle was briefly mooted in 45 ACP, but it is also apparent that none was ever made; fully-automatic variations of the basic design were also considered, although none progressed past the experimental stage.

Length: 33.25in (845mm). **Weight unloaded:** 8lb 10oz (3.92kg). **Barrel:** 9.75in (247mm), 6 grooves, right-hand twist. **Magazine:** 20-round detachable box. **Muzzle velocity:** c.1240 ft/sec (378 m/sec).

• Reising Self-loading Carbine Model 60
Harrington & Richardson Arms Company, Worcester, Mass.
45 ACP

The Reising Model 60 bears considerable resemblance to the Model 50 submachine gun and is virtually the same weapon with an extended barrel, and with the mechanism altered to restrict operation to single-shot fire; like the Model 50, it operates on a retarded blowback system, the bolt being 'locked' into a recess in the receiver.

The Model 60 was developed primarily as a police weapon; since it fired a pistol cartridge it found no application as

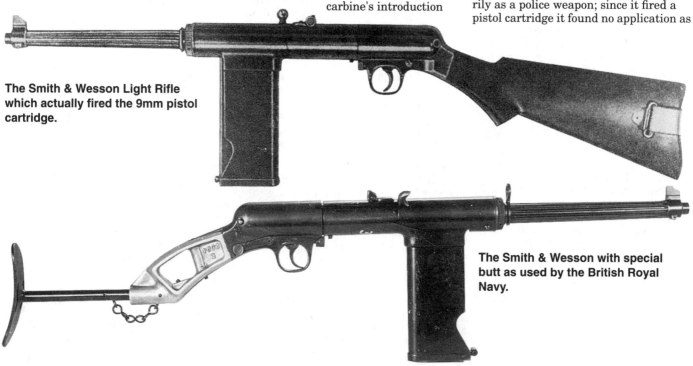

The Smith & Wesson Light Rifle which actually fired the 9mm pistol cartridge.

The Smith & Wesson with special butt as used by the British Royal Navy.

The Reising Model 60 was simply the Model 50 sub-machine gun with the automatic fire ability removed.

a military self-loading rifle; it was, however, tested by a number of military agencies and was adopted in some quantity by security guards and police in the USA during World War II.

• US Carbine, Caliber 30, M1

General Motors Corporation, Saginaw Steering Gear Division, Grand Rapids and Saginaw, Mich.; General Motors Corporation, Inland Manufacturing Division, Dayton, Ohio; International Business Machine Corporation, Poughkeepsie, N.Y.; National Postal Meter Company, Rochester, N.Y.; Quality Hardware and Machine Company, Chicago, Ill.; Rochester Defense Corporation, Rochester, N.Y.; Rock-Ola Manufacturing Corporation, Chicago, Ill.; Standard Products Company, Port Clinton, Ohio; Underwood-Elliot-Fisher Company, Hartford, Conn.; Winchester Repeating Arms Company, New Haven, Conn.

30 M1 Carbine

The Carbine, Caliber 30, MI, the most prolific American weapon of World War II, began as a 1938 request for a light rifle suitable for arming machine-gunners, mortarmen, clerks, cooks and similar grades. The request was refused but, resubmitted in 1940, it met with a more favorable reception. In October 1940, specifications were issued to 25 manufacturing companies, although their work was delayed until Winchester had produced the ammunition. The new round was developed by them to another army specification, with a 110-grain bullet giving a muzzle velocity of 1860 ft/sec (567 m/sec) from an 18-inch (457mm) barrel.

Testing began in May 1941, after some 11 different makers had submitted designs, among them a Springfield Armory weapon designed by John Garand. Some of the submissions were rejected on the spot, but others showed sufficient promise for their makers to be given the chance to modify them and to remedy defects; a final trial took place in September 1941. The result was the adoption of the Winchester designed prototype, which was adopted as the Carbine M1.

Contrary to accepted legend, David 'Carbine' Williams had little or nothing to do with the design of this weapon. It had actually begun early in 1940 as a spare-time occupation of two employees in the Winchester tool-room, who were intending it as a lightweight hunting rifle. It had attracted the attention of Mr. Pugsley, the general manager, who allowed them to continue when nothing better was to hand. When the military request appeared in 1941, Pugsley recalled this rifle, called up the two developers, handed them the Army cartridge and specification, and invited them to modify their design accordingly, and as fast as possible. Since the Williams gas-tappet was used in the design, it was felt politic, and good propaganda, to attribute the whole thing to Williams, from which the legend arose. But it was this early in-house work which enabled Winchester to produce a tested and reliable weapon in the short time allowed for development.

The M1 carbine is a semi-automatic light rifle utilizing a unique operating system. A gas port in the barrel leads to a chamber containing a tappet (or short-stroke piston); when impelled by a rush of gas, this tappet is driven violently back for about 0.32-inch (8mm) and the end outside the gas chamber—which is in contact with the operating slide—drives the slide back. The rear end of this slide has a cam track which, acting on a lug on the bolt, cams the bolt round to unlock and then opens it to extract the empty case. A return spring then drives the slide back, taking the bolt with it to load a fresh round from the magazine and rotate the bolt to lock. During the rearward stroke of the bolt the firing hammer has been cocked, and the weapon is thus ready for the next shot.

Length: 35.65in (905mm). **Weight unloaded:** 5lb 7oz (2.48kg). **Barrel:** 18.00in (457mm), 4 grooves, right-hand twist. **Magazine:** 15- or 30-round detachable box. **Muzzle velocity:** c.1950 ft/sec (593 m/sec).

• US Carbine, Caliber 30, M1A1

This was the same basic weapon as the M1, with the addition of a folding metal stock for the convenience of parachute and airborne troops.

• US Carbine, Caliber 30, M2

The original specification for the Carbine M1 demanded provision for selective fire capability, but this was dropped during the course of development, and in due course, the production guns were capable only of semi-automatic fire. But after the M1 had been in service for a short time, a demand arose from the users for an automatic capability,

The M1 carbine in its original form, with 15-round magazine and magazine pouch attached to the butt.

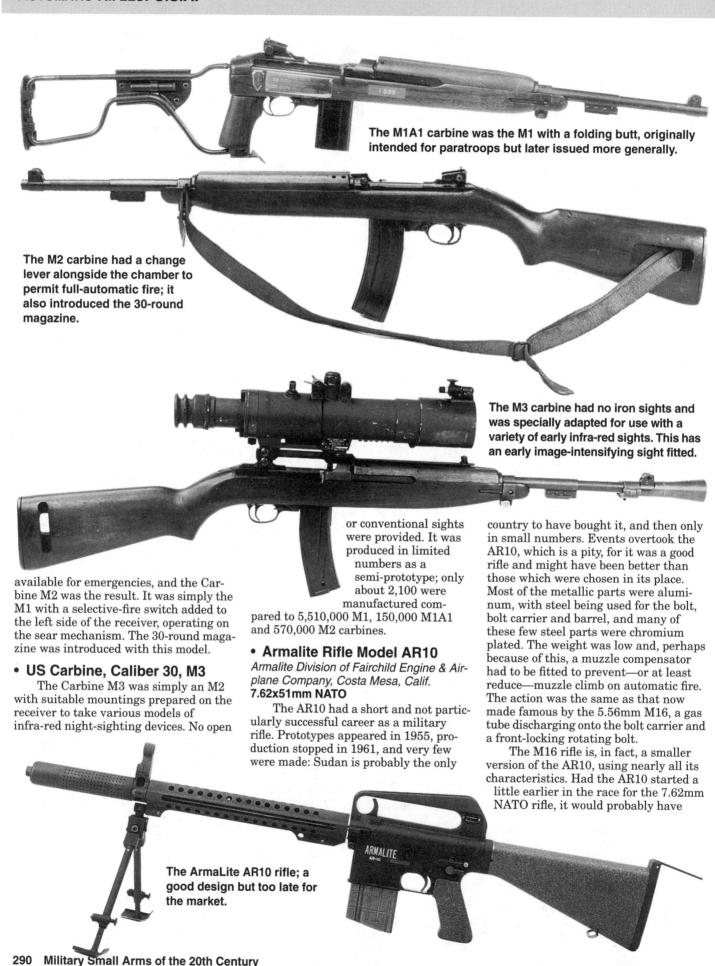

The M1A1 carbine was the M1 with a folding butt, originally intended for paratroops but later issued more generally.

The M2 carbine had a change lever alongside the chamber to permit full-automatic fire; it also introduced the 30-round magazine.

The M3 carbine had no iron sights and was specially adapted for use with a variety of early infra-red sights. This has an early image-intensifying sight fitted.

available for emergencies, and the Carbine M2 was the result. It was simply the M1 with a selective-fire switch added to the left side of the receiver, operating on the sear mechanism. The 30-round magazine was introduced with this model.

• US Carbine, Caliber 30, M3

The Carbine M3 was simply an M2 with suitable mountings prepared on the receiver to take various models of infra-red night-sighting devices. No open or conventional sights were provided. It was produced in limited numbers as a semi-prototype; only about 2,100 were manufactured compared to 5,510,000 M1, 150,000 M1A1 and 570,000 M2 carbines.

• Armalite Rifle Model AR10
Armalite Division of Fairchild Engine & Airplane Company, Costa Mesa, Calif.
7.62x51mm NATO

The AR10 had a short and not particularly successful career as a military rifle. Prototypes appeared in 1955, production stopped in 1961, and very few were made: Sudan is probably the only country to have bought it, and then only in small numbers. Events overtook the AR10, which is a pity, for it was a good rifle and might have been better than those which were chosen in its place. Most of the metallic parts were aluminum, with steel being used for the bolt, bolt carrier and barrel, and many of these few steel parts were chromium plated. The weight was low and, perhaps because of this, a muzzle compensator had to be fitted to prevent—or at least reduce—muzzle climb on automatic fire. The action was the same as that now made famous by the 5.56mm M16, a gas tube discharging onto the bolt carrier and a front-locking rotating bolt.

The M16 rifle is, in fact, a smaller version of the AR10, using nearly all its characteristics. Had the AR10 started a little earlier in the race for the 7.62mm NATO rifle, it would probably have

The ArmaLite AR10 rifle; a good design but too late for the market.

The US M14 rifle was really a Garand with a 20-shot removable magazine and a few other minor refinements.

been most successful; as it was, it came too late and never made the grade with any country.

Length: 40.00in (1016mm). **Weight unloaded:** 7lb 8oz (3.40kg). **Barrel:** 20.00in (508mm), 4 grooves, right-hand twist. **Magazine:** 20-round detachable box. **Cyclic rate:** 700 rds/min. **Muzzle velocity:** c.2500 ft/sec (761 m/sec).

• US Rifle, Caliber 7.62mm NATO, M14

Springfield Armory, Springfield, Mass.; Harrington & Richardson Arms Company, Worcester, Mass.; Winchester-Western Arms Division of Olin-Mathieson Corporation, New Haven, Conn.; Thompson-Ramo-Woolridge, Cleveland, Ohio.
7.62x51mm NATO

When the NATO nations decided to adopt a common cartridge in 1953, it became a matter of urgency for them all to find new weapons to fire it. The majority of the Europeans opted for versions of the FN light rifle, but in the United States at that time it was unthinkable for a foreign design to be accepted. The resultant American design, which became the Rifle M14, was simply a modernized and improved Rifle M1 (Garand). There are a number of physical differences from the Garand, but the parentage is quite obvious. The M14 is, though, capable of both semiautomatic and fully automatic fire and in this it was the first American rifle to do so other than the early versions of the BAR. The 20-round magazine is a great improvement on the 8-round magazine on the Garand, and there is a light bipod for use when the rifle is intended as a squad automatic.

The M14 is generally used with the selector locked in the semi-automatic role. It is a little too light to be effective as a fully automatic weapon, and as the barrel is not interchangeable there is a danger of it overheating. There have been several variations on the basic design, including at least two varieties of folding stock, and a special model for snipers known as the M21. This latter is most carefully selected and assembled and is fitted with the Leatherwood Redfield telescope sight with rangefinding

reticle. It is an extremely accurate weapon which saw considerable combat use in Vietnam. Mass production of the M14 ended in 1963, when roughly, 1,380,000 had been made. The production machinery was sold to Taiwan in 1967 and the rifle went into production there as the 'Model 57', about a million being made before production ceased in the late 1980s.

Length: 44.00in (1117mm). **Weight unloaded:** 8lb 9oz (3.88kg). **Barrel:** 22.00in (558mm), 4 grooves, right-hand twist. **Magazine:** 20-round detachable box. **Cyclic rate:** 750 rds/min. **Muzzle velocity:** c.2800 ft/sec (853 m/sec).

• Rifle Automatic 7.62mm M14A1

Springfield Armory, Springfield, Mass.
7.62x51mm NATO

The M14A1 was a variant of the standard M14 rifle and was intended to be usable as a light machine gun and thus add some extra firepower to the infantry squad. The gun used the standard action and barrel of the M14 mounted in a stock which had a pistol grip for the right hand and a straighter butt. The latter was a gesture towards controlling the movement of the gun when firing automatic. A further attempt to reduce recoil is the fitting of a light sheet-metal sleeve over the muzzle which acted as a compensator. Beneath the forend of the stock was a folding grip for the left hand and a light bipod was clipped to the gas regulator. These additions do not make a machine gun of what

was basically a semi-automatic rifle, and only small numbers of the M14A1 were made and issued to the US Army. Data for the M14A1 is the same as for the M14 except that weight was 12lb 12oz (5.78kg).

• US Rifle, Caliber 5.56mm, M16 and M16A1

Colt's Patent Firearms Manufacturing Company, Hartford, Conn. (now known as Colt's Manufacturing Co. Inc.)
5.56x45mm M193

Eugene Stoner, a prolific and talented inventor of small arms, produced the Armalite while he was employed by the Fairchild Engine and Airplane Company in the late 1950s. The rifle was developed in 1956 to an army specification, and Stoner chose to use the existing 222 Remington cartridge with an improved bullet, and in many ways the rifle is a scaled-down AR10—as already noted in the section on that gun. In July 1959, production of the rifle was licensed to Colt, and the AR15 made its name by being adopted by the smaller nations of Southeast Asia in the early 1960s. The AR15 was an ideal size for smaller men to carry in the jungle, and from this beginning it gradually came to be used and finally accepted by the United States forces operating in Vietnam. It eventually became the standard rifle of the United States Army.

The AR15 mechanism used a direct gas tube which delivered a blast of gas from the barrel to the front face of the bolt carrier. This moved back under the gas

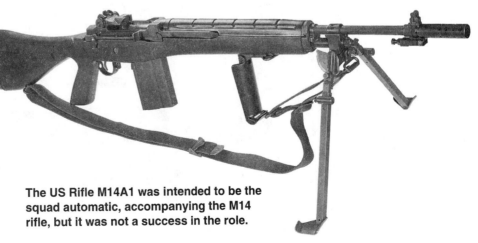

The US Rifle M14A1 was intended to be the squad automatic, accompanying the M14 rifle, but it was not a success in the role.

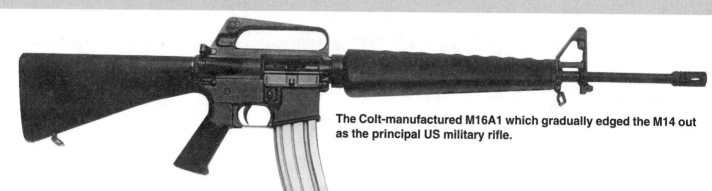

The Colt-manufactured M16A1 which gradually edged the M14 out as the principal US military rifle.

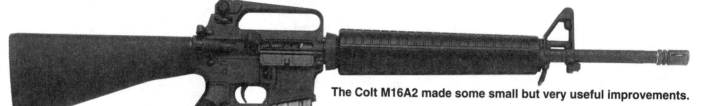

The Colt M16A2 made some small but very useful improvements.

impulse and, by means of a cam, rotated that bolt inside the carrier, so the its lugs unlocked from the chamber. The carrier and bolt then ran back, compressing a return spring. The spring then thrust carrier and bolt forward, stripping a round out of the magazine as they did so, chambering the round and finally closing the breech. The final movement forward of the bolt carrier rotated the bolt into the locked position. The rearward stroke of the carrier had also cocked the firing mechanism.

When the rifle was first adopted, problems appeared in service in Vietnam. As originally designed, the gas system had been 'tuned' to the then-standard military rifle powder, but the US Army then changed the powder specification to a formula which generated excessive fouling in the M16. This, together with some ill-advised instructions about minimal maintenance, led to the M16 acquiring a reputation for jamming, but common-sense instruction on the need for daily maintenance and cleaning eventually cured the problem.

The basic M16 was soon modified into the M16A1, the principal change being a positive bolt closure device which helped overcome a tendency for cartridges to stick as they were being loaded. This was standardized in 1967 and remained the principal US Army rifle until supplanted by the M16A2 in 1983.

Length: 39.00in (990mm). **Weight unloaded:** 6lb 5oz (2.86kg). **Barrel:** 20.00in (508mm), 4 grooves, right-hand twist. **Magazine:** 30-round detachable box. **Cyclic rate:** 800 rds/min. **Muzzle velocity:** c.3250 ft/sec (988 m/sec).

• US Rifle, M16A2/A3
Colt Industries, Hartford, Conn.
5.56x45mm NATO

This is an improved version of the M16A1 design. The changes consist of a three-round burst facility in addition to the automatic and single-shot options; a heavier barrel with a rifling twist of one turn in 7 inches, the optimum for the new NATO standard bullet; a new rear sight incorporating adjustments for windage and elevation; buttstock, handguard and pistol grip of new, stronger, plastic materials, and a new combined flash suppresser and compensator which omits the bottom vent used on the M16A1 so as to reduce muzzle climb and dust dispersion. An unusual feature is a molded excrescence on the right side of the receiver, behind the ejection port, which is a cartridge deflector to prevent ejected cases being flung into the face of left-handed shooters.

The M16A3, introduced in 1996, is a modification of the M16A2 in which the carrying handle can be removed to expose a low-set mounting rail for a variety of optical and electro-optical sights.

Length: 39.625in (1006mm). **Weight unloaded:** 7lb 14oz (3.58kg). **Barrel:** 20.0in (508mm), 6 grooves, right-hand twist. **Magazine:** 30-round detachable box. **Cyclic rate:** 600-940 rds/min. **Muzzle velocity:** 3260 ft/sec (99l m/sec).

• Port Firing Weapon M231
Colt Industries, Hartford, Conn.
5.56x45mm

This is a highly modified M16A1 rifle, designed solely for use in the firing ports of the US M2 Bradley Infantry Fighting Vehicle. The mechanism is that of the M16A1 rifle except that it fires from an open bolt, and most parts are interchangeable; it uses the M16A1 magazine. There is a quick-lock collar around the barrel which engages in the firing port, so that the firer is inside the protection of the armored vehicle; there are no sights on the weapon, since sighting is done through a periscope or vision block in the vehicle and fire is corrected by observing tracer bullets. In an emergency the weapon can be removed from the firing port mount and can be fired as a personal weapon, using the carrying handle as a rudimentary sight.

Length: 28.4in (710mm). **Weight, unloaded:** 8lb 8oz (3.90kg). **Barrel:** 14.5in

The M231 Firing Port Weapon is a stripped-down M16 design with a special fitting to allow firing through the side ports of the Bradley fighting vehicle.

(368mm), 6 grooves, right-hand twist. **Magazine:** 30-round detachable box. **Cyclic rate:** 1100-1300 rds/min. **Muzzle velocity:** 3000 ft/sec (914 m/sec).

• Advanced Combat Rifle (ACR)

In the late 1970s the US Army began looking forward to its next generation infantry rifle, to be fielded some time in the mid-1990s. It issued contracts for a caseless solution and sat back to await developments. In the early 1980s it had second thoughts and issued further contracts for non-caseless solutions, just to make sure that no idea, however outlandish, would be overlooked. Finally, it selected four designs, by AAI, Colt, Heckler & Koch and Steyr-Mannlicher, as being feasible and asked for prototypes to be made. They then arranged a complex and exhaustive testing program, with the Colt M16A2 as the 'control' weapon. The object in view was to finish up with a rifle which would offer a 100 percent improvement in first round hit probability. Tests were conducted in 1989/90. The final word was that none of the contestants produced the desired degree of improvement, and the program was closed down.

Although the rifles never reached production, they are included here since they give a valuable pointer to possible 21st century designs. Note also that some details of the weapons have never been released to the public. The Steyr rifle will be found under 'Austria'.

• AAI ACR

AAI Corporation, Hunt Valley, Md.
5.56mm Flechette

This was a gas-operated rifle firing a flechette cartridge. It is perhaps more conventional than the Steyr or H&K entrants, and had a long unobstructed top surface to act as an aid to quick alignment. It was a modified version of a 'serial bullet rifle' developed in the mid-1970s and it is believed to have used a triple-chamber breech unit formed as a segment of a circle and pivoted so that the three chambers swing past the rear end of the barrel and fire in rapid succession. The closed-bolt mechanism had a two-position selector for single shots or three-round bursts; there was no provision for automatic fire. The flechette cartridge used the standard 5.56x45mm case. The gas characteristics of this round demand that the gas tap for the rifle's action be closer to the chamber than is customary; a slight drawback was that the chamber would accept conventional 5.56mm rounds, but if these were to be fired, the very different gas characteristics could cause dangerous malfunctions. For safety purposes, therefore, the magazine interface would not accept any conventional rifle magazine, and the dedicated magazine would not accept conventional bulleted cartridges. The rifle was provided with optical and iron sights, with a quick-release lever to permit the optical sight to be removed and another type of sight fitted to the mounting.

Length: 40.0in (1016mm). **Weight unloaded:** 7lb 12oz (3.53kg). **Barrel:** not known. **Magazine:** 30-round detachable box. **Muzzle velocity:** 4600 ft/sec (1402 m/sec).

• Colt ACR

Colt's Industries, Firearms Division, Hartford, Conn.
5.56x45mm NATO or Duplex

The Colt ACR was a gas-operated weapon derived from the existing M16A2. The handguard, pistol grip and stock were redesigned and the butt telescoped and incorporated a cheekpiece. The operating system was the same as that of the M16A2 but the barrel had an advanced muzzle brake/compensator to improve control and reduce recoil. There was an ambidextrous fire selector giving single shot and full automatic modes. There were iron sights and also a 3.5-power optical sight; this could be removed, leaving a mount which would accept other types of optical or electro-optical sights. For instinctive shooting, there was a long shotgun-type rib along the top of the weapon. The Colt ACR fired the NATO standard 5.56x45mm round, but was particularly designed for a new Duplex cartridge developed by Colt and Olin Industries (Winchester). Both rounds used the same cartridge case, but the Duplex round carried two projectiles, one behind the other, each using a hard steel core in a gilding metal jacket. The two bullets weighed 2.26g (front) and 2.14g (rear) and this round was specifically designed for use at ranges up to 325m. The leading bullet would go to the point of aim, while the other would have a slight random dispersion around the point of aim to compensate sighting errors.

Length: 40.60in (1031mm). **Weight unloaded:** 7lb 5oz (3.31kg). **Barrel:** not known. **Magazine:** 30-round detachable box. **Muzzle velocity:** 3110 ft/sec (948 m/sec).

• Heckler & Koch ACR

Heckler & Koch GmbH, Oberndorf-am-Neckar, Germany
4.92x34mm Caseless

This is obviously based upon the G11 rifle, though there may have been slight internal differences. It was a

The AAI Advanced Combat Rifle, with optical sight.

The Colt Advanced Combat Rifle had a lot in common with the M16 family.

The Heckler & Koch Advanced Combat Rifle was the German G11 caseless cartridge weapon in a new suit.

gas-operated bullpup with the options of single shots, three-round bursts and full automatic fire. For a general description of the system, reference should be made to the entry on the G11 rifle under 'Germany'. The US version was described as being 4.92mm caliber, but it should be pointed out that this notation is peculiar to this rifle and is arrived at by measuring the bore diameter from the bottom of the grooves; every other rifle measures diameter from the surface of the lands, and by this notation this is a 4.7mm rifle, using exactly the same ammunition as the German G11.

Length: 29.53in (750mm). **Weight, unloaded:** 8lb 9oz (3.90kg). **Barrel:** not known. **Magazine:** 50-round detachable box. **Muzzle velocity:** 3000 ft/sec (914 m/sec).

• Stoner Automatic Rifle M63A1
Cadillac Gage Company, Detroit, Mich.
5.56x45mm

The Stoner rifle was part of the Stoner System of small arms, a system which was unique at the time of its introduction. The idea was to have a number of 'modules' which could be combined and permutated to construct a number of different weapons; this idea has since been employed by several designers (eg the Steyr AUG) but in 1963 it was entirely novel.

The Stoner system consisted of fifteen assemblies and a machine gun tripod from which a complete small arms series could be constructed. The assault rifle was the second in the series, coming after the carbine; it was an attractive weapon, robust and well made, but the idea of interchangeability had yet to appeal to an army. The United States Marine Corps did, however, carry out extensive testing with Stoner weapons and some changes and improvements were made to the basic model. The rifle eventually had a light bipod fitted to it which folded under the handguard, and a more positive action in folding the stock. The operating system of the Stoner patterns was similar to that of the Armalite series, using direct gas action from a port near the muzzle, and a rotating bolt with forward locking lugs. The barrels of all the Stoner variants were easily removed and, although this is of no great importance to the rifle, it was needed in the light machine gun role. Inevitably in a system such as this, where one set of components has to be rearranged to fulfil several tasks, there must be some compromise and it is noticeable that the carbine and rifle versions were a little heavier than some other designs specifically produced for one job. The Stoner weapons never entered service with any army in more than trial quantities, and the inventor turned to other things, but there were signs of a revival of interest in the system shortly before his death in 1997.

Length: 40.25in (1023mm). **Weight unloaded:** 7lb 12oz (3.51kg). **Barrel:** 20.00in (508mm), 6 grooves, right-hand twist. **Magazine:** 30-round detachable box. **Cyclic rate:** 700 rds/min. **Muzzle velocity:** c.3250 ft/sec (988 m/sec).

• Armalite Combat Rifle 5.56mm AR18
Armalite Inc., Costa Mesa, California; Sterling Armaments Ltd., Dagenham, Essex
5.56mmx45mm

This rifle was developed as a result of the experience gained by the Armalite company in the production of other rifles in the series. There was a growing realization that the 5.56mm cartridge was a feasible military round and that the lighter weapons were attractive. But the AR15 was not easy to make without modern plants and machinery, and Armalite realized there were many potential customers who would wish to make the rifle under license but who did not have the necessary industrial capacity. The AR18 was therefore designed to be easily manufactured on relatively simple machinery; it also incorporated improvements which offered the maximum simplicity in both manufacture and maintenance. In some respects the AR18 was similar to the AR15, though the systems are really very different, particularly in using a gas piston system instead of direct gas. The AR18 uses steel stampings instead of the alloy forgings of the AR15, thus considerably reducing the cost of manufacture. The design was simplified, leading to greater reliability and easier cleaning and handling. It was tested by the US Army who decided that it had military potential but, having settled on the M16, they did not adopt it. Production was subsequently licensed to Howa Machinery in Japan, NWM in Holland and Sterling Armaments in Britain. No military contracts were forthcoming, however, since countries which might, in the past, have bought the rifle were now more intent upon setting up their own facilities and making their own weapons. A commercial semi-automatic version, the AT180, was made from 1967 to 1973 in Japan, and in the late 1970s by Sterling, but relatively few were sold

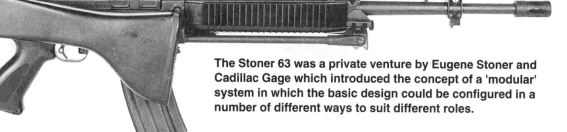

The Stoner 63 was a private venture by Eugene Stoner and Cadillac Gage which introduced the concept of a 'modular' system in which the basic design could be configured in a number of different ways to suit different roles.

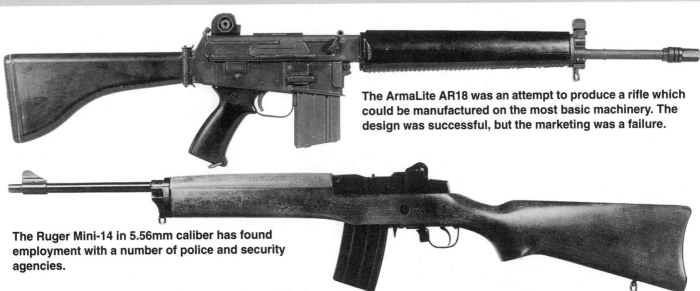

The ArmaLite AR18 was an attempt to produce a rifle which could be manufactured on the most basic machinery. The design was successful, but the marketing was a failure.

The Ruger Mini-14 in 5.56mm caliber has found employment with a number of police and security agencies.

and the license eventually passed to a company in the Philippines, who have never got any further with it.

Length, stock extended: 38.00in (965mm). stock retracted: 28.75in (730mm). **Weight unloaded:** 6lb 11oz (3.04kg). **Barrel:** 18-25in (463mm), 4 grooves, right-hand twist. **Magazine:** 20-round detachable box. **Cyclic rate:** 750 rds/min. **Muzzle velocity:** c.3250 ft/sec (990 m/sec).

• Ruger Mini-14
Sturm, Ruger & Co., Southport, Conn.
5.56x45mm

This rifle was introduced by Sturm, Ruger & Co. in 1973; it is mechanically much the same as the US M1 Garand, a gas-actuated rifle with rotating bolt, but due to ballistic considerations it is by no means a simple scale-down job. One of the principal attractions of this rifle is that, due to the lower recoil force derived from the 5.56mm bullet, it becomes possible to develop a light rifle which can be fired at full automatic and still give a reasonable chance of hitting the target. The gas system uses a cupped piston head surrounding the gas outlet from the barrel, so that the piston is given a brief impulse before the gas is exhausted to atmosphere; the piston thereafter relies upon its own momentum to rotate and open the bolt. At the same time the hammer is cocked and held by the sear. A return spring closes the bolt and the hammer is released by the trigger in the conventional manner

Variations of the Mini-14 include a stainless steel version; the Mini-14/20GB infantry rifle which has a bayonet

lug and flash suppresser; and the AC-556 described below.
Length: 37.25in (946mm). **Weight:** 6lb 6oz (2.90kg). **Barrel:** 18.50in (470mm), 6 grooves, right-hand twist. **Magazine:** 5-, 10-, 20- or 30-round detachable box. **Muzzle velocity:** 3300 ft/sec (1005 m/sec).

• Ruger AC-556
Sturm, Ruger & Co., Southport, Conn.
5.56x45mm

The AC-556 has been specially designed for military and law enforcement use and though it resembles the other 5.56mm rifles in the Ruger range, it has certain significant differences. It is fully selective and incorporates a 3-round burst counter. The glass fiber handguard is heat-resistant and ventilated. The front sight is fully protected and carries a bayonet lug, while the muzzle has a flash suppresser. The rifle is intentionally robust and capable of withstanding rough treatment without degrading the performance or endangering the firer. The AC-556 is in production and foreign sales have been made.
Length: 38.75in (984mm). **Weight unloaded:** 6lb 6oz (2.89kg). **Barrel:** 18.50in (470mm), 6 grooves, right-hand

twist. **Magazine:** 20- or 30-round box. **Cyclic rate:** 750 rds/min. **Muzzle velocity:** 3394 ft/sec (1058 m/sec).

YUGOSLAVIA

• M59/66
Zavodi Crvena Zastava, Kragujevac
7.62x39mm Soviet

This closely resembles the Soviet SKS from which it was derived, by way of the earlier M59 rifle, a direct SKS copy. The principal change lies in the forming of the muzzle into a spigot-type grenade-launcher and a ladder-type grenade-firing sight, behind the launcher, which folds down flat behind the front sight when not required. As with the SKS there is a folding bayonet beneath the barrel, but due to the length of the grenade-launcher there is less free blade in front of the muzzle when the bayonet is fixed.

Length: 44.10in (1120mm). **Weight unloaded:** 9lb 1oz (4.10kg). **Barrel:** 19.70in (500mm), 4 grooves, right-hand twist. **Magazine:** 10-round integral box. **Muzzle velocity:** c.2720 ft/sec (735 m/sec).

The Ruger AC-556 is really a highly militarized version of the Mini-14, but it appears not to be as popular as the standard Mini-14.

• Rifle Model 64, Model 64B, and Model 70

Zavodi Crvena Zastava, Kragujevac
7.62x39mm Soviet M43

The Automatic 64 series are assault rifles, based on the Soviet Kalashnikov and developed at the Yugoslav State arms factory at Kragujevac. The M64 is a straight copy of the AK47, although the Yugoslavs have added an integral grenade-launcher sight mounted on top of the gas-tube assembly; in order to use the grenade launcher, a special muzzle attachment must be substituted for the flash-suppresser/compensator unit. The M64A and the M64B are also similar in design to the AK, although the Yugoslav derivatives have shorter barrels of 14.75in (375mm) instead of the original 16.50in (419mni) barrel of the AK and the M64. Grenade launchers are also fitted to both the M64A and the M64B, although the muzzle attachments still have to be altered, and the M64B also has a folding stock which swings up and over the top of the receiver.

The Model 70 differs very slightly in a few minor components, the most noticeable being the pistol grip, which is straight—the 64 had finger serrations.

(M64A)

Length, including flash-suppresser: 37.68in (957mm). **Weight unloaded:** 8lb 5oz (3.75kg). **Barrel:** 14.75in (375min), 4 grooves, right-hand twist. **Magazine:** 30-round detachable box. **Cyclic rate:** c.600 rds/min. **Muzzle velocity:** c.2300 ft/sec (700 m/sec).

• M70B1, M70AB2

Zavodi Crvena Zastava, Kragujevac
7.62x39mm Soviet

This is the most recent in a series of Kalashnikov copies, beginning with the M64 and M70. The M70B1 is based on the Soviet AKM, while the M70AB2 is a folding stock model based on the AKMS. The only significant difference is that these weapons are provided with a grenade-launcher unit which can be readily attached to the muzzle when required, and have a ladder-type grenade sight attached to the front end of the gas cylinder and coupled to the gas regulator. The sight normally lies flat on the gas tube, and when required is lifted to the vertical position; this movement automatically shuts off the gas supply to the gas cylinder, so ensuring that all the power of the cartridge is used in propelling the grenade.

(M70B1)

Length: 35.43in (900mm). **Weight unloaded:** 8lb 2oz (3.70kg). **Barrel:** 16.34in (415mm), 4 grooves, right-hand twist. **Magazine:** 30-round detachable box. **Cyclic rate:** c.640 rds/min. **Muzzle velocity:** c.2300 ft/sec (720 m/sec).

• M76 Sniping rifle

Zavodi Crvena Zastava, Kragujevac
7.92x57mm Mauser

This uses the same basic Kalashnikov mechanism as the M70 rifles but is more robust and larger, as required by the more powerful 7.92mm Mauser cartridge and fires only in the semi-automatic mode. It is standard issue to snipers of the Yugoslav Army and variant models chambered for the 7.62x51mm NATO and 7.62x54R Soviet cartridges have been developed for export. The rifle is fitted with the usual type of iron sights associated with the Kalashnikov family of weapons, but in addition has a mount on the receiver top to accept a telescope sight which appears to be closely modeled on the Soviet PSO-1. It has also been seen with electro-optical image-intensifying sights attached to the same mount.

Length: 44.68in (1135mm). **Weight unloaded:** 9lb 4oz (4.20kg). **Barrel:** 21.65in (550mm), 4 grooves, right-hand twist. **Magazine:** 10-round detachable box. **Muzzle velocity:** c.2300 ft/sec (720 m/sec).

• Rifle Model 80, Model 80A

Zavodi Crvena Zastava, Kragujevac

5.56x45mm

These rifles resemble the M70 series in being Kalashnikov copies, but they are chambered for the 5.56x45mm cartridge and may be rifled either one turn in 178mm for use with the US M193 cartridge or one turn in 305mm for use with the NATO-standard SS109 bullet. The gas regulator has been redesigned so as to give consistent performance with ammunition of varying energy levels, and the muzzles carry closed-prong flash hiders. Accessory grenade-launchers and sights are available. These weapons were not issued to Yugoslav forces but were developed solely for export. The M80 has a fixed wooden butt; the M80A has a folding steel butt which hinges down and forward to fold beneath the receiver.

(M80)

Length, fixed stock: 38.97in (990mm). **Weight unloaded:** 7lb 14oz (3.60kg). **Barrel:** 18.11in (460mm), 6 grooves, right-hand twist. **Magazine:** 20- or 30-round detachable box. **Cyclic rate:** 600 rds/min. **Muzzle velocity:** 3182 ft/sec (970 m/sec).

The Yugoslavian M59/66A1 is based on the Russian SKS but has the muzzle shaped into a grenade launcher and carries a special grenade-firing sight.

The Yugoslavian M76 sniping rifle is a long-barreled copy of the Kalashnikov design, chambered for the 7.92x57mm Mauser.

MACHINE GUNS

THE HISTORY OF the machine gun can be considered in three periods—the 'mediaeval' period of battery guns, which began in the 14th century and lasted until the 1860s; the 'mechanical' period of hand-cranked guns which lasted a mere thirty years from 1860 to 1890; and the 'automatic' period which began with Maxim's first successful gun of 1884 and is likely to last for a very long time to come.

A few of the hand-operated guns, such as the Gatling, Gardner and Nordenfelt, remained in military inventories into the first few years of the 20th century, principally in fortifications, but they were obsolete holdovers and are not further considered here. By the turn of the century the Maxim had gained a firm foothold, although their tactical handling remained the subject of debate and trial. The same could be said of the few competing designs such as the Colt and Skoda.

One early design which differed greatly from all the others was the Danish Madsen; by modern definition, the Madsen was a 'light' machine gun, capable of being carried by one man and operated by two, supported on a bipod, fired from the shoulder and fed from a box magazine above the gun. It had actually begun life as a semiautomatic rifle, but was not successful in that role and had been redesigned into a more practical weapon. But practical for what? That was the tactical problem facing the Madsen gun.

The debate was fueled further by the Russo-Japanese War of 1904. Here the Russian infantry had the Maxim, their cavalry the Madsen, and the Japanese had the Hotchkiss. As it happened, the Russian cavalry made very little impression on the course of the war, and their use of the Madsen went more or less unregarded. So far as the Maxim and Hotchkiss were concerned, it began to be realized that there was a place for the machine gun in the attack; hitherto, it had been largely considered as a defensive weapon, and had been handled as a form of miniature artillery. European armies decided that two Maxims—or their equivalent—per infantry battalion would be about right, giving them a base of covering fire during an attack and a solid addition to the rifle power in the defense.

The first decade of the century saw a few more new designs appear, notably the light Hotchkiss of 1909 (known as the Benet-Mercie in the US Army), the Bergmann, and the Vickers and Parabellum modifications to the original Maxim. Other designs were still in the exploratory stage when war broke out in 1914 and the world's machine gun factories were snowed under by orders for increased production. The Lewis light machine gun had also appeared in Europe just before the war and this was also called into production, not so much for its tactical possibilities, but for the simple fact that it took a great deal less material and time to make a Lewis than it did to make a Maxim or Vickers gun.

The machine gun came to dominate No Man's Land, in conjunction with wire, although it was never the major casualty-producer—that role was, as always, occupied by artillery. But as a defensive weapon it was supreme and certainly did great execution. The Lewis was also a useful defensive weapon but it soon became apparent that it was also the perfect accompaniment to the infantry section or squad in the attack, and from about mid-1915 the light machine guns began to increase in quantity, even though some of them were not as light as they ought to have been. The US Army was unfortunate in that it either chose or was forced to select a notably unsuccessful French design which probably influenced their thinking for the next thirty years. As a result the American authorities turned to John Browning's very attractive automatic rifle, which seemed to offer everything that the unreliable French machine guns did not. The BAR stayed in their infantry until replaced in the early 1950s by the M60, although it was never particularly successful in the light machine gun role.

The post-1918 years saw most European armies searching for the ideal light machine gun, since none of the wartime expedients had been thoroughly satisfactory. The French, who probably had the worst wartime collection, wisely began by discarding their 1886 cartridge and designing a new 7.5mm rimless round; that done, they then developed a light machine gun to fire it. The British, on the other hand, eventually settled on a Czech gun in 7.92mm caliber but demanded that it be redesigned to take their equally elderly rimmed 303-caliber cartridge; it is to the eternal credit of the Czech designer that he achieved the transition without losing the reliability of the original design. The result was, of course, the Bren, which, in either the original Czech or the modified British pattern, was probably the finest light machine gun of all time. and certainly the best of World War II.

After 1945 there was less urgency about replacing machine guns; the wartime models had almost all worked perfectly well and there was no great imperative for change. But in the 1950s came the first great caliber change, when NATO settled on the 7.62x51mm and the Soviet Bloc on the 7.62x39mm cartridge. With this change in prospect, new designs of machine guns could be contemplated, and this gave the theorists the chance to advance the claims for the General Purpose Machine gun (GPMG). This idea had been born in Germany before the war, but the point had been completely missed by everybody else until the war was almost over. The theory was that the same machine gun could serve both as a light weapon—mounted on a bipod and given a butt—or as a medium or 'sustained fire' weapon when mounted on a tripod. The sustained fire role calls for the ammunition to be supplied in belts, and thus in both roles the gun has to be belt-fed. (This, of course, delights those macho types who like to race into action draped in belts of ammunition, a glittering target which is God's gift to every rifleman within sight and with any pretensions towards marksmanship.) The idea has some definite plus points: one weapon to train on, one weapon to manufacture, maintain and supply, one cartridge for all weapons. But as time was to demonstrate, a belt-fed light machine gun is a contradiction in terms, and trying to run with a light machine gun and a dangling belt or a clamped-on belt box was a painful and frustrating exercise.

The second great caliber change in the 1980s, when the 7.62x51mm group shifted down to 5.56x45mm and the 7.62x39mm people changed to 5.45x39mm, gave everybody some pause for thought. If the infantry rifle was to be 5.56mm or 5.45mm, where did this leave the GPMG? The small calibers lost their authority after about 400 meters or yards of flight, and the machine gun is expected to be able to put down effective fire at greater ranges than that. But for the sake of convenience in supply, the rifle and the squad machine gun should fire the same ammunition.

Early attempts at a 5.56mm machine gun were bedeviled by wear problems, with guns shooting out their rifling within 5000 rounds or even less, and it took some years of trials to settle upon the correct form and twist of rifling and other features before the 5.56mm LMG was a reliable weapon. It was eventually achieved, after which the armies had to be persuaded to try the idea, but by the end of the 1980s the small-caliber light machine gun was a reality in several armies, while

the support gun has tended to remain with the larger and more powerful cartridge. Indeed, the Russians have yet to be persuaded to give up using their 7.62x54R rimmed cartridge from the 1890s in the machine gun role.

For those who wonder about the machine gun and the caseless cartridge, be assured that the designers have settled that question. Both Heckler and Koch of

Germany and Giat of France have developed workable designs for firing caseless ammunition, but the likelihood of these designs ever appearing in the flesh is remote in the extreme. If armies cannot afford caseless rifles, and consider them to show no technical advance over their existing weapons, there is not much chance that a caseless machine gun is ever going to see the light of day.

AUSTRIA-HUNGARY/ AUSTRIA

• Skoda machine guns, 1888--1913

Waffenwerke Skoda, Pilsen, Bohemia
8mm Patrone M90 and M93

The Skoda machine-guns were based on a patent granted in 1888 to Karl Salvator—an Austrian archduke—and Georg Ritter von Dormus, who was at that time a major in the army of Austria-Hungary. The guns relied upon an unusual system of delayed blowback operation in which resistance to the opening of the breech was afforded by a system of pivoting blocks and a large coil spring housed in the tube at the rear of the receiver; the principal locking member was, in fact, reminiscent of the Martini dropping block which had undergone considerable vogue during the period 1870-90, and which had seen considerable military application.

A special feature of the early Skoda models was the provision of a 'rate regulator' which, in the form of a pendant lever fitted with a sliding weight, hung below the receiver where it oscillated as the weapon fired. Through the variable center of gravity of the pendant lever, and the frictional forces inherent in the mechanism, it was possible to vary the cyclic rate to enable between 180 and 250 rounds to be fired in one minute.

Model 1893

The M93 was the first machine gun to be adopted by the authorities of Austria-Hungary when the Skoda weapon was adopted for the use of the navy and of personnel engaged in manning land fortifications; in these guises the gun generally appeared on a pedestal mount. The external appearance of the M93 was more than a little strange: apart from the pendant lever assembly protruding beneath the receiver and the spring housing (to which a shoulder stock was

usually fitted) extending rearwards, the mechanism was fitted with a skeletal top-mounted gravity-fed box magazine clamped to the receiver's left side. The M93 guns saw little action during the decade in which they served, apart from the handful present in the Boxer Rebellion of 1900 where they were used in the defense of the Austro-Hungarian legation at Peking. The gun's principal advantage was in the few working parts and—for their day they were quite reliable, but the design of the action precluded the use of all but the lowest-powered of service cartridges, and the top-mounted magazine was very prone to damage and malfunction.

Model 1902

The water-cooled M02 was a modified version of the M93, intended for more widespread land service and generally mounted on an unusual cranked tripod to which an armored shield was often added. The shield was almost essential to compensate for the very high mounting made necessary by the pendant lever. Much redesign was done to the feed and rate mechanisms to eliminate—with no great success—the more undesirable features of the earlier gun. A much stronger 30-round magazine was provided to reduce the feed problems, but the gravity system defied the efforts and was replaced on later weapons by an equally strange belt feed. Few M02 guns saw service, for during the same period the Schwarzlose was developed and brought to an end the aspirations of the Skoda company.

Model 1909

To compete with the Schwarzlose-system guns, which had been adopted in 1905 as the official machine gun of the Austro-Hungarian services, Skodawerke entirely redesigned their gun and the M09 was the result. The external pendant lever was discarded and the components of the M02 lock were redesigned, although the principle remained the same; a lubricator was added to the mechanism to oil the cartridges before they were chambered (just as in the Schwarzlose), which permitted an increase in the cyclic rate to

The Skoda M1909 machine gun with its peculiar belt feed.

The Schwarzlose machine gun.

425 rds/min. The gravity feed was replaced by a system making use of a 250-round fabric belt which entered the left underside of the receiver and emerged from the left top which must have done little to alleviate feed troubles. An improved optical sighting device was provided to replace the leaf sights of the earlier models.

Model 1913

The M13 was the last of the long-obsolescent Salvator-Dormus system guns; it saw limited service in World War I—with unspectacular results—in the hands of the Reserve and was thereafter replaced by supplies of the Schwarzlose M07/12. The Skoda M13 was mechanically similar to the earlier M09 with slight alterations made to the feed unit. A new heavy-duty tripod—the Dreifuss 13, smaller than those of 1902 and 1909—was introduced to lower the unit's silhouette, although in most instances, the armored shield was retained.

• Schwarzlose Models 05, 07, 07/12 and 07/16

Osterreichische Waffen-Gesellschaft, Steyr
8mm Mannlicher (Austrian), 7.92mm Mauser (German), 6.5mm Mauser (Dutch)

The Schwarzlose machine gun was the only unlocked-breech design (the FIAT-Revelli had a form of locking wedge) to see widespread service use. It relied entirely upon the mass of the breechblock and a toggle lever which worked at a severe mechanical disadvantage when the breechblock first started to open. The barrel was short to ensure that the breech pressure dropped as soon as possible, and this affected the muzzle velocity and maximum range.

The first models of 1905 and 1907 were fitted with an oil pump to lubricate the rounds as they were fed into the breech, but by 1912, this had been abandoned and more weight was added to the bolt in order to force the dry rounds into the chamber. There are disadvantages to the blowback method of operation for medium machine guns, but the Schwarzlose was popular for its simplicity and strength. It was, however, sensitive to adverse conditions and ammunition variations. It was sold commercially throughout Europe until 1918 and was adopted by several mid-European countries. It was still in use in Italy and Hungary in 1945 as a second-line weapon. A lightened version of the basic design—sometimes called the Maschinengewehr 07/16—was also manufactured for aircraft use during World War I: largely owing to the low cyclic rate and the short barrel, it was not a success.

Length: 42.00in (1066mm). **Weight unloaded:** 44lb 0oz (19.9kg). **Barrel:** 20.75in (526mm), 4 grooves, right-hand twist. **Magazine:** 250-round fabric belt. **Cyclic rate:** 400 rds/min. **Muzzle velocity:** c.2050 ft/sec (625 m/sec).

• Armee Universal Gewehr, Heavy Barrel (AUG/HBAR)

Steyr-Mannlicher AG, Steyr
5.56x45mm

This is basically the AUG rifle (described in the 'Automatic Rifles' section), but fitted with a heavy barrel and a bipod to act in the light automatic role. The barrel is supplied in either 178mm, 228mm or 305mm pitch of rifling, and a muzzle attachment acts as a flash hider and reduces recoil and muzzle climb during automatic firing.

There are two different versions, the HBAR and HBAR/T: the former has the carrying handle with built-in optical sight as on the AUG rifle; the latter has a mounting bar on which any sighting telescope or night vision sight can be fitted. Both the HBAR and the HBAR/ T can, if required, be further modified to fire from an open bolt; a new hammer assembly is inserted into the butt and a new cocking piece is fitted to the bolt assembly. This modification can be made retrospectively to weapons already issued to military forces. Changing to open-bolt firing does not change any of the firing characteristics.

Length: 35.43in (900mm). **Weight unloaded:** 10lb 12oz (4.90kg). **Barrel:** 24.45in (621mm), 6 grooves, pitch of rifling variable (see text). **Magazine:** 30- or 42-round detachable box. **Cyclic rate:** 680 rds/min. **Muzzle velocity:** c.3280 ft/sec (1000 m/sec).

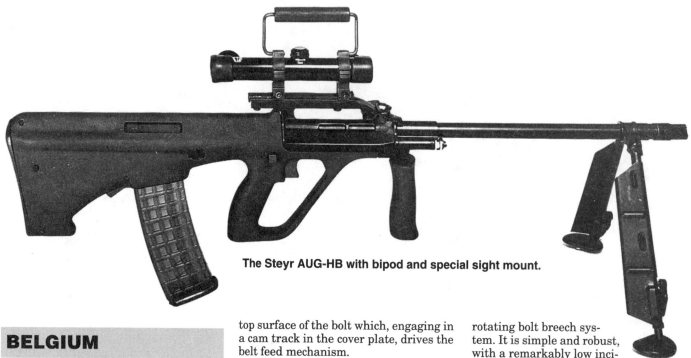

The Steyr AUG-HB with bipod and special sight mount.

BELGIUM

• Mitrailleur d'Appui Generale (MAG)
FN Herstal SA, Liege
7.62x51mm NATO

Like most Fabrique Nationale designs, the MAG machine gun is a sound, reliable and well engineered weapon which has been adopted—especially by NATO-aligned countries—throughout the world. In common with many other manufacturers, FN had looked at the numerous designs which World War II had thrown into prominence and, also like many others, were impressed by the simple and effective feed systems developed for the German MG42. Fabrique Nationale had been involved with Browning designs for so many years that it is hardly surprising to find that the gas operation of the MAG is basically that of the Browning Automatic Rifle. The principal difference lies in the inversion of the bolt so that the locking movement is in a downward direction. This permits a lug to be formed on the top surface of the bolt which, engaging in a cam track in the cover plate, drives the belt feed mechanism.

There are minor variations in the appearance of various models of MAG—finned barrels, smooth barrels, stocks, spade grips and so forth—which largely reflect the national preference of the customers. They all employ the same basic mechanism.

Length: 49.41in (1255mm). **Weight unloaded:** 24lb 4oz (11.0kg). **Barrel:** 21.46in (545mm), 4 grooves, right-hand twist. **Magazine:** metallic link belt. **Cyclic rate:** 650 to 1000 rds/min according to gas setting. **Muzzle velocity:** c.2800 ft/sec (853 m/sec).

• FN Minimi
FN Herstal SA, Liege
5.56x45mm NATO

The Minimi is a gas-operated weapon with a variable gas supply and a rotating bolt breech system. It is simple and robust, with a remarkably low incidence of stoppages during many military trials. The barrel is heavy and easily changed, features which permit sustained fire without a reduction in accuracy due to wear. The feed system is unusual in being able to fire from a belt or from an M16-type magazine without the need for adjustment. On top of the receiver is the usual belt feed which draws the belt through from the left side and strips the rounds out, feeding them into the chamber by two horns on top of the bolt. There are also two more horns on the lower left side of the bolt and these line up with a magazine housing below the belt aperture. When a magazine is inserted the lower horns load the cartridge into the chamber. There is a difference in the rate of fire, since when a belt is used

The FN MAG general purpose machine gun.

The FN Minimi, feeding from a belt and belt box.

The Minimi feeds equally well from an M16-type magazine.

The Minimi field-stripped.

The original FN 15mm BRG heavy machine gun.

the gun mechanism needs to lift the weight of the free portion of the belt; with a magazine there is no such load and thus the gun fires rather faster. There is a magazine cover which closes the magazine housing when a belt is being used, and closes off the belt aperture when opened to permit insertion of a magazine.

The Minimi has been adopted by the US Army as their M249 machine gun; it is also used by the Belgian, Australian, Canadian, Italian and other armies. A 'Paratroop' model with shorter barrel and telescoping butt is also made, for those requiring a more compact weapon. The design has also attracted copyists, not always with benefit of license.

Length: 40.94in (1040mm). **Weight unloaded:** 15lb 1oz (6.83kg). **Barrel:** 18.35in (466mm), 6 grooves, right-hand twist. **Magazine:** 100- or 200-round disintegrating link belt or 30-round (M16) box magazine. **Cyclic rate:** 700 to 1000 rds/min. **Muzzle velocity:** 3035 ft/sec (925 m/sec).

• FN-BRG-15 Heavy Machine Gun (1)

FN Herstal SA, Liege
15x115mm

This machine gun was first announced in October 1983 and was a new design intended to replace the Browning 50-caliber HB as a heavy machine gun. The weapon was gas-operated, the piston acting on a bolt carrier holding a rotating bolt which locked by four lugs into the barrel extension. The receiver was of pressed sheet steel and incorporated an integral elastic cradle which, when tripod or vehicle mounted, reduced the recoil force to 125kg. The weapon had dual feed, an ammunition belt entering each side of the receiver, and a selector lever at the rear permitted the gunner to select which belt he required. There was also a single-shot selector which was intended for use with specialized types of ammunition, such as discarding sabot armor-defeating rounds. The belts used disintegrating links and feed into the weapon from the top. The weapon was cocked by pulling on a cocking handle at the rear which was connected by a flexible cable to the bolt carrier.

Four safety devices were incorporated: a manual bolt lock in the rotary feed selector; a neutral position of the feed selector which threw both belts out of engagement; a safety catch under the bolt carrier which automatically functioned if the working parts failed to recoil completely to the rear; and a mechanism which prevented the firing pin from striking the cartridge unless the bolt was fully closed and locked.

The gun was fitted with simple mechanical sights, but provision was made for fitting whatever optical or night vision sight may be required. The ammunition fired by this gun was of totally new design; only API, tracer and practice bullets were manufactured, but designs of APDS, APFSDS and explosive projectiles were perfected for production at a later date. The standard API bullet weighed 50g (1.76oz or 770gr) and could penetrate a 10mm steel plate, inclined at 35°, at a range of 1350m. It was commonly said that the bullet would go through both sides of an armored personnel carrier at 1000 meters range.

Unfortunately the design ran into problems of barrel wear and inaccuracy which were even-

The dual-feed system of the 15mm BRG. The tuning-fork-shaped selector lever is across to the right and the right belt is feeding.

The later 15.5mm version of the FN BRG gun.

The dual feed of the 15.5mm BRG.

tually traced to the ammunition design. The 15mm design was abandoned and work began on a new model.

Length: 78.7in (2.00m). **Weight unloaded:** 121.2lb (55.0kg). **Barrel:** 53.14in (1.35m). **Magazine:** Dual, disintegrating link belts. **Cyclic rate:** 750 rds/min. **Muzzle velocity:** 3314 ft/sec (1010 m/sec).

• FN BRG-15 Heavy Machine Gun (2)

FN Herstal SA, Liege
15.5x106mm

The redesign of the BRG-15 amounted to a redesign of the ammunition; instead of adopting the configuration of a small arms bullet, it changed to a design using a driving band, similar in principle to a cannon shell. To obtain the desired ballistic characteristics with the new projectile a change of caliber to 15.5mm was necessary, and hence the gun had to be redesigned to suit the new caliber and also a new cartridge case. Otherwise the mechanism and appearance remained the same, with the same gas operation, rotating bolt, dual feed and safety systems.

Unfortunately, just as the design had been perfected, FN ran into organizational and financial problems, and in 1991 the decision was taken to shelve the BRG-15 and concentrate upon perfecting and marketing the P-90 personal defense weapon. The design has not, though, been abandoned and it is doubtless waiting its opportunity. This will undoubtedly come one day, because the BRG-15 can outperform every other machine gun in existence, and the Browning can't last for ever.

Length: 86.65in (2.15m). **Weight unloaded:** 132lb 4oz (60.0kg). **Barrel:** 59.05in (1.50m). **Magazine:** Dual, disintegrating link belts. **Cyclic rate:** 600 rds/min. **Muzzle velocity:** 3460 ft/sec (1055 m/sec).

The Uirapuru machine gun in its company support role, tripod-mounted.

BRAZIL

• Uirapuru Mekanika
Mekanika Industria Commercio Lda,
7.62x51mm NATO

This weapon began as a Brazilian Army research project in 1969; some prototypes were built but did not work very well, and in 1972 the Army, with other things to worry about, handed it over to private enterprise. This produced no results, and the project was given to a member of the original design team who produced a highly modified but successful weapon in 1976. After extensive trials it was approved for the Brazilian Army in 1979 and manufacture has continued since then.

The Uirapuru is a general-purpose machine gun capable of operating in the light, medium, or vehicle-mounted roles. It is gas-operated, the gas piston lying in the barrel cradle to the right side of the barrel and controlling the movement of a bolt with a dropping lever locking system. There is a quick-change barrel with carrying handle, and feed is by means of a disintegrating-link belt. The barrel has a very efficient muzzle brake.

Length: 51.18in (1300m). **Weight unloaded:** 21.75lb (9.90kg). **Barrel:** 23.50in (597mm). **Magazine:** Disintegrating link belt. **Cyclic rate:** 700 rds/min. **Muzzle velocity:** 2788 ft/sec (850 m/sec).

CANADA

• Huot Light Machine gun
Dominion Rifle Factory, Quebec
303 British

When the Mark 3 Ross rifle was replaced by the SMLE in 1916, some concern was expressed at the quantity of serviceable weapons being put into store for which no useful future could be foreseen. At that time, the labor force at the Dominion factory became short of work. In an effort to correct both of these deficiencies, plans were made for the factory to convert the Ross rifle to a light machine gun which became known as the Huot, after one of the designers.

The barrel was shortened and a bracket was screwed to the muzzle to take the cylinder and piston. A gas regulator was also fitted, and the barrel was covered by a sheet-steel tubular guard that extended back to the breech. The piston rod was linked to the bolt handle by a

The Uirapuru on a bipod as the squad automatic.

Canada's C7 Light Support Weapon, the Colt machine gun.

collar and acted directly upon it. As the Ross was a straight-pull action, there was no need for a cam to open the bolt; a simple reciprocating motion was sufficient. A buffer was fitted behind the breech to absorb the energy of the piston, and this too was covered with a sheet-steel casing, A drum magazine was added. The overall effect was ungainly and heavy-looking, but the gas action worked surprisingly well, and at a quoted cost of $50.00 per gun the Huot had distinct attractions as an adjunct to the Lewis gun—which, in 1917, was costing $1000. A prolonged trial at Hythe and Enfield showed that it had promise, although continuous firing did bring about several stoppages and some cook-offs. These, however, were to be expected from such a light weapon. The barrel wore out quickly, but even so, it lasted for 8000 rounds—which would have been adequate for a weapon in mass-production. In the event, the war ended before the gun could be made in quantity and the Huot was quickly dropped in the post-war disarmament rush.

Length: 47in (1193mm). **Weight unloaded:** 20lb (9.06kg). **Barrel:** 25in (635mm), 4 grooves, left-hand twist. **Magazine:** 25-round circular box. **Cyclic rate:** 475 rds/min. **Muzzle velocity:** c.2400 ft/sec (730 m/sec).

• C7 Light Support Weapon
Diemaco, Kitchener, Ontario.
5.56x45mm NATO

This weapon was developed by Diemaco of Canada in conjunction with Colt, and is also known as the Colt Model 715 and as the M16 light machine gun. It is basically a heavy-barreled M16 rifle with selective fire, a large forend/handguard and forward grip, bipod, and a hydraulic recoil buffer. It will accept any magazine with the standard M16 interface. The C7 normally uses the standard aperture rear sight as provided for the M16A2 rifle, but there is also a C7A1 variant which uses an optical sight. The C7A1 was adopted by the Netherlands Marine Corps in the late 1990s, and the weapon is currently under evaluation by several other countries.

Length: 40.16in (1020mm). **Weight unloaded:** 12lb 12oz (5.80kg). **Barrel:** 20.0in (510mm), 6 grooves, right-hand twist. **Magazine:** 30-round detachable box or other M16 type. **Cyclic rate:** 625 rds/min. **Muzzle velocity:** c.3035 ft/sec (925 m/sec).

CHINA

• Light Machine Gun, Type 67
State Arsenals
7.62mm x 54R

This is of local design and has replaced earlier copies of Soviet weapons in first-line formations. It was developed in the early 1970s and was used in Vietnam. It is gas-operated and belt-fed and can be fired from a bipod or tripod. The design is based on a number of features of earlier weapons: the bolt is tilted to lock in the manner of the Czech ZB26 and Bren guns, the belt-feed mechanism is basically Maxim, and the quick-change

The Chinese Type 67m an interesting mixture of features from other weapons.

barrel is taken from the Soviet SG43. The gas regulator is based on the Soviet RPD and allows three settings to compensate for fouling or lack of lubrication.

Length: 45.0in (1,143m). **Weight unloaded:** 21lb 12oz (9.90kg). **Barrel:** 23.5in (597mm). **Magazine:** 100-round metal belt. **Cyclic rate:** 650 rds/min. **Muzzle velocity:** c.2740 ft/sec (835 m/sec).

The Chinese Type 71 was made for the export market.

• Type 74
State Arsenals
7.62x39mm M1943

This weapon was first seen in 1988 and is a gas-operated light machine gun, bipod-mounted and fed from a drum magazine, though it is also possible to use the Type 56 rifle magazine in place of the drum. The breech is closed by a laterally-locking bolt in a similar manner to the Soviet SG43, and the gas system has a four-position regulator on the forward end of the cylinder. Both barrel and chamber are chrome-plated.

Length: 43.62in (1108mm). **Weight unloaded:** 14lb 2oz (6.40kg). **Barrel:** not known. **Magazine:** 101-round drum. **Cyclic rate:** 750 rds/min. **Muzzle velocity:** c.2410 ft/sec (735 m/sec).

• Type 80
State Arsenals
7.62x54mm Soviet

Described as a general-purpose machine gun, the Type 80 is actually a Chinese copy of the Russian PK, a gas-operated rotating bolt belt-fed weapon which can be used either on a bipod or tripod.

Length: 46.93in (1192mm). **Weight, unloaded:** 17lb 6oz (7.90kg). **Barrel:** 26.57in (675mm), 4 grooves, right-hand twist. **Magazine:** 50-round drum, or 100- or 200-round metal link belt. **Cyclic rate:** 650 rds/min. **Muzzle velocity:** 2706 ft/sec (825 m/sec).

• Type 81
State Arsenals
7.62x39mm M1943

This is another gas-operated light machine gun which was probably produced for export and was not adopted in any quantity by the Chinese Army. It used an adaptation of the rotating bolt breech mechanism used in the Type 68 rifle. Feed is from a drum magazine, but of a different pattern than used with the Type 74 machine gun, and it also accepts the box magazine from the Type 81 rifle. Several of the component parts of the Type 81 machine gun and the Type 81 rifle are interchangeable.

Length: 40.31in (1024mm). **Weight:** 11lb 6oz (5.15kg). **Barrel:** not known. **Magazine:** 75-round drum or 30-round box. **Cyclic rate:** 650 rds/min. **Muzzle velocity:** 2411 ft/sec (735 m/sec).

• Type 77
State Arsenals
12.7x107mm Soviet

This first appeared in the late 1980s and was designed principally for air defense purposes, though it is also

The Chinese Type 74 with drum magazine.

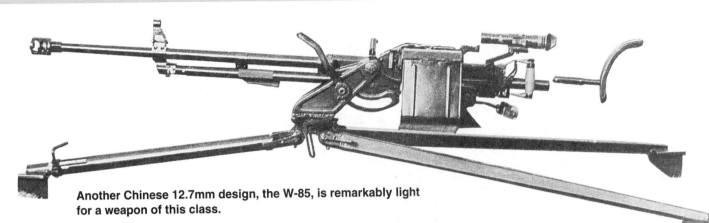

Another Chinese 12.7mm design, the W-85, is remarkably light for a weapon of this class.

capable of operating as a ground gun. It uses a direct gas system, most unusual for a weapon of this caliber, with a gas tube running from the barrel take-off and regulator at the front of the receiver and delivering the gas directly to the lower portion of the bolt carrier. Breech locking is a modified form of the Kjellman flap, the two flaps being operated by the bolt carrier so as to move outwards and lock into recesses in the receiver walls. The weapon is fed by belt, from a box carried on the left side. An optical anti-aircraft sight is standard and there is also a somewhat complex tripod air defense mount.

Length: 84.65in (2150mm). **Weight:** 123lb 11oz (56.10kg) with tripod. **Barrel:** 40.0in (1016mm), 8 grooves, right-hand twist. **Magazine:** 60-round metal belt. **Cyclic rate:** 700 rds/min. **Muzzle velocity:** 2625 ft/sec (800 m/sec).

• Type W-85
State arsenals
12.7x107mm Soviet

As with all other Chinese heavy machine guns this is a dual-purpose weapon for anti-aircraft and ground fire. It is gas operated, though the method of bolt locking is not known, and is exceptionally light for a weapon of this class.

The tripod adjusts for ground or aerial fire, and a telescope sight is fitted.

Length: 37.60in (1995mm). **Weight gun:** 40lb 12oz (18.50kg); mounting: 34lb 3oz (15.50kg). **Barrel:** not known. **Magazine:** 60-round metal link belt. **Cyclic rate:** 600 rds/min. **Muzzle velocity:** 3182 ft/sec (800 m/sec).

• Type 75-1
State arsenals
14.5x114mm Soviet

This is a Chinese copy of the Soviet KPV machine gun, differing from it in details of the belt feed and in the provi-

The Type 77m, a heavy machine gun using direct gas action.

The 14.5mm Type 75 is primarily an air defense weapon, and is based on the Russian KPV.

sion of cooling fins on the barrel. The standard mounting is an air defense tripod which also has two small wheels allowing the tripod to convert to a lightweight carriage which can be towed behind a vehicle. The tripod has mechanical elevating and traverse controls and a parallelogram-mounted optical air defense sight. Photographs of this gun have been seen showing an electro-optical sight in use, presumably for ground firing.

Length: 94.10in (2390mm). **Weight,** with mounting: 363lb 12oz (165.0kg). **Barrel:** not known. **Magazine:** 80-round metal link belt. **Cyclic rate:** 550 rds/min. **Muzzle velocity:** 3265 ft/sec (995 m/sec).

CZECHOSLOVAKIA

• ZB vz/26
Ceskoslovenska Zbrojovka, Brno
7.92x57mm Mauser

The Czech armament firm commonly known as ZB was formed after World War I, and the ZB vz/26 was its first original design. The gun was an immediate success and, together with its later variants, it sold in large numbers throughout Europe. The vz/26 was similar in concept to many other light guns being produced at the same time, but it was far better than the majority. The gas cylinder was unusually long, running under the barrel nearly to the muzzle, but this feature led to a slower and more easily controlled rate of fire and less strain on the working parts because the action was not so fast nor so violent. The piston and cylinder were made in stainless steel to prevent corrosion, and the barrel could be quickly and easily changed by a rotating collar and a carrying handle. A tripod mounting was avail-

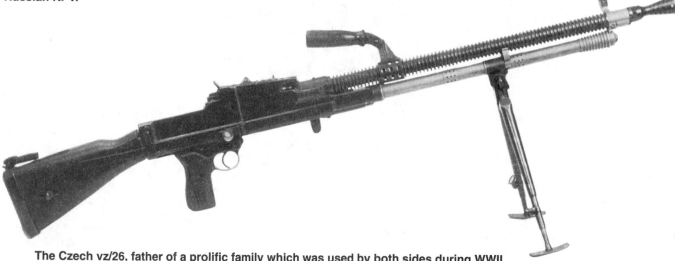

The Czech vz/26, father of a prolific family which was used by both sides during WWII.

The ZGB33 was a vz/30 modified to suit British 303 ammunition; it led to the Bren gun.

able as an extra which helped to give the gun some measure of stability in sustained-fire. Many Czech vz/26 guns served the German Army during World War II, where they were known as the 'MG 26(t)'.

Length: 45.75in (1,161 mm). **Weight unloaded:** 21lb 5oz (9.60kg). **Barrel:** 26.50in (672mm), 4 grooves, right-hand twist. **Magazine:** 30-round detachable box. **Cyclic rate:** 500 rds/min. **Muzzle velocity:** c.2500 ft/sec (762 m/sec).

• ZB vz/30

Ceskoslovenska Zbrojovka, Brno
7.92x57mm Mauser and others

As its title suggests, the vz/30 was a direct descendant of the ZB vz/26, incorporating certain internal improvements although the two guns are difficult to tell apart. The changes were in the cam surfaces which worked the bolt, and in a different method of striking the firing pin. A few changes in the machining operations of manufacture were also made, so that the gun was marginally easier to make and more reliable to use. In fact, both the vz/30 and the vz/26 were expensive to make, as they were designed to be built from expensive and time-consuming milling operations in which quite large blocks of metal were cut away until only a shell remained. This gave great accuracy of dimension and could be done with lower capital costs in equipment, but it made heavy demands on the skill of the workmen and the diligence of the inspectors. China liked the gun, whatever its manufacturing difficulties, and made it in substantial numbers in the 1930s. Britain was also interested and adopted a variant of it as the well-known Bren light machine gun.

Production continued in Czechoslovakia throughout World War II, and the German Army used the gun as a second-line equipment under the title 'MG 30(t)'. The vz/30 was also made in Iran, and a variant made in Spain was known as the FAO—after its manufacturer, Fabrica de Armas de Oviedo. The Spanish also developed an improved belt-fed version in 7.62mm NATO, but never produced it in quantity.

Length: 45.75in (1,161 mm). **Weight unloaded:** 21lb 5oz (9.60kg). **Barrel:** 26.50in (672mm), 4 grooves, right-hand twist. **Magazine:** 30-round detachable box. **Cyclic rate:** 500 rds/min. **Muzzle velocity:** c.2500 ft/sec (762 m/sec).

• ZGB 33

Ceskoslovenska Zbrojovka, Brno
303 British

The ZGB 33 is extremely rare. Exactly how many were made is no longer clear, but it is unlikely to have been more than ten or twelve. It was nothing more than the vz/30 incorporating the alterations desired by the British to bring it to their acceptance standards; the gun was chambered for 303-caliber rimmed ammunition, the barrel was shortened, the gas port brought nearer the breech and the sights regraduated in yards. The gun was then tried by the British, and from it the specification of the Bren was drawn up and the pattern sealed. The ZGB 33 never saw service—it was really little more than a design sample—but it deserves mention because of the importance of the weapon which sprang from it and the evidence which it supplies of the application and attention to detail so characteristic of the Brno company.

Length: 45.50in (1,156mm). **Weight unloaded:** 22lb 2oz (10.03kg). **Barrel:** 25.00in (635mm), 6 grooves, right-hand twist. **Magazine:** 30-round detachable box. **Cyclic rate:** 550 rds/min. **Muzzle velocity:** c.2450 ft/sec (745 m/sec).

• ZB 53 (or vz/37)

Ceskoslovenska Zbrojovka, Brno
7.92x57mm Mauser

The ZB 53 was produced in 1937 and is generally known in military circles as the vz/37, under which guise it was accepted by the Czech Army. However, the factory always knew it as the ZB 53 and it was exported under that title. It is an air-cooled gas-operated weapon of robust and simple design, belt-fed and having two rates of fire. It was made in large quantities for export by the firm, and was built under license (in 7.92mm caliber) in Britain as a tank gun, where it was known as the Besa. In some respects, the action resembles that of the ZB light guns, although the forward motion of the piston lifts the rear of the breech block and engages it with lugs in the barrel extension - thus, unlike the light guns, barrel and block can move together. After firing, the two recoil together until the piston unlocks the block and the barrel stops moving. The block then continues back, to be returned by a spring to load the next round and lock again. Barrel and block now run forward and the gun fires during this movement so that the recoil force must first arrest the forward movement before it can begin the recoil cycle once more. The idea is unusual but good; despite the apparent complication, the gun was highly reliable and the barrel could be removed without much difficulty (and changed if the fire mission is a long one). The gun was mounted on a tripod of rather complicated design. The ZB 53 was used during World War II by the Germans as a substitute standard gun, the 'MG 37(t)'.

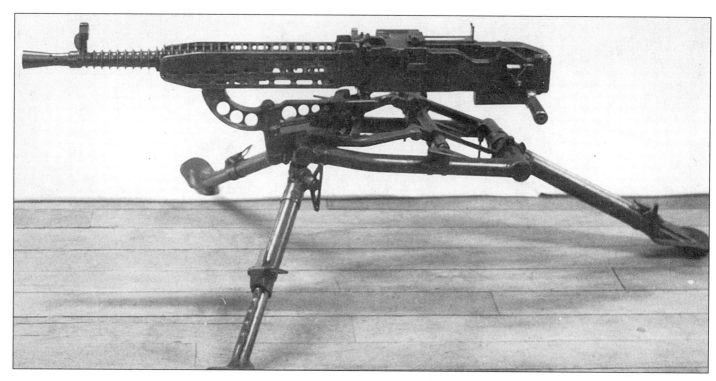

The vz/37 or ZB 53, another Czech design which has seen wide use.

Length: 43.50in (11(gmm). **Weight unloaded:** 41lb 0oz (18.60kg). **Barrel:** 26.70in (678mm), 4 grooves, right-hand twist. **Magazine:** 100-round belt. **Cyclic rate:** 500 or 700 rds/min (adjustable). **Muzzle velocity:** c.2600 ft/sec (792 m/sec).

• vz/52, vz/52-57
Ceskoslovenska Zbrojovka, Brno
7.62x45mm vz/52, 7.62x39mm Soviet M43

Although classed as a light machine gun and bearing obvious affinities with the ZB 26 design, this weapon leans more to the general purpose machine gun concept in its ability to fire from magazine or metallic belt without requiring any adjustment or modification.

Chambered for the Czech 7.62mm vz 52 'Intermediate' round, selection of semiautomatic or full-automatic fire is by a dual trigger system—pressure on the lower portion gives automatic fire; pressure on the top portion gives semi-automatic fire. The operating system relies upon gas, with a piston and bolt assembly very like the ZB 26 but locking into the body in a slightly different way. The barrel can be easily changed, using the maga-

zine port cover as an unlocking lever. The gun body is largely stamped out, with a machined receiver inserted in the appropriate space—an interesting essay in production engineering and cheaper to produce, but otherwise of doubtful value.

A later version of this weapon, the vz/52-57, was produced in small numbers. This was chambered for the Soviet M43 short cartridge,

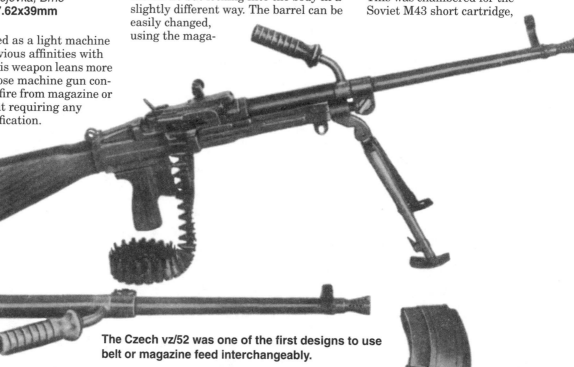

The Czech vz/52 was one of the first designs to use belt or magazine feed interchangeably.

The Czech M59 dispensed with the magazine-feed option.

but in all other respects, it is identical with the vz 52.

Length: 41.00in (1041mm). **Weight unloaded:** 17lb 9oz (7.96kg). **Barrel:** 27.00in (686mm), 4 grooves, right-hand twist. **Magazine:** 25-round detachable box or 100-round belt. **Cyclic rate:** 900 rds/min (belt) or 1150 rds/min (magazine). **Muzzle velocity:** c.2450 ft/sec (746 m/sec).

• vz 59
Ceskoslovenska Zbrojovka, Brno
7.62x54R Russian or 7.62mm NATO

The dual feed (magazine or belt) capability of the vz 52 appears to have introduced more trouble than it was worth. The vz 59, therefore, did away with the magazine feed and was belt-fed only. In most respects, it is no more than an improved vz 52 but, while dispensing with the magazine, the general purpose concept is retained and improved. This model is provided with two alternative barrels: a light one with bipod attached for use in the squad light machine gun role, and a heavy barrel, some four

inches longer, for use in the sustained fire role, in which the gun is mounted on a tripod of unusual appearance and design.

An unusual ballistic reversion is evident: the model vz 52 was chambered for the Czech intermediate cartridge, but the vz 59 is chambered for the Russian 7.62x54R M1891 rimmed rifle round; it seems that the Czechs are willing to encumber the squad light machine gun with a non-universal cartridge (for the remainder of the squad weapons use the intermediate round) so that, in the medium machine gun role, it can be provided with a round having a heavier bullet and longer range.

A light barrel version of the vz 59 was manufactured as the CZ vz 59L, and a version was made for export—in 7.62mm NATO—as the CZ vz 68H. A tank version known as the vz 59T makes use of a firing solenoid.

Length: 48.00in (1220mm). **Weight unloaded, heavy barrel:** 21lb 0oz (8.60kg). **Weight unloaded,** light barrel: 191b 0oz (9.60kg). **Barrel,** heavy: 27.30in (694mm), 4 grooves, right-hand twist. light: 23.30in (591mm), 4 grooves, right-hand twist. **Magazine:** 50-round belt. **Cyclic rate:** 750 rds/min. **Muzzle velocity:** c.2700 ft/sec (823 m/sec).

• CZ 2000
Ceska Zbrojovka, Uhersky Brod
5.45x39.5mm Russian;
5.56x45mm NATO

This first appeared in 1993 as part of the 'Lada' family of weapons, but that name was dropped in 1995 and it became

The latest Czech design, the CZ 2000, is simply a heavy-barreled rifle.

the CZ 2000. It is actually a heavy-barrel version of the CZ 2000 assault rifle and is hence a selective fire gun with a rotating bolt powered by a gas piston. The barrel is longer and heavier than the rifle, there is a bipod attached, and a special 75-round drum magazine is provided, though the standard 30-round plastic rifle magazine will also fit. The tubular butt folds to the right side of the receiver. Whether this will be adopted by the Czech army remains to be seen; at present it seems to be in limbo awaiting a financial decision, though it is being offered for export in either caliber. Should the Czech Army succeed in joining NATO, then presumably it will go into service in the NATO caliber.

Length: 41.34in (1050mm). **Weight unloaded:** 9lb 0oz (4.10kg). **Barrel:** 22.72in (577mm), 6 grooves, right-hand twist. **Magazine:** 30-round box or 75-round drum. **Cyclic rate:** 800 rds/min. **Muzzle velocity:** c.3150 ft/sec (960 m/sec).

DENMARK

• Madsen, c.1904
Dansk Rekylriffel Syndikat AS 'Madsen', Copenhagen.
8mm Patron m/89 and many others

The Madsen is a remarkable gun in almost every respect. It was undoubtedly the first light machine gun ever to be produced in quantity; the same model continued to be produced with only minor variations for over fifty years and it featured in innumerable wars both large and small. Special models were fitted in tanks, armored cars and airplanes—yet it was never officially adopted by any major country. Finally, it possessed a mechanism which, although compact and light, exceeded most others in ingenuity and complexity. As the late Major Frank Hobart once said, the amazing thing about the Madsen was not that it worked well, but that it worked at all.

The Madsen was really an automatic form of the Peabody-Martini hinged-block action, and as such, it had several peculiarities. With no bolt to move the cartridges in and out of the breech, the Madsen was provided with a separate rammer and a powerful extractor. The action worked by recoil, part long and part short, and the movement of the hinged breechblock was controlled by a system of cams and lugs on the block and on a plate in the side of the receiver. The overhead box magazine was another 'first' and was used as a model by other designs which followed.

Despite the complexity, which might appear to be a drawback, the Madsen was remarkably successful and was sold in at least thirty-four countries, remaining in production until the late 1950s. Its manufacturers were quick to appreciate that the experience of World War I indicated that it was desirable in some circumstances to have a machine gun which combined the characteristics of a light weapon when mounted on a bipod, with those of a medium gun when mounted on a tripod. The Madsen was offered with these possibilities and the necessary associated equipment. It was accepted by most of the Latin-American countries and bought by them in quantity. In British service (principally in the early tanks), the Madsen gun gained a reputation for jamming frequently, which was due to the rimmed 303 British cartridge. With rimless ammunition, however, the guns' performance was excellent. Apart from the 303 British cartridge, Madsen guns were offered in a wide variety of calibers—including 7.92mm, 7.65mm, 7mm and 6.5mm rimmed.

(303-caliber model)
Length: 45.00in (1143mm). **Weight unloaded:** 20lb 0oz (9.07kg). **Barrel:** 23.00in (584mm), 4 grooves, right-hand twist. **Magazine:** 25-, 30- or 40-round detachable box. **Cyclic rate:** 450 rds/min. **Muzzle velocity:** 2350 ft/sec (715 m/sec).

• Madsen-Saetter
Dansk Industri Syndikat AS 'Madsen', Copenhagen
7.62x51mm NATO

This, the last of the Madsen line of weapons, was a general purpose machine gun which could be used as a man-portable light gun or as a tripod-mounted sustained-fire support gun. It was made in a variety of calibers, though chiefly 7.62mm NATO, and it could be quickly changed to accept other calibers with a similar case base diameter, simply by substituting the appropriate barrel. If the case diameter dif-

A later Madsen, right side, showing the magazine retaining clip, and also showing the design didn't change much over the years.

An early Madsen, right side, showing the cocking handle and folded bipod.

The Madsen-Saetter machine gun, a sound design which failed to attract customers, was Madsen's last venture in the armaments market.

fered, then a new bolt was also required. The rate of fire was adjustable to any speed between 650 rds/min and 1,000 rds/min. By using two barrels and changing them at the correct intervals, the manufacturers claimed that a sustained rate of 7,000 or 8,000 rounds per hour could be maintained. Simple production techniques were predominantly used, and much of the gun was made by punching, turning and precision casting. The bore was chromium-plated to prolong barrel life, and was locked to the gun by a quick-release handle. The gun operated by gas action, and locked by lugs being forced into recesses in the receiver wall. It fired from an open bolt, so giving the breech the best possible chance of cooling between shots. As a light machine gun, the Madsen-Saetter was adopted and produced by Indonesia, but it failed to find favor elsewhere. A prototype 50-caliber machine gun employing the same basic mechanism showed promise but failed to attract any buyers, and in the mid-1970s Madsen left the firearms business for more profitable fields.

Length: 45.90in (1165mm). **Weight unloaded:** 23lb 8oz (10.65kg).

Barrel: 22.20in (565mm), 4 grooves, right-hand twist. **Magazine:** 49-round belt. **Cyclic rate:** 650 rds/min to 1000 rds/min (adjustable). **Muzzle velocity:** c.2800 ft/sec (853 m/sec).

EGYPT

• ALFA Model 44, Egyptian Pattern
Fabrica de Armas de Oviedo, Oviedo, Spain
7.92x57mm Mauser

The Egyptian model of the ALFA Model 44 differed slightly from the standard Spanish version. It was a medium machine gun with the same operating system, but certain modifications were introduced, either as a result of experience with the original gun or to suit the conditions of the Egyptian army. The most obvious difference was in the cooling fins on the barrel. They were aluminum and they covered the entire length of the barrel. For the carrying handle, the aluminum was cut away mid-way up the length, and the handle was clamped to the steel barrel. The other difference—a less noticeable one—was in the holes for the escaping gas in the operating cylinder. They were enlarged and slotted, which may have been done to prevent fouling from clogging of the holes after prolonged firing.

Apart from these two features and the fact that it was engraved with Arabic characters, the Egyptian pattern was identical with the standard Spanish ALFA.

FINLAND

• Lahti-Saloranta M/26
Valtion Kivaarithedas (VKT), Jyvaskyla
7.62x54R Russian

Designed in 1926 by Aimo Lahti, the M26 is a good example of the type of machine gun produced in the aftermath

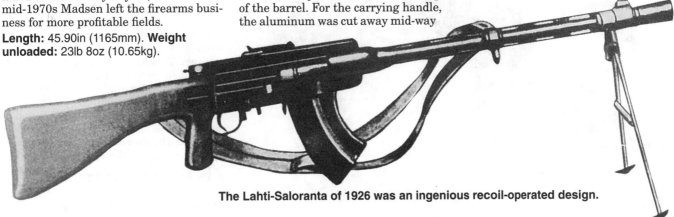

The Lahti-Saloranta of 1926 was an ingenious recoil-operated design.

of World War I: simple, strong, and not too heavy. It was hoped to recoup some of the development costs by selling the gun in Europe, but the Depression years were no time to try selling machine guns and only the Finnish Army ever employed it. It was used extensively in the Russo-Finnish 'Winter War' of 1939/40 and did not pass out of service until the late 1940s when Soviet equipment was introduced.

The M26 was a recoil-operated gun which fired from an open bolt. Barrel and bolt recoiled, locked together, until the bolt was unlocked by a cam on the receiver wall striking a stud on the bolt and lifting it out of engagement with the barrel. An accelerator then flings the bolt back while the barrel is halted; on the return stroke the bolt chambers a round and then re-engages with the cam which forces the lug down to lock, after which bolt and barrel run back into the firing position, the cartridge firing just before the barrel comes to rest. Thus the recoil has to halt the forward movement before reversing it, so absorbing a proportion of the recoil force. The feed system could use either a box magazine or a drum, both of which fitted below the receiver. The barrel could be quickly removed, but the bolt had to come out with it, which was not always desirable in the field. Single shot or automatic fire could be selected, and the rate of fire was reasonably low, giving good control.

Length: 46.50in (1180mm). **Weight unloaded:** 19lb 0oz (8.60kg). **Barrel:** 22.3in (566mm) approximately, 4 grooves, right-hand twist. **Magazine:** 20-round detachable box or 75-round drum. **Cyclic rate:** 500 rds/min. **Muzzle velocity:** c.2630 ft/sec (800 m/sec).

• Valmet Model 62
Valmet Oy, Helsinki
7.62x39mm Soviet M43

This gas-operated light machine gun has been in service with the Finnish Army since 1966, when it replaced the elderly Lahti-Saloranta. The Model 62 has affinities with the Czech ZB 26 series, using the same type of vertically-cammed bolt which locks into a recess in the roof of the receiver. It uses a belt feeding into the right side of the receiver from a clip-on belt box and has a quick-change barrel fitted with a flash-hider. In addition to use in Finland, numbers were sold to the armed forces of Qatar.

Length: 42.70in (1085mm). **Weight:** 18lb 5oz (8.30kg). **Barrel:** 18.50in (470mm), 4 grooves, right-hand twist. **Magazine:** 100-round belt. **Cyclic rate:** c.1000 rds/min. **Muzzle velocity:** 2345 ft/sec (730 m/sec).

FRANCE

• Mitrailleuses Hotchkiss, 1897-1918
Société de la Fabrication des Armes A Feu Portatives Hotchkiss et Cie, St Denis
8x50R Lebel; 7x57mm Mauser for export

The Hotchkiss machine gun was a significant advance in the design of repeating arms at a time when most of the systems of operation were carefully covered by patents which almost totally precluded evasion. By

1893, only Maxim and Browning had produced truly workable machine guns (although others had tried), and both had used barrel recoil to drive the mechanism. In the same year, however, an Austrian cavalry officer, Baron von Odkolek, brought to Hotchkiss & Cie a prototype of a gas-operated machine gun; seeing the potential of the weapon, although it required considerable development, the Hotchkiss organization promptly acquired the rights in a manner none too satisfactory from the viewpoint of the luckless inventor. Hotchkiss & Cie would countenance only a straight cash payment, with exclusion of such things as royalties from the contract, with the result that Odkolek scarcely benefited from the transaction.

The heart of Odkolek's weapon was his idea of drilling a hole in the gun barrel so as to divert some of the propellant gas into a tube mounted below the barrel. Here it expanded and drove a piston backwards; a rod attached to the piston then operated the bolt to open and close the breech. This, of course, is so commonplace today that some people cannot imagine a machine gun working in any other way, but in the early 1890s it was entirely new. Although Odkolek's gun worked, it did so intermittently and when it did work it overheated badly, and Lawrence V. Benet, an American who was chief

engineer at the Hotchkiss factory, set about improving it.

The Hotchkiss gun first appeared in 1895—a gas-operated pattern locked by a pivoting locking lug which was raised from the bolt to lock into the top of the receiver. This Mle 95 worked well enough but still suffered from overheating, and Benet eventually produced a barrel with five large radial fins which, by increasing the radiating area, kept the barrel to a reasonable temperature. This was submitted to the French Army and accepted for service as the Model 1897.

• Hotchkiss Meypodel 1897
The first of the official patterns, the Mle 97 was closely based on the experi-

The Valmet Model 62 is based on the tilting bolt of the CZ26 design.

mental Mle 95; brass cooling fins were added to the barrel in an attempt to cure overheating problems inherent in the experimental weapons, but although this improved the situation, the guns were still notorious for the rapidity with which the barrel warmed up. The Mle 97 used a normal Hotchkiss feed—perhaps the greatest single failing of the design—of metallic (originally brass but later steel) strips, holding either 24 or 30 8mm rounds. These were inserted into the gun from the left side and the empty strip was

The Hotchkiss 'Portative' of 1909 which also appeared elsewhere as the Benet-Mercie and as the Hotchkiss Mark 1.

ejected from the right. A second failing of the Mle 97 lay in the design of the mounting, a spindly tripod known as the Affut-Trépied Mle 97, which had provision for neither elevation nor traverse. The gun weighed 56lb 0oz (25.50kg) and the mount contributed a further 36lb 7oz (16.50kg).

• Hotchkiss Model 1900

A modified pattern of the Mle 97, the principal recognition feature of the Mle 00 was the steel-finned barrel substituted in yet another attempt to improve barrel heat dispersion A new type of mount - the Atlut-Trépied Mle 00 - was provided with elevation and traverse, and either of the two patterns of machine gun could be mounted on it. The later Affut Mle 07 could also be adapted to the gun.

After the Hotchkiss had seen service for several years, the French designers attempted to improve it by adding such

things as a variable-fire rate device and returning once again to brass cooling fins. The results of their deliberations, the machine guns Mle 05 ('Puteaux') and Mle 07 ('Saint-Etienne') are separately described: both were failures, and the authorities returned to the proven Hotchkiss.

• Hotchkiss Model 1909

The Mle 09 was originally designed in an attempt to provide a light automatic arm which fitted the French theories of 'assaulting at the walk', but which ultimately proved to be too heavy and was therefore relegated to tanks, aircraft and fortifications. The Mle

09 deviated from the normal Hotchkiss guns in the design of the locking mechanism—the new pattern was, as a result, often called the 'Hotchkiss-Mercié' or the 'Bénét-Mercié'—which replaced the well-tried locking flap by a *'fermeture nut'* which locked the bolt and barrel together and was rotated out of alignment by gas pressure. At the same time, the opportunity was taken of reversing the feed unit so that the cartridges were on the underside of the feed strip, greatly complicating the problems of feeding ammunition to the weapon. These strictures apart, the mechanism was relatively simple although not as efficient as some competing designs. The Mle 09 was actually adopted by the United States of America as the

'Machine Rifle, Bénét-Mercié, Caliber .30 M1909', and by Great Britain as the 'Gun, Machine, Hotchkiss Mark 1'.

(Bénét-Mercié M1909)

Length: 46.75in (1187mm). **Weight:** 27lb 0oz (12.25kg). **Barrel:** 23.50in (596mm), 4 grooves, right-hand twist. **Magazine:** 30-round metal strip. **Cyclic rate:** 600 rds/min. **Muzzle velocity:** 2788 ft/sec (850 m/sec) (with US 30-06 cartridge).

• Hotchkiss Model 1914

The Mle 14 was no more than a slightly redesigned version of the original Mle 00, with the elimination of the safety

The 1914 Hotchkiss, easily recognized by the large brass fins.

system and the revision of certain action components. The feed was now from 25-round strips or from an 'articulated belt' which was simply a series of three-round metallic strips linked together to make up a 249-round 'belt'. Various manufacturing short cuts were introduced, but the result was reliable and well-liked, even if it was a trifle over-weight. Numbers were still in use by the French Army in 1940, and many were assimilated by the German Army and deployed for the defense of the French coast.

Length: 51.60in (1310mm). **Weight:** 55lb 11oz (25.26kg). **Barrel:** 31.0in (787mm), 6 grooves, right-hand twist. **Magazine:** 24- or 30-round metal strip, or 250-round articulated strip belt. **Cyclic rate:** 500 rds/min. **Muzzle velocity:** 2325 ft/sec (708 m/sec).

Hotchkiss heavy machine guns were exported in 7mm caliber to Brazil, Mexico and Spain, where the guns were extensively used by their armies. The 8mm French version was used by Greece and other Balkan states, and the American Expeditionary Force to Europe in 1917 used Hotchkiss guns on a divisional basis.

• Hotchkiss, 'Modéle de Ballon', 1917

The Hotchkiss 'Balloon model' was used to combat the menace of the Ger-

man observation balloons which had proved so useful to the Germans' artillery fire control, although it had originally been conceived as a heavy infantry machine gun. It used a similar operating system to the lighter Hotchkiss weapons but was chambered for a special 11mm round developed from the old 11mm Gras rifle cartridge and carrying an incendiary bullet to ignite the hydrogen-filled balloons. The gun was relatively heavy and immobile and its use did not continue into the postwar years, though the Americans adapted the cartridge to a special version of the Vickers gun for use in a similar role and continued the development into the 1920s, eventually abandoning it when the 50-caliber Browning began to show promise.

• Mitralleuse Modéle 1905 Puteaux
Manufacture d'Armes de Puteaux, Paris
8x50R Lebel

The Puteaux machine gun was an abject failure and lasted in service for just two years before it was relegated to static and reserve use. The design began as an attempt to provide the French Army with a gun superior to the Hotchkiss patterns then in service. The Modéle 1905 was hardly an improvement on its predecessors and, when compared to the work progressing in other European countries at the time, well illustrates the

ineptitude of the French ordnance personnel at that time.

The Puteaux operated in similar fashion to the gas-operated Hotchkiss to which it bore several affinities and with which it shared the same 24- or 30-round strip feed, the first feature which should have been discarded. The normal cyclic rate was 500 rds/min, but the French incorporated a rate regulator theoretically capable of infinitely varying the rate between 8 rds/min and 650 rds/min; the device (a poor copy of Maxim's 1884 device) was all but useless.

The external appearance of the Puteaux foreshadowed the Mitrailleuse Mle 07 ('Saint-Etienne') for which it served as a prototype, but the barrel of the Puteaux was entirely covered by brass cooling fins which, in the event, rapidly overheated. Owing to the many deficiencies in the design, the Puteaux was withdrawn and supplied to fortresses as a defensive gun in order to camouflage the troubles discovered in the field. In this guise it was known as the 'Mitrailleuse de la Fortification Mle 07'.

• Mitrailleuse Mle 1907 Saint-Etienne
Manufacture d'Armes de Saint-Etienne, Saint-Etienne
8x50R Lebel

This gun represents a hopelessly unsuccessful attempt to improve upon the abortive Mle 05 Puteaux—itself an attempt to improve upon the Hotchkiss types then in French service. The Mle 1907 was designed by a small group working at the French Government arsenal at Saint-Etienne, all of whom seem to have been poorly versed in the operating principles of automatic weapons. The group began with the Puteaux and promptly reversed the piston operation so that, instead of moving backwards, it moved forwards and so a rack-and-pinion mechanism had to be introduced to reverse the motion so as to drive the bolt back. The bolt was locked by an over-center cam lever instead of the Hotchkiss lug, and the gas cylinder could be varied in volume to adjust the cyclic rate. It was hardly worth the trouble as it further complicated the mechanism and gave rise to still further stoppages. The return spring was placed below the barrel, but the

The St-Etienne was an attempt to improve on the Hotchkiss; it failed.

temper in the spring was quickly destroyed by heat if enclosed and so it was consequently exposed to the elements. In the trenches of the Western Front, the Saint-Etienne's deficiencies were quickly evident, particularly as the exposed spring rapidly clogged with mud, and the guns were promptly replaced by the Hotchkiss.

Modifications were made to the gun in an attempt to improve it, including the substitution of new patterns of gas pressure regulator, firing pin and front sight, and a form of drum sight replaced the old type of leaf rear sight—if such a peculiar assembly could be so called—and the altered weapon was called the 'Modéle 1907 transformée 1916' (Mle 07T16, or simply Mle 07T). After tests, the French military decided that the Saint-Etienne was suited to arid regions—another way of ridding themselves of the gun without actually saying so—whereupon most were shipped to France's African colonies.

Length: 46.50in (1180mm). **Weight unloaded:** 56lb 12oz (25.73kg). **Barrel:** 28.00in (710mm), 4 grooves, right-hand twist. **Magazine:** 24- or 30-round metallic strips. **Cyclic rate:** 400-500 rds/min. **Muzzle velocity:** c.2300 ft/sec (700 m/sec).

• CSRG (or Chauchat) Mle 1915 Machine Rifle, Chauchat, Caliber 30, M1918
Manufacturers unknown
8x50R Lebel; 30-06 Springfield

The CSRG light machine gun was accepted by a four-man commission before 1914, and like most commission-instigated weapons, the result was nothing to be admired; it has been described as the worst design of machine gun ever formulated and it was universally execrated by those who used it. (There has been a recent move to decry this verdict and to assert that the CSRG was, in fact, one of the finest weapons

ever conceived. There are also people who believe the earth is flat.)

To start with, it is a long-recoil weapon in which the barrel and bolt are locked together for the full stroke; the bolt is then held and the barrel is returned to battery. Once the barrel has returned, the bolt is released to chamber and fires the next round. It is not a system that readily lends itself to a light weapon where steadiness of aim is all-important and, to compound the mischief, the CSRG was poorly manufactured of inferior material and thus the moving surfaces rapidly wore away. Made mostly from sheet steel and drawn tubing, it foreshadowed later production techniques; but its issue to the troops was an unending tale of malfunction.

The peculiar semicircular magazine was forced upon the French designers by the abrupt taper of the 8mm Lebel cartridge; they do not seem to have thought of using a different round. When the United States Army arrived in France in 1917, approximately 16,000 of the CSRG Mle 15 were passed to them; in order to rationalize the ammunition supply the gun was redesigned to accept the American 30-06 Springfield round and the resulting weapon, slightly over 19,000 of which were supplied to the luckless American troops, was called the M1918. The principal difference between the two models lies in the design of the magazine, as the M1918 was fitted with a straight box magazine suited to the 30-caliber round. Although the rechambering was theoretically advantageous, the more powerful 30-06 Springfield cartridge merely shook the gun to pieces that much quicker, and components often expired through over-loading.

In spite of the poor combat showing, the CSRG was briefly adopted by Greece and by Belgium (both in 8mm caliber). The Greeks listed the weapon as the 'Gladiator' and the caliber as 7.8mm but, as this was their term for the French

8mm cartridge, the weapons were neither rechambered nor rebarreled. Some 5000 were shipped from Poland to Spain during the Spanish Civil War, though where the Poles got them is far from clear, and reliable reports have been read of the odd one or two turning up in Vietnam in the 1960s. It would appear that for all its shortcomings the Chauchat managed to survive and baffle at least three generations of soldiers.

(Mle 1915)
Length: 45.00in (1143mm). **Weight unloaded:** 20lb 06z (9.07kg). **Barrel:** 18.50in (469mm), 4 grooves, right-hand twist. **Magazine:** 20-round detachable box. **Cyclic rate:** 250 rds/min. **Muzzle velocity:** c.2300 ft/sec (700 m/sec).

• Darne Modéle 1918
Manufactured by Unceta y Compania, Guernica (Spain) for R. & P. Darne et Cie, Saint-Etienne
8x50R Lebel

The Darne company, long renowned as the manufacturers of a variety of sporting weapons, became interested in the machine gun as a result of a World War I contract to produce Lewis guns for the French government. However, unlike many traditional manufacturers, they saw no need to spend excessive amounts of time and money on applying commercial standards of finish to a military weapon whose service life was likely to be short, and they succeeded in producing one of the cheapest and crudest machine guns ever marketed. Although their name is attached to the weapon by virtue of their having designed it, the vast majority of the Darne guns came from Unceta's Spanish factory where they were made on subcontract at an even lower price than that at which the

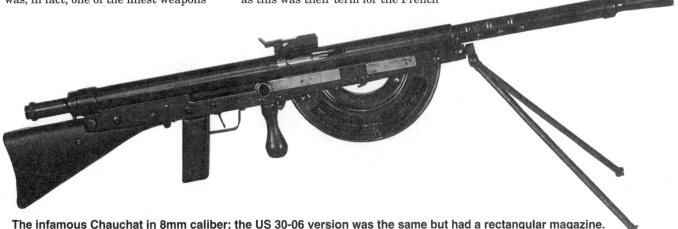

The infamous Chauchat in 8mm caliber; the US 30-06 version was the same but had a rectangular magazine.

The Darne was a successful aircraft gun, but this ground conversion was less popular.

original French firm could have produced them.

For all its cheapness, the gun was undeniably efficient, serving the French and other European nations as an aircraft gun throughout the 1930s. The Darne was among several weapons evaluated by the Royal Air Force just prior to World War II, but it was turned down in favor of the Browning. Gas-operated and belt-fed, it had the high rate of fire desirable in an aircraft weapon, although this was one of the features which prevented it from gaining wide following as an infantry accompanying gun.

It is also recorded that the Darne gun was manufactured in Czechoslovakia prior to the appearance of the vz/26; it is thought that these guns were made in 7.92mm caliber.

Length: 36.89in (937mm). **Weight:** 15lb 7oz (7.0kg). **Barrel:** 25.98in (660mm), 4 grooves, right-hand twist. **Magazine:** cloth belt. **Cyclic rate:** 1100 rds/min. **Muzzle velocity:** 2300 ft/sec (700 m/sec) (8mm Lebel).

• Hotchkiss Light Machine gun, 1922-6

Société de la Fabrication des Armes A Feu Portatives Hotchkiss et Cie,
Saint-Denis, and others
Various calibers

This Hotchkiss light gun was offered commercially in the immediate post-war years. The gun was a standard type of gas-operated weapon, locked by a tilting flap, although it incorporated a rate-reducing mechanism in a housing in front of the pistol grip/trigger assembly. Versions of the basic design were made, using either a top-mounted box magazine or a side-feeding metallic strip, in standard Hotchkiss fashion; in the latter case there is also evidence that a belt,

consisting of short three-round sections of strip joined together to form an articulated belt, was also developed. Other features of the light Hotchkiss were the 'rocker-feet' bipod and the muzzle compensator/flash suppressor which was cut obliquely to provide the necessary downward thrust—but whether this in any way helped to stabilize the gun is not recorded.

The gun saw little use: apart from some 303 British examples tested during the period 1922-3 by the British authorities (when the gun was tried and found wanting), 1,000 were used in Czechoslovakia in 1924 for extended trials. The Czech guns, in 7.92mm caliber and manufactured by Hotchkiss of Saint-Denis, were rejected in favor of the ZB vz/26. It

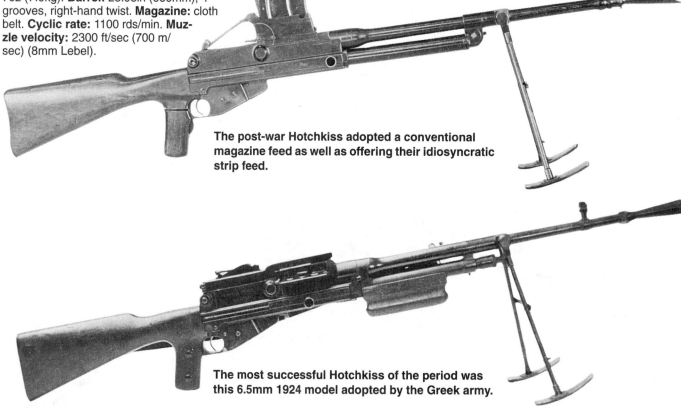

The post-war Hotchkiss adopted a conventional magazine feed as well as offering their idiosyncratic strip feed.

The most successful Hotchkiss of the period was this 6.5mm 1924 model adopted by the Greek army.

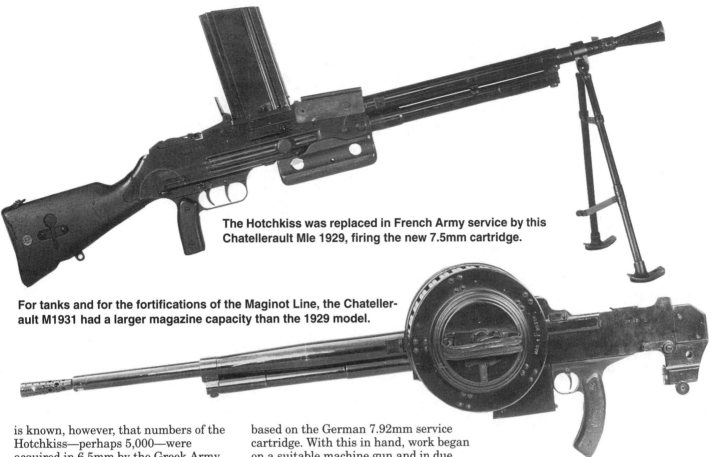

The Hotchkiss was replaced in French Army service by this Chatellerault Mle 1929, firing the new 7.5mm cartridge.

For tanks and for the fortifications of the Maginot Line, the Chatellerault M1931 had a larger magazine capacity than the 1929 model.

is known, however, that numbers of the Hotchkiss—perhaps 5,000—were acquired in 6.5mm by the Greek Army, and used in Greece for several years; 7mm examples were also used in the Dominican Republic and Brazil, which suggests that Hotchkiss found the markets sufficiently lucrative to produce the guns (as the Modéle 1924) for several years.

(Greek M1926)

Length: 47.75in (1214mm). **Weight unloaded:** 21lb 0oz (9.52kg). **Barrel:** 22.75in (577mm), 4 grooves, right-hand twist. **Magazine:** 25-round strip feed. **Cyclic rate:** c.450 rds/min. **Muzzle velocity:** c.2450 ft/sec (745 m/sec).

• Chatellerault Models 1924, 1924/29 and 1931
Manufacture d'Armes de Chatellerault; Manufacture d'Armes de Saint-Etienne
7.5mm Cartouche Mle 24 (Mle 24), 7.5mm Cartouche Mle 29 (Mles 24/29 and 31)

The French light machine gun at the end of World War I was the infamous Chauchat, and it was patently obvious that something better was vitally necessary. Since the 8mm rimmed Mle 86 (Lebel) cartridge was of an awkward size and shape for use in automatic weapons, the French began very wisely by developing a new 7.5mm rimless round broadly

based on the German 7.92mm service cartridge. With this in hand, work began on a suitable machine gun and in due course a limited number—known as the Mle 1924—were produced for trials. This gas-operated weapon was based on the Browning Automatic Rifle and used a similar form of tilting bolt breech locking.

The gun was far better than its predecessor (although still some way from perfection) but the cartridge had some ballistic shortcomings, and it was redesigned with a shorter case. The gun was modified to suit, and was tested c.1928 with the new round. The combination was found to be successful and the weapon was standardized for issue as the Mle 24/29.

In 1931, a slightly modified version was issued for use in fixed defenses—notably along the Maginot Line—and this was later adopted as a tank gun. This, the Mle 31, was distinguished by its peculiar butt and handgrip, and the 150-round drum magazine mounted vertically on the left side.

The Chatellerault guns remained in the hands of the French Army until the middle 1950s; indeed, during World War II, numbers were seized by the German Army and put to use, principally in the anti-invasion defenses on the coasts of France and the Channel Islands.

Length: 42.60in (1082mm). **Weight unloaded:** 20lb 4oz (9.24kg).

Barrel: 19.70in (500mm), 4 grooves. **Magazine:** 25-round detachable box. **Cyclic rate:** 500 rds/min. **Muzzle velocity:** c.2700 ft/sec (823 m/sec).

• Arme Automatique Transformable Modéle 52 (AAT 52)
Manufacture d'Armes de Saint-Etienne, Saint-Etienne
7.62x51mm NATO

The AAT-52, or Arme Automatique Transformable Modéle 52 (AAT Mle 52) is the French entry in the general purpose machine gun field. It is a considerable improvement on earlier French designs, but still manages to exhibit that flair for *'la différence'* which characterizes most French weapons.

Normally used with a light barrel and bipod as a light machine gun, it can also be fitted with a 23.50in (596mm) heavy barrel, and mounted on a tripod to act as a sustained fire weapon. In the light machine gun role it also boasts that favorite and useless European appendage, a butt monopod. The belt feed system owes a good deal to the MG42 while the general system of operation stems from Hungary by way of Kiraly's two-part bolt (as seen in the Hungarian 39M submachine gun). The AAT 52 operates by delayed blowback, using a

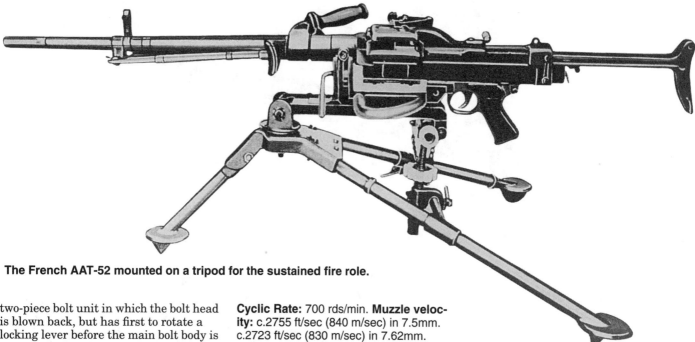

The French AAT-52 mounted on a tripod for the sustained fire role.

two-piece bolt unit in which the bolt head is blown back, but has first to rotate a locking lever before the main bolt body is permitted to recoil. Like all blowback guns, the extraction of the empty case is liable to be violent and—in order to prevent sticking and possible separations—the chamber is fluted to float the case on a layer of gas. In spite of this, the system is taxed to its utmost and a random handful of empty cases will inevitably exhibit a number of expansions and splits. The AAT 52 works—but only just.

The gun was originally produced, in the 1950s, in 7.5mm caliber. With the adoption of NATO standardization most of these guns were converted to 7.62x51mm chambering, and all subsequent production has been to this caliber. In this guise the gun is known as the AA 7.62 NF-1. The dimensions of the two models are the same, but the ballistic performance differs.

Length: 39.00in (990mm). **Weight unloaded,** light barrel: 21lb 12oz (9.88kg). **Barrel:** 19.30in (488mm), 4 grooves, right-hand twist. **Magazine:** 50-round belt.

Cyclic Rate: 700 rds/min. **Muzzle velocity:** c.2755 ft/sec (840 m/sec) in 7.5mm. c.2723 ft/sec (830 m/sec) in 7.62mm.

GERMANY (PRE-1945)

• Maxim MG08 and variants
Königlich Gewehr- und Munitionsfabrik Spandau; Deutsche Waffen-und-Munitionsfabriken AG, Berlin
7.92x57mm Mauser and various calibers for export

German experiments with machine guns began in 1887 with the demonstration by Hiram Maxim of his automatic gun; as a result of this extensive field trials were held from 1890 to 1894. Limited quantities of Maxim guns had, however, been purchased in 1895 by the army and in 1896 by the navy. Wide-spread trial issue in 1899 was followed in 1901 by the official introduction of the gun to the German Army.

The perfected Maschinengewehr 08 was the ultimate outcome of the German trials and was

promptly issued to the German Army. The MG08 is of typical Maxim design, working on short-recoil principles in which the barrel and breechblock move approximately .70-inch (18mm) securely locked together. The barrel is then halted and the toggle locking the breechblock breaks to permit the block to continue towards the rear; the recoil spring then halts the movement and propels the breechblock back into battery, having stripped a round from the belt. The toggle then locks once again. In 1915, many MG08 guns were fitted with muzzle boosters to increase the cyclic rate, giving an additional thrust to the recoiling barrel by deflecting some of the propellant gases to impinge upon it. This increased the cyclic rate by approximately 45%, and weapons so modified were called *'MG08 mit Rilckstorsverstärker S'*. The MG08 was originally issued with a heavy sledge mounting called the *'Schlitten 08'*,

The AAT-52 with bipod and monopod in the squad automatic role.

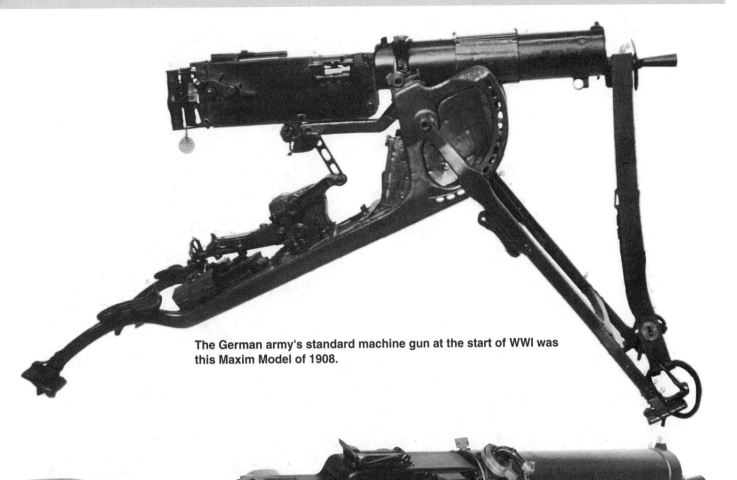

The German army's standard machine gun at the start of WWI was this Maxim Model of 1908.

A 'Light' machine gun in name only—the Maxim 08/15 was simply the 1908 divorced from its tripod.

but this made the combination heavy—as the basic gun weighed 58lb 5oz (26.50kg) unloaded (but with 4 liters of coolant in the water jacket) and the sledge weighed 70lb 8oz (32.00kg). Together with the two extra barrels and the two extra locks which made up the 'Maschinengewehr-Gerät 08 (System Maxim)' this meant a total weight of about 137lb (62kg).

As a result, the German authorities issued a lighter pattern of the MG08—the MG08/15—which was fitted with a light bipod, a pistol grip and a shoulder stock; the weapon weighed some 39lb 0oz (18.00kg) with the bipod, but with an empty water jacket, which was too heavy for a true light machine gun. At the same time, a lightened version, the IMG08/15 (the 'I' for *'Luftgekühlt'*—'air-cooled') was supplied as an airplane gun; it was fitted with a skeleton jacket suited to air cooling and could also be adapted for the

German interrupter gear for firing through a rotating propeller.

In 1916, a tripod, the 'Dreifuss 16', was introduced to replace the sledge mounting of the MG08; assorted Maxim-system weapons captured in Belgium and Russia were also converted for this mounting.

The last of the wartime guns, the Maschinengewehr 08/18, was introduced as a last attempt to make a light machine gun from the MG08 in which the water jacket of the MG08/15 was discarded and a light casing adopted instead. The MG08/18—1kg (2.2lb) lighter than the MG08/15—was not supplied with a readily removable barrel, greatly restricting the volume of fire which could be delivered because the barrel soon overheated. In an attempt to avoid this,

the Germans often grouped the guns in threes and advised alternate use of them.

The MG08 continued to be issued to the German Army until the 1930s when the MG34 was perfected. Many MG08 guns remained, however, in the hands of the reserve formations and the German police forces until 1945.

(MG08)

Length: 46.25in (1175mm). **Weight:** Gun 58lb 5oz; (26.50kg); tripod 70lb 8oz (31.97kg). **Barrel:** 28.35in (720mm), 4 grooves, right hand twist. **Magazine:** 250-round cloth belt. **Cyclic rate:** 450 rds/min. (with muzzle booster). **Muzzle velocity:** c.2838 ft/sec (865 m/sec).

(MG08/15)

Length: 56.90in (1445mm). **Weight:** 31lb 0oz; (14.06kg). **Barrel:** 28.30in (720mm), 4 grooves, right-hand twist. **Magazine:** 250-round cloth belt. **Cyclic rate:** 450 rds/min. **Muzzle velocity:** c.2838 ft/sec (865 m/sec).

The Maxim '08 survived into the early days of the Wehrmacht; here it is in the air defense role during exercises in 1933.

• Bergmann MG10, MG15, MG15 Neuer Art (MG15 nA)

Theodor Bergmann Waffenbau AG, Suhl
7.92x57mm Mauser

These guns were recognized as the work of the noted designer Theodor Bergmann, although it is quite probable that they were due to Louis Schmeisser. The first Bergmann machine gun was patented in 1900 and the first production—on a limited scale—was undertaken as the Bergmann Maschinengewehr Modell 02; a slight modification appeared in the following year and the first model to achieve reasonable success was the MG10, extensively tested by the German Army.

The MG10, and its wartime successors the MG15, are water-cooled guns, belt fed and utilizing short-recoil principles to operate the mechanism; the recoiling components travel approximately .50-inch (12.70mm) rearwards before a locking block is cammed downwards from the underside of the breechblock, thereafter permitting the block to continue in its travel. (There is a distinct similarity here with Bergmann's 1910 Bergmann-Bayard pistol.) The action of the recoil spring then returns the breechblock and cams the vertically swinging locking-piece back into place. A notable feature of the water-cooled MG10 and MG15 is the provision of a quickly removable barrel, remarkable in weapons of this class.

A much-lightened version of the basic design, the MG15nA (nA represents *'neuer Art'*, 'new pattern'), was issued in 1916 to troops on the Italian front. The MG15nA discarded the water jacket of the MG10 and MG15, and instead adopted a pierced casing suited to air cooling. A bipod, a pistol grip, and a shoulder pad—hardly a stock in the conventional sense—were added, and the weapon fed from a belt box fixed to the right side of the receiver. The MG15 nA weighed 28lb 8oz (12.92kg) unloaded.

The Bergmann designs never gained the acceptance they perhaps deserved, particularly as they incorporated several advanced features (among which was a disintegrating aluminum link belt—a definite advance over the canvas belts of most contemporaries). It is perhaps fair to say that the success of the Maxim pattern MG08 blinded the German authorities to the features of the Bergmann which was, after all,

The Bergmann was overshadowed by the Maxim until war came, after which the German army could not get enough of this MG15 model.

The Bergmann lent itself easily to conversion into this MG15nA light version.

an indigenous product. In retrospect, however, the authorities deserve recognition for eschewing chauvinism and not veering from the MG08 at a time when such a change was at best ill-advised.

(Bergmann 15nA)

Length: 44.13in (1121mm). **Weight unloaded,** without mount: 28lb 8oz (12.92kg). **Barrel:** 28.50in (726mm), 4 grooves, right-hand twist. **Magazine:** 200-round belt. **Cyclic rate:** c.500 rds/min. **Muzzle velocity:** c.2925 ft/sec (892 m/sec).

• Parabellum Model 14, Light Parabellum Model 1914, Parabellum Model 1917

Deutsche Waffen-und-Munitionsfabriken AG, Berlin

7.92x57mm Mauser

The Parabellum light machine gun was the standard aircraft flexible gun, and was mounted singly or in pairs on many German airplanes. It was also used as a Zeppelin gun and occasionally appeared in a ground role; this was particularly the case during 1918 when the Germans were experiencing a very severe arms shortage.

The Parabellum arose from a 1909 specification for a weapon suited to aircraft use and much lighter than the service MG08: at that time none of the government arsenals was capable of designing and manufacturing such a gun and so the authorities turned to the Berlin firm of DWM, who were then producing Mauser rifles. The project was

assigned to Karl Heinemann who, after two years' work, produced the Parabellum in 1911, having taken the Maxim design as his starting point. The Parabellum was a much-lightened Maxim with the toggle inverted so that it broke upwards—in the manner of the Parabellum pistol and the British Vickers—rather than downwards as in the original MG08. The Parabellum MG was otherwise operated by short-recoil principles, although careful attention to the mechanism's size, weight and fit gave a cyclic rate of 700 rds/min without recourse to a muzzle booster.

The most common guise of the Parabellum MG is that of the aircraft flexible gun (lMG14), with a pistol grip and a shoulder stock; the weapon was drum-fed from the right side of the receiver. Some of these appeared with a large barrel casing and others (the so-called MG17 or MG14/17) with one of much slimmer pattern. Most of the heavier Zeppelin guns (MG14) were watercooled to prevent the too-ready dissipation of heat to the inflammable surroundings. Optical sights sometimes appeared on the airborne weapons, and ground guns were provided with simple bipods, with which they weighed about 23lb (11.00kg).

The Parabellum MG was an efficient gun—the best, perhaps, of the flexible guns produced during World War I and lacked only a readily-changeable barrel . Rather than bothering to convert the MG08 to a light machine gun (as the MG08/15 and MG08/18) it might well have paid the Germans to have concen-

trated on the lighter Parabellum; the majority of such weapons were, however, required for air use.

Length: 48.13in (1223mm). **Weight unloaded,** without bipod: 21lb 9oz (9.80kg). **Barrel:** 27.75in (705mm), 4 grooves, right-hand twist. **Magazine:** 250-round belt. **Cyclic rate:** 650-750 rds/min. **Muzzle velocity:** c.2925 ft/sec (892 m/sec).

• Dreyse-Maschinengewehr Modell 10, Dreyse-Maschinengewehr Modell 15

Rheinische Metallwaaren-und-Maschinenfabrik AG, Sömmerda

7.92x57mm Mauser

The 'Dreyse' machine guns were based on the 1907 patents granted to Louis Schmeisser and they were manufactured by RM&M of Sömmerda. The name ascribed to the design is confusing as Johann Niklaus von Dreyse, the inventor of the Needle Gun and whose name had been chosen to grace the machine guns, had died some forty years before Schmeisser's patents were granted. In fact, RM&M had acquired von Dreyse's weapons business in 1901 and from then on named their small arms in honor of the famous connection.

Like the Bergmann designs the Dreyse guns, although possessing advanced features, found little success in view of the successful MG08. Both the Dreyse MG10 and the Dreyse MG15 were water-cooled weapons; the former was mounted on a tripod for use in a

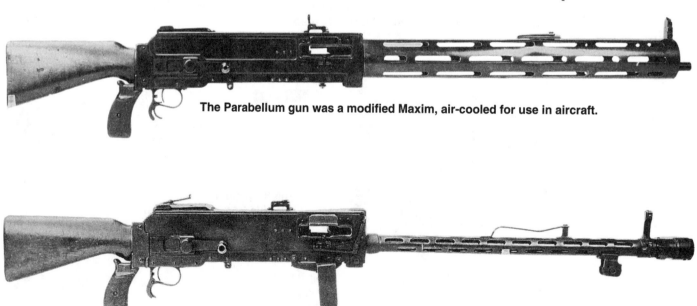

The Parabellum gun was a modified Maxim, air-cooled for use in aircraft.

With a little modification the Parabellum MG17 came into existence, mainly for aircraft gunners but also for ground use.

The remarkable twin Gast, which used the recoil of one barrel to fire the other; the object being to obtain a high rate of fire for aircraft use.

sustained-fire role and the latter was provided with a light bipod fixed to the breech end of the water jacket. The MG15 was also provided on occasion with a crude monopod which, positioned beneath the receiver in line with the cocking handle, was sometimes needed to prevent the gun from resting on the spade grips, as no shoulder stock was provided. The MG15 was a reworked version of the MG10 intended to supply a somewhat rudimentary light machine gun for use in Palestine, Turkey and Mesopotamia but the improvements were at best marginal.

Both patterns operated by short recoil with a hinging breechblock cammed upwards at the rear by tracks cut in the receiver, and consequently lowering the front or locking portion of the block. Further rearward travel of the block permits the novel three-claw feed unit to remove a cartridge from the belt; the recoil spring then returns the breechblock and cams the lock upwards. The guns are hammer-fired, and an accelerator augments the recoil which is then checked by a buffer, resulting in a cyclic rate higher than many contemporary weapons of comparable class.

Although taken into service in reasonable numbers during World War I, most surviving Dreyse guns were converted in 1933-4 to the MG13 (q.v.) and ultimately sold to Spain or Portugal.

• Gast-Maschinengewehr, 1917-1918

Vorwerk, Barmen
7.92x57mm Mauser

The Gast-MG can rightly be described as one of the oddities produced during World War I, although it was, nevertheless, a remarkable development. The gun was designed in response to a 1917 request from the military authorities for a machine gun capable of a high rate of fire and therefore suited to the flexible armament of aircraft, as the single-mounted Parabellum aircraft gun had a cyclic rate of only 700 rds/min, which was held to be too low. The Gast-MG was the design of Ingenieur Carl Gast and was in direct competition with such weapons as the Siemens powered machine gun, which was never satisfactorily developed. Gast's solution was to provide two barrels on a single mounting and controlled by a single trigger unit. The units are recoil-operated and are cross-connected so that the recoil of one barrel unit provides the power for the other's feed cycle; large spring-operated drum magazines were placed on either side.

The Gast-MG was secretly developed and tested in the spring of 1918 and it was not until the war had been over for some months that the Allied disarmament commissions heard of it: it was even longer before they each managed to obtain an example of the gun. Each nation then tested the design, and all expressed themselves amazed at the gun's performance and reliability. However, no further development was forthcoming and the Gast-MG was forgotten.

It is possible that the drum magazines would have provided a weakness to the gun as the springs aged, but none of the post-war trials showed this—possibly because few of them used more than 4,000 rounds in the course of tests.

Length: 54.72in (1390mm). **Weight unloaded:** 40.78lb (18.5kg). **Barrel:** 28.34in (720mm), 4 grooves, right-hand twist. **Magazine:** 2 x 192-round drums. **Cyclic rate:** 1300 rds/min. **Muzzle velocity:** c.3000 ft/sec (915 m/sec).

• Maschinengewehr Modell 13 (MG13)

Rheinische-Metallwaaren-und-Maschinenfabrik, Sömmerda
7.92x57mm Mauser

The MG13 was a light machine gun constructed by rebuilding the old 1918 model Dreyse guns left over after World War I. The only significant change was the adaptation to air-cooling by using a perforated barrel jacket and mounting a

The Dreyse MG13 was long-lived; this one was used in Angola in the 1980s.

Another aircraft gun pressed into ground service, the MG15 was one of the first 'straight-line' designs.

The MG15 led, eventually, to the MG34, the first German attempt at the general purpose machine gun.

bipod at the front. When sufficient quantities of the much more efficient MG34 became available, the majority of the remaining MG13 guns were sold in 1938 to Portugal where the design was adopted as the Metralhadora M938, and remained there in service until the late 1940s.

Length: 57.75in (1466mm). **Weight unloaded:** 23lb 15oz (10.89kg). **Barrel:** 29.25in (717mm), 4 grooves, right-hand twist. **Magazine:** 25-round detachable box or 75-round saddle drum. **Cyclic rate:** 650 rds/min. **Muzzle velocity:** c.2700 ft/sec (823 m/sec).

• MG15

Rheinmetall-Borsig AG, Düsseldorf
7.92x57mm Mauser

The MG15 was an aircraft gun which was pressed into ground service when Germany began to run short of weapons and replacements in the late stages of World War II. The background of the MG15 is of interest because from it evolved another and more widely used gun, the MG34.

During the inter-war years, Rheinmetall acquired control of the Solothurn company in Switzerland, in which they then had an outlet unrestricted by the provisions of the Treaty of Versailles. The Rheinmetall designers, through Solothurn, developed a variety of machine guns and other weapons and in 1930 produced the Model 30 machine gun for aircraft installation.

In 1932, Rheinmetall produced in Germany an improved version firing from an open bolt, later known as the MG15. The design had been lightened, the locking system was a variation on the Hotchkiss *fermeture* nut, it was capable only of automatic fire and it used a 75-round saddle-drum magazine which fed rounds from each side alternately so that the balance of the weapon did not change as the ammunition was expended.

The first experimental version was known as the T6-200 and was for fixed installation. It was soon followed by the T6-220 for flexible application, but this terminology was dropped on the military acceptance of the weapons and both versions became the MG15. An open-bolt weapon, however, is inconvenient for synchronization with a revolving propeller and a new model firing from a closed bolt—the MG17—superseded the MG15 in fixed installations.

When adapted to the ground role, a stock was clamped to the receiver, a bipod was pinned to the barrel and simple sights were fitted to the barrel jacket. The resulting gun was long, rather heavy, and definitely clumsy. It was not issued in large numbers.

Length: 52.50in (1334mm). **Weight unloaded:** 29lb 0oz (12.70kg).

Barrel: 23.50in (595mm), 4 grooves, right-hand twist. **Magazine:** 75-round saddle drum. **Cyclic rate:** 850 rds/min. **Muzzle velocity:** c.2480 ft/sec (755 m/sec).

• Maschinengewehr Modell 34 (MG34)

Mauser-Werke AG, Berlin, and others
7.92x57mm Mauser

The MG34 was derived from the Swiss-developed (but German-designed) Solothurn MG30. Simply by changing the type of mount, the MG34 could be used in a number of widely-differing roles; a bipod, which was adjustable for height, could be attached to the muzzle to make a light machine gun, and a light tripod called the Dreifuss 34 was issued to convert it to a light anti-aircraft machine gun. A heavy sprung-cradle tripod, the MG Mounting 34, was used to turn the gun into a heavy machine gun, in which role only the belt-feed could be used owing to the form of the mount; an anti-aircraft adapter could also be supplied for the MG-Lafette 34.

The MG34 was brought into service in 1936, and although officially superseded in 1943 by the MG42, supplies of the earlier weapon were never withdrawn. The gun introduced two radical ideas: the concept of a general or multi-purpose machine gun, and the use of a belt feed in a 'light' gun. The MG34 was manufactured to a high standard of

The MG34 in the air defense role during maneuvers in 1935.

The ultimate German machine gun, the MG42 on its sustained-fire tripod with optical sight.

tolerance and finish—a factor which greatly contributed to its being superseded by the MG42, as the factories (originally Mauser-Werke, but later including such companies as Steyr-Daimler-Puch AG and Waffenwerk Brünn) could not keep pace with demand arising from the greatly enlarged German Army and the wartime rate of attrition. Too much effort was required to produce the MG34, although this made for an excellent result.

The trigger was large and rocked about its center; pressure on the upper portion gave semiautomatic fire, and pressure on the lower half gave automatic fire. It was recommended that the barrel be changed after firing 250 rounds at the rapid rate, and this was done by unlatching the receiver, swinging it through 180°—so exposing the breech—and withdrawing the barrel to the rear: not the easiest of tasks with a hot barrel.

The normal feed was by 50-round belts which could be linked together to give 250 rounds, but a special feed cover allowed the use of the 75-round saddle drum of the MG15, which was normally fitted for anti-aircraft work as the magazine was convenient for such use, and the

reduced effort due to not having to lift a loaded belt served to increase the cyclic rate.

The MG34 utilized short-recoil operation, with an additional thrust imparted to the mechanism by a muzzle booster. The bolt was locked by means of an interrupted screw rotated by cam faces on the receiver walls which revolved it through 90° to lock into the barrel extension.

On the infantry tripod (MG-Lafette 34) the gun was steady and effective to 3800 yards, but on the bipod it was by no means so efficient and was accurate only when firing single shots. The gun was strong, but suffered from a tendency to jam in dust, dirt and snow; despite this, it lasted throughout the war in large numbers and was, at some time, present in practically every German first-line unit.

Length: 48.00in (1219mm). **Weight unloaded:** 26lb 11oz (12.10kg). **Barrel:** 24.75in (627mm), 4 grooves, right-hand twist. **Magazine:** 50-round belt or 75-round saddle drum. **Cyclic rate:** 800-900 rds/min. **Muzzle velocity:** c.248(f ft/sec (755 m/sec).

• MG 34S, MG 34/4I.

Apparently the MG34S served as a prototype for the 1941 modification which was intended to provide a higher rate of fire. The MG34/41 used the shortened barrel of the MG34 and a modified bolt lock in which lugs replaced the interrupted threads; the trigger mechanism was altered to eliminate single-shot fire, and the gun was capable of using only the belt feed. There were numerous internal modifications which led to non-interchangeability between parts of the designs of 1934 and 1941. Although mooted as a replacement for the MG34, the advent of the MG42—which was, above all, a much more simple manufacturing proposition—spelled the end of the MG34/41's career, and official adoption was not forthcoming.

• Maschinengewehr Modell 42 (MG42)
Mauser-Werke AG, Berlin, and others
7.92x57mm Mauser

Faced in 1941 with a critical shortage of infantry weapons, Germany looked for a machine gun that could be produced more easily and more quickly than the M634, yet still retain its more admirable characteristics. A new gun was conceived, using the MG34 as its basis, but introducing certain changes and employing, to some extent, the manufacturing techniques of the equally successful MP40 submachine gun: as much metal stamping as possible was used in production, and the finish on the MG42 never equaled that of its predecessor. Despite this, however, it was a better gun and became most popular in the Wehrmacht. Like the MG34, the MG42 was a general-purpose weapon meant to be used from either a bipod or a tripod, and it used the same ammunition, belts and ammunition carriers as the preceding design. Some major mechanical changes were introduced: the locking system was entirely new and used locking rollers forced outwards into the receiver walls by the bolt. The locking action was much smoother and easier, and the rate of fire was increased to the remarkable figure of 1200rds/min. At such a high rate, the barrel quickly heated and a second innovation was an excellent and simple barrel change. The barrel casing was as square in outline as the receiver, the right-hand side was cut away for most of its length, and the barrel was held at the breech by a yoke, and at the muzzle by a simple bearing. The yoke was located by a latch and this swung forwards both to release the breech end of the barrel and to allow the entire barrel to be pulled out to the right and to the rear, clear of the gun. A fresh barrel entered in the reverse direction and the entire change could be completed by a trained gunner in five or six seconds.

The high rate of fire also made the gun difficult to control in the bipod role, but the Germans felt that any loss of accuracy was more than compensated by the resultant fire-power. More reliable than the MG34 and better able to resist dirt and rough treatment, the MG42 made an enviable name for itself with both the Wehrmacht and the Allies—the latter treated it with great respect. By the end of the war, over 750,000 had been made and many were sold by the Allies to countries in need of small arms. In 1957,

the design was revived in NATO 7.62mm caliber for the Federal German Army, after which it was adopted by several other countries and is still in use by all of them.

Length: 48.0in (1219mm). **Weight unloaded:** 25lb 8oz (11.50kg). **Barrel:** 21.00in (533mm), 4 grooves, right-hand twist. **Magazine:** 50-round belt. **Cyclic rate:** 1200 rds/min. **Muzzle velocity:** c.2480 ft/sec (755 m/sec).

• Knorr-Bremse Model 35
Knorr-Bremse AG, Berlin-Lichtenburg
7.92x57mm Mauser

This weapon first appeared in the early 1930s as a Swedish design called the 'LH33' in 6.5mm caliber. It was intended as a simple and cheap light machine gun, and after the Swedish Army bought a few for evaluation, the inventor made some small improvements and looked around for an export market. He tried the Norwegians but they declined the weapon, and he then sold his patents to the German Knorr-Bremse company who—as their name implies—were in the automobile brake business. They appear to have rushed blindly into the arms trade in the hopes of a lucrative German Army contract, and in 1935 they began manufacture of a slightly simplified version of the LH33 under their own name.

The modified weapon was capable of automatic fire only and discarded the double trigger of the original LH33. Feeding from a box magazine on the left side, the Knorr-Bremse had one or two odd features. The barrel was retained by a quick-release nut and for no apparent reason the rifling ended three inches from the muzzle. The safety catch was a trap for the unwary since, if wrongly applied, it would hold the bolt three-quarters cocked without engaging the sear; releasing the safety thus released the bolt and fired the gun. The butt was secured by a metal clip plate which

vibrated loose so that the butt dropped off during firing—which is, to say the least, disconcerting.

Although the gun worked, the general standard of design and manufacture was poor, even allowing for the intention to keep it cheap. The Waffen-SS purchased a few which were used for training and then unloaded onto the various 'legions' of foreigners formed in the war, principally the Latvian Legion. Apart from this, the only major sales were in 1940 to the hard-pressed Finns—who were glad of anything—and a few more to Sweden, where it was adopted as the m/40. Thereafter, production ceased.

Length: 51.48in (1308mm). **Weight unloaded:** 22lb 0oz (10.00kg). **Barrel:** 27.25in (692mm), 4 grooves, right-hand twist. **Magazine:** 20-round detachable box. **Cyclic rate:** 490 rds/min. **Muzzle velocity:** c.2600 ft/sec (792 m/sec).

GERMANY (FEDERAL REPUBLIC)

• MG1 - MG3A1 MG42/59
Rheinmetall GmbH, Düsseldorf
7.62x51mm NATO

The German Army's MG1 series all derive from the wartime MG42, although the caliber has been changed from 7.92mm to 7.62mm NATO. The MG1, commercially known as the MG42/59, was re-engineered from an actual specimen of the MG42 as the original manufacturing drawings had disappeared in the aftermath of World War II; there are, consequently, a few minor departures from the original design, and more modifications have been made in the light of service experience. The operation of the weapon, however, remains unchanged from the MG42—although in some weapons, the rate of fire can be altered by changing the bolt and buffer:

The Knorr-Bremse light gun, used principally as a training weapon.

The present-day MG3 is simply the wartime MG42 in 7.62mm caliber.

The MG3 on tripod with optical sight.

Rheinmetall's Type N buffer and light bolt V550 (which weighs 550gm) give a fire-rate of 1150-1350 rds/min, while the Type R buffer and heavy bolt V950 (weight 950gm) gives a cyclic rate of 750-950 rds/min.

The variants of the basic design are as follows:

7.62mm MG1. The initial design reconstructed from the MG42, the MG1 is virtually identical with its predecessor; the bolt and feed unit have been slightly modified, but the two guns are externally virtually indistinguishable. The old pattern of muzzle booster, with fins and gas ports, is fitted.

7.62mm MG1A1 and 1A2. Both of these are experimental weapons which were not taken into service; the MG1A1 had a slightly modified trigger mechanism, a chromed bore and modified sights. The

MG1A2 served as a prototype for the MG3, and had the feed unit suitably modified to accept the American M13 disintegrating link belt.

7.62mm MG1A3. A developed form of the MG1, alterations were made to the bolt, the trigger, the bipod and the feed mechanism. A new type of muzzle booster was added which was integral with the flash hider. The MG1A3 could be used in an anti-aircraft role by discarding the shoulder stock in favor of a rubber pad and using a special mount.

7.62mm MG1A4. The fixed gun version of the basic MG1, the bipod and carrying strap were discarded along with the anti-aircraft sight, and the rubber shoulder pad was fitted as standard. A third pattern of muzzle booster was fitted.

7.62mm MG1A5. A conversion of the MG1A3 to MG1A4 standards, it was fitted with the third pattern muzzle booster.

7.62mm MG2. A conversion of wartime examples of the MG42 from 7.92mm to 7.62mm NATO, with the attendant alterations to the barrel, feed system and bolt. These guns can easily be recognized by the appearance on the receiver of dates prior to 1945.

7.62mm MG3. An improved version of the MG1 based on the experimental MG1A2, the feed unit was modified to accept the German DM1 continuous belt, the DM13 disintegrating link belt or the American M13 disintegrating link belt. Provision was made for the attachment of a 100-round magazine case to the receiver, and a larger ejection port was added. The barrel is externally tapered and has been given a chromed bore lining. Data: essentially similar to MG42 (q.v.).

7.62mm MG3A1. The fixed version of the MG3, the gun has been modified in a similar fashion to the MG1A4.

• HK11A1, 11E

Heckler & Koch GmbH,
Oberndorf-am-Neckar
7.62x51mm NATO

The HK11A1 is simply a magazine-fed version of the HK21A1. The belt feed unit of the latter is hinged at the forward end so as to drop down and

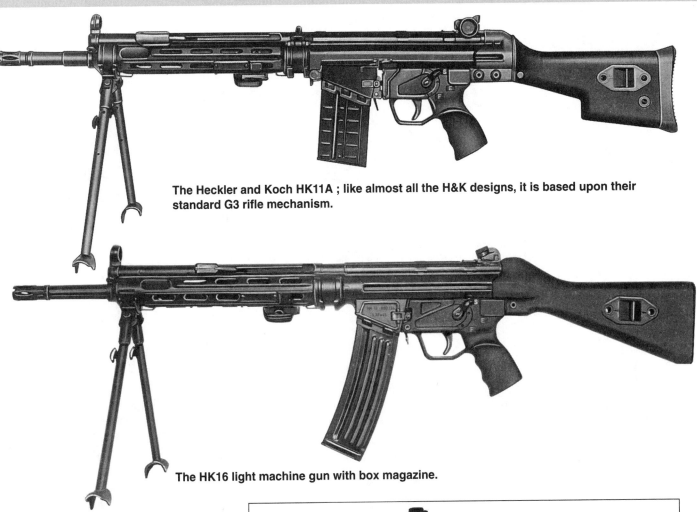

The Heckler and Koch HK11A ; like almost all the H&K designs, it is based upon their standard G3 rifle mechanism.

The HK16 light machine gun with box magazine.

facilitate quick insertion or removal of the belt; by removing the hinge bolt the entire unit can be taken off the gun and a magazine housing unit can be fitted into place to accept the standard 20-round rifle magazine. The HK11A1 was bought by Greece and by un-named countries in Africa and Asia.

The HK11E is the improved version of the 11A1, with the usual; 'E' modifications—three-round burst control, drum sight, lengthened receiver, Still magazine-fed, it can be converted back to belt feed by simply reversing the operation which converted it in the first place. **(HK11E)**

Length: 40.55in (1030mm). **Weight unloaded:** 17lb 15oz (8.15kg). **Barrel:** 17.71in (450mm), 4 grooves, right-hand twist. **Magazine:** 20-round detachable box or 50-round drum. **Cyclic rate:** 800 rds/min. **Muzzle velocity:** c.2625 ft/sec (800 m/sec).

• Heckler & Koch HK13
Heckler & Koch GmbH,
Oberndorf-am-Neckar
5.56x45mm

The HKI3 is a light machine gun capable of both fully automatic fire and

The HK13 stripped, showing the dual-feeding drum magazine.

semiautomatic fire, and it is intended to provide the main firepower of an infantry squad equipped with 5.56mm weapons. The general design and system of operation has been derived from the highly successful Heckler & Koch rifles, and the

action closely resembles that of the 7.62mm G3 rifle. It has a semi-rigid bolt, sliding locking rollers, and feed is by a 25-round magazine.

Despite a promising start, this gun showed itself in need of several

The HK21 with bipod and belt feed.

modifications, particularly in respect of the feed, where failures were not unknown, and the firm continued with a program of improvement and adaptation. The design of the gun was extremely good and manufacture was to a high standard, using many precision stampings or pressings; it bore a distinct external resemblance to the G3 and was as robust and practical.

Length: 38.58in (980mm). **Weight unloaded:** 11lb 14oz (5.4kg). **Barrel:** 17.7in (450mm), 4 grooves, right-hand twist. **Magazine:** 25-round detachable box. **Cyclic rate:** 750 rds/min. **Muzzle velocity:** 3115 ft/sec (950 m/sec).

• HK13E
Heckler & Koch GmbH, Oberndorf-am-Neckar
5.56x45mm

The HK13E is the HK13 re-designed to the 'E' or export standard by adding three-round burst control, drum-pattern rear sight, front handgrip and longer receiver.

Normally using a 20-round magazine, it will also accept the 30-round magazine of the G41 rifle. It is in military service with a number of undisclosed armies.

Length: 40.55in (1030mm). **Weight unloaded:** 17lb 10oz (8.0kg). **Barrel:** 17.7in (450mm), 4 grooves, right-hand twist. **Magazine:** 20- or 30-round detachable box. **Cyclic rate:** 750 rds/min. **Muzzle velocity:** 3115 ft/sec (950 m/sec).

• Heckler & Koch HK73
Heckler & Koch GmbH, Oberndorf-am-Neckar
5.56x45mm

Introduced in 1984, this was a variant of the HK13E machine gin, the difference being that the HK73 had a linkless ammunition feed system which combined the reliability of a magazine with the

high volume of fire of a belt. The feed system was a completely autonomous unit with a container for 200 rounds which could be loaded from clips or with loose rounds and without having to remove the container from the weapon. It could be 'topped up' when the container was partly empty. As an alternative, there was also a 50-round drum magazine available. In spite of these advantages, there appears to have been little military interest and the weapon was dropped from the Heckler & Koch line in 1986. Data as for the HK23E machine gun except that the empty weight was 14lb 5oz (6.49kg).

• Heckler & Koch HK21
Heckler & Koch GmbH, Oberndorf-am-Neckar
7.62x51mm NATO

The HK21 is a selective-fire light machine gun. Like the others in Heckler & Koch's weapon family, it is a delayed blowback gun with a fixed barrel. Automatic fire is from an open bolt, in order to keep the breech cool between bursts. The barrel is easily changed by means of a handle on its right side: lifting the handle unlocks the barrel from the body and it is then pushed forward to clear the housing, drawn to the right and pulled back clear of the gun. The action is both simple and fast to perform. The gun is meant to feed from a belt, but the feed mechanism can be easily removed and replaced by a special magazine adapter which accepts the

normal range of Heckler & Koch magazines. The bipod can be either at the front or at the rear of the barrel casing—which allows flexibility in mounting the weapon. The HK21 shares 48% of its components with the original G3 rifle and there is full interchangeability between HK21 parts. Another useful item is a recoil booster which allows the gun to operate with blank cartridges. The HK21 ceased in production in Germany in the early 1980s but was manufactured under license in Portugal for some years thereafter.

Length: 40.00in (1016mm). **Weight unloaded:** 14lb 9oz (6.60kg). **Barrel:** 17.70in (448mm), 4 grooves, right-hand twist. **Magazine:** 50-round metallic belt, or 20- or 30-round box. **Cyclic rate:** c.750 rds/min. **Muzzle velocity:** c.2625 ft/sec (800 m/sec).

• Heckler & Koch HK21A1
Heckler & Koch GmbH, Oberndorf-am-Neckar
7.62x51mm NATO

This is an improvement on the original HK21; the principal change is that the magazine-feed option has been dropped and the belt-feed mechanism can be hinged down to permit faster loading of the belt. It is also possible, by changing the barrel, bolt and feed unit, to fire 5.56x45mm ammunition. Either jointed or disintegrating metal belts can be used, and the gun now fires from a closed bolt.

The HK21A1 was tested by the US Army as a candidate for the future Squad Automatic Weapon, but was not adopted. It is currently in production for undisclosed armies.

Length: 40.55in (1.030m). **Weight unloaded:** 18lb 5oz (8.3kg). **Barrel:** 17.7in (450mm). **Magazine:** metallic link belt. **Cyclic rate:** 900 rds/min. **Muzzle velocity:** 2625 ft/sec (800 m/sec).

The HK21 on tripod.

• Heckler & Koch HK21E
Heckler & Koch GmbH,
Oberndorf-am-Neckar
7.62x51mm NATO

This is the most recent development of the HK21 design, the 'E' indicating 'Export'. Based on stringent testing and practical experience, the changes include a 94mm extension of the receiver, giving a longer sight radius; a reduction in recoil force, the addition of a three-round burst facility, longer barrel, improved quick-change barrel grip, winter trigger, and drum rear sight with adjustments for windage and drift. The belt feed mechanism has been changed so that half the feed action is carried out on the rearward stroke of the bolt and half on the forward stroke, leading to lower stresses in the mechanism and a smoother feed. It is in service with the Mexican Army (manufactured in that country under license) and undergoing evaluation elsewhere.

Length: 44.88in (1.140m). **Weight unloaded:** 20lb 8oz (9.30kg). **Barrel:** 22.04in (560mm), 1 turn in 310mm, right-hand twist. **Magazine:** metallic link belt. **Cyclic rate:** 800 rds/min. **Muzzle velocity:** c.2755 ft/sec (840 m/sec).

• Heckler & Koch HK23
Heckler & Koch GmbH,
Oberndorf-am-Neckar
5.56x45mm M193

The HK23 is a direct descendant of the HK13, from which it differs only slightly. It is a light, belt-fed, air-cooled machine gun of modern conception and manufacture, incorporating several advanced features. It retains the distinctive delayed blowback system of operation with its locking rollers, and the overall outline shape closely resembles the previous model. However, the feed is changed to a belt which is pulled through the receiver by a stud working in a channel in

An ornate field mount with recoil buffer, carrying an HK21E machine gun with belt box.

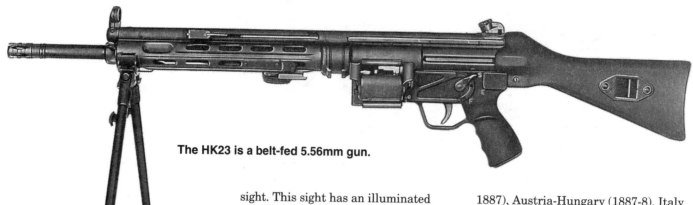

The HK23 is a belt-fed 5.56mm gun.

the bolt. The channel is angled and the stud moves from side to side as the bolt reciprocates. This motion is transferred to two star wheels which engage with rounds in the belt. There is adequate power to drive the feed mechanism and also to ensure that the gun works in adverse conditions.

The HK23 was highly regarded, but the manufacturers decided to subject it to the same modernization program as the HK13E and production was ended in the late 1970s.

Length: 40.00in (1016mm). **Weight unloaded:** 17lb 10oz (7.99kg). **Barrel:** 22.0in (558mm), 6 grooves, right-hand twist. **Magazine:** 50-round belt. **Cyclic rate:** c.600 rds/min. **Muzzle velocity:** 3250 ft/sec (990 m/sec).

• Heckler & Koch HK23E

Heckler & Koch GmbH, Oberndorf-am-Neckar
5.56x45mm NATO

This is the HK23 (above) improved in the same way as the HK21E, by having a new feed mechanism, three-round burst facility and new rear sight.

Length: 40.55in (1.033m). **Weight unloaded:** 18lb 5oz (8.75kg). **Barrel:** 17.7in (450mm), one turn in 178mm or one turn in 305mm (optional). **Magazine:** metallic link belt. **Cyclic rate:** 750 rds/min. **Muzzle velocity:** c.3115 ft/sec (950 m/sec).

• Heckler & Koch GR6

Heckler & Koch GmbH, Oberndorf-am-Neckar
5.56x45mm NATO

This is a further variation on the HK23E; it differs by using the linkless ammunition feed system as described above on the HK73 machine gun, and by being permanently fitted with an optical

sight. This sight has an illuminated reticle and a very short-based iron sight above the telescope casing for emergency use. An infra-red laser sight can be provided; this clips to the front of the receiver and emits a beam of light invisible to the naked eye, but the spot projected on the target can be detected by a gunner wearing night vision goggles, allowing engagement of targets in complete darkness.

Data as for the HK23E.

• HK MG36

Heckler & Koch GmbH, Oberndorf-am-Neckar
5.56x45mm

This is derived from the G36 rifle, and like that weapon breaks with the H&K delayed blowback tradition by being gas operated. It has a somewhat heavier barrel, and is fitted with a bipod, but apart from these features it is precisely the same as the rifle. A variant mode, the **MG36E**, is offered for export; it differs from the German service G36 only in the optical sight, which is of 1.5x magnification instead of 3x.

Length: 39.29in (998mm). **Weight unloaded:** 7lb 14oz (3.58kg). **Barrel:** 18.90in (480mm), 6 grooves, right-hand twist. **Magazine:** 30-round detachable box. **Cyclic rate:** 750 rds/min. **Muzzle velocity:** c.3018 ft/sec (920 m/sec).

GREAT BRITAIN

• Maxim Machine guns, 1884-c.1925

Albert Vickers Ltd, Crayford, Kent (later known as Vickers' Sons & Maxim Ltd and then simply as Vickers Ltd)
303 British and others

Hiram Maxim was one of the geniuses produced by the nineteenth century: his inventions, an astonishing list, covered many fields. The one for which he is most remembered is his machine gun pattern, first demonstrated in 1884 and later adopted by many nations. Among the countries to test the Maxim Gun were the United Kingdom (first trial

1887), Austria-Hungary (1887-8), Italy (1887), Germany (1887), Russia (1897), Switzerland (1887), and the United States of America (1888). Most of the trials were successful although few of those countries who tried the Maxim adopted it much before 1900, largely owing to the prevalent conservatism existing in the minds of the contemporary military authorities. In 1889, however, the Maxim Gun had been issued to British troops and had proved its effectiveness in combat; adoption of the weapon by Switzerland followed in 1894, and the U.S. Navy took a limited number in 1896.

Most of the earlier guns were manufactured in the United Kingdom by Vickers, who held most of the patents. The parent company later developed a modified design—usually known as the 'Vickers' or -the 'Vickers-Maxim'—which ultimately supplanted the Maxim in many armies.

Some nations produced Maxim-system machine guns in their own plants, especially Germany and Russia. Apart from the infantry machine guns, assorted Maxim-system arms were made in calibers as large as 37mm.

• Gun, Maxim, .303in Mark 1

The first British Maxim guns were in 45-caliber, using the Martini-Henry rifle cartridge, but the .303 Mark 1 appeared in June 1889. These were to the standard Maxim pattern, recoil-operated and with a smooth phosphor-bronze water jacket. The breech was locked by a toggle system; on firing, the barrel and breechblock recoiled together, the block being held closed by a toggle strut lying between the block and the barrel extension. As the unit recoiled, the hinge of the toggle struck a ramp and was broken downwards; this allowed the block to part company with the barrel and extract the spent case. At the same time a fresh round was withdrawn from the cloth feed belt and positioned in the feedway, and a 'fusee spring' was tensioned by the rotation of the toggle anchorage.

Once recoil stopped, the spring drove the toggle upwards, forcing the block for-

Hiram Maxim's first model gun of 1884.

Early machine guns were treated as a form of artillery: a British Maxim 45 on field carriage, 1895.

Victorian engineering: a 45-caliber Maxim of the 1880s with phosphor-bronze water jacket and belt feed guides, all highly polished.

ward to chamber the round, after which the toggle snapped into the rigid position and the barrel and breech slid back into the firing position. The earliest guns were issued on wheeled carriages or on a peculiar 'overbank' carriage which allowed the gun to be fired over high breastworks, but these were soon replaced by the familiar type of tripod with a bicycle-type saddle for the gunner.

Although replaced by the Vickers gun from about 1911 onwards, the Maxim remained in service into World War I and was not officially declared obsolete until 1928. In 1912 its replacement price in the 'Vocabulary of Army Ordnance Stores' was £64.15.0d (£64.75 or about $255 at the then-current rate of exchange).

Length: 42.38in (1076mm). **Weight:** 60lb (27.20kg). **Barrel:** 28.0in (1102mm), 5 grooves, right hand twist. **Magazine:** 250-round cloth belt. **Cyclic rate:** 400 rds/min. **Muzzle velocity:** c.1800 ft/sec (548 m/sec).

• Laird-Mentayne Machine gun, 1908-1914

Coventry Ordnance Works, Coventry
303 British

The Laird-Mentayne machine gun was produced in England by the Coventry Ordnance Works to the designs of Mentayne and Degaille, whose patents were taken out in 1908. Laird was a later co-patentee with Mentayne in respect of one or two very minor modifications to the original designs, and one is inclined to feel that Laird's name is attached to the gun out of courtesy in return for his assistance in producing the weapon.

The gun was a long-recoil type, using the firing pin to lock the bolt: when fired, the barrel and bolt recoiled for the full stroke, the firing pin was held and the barrel and bolt began to move forward again. This withdrew the firing pin and unlocked the bolt, which was then held while the barrel returned. Feed was from a bottom-mounted box magazine, and the gun could be fitted to a tripod, although versions were also submitted with a light folding bipod under the barrel. The barrel was designed to be quickly interchanged when overheated and, reading the trial reports of the period, one has the impression that here was a fairly sound and serviceable light machine gun—certainly better-designed than some which followed. The military of the time were regrettably unaware of the light machine gun concept: machine guns, as everyone well knew, were large pieces, water-cooled and fired from tripods.

Tested in 1912 by the British Army, the 303 British version weighed 17lb (7.71 kg) and fired from an interchangeable 25-round magazine. It survived its trials reasonably well, with slight feed troubles, but the eventual conclusion was: 'The Committee do not consider this gun would meet any want except possibly for mounting in airplanes, for which purpose it would require considerable modification, as at present it is not adapted to a central pivot.' Had there been the necessary recognition, the tactics of World War I might well have been considerably revised.

• Gun, Machine, Hotchkiss, .303in Marks 1and 1*

Royal Small Arms Factory, Enfield Lock, Middlesex (?)
303 British

During World War I, the supply of machine guns for the British Army was augmented by purchasing the rights to the Hotchkiss gun and manufacturing it in Britain in 303 British caliber. The result was basically the French Army's 'Fusil Mitrailleur Mle 09' and it was known to the British as the Mark 1, introduced in March 1916. Fitted with a butt and bipod it became a useful light machine gun.

The basic design was then altered to ensure that the gun could be loaded either from the standard metallic strips or from a form of 'belt-feed' which consisted of no more than a series of short three-round strips hinged at their joints. This was primarily accomplished in order to use the guns for tank weapons, and was based on similar French developments. The revised gun, known as the Mark 1*, was introduced in June 1917.

Although superseded by the Lewis Gun and later by the Bren Gun, the Hotchkiss was retained in service throughout World War II as a reserve and Home Defense gun and was not declared obsolete until June 1946. In c.1926, however, the guns had become the 'Guns, Machine, Hotchkiss, .303in Number 2, Marks 1and 1*'

Length: 46.75in (1187mm). **Weight unloaded:** 27lb 0oz (12.25kg). **Barrel:** 23.50in (596mm), 4 grooves, right-hand twist. **Magazine:** 30-round metallic strip. **Cyclic rate:** c.500 rds/min. **Muzzle velocity:** c.2425 ft/sec (739 m/sec).

• Lewis Machine gun

Birmingham Small Arms Company Ltd, Birmingham
303 British

The Lewis light machine gun was the first light automatic to be used on a large scale in time of war. It was adopted by the Belgian Army in 1913 and soon afterwards, the British Army expressed an interest and BSA obtained manufacturing rights. The first combat use of the gun occurred in the 1914 retreats of the Belgian Army, though small numbers were already in the hands of the contemporary British Army. It was made in large numbers throughout the war, one reason for its success being that six Lewis Guns could be made for the time and expense involved in making one Vickers gun. The other reason was that it could be carried by one man, fast enough to keep up with an infantry battle. It was, of course, extensively adopted as an aircraft gun.

The original design was evolved from the designs of one Samuel Maclean by Colonel Isaac Lewis (of the US Army) and, as originally patented, was intended for production as a heavy or medium gun cooled either by air or water and mounted on a tripod; it had the distinctive Lewis action and drum feed, but it was without the peculiar cooling system later added when the gun was transformed into a light weapon.

The action is based on a turning bolt with rear locking lugs, and is somewhat similar to the Swiss Schmidt-Rubin rifle action, from which Maclean perhaps drew inspiration. A post on the gas piston extension engages in a helical slot in the bolt and also carries the striker, riding within the bolt. With the gun cocked, and the piston to the rear, pressure on the trigger releases the piston which is driven forward by the helical return spring—another distinctive Lewis feature. As the piston moves so the post carries the bolt forward, chambering a round, rotating the bolt by the helical slot until the lugs engage in the receiver body, and finally carrying the striker on to the cartridge cap. After firing, gas pressure on the piston drives it to the rear, withdrawing the striker, unlocking the bolt and opening it, ejecting the spent case and rewinding the helical return spring.

Cooling of the barrel is accomplished by forced draught, as the barrel is in contact throughout its length with a finned aluminum radiator enclosed in a cylindrical steel casing which is open at the rear but which projects some distance in front of the muzzle. The expansion of propellant gases at the muzzle induces a flow of air into the rear opening and along the aluminum radiator. When the gun was adapted to aircraft installation, this device, held to be unnecessary, was abandoned, and during World War II, when many of these aircraft guns were put to ground use, they seemed to work as well as the forced-cooling type—though prolonged firing might well have shown the difference. The general opinion, though, was that it appeared that soldiers had

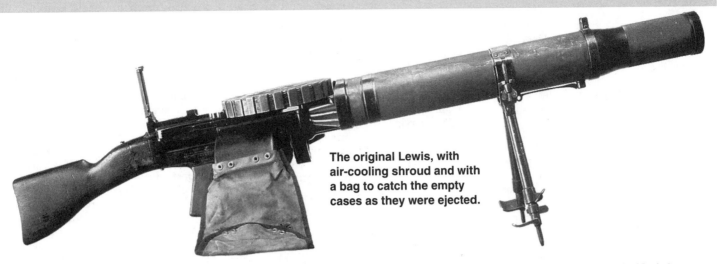

The original Lewis, with air-cooling shroud and with a bag to catch the empty cases as they were ejected.

been carrying a few pounds of excess weight around for several years to no very good purpose.

Although Colonel Lewis had energetically promoted his invention to various American authorities, and tests had been made, it was not until the gun had been produced in tens of thousands in Europe and proved in war that it was finally adopted in the land of its inception. In spite of subsequent combat experience, the United States Army retained only a small number after the war for training purposes, though the Army Air Service adopted the gun as a standard aircraft weapon. The truth of the matter will probably never be known, but it seems almost certain that a personality clash between Lewis and General Crozier, Chief of Ordnance, lay at the bottom of it, and Crozier had enough influence to block any move to adopt the Lewis gun until his retirement in 1918.

The Lewis Gun continued in service with many European and Asian countries until World War II. By that time, the British Army had replaced it in first line service with the Bren gun, but after Dunkirk, the many weapons in reserve stores were issued to units as a temporary measure until sufficient Brens were available; they continued to be used

for the remainder of the war by the Home Guard and the Merchant Marine.

The Lewis Gun's principal virtue was that it was the first in the field: its drawbacks lay in the excessive weight and the astounding variety of malfunctions and stoppages which could result from its not particularly complicated mechanism.

The following list gives the nomenclature and distinctive features of the various models of Lewis Gun from 1915 to post-World War II.

Gun, Machine, Lewis .303in Mark 1

(introduced on 15 October 1915). This is the original model, sighted to 2000 yards and supplied with a 47-round magazine. It was officially declared obsolete on 16 August 1946, though none had been seen in use for years.

Length: 50.50in (1283mm). **Weight unloaded:** 26lb 0oz (11.80kg). **Barrel:** 26.25in (666mm), 4 grooves, left-hand twist. **Magazine:** 47-round or 97-round pan drum. **Cyclic rate:** 550 rds/min. **Muzzle velocity:** c.2450 ft/sec (745 m/sec).

Gun, Machine, Lewis .303in Mark 2

(introduced on 10 November 1915). The Mark 2 differed from Mark I in having the cooling arrangements removed for aircraft use, leaving the barrel and gas cylinder exposed. A spade grip was fitted in place of the butt. The 97-round magazine was introduced for this gun in November 1916.

Gun, Machine, Lewis .303in Mark 2*

(introduced on 13 May 1918). This differed from Mark 2 in having a larger gas port and certain other parts modified to produce a faster rate of fire. Mark 2* guns were modified from existing weapons.

Gun, Machine, Lewis .303in Mark 3

(introduced on 13 May 1918). The Mark 3 was exactly the same as Mark 2* but of new manufacture and not a modification of existing weapons.

Gun, Machine, Lewis .303in SS

(introduced on 27 August 1942). For naval use 'to guide modification of existing guns to Shoulder Shooting'—so said the official announcement. The modification consisted of removing the radiator assembly and fitting a new short butt and a muzzle compensator, and adding a cylinder guard and foregrip. It could be applied to any Mark, whereupon the Mark had a 'star' added to the nomenclature; these guns, however, were also referred to rather indiscriminately as the 'Mark XI SS', which tended to confuse matters.

The aircraft model Savage-Lewis modified for ground use by the British Army in 1940. It carries the 97-round magazine.

Gun, Machine, Lewis .303in Mark 1*

(introduced on 16 August 1946). A conversion of Mark 1 guns to Mark 4 standard. It is doubtful if any were ever converted, for they were declared obsolete on the day of approval.

Gun, Machine, Lewis .303in Mark 4

(introduced on 16 August 1946). A conversion of Mark 3 guns to simplify manufacture. Again, it is doubtful if any were ever made, as the gun was declared obsolete on the day it was approved.

Gun, Machine, Savage-Lewis .30in.

This was the American 30-caliber Lewis aircraft gun made by the Savage Arms Corporation, purchased sometime in 1940 for British naval use (although it was later taken into use by the Home Guard). As supplied, they had no adjustable sights, but were later fitted with simple battle sights zeroed to 400 yards; the spade grip originally provided was extended into a skeleton butt by welding strip metal on and adding wooden shoulder and cheek pieces. Some of the first guns were provided with spare standard

wooden butts from store, but the welded model was developed when this supply ran out.

The name 'Savage-Lewis' was adopted by the naval authorities to distinguish the guns from the British 303-caliber versions. In addition, a two-inch wide red band was painted around the body in front of the magazine post, and the rear half of the magazine center disc was painted red, to remind users of the 30-06 Springfield caliber.

• The Vickers Gun, 1915-67

Manufactured in Royal Ordnance Factories, and by Vickers' Sons and Maxim (later 'Vickers-Armstrongs Ltd)

303 British

The Vickers machine gun was an improvement on the original Maxim. The main difference lies in the fact that the toggle locking action was inverted, but the weight was also considerably reduced by careful stress calculations and by the use of good grade steel and aluminum. The gun was adopted by the British Army in November 1912, and remained

as the standard support-fire machine gun until the middle 1960s, when it was replaced by the L7A1 GPMG. In its time, the Vickers pattern went through twelve or more modifications—mostly minor—and was substantially the same gun after fifty years of service. It was heavy, fairly slow-firing, prone to a number of stoppages from the ammunition, but reliable in itself and well loved by all. It worked in the most adverse conditions, and its water-cooled barrel ensured a long life for the bore. It was used in aircraft (for which it was air-cooled), in ships, in tanks, as a ground AA gun, on armored trains, on armored cars, and in a host of other roles. While firing the standard types of 303-caliber ammunition, a special round was developed for the Vickers—the boat-tailed Mark 8z—and this round added an extra 1000yds (914m) to the maximum range.

Gun, Machine, Vickers, .303in Mark 1

(introduced in 1912). This, the standard water-cooled weapon described above, remained in service until 1965. It was finally declared obsolete in 1968.

The Vickers Mark 1, complete with water can, condensing hose and collimating sight. Note the muzzle booster to improve the rate of fire, and the canvas jacket to reduce heat radiation in the line of sight.

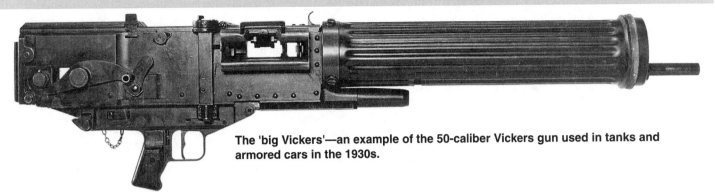

The 'big Vickers'—an example of the 50-caliber Vickers gun used in tanks and armored cars in the 1930s.

Length: 45.50in (1155mm). **Weight unloaded:** 40lb 0oz (18. 10kg). **Barrel:** 28.50in (723mm), 4 grooves, right-hand twist. **Magazine:** 250-round fabric belt. **Cyclic rate:** 450 rds/min. **Muzzle velocity:** c.2450 ft/sec (745 m/sec).

Gun, Machine, Vickers, .303in Mark 1*

An air-cooled aircraft gun, introduced in 1916. The barrel jacket was louvered to permit the circulation of air around the barrel, and the entire machine gun, excluding the Constantinesco interrupter gear, weighed 28lb (12.70kg).

Gun, Machine, Vickers, .303in Mark 2

(1917). A minor variant of the Mark 1* and also intended for air service; a smaller casing pierced with holes was fitted, and the unit weighed 22lb (10kg).

Gun, Machine, Vickers, .303in Mark 2*

(1927). Identical with the Mark 2, but with slightly different feed arrangements; the Mark 2* 'A' was provided with a left-side feed and the Mark 2* 'B' with a right-side feed.

Gun, Machine, Vickers, .303in Mark 3

(c. 1928). Another of the aircraft guns, the Mark 3 was virtually the Mark 2* with an elongated flash-hider designed to protect the aircraft's engine cowling.

Gun, Machine, Vickers, .303in Mark 4

(c. 1929-30). An experimental armored vehicle machine gun derived from the Mark 1; it was never adopted and remained in the prototype stage.

Gun, Machine, Vickers, .303in Mark 4B.

An armored vehicle gun manufactured with a suitably modified barrel casing and provided with an integral block carrying the mounting trunnions.

Gun, Machine, Vickers, .303in Mark 5

(c.1932). An aircraft gun similar in design to the Mark 3, but with a modified method of opening the body.

Gun, Machine, Vickers, .303in Mark 6

(1934). A gun similar to the Mark 4B and similarly intended for use in armored vehicles. It was given a better mount and had a corrugated barrel casing; versions existed with left- or right-side feed.

Gun, Machine, Vickers, .303in Mark 6*

(1938). Similar to the Mark 6, but with inlet and outlet pipes attached to the barrel casing to allow attachment to a header tank—or some similar reservoir—in the vehicle.

Gun, Machine, Vickers, .303in Mark 7.

Another of the vehicle guns, and again, similar to the Mark 6; the mounting, which seems to have given constant trouble, was once again strengthened. A thicker barrel casing was used and the surface left plain; the machine gun weighed 48lb (21.75kg).

Marks 4 to 7 were declared obsolete in 1944 and none of the aircraft guns saw service in World War II.

Vickers-system medium machine guns were also used by the US Army under the title **US Machine gun, Caliber .30in, M1915.** They were made by Colt's Patent Firearms Manufacturing Company, of Hartford, Connecticut, to a license granted by Vickers and were chambered for the Cartridge .30 M1906 (30-06 Springfield). Some were commercially marketed after World War I in a variety of calibers, and some in 30-caliber were purchased c.1922 by the Mexican Army—where they were known as the 'Ametrallador Modelo 1915'.

Vickers themselves are also known to have marketed commercial machine guns in various calibers, including 7.65mm Mauser. Guns in this caliber are known to have been supplied to Bolivia and Paraguay, and possibly to Argentina.

• Beardmore-Farquhar .303in Experimental, c.1917-1924
Beardmore Engineering Company
303 British

The Beardmore-Farquhar machine gun designed by the Farquhar of the Farquhar-Hill rifle and manufactured by Beardmore—was developed during World War 1, but did not reach a suitable standard for testing until the war was over. Thus, with the immediate urgency removed, the gun was somewhat more stringently examined than might have been the case had it been ready more quickly. It was an early contender in the light machine gun field,

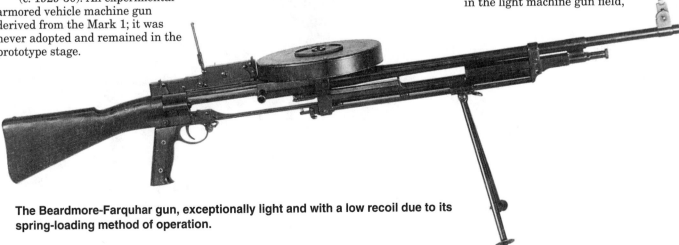

The Beardmore-Farquhar gun, exceptionally light and with a low recoil due to its spring-loading method of operation.

for it must be borne in mind that until World War I was into its third year, the light machine gun had little or no place on the battlefield, and it was not until the Lewis had been demonstrated as a useful adjunct to the rifle section that the philosophy took firm hold.

In addition to its possible use as an infantry weapon, this model was also proposed as an aircraft observer's gun and it was in this role that it was first tested. The report on the tests was favorable; indeed, had finance been available at the time and had World War I lasted longer, there is every reason to suppose that the Beardmore would have been accepted as a service weapon. As it was, circumstances militated against it and the Beardmore-Farquhar was not adopted. Nevertheless, its inventor kept making small improvements and offering his gun to the War Department through the 1920s and early 1930s. His final appearance was in the early 1940s, by which time his gun was obsolete and no longer of any value in either the air or the infantry roles, and, reading between the lines of the Ordnance Board's reports, one is inclined to think that they were by that time heartily fed up with Mr. Farquhar and his gun.

The principle of operation in this gun is quite unusual. Most gas-operated guns rely on the push of a gas piston to operate directly on the bolt, but here the piston actually compresses a powerful spring and the pressure generated by this spring upon the bolt is very carefully balanced against the pressure placed on the bolt by the exploding cartridge. Until the chamber pressure—and thus the pressure on the bolt—has dropped to a safe level, the spring pressure is not sufficient to unlock the bolt. Once the pressure has dropped, the spring performs the unlocking and bolt retraction with a very smooth movement unlike the usual 'slam-bang' action of a gas piston. The result is a smooth action with less liability to stoppages and difficult extraction, and a slower rate of fire than any of its contemporaries. Moreover, owing to the

gentle action and low recoil forces developed by this system, the whole weapon was considerably lighter—without sacrificing the robustness demanded in military service—than had previously been thought possible.

Length: 49.5in (1258mm). **Weight unloaded:** 19lb 0oz (8.62kg). **Barrel:** 26.5in (673mm), 4 grooves, right-hand twist. **Magazine:** 91-round drum. **Cyclic rate:** 500 rds/min. **Muzzle velocity:** 2440 ft/sec (744 m/sec).

• Vickers-Berthier Machine Guns, 1925-1945

Vickers-Armstrong Limited, Crayford, Kent; Ishapore Rifle Factory, India.
303 British

The gun which eventually became the Vickers-Berthier was designed by the Frenchman Adolphe Berthier prior to 1914, and he spent the war years perfecting the design to the point where the US Army provisionally approved the gun for issue as the US Machine Gun, Light, M1917. Unfortunately, the manufacturing facilities were not readily available, and before they could be arranged and production begun, the war ended. Subsequent closer and more searching trials of the gun

indicated that it was not sufficiently developed to be a serviceable weapon, the contract was canceled, and that was that.

Berthier then went to Britain and patented an improved gun in the early 1920s; manufacturing rights were acquired by Vickers in 1925 and the design was perfected and put into production. Limited numbers were made in the United Kingdom and a few sales were made to minor powers, including Bolivia, during the first years of the 1930s. In 1933, the Indian government adopted the Vickers-Berthier as their army's standard light machine gun, replacing the Lewis and the Hotchkiss. It is also probable, but for the appearance in 1932/3 of the original models of the Bren gun, that the Vickers design would have been adopted by the British army.

The VB was a gas-operated gun with few moving parts, a smooth action and the ability to be dismantled and assembled without special tools. The action locked by the tilting of the bolt into a recess in the top of the receiver; it was said to be reliable and trouble-free in adverse conditions.

Variants of the VB were:

Mark 1. Introduced in 1928, this was the first model, and could be recognized by a slab-sided forend under the receiver. The barrel was finned.

The Vickers-Berthier Mark 1, with rear monopod and finned barrel.

The Vickers-Berthier Light Mark 2 as adopted by the Indian Army.

Mark 2 (c.1929/30). Essentially similar to the Mark 1, the forend was rounded and extended forward of the receiver. A bipod and a butt monopod were fitted, similar in pattern to those of the Mark 1.

Light Mark 2. Produced in 1931 as an experiment for the Indian government. The gun had a smooth barrel, a light forend, no monopod and a cutaway butt.

Mark 3 and Mark 3B. The Mark 3 was adopted in 1933 by the Indian authorities, and was basically a heavier-looking version of the Light Mark 2. The gun, made by the rifle factory at Ishapore, was officially known as the 'Gun, Machine, .303in Vickers-Berthier, Indian Mark 3'; the Mark 3B was a minor variant in which alterations were made to the gas system to improve reliability.

Length: 46.50in (1180mm). **Weight unloaded:** 20lb 14oz (9.4kg). **Barrel:** 23.9in (607mm), 5 grooves, right-hand twist. **Magazine:** 30-round box. **Cyclic rate:** 450-500 rds/min. **Muzzle velocity:** c.2450 ft/sec (745 m/sec).

• Vickers 'K' (or VGO)
Vickers-Armstrong Ltd, Crayford, Kent
303 British

The Vickers 'K' was an aircraft gun derived from the Vickers-Berthier in 1935; it used the same general principles but it was more robust and thus heavier. This was done deliberately in order to increase the rate of fire. To distinguish it from other Vickers guns then in service it was generally known as the Vickers Gas Operated (VGO). It served with the RAF as an observer's gun until the general introduction of power-operated turrets in 1941 when the remaining VGOs were offered to the Army. The VGO was used by various units, including the newly-formed SAS who mounted them on jeeps in the desert. It was found that the VGO stood up to desert conditions very well and the high rate of fire was ideally suited to the hit-and-run raids undertaken by the SAS. A few remained in use for the same purpose until the mid-1960s.

Length: 40.00in (1016mm). **Weight unloaded:** 19lb 8oz (8.86kg). **Barrel:** 20.00in (508mm), 5-grooves, right-hand twist. **Magazine:** 100-round flat drum (non-rotating). **Cyclic rate:** 1050 rds/min (modified on later guns to 950 rds/min). **Muzzle velocity:** c.2450 ft/sec (745 m/sec).

• Gun, Machine Bren, .303in, Marks 1-4; Gun, Machine, 7.62inm Bren, L4A1-L4A6; c.1935-1971
Royal Small Arms Factory, Enfield Lock, Middlesex; J Inglis & Co, Montreal, Canada.
303 British (Marks 1-4), 7.62mm NATO (L4A1-L4A6); 7.92x57mm Mauser (Inglis)

During the early 1930s, the British Army was searching for a light machine gun which would show some improvement on the Lewis. The Vickers-Berthier was the strongest contender, but before a decision had been taken, a British military attaché brought the Czech ZB vz/26 machine gun to the army's attention. Specimens of the gun were obtained and it performed so creditably under test that it was adopted for service forthwith. The only difficulty was that the ZB vz/26 had been designed for the 7.92mm rimless Mauser cartridge, and so it had to be redesigned to accommodate the 303 British rimmed round, which accounts for the characteristic curved magazine of the Bren. Once the necessary modification had been made, the gun went into production at the Royal Small Arms Factory at Enfield Lock in 1937. In subsequent years, large numbers were made in Canada, including a quantity redesigned to the original 7.92mm chambering for supply to Nationalist China.

Without doubt, the Bren is one of the finest light machine guns ever made. Gas-operated, its mechanical components are simple and easily understood; it can be stripped and assembled by a trained soldier in a very short time indeed. There are only a few possible stoppages, and the Bren built up an enviable reputation for accuracy and reliability during World War II.

Gun, Machine, Bren, .303in Mark 1
(Officially introduced in August 1938). This was a direct copy of the original design and was equipped with a rather luxurious drum-pattern rearsight. The butt was fitted with a strap to go over the firer's shoulder and a pistol grip beneath it for his non-firing hand; this particular style of grip did not commend itself to the British soldier, and when modification and simplification were called for, the butt fittings were the first to go.

Length: 45.25in (1150mm). **Weight unloaded:** 22lb 5oz (10.15kg). **Barrel:** 25.00in (635mm), 6 grooves, right-hand twist. **Magazine:** 30-round detachable box. **Cyclic rate:** 500 rds/min. **Muzzle velocity:** c.2400 ft/sec (73 m/sec).

Gun, Machine, Bren, .303in Mark 2.
In June 1941, the Mark 2 was introduced. This changed the rear sight to a more conventional leaf type; the telescopic bipod was replaced by one of fixed length; the butt was simplified; the cocking handle did not fold, and certain lightening grooves in the original body design were omitted in the interests of faster production in wartime.

The Bren Mark 1, as developed by the Czechs and adopted by the British Army in 1938.

A Vickers GO (gas operated) gun, minus its drum magazine.

The Bren Mark 3 was considerably simplified and had a shorter barrel.

Gun, Machine, Bren, .303in Marks 3 and 4.

These were introduced in July 1944. The Mark 3 was similar to the Mark 1but was generally lighter and had a shorter barrel. The Mark 4 was a similar conversion of the Mark 2.

Gun, Machine, Bren, .303in Mark 2/1.

Introduced in 1948, the Mark 2/1 was the same as the Mark 2 but with a new cocking handle and slide assembly.

• 7.62mm Machine guns L4A1-L4A6.

When the 7.62mm NATO cartridge was adopted by the British Army, the Bren L4 series was introduced. By and large this consists of conversions of later Marks of Bren to the new cartridge, but there are a number of distinct models:

The **L4A1** was a conversion from Mark 3 by the fitting of a new barrel with slotted flash eliminator, new ejector assembly, a Canadian 7.92mm Bren extractor and a suitably modified Canadian 7.92mm breechblock; the body and magazine cover were altered to suit the new straight 30 round magazine.

The **L4A2** was the L4A1 with some minor design improvements.

The **L4A3** was a conversion of Mark 2 models by modification of the body and the fitting of a new barrel, the interior of which was chromium-plated, a step which so extended the life of the barrel that the provision of a spare barrel was unnecessary.

The **L4A4** was a conversion of the Mark 3 Bren using a chrome-plated barrel.

The **L4A5** was similar to the L4A3 except that the barrel was not chrome-plated and therefore two barrels were issued with each gun.

The **L4A6** was a conversion of the L4A1 by replacing the barrel with a chromium-lined one which obviated the need for a spare barrel.

The **L4A7** was a conversion of the Mark 1 Bren; drawings were prepared for the Indian Army, but none were ever manufactured.

• Gun, Machine, Besa, 7.92mm, Marks 1-3/3, c.1939-1965

Birmingham Small Arms Company Ltd, Redditch
7.92x57mm Mauser

After purchasing the vz/26 design from Czechoslovakia, the British authorities were offered a tank machine gun, the ZB vz/53, from the same source. This weapon was accepted in 7.92mm chambering and in view of the trouble which had arisen in converting the vz/26 design from the 7.92mm rimless round to the 303 British rimmed round (after which it became the Bren Gun), it was felt preferable to retain the original caliber of the gun and place a quantity of ammunition under manufacture in Britain. This course was acceptable since the gun was intended solely for use in armored vehicles, and the logistic problem was not therefore of the proportions which would have arisen had the gun been in general service.

When modified to suit production techniques and placed in production by the Birmingham Small Arms Company, the gun became known as the Besa. It is gas-operated, but it is unusual in having a recoiling barrel as well, the movement of which provides a system of recoil control known as the differential system. The point of it is that the cartridge is inserted into the chamber while the weapon is recoiled and is fired while the barrel is still moving forward into battery; the resultant recoil force has first to arrest the forward motion of the barrel before causing it to recoil. This enforced change of direction absorbs a good deal of the recoil energy and reduces the stresses on

The Bren still flourishes, 61 years after its adoption, as the L4A1 gun in 7.62mm NATO caliber.

the rest of the gun. Whether or not this system was responsible for it, the Besa was renowned in the British Army for the accuracy of its shooting.

Gun, Machine, Besa, 7.92mm, Mark 1

This was officially introduced in June 1940, although numbers were in use well before that date. It was declared obsolete on the day of its introduction. The Mark 1 was a direct copy of the original Czech design, differing only in having solid side-plates instead of perforated. The gun was gas-actuated, using a very short gas cylinder so that after the initial impulse, the piston moved out of the cylinder and the gas was vented to the air. This also blew out any possible fouling and was instrumental in making the gun exceptionally reliable. The breech was locked by the lifting of the breechblock, in a similar manner to the ZB26 series, but in this case it locked into the barrel extension, allowing barrel and breechblock to recoil inside the receiver while still locked together. This model had two rates of fire, adjustable by varying the bolt stroke and buffer strength by means of a control known as the 'accelerator'.

Length: 43.50in (1105mm). **Weight unloaded:** 47lb 0oz (21.46kg). **Barrel:** 29.00in (736mm), 4 grooves, right-hand twist. **Magazine:** 225-round belt. **Cyclic rate, low:** 450-500 rds/min. **Cyclic rate, high:** 750-850 rds/min. **Muzzle velocity:** c.2700 ft/sec'(823 m/sec).

Gun, Machine, Besa, 7.92mm, Mark 2

This variant was introduced on the same day as the Mark 1. The differences between the Marks 1and 2 were relatively minor. In the Mark 2, the accelerator was cranked to the rear instead of forward; the barrel sleeve was shorter; the flash guard had no vent holes, and there were minor changes in the body and cover to facilitate production. At 48lb (21.84kg), the Mark 2 weighed 1lb (0.46kg) more than the Mark 1.

Gun, Machine, 7.92mm, Besa, Marks 2*, 3 and 3*

In August 1941, the Marks 2*, 3 and 3* guns were introduced. The Mark 2* was a transitional model between the Mark 2 and the Mark 3. Some components were of simplified pattern, but all were interchangeable with Mark 2 guns; the Mark 3 was a simplified design, components of which were not interchangeable with earlier Marks. The greatest change in the Mark 3 was that the rate-of-fire selector was omitted: consequently, only the high rate of fire 750 rds/min to 850 rds/min was available. The Mark 3*, on the other hand, had the rate of fire fixed at the low level of 450 rds/min to 550 rds/min. Except for this, there was no difference between the two guns.

Gun, Machine, 7.92mm, Besa, Marks 3/2 and 3/3

The Besa design remained stationary until 1952 when the Mark 3/2 was introduced, which was simply a conversion of the Mark 3* gun to accept a new bracket and cover. Then in 1954 came the Mark 3/3, which differed from the Mark 3/2 in having a new pattern of barrel and sleeve and a new gas cylinder with larger gas vents. It was introduced in order to ensure that guns using belts of mixed ammunition would function satisfactorily. A number of existing Mark 3/2 guns were modified to Mark 3/3 pattern but, so far as can be ascertained, no new manufacture to this mark ever took place.

All Besa guns were declared obsolete in 1969.

• Gun, Machine, Besal, .303in Marks 1 and 2, c.1940

Birmingham Small Arms Co. Ltd., Birmingham
303 British

During World War II, the Bren gun was exclusively produced in Britain by the Royal Small Arms Factory at Enfield Lock. During the early days of the war it became blatantly obvious that one large air-raid on the plant would completely disrupt production for some time. BSA were consequently asked to prepare an alternative design capable of rapid and uncomplicated production by almost any engineering shop. The resultant design was known as the Besal, but was later rechristened the Faulkner in recognition of the gun's designer. In many ways, the Besal was a simplified Bren designed with production limitations in mind; the body and gas cylinder were simple pressings, the trigger mechanism is basic in the extreme, and the piston and breechblock—devoid of any frills—are of square section. The block locks by two lugs which are forced by a ramp into recesses cut in the receiver, and the return spring is contained in the piston and retained by a removable pin pushed up from underneath. Cocking was achieved by pulling the pistol grip to the rear. The gas regulator was a finned cylinder providing four sizes of port, which could be changed by rotating the unit with a bullet nose. A handle projected from the left side of the barrel and was used as a handgrip when changing the barrel unit: it was of little value as a carrying handle as it did not rotate. The rear sight had two positions only, and the legs of the bipod were not adjustable for height, but the Besal was, nevertheless, an impressive gun, and on trial, it shot well with few stoppages.

Only a few pilot models were made, as Bren production at Enfield was never seriously impaired.

Length: 46.63in (1185mm). **Weight unloaded:** 21lb 8oz (9.74kg). **Barrel:** 22.00in (558mm), 4 grooves, right-hand twist. **Magazine:** 30-round detachable box (Bren). **Cyclic rate:** 600 rds/min. **Muzzle velocity:** c.2450 ft/sec (745 m/sec).

The Besal, or Faulkner, gun was designed as a cheap emergency alternative to the Bren gun, capable of being made in any workshop. The design was perfected but never put into production.

The only surviving specimen of the Rolls-Royce machine gun.

• Gun, Machine, Besa, 15mm Mark 1, 1940

Birmingham Small Arms Co., Ltd., Redditch

15x103mm Besa

The Besa 15mm Mark 1, introduced in June 1940, was another Czech design—a modification of the ZB vz/60. Basically it was an enlargement of the 7.92mm weapon and, like it, was destined solely for use in armored vehicles. It had, however, one additional feature in that it was possible to fire single shots from it.

Only one Mark was ever introduced, and the 15mm Besa never seems to have been very popular; in 1942 there was even an abortive attempt to redesign it to 20mm caliber, in order to use Hispano-Suiza ammunition. It was declared obsolescent in 1944 and obsolete in 1949. The design's principal drawback was said to be its weight and size, but it is of interest to see that similar heavy machine guns now form the armament of armored personnel carriers of other countries and it has also been said that the 15mm Besa would have been well-suited to such employment had it remained in service, although in British service this particular role has been taken over by the 30mm Rarden cannon.

Length: 80.70in (2050mm). **Weight unloaded:** 125lb 8oz (56.9kg). **Barrel:** 57.60in (1462mm), 8 grooves, right-hand twist. **Magazine:** 25-round belt. **Cyclic rate:** 450 rds/min. **Muzzle velocity:** c.2900 ft/sec (884 m/sec).

• Gun, Machine, Rolls-Royce Experimental, 1941

Rolls-Royce Ltd, Derby

50 Browning and 55-caliber Boys

Although their design was never finally developed as a service weapon, the fact that Rolls-Royce once made the venture into the machine gun field is felt to be of sufficient interest to warrant a mention here.

In 1941 Rolls-Royce began to develop a gas-operated machine gun for use in aircraft turrets; it was intended to fire the standard American 50 Browning cartridge. In order to reduce weight and size to a level suited to aircraft use, the barrel was some 5inches (126mm) shorter than that of the Browning, and the body and cover of the gun were to be made from RR50 aluminum alloy. As finally developed, the gun was recoil-operated and used a breech-locking system based on the Friberg-Kjellman-Degtyarev system with refinements by Rolls-Royce. As the barrel and breechblock recoiled, a pair of accelerator levers carried back a wedge-like 'balance piece' and retracted the striker. The withdrawal of this balance piece allowed the bolt-lock arms to fold in and unlock the breech, after which, the accelerators threw the block back at high speed to strike an oil buffer at the rear of the body. At the same time, a feed claw withdrew the next round from the belt and this was guided down and back to rest on guide lips ready to be rammed into the chamber. The barrel returned into battery under the power of its own return spring, while the bolt was returned not by a spring, but by the pressure of the oil in the buffer, collecting the fresh round en route and loading it. As the mechanism went forward, the balance piece opened out the breech locks and then carried the firing pin on to the cap to fire the round.

In March 1941, the gun was delivered for trial at the Proof and Experimental Establishment, Pendine. Owing to the short barrel, a long flash-hider had to be used—which rather detracted from the original intentions—and the trial was bedeviled by minor stoppages, culminating in the breaking of the extractors. A month later, Rolls-Royce decided to redesign the gun around the high-velocity belted 55-caliber round from the Boys anti-tank rifle, the result of which would have produced a very formidable weapon. The Ordnance Board agreed that the idea showed promise, and furnished 2000 rounds for use in preliminary trials, but it would seem that shortly after this Rolls-Royce decided that they had enough to occupy their minds in the matter of making airplane engines, and in 1942 came notification that the development had been dropped.

Length: 50.00in (1270mm). **Weight unloaded:** 49lb 0oz (22.22kg). **Barrel:** 40.00in (1016mm), 6 grooves, right-hand twist. **Magazine:** 250-round belt. **Cyclic rate:** 1000 rds/min. **Muzzle velocity:** c.2340 ft/sec (712 m/sec).

• Gun, Machine, Hefah V .303in Mark 1 (1942)

Ductile Steel Company, Short Heath, Staffs., (originally); Hefah & Co, Wednesfield, Staffs. (finally) -

303 British

The Hefah machine gun was developed as a private venture by the Ductile Steel Company in 1940, and was first submitted for trial in June of the same year. It was basically a modified Lewis action, simplified to facilitate rapid manufacture. The breechblock used only one locking lug, a slightly altered Bren drum magazine was fitted beneath the gun, and the return spring was contained within a tube projecting from the rear of the receiver. On trial, it was noted that this return spring housing tended to bruise the cheek of the firer, and with the gun resting on bipod and butt, there was only a bare half-inch clearance beneath the magazine.

The Hefah V machine gun; it was normally fitted into a multiple-gun mounting for air defense on ships.

Although these faults weighed against it when considered for use as an infantry squad weapon, the Director of Naval Ordnance—who was desperate for anti-aircraft machine guns for small coastal vessels—felt that the simple design was of value in view of the production capacity available at that time, and he recommended its adoption. The Director General of Munitions Production, however, suspended all work on the gun for some months because there was no factory available to make the rifled bar-

General Purpose Machine gun, 7.62mm, L7A1 (GPMG).

This is the basic model, with a pistol grip, a butt and a stamped-steel bipod; the action is fed from the right side by means of a disintegrating-link metallic belt, which usually contains 250 rounds of ammunition.

General Purpose Machine gun, 7.62mm, L7A2.

The L7A2 differs from its predecessor only in the provision of mounting points for a box containing a 50-round belt, and the provision of double feed pawls in the mechanism.

Length: 48.50in (1232mm). **Weight unloaded:** 24lb 0oz (10.9kg). **Barrel:** 23.50in (597mm), 4 grooves, right-hand twist. **Magazine:** metal belt. **Cyclic rate:** 750-1000 rds/min. **Muzzle velocity:** 2750 ft/sec (838 m/sec).

The British L7 general purpose machine gun (GPMG) with bipod.

The GPMG in the sustained fire role on a tripod.

rels. Capacity was eventually found, and the Hefah, by this time the product of the Hefah Company of Wednesfield, went into production for the Royal Navy, formally approved for service as the 'Gun, Machine, Hefah V, .303in Mark 1' in May 1942.

The gun's subsequent employment is not entirely clear, although it seems that only a limited number were made; it was declared obsolete in November 1944.

Length: 48.0in (1220mm). **Weight:** 15lb 2oz (6.85kg). **Barrel:** 24.50in (622mm), 4 grooves, right-hand twist . **Magazine:** 60-round drum. **Cyclic rate:** 600 rds/min. **Muzzle velocity:** 2500 ft/sec (762 m/sec).

• General Purpose Machine Gun, 7.62mm L7 Series
Royal Small Arms Factory, Enfield Lock, Middlesex
7.62x51mm NATO

The L7 series of machine guns is basically Fabrique Nationale's MAG pattern with many minor modifications made by the Royal Small Arms Factory to suit production to British methods; the operation, however, remains unchanged—a gas-operated tipping-bolt design. Among the British variants are the following:

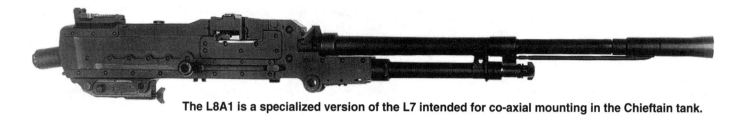

The L8A1 is a specialized version of the L7 intended for co-axial mounting in the Chieftain tank.

The L37A1 is the version of the L7 intended for use in tanks other than the Chieftain, armored personnel carriers and armored cars.

The British army's 5.56mm squad automatic is this L86A1 'Light Support Weapon'.

Tank Machine gun, 7.62mm, L8A1

Intended for use in the Chieftain tank, this weapon is fitted with a bore evacuator to keep the tank's interior free of fumes. It is also fitted with a variable-aperture gas regulator and has provision for a firing solenoid.

Tank Machine gun, 7.62mm L8A2

An improved version of the L8A1 specifically adapted to fitting into the Challenger tank.

General Purpose Machine gun, 7.62mm, L19A1

The L19 was a version of the L7 fitted with a heavier barrel to reduce the number of changes of barrel necessary when the gun is used for prolonged firing. It is not a general-issue weapon.

General Purpose Machine gun, 7.62mm, L20A1

The L20 is intended for pod-mounting on the army's helicopters and light aircraft; and is fitted with an L8 gas regulator and an L7 barrel (which lacks the bore evacuator). The gun is capable of either left or right side feed. The gun is fired electrically, and there are no sights fitted.

General Purpose Machine gun, 7.62mm, L20A2

A slightly improved version of the L20A1.

Tank Machine gun, 7.62mm, L37A1

This weapon is a version of the basic design intended for use in tanks other than the Chieftain and sundry other armored vehicles. It is basically a mix of L7 and L8 components with a special barrel designed to withstand a high proportion of tracer ammunition being fired through it for ranging purposes, and can be sometimes found with a folding pistol grip unit which, together with the bipod, butt and trigger assembly carried in the vehicles, enables the L37 to be dismounted in an emergency to do duty as a standard ground gun.

• 5.56mm L86A1 Light Support Weapon

Royal Small Arms Factory, Nottingham
5.56x45mm NATO

The Light Support Weapon (LSW) is the LMG version of the 5.56mm L85 rifle, and as the differences are only slight, reference should be made to that entry for full details.

The LSW uses 80% of the rifle components, differing mainly in that it has a heavier and longer barrel, some changes in the trigger mechanism, a light bipod, and a longer magazine. However, the magazines on the two weapons are interchangeable. The heavy barrel permits automatic fire in the support role, and gives the bullet a greater effective range than from the rifle. It is unusual among British LMGs in being fixed to the body, and is not capable of being changed. The mechanism is virtually identical with that of the rifle, but the bolt is held back by a rear sear when firing automatic, thus helping to cool the breech and avoid cook-offs. Single shots are fired from a closed breech.

Length: 35.4in (900mm). **Weight unloaded:** 11lb 14oz (5.40kg). **Barrel:** 25.43in (646mm), 6 grooves, right-hand twist. **Magazine:** 30-round box. **Cyclic rate:** 610-775 rds/min. **Muzzle velocity:** 3182 ft/sec (970 m/sec).

INDIA

• INSAS
Indian Small Arms Factory, Kanpur
5.56x45mm

This is the heavy-barreled version of the INSAS (Indian Small Arms System) assault rifle, described elsewhere. It is gas-operated, using a rotating bolt, and can deliver single shots or automatic fire. The barrel is heavier than that of the rifle, is chromed internally, and has a different rifling contour to develop better long-range ballistic performance. The weapon is sighted up to 1000 meters. The muzzle is formed to the NATO-standard 22mm diameter for grenade launching, and a bayonet can be fitted. The bipod is instantly recognizable as that produced in the Indian factories for the Bren and Vickers-Berthier machine guns during World War II. The Indians obviously see no point in reinventing the wheel.

At the time of writing the INSAS LMG has been approved for service with the Indian Army, but, like the rifle, issue has been held up until the ammunition production has been organized.

Length: 41.34in (1050mm). **Weight unloaded:** 13lb 11oz (6.23kg). **Barrel:** 21.06in (535mm), 4 grooves, right-hand twist. **Magazine:** 30-round detachable box. **Cyclic rate:** 650 rds/min. **Muzzle velocity:** c.3035 ft/sec (925 m/sec).

IRAQ

• Al-Quds machine rifle
State factories
7.62x39mm Russian

The Al-Quds is a heavy-barreled version of the standard Kalashnikov AKM rifle. The barrel is longer than normal and has cooling fins on that portion beneath the gas cylinder.

There is a detachable bipod, and the normal 30-round rifle magazine is used.

Length: 40.35in (1025mm). **Weight unloaded:** 11lb 0oz (5.0kg). **Barrel:** 21.34in (542mm), 4 grooves, right-hand twist. **Magazine:** 30-round detachable box. **Cyclic rate:** 600 rds/min. **Muzzle velocity:** c.2450 ft/sec (745 m/sec).

ISRAEL

• Dror
Israel Military Industries, Ramat Ha Sharon
7.92x57mm Mauser

This weapon, resembling the Johnson light machine gun of 1944, was developed by the Israeli Army in the early 1950s. Although a sound weapon, only a small quantity was produced and it seems likely that the Israeli government found it more economical to buy a foreign design of proven worth and commercial availability rather than involve themselves in the considerable expense of laying out a plant to produce the relatively small numbers they required.

The Dror is recoil-operated, an unusual feature in a light machine gun, and magazine-fed. The usual quick-change barrel and bipod are fitted. Difficulties with barrel stability in the original Johnson design dictated that the Dror should have a longer barrel support. The modified gun was not completely successful under harsh Middle East conditions.

• Negev
Israel Military Industries, Ramat Ha Sharon
5.56x45mm

The Negev is a multi-purpose weapon which can feed from standard belts, drums or box magazines and can be fired from a bipod, tripod or vehicle mounts. The standard barrel is rifled for SS109 ammunition; an alternative barrel is rifled for US M193 ammunition. The weapon is gas operated with a rotating bolt which locks into the barrel exten-

sion, and fires from an open bolt. The gas regulator has three positions, allowing the rate of fire to be changed from 650-800 rds/min to 800-950 rds/min or the gas supply cut off to permit launching grenades from the muzzle. The weapon will fire in semi or full-automatic modes, and by removing the bipod and attaching a normal forend and short barrel it can be used as an assault rifle. The Negev was introduced in 1988 and has been adopted by the Israel Defense Force.

Length, butt extended: 40.16in (1020mm); butt folded: 30.71in (780mm). **Weight unloaded:** 16lb 8oz (7.50kg). **Barrel:** 18.11in (460mm), 6 grooves, right-hand twist. **Magazine:** 30- or 35-round box, link belt or drum. **Cyclic rate:** 800 rds/min. **Muzzle velocity:** c.3117 ft/sec (950 m/sec).

ITALY

• Perino machine gun, 1900-1913
Manufacturer unknown
6.5x52mm Mannlicher-Carcano

The Perino machine gun, patented in 1900 by Guiseppe Perino, was an interesting weapon with several creditable features. It was operated by a combination of recoil and gas action, in reality, a recoil gun augmented by impinging the muzzle gases on a fixed muzzle section, which thus boosted the recoil of the moving portion of the barrel. The breech locking was achieved by a bell-crank lever system which gave a very positive action. The feed unit was originally a metal chain carried on a drum on the side of the gun (each link of the chain carried a cartridge), but this was later replaced by a feed box carrying five trays of twelve rounds, similar to the feed system used on many Italian machine-guns in later years.

A notable feature was the enclosure of the recoiling barrel within a sleeve; the barrel was carried on two piston rings which—working in the

The Israeli Dror of the 1940s closely resembled the Johnson M1944 but has a bipod rather than a monopod and a much longer barrel jacket.

The Israeli Negev 5.56mm machine gun with belt feed.

The Negev will also feed from a Galil rifle box magazine.

The Commando assault model of the Negev with short barrel and folded stock.

A rare surviving example of the SIA machine gun; the 'horns' at the left end are the supports for a conventional spade grip— the grips have vanished over the years.

sleeve—acted as an air pump to force cool air through ports alongside the breech, which were themselves angled to direct a flow of cooling air into the chamber every time the bolt was opened. A modified version was also produced in which the whole length of the barrel was covered by a casing and water was pumped around the barrel by the same piston ring arrangement. A further refinement, common in that era, provided for the alteration of the fire-rate by controlling the return of the bolt.

It has frequently been said that the highly-esteemed Perino was treated with considerable secrecy by the Italian government and this may be so, as far as service adoption is concerned, but the gun was commercially available to everyone and, in 1911, an improved version was offered to the British Army by the English importer. This was somewhat modified from Perino's original design, water-cooled by an external pump and having the tray-feed system. The trials showed that the gun was robust and reliable, although owing to the large proportion of sliding mechanical components, it was thought likely to give trouble in dusty or sandy climates. The main drawback was one of weight, almost fifty pounds without water or tripod, and this was sufficient to lead the trials committee to the conclusion that it showed no advantage over the Vickers-Maxim. In 1913, the agents returned with news of an improved '1913 Model' which, they claimed, was simpler in its mechanism

The Fiat-Revelli water-cooled gun of 1914.

and more reliable than any other known machine gun, and reduced in weight to a few ounces under thirty pounds; it is not known whether trials were ever made of this version, and the details of how it differed from the earlier model are not clear.

The Italian government were much taken with the idea of promoting indigenous inventions—and rightly so, for the Perino was quite a serviceable weapon for its day—but they wasted too much time in endless trials against Maxim, Vickers, Colt and other weapons, without committing themselves to production. When they had finally decided, World War I was upon them and they were forced to take what they could get instead of having a Perino production line ready. Unfortunately, no dimensions of the Perino have been discovered.

• Light Machine Gun SIA, System Agnelli, c.1913-1925
SIA: Societa Italiana Ansaldo, Armstrong & Co., Rome
6.5x52mm Mannlicher-Carcano

The SIA machine gun was a relatively simple light machine gun of dubious value. There is no evidence to suggest

that it was ever accepted into military service in any numbers, though it appears to have been employed by the Italians as a training weapon in the 1930s.

The design is a questionable form of retarded blowback based upon the patents of Giovanni Agnelli, which relate to a system of locking the rotating breech-bolt by using a positively-located firing pin with a lug riding in helical grooves within the breech-bolt. Thus, as the pin went home under the pressure of the return spring, the bolt was revolved to lock to the breech, but the pin was held clear of the cartridge cap by an auxiliary spring which was overcome only by the blow of the firing hammer. Like every other inventor of a blow-back gun, Agnelli had his share of troubles owing to sticky extraction of the bottlenecked cartridge case, and he must be credited as the first patentee of the idea of machining flutes in the chamber in order to equalize the pressure on each side of the case and thus overcome this problem.

The Ansaldo-Armstrong combine took over the Agnelli patents and produced a gun shortly before World War I, but it was not developed into a workable proposition until the 1920s, by which time there were many other and better ideas available. Probably the worst feature of the SIA was the open-sided magazine which allowed the dust and dirt roused by firing to thoroughly coat the rounds waiting to be fed into the chamber, which may account for the rest of Agnelli's extraction troubles. As with the Perino, no reliable dimensions can be discovered.

The Breda Model 30 had some peculiar design features.

Length: 46.50in (1180mm.). **Weight unloaded:** 37lb 8oz (17.00kg). **Barrel:** 25.75in (654mm), 4 grooves, right-hand twist. **Magazine:** 50-round strip-feed box. **Cyclic rate:** 400 rds/min. **Muzzle velocity:** c.2100 ft/sec (640 m/sec).

• Machine Gun, System Revelli Model 14 ('FIAT-Revelli')

FIAT SpA, Turin
6.5x53mm Mannlicher-Carcano

The Model 1914 Revelli was the first Italian-designed machine-gun to appear in any numbers. It was chambered for the under-powered 6.5mm M95 rifle round, but was as heavy as any of the more powerful Maxims to which it bore a considerable resemblance. The action was novel, for it worked by a retarded blowback system in which the barrel recoiled for a short distance before the bolt moved away from the breech. This arrangement did not allow for any primary extraction and, to ensure that the cartridge cases did not rupture, each round was oiled as it was fed into the chamber, the oil being kept in a reservoir on top of the receiver. Another curiosity was a buffer rod attached to the top of the bolt and working outside the receiver on the top surface. This rod buffered against a stop immediately in front of the firing handles, in which position it was a constant source of danger while the gun was firing—and where it also picked up grit and dust and fed it into the mechanism. In any case, the oiled cartridges attracted dirt and the gun was noted for stoppages.

The Model 14 was fitted with an extraordinary pattern of magazine containing ten compartments, each of five rounds. As the device emptied, a projection at the rear of each compartment raised a pawl to allow an arm to push the magazine to the right, in so doing, presenting the next of the magazine compartments to the feed. The peculiar feed arrangements constituted an example of the needless mechanical complexity usually evident in Italian machine gun design but, even so, it survived in first-line use throughout World War II (although many were modernized in 1935).

• Machine guns, System Breda, 1925--1938

Societa Anonima Ernesto Breda, Brescia
6.5x53mm Mannlicher-Carcano; 7.35x51mm Breda; 8x59RB Breda M35; 13.2x99mm Breda

The Breda company produced a number of machine-guns for the Italian Army which, for the sake of convenience, might be considered together. The first design produced by the Breda company was the Mitragliatrice Sistema Breda Modello 1924, which was little different from the succeeding pattern of 1930, adopted on a large scale by the army.

Breda Model 30

The design of 1930 was the result of trials undertaken with the earlier machine guns of 1924 (known commercially as the Mitragliatrice Breda tipo 5C), 1928 and 1929. It was an ungainly-looking weapon which must have been difficult to clean and maintain in dusty conditions. Like its predecessors, the Model 30 was blowback-operated, and since blowback operation invariably means difficult extraction, the gun carried an oil pump to lubricate the rounds prior to chambering. The magazine on the right side of the receiver hinged forward, in which position it could be loaded from rifle chargers. This design offered a theoretical advantage in that the lips could be properly machined and were therefore less liable to damage than those of detachable magazines. But there were disadvantages, principally that the rate of fire was greatly reduced owing to the difficulties of loading and—should the magazine become in any way damaged—the gun could be put out of action. The barrels of these guns could be changed quite rapidly, but it is notable that there was no form of handle or grip with which to hold the hot barrel; nor, indeed, was there any carrying-handle,

and so the unfortunate gunner had either to carry the gun across his shoulder or cradle it in his arms.

The Model 30 differed from the earlier 1924 design in having a bipod instead of a tripod, and in being given a pistol grip and shoulder stock in place of spade grips and a thumb trigger.

Length: 48.40in (1230mm). **Weight unloaded:** 22lb 8oz (10.20kg). **Barrel:** 20.50in (520mm), 4 grooves, right-hand twist. **Magazine:** 20-round box. **Cyclic rate:** 475 rds/min. **Muzzle velocity:** c.2000 ft/sec (609 m/sec).

Breda Model 31

In 1931, the Italians introduced a 13.2mm heavy machine-gun intended primarily as a tank gun, although it could be mounted on a tripod and issued in an infantry support role. It has few unusual features apart from some exceptionally sensitive explosive bullets, although from a design aspect, it seems to have been an intermediate step towards the development of the Model 37.

Breda Model 37

The Model 37, which became the standard Italian Army machine-gun in World War II, was a fairly conventional gas-operated pattern with several unusual features which placed it in a class of its own. The design of the mechanism was such that the cartridges were not given a primary extraction movement to loosen them in the chamber prior to ejection: it was still necessary, therefore, to oil the rounds before they were fed into the mechanism. The second unusual feature was the system of feeding the rounds into the gun from a series of trays inserted from the side; the action of the gun was to remove the cartridge from the feed-tray, chamber and fire it, and then to extract the empty case and replace it in the tray. The full tray fed into one side of the gun and appeared at the other loaded with empty cartridge cases. The reason for this complication was that the gun

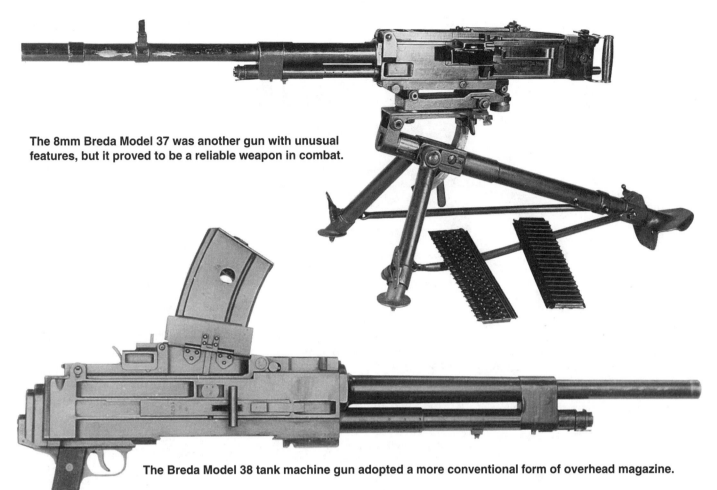

The 8mm Breda Model 37 was another gun with unusual features, but it proved to be a reliable weapon in combat.

The Breda Model 38 tank machine gun adopted a more conventional form of overhead magazine.

was originally designed for use in tanks, and there was a great fear that a carelessly ejected cartridge case might fall into some part of the machinery of the tank and jam the turret or some of the driving controls; and having designed it so, there was no great incentive to re-design it when the gun was adopted for field use. But whatever the employment, the principal drawback was simply that the poor gunner was forced to pull the empties from the tray before he could attempt to reload it.

In spite of this, the Model 37 managed to stay in front-line service throughout World War II, and emerged from it with a reputation for reliability.

Length: 50.00in (1270mm). **Weight unloaded:** 43lb 0oz (19.50kg). **Barrel:** 26.75in (679mm), 4 grooves, right-hand twist. **Magazine:** 20-round strip. **Cyclic rate:** 450 rds/min. **Muzzle velocity:** c.2600 ft/sec (791 m/sec).

Breda, caliber 8mm, Model 38

This was the basic small-caliber tank and armored vehicle gun, and was a far more sensible design than some of its predecessors, using a top-mounted spring-fed box magazine and supplied with a heavy barrel which was capable of sustained fire.

Breda, caliber 7.35mm, Model 38

In 1938, the Italians introduced a new 7.35mm cartridge in an attempt to improve the efficiency of their rifles; at the same time, they took the opportunity of rechambering some of the Breda Model 30 guns for the larger round, and the Model 38 was the result. The 6.5mm and 7.35mm cartridge cases were almost identical except for the size of the case-mouth, so apart from the barrel, few changes were necessary to execute the conversion.

• Machine gun, System Scotti, Model 28

Isotta-Fraschini SpA, Turin
7.7mm (303 British)

The Scotti light machine gun was one of a range of weapons designed by Alfredo Scotti of Brescia. He was a freelance designer associated, for the most part, with the Italian aircraft firms and most of his weapons were intended for use in air warfare, although he also produced some machine guns and a few light guns for infantry use. The pattern of 1928 was the best of his light infantry guns. It utilized the Scotti patent principle of operation, which is a form of locked blowback. Gas is tapped from the barrel and used to unlock the bolt, which is then carried to the rear by residual pressure in the breech. Both belt and drum feed were offered, but the design was not taken up by anyone and few were made. The gun is included here because it shows a different approach to the problem of operating the mechanism. In larger form, as a 20mm cannon, the Scotti system was used by the Italian Air Force in World War II.

Length: 42.00in (1068mm). **Weight unloaded:** 27lb 0oz (12.25kg). **Barrel:** 25.00in (636mm), 4 grooves, right-hand twist. **Magazine:** 250-round belt. **Cyclic rate:** 500 rds/min. **Muzzle velocity:** c.2400 ft/sec (731 m/sec).

• Fiat-Revelli Model 35

FIAT SpA, Turin
8x59RB Breda M35

The Model 35 is actually the 1914 gun brought up to date. The water-cooled barrel gave way to an air-cooled one, the feed was changed to a belt, the oiler was discarded and a fluted chamber substituted, and the caliber was changed to

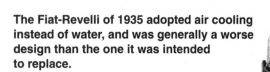

The Fiat-Revelli of 1935 adopted air cooling instead of water, and was generally a worse design than the one it was intended to replace.

8mm. This should have insured some success, but sadly, it did not. There were too many of the old Revelli features left to allow the gun to work well. Despite the fluted chamber, the cartridge cases still stuck and, in the end, either the oiler had to be reinstated or the rounds had to be greased before going into the belt. The gun fired from a closed bolt, which is always undesirable in a sustained-fire weapon, and it led to premature ignitions ('cook-offs') when the breech got hot. In fact, the Modello 35 was actually a worse gun than the one upon which it supposedly improved. It lasted throughout the war but went out of service immediately afterwards.

Length: 50.00in (1270mm). **Weight unloaded:** 40lb 0oz (18.10kg). **Barrel:** 25.75in (653mm), 4 grooves, right-hand twist. **Magazine:** 50-round belt. **Cyclic rate:** 500 rds/min. **Muzzle velocity:** c.2600 ft/sec (792 m/sec).

• Beretta M70/84
Pietro Beretta SpA, Gardone Val Trompia
5.56x45mm

This light machine-gun was derived from the Beretta AR-70/223 rifle, and many of the components were interchangeable. The principal difference lay in the adoption of a heavy barrel with quick-change facility. A bipod capable of adjustment for height was fitted, and the muzzle was shaped to form a combination brake and grenade launcher. Each barrel carried its own sight, which was adjustable, so that each barrel could be zeroed-in independently. The M70-78 was brought to the final stages of development but by that time the rifle had shown one or two deficiencies and a completely new system (the 70/90) was about to begin development, so this machine gun was never placed in production.

Length: 37.6in (955mm). **Weight unloaded:** 11lb 11oz (5.3kg). **Barrel:** 17.72in (450mm), 6 grooves, right-hand twist. **Magazine:** 30- or 40-round detachable box. **Cyclic rate:** 670 rds/min. **Muzzle velocity:** 3180 ft/sec (980 m/sec).

• Beretta AS 70/90
Pietro Beretta SpA, Gardone Val Trompia
5.56x45mm NATO

This is the squad automatic version of the 5.56mm AR70-90 assault rifle. It uses the same gas-operated rotating bolt system as the rifle but fires from an open bolt, and has a heavy barrel which cannot be quick-changed. The butt is cut away to provide a firm grip and has an over-shoulder strap, and there is a long, perforated barrel jacket. The bipod is articulated and can be adjusted for height. A carrying handle is fitted and,

The Beretta 70-78 light machine gun; the handle above the magazine locks the removable barrel in place.

The Beretta 70-90 is simply a heavy-barrel version of the 70-90 rifle.

like that of the rifle, it can be easily removed to expose a mount for optical sights. The AR70-90 has been extensively tested by the Italian Army but as yet no decision has been taken about adopting a 5.56mm machine gun in their service.

Length: 39.37in (1000mm). **Weight unloaded:** 11lb 12oz (5.34kg). **Barrel:** 18.30in (465mm), 6 grooves, right-hand twist. **Magazine:** 30-round detachable box. **Cyclic rate:** 800 rds/min. **Muzzle velocity:** 3180 ft/sec (980 m/sec).

JAPAN

• Machine gun Taisho 3 (1914)
Koishikawa Arsenal, Tokyo
6.5x50SR Arisaka

The Taisho 3 is really a Japanese version of the Hotchkiss. During the Russo-Japanese war of 1904-5, the first in which machine guns were employed by both sides in significant numbers, the Japanese Army used the French Hotchkiss to great effect. Kijiro Nambu then used the 1914 pattern Hotchkiss to design a gun suitable for Japanese manufacture, and the resulting close copy of the original is chambered for the 6.5mm Arisaka rifle cartridge. The only obvious external differences lie in the barrel finning and the fittings on the tripod. It was adopted in 1914, and some of the original weapons continued in service throughout World War II. The Taisho 3 inherited from its French ancestor the merits of reliability and strength, although the necessity to oil the cartridges was always a possible source of trouble in dusty conditions. Like the models which followed it, the Taisho 3 had sockets in the tripod feet through which the crew passed poles so that they could carry the gun and tripod in one lift—something unique to Japanese machine-guns.

Length: 45.50in (1156mm). **Weight unloaded:** 62lb 0oz (28.10kg). **Barrel:** 29.50in (749mm), 4 grooves, left-hand twist. **Magazine:** 30-round metal strip. **Cyclic rate:** 400 rds/min. **Muzzle velocity:** c.2400 ft/sec (731 m/sec).

• Type 11, (1922)
State manufacture
6.5x51SR Arisaka, reduced load

The Type 11 was brought into service in 1922 as the first light machine gun the Japanese had designed themselves. It was unusual in several ways and was probably never entirely satisfactory, but it survived until 1945 and gave a good account of itself. Apart from its ungainly outline and angular shape, it possessed some features seldom found in other machine guns. The chief of these was the feed system, in which a hopper on the left of the gun accepted clips for the 38th Year Arisaka rifle, stripped the rounds out and fed them into the breech. Thus any rifleman could provide ammunition for the gun without having to load a magazine or a belt. However, the system was complicated and led to stoppages. Another feature of the feed was that the rounds were oiled as they passed into the breech, for the Type 11 had no primary extraction and without some sort of lubrication the empty case could not easily be withdrawn from the chamber. A special cartridge loading, somewhat less powerful than the standard infantry rifle round, was generally used to prevent case ruptures. The Type 11 was only capable of automatic fire.

Length: 43.50in (1104mm). **Weight unloaded:** 22lb 8oz (10.19kg). **Barrel:** 19.00in (482mm), 4 grooves, right-hand twist. **Magazine:** 30-round hopper. **Cyclic rate:** 500 rds/min. **Muzzle velocity:** 2300 ft/sec (701 m/sec).

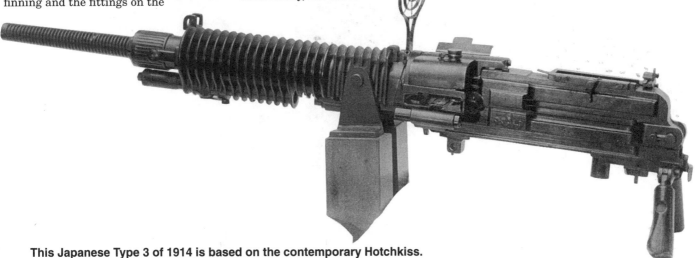

This Japanese Type 3 of 1914 is based on the contemporary Hotchkiss.

The Japanese 11th Year gun used an unusual feed hopper.

• Type 91, (1931)
State manufacture
6.5x51SR Arisaka

The Type 91 was the tank version of the Type 11. It differed very little from the earlier gun except for the feed: it was found necessary to give the tank gunner more than 30 rounds at one filling of the hopper and so this was enlarged to almost twice the original size. This cannot have been such a great advantage, as the gunner still had to refill it with clips in the confined space of the turret. It does not seem that the Type 91 was in service for long, although some were converted to infantry use by fitting a bipod and also, in many cases, a long telescope sight. They can hardly have been popular in the infantry role since they were heavier than any other Japanese 'light' machine gun and no more effective. It is not recorded if the larger hopper conferred any advantage in the infantry role.

Length: 42.00in (1066mm).
Weight unloaded: 24lb 7oz (11.00kg).
Barrel: 19.20in (488mm), 4 grooves, right-hand twist. **Magazine:** 50-round hopper. **Cyclic rate:** 500 rds/min. **Muzzle velocity:** c.2300 ft/sec (700 m/sec).

• Type 92, (1932)
State manufacture
7.7x58SR Type 92 and 7.7x58mm Type 99

The Type 92 is no more than an improved Type 33 and in all aspects except the ammunition, barrel and breech it is the same gun. It was recognized in the late 1920s that the 6.5x51SR Arisaka round was inadequate for machine-gun use and the more powerful 7.7mm was introduced in 1932—hence Type 92, from the equivalent year of the Japanese calendar. Strangely, the 7.7mm round still needed to be oiled and the opportunity was lost to abandon this undesirable feature. The Type 92 round was semi-rimless and its successor, the Type 99, was rimless. The Type 92 gun was fortunate in being able to fire both kinds, and it became one of the most widely used guns in the Japanese Army during World War II. The rate of fire was low, and because of a curious stuttering effect in the firing, the gun was nicknamed the 'woodpecker'—although the sound hardly resembles that bird. Examples of the Type 92 remained in use with some armies in the Far East until the early 1970s.

A modified version was introduced in 1941 and was rather confusingly known as the Type 1. It was a little lighter than the Type 92, the barrel could be removed more easily and it fired only the Type 99 ammunition.

Length: 45.50in (1156mm). **Weight unloaded,** with tripod: 122lb 0oz (55.30kg). **Barrel:** 27.50in (698mm), 4 grooves, right-hand twist. **Magazine:** 30-round strip. **Cyclic rate:** 450 rds/min. **Muzzle velocity:** c.2400 ft/sec (732 m/sec).

The Type 92 was simply a Type 3 in 7.7mm caliber.

The Type 96 improved the method of feed but in other respects was similar to the earlier Type 11.

• Type 96, (1936)
State manufacture
6.5x51SR

The Type 96 was introduced in 1936 as an improvement on the Type 11. The cartridge hopper was replaced by a box magazine holding 30 rounds of the same 6.5mm ammunition and the cartridge oiler was abolished. The rounds were still oiled, with all the objections that accrue from doing it, but in the Type 96, the oil was introduced in the magazine loader and so the pump was divorced from the gun; the barrel was thus easier to change, which was a distinct advantage, but apart from these small advances, the Type 96 was little better than the Type 11 which it was meant to replace. In fact, the Type 96 never did replace the 11 because Japanese arms manufacture could not possibly satisfy the demands made upon it. The two versions therefore existed alongside each other for the whole war.

One feature of the Type 96 rarely found on other machine guns is the sight, for in many cases a low-power telescope sight was fitted. The exact reason for this is no longer clear, since the inherent lack of consistent accuracy in the gun makes the use of a telescope largely unnecessary.

The standard ammunition for the Type 96 was a reduced-charge version of the standard Meiji 30 infantry cartridge: the lower charge was essential in preventing case ruptures and head separations.
Length: 41.50in (1054mm). **Weight unloaded:** 20lb 0oz (9.07kg). **Barrel:** 21.70in (552mm), 4 grooves, right-hand twist. **Magazine:** 30-round detachable box. **Cyclic rate:** 550 rds/min. **Muzzle velocity:** c.2400 ft/sec (732 m/sec).

• Type 97 tank machine-gun (1937)
State manufacture
7.7x58SR Type 92

The Type 97 is the successor to the Type 91, and not to the Type 96 as one might be led to imagine from the numbering. A tank machine-gun, it was used throughout World War II alongside the Type 91, although it never replaced it as it was obviously meant to do. It is a straightforward copy of the Czech ZB vz/26 firing the Japanese 7.7mm round, and it retains almost all the characteristics of the Czech weapon. It can hardly have been a success in a tank since the feed is by a box magazine, although this is undeniably better than the old hopper. The barrel is too light for the sort of shooting required of a tank gun, and this means that the gunner was restricted in the rate at which he could fire his magazine, or that the barrel would rapidly overheat and be shot out—the latter fault being the most likely. In fact, an improved Browning-system gun (the '4 Shiki Sensha Kikaniu') was designed

as a future replacement but no more than the prototypes and a few pre-production guns were completed by Japan's fall.

Length: 34.00in (864mm). **Weight unloaded:** 24lb 0oz (10.88kg). **Barrel:** 28.00in (711mm), 4 grooves, right-hand twist. **Magazine:** 30-round detachable box. **Cyclic rate:** 500 rds/min. **Muzzle velocity:** c.2400 ft/sec (732 m/sec).

• Type 99, (1939)
State manufacture
7.7x58mm Type 99

When the decision was taken in 1939 to introduce the 7.7mm Type 99 rimless round, the Japanese Army had no light machine-gun to accommodate it; the Type 99 machine gun was therefore designed for it. Since time was short, the design team worked from modifications to existing service guns and the accepted Type 99 was a development of the Type 96, itself a new weapon at that period. The Type 99 was a great improvement on its predecessors and more nearly resembled the light machine guns which were in use in Europe. The new rimless round did not require oiling, there was adequate primary extraction to reduce stoppages, tolerances were held to fine limits, and a new pattern of barrel change was used. It was a good gun, but it came too late to be effective and never saw service in large numbers. Japanese industry was overloaded when it appeared, and the factories never caught up with the demand. There was more than a hint of

The Type 97 was a tank gun but had more than a hint of the Czech zb/26 about its mechanical design.

The Type 99 is little more than a Type 96 in 7.7mm caliber, though it was built to closer tolerances and had a monopod underneath the butt.

Another view of the Type 99, this time with a bayonet fitted; not an attachment commonly seen on machine guns.

the ZB vz/26 in its outline, although the Type 96 ancestry was also clear. A small monopod was fitted to the toe of the butt to allow the gun to be used for firing on fixed lines, somewhat after the manner of a tripod-mounted gun; this has been used on some other guns, but it is not stable or accurate enough to be of great value. The virtues of the Type 99 lay in its powerful ammunition and its magazine feed. In common with the majority of Japanese machine guns, it was capable of only automatic fire.

Length: 46.50in (1181mm). **Weight unloaded:** 23lb 0oz (10.43kg). **Barrel:** 21.50in (545mm), 4 grooves, right-hand twist. **Magazine:** 30-round detachable box. **Cyclic rate:** 850 rds/min. **Muzzle velocity:** c.2350 ft/sec (715 m/sec).

• Model 62 machine gun, (1962)

Sumitomo Heavy Industries, Tokyo
7.62x51mm NATO

The Model 62 is a general purpose machine gun similar in outline and performance to the many that exist in NATO and those that have emanated from Europe. The specification which led to the Model 62 was laid down in the same period as elsewhere—the mid-1950s—and the gun was adopted in 1962. In appearance it is similar to the MAG of Fabrique Nationale, and the mechanisms uses a similar tipping bolt to lock the breech. The Model 62 is a simple gas-operated gun of good design and of high quality finish, which can fire both the full charge round and a reduced charge version using the United States disintegrating metal link belt. The Model 62 is also fitted onto the American M2 buffered tripod when used as a support gun. There is no selector lever, as the gun is only capable of automatic fire, and it has a quick change barrel.

Length: 47.24in (1200mm). **Weight unloaded:** 23lb 8oz (10.7kg). **Barrel:** 20.6in (524mm), 4 grooves,

The modern Japanese Self-Defense Force adopted this M62 as their standard machine gun.

The M74 is the tank and armored vehicle version of the Japanese M62 gun.

right-hand twist. **Magazine:** metallic link belt. **Cyclic rate:** 600 rds/min. **Muzzle velocity:** 2805 ft/sec (855 m/sec).

• Model 74 Machine Gun (1974)
Sumitomo Heavy Industries, Tokyo, Japan
7.62x51mm NATO

This is a variation on the Model 62 which was developed for use in armored vehicles and adopted in 1974. The operation is the same gas system as the Model 62 but the gun is generally more robust and has a longer and much heavier barrel, allowing sustained fire without the need to change barrels. It can be fired by a manual trigger or by the usual solenoid system, and a selector lever allows a choice of two rates of fire.

Length: 42.72in (1085mm). **Weight unloaded:** 45lb 0oz (20.4kg). **Barrel:** 32.48in (825mm), 4 grooves, right-hand twist. **Magazine:** metallic link belt. **Cyclic rate:** 700 or 1000rds/min. **Muzzle velocity:** 2805 ft/sec (855 m/sec).

KOREA, SOUTH

• Daewoo K3
Daewoo Precision Industries Ltd., Kumjeong
5.56x45mm M193 or NATO

The K3 is a lightweight, gas-operated, full-automatic machine gun which appears to have drawn a good deal of its inspiration from the FN Minimi. It uses a similar system of belt or magazine feed and is fitted with a bipod for the squad automatic rifle, though it can also be tripod-mounted for use in the sustained fire support role. The rear sight is adjustable for elevation and windage, and the front sight can be adjusted in elevation for purposes of zeroing. The barrel is fitted with a carrying handle and can be quickly changed in action so as to permit sustained fire; as the barrel also carries the front sight it follows that each can be individually zeroed. The action is gas piston driven, using the usual rotating bolt in a bolt carrier.

Length: 37.6in (1030mm). **Weight unloaded:** 11lb 11oz (6.85kg).

Barrel: 17.7in (533mm), 6 grooves, right-hand twist. **Magazine:** 30-round detachable box or 250-round metal belt. **Cyclic rate:** 700rds/min (belt), 1000 rds/min (magazine). **Muzzle velocity:** 3180 ft/sec (960 m/sec) with M193 round.

MEXICO

• Mendoza Model B (1933)
Fabrica de Armas Nacionales, Mexico City
7x57mm Spanish Mauser

Mexico has been fortunate in having the talented arms designer Rafael Mendoza as the driving force behind small arms production in the country, which has enabled Mexico to develop a range of cheap weapons for her own specialized uses. The Model B 1933 machine gun is an original design, but it owes something of its inspiration to both the Hotchkiss light machine gun and the Lewis. The bolt-locking

The South Korean K3 has more than a passing resemblance to the FN Minimi; here it is in the squad role, using a magazine.

And here is the M3 on a tripod, belt fed, in the supporting role.

Mexico's Mendoza M45 fired the potent 30-06 Springfield cartridge and needed a muzzle brake.

action is of improved Lewis type, with some of the locking friction in the system diminished by using two cam slots. The gas cylinder is broadly of Hotchkiss form, though with improvements. The overall layout, the feed system and the quick-change barrel are purely of Mendoza's conception. The operating stroke of the piston is short, and the gas is quickly released to the atmosphere. The bolt then continues under its own momentum.

The gun was much lighter than its contemporaries, provision was made for selective fire and the magazine was small and easily handled. At the time it was produced it represented an advance on most other similar guns in the world. It was taken into service in the Mexican Army, and remained in first line use until after 1945.

Length: 46.00 (1168mm). **Weight unloaded:** 18lb 8oz (8.39kg). **Barrel:** 25.00in (635mm), 4 grooves, right-hand twist. **Magazine:** 20-round detachable box. **Cyclic rate:** 450 rds/min. **Muzzle velocity:** c.2700 ft/sec (822 m/sec).

• Mendoza Model 45
Fabrica de Armas Nacionales, Mexico City
30-06 Springfield (30-caliber M1906)

By 1945, it had become apparent that the 7mm cartridge was becoming outdated, and at the same time, great quantities of United States 30-06 Springfield ammunition existed. Mexico has always enjoyed a close relationship with the United States and it became expeditious, as well as good sense, to develop weapons which could take advantage of common calibers. Mendoza took the opportunity to improve his 1933 design while retaining the main features. The Model 45 had a slightly shorter barrel, a perforated muzzle brake and a simplified receiver. There was also a slight cleaning-up of the outline, but it was otherwise the same gun as the 1933 type.

Length: 45.00in (1142mm). **Weight unloaded:** 18lb 0oz (8.15kg). **Barrel:** 24.50in (622mm), 4 grooves, right-hand twist. **Magazine:** 20-round detachable box. **Cyclic rate:** 500 rds/min. **Muzzle velocity:** c.2750 ft/sec (837 m/sec).

• Mendoza Model RM2
Productos Mendoza SA, Mexico City
30-06 Springfield (30-caliber M1906)

The RM2 was the last of the Mendoza machine gun designs and its main features were low cost and simplicity of manufacture. It was also remarkably light—so light that it could almost be considered as an automatic rifle roughly in the same class as the BAR. The RM2 did not have a readily detachable barrel and, in a light machine gun, this is a distinct drawback since it denies the gunner the ability to fire more than a small number of magazines before having to stop to let the barrel cool down. One feature of the gun which was an advance on others was its method of stripping, the rear of the receiver being hinged so as to fold downwards and allow the working parts to be easily and quickly withdrawn. This method is reminiscent of the Fabrique Nationale's series of rifles, and the inspiration for it may have been drawn from there. So far as is known, the RM2 did not appear in large numbers.

The Mendoza designs served for several years but were

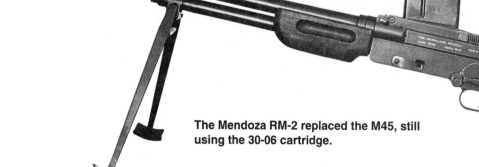

The Mendoza RM-2 replaced the M45, still using the 30-06 cartridge.

replaced in the 1980s by the 5.56mm Ameli and the 7.62mm FN-MAG.

Length: 43.00in (1092mm). **Weight unloaded:** 14lb 0oz (6.30kg). **Barrel:** 24.00in (609mm), 4 grooves, right-hand twist. **Magazine:** 20-round detachable box. **Cyclic rate:** 600 rds/min. **Muzzle velocity:** c.2750 ft/sec (837 m/sec).

NEW ZEALAND

• Charlton Light Machine-gun
Charlton Automatic Arms, Hastings, New Zealand
303 British

During World War II, New Zealand provided one of the proportionately largest armed forces in relation to population of any of the Commonwealth countries. The equipment for it came from other countries and in 1942, when the Japanese gave every sign of invading both Australia and New Zealand, the only arms available to defend the country were SMLE rifles. The firm of Charlton in Hastings, New Zealand, was directed by an inventive and energetic man who turned his efforts to conceiving some sort of automatic weapon for home defense. After several attempts he produced the Charlton Light Machine Gun—a weapon that today might more correctly be called a machine rifle. Within a very short time, limited series production was begun in Australia, as New Zealand lacked the necessary machine shops, and the contract went to a firm that in peacetime had made vacuum cleaners and similar light engineering products. The work force was mostly women and the greatest part of the manufacturing process was hand-work with simple tools.

The basis was the SMLE rifle, which was completely dismantled to provide the parts from which was constructed a crude gas-operated LMG. The gas system was made up from simple turned parts, and the magazine was that of the Bren—which was made in Australia. Although the initial order

was for 4,000 Charltons, production was stopped after a few hundred had been completed, and the plant was turned over to Owen guns.

The finished Charltons were issued for home defense, but were retained in service for only a short time. The design was very simple: the barrel was left screwed to the receiver; cooling fins were added to it, a gas port and gas block were fitted, and a bipod was clamped just forward of that. The cylinder was a straight tube and the piston was a simple rod. The return spring was housed in a second tube, below the cylinder. The bolt handle was cut off with a hacksaw and the long locking lug was cut to accommodate a large curved cam that arched over the entire bolt and ran in a groove cut along the left side of the receiver. This cam was entirely cut by hand from a solid block of steel, there being no signs of any milling work on it. The piston forced the cam to the rear and the cam rotated the bolt and opened it. The reverse action took place on run-out. A substantial buffer was provided to slow down the considerable weight of reciprocating metal. Locking was as for the SMLE. A spring-loaded ejector was fitted on the left-hand side of the receiver, and the empty cases were ejected with some velocity.

A small sheet-metal stock was provided at the point of balance so that the gun could be carried with a hot barrel, and there was a forward pistol grip that was necessary when firing from any position. Because of its low weight, the Charlton was inclined to 'walk away' from the firer unless held very firmly. Some models were fitted with a tubular flash eliminator that may also have had some effect as a muzzle brake, but it was not by any means a standard feature. Indeed, there were many variations between batches of guns, as the factory incorporated new ideas or changed its production methods. The butt was a standard SMLE somewhat cut down. A simple change lever

allowed semi or full automatic fire, and the cyclic rate was probably kept low by the weight of the moving parts. Sights were SMLE with the front sight protectors cut down, and even the sling swivels were retained. So far as is known, no Charlton was ever used outside New Zealand; and very, very few have survived. The gun was an almost incredible feat of adaptation, and there is no doubt that for limited use—which was all that it had been intended for—it would have been highly successful. Its production, issue, and subsequent decline is one of the obscure sagas of the war.

Length: 44.87in (1142mm). **Weight unloaded:** 15lb 8oz (7.05kg). **Barrel:** 23.5in (596mm), 5 grooves, left-hand twist. **Magazine:** 30-round detachable box. **Cyclic rate:** c.500 rds/min. **Muzzle velocity:** c.2450 ft/sec (745 m/sec).

RUSSIA

• Maxim 1910, and variants
State factories
7.62x54R Russian

The first automatic machine guns in service with the Tsarists were supplied by the Vickers' Sons & Maxim Machine Gun Company from England, but by the end of the Russo-Japanese War in 1905, the indigenous arms industry was capable of producing its own weapons and production was started at the Tula Arsenal. The first machine gun was a Maxim with minor variations called the PM ('Pulemyot Maxima') 1905; it had a bronze water jacket for the barrel. The next model was the PM 1910 and on this the water jacket reverted to the sheet-steel used by all other countries, and opportunity was also taken to make a slight alteration to the feed. A later variant of this model had a fluted water jacket, and the last version had a distinctive big water-filling port to facilitate rapid refilling or topping-up with

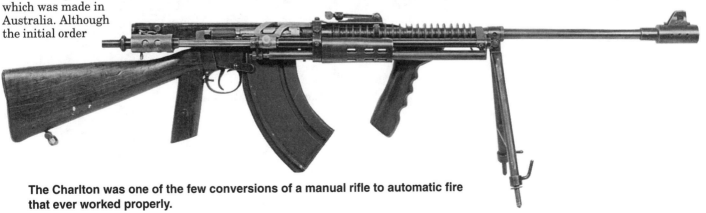

The Charlton was one of the few conversions of a manual rifle to automatic fire that ever worked properly.

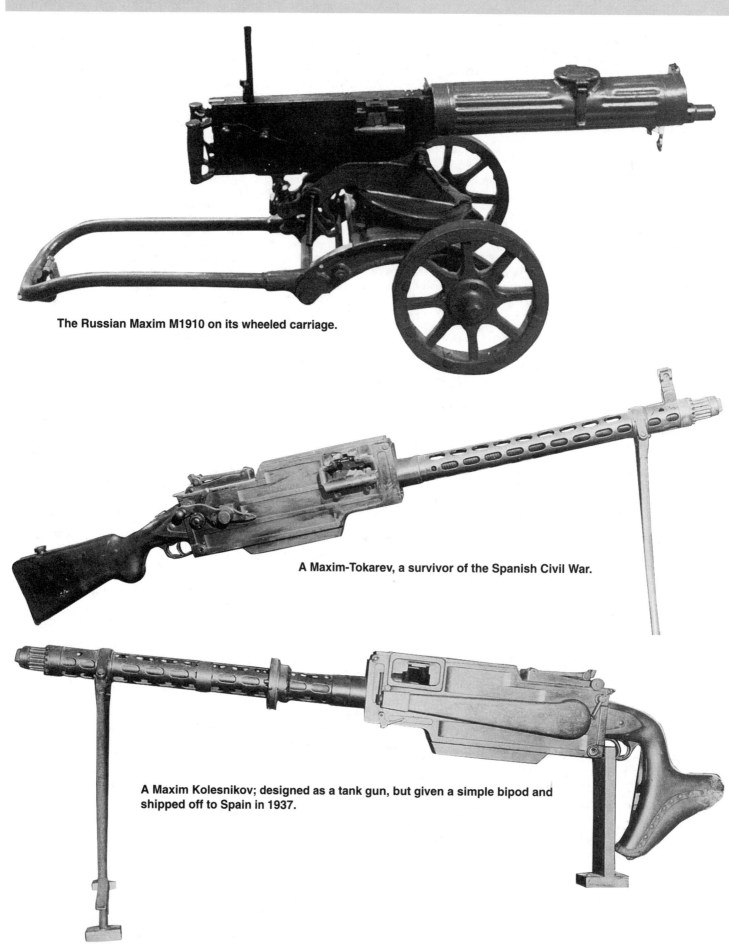

The Russian Maxim M1910 on its wheeled carriage.

A Maxim-Tokarev, a survivor of the Spanish Civil War.

A Maxim Kolesnikov; designed as a tank gun, but given a simple bipod and shipped off to Spain in 1937.

handfuls of snow. This last version of the PM 1910 was produced in vast numbers and remained in front-line service with the Soviet Army until replaced by the SG43. It is still to be seen in the hands of troops in various Asian armies, and is in second-line service with several armies in the Eastern bloc. It is probably the longest-lived of the Maxim variants.

In the late 1920s, the Red Army attempted to lighten and improve the design in the hope of producing a light machine gun, for infantry use, which could be manufactured by the machinery used for the medium gun. There were two trial types, one designed by Tokarev and called the MT and another designed by Kolesnikov, whose product was called the MK. Neither was a success and the idea was abandoned as impracticable, though several thousand guns were made, most of which were off-loaded to the Republicans during the Spanish Civil War. In the end, Degtyarev produced a design which became the DP light gun of 1928. Redesigned and air-cooled, it was used by the Red Air Force as PV-1.

Most Soviet Maxims are seen with the 'Sokolov' mounting, a pair of wheels supporting a large turntable (to allow traversing) and a U-shaped trail. Early models had two extra legs

which folded underneath when the gun was being moved, but could be put out in front for extra stability or to raise the gun well clear of the ground to shoot over high cover. Sometimes a steel shield was fitted, but this was unpopular because of its weight and the marginal protection that it offered. For winter warfare there was a sled fitting, and all models could be fitted with drag ropes.

Length: 43.60in (1107mm). **Weight unloaded:** 52lb 8oz (23.80kg). **Barrel:** 28.40in (721mm), 4 grooves, right-hand twist. **Magazine:** 250-round fabric belt. **Cyclic rate:** 520-580 rds/min. **Muzzle velocity:** c.2830 ft/sec (863 m/sec).

• 7.62mm Degtyarev DP
State manufacture
7.62x54R Russian

The DP was adopted by the Soviet Army in 1928 after two years of trials, and it was the first truly original development in Russia. It is extremely simple, yet remarkably reliable and robust. It remained the standard light gun until the 1950s and huge numbers were made, many of which survive today in the Eastern bloc countries and in Asia. The secret of the DP was the simple locking system, a modification of one of the earliest known types—the Friberg-Kjellman—which makes use of locking flaps on the bolt, pushed out by the firing pin. The DP

proved to be resistant to dust and dirt and free from any serious vices. Its weak point was the ammunition, as the long Russian 7.62mm rimmed cartridge was difficult to load into an automatic gun without jamming. The distinctive flat pan magazine almost overcame this fault, but was itself liable both to damage and to distortion. The operating spring was housed beneath the barrel in the piston tube, but it tended to lose its tempering when the barrel became hot. The gun was capable of automatic fire only, and the bolt remained open between bursts to allow the chamber to cool. The success of this weapon brought about a series of similar guns which were derived from it, all of which proved to be equally good.

Length: 50.80in (1290mm). **Weight unloaded:** 20lb 8oz (9.12kg). **Barrel:** 23.80in (605mm), 4 grooves, right-hand twist. **Magazine:** 47-round drum. **Cyclic rate:** 500-600 rds/min. **Muzzle velocity:** 2760 ft/sec (840 m/sec).

• 7.62mm Degtyarev DT
State manufacture
7.62x54R Russian

The DT is one of the variants of the original DP and was designed for the armament of tanks and armored cars. The stock is made of metal and can be telescoped to reduce the inboard length, and there is an added pistol grip for greater control when the stock is not used. The barrel is a little heavier than on the DP and it cannot be quickly replaced. The drum magazine remained, which is an undesirable feature in an armored vehicle, but it was of a smaller diameter and greater

The Degtyarev DP was the standard infantry light machine gun of the 1930s.

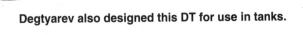
Degtyarev also designed this DT for use in tanks.

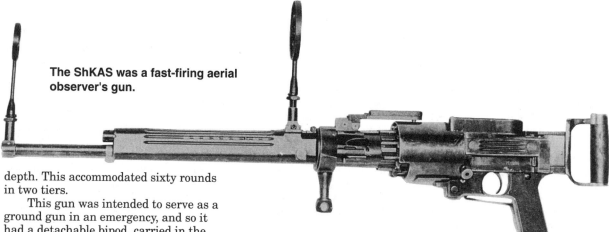

The ShKAS was a fast-firing aerial observer's gun.

depth. This accommodated sixty rounds in two tiers.

This gun was intended to serve as a ground gun in an emergency, and so it had a detachable bipod, carried in the vehicle, and a removable front sight. As with the DP, the return spring gave trouble through overheating. There was also an aircraft version which appeared in two forms—as a single machine gun and as a twin-coupled gun. The first was designated DA ('Degtyaryova aviatsionnyi), the second, DA-2.

Length: 47.00in (1193mm). **Weight unloaded:** 28lb 0oz (12.70kg). **Barrel:** 23.80in (605mm), 4 grooves, right-hand twist. **Magazine:** 60-round drum. **Cyclic rate:** 650 rds/min. **Muzzle velocity:** c.2750 ft/sec (840 m/sec).

• 7.62mm ShKAS Aircraft Guns, 1932-1941
State manufacture
7.62mm SHKAS M1933

There were four models in the ShKAS series—KM33, KM35, KM36 and KM41—starting in 1933 and ending in 1941. The gun was designed by two men, Shpitalny and Komaritsky, from whose names the first letters of the title are derived. The 'AS' was added to show that the gun was for aircraft use and capable of a high rate of fire. It was a complicated and expensive gun, but had the necessary high rate of fire and a good reputation for reliability. It may be that the early guns were all hand-made, and it is distinctly possible that mass-production in the normally accepted sense was never achieved with the ShKAS designs. The gun is gas-operated and belt fed, but the belt is picked up by a rotating mechanism sometimes called a 'squirrel cage', and the rounds are taken out and fed to the breech. The same mechanism takes the empty cases and ejects them in two stages forward out of the gun. The intention was to keep the cockpit clear of spent brass, and the gun is highly unusual in going to such trouble to achieve this. The concept of the gun incorporates

several systems from other guns but these are skillfully combined to produce an harmonious (if involved) whole.

ShVAK

This was a development of the SHKAS and was intended for vehicle use, but some were mounted on aircraft, though with what success is not known. The gun was similar in all respects to the ShKAS, but was of a larger caliber, and therefore larger in every other dimension. Two versions were made, in 12.7mm and 20mm, neither in very large numbers.

The development of this gun was undertaken by Shpitalny and Vladimirov, who later designed the KPV, and perhaps his influence and experience brought about the increase in caliber. At the time of going to press there is no reliable data on either gun.

(ShKAS)
Length: 36.81in (935mm). **Weight unloaded:** 23.50lb (10.66kg). **Barrel:** 26.5in (675mm). **Magazine:** 250-round belt. **Cyclic rate:** 2000 rds/min. **Muzzle velocity:** c.2430 ft/sec (740 m/sec)

• 12.7mm DShK 1938 and DShKM 1938/46
State manufacture
12.7x107mm Soviet

The DShK is still in service in the Soviet Army; it started in 1938 as a joint design by Degtyaryov and Shpagin, using Degtyaryov's gas operation and locking system, and a feed mechanism by Shpagin. The feed had a rotating cylinder which extracted the rounds from the belt and fed them into the chamber, though the latest model (the DShK 1938/46 or

The 12.7mm DShK 38 on a wheeled carriage.

The breech area of the 12.7mm DShK 38/40, showing the different outline due to the adoption of a simpler feed system.

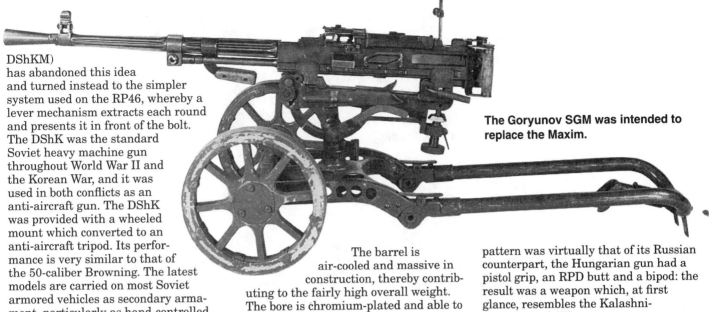

The Goryunov SGM was intended to replace the Maxim.

DShKM)
has abandoned this idea
and turned instead to the simpler
system used on the RP46, whereby a
lever mechanism extracts each round
and presents it in front of the bolt.
The DShK was the standard
Soviet heavy machine gun
throughout World War II and
the Korean War, and it was
used in both conflicts as an
anti-aircraft gun. The DShK
was provided with a wheeled
mount which converted to an
anti-aircraft tripod. Its performance is very similar to that of
the 50-caliber Browning. The latest
models are carried on most Soviet
armored vehicles as secondary armament, particularly as hand-controlled
anti-aircraft guns, and, in some cases,
they are turret-mounted as co-axial guns.
Both the DShK and the DShKM are
widely distributed throughout the Eastern bloc and Asia.

Length: 62.50in (1586mm). **Weight
unloaded:** 78lb 8oz (35.50kg). **Barrel:**
42.00in (1066mm), 4 grooves, right-hand
twist. **Magazine:** 50-round belt. **Cyclic
rate:** 550 rds/min. **Muzzle velocity:** c.2825
ft/sec (860 m/sec).

• 7.62mm Goryunov 1943 (SG43)
State manufacture
7.62x54R Russian

The Goryunov was developed during
World War II as a replacement for the
PM1910 (Maxim). An earlier replacement gun, the DS of 1939 designed by
Degtyarev, had failed to meet its specifications and by 1942, a modern medium
machine gun, easy to manufacture and
simple to use, was urgently needed in the
U.S.S.R. Goryunov used some of the features of the unsuccessful Degtyarev gun
in order to save time, but the design of
the locking system was radically
changed. A tilting breechblock was used,
similar to that of the Bren machine gun,
but moving sideways instead of vertically
and locking into the side of the receiver.

The feed is not straightforward, as
the gun fires the 7.62mm rimmed rifle
round, and this has to be withdrawn
rearwards from the belt before ramming
into the breech. The reciprocating motion
is achieved by using two claws to pull the
round from the belt, and then an arm
pushes the round into the cartridge guide
ready for the bolt to carry it to the
breech: despite this complication, the
Goryunov is remarkably reliable and feed
jams are apparently few.

The barrel is
air-cooled and massive in
construction, thereby contrib-
uting to the fairly high overall weight.
The bore is chromium-plated and able to
withstand continuous fire for long periods, although the barrel can be easily
changed by releasing a simple barrel lock
and the carrying handle allows a hot barrel to be lifted clear without difficulty.
The wartime version of the gun had a
smooth outline to the barrel, and the
cocking handle was under the receiver.
This gun was produced in limited quantities before 1945, but it never entirely
replaced the Maxim.

The **SG43** was the original version of
the design, with a smooth barrel, a plain
barrel lock, no dust covers to the feed and
ejection ports, and an operating handle
between the spade grips.

The **SG43M** represents the first
improvements to the original gun; dust
covers were added to the feed and ejection ports, and a new pattern of barrel
lock was fitted. A fluted barrel was fitted
to improve cooling, and an operating handle appeared on the right-hand side of
the receiver. There is a little confusion
over the designation of this gun, as the
term SG43M is sometimes used to denote
a variation of the SG fitted with the new
micrometer barrel lock and dust covers to
the ports. As it is also possible to find
early variations of the SGM without the
dust covers, it is thought that there are
not two separately recognized patterns.

SGMT and **SGMB**. These are,
respectively, the tank and vehicle versions of the basic SG43 design; the tank
version has a firing solenoid mounted on
the backplate, the vehicle gun appears in
a special cradle mounting.

It must also be noted that several of
the satellite countries, including Hungary, and the People's Republic of China,
manufactured their own guns to the
basic SG design. Although the Chinese

pattern was virtually that of its Russian
counterpart, the Hungarian gun had a
pistol grip, an RPD butt and a bipod: the
result was a weapon which, at first
glance, resembles the Kalashni-
kov-designed PK.

(SGM)
Length: 44.10in (1120mm). **Weight
unloaded:** 29lb 14oz (13.60kg). **Barrel:**
28.30in (719mm), 4 grooves, right-hand
twist. **Magazine:** 250-round pocketed belt.
Cyclic rate: 650 rds/min. **Muzzle velocity:**
2624 ft/sec (800 m/sec).

• 7.62mm DPM
State factories
7.62x54R Russian

The Degtyarev DPI928 was not without certain faults; the return spring
weakened with the heat from the hot barrel, and the bipod legs bent and broke
from rough handling. Heavy use during
the German invasion of Russia made
these drawbacks particularly noticeable,
and a modified gun was built. This was
the DPM, 'M' representing 'modernized'.
The Red Army began to take delivery of
these in 1945. The return spring was
moved to the rear of the bolt and protruded over the small of the butt in a
cylindrical housing, where it prevented
the gunner from grasping the gun in the
usual way, and so induced the fitting of a
pistol grip.

The bipod, which had been the cause
of continuous complaint, was replaced by
a stronger version attached to the barrel
casing. This raised the roll center of the
gun and made it easier to hold upright.
The grip safety was replaced by a conventional safety lever, but apart from these
changes, no others were made. The
resulting gun was apparently popular
with the troops and was said to be more
accurate and easier to hold and shoot
than the original of 1928.

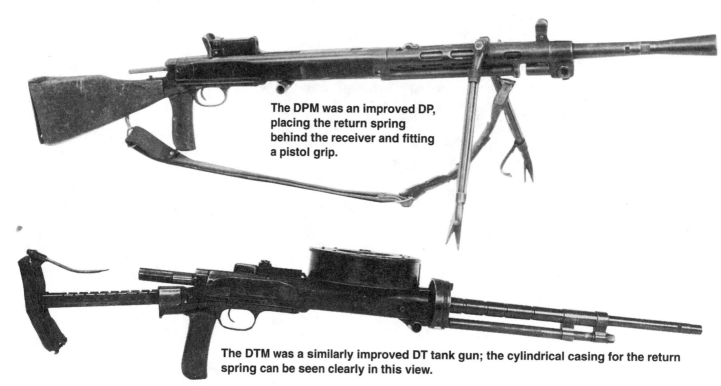

The DPM was an improved DP, placing the return spring behind the receiver and fitting a pistol grip.

The DTM was a similarly improved DT tank gun; the cylindrical casing for the return spring can be seen clearly in this view.

Length: 49.80in (1265mm). **Weight unloaded:** 26lb 13oz (12.20kg). **Barrel:** 23.80in (605mm), 4 grooves, right-hand twist. **Magazine:** 47-round detachable pan. **Cyclic rate:** 520-580 rds/min. **Muzzle velocity:** c.2770 ft/sec (844 m/sec).

• 7.62mm DTM
State factories
7.62x54R Russian

The DTM is simply the tank version of the DPM, and the same remarks apply to it. Apart from the position of the return spring, it is almost exactly the same gun as the original DT of 1929, and it was fitted with the same 60-round pan magazine.

Length, stock extended: 46.50in (1181mm). **Weight unloaded:** 28lb 6oz (12.90kg). **Barrel:** 23.50in (597mm), 4 grooves, right-hand twist. **Magazine:** 60-round detachable pan.

Cyclic rate: 600 rds/min. **Muzzle velocity:** c.2755 ft/sec (839 m/sec).

• 7.62mm RP46
State manufacture
7.62x54R Russian

The RP46 is a second modernization of the DP, intended for use as a company level sustained-fire support gun. It is capable of delivering a high volume of fire, but it is not so portable as the original DP and DPM light guns. It has a heavier barrel, and a belt feed system.

There is a carrying handle (conspicuously absent from the DP) and an improved barrel change. Despite the belt feed, it is still possible to fit the 47-round pan if required. This gun has now been replaced in first-line service, but it

undoubtedly remains in second-line service in many parts of the world.

Length: 50.00in (1270mm). **Weight unloaded:** 28lb 12oz (13.00kg). **Barrel:** 23.80in (605mm), 4 grooves, right-hand twist. **Magazine:** 50-round belt or 47-round drum. **Cyclic rate:** 650 rds/min. **Muzzle velocity:** c.2755 ft/sec (840 m/sec).

• 7.62mm RPD
State manufacture
7.62x39mm M1943

The Ruchnoy Pulemyot Degtyarev (Degtyarev light machine-gun, or RPD) was for some years the standard light machine-gun of the Soviet Army, having been introduced in the 1950s as the complementary squad weapon to the AK rifle. It was the logical development of the earlier DP (1928) and DPM (1944), and it was progressively improved during

The RP-46 company machine gun.

Degtyarev improved his DP/DT design to fire the new 7.62x39 cartridge and produced this RPD gun.

The 12.7mm NSV machine gun has gradually replaced the DShK series.

its life. The original model used a cup-type piston head, had a straight cocking handle which oscillated back and forth as the gun fired, and was without a dust cover. The piston was then modified to the more usual plunger pattern and the dust cover added, and then came a change in the cocking handle to a folding type which remained still as the gun was fired. The fourth modification had a longer gas cylinder, and a recoil buffer incorporated in the butt—measures intended to improve stability, which was always a problem with this somewhat light weapon, and also to try and improve the reserve of power available to lift the feed belt.

The final version was very slightly changed, having a combined magazine bracket/dust cover, and a sectional cleaning rod housed inside the butt. The RPD fired the 7.62mm M43 'intermediate' round and was belt-fed from a drum clipped beneath the gun at the center of gravity. The mechanism had therefore to lift the belt up to the breech, and there is evidence that the power available to do this was barely sufficient even after the changes incorporated

in the fourth modification, giving rise to malfunctions under adverse conditions.

The replaceable barrel of the DP was abandoned in this fresh design, and it became a matter of drill and training for the gunner to avoid firing more than 100 rounds in one minute to prevent overheating the barrel. The remainder of the mechanism was similar to the DP, suitably scaled down for the smaller ammunition, and, like its predecessor the DP, the RPD was capable of automatic fire only.

Length: 41.00in (1041mm). **Weight unloaded:** 15lb 7oz (7.00kg). **Barrel:** 20.50in (520mm), 4 grooves, right-hand twist. **Magazine:** 100-round belt. **Cyclic rate:** 700 rds/min. **Muzzle velocity:** c.2410 ft/sec (734 m/sec).

• NSV Heavy Machine Gun
State manufacture
12.7x107mm Soviet

This weapon was developed from 1960 onwards by Nikitin, Sokolov and Volkov. As a ground gun it is known as the 'NSV-12,7' and is fired from a tripod. It has a skeleton shoulder stock which probably folds, a pistol grip, optical and

iron sights. When used on armored vehicles it is known as the 'NSVT-12,7' and the pistol grip is replaced by a solenoid-controlled firing unit. The gun is gas-operated, belt-fed from the right side, and has a horizontal sliding breech-block. Only automatic fire is possible.

Length: 61.42in (1560mm). **Weight:** 55lb 2oz (25.0kg). **Barrel:** 44.48in (1130mm). **Magazine:** Metallic link belt. **Cyclic rate:** 750 rds/min. **Muzzle velocity:** 2770ft/sec (845 m/sec).

• KPV Heavy Machine Gun
State manufacture
14.5x114mm Soviet

The KPV is an anti-aircraft machine gun of a sophisticated and advanced design. It came into service in the 1950s, when there was a general overhaul of Soviet equipment, and it has since appeared on a number of wheeled mountings in single (ZPU1), twin (ZPU2) and quadruple (ZPU4) form. It is now being mounted on Soviet armored personnel carriers and some other vehicles. It is widely used in the Eastern bloc countries, and some of the anti-aircraft mounts have been installed in North Korea. The gun is unusual in Soviet designs, in that it operates by recoil and

The 14.5mm KPV is a heavy recoil-operated weapon.

The KPV on its usual mounting, the ZPU, for air defense firing.

the bolt is locked by turning to engage two projections on the outer surface of the breech. The chromium-lined barrel can be easily and quickly changed, and the number of parts in the mechanism is small. The ammunition was originally used in the Soviet PTRS and PTRD anti-tank rifles of World War II, and has been developed to include a variety of different types.

Length: 78.80in (2002mm). **Weight:** 108lb 0oz (48.97kg). **Barrel:** 53.10in (1349mm), 8 grooves, right-hand twist. **Magazine:** 100-round belt. **Cyclic rate:** 600 rds/min. **Muzzle velocity:** c.3250 ft/sec (988 m/sec).

• 7.62mm RPK, RPKS
State manufacture
7.62x39mm M1943

The RPK is replacing the RPD, and may have already replaced it, as the standard light gun of the Soviet infantry. It can really be regarded as an enlarged AK assault rifle since it uses most of the same parts and spares in its manufacture. The system of operation is the same as the AK, and the gun accepts the magazines from the AK as well as those

The RPK is based on the Kalashnikov rifle action.

The PKM with 100-round belt box.

The PKT is the electrically-fired tank version of the PK family.

designed
especially for
it. Like the RPD, the barrel is fixed so that tactical use of the gun is to some extent restricted, but as Soviet squad members all carry AKs, the limitation is perhaps not so critical since the combined volume of fire is high. The finish on the RPK is good and, like the AK, the bolt and bore are chromium-plated to reduce wear.

Length: 41.0in (1041mm). **Weight unloaded:** 10lb 8oz (4.76kg). **Barrel:** 23.20in (589mm), 4 grooves, right-hand twist. **Magazine:** 30- or 40-round detachable box, or 75-round drum. **Cyclic rate:** 600 rds/min. **Muzzle velocity:** c.2400 ft/sec (734 m/sec).

• 7.62mm PK Family
State manufacture
7.62x54R Russian

The PK is a true general purpose machine gun—the first to be seen in Soviet service. It replaced the elderly RP46 and

it uses the same 7.62mm long rimmed cartridge; in this respect it is remarkably old-fashioned, because this round dates back to 1891 (although a similar stricture can be applied to others) and the rim gives rise to feed complications. As in the RP46, each cartridge has to be taken from the belt before it can be rammed into the breech; there are, presumably, sufficiently large stocks of the 7.62mm rifle round to make it uneconomical to change to another. The PK is intended as a company support gun and so requires a more powerful round than the M43 'Intermediate' round of the assault rifles and light machine guns. The mechanism is a clever combination of that of the AK together with an original feed system, the barrel is replaceable, the gas regulator can be adjusted without tools, the finish is very good and the weight low; it is an impressive gun. There are versions of it for use in armored vehicles, and a tripod is supplied for the sustained-fire role, when the gun is known as the **PKS**. When mounted on the tripod, the box

holding the belt is attached to the left-hand side of the receiver; in the bipod role this box clips underneath the receiver, as in the RPD, and centralizes the center of gravity. A tank machine gun—the **PKT**—is also manufactured; it, of course, lacks the shoulder stock and pistol grip assemblies.

Length: 47.00in (1193mm). **Weight unloaded:** 19lb 12oz (8.90kg). **Barrel:** 26.00in (660mm), 4 grooves, right-hand twist. **Magazine:** 100-, 200- or 250-round belt. **Cyclic rate:** 650 rds/min. **Muzzle velocity:** c.2700 ft/sec (822 m/sec).

• 5.45mm RPK74
State factories
5.45x39.5mm Soviet

The light machine-gun version of the AK74 small caliber rifle took longer to be recognized, and it was not until the middle of 1985 that the identification was certain. It follows exactly the same line of development as with the RPK and is simply a heavy-barreled AK74 fitted with a light bipod. All indications are that the

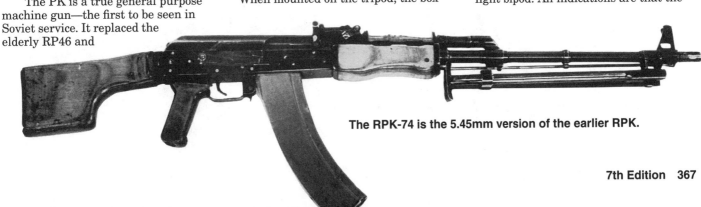

The RPK-74 is the 5.45mm version of the earlier RPK.

furniture is once again the same as for the 7.62mm version, including the distinctive butt with the curved lower edge. The bipod is also the same. There is a slight re-shaping of the wooden forend, but this is not extensive and could have been just a variation on those already in stock. In all other respects the weapon appears to be unchanged from the RPK. The unusual muzzle brake of the rifle is not fitted. We have no data yet, but it appears that the barrel is roughly 60 per cent longer than that of the rifle, making it about 25 inches long.

SINGAPORE

• Ultimax 100 Light Machine-gun
Chartered Industries of Singapore, Singapore
5.56x45mm

Design of this weapon began in 1978 with the intention of providing a one-man weapon with high reliability, good firepower and ease of handling. It was announced in 1982 and is in use by the Singapore Armed Forces.

The Ultimax 100 is a gas-operated weapon using a rotating bolt; it can be fired from the shoulder, the hip, or from a bipod. It fires only in the automatic mode, from an open bolt, and feeds from a special 100-round drum or from 20- or 30-round box magazines. The barrel has a quick-change facility, and the flash hider also functions as a grenade-launching spigot. The rear sight is fully adjustable to 1200m range and for windage; the front sight is adjustable for elevation and windage and thus all barrels can be zeroed to the weapon. The buttstock can be removed and a short 'Para-barrel' fitted when required.

Length: 40.55in (1030mm). **Weight unloaded:** 10lb 8oz (4.79kg). **Barrel:** 20.0in (508mm), 6 grooves, right-hand twist. **Magazine:** 100-round drum, or 20- or 30-round box. **Cyclic rate:** 540 rds/min. **Muzzle velocity:** 3180 ft/sec (970 m/sec).

• CIS 50MG
Chartered Industries of Singapore
50 BMG (Browning)

In view of the age of the 50-caliber Browning and its known drawbacks—lack of a quick-change barrel and need for frequent headspace adjustment—CIS began development of a new 50-caliber weapon in 1983. In addition they aimed at a simpler and lighter weapon so as to improve portability and reduce maintenance demands. The CIS 50 BMG is modular in construction, with five basic groups. It is gas operated and fires from the open bolt position. The locking system is the now-familiar bolt carrier and rotating bolt, the firing pin being part of the carrier assembly and driven onto the cap by the final forward movement of the gas piston; there are actually two gas pistons and cylinders, disposed below the barrel so as to obviate any torque twisting. The barrel is a quick-change pattern and is fitted with an efficient muzzle brake. Feed is by two belts, entering one on each side of the receiver, and the gunner can select either belt instantly as required. The gun can be provided with either a tripod mount or a pintle mount

The Ultimax 100 from Singapore, with its 100-round drum magazine.

The CIS50 is the Singapore 50-caliber heavy machine gun.

The South African SS-77 uses a laterally-shifting bolt.

for fitting into APCs. The CIS 50 BMG was taken in use by the Singapore armed forces; it was also evaluated elsewhere and production has continued, though sales have not been publicized.

Length: 70.0in (1778mm). **Weight unloaded:** 66lb 2oz (30.0kg). **Barrel:** 45.0in (1143mm), 8 grooves, right-hand twist. **Magazine:** dual disintegrating link belt. **Cyclic rate:** 600 rds/min. **Muzzle velocity:** c.2920 ft/sec (890 m/sec).

SOUTH AFRICA

• Vektor SS77
Vektor Division of Denel (Pty), Lyttleton
7.62x51mm NATO

Development of this weapon became necessary due to the UN embargo upon the export of weapons to South Africa which cut off the hitherto normal supply of weapons such as FN-FAL rifle and FN-MAG machine gun. Work began in 1977 and first issues were made in 1986. The SS-77 (from the names of the designers, Smith and Soregi, and the year it began) is gas operated and uses a breech-block which swings sideways into a recess in the receiver wall to lock, a method very similar to that used by the Soviet Goryunov. After firing, gas drives the piston back and a post on the piston extension rides in a cam groove in the block and swings it out of engagement, then withdraws it to extract the empty case. During this movement a post on top

of the block engages with a belt feed arm in the top cover, and this moves the ammunition belt a half-step inwards. On the return stroke the belt is moved a further half-step and the block strips out the fresh cartridge and chambers it. The final forward movement of the piston forces the block back into engagement with the receiver recess; the piston post then strikes the firing pin to fire the next round. The barrel has a quick-change facility and is externally fluted to save weight and also increase the cooling surface. The gas regulator is adjustable and also has a position which closes the exhaust to give minimal emission of gas, allowing the gun to be safely fired in enclosed spaces. There is an adjustable bipod and a carrying handle.

Length, butt extended: 45.47in (1155mm); butt folded: 37.0in (940mm). **Weight unloaded:** 21lb 3oz (9.60kg). **Barrel:** 21.65in (550mm), 4 grooves, right-hand twist. **Magazine:** disintegrating or non-disintegrating metal link belt. **Cyclic rate:** 800 rds/min. **Muzzle velocity:** c.2756 ft/sec (840 m/sec).

• Vektor Mini-SS
Vektor Division of Denel (Pty), Lyttleton
5.56x45mm

The Mini-SS is simply the SS-77 (above) modified by means of a parts kit to fire the 5.56mm cartridge. The kit includes a new chromed barrel, new bolt, feed cover, gas piston and some minor components and the change-over can be

accomplished fairly easily and without recourse to expensive workshop facilities. The barrel is fitted with a flash hider and bipod and a folding butt may be used in place of the normal fixed model. Being somewhat heavier than the general run of 5.56mm machine guns, this ought to be a very stable and accurate weapon. It is in use by the South African Army.

Length: 39.37in (1000mm). **Weight unloaded:** 18lb 3oz (8.26kg). **Barrel:** 20.20in (513mm), 6 grooves, right-hand twist. **Magazine:** 100-round metal belt. **Cyclic rate:** 800 rds/min. **Muzzle velocity:** 3180 ft/sec (980 m/sec).

• Vektor MG4
Vektor Division of Denel (Pty), Lyttleton
7.62x51mm NATO

The MG4 is based on the Browning M1919A4, converted from 30-06 Springfield to 7.62x51mm chambering. In addition, opportunity has been taken to modify the feed mechanism to accommodate a disintegrating-link belt, and modify the firing mechanism to permit firing from an open bolt. A safety catch has also been incorporated in the design, and several minor components have been strengthened or modified in the light of considerable user experience in the harsh conditions of the South African bush. As well as producing complete guns, the makers have also produced a conversion kit which can be applied to any M1919A4, and are offering it on the export market.

The South African R4 is a Browning M1919 modified to fire the 7.62mm NATO cartridge.

The MG4 is normally tripod-mounted for infantry use, but it can also be configured for vehicle mounting and as a dedicated anti-aircraft gun on a special mount with a tachometric sight.
Length: 37.0in (940mm). **Weight unloaded:** 33lb 11oz (15.3kg). **Barrel:** 23.43in (595mm), 4 grooves, right-hand twist. **Magazine:** disintegrating link belt. **Cyclic rate:** 700 rds/min. **Muzzle velocity:** 2756 ft/sec (840m/sec).

SPAIN

• ALFA Model 44, Model 55
Fabrica de Armas de Oviedo, Oviedo
7.92x57mm Mauser (M44), 7.62x51mm NATO (M55)

The Alfa Model 44 was a medium machine gun usually found mounted on a tripod. It was gas-operated and belt fed,

feeding from a fixed cartridge box on the left-hand side. The operation was quite conventional in that a gas piston in a cylinder beneath the barrel was employed to unlock the bolt and drive it back while operating the belt feed mechanism and cocking the weapon. A return spring then sent the bolt back into battery, locking it and preparing it to fire the next round. A selector mechanism permitted the firing of single shots.

A 1955 model also existed which was no more than the 1944 type chambered for the 7.62mm NATO round. Both types were replaced in the early 1960s by the German MG42/59.

Length: 57.00in (1447mm). **Weight unloaded:** 28lb 8oz (12.92kg). **Barrel:** 29.50in (750mm), 6 grooves, right-hand twist. **Magazine:** 100-round metal link belt. **Cyclic rate:** 800 rds/min. **Muzzle velocity:** c.2500 ft/sec (761 m/sec).

• CETME Ameli
Assault Machine gun
Empresa Nacional 'Santa Barbara', Oviedo
5.56x45mm

This design appeared in 1982 and is a light machine gun using delayed blow-back action by means of a bolt with rollers, as used in the CETME and Heckler & Koch rifles (q.v.). There is some interchangeability of components between the Ameli machine gun and the Model L rifle.

As can be seen, the design is strongly reminiscent of the MG42, which is manufactured under license in Spain, and incorporates a similar method of barrel changing. Feed is by a disintegrating link

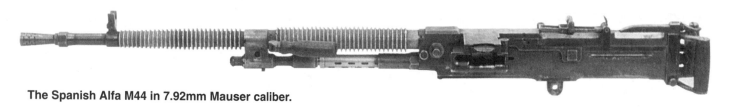

The Spanish Alfa M44 in 7.92mm Mauser caliber.

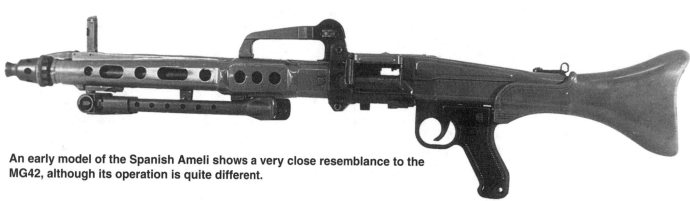

An early model of the Spanish Ameli shows a very close resemblance to the MG42, although its operation is quite different.

A special lightweight Ameli has a different muzzle and butt to the standard gun.

belt, and a small internal change enables the rate of fire to be selected at either 900 or 1250 rds/min. A tripod is available, though bipod use appears to be more common. The Ameli has been placed in service by the Spanish and Mexican Armies, and has been sold to other countries.

Length: 38.58in (980mm). **Weight unloaded:** 12lb 9oz (5.70kg). **Barrel:** 15.7in (470mm), 6 grooves, right-hand twist. **Magazine:** disintegrating link belt. **Cyclic rate:** 900 or 1250 rds/min. **Muzzle velocity:** 2870 ft/sec (875 m/sec).

SWEDEN

• Kjellman, c.1907

Manufacturer unknown (Husqvarna Vapenfabrik?)

6.5x55mm Swedish Mauser

The Kjellman machine gun was never adopted for service, but it deserves a place in history for it pioneered a locking system that has since become widely used and well known. The original idea was conceived by a Swedish officer named Friberg, but it was not developed for over twenty years until it was incorporated into a gun designed in 1907 by Rudolf Kjellman. The locking system utilized two pivoting locking lugs which were forced into recesses in the receiver as the firing pin moved forward. The moving masses were thus kept light and could move quickly. At the same time, the gun could not fire until the breech was locked since the pin could not reach the base of the cartridge until the lugs had been pushed out of the way. The system was used in the Russian Degtyarev light machine guns and also, in a modified form, in the

The Swedish Kjellman of 1907 on its field tripod.

German MG42, which had an impressively high rate of fire. The Kjellman gun was produced both as a light machine gun on a bipod mount with a box magazine and as a tripod-mounted gun with belt feed.

SWITZERLAND

• Model 25 (IMG25 or 'Fürrer')
Waffenfabrik Bern, Bern
7.5x55mm M1911

This Swiss design, taken into service as the lMG25, is typical of its origin: exceptionally well conceived, beautifully made, and far too expensive to be considered as a mass-production weapon. It was designed by Colonel Adolf Furrer, Superintendent of the Waffenfabrik Bern and a man with an astonishing passion for the toggle lock system of operation.

It is a recoil-operated gun which, not to put too fine a point on it, is virtually the Parabellum pistol turned on its side, insofar as the locking system used is the Parabellum's toggle joint. (This, of course, led to the need to feed the ammunition from a side-mounted magazine.) However, Fürrer took a leaf from the submachine gun world and used the differential recoil theory to produce a weapon with a very light recoil. Basically, the system is so arranged as to fire the weapon while substantial portions of the recoiling mass are still moving forward, so that the recoil force of the exploding cartridge is largely absorbed in bringing the mass to rest, and then reversing its direction of motion. Most applications of this system are in the blowback weapons in which firing takes place while the heavy bolt is still moving. In the Fürrer, however, the breech toggle is closed and locked while the entire barrel and action unit are still moving forward into battery. The sear is released during this movement, so that the entire mass of the barrel and bolt must be stopped before recoil can begin. Although a very effi-

The Kjellman mounted on a shielded pedestal for shipboard or fortress use.

cient system, it demands careful manufacture—which is why the Fürrer never achieved success outside Switzerland.

A twin-barrel weapon for aircraft use was also designed by Furrer, and he even went as far as developing 20mm and 37mm anti-aircraft and anti-tank weapons using the same system of operation.

Length: 45.80in (1163mm). **Weight unloaded:** 23lb 6oz (10.59kg). **Barrel:** 23.00in (583mm), 4 grooves, right-hand twist. **Magazine:** 30-round detachable box. **Cyclic rate:** 450 rds/min. **Muzzle velocity:** c.2450 ft/sec (746 m/sec).

• Solothurn MG30
Waffenfabrik Solothurn AG, Solothurn
7.92x57mm Mauser

The Solothurn firm was originally a watch manufacturing concern, but it was bought and converted to arms manufacture in the 1920s. In 1929, Rheinische Metallwaaren und Maschinenfabrik AG gained control of Waffenfabrik Solothurn and it seems that they used the Solothurn factory as a research and development shop for their own designs. The first of these was the Model 29, which was quickly changed to the Model 30 and sold in Austria and Hungary, The Model 30 had a quick-change barrel which was removed by rotating the stock and pulling it off. The main spring and guide stayed with the stock. Barrel and bolt could then be shaken out of the receiver and another barrel inserted. Another feature was a rocking trigger: pressure on the top half gave single shots, and pressure on the lower half gave automatic fire. On firing, the barrel recoiled a short way and the bolt rotated to unlock. The barrel then returned to battery and the bolt continued rearwards until returned by the main spring. It was a simple and rapid action with low iner-

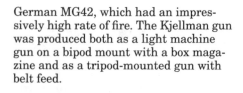

The Swiss M25 light machine gun.

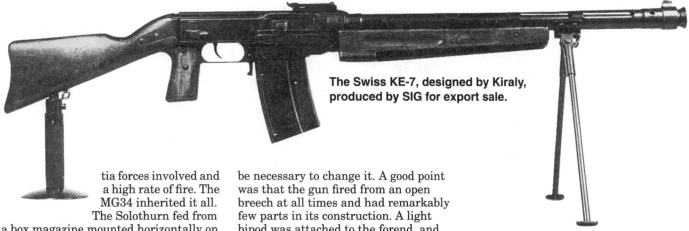

The Swiss KE-7, designed by Kiraly, produced by SIG for export sale.

tia forces involved and a high rate of fire. The MG34 inherited it all.

The Solothurn fed from a box magazine mounted horizontally on the left of the receiver, an unusual idea which is rarely seen because of the changing center of gravity as the magazine is emptied. However, whatever the disadvantages of the gun, 5,000 were made between 1930 and 1935; and of these, a large proportion must have seen service during World War II. The real significance of the Model 30 is that it acted as the starting point for the MG15 and MG34.

Length: 46.25in (1174mm). **Weight unloaded:** 17lb 4oz (7.80kg). **Barrel:** 23.50in (596mm), 4 grooves, right-hand twist. **Magazine:** 25-round detachable box. **Cyclic rate:** 800 rds/min. **Muzzle velocity:** 2500 ft/sec (761 m/sec).

• SIG Model KE7 (c.1936)
Schweizerische Industrie-Gesellschaft, Neuhausen-am-Rheinfalls
7.92x57mm Mauser

Developed before World War II in the late 1930s, the KE7 was a purely commercial venture of SIG and the designers Kiraly and Ende, unsupported by the Swiss Army. It was an attempt to produce a practical light machine gun at a realistic price. However, it had only limited success in overseas sales although China took several large consignments, and it was not manufactured after the war.

The KE7 was an interesting recoil-operated design, and although few light machine guns have used this system, it has some advantages over gas, particularly in barrel changing, fouling of the working parts and simplicity. Recoil operation is less successful in that the power of the mechanism cannot be easily altered to compensate for ammunition of varying characteristics. The KE7 was very light for a full-power light machine gun—even lighter than the Browning Automatic Rifle—and it was probably difficult to control in continuous fire but, as the magazine only held 20 rounds, there would not be many bursts before it would

be necessary to change it. A good point was that the gun fired from an open breech at all times and had remarkably few parts in its construction. A light bipod was attached to the forend, and there was an optional large tripod not unlike that provided for the MG34 or the Bren. This tripod gave the weapon a measure of stability for fixed fire tasks, but the construction of the gun would not really allow it to be employed in support fire roles since the barrel was too light. Another inconvenience would have been the constant replacement of the small magazines.

Length: 46.87in (1190mm). **Weight unloaded:** 17lb 4oz (7.80kg). **Barrel:** 23.63in (600mm), 4 grooves, right-hand twist. **Magazine:** 20-round detachable box. **Cyclic rate:** 550 rds/min. **Muzzle velocity:** c.2450 ft/sec (746 m/sec).

• SIG MG51
Schweizerische Industrie-Gesellschaft, Neuhausen-am-Rheinfalls
7.5x55mm M1911 (Swiss), 30-06 Springfield (Denmark)

The MG51 was developed from the German MG42 during the immediate post-war years. It was only used in Switzerland in small numbers and the only sale of any significance was to Denmark, who equipped her army with it. The MG51 was a heavy gun, as it was milled from solid metal rather than stamped from sheet like the MG42. Another minor change was the introduction of locking flaps on the bolt rather than the rollers of the MG42. These changes did not affect its performance and the gun was both reliable and fast-firing; it was usually mounted on a robust tripod which was provided with carrying straps and back pads. It has now been replaced by the German MG42/59 firing NATO 7.62mm ammunition.

Length: 50.00in (1270mm). **Weight unloaded:** 35lb 6oz (16.00kg). **Barrel:** 22.20in (564mm), 4 grooves, right-hand twist. **Magazine:** 250-round belt. **Cyclic rate:** 1000 rds/min. **Muzzle velocity:** c.2600 ft/sec (792 m/sec).

• SIG MG710-1, MG710-2
Schweizerische Industrie-Gesellschaft, Neuhausen-am-Rheinfalls
7.62x51mm NATO, 7.92x57mm Mauser

The SIG 710 series of machine guns were developed in the post-war years, not only for service in the Swiss Army, but also for sale abroad. They bear certain likenesses to the last models of the MG42, and are direct derivations from the Stgw57 assault rifle. The rifle's delayed blowback locking system is once again employed and, despite apparent complication, it is successful. The Models I and 2 differ in respect of the barrel change; the 710-1 has a perforated barrel jacket with flash-hider and looks very much like the MG42; the barrel is changed by swinging it to the right and withdrawing to the rear, clear of the gun. The 710-2 barrel has no jacket and a vertical carrying handle which is turned and pushed forward to remove the barrel.

The guns are offered with a wide range of extras including a tripod, a drum magazine, and a carrying attachment. They are remarkably well made weapons, and are finished to very fine limits. The 710-1 and 710-2 were not adopted by the Swiss Army, which was already well-equipped, and their sales abroad seem to have been affected by the later Model 710-3.

(MG710-1)

Length: 46.85in (1189mm). **Weight unloaded:** 25lb 0oz (11.30kg). **Barrel:** 19.75in (500mm), 4 grooves, right-hand twist. **Magazine:** 200-round belt. **Cyclic rate:** 750-1400 rds/min. **Muzzle velocity:** c.2600 ft/sec (792 m/sec).

(MG710-2)

Length: 46.75in (1190mm). **Weight unloaded:** 24lb 0oz (10.90kg). **Barrel:** 21.75in. (550mm), 4 grooves, right-hand twist. **Magazine:** 200-round belt. **Cyclic rate:** 750-1400 rds/min. **Muzzle velocity:** c.2600 ft/sec (792 m/sec).

The SIG 710-3 machine gun was based on the improved German MG 42.

• SIG MG 710-3
Schweizerische Industrie-Gesellschaft, Neuhausen-am-Rheinfalls
7.62x51mm NATO

The 710-3 was the last in the 710 series, still using the same method of operation as the preceding two types, but with a less expensive form of manufacture. It is also slightly lighter: In this gun steel stampings are used as much as possible and this has resulted in a small change of outline. Once again, the barrel change has been altered, returning to one similar to the 710-1, in which the barrel is held in a jacket extending more than half-way along its length, and providing a front bearing for the barrel. The barrel has a large plastic handle on the right-hand side, and this permits a hot barrel to be taken off the gun by pulling to the right and to the rear, as on the 710-1; the barrel itself is held by a simple latch.

The basic gun was offered with many extras and, like the others in the series, it was meant to be used as a general purpose gun. It was remarkably well made but expensive, though some sales were made, particularly in South America.

Length: 45.00in (1146mm). **Weight unloaded:** 21lb 4oz (9.65kg). **Barrel:** 22.00in (560mm), 4 grooves, right-hand twist. **Magazine:** 200-round belt. **Cyclic rate:** 900 rds/min. **Muzzle velocity:** c.2600 ft/sec (792 m/sec).

TAIWAN

• Type 74
State arsenal
7.62x51mm NATO

Apart from the shape of the butt and the presence of cooling fins on the barrel this could easily be mistaken for the FN MAG general-purpose machine gun; probably because it was copied from the FN MAG. So far as can be ascertained the dimensions and performance are the same.

• Type 75
State arsenal
5.56x45mm NATO

This appears to be a direct copy of the FN Minimi—and not a licensed copy either, to the best of our knowledge. As with the Type 74, so far as we can discover the dimensions are the same as those of the Minimi.

U.S.A.

• US Colt-Browning Machine Guns, 1895-1917
Colt's Patent Firearms Manufacturing Co., Hartford, Conn.
30-caliber US Service, and others

The original Colt machine gun of 1895 was developed by John Browning from an action based on a rifle he had produced while experimenting to determine whether the muzzle blast of a weapon could be put to some practical use. The unique feature of this gun was a swinging arm beneath the barrel. Gas was tapped off at a point just before the muzzle to drive the end of this arm down and back through an arc of about 170°. The arm was connected to a linkage which opened the breech, extracted the spent case and loaded the new one into the chamber. The action of the arm led to the gun being called the 'potato digger' and, of course, prevented it from being used too close to the ground without first digging a pit. However odd this action may appear, there is no doubt that, owing to the mechanical linkage, it produced a very progressive and gentle movement of the bolt which gave particularly effective and clean extraction and kept the rate of fire down to a practical value.

Numbers of these guns were purchased by the United States Navy in the 1890s, in 6mm (0.236-inch) caliber, and large numbers were sold by Colt to various other countries in various national calibers. The gun first saw action with the

The Colt-Browning 'Potato Digger' of 1895.

The Colt, converted, became the Marlin M1917.

United States Marine Corps at Guantanamo Bay, Cuba, in 1898. It was later used by the United States Army in both 30-40 Krag and 30-06 Springfield calibers, but was largely relegated to use as a training weapon. A very few were used in action during World War I. By that time it had, of course, been obsolete for many years, but it was taken as the starting point for improvements which later led to the Marlin machine gun. The gun was extensively used by Spain (7x57mm caliber) and Italy (6.5x52mm).

• US Tank Machine Gun, Caliber 30 M1918 ('Marlin')

Marlin-Rockwell Corporation, New Haven, Conn.
30-06 Springfield

The Marlin gun was a variation of the original Colt gas-operated light gun of 1895 (the 'potato digger'). During World War I, the Marlin-Rockwell Company were given a contract to make the

Colt design, and they produced the modification for aircraft use. The pendant lever below the barrel was replaced by a piston, and several other alterations were also incorporated. The Marlin version was much lighter than the Colt and it was undoubtedly a better gun. As an aircraft gun (M1916 and M1917) it remained in use with the United States Air Corps throughout World War I and for several years afterwards. Altogether, 38,000 aircraft guns and 1,470 tank machine guns were made, the latter differing slightly from the aircraft gun in having an armored barrel jacket. There was also a projected version for infantry use as a light machine gun but this was not pursued. In 1941, when Britain was desperately short of all types of weapons, several thousand Marlins were supplied by the United States, all of them dating from World War I. These

guns were used for anti-aircraft defense on small merchant ships. In this role, the Marlin was valuable though inconspicuous. It was not used to any extent elsewhere.

Length: 40.00in (1016mm). **Weight unloaded:** 22lb 8oz (10.20kg). **Barrel:** 28.00in (711mm), 4 grooves, right-hand twist. **Magazine:** 250-round cloth belt. **Cyclic rate:** 600 rds/min. **Muzzle velocity:** c.2800 ft/sec (853 m/sec).

• Browning Machine Guns

Various manufacturers
30-06 Springfield, 50 BMG

After experimenting with gas-operation, John Browning came to the conclusion that recoil offered the greater possibilities and as early as 1900, therefore, he began to take out patents which

covered the operating system later developed in his machine guns.

The Browning guns utilize the recoil force of the expanding powder gases to push the barrel and the bolt to the rear; after a short recoil, the bolt is unlocked and the barrel is halted. An accelerator then throws the bolt to the rear and the movement of the bolt, by cam surfaces, operates the belt-feed mechanism. The bolt is then returned by the recoil spring until it once again joins the barrel, when the parts are once again locked together and return to battery.

Although the design was fully developed by c.1910, it was not until America's entry into World War I in 1917 that Browning was able to interest the authorities in his design, which was very promptly accepted as the Model 1917.

US Machine Gun, Caliber 30, M1917

In appearance, the M1917 is similar to the Maxim and Vickers patterns, tripod mounted with a water jacket of conventional form and belt fed, although the pistol grip at the rear of the receiver casing readily distinguishes the Browning design. Slightly more than 68,000 of the M1917 were manufactured before the close of World War I by the Remington Arms-Union Metallic Cartridge Co., Colt's Patent Firearms Manufacturing Co., and the New England Westinghouse Co. As a result of combat experience the M1917 underwent several small modifications during the early 1920s and, in 1936, the opportunity was taken of revising the basic design with the consequent appearance of the M1917A1.

The stark simplicity of the Browning M1917.

US Machine Gun, Caliber 30, M1917A1 (1936).

The M1917AI was virtually identical with the M1917 from which it was modified; alterations were made to the feed unit, the sights were re-graduated, and the tripod was altered. Service weapons were reworked by Rock Island Arsenal in 1936-7, and further small modifications were made to them between 1942 and 1944 as a result of further field experience.

Length: 38.50in (978mm). **Weight unloaded:** 32lb 10oz (14.97kg). **Barrel:** 24.00in (610mm), 4 grooves, right-hand twist. **Magazine:** 250-round fabric belt. **Cyclic rate:** 500 rds/min. **Muzzle velocity:** c.2800 ft/sec (853 m/sec).

US Machine Guns, Caliber 30, M1918 and M1918M1

The M1917 was a water-cooled gun, and, consequently, was ill-suited to air-craft use. Modified patterns were therefore designed by discarding the water jacket in favor of light pierced casings, and by lightening components where at all possible. The M1918 designs led to the introduction of the M1919.

US Machine Gun, Caliber 30, M1919.

Intended to be the definitive Browning-type tank gun of World War I (but appearing too late), it was fitted with a heavier barrel than that of the M1917

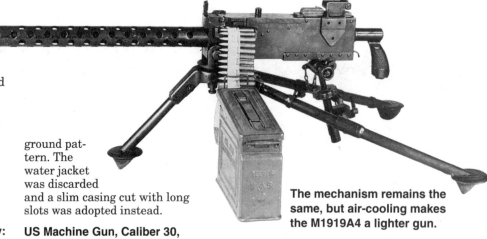

ground pattern. The water jacket was discarded and a slim casing cut with long slots was adopted instead.

US Machine Gun, Caliber 30, M1919A1

A variant of the M1919 intended to be mounted in the Mark VIII tank, suitable modifications were made to the mounting.

US Machine Gun, Caliber 30, M1919A2

A version of the M1919 intended for the use of mounted cavalry, the M1919A2 was fitted with an especially-small tripod and could be packed on to a special saddle for mule-pack carriage.

US Machine Gun, Caliber 30, M1919A3

A general-purpose derivative of the basic M1919, it served as a prototype for the M1919A4.

The mechanism remains the same, but air-cooling makes the M1919A4 a lighter gun.

US Machine Gun, Caliber 30, M1919A4.

This gun was issued in fixed and flexible forms; the fixed gun was intended to be used in tank and multiple anti-air-craft gun installations, and the flexible pattern was intended for use in other combat vehicles or—mounted on a tripod—for infantry use.

Length: 41.00in (1041mm). **Weight unloaded:** 31lb 0oz (14.05kg). **Barrel:** 24.00in (610mm), 4 grooves, right-hand twist. **Magazine:** 250-round fabric belt. **Cyclic rate:** 500 rds/min. **Muzzle velocity:** c.2800 ft/sec (853 m/sec).

The M1919A4 in action.

The M1919A6 was, like the Mauser 098/15, an attempt to turn a medium machine gun into a light one. It had no better success.

US Machine Gun, Caliber 30, M1919A4E1

A post-World War II version of the M19l9A4, this had the slide retracting mechanism of the M1919A5.

US Machine Gun, Caliber 30, M1919A5

This was a special weapon intended to be mounted in the Light Tank M3: a special bolt-retracting slide was fitted.

US Machine Gun, Caliber 30, M1919A6

Adopted in April 1943, the M1919A6 is essentially similar to the M1919A4 with the addition of a shoulder-stock, a bipod, a carrying handle, a lighter barrel and a flash suppresser.
Length: 53.00in (1346mm). **Weight unloaded:** 32lb 8oz (14.73kg). **Barrel:** 24.00in (610mm), 4 grooves, right-hand twist. **Magazine:** 250-round fabric belt. **Cyclic rate:** 500 rds/min. **Muzzle velocity:** c.2800 ft/sec (853 m/sec).

US Machine Gun, Caliber 30, M37

A tank version of the basic M1919 series, the feed mechanism was changed to permit either left- or right-hand feed. An ejection chute was also added for the metallic-link belt.

US Machine Gun, Caliber 30, M2

This version was designed specifically as an aircraft weapon; the principal differences between the M2 and the earlier M1918 lie in the provision of a special retracting mechanism. A solenoid sear-release mechanism was supplied for fixed aircraft guns, and spade grips could be fitted to the flexible guns.
Length: 39.90in (1014mm). **Weight unloaded:** 23lb 0oz (10.48kg). **Barrel:** 23.90in (608mm), 4 grooves, right-hand twist. **Magazine:** 250-round metallic link belt. **Cyclic rate:** 1200 rds/min. **Muzzle velocity:** c.2800 ft/sec (853 m/sec).

US Machine Gun, Caliber 7.62mm NATO, Mark 1-1 Model 0

This strangely named gun is a conversion of the M1919A4 intended for the United States Navy. Apart from the rechambering of the gun with the appropriate barrel and feed modifications, it is a standard M1919A4.

• US Machine Guns, Caliber 50

All the foregoing Browning weapons were of 30-caliber but, during the latter days of World War I, a request was made for a weapon comparable in power to the French 11mm Hotchkiss machine gun, and capable of attacking observation balloons and aircraft. After some experimentation, a Browning-system machine gun was developed in 50-caliber and eventually introduced to the service as the '**US Machine Gun, Caliber 50, M1921**', a modified form of which later appeared as the **M1921A1**. During the 1930s, the M2 version appeared, in which provision was made to enable the water to constantly circulate through the water jacket, which greatly helped dissipate the heat produced during long periods of sustained fire.

After this gun had been developed, an air-cooled version—which was still called the M2—also appeared, having been developed for aircraft use. Like the 30-caliber M2, this also came in fixed and flexible guise. The cooling of the 50-caliber M2 barrel was soon overtaxed by the

Two Browning 50-caliber guns: top, the fixed gun for aircraft mounting, below the flexible gun for use by aerial gunners.

A 50 Browning with quick-change barrel, by Manroy Engineering of Britain.

Left side view of the QCB 50 Browning, showing belt feed.

power of the cartridge, and no more than a 75-round burst could be fired without stopping to allow the barrel to cool. Such a restriction was unacceptable for ground use and so the M2HB ('Heavy Barrel') was developed; this was supplied with a much thicker barrel which permitted faster dissipation of heat (and, of course, was capable of absorbing proportionately more heat) and therefore allowed firing over a long period without the danger of overheating the barrel. This was again made available in fixed, flexible and anti-aircraft form: the fixed gun was mounted in the bows of the heavy Tank M6 and in multiple-gun anti-aircraft units, while the flexible gun was used on combat vehicles' turret tops or as a heavy ground-support gun.

(M2 water-cooled)
Length: 66.00in (1666mm). **Weight unloaded:** 100lb 0oz (45.35kg). **Barrel:** 45.00in (1143mm), 8 grooves, right-hand twist. **Magazine:** 110-round metallic link belt. **Cyclic rate:** 600 rds/min. **Muzzle velocity:** c.2900 ft/sec (884 m/sec).

(M2 air-cooled)
Length: 57.00in 1447mm. **Weight unloaded:** 65lb 2oz (29.53kg). **Barrel:**

36.00in (914mm), 8 grooves, right-hand twist. **Magazine:** 110-round metallic link belt. **Cyclic rate:** 800 rds/min. **Muzzle velocity:** c.2900 ft/sec (884 m/sec).

(M2HB)
Length: 65.10in (1653mm). **Weight unloaded:** 84lb 0oz (38.22kg). **Barrel:** 45.00in (1143mm), 8 grooves, right-hand twist. **Magazine:** 110-round metallic link belt. **Cyclic rate:** 500 rds/min. **Muzzle velocity:** c.2950 ft/sec (898 m/sec).

During and after World War II, several attempts were made to improve the basic Browning designs: none was particularly successful, and the Browning-designed machine guns continue to serve all over the world.

• Johnson Light Machine Guns Models 1941 and 1944
Cranston Arms Company, Providence, R.I.
30-06 Springfield
The Johnson light machine gun was developed between 1936 and 1938 from the rifle of the same designer. The United States Marine Corps tried it without adoption, and the only sizable order the company ever received came from the Dutch armies in the Netherlands East Indies. Before this could be entirely

fulfilled, the Japanese invaded and the orders ceased, although use by the United States Army Rangers and Special Services ensured that a small continuous output emanated from the factory.

The Johnson was one of the few light machine guns to operate on recoil principles and, although an elegant design manufactured to a high standard, it was too flimsy and too prone to jamming for prolonged field use. An interesting milestone in the history of arms designs, it perhaps deserved a better fate, but the gun appeared at a time when the army had made up its mind regarding light machine-gun policy and had settled upon the Browning Automatic Rifle and the machine-gun M1919A4. The Johnson possessed a number of unusual features, including firing from an open bolt in the automatic mode and from a closed bolt for single shots. The box magazine was on the left side of the gun, but it was also possible to reload the magazine through the right side of the action without removing the box; standard five-round chargers or single rounds could be utilized, which was Melvin Johnson's method of overcoming the authorities' demands for a belt-fed gun. The cyclic rate could he altered by changing the

The Johnson machine guns: top, the M1941; below, the M1944.

tension in the buffer spring, and was theoretically variable between 300 and 900 rounds per minute.

Two basic models were manufactured by the Cranston Arms Company, the M1941 and the M1944. The earlier pattern was provided with a bipod and a wooden butt, whereas the 1944 pattern was marketed with a light tubular monopod and a 'butt' made from two parallel pieces of tubing finished by a buttplate.

Length: 42.00in (1066mm) **Weight unloaded:** 14lb 5oz (6.48kg). **Barrel:** 22.00in (558mm), 4 grooves, right-hand

eral purpose machine gun of the United States Army. It was designed during the last years of the 1950s and has been in service since the early 1960s. The M60 is interesting in that it uses the feed system of the German MG42 and the bolt and locking system of the FG42, an impressive example of imitation being the sincerest form of flattery. Much expense and effort went into producing the gun which in its original form barely justified the work. Despite its illustrious forebears, the original M60 had some serious drawbacks, the most noticeable of which was in the barrel change. Each barrel had its

M60E1 more into line with current practice, and gave it improved reliability. A feature of both models was the Stellite lining to the barrels which prolonged their lives beyond that normally experienced with unprotected steel, and both models had a constant-energy gas system to work the piston.

Length: 43.5in (1.10m). **Weight unloaded:** 23lb 3oz (10.51kg). **Barrel:** 22.04in (560mm), 4 grooves, right-hand twist. **Magazine:** Disintegrating link belt. **Cyclic rate:** 550 rds/min. **Muzzle velocity:** 2805 ft/sec (855 m/sec).

The US M60 general purpose machine gun.

twist. **Magazine:** 20-round detachable box, with a further 5 in the action. **Cyclic rate:** 300-900 rds/min. **Muzzle velocity:** c.2900 ft/sec (853 m/sec).

• US Machine Gun, Caliber 7.62mm NATO, M60 and M60E1
Bridge Tool & Die Manufacturing Company, Philadelphia, and Inland Manufacturing Division of General Motors, Dayton, Ohio
7.62x51mm NATO

The M60, with its modified successor the M60E1, is the standard squad gen-

own gas cylinder and bipod attachment to it—but no handle. It was, therefore, not only an expensive item but also unnecessarily heavy and dangerous to handle when hot. An asbestos glove formed part of the gun's equipment, and since the bipod vanished with the barrel, the poor gunner had to hold the gun up in the air while the barrel was changed.

The later M60E1 had a simpler barrel with the gas cylinder and bipod fixed to the gun, and it also has a handle for barrel changing. There were other less important changes which brought the

The M60E3 lightened the overall gun and made improvements to the gas system and barrel changing.

• Maremont Lightweight Machine gun M60

Saco Division, Maremont Corporation, Saco, Maine
7.62x51mm NATO

This weapon was developed by Saco to provide a lighter and more versatile M60 which retained the firepower of its parent. Generally similar to the M6E1, it had the bipod permanently mounted to the receiver, had a carrying handle which doubled as a barrel-changing handle, and had a forward pistol grip with heat shield instead of the forend of the standard M60. The feed mechanism was altered to simplify charging the weapon, the front sight was fully adjustable so that each barrel could be pre-zeroed to the receiver, and the gas system was simplified. All the operating group was common to this and to the standard M60 and the major sub-assemblies were interchangeable. The Lightweight M60 underwent a great deal of field testing and formed the basis of the M60E3.

Length: 42.00in (1070mm). **Weight unloaded:** 19.0lb (8.68kg).

Barrel: 22.04in (560mm), 4 grooves, right-hand twist. **Magazine:** Disintegrating link belt. **Cyclic rate:** 550 rds/min. **Muzzle velocity:** 2820 ft/sec (860 m/sec).

• US Machine Gun M60E3

Saco Defense Inc., Saco, Me.
7.62x51mm NATO

This was the further development of the Saco Lightweight design and generally follows the same lines, with a forward handgrip. The barrel may be a short assault barrel or a longer and heavier one for sustained fire missions. The feed cover has been modified to permit it being closed whether the bolt is forward or back, and the bipod is attached to the receiver. A winter triggerguard allows firing when wearing heavy gloves. The M60E3 was taken into use by the US Navy and Marine Corps and sold to several other countries.

Length: 42.40in (1077mm). **Weight unloaded:** 19lb 6oz (8.80kg). **Barrel:** 22.0in (558mm), 4 grooves, right-hand twist. **Magazine:** disintegrating link belt. **Cyclic rate:** 600 rds/min. **Muzzle velocity:** 2800 ft/sec (853 m/sec).

• US Machine Gun M60E4

Saco Defense Inc., Saco, Me.
7.62x51mm NATO

The M60E4 is simply an improved M60E3; it follows the same general lines but now has three alternative barrels: a short heavy sustained fire barrel, a long heavy sustained fire barrel, and a short lightweight assault barrel. All barrels fit all guns, but generally the squad light machine gun uses the short heavy barrel, while the long heavy is normally used when the gun is working in the coaxial role or in a vehicle mount. Modifications to the feed mechanism have improved the belt lifting capability, and several minor parts have been strengthened or re-designed. The gun has been adopted by the US Navy.

Length, short barrel: 37.72in (958mm); standard barrel 42.40in (1077mm); assault barrel 37.0in (940mm). **Weight unloaded,** short barrel : 22lb 8oz (10.20kg); long barrel: 23lb 2oz (10.50kg); assault barrel: 21lb 3oz (9.90kg). **Barrel,** standard: 22.0in (560mm); short: 17.36in (441mm); assault: 16.65in (423mm). **Magazine:** disintegrating link belt. **Cyclic rate:** 600 rds/min. **Muzzle velocity:** 3180 ft/sec (853 m/sec).

The M60E4 was a further advance on the M60 design.

• M249 SAW (Squad Automatic Weapon)

FN Manufacturing Inc, Columbia, SC.
5.56x45mm NATO

The M249 is the FN Minimi with sundry small changes to meet the US Army's requirements for a light machine gun. It was approved in 1982 but did not enter production until the early 1990s due to a long drawn-out period of testing and modification before the requirements were satisfied. As a result the US Army had to purchase 1000 Minimi guns rather rapidly in 1992 when the Gulf Live-Firing Exercise took place.

The changes were largely to suit US manufacturing methods and were relatively small, though nonetheless important; the principal exterior difference is the presence of a heat shield above the barrel. All other characteristics of the Minimi are unchanged.

Length: 40.95in (1040mm). **Weight unloaded:** 15lb 2oz (6.85kg). **Barrel:** 20.60in (523mm), 6 grooves, right-hand twist. **Magazine:** 30-round detachable box or 200-round metal belt. **Cyclic rate:** 750 rds/min. **Muzzle velocity:** 3000 ft/sec (915 m/sec).

• US Machine Gun M240 series

FN Manufacturing Inc, Columbia, SC.
7.62x51mm NATO

The M240 was purchased from FN Herstal in 1976 as a co-axial machine gun for armored vehicles, and it is, in fact, the FN MAG. Subsequently produced in the USA under license, it was fitted to M60 and M1 Abrams tanks. This was followed by the M240C, which differed in feeding in from the right side so as to suit the location of the gun in the M2 Bradley IFV.

The gun rapidly acquired a formidable reputation for reliability, as a result of which the US Marines demanded it as their sustained fire machine gun to replace the M60. Acquiring a number of surplus M240 guns, they converted them into ground weapons, suitable for use on the M122E1 tripod or with a fitted bipod, the result being called the M240G and issued to the Fleet Marine Force in 1994.

Having watched this transition with interest, the US Army now conducted their own conversion, calling it the M240E4 and, after trials, renamed it the M240B and took it into service in 1995. The only visible difference between the M240B and M240G is the presence of a handguard over the barrel on the Army model. Finally, in 1997, FN Manufacturing Inc. was awarded a contract for the supply of 8160 M240B guns and a similar number of mountings, the order to be completed by mid-2002. Whatever the terminology, it remains the standard FN MAG; gas operated, with a tipping bolt, belt fed, and as reliable as a railroad watch.

Length: 48.03in (1220mm). **Weight unloaded:** 25lb 13oz (11.70kg). **Barrel:** 24.69in (627mm), 4 grooves, right-hand twist. **Magazine:** disintegrating link belt. **Cyclic rate:** 750-950 rds/min. **Muzzle velocity:** 2800 ft/sec (853 m/sec).

• US Machine Gun M73

General Electric Company, New York
7.62x51mm NATO

The M73 machine gun was designed as a tank weapon, with the specific aim of producing a gun with short inboard length and one in which all the necessary immediate actions and maintenance, including barrel changes, could be done from inside the vehicle. Another important design consideration was the necessity to avoid powder fumes inside the turret. The design is attributed to Russell Robinson, an Australian who had worked with the British during the post-war years, and uses a horizontal sliding breechblock instead of the more usual axially-moving bolt; it is this feature which gives the desired shortness of body. Other advantages in tank use accrue from the fact that the top cover is side-hinged and thus demands less headroom when opened, and the entire body section can be swung to one side to allow the barrel to be withdrawn from its jacket while inside the tank.

Length: 34.75in (883mm). **Weight unloaded:** 28lb 0oz (12.70kg). **Barrel:** 22.00in (558mm). **Magazine:** 250-round

disintegrating belt. **Cyclic rate:** 500 rds/min. **Muzzle velocity:** c.2800 ft/sec (853 m/sec).

• US Machine gun M85

General Electric Company (USA), Burlington, Vermont
12.7x99mm (50 Browning)

Designed by the Aircraft Armament Corporation (AAI), this gun was designed to replace the 50-caliber Browning as the tank co-axial or cupola machine gun in US service. It is a recoil-operated gun using a bolt and bolt carrier; the movement of the bolt carrier cams locking lugs into recesses in the receiver to lock the bolt. On firing, the barrel and barrel extension recoil in the receiver; an accelerator throws the bolt carrier back and this movement cams in the locking lugs and then retracts the bolt. Feed is by a disintegrating link belt and, due to the lightness of the recoiling parts, the rate of fire is about 1050 rounds per minute. For occasions where this rate would be too high, a rate regulator can be switched in; this delays the return of the bolt and reduces the rate to about 400 rounds per minute.

Length: 54.50in (1384mm). **Weight:** 61lb 8oz (27.90kg). **Barrel:** 34.00in (914mm). **Magazine:** Disintegrating link belt. **Cyclic rate:** 1050 or 400 rds/min. **Muzzle velocity:** 2840 ft/sec (866 m/sec).

• Stoner Light Machine Gun M63A1

Cadillac Gage Company, Detroit, Mich.
5.56mmx45mm

The M63A1 light machine gun was the last weapon in the Stoner small-arms system. When assembled into the machine gun form, the weapon fired from an open bolt and was only capable of automatic fire. The method of operation was by a conventional gas system, with the piston and gas port on the underside of the barrel. The gun could be fed either from a box magazine or from a belt. If the magazine was used, it fed vertically downwards; for belt feeding, a different receiver cover had to be fitted in order to incorporate the feed

The M85 tank gun.

The Stoner 63A1 as a light machine gun, with belt box.

The Stoner 63A1 tripod-mounted for sustained fire.

pawls and stops. It will be noticed that the box was clipped under the center of the receiver, with the feed coming up under a cover. There were several extras offered with this gun, including different varieties of ammunition box and methods of attachment.

The Stoner was a most attractive system with much to recommend it, but it never managed to sell in large numbers although it underwent evaluation by the United States Marine Corps in Vietnam.

Length: 40.24in (1622mm). **Weight unloaded:** 12lb 8oz (5.65kg). **Barrel:** 21.69in (551mm), 4 grooves, right-hand twist. **Magazine:** 30-round box, or belt. **Cyclic rate:** 700 rds/min. **Muzzle velocity:** c.3250 ft/sec (990 m/sec).

• General Purpose Heavy Machine Gun (GPHMG)

US Army Armament Research & Development Command (ARRADCOM) Dover, N.J.
12.7x99mm (50-caliber Browning)

This weapon was developed in the mid-1980s as a design capable of being utilized in calibers from 12.7 to 25mm, and was originally known as the 'Dover Devil'. It was a gas-operated, fully automatic, belt-fed weapon which fired from an open bolt. It was modular in construction, being built up from six basic assemblies.

The receiver consisted of two steel tubes mounted in a vertical plane and joined by an aluminum end cap. Inside each tube was a short-stroke gas piston which drove an operating rod. These rods struck the bolt carrier, which contained the bolt; the movement of the bolt carrier caused the bolt to revolve, by means of a cam track and pin, so as to lock with three lugs into the rear of the barrel. As the carrier continued forward after loading a round and locking the bolt, a fixed firing pin was driven forward and struck the cap. The use of two pistons and two operating rods distributed the load evenly and obviated stress.

The gun fed from the left side, using a sprocket-driven disintegrating link belt. There was a neutral selector lever which disengaged the feed mechanism and permitted single shots to be fired. The reciprocating bolt group also drove the feed mechanism, operated a rammer which withdrew the cartridge from the belt, and an extractor which removed and ejected the spent case. The working parts were protected by a dust cover, but this was not essential to the operation of the weapon.

Length: 72.0in (1.829m). **Weight, unloaded:** gun: 47lb 0oz (21.32kg); tripod: 19lb 0oz (8.60kg). **Barrel:** 36.0in (914mm).

Magazine: Disintegrating link belt. **Cyclic rate:** 400 rds/min. **Muzzle velocity:** c.2837 ft/sec (865 m/sec).

• General Purpose Heavy Machine Gun (GPHMG)
AAI Corporation, Baltimore, Md.
12.7x99mm (50-caliber Browning)

This, though developed by a private concern, is very similar in concept to the ARRADCOM design (above). It used a three-tube configuration for the receiver which added strength to the design and made it easier to incorporate dual feed. There were two operating rods, driven by gas pistons, which controlled a bolt carrier and three-lug rotating bolt. Feed was performed from both sides of the gun and a selector lever allowed the gunner to choose which belt to use. It could also be set in a neutral position, preventing either belt from feeding, and acting as a positive safety. There was a quick-change barrel. The manufacturer claimed that this gun could be made for some 30 percent less than the current M2HB Browning.

Although both these GPHMGs proved out quite well in their initial tests, the army decided that other weapons had a greater priority and a better claim on the available finance, and the development program was closed down in about 1988.

Length: 61.0in (1549mm). **Weight unloaded:** 55lb 0oz (24.50kg). **Barrel:** not known. **Magazine:** Dual disintegrating link belts. **Cyclic rate:** 400 rds/min. **Muzzle velocity:** not known.

• Minigun M134
General Electric Company (USA), Burlington, Vt. (originators); Lockheed Martin Armament Systems, Burlington, Vt. (current production)
7.62x51mm NATO

This multiple-barrel 'Gatling-type' machine gun is based on the 20mm Vulcan development, and was specifically designed for use in helicopters in Vietnam. Due to its demands for power and ammunition, its application is limited to helicopters or vehicle mounts which provide the necessary space. The six barrels are revolved by an electric motor; they are normally parallel but can be clamped into various degrees of convergence if required. The action body, behind the barrels, carries six bolts in a rotating unit; these bolts lock into the barrels by rotation of their heads. The ammunition is belt-fed into the action body, the rounds are stripped out and located in front of the bolts, and as the bolt unit revolves so each round is cham-

bered; at the uppermost position the firing pin is released and the round fired, after which the empty case is extracted and the bolt makes a complete circuit to pick up another round. When the trigger is released, the ammunition feed is isolated so that there is no danger of a cook-off during the short time the barrel and bolt assembly is coming to rest.

Length: 31.50in (800mm). **Weight unloaded:** 35lb 0oz (15.90kg). **Weight with power supply:** 59lb 0oz (26.8kg). **Barrels:** 22.00in (559mm), 4 grooves, right-hand twist. **Magazine:** 4000-round linked belt. **Cyclic rate:** c.6000 rds/min. **Muzzle velocity:** 2850 ft/sec (869 m/sec).

• Hughes Chain Gun EX34
Hughes Helicopters & Ordnance Systems, Culver City, Calif. (originators); McDonnell Douglas Helicopter Systems, Mesa, Ariz. (current production).
7.62x51mm NATO

The Hughes Helicopter Company spent several years developing their Chain Gun, concentrating on 25mm and 30mm weapons for aircraft armament. After perfecting these, they turned to a rifle-caliber weapon as a potential tank armament.

The Chain Gun derives its name from the use of a conventional roller chain in an endless loop which drives the

bolt. The chain is driven by an electric motor, and a shoe on the chain engages in the bolt, carries it forward to chamber a round, holds it closed, then retracts it to extract the spent case. Cams rotate the bolt head to lock into the barrel and also actuate the firing pin as the bolt locks. A dynamic brake on the motor ensures that when the trigger is released the bolt stops in the open position, so that there is no danger of cook-off. The belt feed is also driven by the motor, independently of the bolt mechanism, so that there is ample power to handle long belts, particularly in a vehicle bounding over rough country. The Chain Gun is particularly well suited to tank installation since case ejection is forward, under control, and the relatively long bolt closure dwell time reduces the amount of fumes released into the vehicle. The Hughes Chain Gun is one of the few new operating principles which have appeared in recent years, but it has not achieved the success it would appear to deserve. Although extensively tested by the US Army and Navy, its only major adoption has been by the British as the co-axial armament for their 'Warrior' IFV and various other light fighting

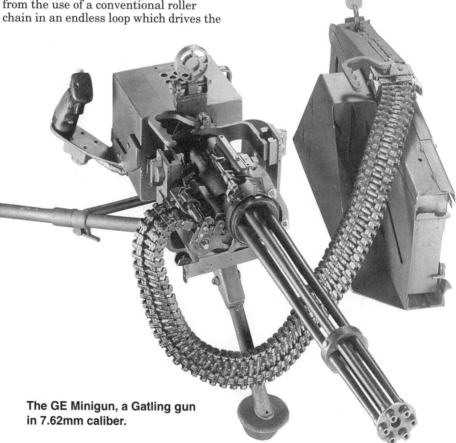

The GE Minigun, a Gatling gun in 7.62mm caliber.

The Hughes Chain Gun, a mechanically-driven gun used in US and British armored vehicles.

First known as GECAL 50, now GAU/19A, the GE three-barrel 50-caliber Gatling gun.

vehicles, and it is currently manufactured under license in Britain as the L94A1.

Length: 49.21in (1250mm). **Weight:** 39lb 6oz (17.86kg). **Barrel:** 27.68in (703mm). **Magazine:** disintegrating link belt. **Cyclic rate:** 520 rds/min. **Muzzle velocity:** 2828 ft/sec (862 m/sec).

• US Machine Gun M219
General Electric Company (USA), Burlington, Vermont
7.62x51mm NATO

The M73 tank machine gun turned out, in service, to be prone to serious mechanical problems; the redesign necessary to correct these faults was so extensive that the end result was virtually a new gun, so it was called the M219. The redesign has involved a new extractor, rammer and feed tray and a complete re-timing of the feed-fire-extract-eject cycle to obviate feed jams. Hence the components of the M13 and M219 are not interchangeable. In spite of all this work, the M219 was still not the best answer, and in 1978 it was decided to replace it by adopting the Belgian FN-MAG as the future US tank machine gun.

Data as for the M73.

• GAU 19/A
Lockheed Martin Armament Systems, Burlington, Vt.
50 Browning

This was originally developed by General Electric and called the 'GECAL 50', gaining its more formal nomenclature after adoption by the US Army. It is a three-barreled Gatling-type weapon requiring an external source of power such as vehicle batteries. Although it produces a much higher volume of fire than a standard M2HB gun, it is only slightly heavier and delivers lesser recoil force to its mounting. It can be adjusted to give two rates of fire.

The mechanism is similar to that of the M134 gun described above, with the three barrels rotating in front of a receiver unit in which cam tracks control the movement of the three bolts. The gun will fire any type of 50 Browning ammunition, including SLAP discarding sabot rounds. A de-linking feed system accepts standard machine gun belts and removes the rounds from the belt prior to feeding into the linkless supply chutes.

Length: 46.50in (1181mm). **Weight unloaded:** 74lb 1oz (33.60kg). **Barrel:** 36.0in (914mm), 8 grooves, right-hand twist. **Magazine:** linkless feed. **Cyclic rate:** Selectable 1000 or 2000 rds/min. **Muzzle velocity:** 2900 ft/sec (884 m/sec).

• Colt M16A2
Colt's Manufacturing Co., Hartford, Conn.
5.56x45mm NATO

Developed in collaboration with Diemaco of Canada, this is based upon the M16A2 rifle. It has a heavier barrel, larger and stronger forend and hand-

The Colt M16A2 machine gun.

guard with carrying handle, an attached folding bipod and a forward assault hand grip. The basic mechanism remains that of the Stoner rotating bolt, driven by gas impingement. The standard 30-round magazine is used, but there are a number of proprietary large-capacity magazines available in the USA which will also fit the magazine housing.

The M16A2 machine gun has been adopted by the US Marines and also by Brazil, El Salvador and other countries.

Length: 39.37in (1000mm). **Weight unloaded:** 12lb 12oz (5.78kg). **Barrel:** 20.0in (510mm), 6 grooves, right-hand twist. **Magazine:** 30-round detachable box. **Cyclic rate:** 700 rds/min. **Muzzle velocity:**-3100 ft/sec (945 m/sec).

YUGOSLAVIA

• Machine Guns M65A, M65B
Zavodi Crvena Zastava, Kragujeva
7.62x39mm M1943 Soviet

The M65A and M65B are the Yugoslavs' standard light machine gun designs, the equivalents of the Soviet RPD and RPK patterns. Both are designed to use as many of the parts as practicable of the Yugoslav M64 assault rifles, which ensures uncomplicated production. Both the M65A and the M65B are fitted with light bipods, and heavier barrels than the assault rifles, although the utility of this is questionable as the barrels are apparently non-interchangeable. This, of course, means that sustained fire from these weapons is impossible; and the 30-round box magazine imposes another shortcoming. The barrels are finned out as far as the gas port to help dissipate the heat.

Length: 43.11in (1095mm). **Weight unloaded:** 12lb 2oz (5.50kg). **Barrel:** 18.50in (470mm), 4 grooves, right-hand twist. **Magazine:** 30-round detachable box. **Cyclic rate:** c.600 rds/min. **Muzzle velocity:** c.2445 ft/sec (745 m/sec).

• Machine Gun M53
Zavody Crvena Zastava, Kragujevac
7.92x57mm Mauser

During the Second World War and afterwards the Yugoslav Army acquired numbers of German MG42 machine guns. They were so satisfied with these that when they began to wear out they simply copied them, called them their M53, and have continued to use them ever since. As with the German weapon, the M53 can be used either as a light squad automatic or as a medium support-gun on a tripod. For details of operation and dimensions, see under MG1 in the German (Federal Republic) section.

• Machine gun M72
Zavodi Crvena Zastava, Kragujevac
7.62x39mm Soviet M43

In spite of their employment of the M53 general purpose machine gun in the squad automatic role, the fact that it demands ammunition not used by the rest of the rifle squad can be an embarrassment at times, and the Yugoslavs have now adopted a light machine gun firing their standard infantry round, the 7.62x39mm cartridge. In fact, the M72 is little more than a strengthened Kalashnikov design and it resembles the RPK used by the Soviet Army. The barrel is heavier than that used with the rifle, and a bipod is fitted, but there is no provision for changing the barrel. which suggests that fire discipline will have to be good in order to avoid overheating.

Length: 40.35in (1025mm). **Weight:** 11lb 2oz (5.00kg). **Barrel:** 21.25in (540mm). **Magazine:** 30 round detachable box. **Cyclic rate:** c. 650 rds/min. **Muzzle velocity:** 2445 ft/sec (745 m/sec).

• M77B1
Zavodi Crvena Zastava, Kragujevac
7.62x51mm NATO

This was produced in the late 1970s and intended for export sales; presumably it sold, since it remained in production until about 1990. In essence it is a heavy-barreled version of the M72B1 assault rifle, gas operated on the Kalashnikov system and provided with a bipod and carrying handle.

Length: 40.35in (1025mm). **Weight:** 11lb 4oz (5.10kg). **Barrel:** 21.05in (535mm), 4 grooves, right-hand twist. **Magazine:** 20-round detachable box. **Cyclic rate:** c.600 rds/min. **Muzzle velocity:** 2756 ft/sec (840 m/sec).

It looks like an MG42; the Yugoslavian M53 is a direct copy of the German wartime gun.

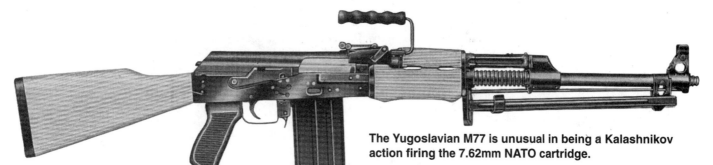

The Yugoslavian M77 is unusual in being a Kalashnikov action firing the 7.62mm NATO cartridge.

The M82A is another Kalashnikov derivative, but this time firing the NATO 5.56mm cartridge.

• M82
Zavodi Crvena Zastava, Kragujevac
5.56x45mm

The M82 is a heavy-barreled model based on the M80 assault rifle; in other words, yet another Kalashnikov derivative, chambered for the 5.56x45mm cartridge in the hope of attracting foreign orders. The weapon uses the standard rifle magazine but is fitted with a bipod, attached just behind the muzzle. The makers claimed that a new design of gas regulator has been fitted so as to maintain performance with varying grades of ammunition. It was first seen in the mid-1980s, but whether it achieved any sales success is not known, since Yugoslavia dissolved into civil unrest shortly afterwards.

Length: 40.16in (1020mm).
Weight: 8lb 13oz (4.0kg). **Barrel:** 21.34in (542mm), 6 grooves, right-hand twist. **Magazine:** 30-round detachable box. **Cyclic rate:** c.750 rds/min. **Muzzle velocity:** 3280 ft/sec (1000 m/sec).

• Machine gun M84
Zavodi Crvena Zastava, Kragujevac
7.62x54R Russian

This is a gas-operated gun using a rotating bolt and belt feed, and appears to have been broadly copied from the Soviet PK model. It is believed to have entered service with the Yugoslav Army in 1985. The gun can be fired from

The Yugoslavian M84 general purpose gun appears to have been based on the Russian PK family and fired the Russian 7.62x54R cartridge.

a bipod or tripod and there is a quick-change barrel facility. It is said to have an effective range of 1000 meters against ground or air targets.
Length: 46.26in (1.175m). **Weight unloaded:** 22lb 0oz(10kg). **Barrel:** 25.9in (658mm), 4 grooves, right-hand twist. **Magazine:** 100- or 250-round belts. **Cyclic rate:** 700 rds/min. **Muzzle velocity:** 2705 ft/sec (825 m/sec).

ANTI-TANK AND ANTI-MATERIEL RIFLES

THE CAREER OF the anti-tank rifle lasted just twenty-seven years, from the tanks of World War I in 1918 to the close of World War II in 1945. The number of designs was small—all but a few rare experimental weapons are shown in the following short section—and it would be possible to house a specimen of every one of them in a relatively small room.

The advent of the tank on the Western Front caused the German army to seek a weapon powerful enough to harm the vehicle, yet light enough to be man-portable; a field-gun would, of course, destroy any of the early tanks by a direct hit but they were nevertheless immune to the impact of small-caliber rifle and machine gun bullets. The answer was the T-Gewehr of 1918, an enlarged bolt-action rifle firing a steel-cored projectile at a velocity in the region of 3,000 ft/sec to penetrate 0.90-inch of hardened plate at 100 yards range (or 22mm at 100 meters).

The interwar years saw little advance on the big Mauser-designed rifle, although some nations made attempts at adding box magazines to the basic pattern. Efforts were aimed more at improving the ammunition and one notable advance was the development of tungsten-cored bullets, which greatly improved penetrative performances. By 1939 most major armies had adopted an anti-tank rifle and, to be honest, at the time of their inception they were quite capable of penetrating any tank then in service and of doing damage to whatever the bullet found behind the armor.

But the thickness of tank armor rapidly increased as the war progressed, and by 1942 it was becoming all too apparent that the anti-tank rifle was no longer a serious threat to the newest tanks. Fortunately, by that time the shaped charge had been perfected to the point where viable weapons were entering service, such as the British PIAT (Projector, Infantry, Anti-Tank) and the American

'Bazooka' (or 2.36-inch Rocket Launcher). Once these and similar weapons became general issue, the anti-tank rifle was withdrawn and scrapped.

Except in the Soviet Army; they had the two most potent weapons of this class, firing a powerful 14.5mm cartridge. It was effective enough, if aimed at a suitably soft part of the tank, and the Russians had enough on their minds without setting up to produce an entirely new type of weapon. So in the Soviet Army the anti-tank rifle continued in service until the end of the war in 1945.

And that, we thought, was that. End of an era. But in 1983, at an American small arms conference, I was surprised to see a British Boys anti-tank rifle. On inquiry I was told that it was re-barreled to fire the ubiquitous 50 Browning machine gun cartridge, and was being suggested as a long range sniping rifle.

Now at that time 'sniping' meant anti-personnel shooting; which raised some questions in my mind, because the stock 50-caliber ball cartridge is by no means accurate enough for anti-personnel sniping at 1000 yards range, which was what was being suggested. It obviously raised the same question in other minds, because within a year or two the anti-personnel aspect was forgotten; the target was now 'high technology' devices close to the front line. Such things as forward airstrips, radar sets, communications systems, fuel and ammunition dumps, vehicle parks and so forth. Equip a specialist team with one of these rifles and some ammunition; they would sneak into enemy territory—or be dropped or landed there by helicopter—and with a few well-placed shots they could wreck several million dollars' worth of jet aircraft or radars or blow up a fuel dump. Highly cost effective for a few rounds of 50-caliber ammunition, even if they had to abandon the rifle. And with targets of that nature, the pinpoint accuracy of anti-personnel sniping was not quite so critical. So by 1985 the 'Anti-Materiel' rifle had been born, and by the end of the century it has gained a considerable degree of acceptance in many military forces. To some degree it is, like the submachine gun in the 1920s, a solution looking for a problem, a weapon looking for a tactical niche in which to fit. For the moment it seems to be earning its keep

"Look at the size of that!" A British tank crew examining the first Mauser anti-tank rifle to be captured in 1918.

as a method of detonating or destroying explosive ordnance devices at long range; an unexploded bomb on an airfield runway or a terrorist bomb in a railway station, both are equally vulnerable to a high-velocity bullet, and in these cases it is generally possible to get close enough to put the bullet exactly where it will do the most good. But for the more aggressive tasks, as outlined above, it looks as if we will have to wait for some time before sufficient experience is gathered to make decisions upon the utility of the heavy rifle as an offensive weapon.

In the data tables which follow each entry the performance of the weapon against armor plate is specified by a sequence of figures, for example '25/300/60'. This is the accepted NATO-standard notation which indicates that the bullet will defeat 25mm of homogenous armor plate at a range of 300 meters, striking at 60° from the surface of the plate. Note that World War II British and US reports give the angle from 'normal', that is from a line drawn at exact right-angles to the face of the plate, in which case the same performance would be given as 25/300/30.

AUSTRIA

• Steyr 15.2mm IWS2000
Steyr-Mannlicher AG, Steyr
15.2mm APFSDS

In the middle 1980s Steyr-Mannlicher saw a gap in the small arms market and set about filling it by developing an 'anti-materiel rifle'. This was intended for the attack of targets which were of high tactical value and high vulnerability which could not be successfully dealt with by the ordinary run of rifles, machine guns or mortars. Things like radar sets, helicopters or fighter aircraft on the ground, communications vehicles, fuel dumps and so on; things which were of vital importance to a modern military force but which could be completely ruined by one or two well-placed heavy-caliber bullets. The result was the Steyr 14.5mm AMR5075 which appeared in 1990. Subsequent development turned it into 15.2mm caliber and the Infantry Weapon System 2000, development of which is still continuing.

The rifle is in bullpup form and semi-automatic in action, operating on the long recoil system. The bolt and barrel recoil together for about 8 inches (200mm); the bolt is then rotated to unlock and is held, while the barrel returns to battery. During this movement the empty case is stripped from the chamber and mechanically ejected, after which the bolt is released and runs forward to chamber the next round and lock.

The barrel is supported in a ring cradle which incorporates a hydro-pneumatic recoil system which, assisted by a high-efficiency muzzle brake, absorbs much of the shock of discharge, making the weapon moderately comfortable to fire; the felt recoil is said to be rather like that of a heavy-caliber sporting rifle.

Much use has been made of synthetic materials and alloys to lighten the parts wherever possible, and the weapon strips into two major groups so that it can be easily carried by a two-man team. There is a bipod and an adjustable monopod under the butt, and a 10x telescope sight is standard.

The current cartridge is an armor-piercing, fin-stabilized, discarding sabot projectile in the shape of a finned tungsten alloy dart weighing 20 grams (308 grains). Fired at 4757 ft/sec (1450 m/sec) this will completely penetrate 40mm or rolled homogenous steel armor at 1000 meters range, and at this velocity the dart never reaches more than 31 inches (80cm) above the direct line of sight; for all practical purposes this can be considered as a flat trajectory.

Length: 70.86in (1800mm). **Weight unloaded:** c.40lb (18kg). **Barrel:** 47.24in (1200mm); smoothbore. **Magazine:** 5-round detachable box. **Muzzle velocity:** 4757 ft/sec (1450 m/sec).

CROATIA

• 12.7mm MACS-M2A
RH-ALAN, Zagreb
12.7x99mm Browning

This is a single-shot bolt action rifle of conventional form, firing the equally conventional (in this role) 50-caliber Browning machine gun cartridge. Half-stocked, with a bipod and a skeleton butt and pistol grip, the recoil is abated by a large muzzle brake. A 10x42 telescope sight is fitted as standard. It is reported that this rifle was in use by the Croatian Army in 1997.

Length: 57.87in (1470mm). **Weight unloaded:** 27lb 5oz (12.40kg). **Barrel:** 31.10in (790mm); smoothbore. **Magazine:** none; single shot. **Muzzle velocity:** 2805 ft/sec (855 m/sec).

• 20mm RH-20
RH-ALAN, Zagreb
20x110mm HS404

This peculiar weapon is said to be in use by the Bosnian Army; but I have to say that I am doubtful whether its performance will actually live up to the claims made for it. It is a single-shot bolt action rifle chambered for the 20mm Hispano-Suiza cannon cartridge, which gives it the ability to fire armor-piercing and high explosive projectiles. It is, in some ways, possible to call it a bullpup design,

The Steyr 15.2mm IWS 2000 anti-materiel rifle.

since the layout of the weapon is such that the shoulder-piece is some distance in front of the chamber, and the bolt actually forms the rear of the weapon. The bolt is, as might be expected, a substantial device with a triple row of locking lugs. There is a pistol grip and a telescope sight, plus the usual bipod and a very large muzzle brake.

Even with this muzzle brake the recoil force would be far too much for a shoulder-fired weapon of this weight, which leads to the most unusual feature of the design. In front of the chamber the barrel is tapped with a ring of 24 holes to release gas into a tubular vent which stretches back over the rear of the weapon and thus over the shoulder of the firer. Who, we might note, is recommended to lie almost at right-angles to the axis of the bore when firing the weapon. Thus, when the rifle is fired the projectile leaves the cartridge case and moves up the bore; once it passes the port, a proportion of the gas is diverted into the 'recoil compensator tube' and vented out to the rear behind the weapon. It is, therefore, similar to a recoilless gun in that some of the propellant energy is sent rearwards to balance the recoil force.

However, it is not, and never can be, a recoilless weapon. Recoil commences as soon as the projectile moves, and in this case it moves some distance before the gas is vented, so that there must be some felt recoil. However, the sudden release of gas into the vent will considerably dimin-

ish the propelling force on the projectile, leading to a drop in the rate of acceleration and hence of the muzzle velocity, and this, in itself, will certainly reduce the recoil effect, since recoil is proportional to the momentum of the projectile. But at the same time this diversion of propelling energy can only reduce the potential performance of the cartridge, which leads to some doubts about the claimed performance of the weapon.

Length: 52.36in (1330mm). **Weight unloaded:** c.42lb 5oz (19.20kg). **Barrel:** 36.22in (920mm). **Magazine:** none: single shot. **Muzzle velocity (claimed):** 2788 ft/sec (850 m/sec). **Maximum effective range (claimed):** 1968yds (1800m). **Absolute maximum range (claimed):** 8750 yds (8000m).

FINLAND

• Lahti Model 39
State arsenals
20x138B Long Solothurn

The Lahti anti-tank rifle was derived directly from the Lahti aircraft cannon of 1937, and as little modification as possible was done to produce the ground weapon. A pistol grip and trigger mechanism were fitted; a muzzle brake, a shoulder-pad, sights and a dual-purpose bipod. A rack and pinion cocking handle was fitted on the outside of the body and a wooden sleeve was put on the forend of the barrel. Most of the triggers were adapted for single-shot, but it seems likely that several were full-automatic fire only. The only buffering was in the shoulder pad, and the effect on the gunner, when firing a burst, must have been alarming.

The bipod always attracts interest since it is the only one ever to have been produced with alternative feet. One set is the usual small spiked variety for hard ground, and the others have short curved plywood skis for use in snow and slush. The legs have small spring dampers to balance the muzzle heavy gun. It seems that few of these guns were ready in time for the Winter War of 1939/40, and there are no records of their performance. Several appeared on the civilian market in the United States after World War II, and were sold together with a box of ammunition, for $99.95.

Length overall: 87.75in (2232mm). **Weight unloaded:** 94lb 9oz (42.10kg). **Barrel:** 54.75in (1393mm), 12 grooves, right-hand twist. **Magazine:** 10-round vertical box. **Cyclic rate:** 500rpm. **Muzzle velocity:** 2950fps (900 m/sec).

• Helenius 12.7mm APH RK97
Helenius, Salo
12.7x108mm Soviet or 50 Browning

Introduced in 1996, this single-shot rifle appears to have been influenced by the German PzB39 in that it uses a vertical sliding breech-block like a miniature artillery breech. Apart from this, it is a conventional heavy-barreled anti-materiel rifle firing either the 50 Browning cartridge or the 12.7mm Russian equivalent, barrels being available in either chambering. The rifle has a butt which is turned up at the rear so as to allow it to lie rather closer to the ground on its bipod and also to put the axis of the bore level with, if not slightly below, the firer's shoulder. This could well reduce the tendency to upwards jump on firing, and might even cause the rifle to sit more firmly into its bipod. In front of the pistol grip is a second vertical handgrip, and

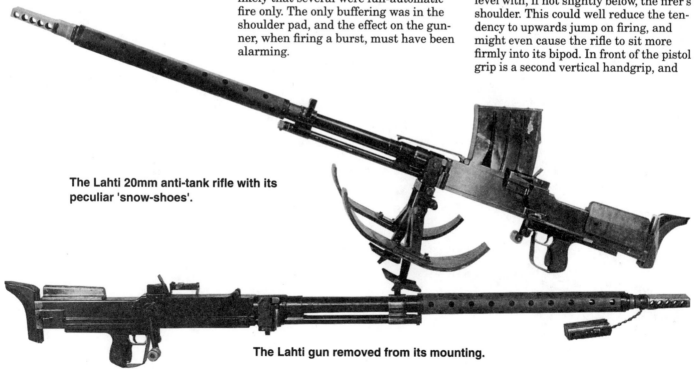

The Lahti 20mm anti-tank rifle with its peculiar 'snow-shoes'.

The Lahti gun removed from its mounting.

The French Hecate II 50-caliber rifle.

this controls the breech block; pushing it forward drops the block and allows a round to be loaded into the chamber, after which pulling on the handle closes the block and cocks the action.

Length: 70.66in (1330mm). **Weight unloaded:** c.30lb 14oz (14kg). **Barrel:** 37.0in (940mm); 8 grooves, right-hand twist. **Magazine:** none: single shot. **Muzzle velocity:** 2870 ft/sec (875 m/sec)

FRANCE

• 12.7mm PGM Hecate II
PGM Precision, Poisy
50 Browning

PGM Precision are well-known makers of sporting rifles, and in the late 1980s they developed a range of sniping rifles, largely adopted by French and other continental police forces. The 'Hecate' is more or less a scaled-up version of their 'Intervention' sniping rifle and is a conventional bolt action repeating rifle. The wooden butt, with cheekpiece, can be removed for transportation and has a monopod beneath it; there is a bipod attached to the receiver forend, and a pistol grip. A large single-baffle muzzle brake reduces the recoil to a reasonable amount, and it can be removed and replaced by a silencer. The rifle has been taken into use by the French Army.

Length: 54.33in (1380mm). **Weight unloaded:** 29lb 12oz (13.50kg).

Barrel: 27.56in (700mm), 8 grooves, right-hand twist.
Magazine: 7-round detachable box. **Muzzle velocity:** 2788 ft/sec (850 m/sec)

GERMANY (PRE-1945)

• 'Tank-Gewehr' Model 1918 (T-Gew')
Waffenfabrik Mauser AG, Oberndorf-am-Neckar
13x92SR T-Patrone

The first anti-tank rifle ever developed was produced in 1918 by Mauser; it was little more than an enlarged Mauser rifle action fitted to a long barrel with a heavy butt and furniture. Supported on a light bipod, it was a one-man weapon firing a 13mm jacketed bullet with an armor-piercing steel core. While the Allied tanks of the time were immune to rifle bullets, they were not proof against such a heavy missile, delivered—thanks to a powerful cartridge and long barrel—at an extremely high velocity. The Mauser of 1918 set the pattern for a number of similar weapons.

Length: 66.13in (1680mm). **Weight unloaded:** 39lb 0oz (17.69kg). **Barrel:** 38.69in (983mm), 4 grooves, right-hand twist. **Magazine:** None, single-shot. **Muzzle velocity:** c.3000 ft/sec (913 m/sec). **Armor penetration:** 25mm/200m/90 .

• SS41
Manufacturer unknown
7.92x95mm Patrone 318

The SS41 is something of a mystery weapon. Very few have survived World War II, and it seems highly likely that only a very small number were ever made. There is little written record of them, and even the precise place of manufacture is not clear. The design is unusual and intriguing.

The SS41 is a single-shot bullpup rifle, firing an armor-piercing 7.92mm bullet from a necked-down 13mm case. The magazine is behind the pistol-grip, and this pistol-grip is attached to a long sleeve which forms the breech and chamber. The sleeve slides on the barrel, but when it is at its rearmost position, it locks to the barrel by lugs. At that same time, it also locks to the face of the breech by the same method. The face of the breech is on the forward face of the shoulder pad. Thus, the barrel and breech face remain stationary at all times, and the chamber slides forward to open the breech.

The sequence of operation is as follows: after firing, the pistol-grip is rotated to the right, which unlocks it from both barrel and breech-face. The pistol-grip is now pushed smartly forward. It slides up the barrel, carrying the breech-sleeve with it and leaving the empty case lying against the breech-face. At the farthest point of motion of the sleeve, the empty case is sprung out to

The original Mauser anti-tank rifle of 1918.

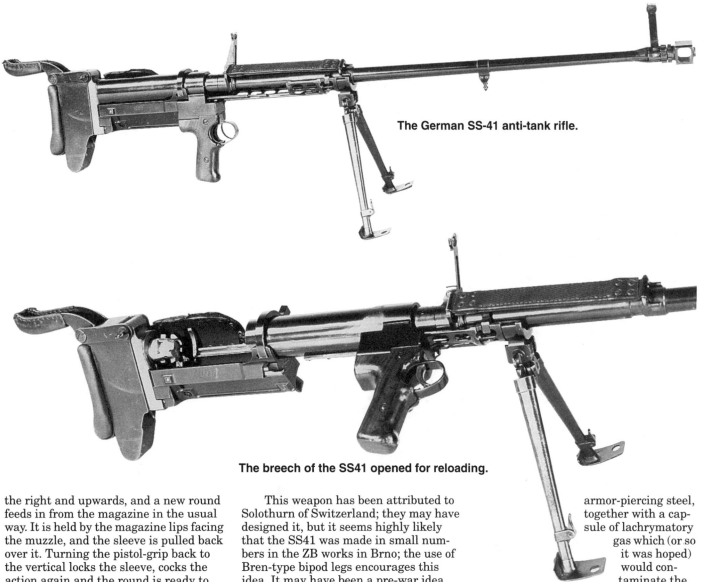

The German SS-41 anti-tank rifle.

The breech of the SS41 opened for reloading.

the right and upwards, and a new round feeds in from the magazine in the usual way. It is held by the magazine lips facing the muzzle, and the sleeve is pulled back over it. Turning the pistol-grip back to the vertical locks the sleeve, cocks the action again and the round is ready to be fired.

This complicated and unusual action was obviously adopted to save weight and to reduce the inordinate length of all anti-tank rifles, but its manufacture must have introduced appalling machining difficulties. Furthermore, the sleeve slides forward along the unprotected outer surface of the barrel, so that it would be highly vulnerable to dirt and dust. Finally, the 7.92mm bullet was known to be ineffective as early as 1938, so its introduction in this sophisticated rifle was already an anachronism.

The magazine fed in from the left side at an angle of about 45°, thereby keeping clear of the firer's right wrist and hand. A light Bren bipod was pinned to the long, unsupported barrel, a small muzzle-brake was put on the muzzle and the well-padded stock had a top shoulder strap.

This weapon has been attributed to Solothurn of Switzerland; they may have designed it, but it seems highly likely that the SS41 was made in small numbers in the ZB works in Brno; the use of Bren-type bipod legs encourages this idea. It may have been a pre-war idea that was resurrected to try and redress the tank/anti-tank conflict which by late 1941 was going strongly against the infantryman. If it was, it was well outdated by the time that it first saw service.

Length overall: 61.05in (1510 mm).
Weight unloaded: 29lb 12oz (13.50 kg).
Barrel: 43.30in (1100mm). **Magazine:** 6-round box, feeding from lower left side.
Muzzle velocity: c.3545 ft/sec (1080 m/sec). **Armor penetration:** 25mm/200m/90 .

• Panzerbuchse Modell 38 (PzB38)
Rheinmetall-Borsig AG, Düsseldorf
7.92mmx95mm Patrone 318

The PzB38 was a much improved weapon compared to the Mauser of 1918, gaining greater velocity and penetrative effect by combining a 7.92mm bullet of new construction with a necked-down cartridge case based on the 1918 Mauser design. The bullet contained a core of

armor-piercing steel, together with a capsule of lachrymatory gas which (or so it was hoped) would contaminate the air inside the tank and either disrupt the crew's effectiveness or force them to leave the vehicle. It was entirely useless in this respect; the bullet had a satisfactory penetrative capability, but none of the victims ever complained of sneezing, and the lachrymatory capsule was not discovered until captured ammunition was examined.

The PzB38 was a single-shot rifle making use of a vertical sliding-wedge breechblock—almost a scaled-down artillery piece in its operation. On firing, the barrel recoiled in the stock and on return operated a cam system to open the breechblock and eject the spent case, the block then remaining open for reloading. Inserting a fresh round caused the block to close.

During the Polish campaign of 1939, the Germans captured numbers of the Polish wz 35 anti-tank rifle and stocks of its ammunition. This was also of 7.92mm

The German PzB 38.

caliber and the bullet carried a tungsten carbide core of much better penetrative power than the original German model; the Polish design was quickly copied.

Length: 51.00in (1295mm). **Weight unloaded:** 35lb 0oz (15.88kg). **Barrel:** 43.00in (1092mm), 4 grooves, right-hand twist. **Magazine:** None, single-shot. **Muzzle velocity:** c.3975 ft/sec (1210 m/sec). **Armor penetration:** 30mm/100m/60 .

• Panzerbuchse Modell 39 (PzB39), Granatbüchse Modell 39 (GrB39)

Rheinmetall-Borsig AG, Düsseldorf, Steyr-Daimler-Puch AG, Steyr, Austria, and others.
7.92x95mm Patrone 318

While the PzB38 was a satisfactory weapon, it was felt to be a little too expensive to manufacture and a slightly simplified version replaced

it. While of the same general appearance, the mechanism was changed by discarding the recoiling barrel and semi-automatic breech and instead, operating the vertical breechblock by the pistol grip, which slid along the receiver. Some small modifications were also made in the interest of simplifying manufacture.

Length: 62.25in (1581mm). **Weight unloaded:** 27lb 4oz (12.35kg). **Barrel:** 42.75in (1086mm), 4 grooves, right-hand twist. **Magazine:** None, single-shot. **Muzzle velocity:** c.4150 ft/sec (1265 m/sec). **Armor penetration:** 30mm/100m/60 .

As the tank gained the ascendancy, and armor improved, so these weapons were withdrawn. Numbers of them were converted to grenade launchers by cutting down the

barrel and fitting a discharger cup (*Schiessbecker*). The modified guns were known as the '**Granatbüchse Modell 39**', or '**GrB39**'.

• Panzerbuchse Modell 41 (PzB41)

Rheinmetall-Borsig AG, Düsseldorf
20x138B Long Solothurn

The origins of this enormous rifle lie in an Erhardt design for a ground-strafing aircraft cannon of 1918. The drawings lay in Holland and Switzerland until resurrected in the 1930s and modernized. From this sprang the idea for a

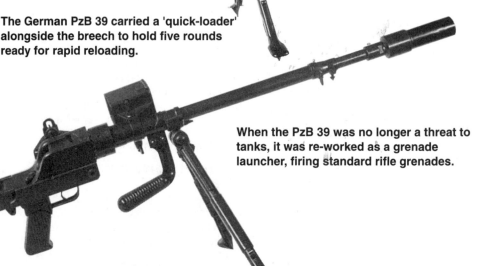

The German PzB 39 carried a 'quick-loader' alongside the breech to hold five rounds ready for rapid reloading.

When the PzB 39 was no longer a threat to tanks, it was re-worked as a grenade launcher, firing standard rifle grenades.

The German PzB 41 was a formidable weapon firing a very powerful cartridge.

semi-automatic anti-tank rifle, and the automatic mechanism was altered by the two Solothurn designers, Herlach and Rakale. As early as 1938, just as the PzB38 was coming into service, it was realized that it could have an effective life of only a year or two, and this design was specified for its successor. The PzB41 ended up as one of the largest anti-tank rifles ever made, and certainly the most complicated.

The system of operation was by recoil, the bolt being locked to the barrel extension by a locking collar. Initial cocking was done by hand winding the handle on the right-hand side of the body, this handle turned a sprocket and pulled in a length of bicycle chain attached to the barrel assembly.

Once cocked, the system re-cocked itself after every shot. The recoil must have been considerable, and to minimize it, a large muzzle brake was fitted. The rear monopod also took some of the shock. The magazine fed in from the left, to reduce the overall height of the weapon.

A very few PzB41s were tried on the Eastern Front and were immediately discarded since they had no effect on the Russian T34. The Italian Army took delivery of a number, and used them in the 1943 campaign, and it is from these that the few existing examples were captured. Like all the anti-tank rifles, the PzB41 was enormously expensive to make, and ineffective in use.

Length: 83in (2108mm). **Weight unloaded:** 97lb (44kg). **Barrel:** 35.43in (901mm), 8 groove, right-hand twist. **Magazine:** 5- or 10-round box. **Muzzle velocity:** 2400 ft/sec (731 m/sec). **Armor penetration:** 30mm/250m/90 .

GREAT BRITAIN

• Rifles, Anti-tank, .55in Boys Mark 1 and Mark 2
Royal Small Arms Factory, Enfield Lock
55 Boys

This weapon was developed in the mid-1930s by the British Small Arms Committee, and one of the principal designers was Captain Boys. The gun was originally code-named 'Stanchion', but Boys died after development had been completed and while the weapon was being prepared for manufacture; as a

The British Boys anti-tank rifle.

An early tank destroyer? A British Bren gun carrier mounting a Bren in the front and a Boys anti-tank rifle on a pedestal; for home defense in 1940.

mark of respect, the Small Arms Committee decided that the weapon should be named after him.

The Boys rifle was an enlarged bolt-action weapon feeding from a top-mounted magazine and equipped with a muzzle brake and a monopod firing support. The barrel was permitted to recoil in a cradle and the butt was heavily padded—both measures to reduce the extraordinary recoil forces. The bullet was steel-cored and was placed in a belted cartridge case, one of the few instances where this case-type has seen military use. The design was originally intended for high-powered sporting rifles, and the belt gave the base immense strength to resist high internal pressure. In 1940, a tungsten-cored bullet in a plastics/aluminum body was approved and issued, but shortly afterwards, the Boys was withdrawn from service and replaced by the Projector, Infantry, Anti-Tank (PIAT) which threw a shaped-charge bomb.

In 1942, the Boys had a brief return to popularity when a short-barrel Mark 2 version was developed for use by airborne troops, but it as belatedly realized that shortening the barrel reduced the velocity and

hence the penetrating power, so the requirement was dropped and the weapon was never adopted. Another attempt to revive it was the 1942 development of a taper-bore version; this was successful in trials as far as its penetrative performance went, but it was a singularly unpleasant weapon to fire (so, too, was the airborne model) and it was not accepted for service.

Length: 63.50in (1614mm). **Weight unloaded:** 36lb 0oz (16.32kg). **Barrel:** 36.00in (915mm), 7 grooves, right-hand twist. **Magazine:** 5-round detachable box. **Muzzle velocity:** c.3250 ft/sec (990 m/sec). **Armor penetration:** 21mm/300m/90 .

HUNGARY

• 12.7mm Gepard M1, M1A1
Technika, Budapest
12.7x107mm Soviet

This is a simple but effective single-shot anti-materiel rifle firing the Russian 12.7mm cartridge. The barrel is carried in a tubular cradle, which also mounts the bipod, and a barrel extension carried the pressed buttplate. The pistol grip acts as the bolt handle; to load, the grip is twisted up, unlocking the interrupted-thread breechblock which can then be withdrawn completely from the rifle. A round is loaded into the chamber and the breech-piece is replaced, and the

pistol grip turned down to lock. A hammer in the pistol grip unit is now manually cocked and the trigger pressed to fire the rifle. Aiming is done by means of a 12x telescope, and the cartridge is sufficiently accurate to deliver a 300mm (11.8 inch) group at 600 meters range. The armor-piercing bullet will defeat 15mm of steel armor at the same range.

The **M1A1** is the same weapon but mounted on a back-pack frame which also serves as a firing mount for use in soft ground or snow; the bipod is still attached to the cradle but folded up when the frame is used. The M1A1 weighs 48lb 8oz (22kg).

Length: 61.81in (1570mm). **Weight unloaded:** c.41lb 14oz (19.0kg). **Barrel:** 43.30in (1100mm), 8 grooves, right-hand twist. **Magazine:** none; single shot. **Muzzle velocity:** 2756 ft/sec (840 m/sec).

• 12.7mm Gepard M2, M2A1
Technika, Budapest
12.7x107mm Soviet

The Gepard M2 is a similar to the M1 described above but is a semiautomatic rifle operating on the long recoil system. The barrel recoils inside a cylindrical jacket and receiver, and uses a rotating bolt to lock the breech. The magazine is oddly placed on the left side of the pistol grip, making it impossible to fire left-handed. A bipod is attached to the barrel jacket, and a telescope sight is standard.

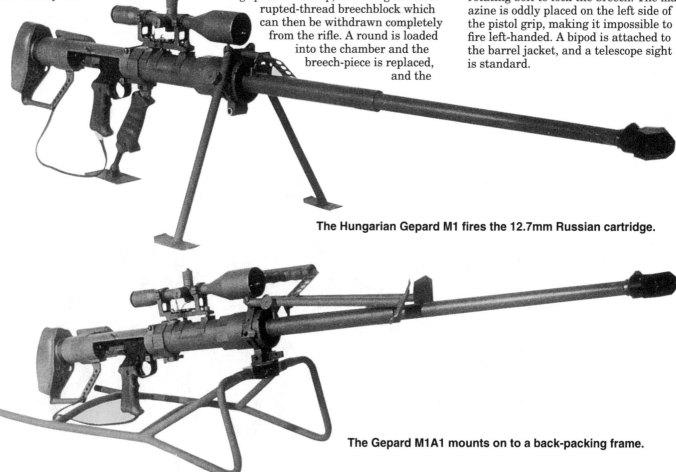

The Hungarian Gepard M1 fires the 12.7mm Russian cartridge.

The Gepard M1A1 mounts on to a back-packing frame.

Gepard M2 is a semi-automatic with the magazine alongside the pistol grip.

Gepard M2A1 is simply a shorter version of the M2.

The Gepard M3 is probably the most powerful anti-materiel rifle currently available in Europe, firing the 14.5mm Russian cartridge.

The breech area of the Gepard M3, showing the pistol grip and magazine.

The Japanese 20mm Type 97 proved to be too powerful as a rifle and eventually went on to a wheeled mounting as an anti-tank gun.

The **M2A1** is simply a short-barreled version of the M2 intended for use by airborne and special forces who require a more compact weapon.

(M2)

Length: 60.23in (1530mm). **Weight unloaded:** 26lb 7oz (12.0kg). **Barrel:** 43.31in (1100mm), 8 grooves, right-hand twist. **Magazine:** 5- or 10-round detachable box. **Muzzle velocity:** 2756 ft/sec (840 m/sec).

(M2A1)

Length: 49.60in (1260mm). **Weight unloaded:** 22lb 1oz (10.0kg). **Barrel:** 32.68in (830mm), 8 grooves, right-hand twist. **Magazine:** 5- or 10-round detachable box (to NATO/M16 standard). **Muzzle velocity:** 2592 ft/sec (790 m/sec).

• 14.5mm Gepard M3

Technika, Budapest
14.5x114mm Soviet

This is more or less an enlarged version of the Gepard M2, with the addition of a hydro-pneumatic recoil system to absorb some of the firing shock and a more effective muzzle brake. Firing the powerful 14.5mm AP bullet it can defeat 25mm of armor plate at 600 meters range.

Length: 74.0in (1880mm). **Weight unloaded:** 44lb 1oz (20.0kg). **Barrel:** 58.27in (1480mm), 8 grooves, right-hand twist. **Magazine:** 5- or 10-round detachable box. **Muzzle velocity:** 3117 ft/sec (950 m/sec).

JAPAN

• Model 97

State arsenals
20x124mm Type 97

The Model 97 represents the zenith of the anti-tank rifle. It was a gas-operated, fully automatic 20mm weapon, often referred to as an anti-tank machine gun. It was by far the heaviest of its breed, and probably the most unpleasant to fire. It fired from a closed breech, the unlocking being by gas, and the remainder of the operating cycle by blow-back. Such a system made no allowance for absorbing the recoil, so the entire barrel and body recoiled along a cradle for a distance of roughly 6 inches . Even so, this was rather more than the lightly-built Japanese soldiers could manage, and the mounting was given an inclined rear monopod leg. This had to be dug into the ground if the firer were not to be pushed violently backwards, and so the weapon could not really be used to engage crossing targets, since it had to be firmly dug in on one line. In the hands of a large and determined gunner, the accuracy was quite good for the first round, but any attempt to fire a burst resulted in the barrel moving off the aiming point.

The Model 97 required a crew of four to man-handle it. Two carrying handles were provided, which looked like bicycle handlebars, and plugged into the bipod and monopod. With these, the crew could move it quite easily. There was also a shield, which was rarely used. Like all the 20mm guns, a muzzle brake was fitted. The ammunition was of two types, a solid AP shot, and an HE shell, both with a tracer element. A small number of Model 97s were used in the Pacific, where they had some slight success against the light tanks of the US Marines, and some were reported to have appeared in China in 1939 and 1940. Apart from these actions, the gun saw very little service.

Length: 82.5in (2095mm). **Weight unloaded:** 152lb (68.93kg). **Barrel:** 47.0in (1195mm). **Magazine:** 7-round vertical box. **Muzzle velocity:** 2000fps (609 m/sec).

It appears that the drawbacks of this weapon were appreciated by the Japanese army, because in 1938 the '**Type 98** anti-tank gun' appeared, which proved to be nothing more than the Type 97 rifle modified to take an even more powerful cartridge (20x142mm) and mounted upon a wheeled carriage which had two trail legs and a front outrigger so as to provide a tripod stabilizing support in addition to the wheels. The wheels could be removed, whereupon the gun had all-round traverse. Complete with elevating and traversing gears and a balancing spring to support the muzzle weight, the Type 98 weighed 836lb (280 kg); not really a small arm, but perhaps the only intelligent solution to the Type 97.

POLAND

• Model 35 'Marosczek' rifle

Fabryka Karabinow, Warsaw
7.92x107mm

Towards the end of 1935, the Polish Army began to take delivery of an anti-tank rifle of conventional bolt-action pattern, generally based on the 1918 Mauser pattern, but stripped of every unnecessary ounce to provide the lightest weapon of the class ever made. The tungsten-cored bullet was fired from an over-sized case, and it has been claimed that it was this which led the Germans and Russians to develop similar cored bullets; it was certainly responsible for a British development in which a 303-caliber cored bullet was married to a necked-down 55 Boys cartridge case for a modified Boys anti-tank rifle.

Loaded from five-round clips, and with a muzzle brake to cut

The Polish Marosczek anti-tank rifle.

down the recoil force, it was ahead of its contemporaries for ease of handling and, owing to the cored bullet, had a slight supremacy in penetrating power. Unfortunately, such virtue had to be paid for somehow—and the price in this case was a barrel life of but 200 rounds, after which, the muzzle velocity had dropped to 3775 ft/sec (1150 m/sec) and penetration began to fall off rapidly.

Length: 69.30in (1760mm). **Weight unloaded:** 20lb 1oz (9.10kg). **Barrel:** 47.25in (1200mm), 4 grooves, right-hand twist. **Magazine:** 10-round detachable box. **Muzzle velocity:** c.4198 ft/sec (1290 m/sec). **Penetration:** 20mm/300m/90 .

In 1939, work began on a coned bore weapon on the Gerlich principle, using a tungsten core surrounded by a soft lead jacket and a cupro-nickel envelope, formed with a raised band around the center. The breech caliber was 11.00mm and the emergent caliber at the muzzle 7.92mm, so that the squeeze action of the bore deformed the raised portion of the bullet and reduced the diameter. This gave a velocity of nearly 5000 ft/sec (15427 m/sec) and almost doubled the penetrative performance. When Poland was overrun, the rifle and drawings were smuggled to France, where development was continued. At the time of the French collapse in 1940, the weapon was undergoing its final tests at Satory, near Versailles, and had been scheduled to go into production and issue later in 1940. In the confusion following the German advance, the rifle was lost; neither it nor the drawings have since been seen, and no specimen is now known to exist.

RUSSIA (and former USSR)

• 14.5mm PTRD41
State manufacture
14.5x114mm

This rifle, which appeared in 1941, fired a 14.5mm bullet (slightly larger than the British 55-caliber) from a massive cartridge case, probably the heaviest 'small arms' round in regular service which, when redundant in its anti-tank role, became a heavy machine gun round. The rifle itself—while it appeared to be simple—was in fact quite an ingenious design by Degtyarev and probably owed something to the German PzB38. The barrel was allowed to recoil in the stock, and during this movement, the bolt rode on a cam which rotated and unlocked it. At the end of the recoil stroke, the bolt was held and the barrel moved back into battery, moving away from the bolt to open the breech and eject the spent case. A fresh round was then inserted and the bolt was manually closed: in some respects this could be described as a 'long recoil' system.

The bullet was originally a steel-cored streamlined armor-piercing type, but this was superseded by a non-streamlined tungsten-cored armor-piercing-incendiary pattern.

Length: 78.7in (2000mm). **Weight unloaded:** 38lb 2oz (17.3kg). **Barrel:** 48.30in (1227mm), 8 grooves, right-band twist. **Magazine:** None, single-shot. **Muzzle velocity:** c.3320 ft/sec (1010 m/sec). **Armor penetration:** 25mm/500m/0 .

• 14.5mm PTRS41
State manufacture
14.5x114mm

This design of Simonov's was a contemporary of the PTRD, and it fired the same ammunition although of a more complex self-loading design. A gas piston acted on a bolt carrier to open the bolt,

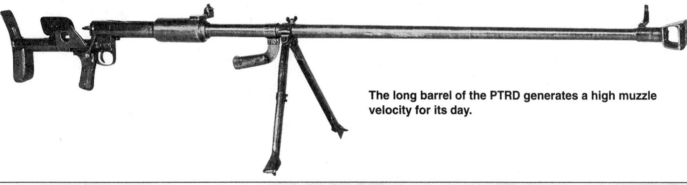

The long barrel of the PTRD generates a high muzzle velocity for its day.

The PTRD in combat; anti-tank rifles are no use for personal defense, hence the bodyguard with the PPSh submachine gun.

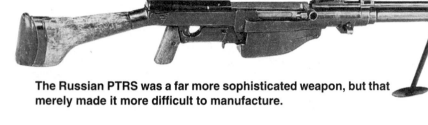

The Russian PTRS was a far more sophisticated weapon, but that merely made it more difficult to manufacture.

eject, and reload in the usual fashion, and the gas regulator could be adjusted to give sufficient force to overcome dirt or freezing conditions. A clip-loaded magazine was fitted.

Despite its theoretical superiority, the PTRS was less robust, much heavier and considerably longer than the PTRD, and fewer of them were issued. Both rifles remained in Soviet service until the end of World War II (long after they had been superseded in other nations) probably because no suitable replacement was forthcoming.

Length: 86.61in (2134mm). **Weight unloaded:** 46lb 3oz (20.86kg). **Barrel:** 48.00in (1220mm), 8 grooves, right-hand twist. **Magazine:** 5-round clip-loaded box. **Muzzle velocity:** c.3320 ft/sec (1010 m/sec). **Armor penetration:** 25mm/500m/0 .

• 12.7mm V-94
Instrument Design Bureau, Tula
12.7x107mm Soviet

This anti-materiel rifle, introduced in 1995, has some affinity with the World War II PTRD insofar as it uses a gas piston to operate a rotating bolt which then requires to be closed by hand after a cartridge has been loaded. It is difficult to see what advantage this system provides, apart from the possibility that it might form the basis for a future semi-automatic design. It also resembles the wartime rifles by having a long and slender barrel, though with a large two-port muzzle brake, and a bipod. The wooden butt has a substantial rubber recoil pad. There are no iron sights, but a telescope

mount for the usual PSO telescope sight is provided.

Length: 70.86in (1700mm). **Weight unloaded:** c.40lb (11.70kg). **Barrel:** 47.24in (1020mm); 8 grooves, right-hand twist. **Magazine:** none; single shot. **Muzzle velocity:** 4757 ft/sec (850 m/sec).

SOUTH AFRICA

• 20mm NTW-20
Mkhonto Arms, Pretoria
20x83mm MG151

Announced in 1993 this is an anti-materiel rifle firing what is perhaps the most powerful 20mm cartridge that can be used in a moderately portable shoulder-fired weapon. Heavier cartridges have been used, as these pages show, but only with heavier and more cumbersome rifles; the level of recoil from the MG151 is about as much as the average soldier can control—or tolerate for long.

Apart from its size, the rifle is conventional enough, a bolt-action repeating type with long, heavy barrel, efficient muzzle brake and a left side mounted magazine. This assembly is carried in a receiver frame with butt so that it is allowed to slide back into the butt against the resistance of a hydro-pneumatic buffer resembling the recoil system of an artillery piece. The combination of buffer, movement and muzzle brake bring the recoil down to a supportable level. The butt is shaped to allow it to be gripped by the non-firing hand, and the rest of the weapon is supported on a

bipod. It can be split into two units for man-carrying.

Length: 70.66in (1795mm). **Weight unloaded:** c.57lb 5oz (26kg). **Barrel:** 39.37in (1000mm); 8 grooves, right-hand twist. **Magazine:** 3-round detachable box. **Muzzle velocity:** 2362 ft/sec (720 m/sec). **Max effective range:** 1500 yds/m.

• 14.5mm NTW-14.5
Mkhonto Arms, Pretoria
14.5x114mm Soviet

This was developed from the 20mm NTW-20 described above, and the principal and obvious difference is that it is chambered for the Russian 14.5mm anti-tank rifle cartridge which first appeared with the PTRS and PTRD weapons in 1941. Improvements on the NTW-20 design include the provision of a folding handle under the butt, which can be lowered to act as an adjustable monopod, and an improved method of removing the barrel for transportation. The barrel is longer, due to the ballistic requirements of the cartridge, and is smooth instead of fluted, and the muzzle brake is rectangular instead of circular.

Length: 70.66in (2015mm). **Weight unloaded:** c.57lb 5oz (29kg). **Barrel:** 39.37in (1220mm); 8 grooves, right-hand twist. **Magazine:** 3-round detachable box. **Muzzle velocity:** 2362 ft/sec (1080 m/sec). **Max effective range:** 2300 yds/m.

SWITZERLAND

• Solothurn S-18/100
Waffenfabrik Solothurn AG, Solothurn
20x105B (Short Solothurn)

The Solothurn company began work on an anti-tank rifle in the early 1930s, their design being derived from the Erhardt 20mm cannon of World War I. In 1934 the S-18/100 appeared and was adopted by Hungary, Switzerland and Italy in small numbers. The gun was recoil-operated to give semiautomatic fire and had a well-padded shoulder-piece above a rear monopod, a combination which managed to absorb much of the recoil force. It fired a base-fused piercing shell, which gave quite good

The South African NTW-20 fires the Mauser MG151 cartridge.

The Swiss Solothurn S18-100 fired a 20mm cartridge and was the fore-runner of the German PzB41.

performance for its day, and it was one of the more powerful anti-tank rifles of the 1930s. Solothurn then developed a more powerful cartridge and a heavier rifle; this became the S-18/1000 and is dealt with in these pages under its German name, the PzB41.

Length: 69.25in (1760mm). **Weight:** 99.2lb (45.00kg). **Barrel:** 35.40in (900mm). **Magazine:** 5- or 10-round detachable box. **Muzzle velocity:** 2500 ft/sec (762 m/sec). **Penetration:** 27mm/300m/90 .

U.S.A.

• Barrett M82A1 'Light Fifty'

*Barrett Firearms Mfg. Co,
Murfreesboro, Tenn.*
50 Browning

The Light Fifty is a semiautomatic heavy sniping rifle, and one of the first of this type to be taken seriously by military establishments. It appeared in the early 1980s and undoubtedly did much to promote the idea of an anti-materiel rifle. It operates on short recoil; barrel and bolt recoil some 25mm locked together, after which the

bolt carrier is unlocked and moved back to rotate the bolt and open the breech. An accelerator is used to transfer much of the barrel's energy to the bolt carrier. After the recoil stroke, a spring returns the carrier and bolt, loading a fresh round as it does so. There is an efficient muzzle brake, which reduces the recoil by about 30 percent. The rifle has a bipod as standard, but it can also be fitted to the US M82 tripod or to any tripod compatible with the M60 machine gun.

Length: 57.0in (1448mm). **Weight:** 28lb 7oz (12.90kg). **Barrel:** 29.0in (737mm), 8 grooves, right-hand twist. **Magazine:** 10-round detachable box. **Muzzle velocity:** 2800 ft/sec (853 m/sec).

• Barrett M82A2

*Barrett Firearms Mfg. Co,
Murfreesboro, Tenn.*
50 Browning

The M82A2 uses the same mechanism as the M82A1 but is lighter and shorter, and built in a bullpup configuration, the object being to make the weapon somewhat easier to carry and to conceal in the field. The pistol grip is moved forward, the magazine housing is shaped to form a shoulder rest, and there is a forward handgrip instead of a bipod.

Length: 69.25in (1409mm). **Weight:** 27lbs (12.24kg). **Barrel:** 20.0in (737mm), 8 grooves, right-hand twist. **Magazine:** 10-round detachable box. **Muzzle velocity:** 2800fps (853 m/sec).

One of the earliest American entrants in the anti-materiel field, the Barrett M82A1 'Light Fifty'.

The Barrett M82A2 is in bullpup form in order to reduce the overall length.

The Barrett M95 is a bolt-action bullpup.

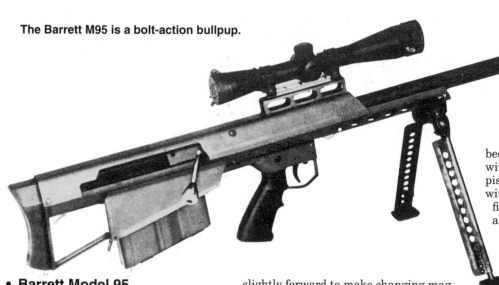

• Barrett Model 95

Barrett Firearms Mfg. Co, Murfreesboro, Tenn.

50 Browning

Introduced in 1990 the Model 90 was designed for those traditionalists who prefer a bolt-action rifle, and in the process of redesigning the breech action several other modifications to the basic M82 design were made, resulting in a much lighter and more handy weapon. It is a bullpup, with the bolt action right at the rear of the receiver and the pistol grip in front of the magazine. There was a highly absorbent butt pad, and a high efficiency muzzle brake, a combination which kept the recoil blow down to an acceptable figure.

After the M90 had seen some use, a few improvements were felt desirable; the bore and chamber were chromed, the pistol grip and trigger were moved slightly forward to make changing magazines easier, the bolt handle and some internal details of the bolt were modified. The resulting weapon became the M95.

Length: 45.0in (1143mm). **Weight:** 22lb (9.98kg). **Barrel:** 20.0in (737mm), 8 grooves, right-hand twist. **Magazine:** 5-round detachable box. **Muzzle velocity:** 2800fps (853 m/sec).

• Harris (McMillan) M87R

Harris Gunworks, Inc, Phoenix, Ariz.

50 Browning

This rifle, and the following Harris models, were previously known by the name of McMillan; the McMillan Gun Works was acquired by the Harris Gunworks in 1995, and the McMillan models were continued in production under their old model numbers.

The M87 rifle was originally a single shot weapon of conventional bolt-action type. It was then given a magazine and became the M87R. It is half-stocked, without being hollowed out to form a pistol grip, and has a very heavy barrel with a pepper-pot muzzle brake. A bipod fits on to the front end of the stock, and a telescope mount is provided. No iron sights are fitted. It is also possible to have the rifle with a synthetic stock, the butt of which has facilities for adjustment for length and rake.

The M87R was adopted by, among others, the French army.

Length: 53.0in (1346mm). **Weight:** 21lb (9.52kg). **Barrel:** 20.0in (737mm), 8 grooves, right-hand twist. **Magazine:** 5-round detachable box. **Muzzle velocity:** 2800 ft/sec (853 m/sec).

• Harris M92

Harris Gunworks, Inc, Phoenix, Ariz.

50 Browning

The M93 is a bullpup version of the M87R , having the same bolt action and barrel but set back into a glass-fiber stock of somewhat ungainly appearance. It is fitted with a bipod and a mounting for optical sights.

Length: 40.0in (1016mm). **Weight:** 24lb (10.90kg) with telescope sight. **Barrel:** 20.0in (737mm), 8 grooves, right-hand twist. **Magazine:** 5-round detachable box. **Muzzle velocity:** 2800 ft/sec (853 m/sec).

The Harris M92 is another bolt-action bullpup design.

• Harris M93

Harris Gunworks, Inc, Phoenix, Ariz.
50 Browning

This is a modified version of the M87R described above, the principle change being the fitting of a hinged buttstock for easier storage and transportation. The magazine capacity was also increased. Like the M87R it was adopted by the French army.

Length, butt extended: 53.0in (1346mm); butt folded: 39.0in (991mm). **Weight:** 21lb (9.52kg). **Barrel:** 20.0in (737mm), 8 grooves, right-hand twist. **Magazine:** 10- or 20-round detachable box. **Muzzle velocity:** 2800 ft/sec (853 m/sec).

• Harris M95

Harris Gunworks, Inc, Phoenix, Ariz.
50 Browning

A further improvement on the M87R, the M95 is generally to the same design but used advanced materials to produce a lighter and stronger weapon. The barrel is forged from a special carbon graphited steel, the bolt uses titanium, and the stock is of synthetic material. The usual pepper-pot muzzle brake is fitted, together with a telescope mount and a bipod.

Length: 53.0in (1346mm). **Weight:** 18lb (8.17kg) with telescope sight. **Barrel:** 20.0in (737mm), 8 grooves, right-hand twist. **Magazine:** 10- or 20-round detachable box. **Muzzle velocity:** 2800 ft/sec (853 m/sec).

• Stoner SR-50

Knights Armament Co., Vero Beach, Fla.
50 Browning

This is probably the last design completed by Eugene Stoner before his untimely death in 1997. It is a semi-automatic rifle operating by direct gas impingement upon the bolt carrier, in the same manner as the AR-15 rifle. The magazine feeds from the left side, allowing the weapon to be positioned closer to the ground than with other rifles of this class, and it also allows the receiver to be shorter since the trigger mechanism and magazine can co-exist side by side rather than being one behind the other. The butt resembles that of the German MG34 and doubtless helps to keep the muzzle from rising too much, and a three-port Solothurn muzzle brake cuts down the recoil. This is a neat and efficient design, and although no official admission has been made, there is reason to believe that it has already been taken into some military service.

Weight: 31lb 8oz (14.28kg) with telescope. **Barrel:** 35.50in (902mm), 8 grooves, right-hand twist. **Magazine:** 10-round detachable box. **Muzzle velocity:** c.2855 ft/sec (870 m/sec).

The Harris M93 is generally similar to their earlier M78 but the butt can be folded to make the weapon more compact for carriage.

The Harris M93 in the process of being folded.

AMMUNITION

By THE BEGINNING of the 20th century, smokeless powder and the jacketed bullet had become the standard military rifle ammunition components, lead bullets surviving only in revolver cartridges. All the ammunition of the period was more or less the same in concept, if not in caliber and appearance, throughout the world; rifle ammunition was powerful and designed to retain its accuracy and lethality well in excess of a thousand yards range, while pistol ammunition was generally of low velocity, using a heavy bullet with ample 'stopping power'. There were exceptions to this generalization, but they were few, and they were regarded with some suspicion by the greater part of the contemporary military establishment.

The first major improvement came with the adoption of pointed bullets for rifle ammunition. Until 1905, the norm was a blunt-nosed, parallel-sided, square-based bullet, but in that year, the German Army introduced a pointed (Spitzer) bullet, a design based on research using the recently developed technique of spark-gap photography, which permitted the air-flow over the bullet to be examined for the first time. This lead was followed by other countries, as with the USA in 1906 and Britain in 1911, though a surprising number of countries ignored it and continued to use blunt bullets for many years.

During the First World War, the increased use of medium machine-guns at long ranges led to more research into bullet design, since the accuracy of the existing bullets at long range was a good deal worse than had been anticipated. It was eventually discovered that the shape of the bullet had considerable bearing on long-range performance. A square-cut base was satisfactory at supersonic velocities since, in that speed range, it was the head shape which mattered, the drag due to the square base being relatively insignificant when weighed against the compression waves produced at the bullet's nose. But once velocity fell into the subsonic region—as it did at the latter part of a long-range flight—these compression waves vanished, and the base drag assumed major importance, upsetting accuracy and detracting from the theoretical maximum range. To counter this, the streamlined or 'boat-tailed' bullet was developed, in which the base of the bullet was given a degree of taper; this allowed the air-flow over the bullet to merge behind the base with less turbulence, and

it improved regularity and maximum range to a remarkable degree. With the American 30-06 bullet, for example, boat-tailing improved the maximum range from 3500 to 5000 yards.

This type of bullet was developed during the 1920s and was generally in service before World War II. But most countries who developed boat-tailed bullets found that the shape gave rise to gas swirl and to heavy erosive wear of the weapons. While this was a stiff price to pay, it was thought to be acceptable in machine guns in order to gain the benefit of the long-range accuracy; and in any case, regular barrel-changing was already an accepted fact in the machine gun world. But in rifles it was unacceptable, and so the streamlined bullet was usually restricted to firing in machine guns only.

The obsession with long-range performance from rifles had been founded in the early days of the century by a strong lobby of long-range target shooters who, having seen their specialty put to use once or twice in the South African War, managed to give it the status of a minor religion, and foist it onto the military. One example of this attitude was the abortive 276-caliber P-13 rifle proposed for the British Army; in an endeavor to produce a weapon capable of accurate fire at 2000 yards and a practically flat trajectory out to 500 yards or more, the designers came up with a 165-grain bullet propelled by 49.5 grains of a particularly 'hot' cordite, a combination which gave a muzzle velocity in the region of 3000 ft/sec and, with it, objectionable muzzle blast, flash and recoil, excessive erosion of the leade, irregular ballistics and severe overheating of the barrel. Fortunately, the coming of World War I gave the practical soldiers an excellent excuse to scrap the whole project and, of course, the war demonstrated that the service 303-caliber rifle and its cartridge were perfectly adequate for the purposes of practical combat.

Indeed, the war showed that the normal type of rifle cartridge was more than enough; with the exception of snipers, it was rare for a front-line soldier to fire at any greater range than 300 yards, and the ballistic potential of the cartridge was largely wasted weight and bulk. Few people, though, seem to have assimilated this lesson, probably because it was widely thought that the conditions obtaining in trench warfare were abnormal, and that future wars might well

revert to the open combat found in South Africa, where the ability to shoot accurately to a thousand yards had some value. But more than sheer ballistics came into this question; there was also the problem of training a wartime conscript, when time was of the essence, to handle these powerful cartridges and shoot accurately with them. The 'old' British Army prided itself on its musketry, and rightly so, but it overlooked the fact that this immaculate riflemanship was the product of long peace-time hours on the ranges, time which could not be spared in war. Another problem which was never mentioned was that of actually seeing and identifying targets at extreme ranges; it was one thing to lie down comfortably at the firing point and take a leisurely aim at a six-foot square white target two-thirds of a mile distant. It was a vastly different thing to throw oneself down into a mud puddle, burdened with sixty pounds of equipment and panting with exertion, to take aim at the slender figure of a man, clothed in field-gray or khaki, merging into his background and flitting among the shadows, at even half that distance.

During the 1930s, a number of German Army officers began to take a critical look at all these aspects of combat rifle shooting, and they came to the conclusion that the standard rifle cartridge could be halved in size and power if a more realistic view were taken of the tactical requirements. Provided the rifle was accurate and lethal to about 500 yards range, this was all that was needed for 95% of the time, and the balance could be taken care of by machine guns or snipers using the old-style cartridge. To achieve their end, they called for a cartridge in which the bullet retained its size and lethality, but in which the cartridge case and propelling charge were smaller. Over and above the tactical advantages, others would then accrue; the soldier could carry more ammunition (there was little likelihood of him being allowed to lessen his burden by carrying the same number of rounds as before), and since the cartridge would be shorter, the weapons designed to use it would also be more compact, since a shorter operating stroke would be needed to reload. Moreover, the smaller impulse derived from the smaller propelling charge would allow lighter weapons to be built and would reduce the recoil and jump and this, in turn, would simplify the problem of training the soldier to shoot well.

The Polte company of Magdeburg were given the task of designing a cartridge to suit these requirements, and they produced a totally new round with a short cartridge case and a 7mm bullet. While this gave admirable ballistics, the imminence of war argued against tooling-up for something completely new, and a modified design using the service 7.92mm bullet was prepared, a design which had the advantage of allowing much of the manufacture to be done on existing machinery. To suit this new round a new rifle, known at first as the MP-43 and later as the 'Sturmgewehr' or Assault Rifle, was developed and the short cartridge was off to a flying start. The Soviets then followed this example, developing a 7.62mm short round originally called the M1943 (though the grounds for such terminology have never been substantiated in public) and which is now used throughout the world as the 7.62x39mm cartridge.

In post-war years, much development on these lines was carried out in several countries, but old ideas die hard, especially among victors, and the British 7mm round proposed for NATO was resisted by the Americans on the grounds, among others, that its long-range performance was not good enough. The eventual compromise was virtually the old 30-caliber M2 bullet in a slightly shorter case, a compromise which had neither flesh, fowl nor good red herring. But because of its NATO acceptance, the 7.62mmx51 cartridge has seen worldwide use in the years since its adoption.

The next move was to the reduction of caliber. This promised several advantages, notably in the reduction of weapon size and recoil, and a list of the number of experimental rounds developed in pursuit of this aim would fill a fair-sized book. The practical result was the adoption of the 5.56x45mm cartridge with the Armalite rifles in the 1960s, and in spite of dubious forecasts, the cartridge proceeded to catch on all over the world. It was considerably aided by its lethality, a fortuitous combination of bullet mass and stability, which resulted in a projectile which tumbled rapidly when it struck its target and delivered up its energy in massive fashion rather than, as with the older, heavier and better-stabilized bullets, passing through the target with minimal energy transfer. This led, of course, to some fearful stories of the effects of micro-caliber bullets and, in turn, to some emotional outbursts from various humanitarian organizations, though the precise aesthetic difference between being decapitated by a flying shard of steel from an artillery shell or by

a tumbling 5.56mm bullet is one I find hard to distinguish.

In 1978-80 a most involved and comprehensive trial took place under NATO auspices, the object being to determine the ammunition to be adopted as standard for the next generation of NATO small arms. In view of the amount of money which had already been invested in production facilities for the 5.56x45mm cartridge, and the prior adoption of that cartridge by the US Army in their M16 rifle, and the amount of weight which the Americans were able to bring to bear on NATO decisions, it was a foregone conclusion that the result would be the 5.56mm cartridge. And so it was, but, rather surprisingly, with a new and heavier Belgian bullet, which improved the down-range performance. The SS109 bullet, though, demanded a slower twist of rifling, and for some time it was thought that there might be a compromise solution to avoid having to rebarrel millions of rifles. But the timing of the trial proved to be fortuitous, since by the early 1980s several armies were contemplating a change of rifle, and even the US Army was about to receive the M16A2, and it was a relatively painless task to change the rifling to suit the new bullet.

As the NATO trial was getting under way, so the news came that the Soviets had a new rifle which fired a 5.45x39mm cartridge. Full information of the round was available fairly rapidly, but information of the rifle took longer to filter through. The only significant reaction was that it strengthened the hand of the micro-caliber Mafia, and cries of 'If the Russians are doing it, it must be right!" were heard once more.

Shortly after the NATO trials had ended, the US Army began their 'Advanced Combat Rifle' project. This began by requests for caseless solutions from three manufacturers, and then a request for non-caseless solutions from a further four. Eventually, at the end of the 1980s, four contestants, one caseless, appeared and a vast and costly comparative trial was conducted. The ammunition was as interesting as the rifles: the caseless rifle (Heckler & Koch's G-11 in a new suit) fired a straightforward ball bullet. The Colt (an M16 in a new suit) fired a Duplex 5.56mm bullet; and the AAI and Steyr designs, which were entirely new, fired flechettes. New materials— and twenty years of study—had improved the flechette designs over those which had been seen in the 1960s, and there appeared to be little to choose between the various projectiles so far as terminal effect was concerned. But the overall performance of the rifles failed to

show sufficient advance upon the existing M16A2 to warrant putting any of them into production, and the ACR program was closed down.

The development of pistol ammunition has been less radical. Already by 1900, the jacketed bullet had been found to be mandatory for the automatic pistol due to the severe treatment suffered during the loading cycle, and in order to reduce the possibility of lead fouling and of the mechanism being jammed by lead fragments. The lead bullet was retained for revolvers, since low velocities were still the order of the day in those weapons, though automatics had begun to explore the possibility of obtaining the necessary impact at the target by stepping up the velocity proportionately as the caliber was reduced. But the lead revolver bullet gave rise to some ethical problems during World War. The British 455-caliber service revolver bullet had gone through some drastic changes during the first few years of the century. In 1898, the Mark 3 bullet, flat-nosed with a hemispherical cavity in both nose and base, had been produced, a bullet well calculated to deal severely with anyone it hit. In spite of earnest protestations that such bullets were solely for warfare against 'uncivilized enemies', the Hague Convention outlawed them, and in 1902, they were declared obsolete. Production reverted to the round-nosed Mark 2 bullet for some years until in 1912, the Mark 4 was issued, a simple flat-fronted lead cylinder of awesome stopping power - indeed, the same bullet was marketed for many years by Webley under the trade-name of 'Manstopper'. But in late 1914, when the Germans began capturing British officers with these bullets in their possession, there was a loud outcry and talk of summary executions. The flat-nosed bullets were withdrawn (though they were never formally declared obsolete until 1946) and the old Mark 2 was re-issued.

When the British Army decided to move to 38-caliber for their next revolver, a 200-grain lead bullet was taken as the standard, and this gave quite reasonable stopping power. But when war loomed closer in the late 1930s, the old arguments about soft lead bullets and inhumanity were raised once more, and in order to avoid any accusations, the bullet was withdrawn and replaced by a jacketed 178-grain design.

Designers of jacketed bullets had, of course, made some attempts to improve on the target performance of their products. Some quite fearsome designs were produced for hunting purposes, notably for the 7.62mm Mauser pistol-carbine, but every suggestion to introduce these things into military use was firmly resisted. The most that could be done was a slight flattening of the nose, as seen in the original, conical, 9mm Parabellum.

Between the wars, there was little of note in the pistol ammunition field, and nothing which affected military applications. The Americans began their progress towards greater power with the introduction of the 357 Magnum cartridge, while in Germany, a move in the other direction took place with the development of the 'Ultra' series of cartridges. These were developed by the Genschow company in an attempt to improve on the conventional 6.35mm, 7.65mm and 9mm Short cartridges used in blowback pocket automatic pistols. The new cartridges, in 6.45mm, 8mm and 9mm calibers, were ballistically superior to the older designs, but before they could be perfected, the war intervened and the project was abandoned.

In post-war years, the American magnums have proliferated, though without much effect on military thinking, while the ultra idea has been revived in so far as both the Soviets and the West Germans have developed improved 9mm cartridges to replace the old 9mm Short. The first to appear was the 9mm Makarov, or 9x18mm, allied with the Makarov automatic pistol. More pistols chambered for this cartridge then appeared, and it gained general acceptance in Soviet satellite countries. In West Germany, the '9mm Police' cartridge (also 9x18mm, a conjunction of measurements which promised untold confusion in the future) was introduced with the SIG-Sauer P-230 pistol. In both cases, the object was the same; the production of a cartridge of the maximum power compatible with a simple blowback pistol, a design philosophy which permits the pistol to be cheap and simple, but which provides sufficient performance to make it a possible combat cartridge. However, the 9mm Police cartridge failed to gain much of a following, largely because no sooner had it appeared than vastly improved pistols in 9mm Parabellum caliber began to make their mark in military and police service.

The next move came in the USA where a 10mm automatic pistol had been struggling for a foothold in the market for some years. One manufacturer had

sufficient faith in the caliber to begin manufacturing ammunition, and although the pioneer pistol went into oblivion, other manufacturers began to take an interest. It became more of an interest in the early 1990s when the FBI decided that it would be their standard caliber in the future.

The drawback to the 10mm auto cartridge was that pistols had to be specially designed for it. The length of the bullet was somewhat greater than the 9mm Parabellum, and this it demanded a new frame and magazine. If a more powerful round of more compact dimensions could be designed.... No sooner the idea than the deed, and the 40 Smith & Wesson cartridge appeared to compete with the 10mm Auto. It was designed so that the frame and magazine opening designed for the 9x19mm round would suit the 40 S&W, so that converting a 9mm Parabellum design to 40-caliber was relatively simple. Before long virtually every 9mm combat pistol had a 40 S&W equivalent, and the 10mm was relegated to second place.

Other, less conventional, designs have come and gone. The 'Gyrojet' rocket-propelled bullet found no military acceptance because of its lack of power at short ranges and poor accuracy at longer ones. Micro-calibers, flechettes and similar solutions touted for rifles are impractical in hand guns, since they demand terminal velocities which cannot be attained from small weapons. So it seems unlikely that there will be any revolutionary thinking in the pistol ammunition field to compare to that going on in rifle circles.

• AMMUNITION DATA

Over the years, the number of cartridges which have actually been manufactured, and had weapons produced to match, runs well into four figures, and it is probable that a large number of them have been fired in combat at some time or other, even if they never figured in a military vocabulary. To make a complete list of all the possible cartridges would, we feel, be a waste of effort and of limited interest. There are, after all, any number of highly specialized books on cartridges which can be studied if great detail is demanded. We have, therefore, confined our attention to those cartridges in common use with the major armies, and mentioned in this book as applicable to weapons featured here. We have been extremely selective in listing variant types of cartridge; there are, for example, scores of minor variants of the 303 British and the German 7.92x57mm, but we cannot see that such fine detail is warranted in these pages.

The cartridges quoted are those specified as standard by the country of origin; they can, and do, vary according to what the precise powder is in the cartridge. Cartridges are commonly loaded to produce a specific velocity and chamber pressure, letting the weight fall as it may. In similar fashion, the muzzle velocities given are those of the country of origin and, where possible, the official specification. But different countries have different ways of specifying their velocities, so a certain amount of variation can be expected in this area as well. To give an example; the US 30-caliber Carbine Ball M1 in US service, carries a 13-grain charge, a 108-grain bullet, and achieves a specified velocity of 1900 ft/sec. The same cartridge manufactured in Britain, to the British Service specification 'Cartridge, .30in Carbine, Ball Mark 1', carries a 15-grain charge, a 111-grain bullet, and is specified at 1970 ft/sec. For all practical purposes they are interchangeable; indeed, it is doubtful if a firer, given a magazine filled with the two types mixed together, would ever notice the difference. But it goes to show that differences between 'identical' cartridges do exist—and that too much should not be made of the fact.

It is also worth noting that 'NATO Standard' appears to mean whatever the speaker wants it to mean. The NATO standards for ammunition are somewhat loosely drawn, and thus the 7.62x51mm or 5.45x45mm cartridges of the different NATO countries show some differences in weight of bullet, propellant charge and velocity. The theory is that any NATO soldier can acquire ammunition from any NATO source; but the British soldier fires a 5.56mm 4 gram bullet at 940 m/sec, while his French counterpart fires a cartridge with a 3.2 gram bullet at 957 m/sec. The difference is slight, and again might not be noticed; standardized they may be, identical they are not.

Pistol and submachine-gun ammunition (dimensions in inches)

Type	Round length	Case length	Rim diameter	Bullet weight	Bullet diameter	Muzzle velocity (fps)	Other
5.45x18mm Soviet	0.98	0.70	.297	40gr	.222	1033	PSM pistol
6.35x16mm Auto Colt	0.91	0.62	.298	50gr	.250	750	Military use rare
7x19.5mm Nambu	1.06	0.78	.359	55gr	.278	1050	
7.62x25mm Tokarev	1.35	0.97	.390	86gr	.307	1500	Type 'P'
7.62x38mm Soviet Revolver	1.51	1.51	.390	108gr	.307	935	Type 'R'
7.63x25mm Mauser	1.36	0.99	.390	85gr	.307	1450	German service
7.63x21mm Mannlicher M1900	1.12	0.84	.334	85gr	.305	1050	Austrian military
7.65x25mm Browning	1.03	0.68	.354	72gr	.310	875	or 32 Colt
7.65x19.5mm Longue	1.19	0.78	.337	85gr	.310	1175	
7.65x21.5mm Parabellum	1.15	0.75	.391	93gr	.307	1200	DWM Manufacture
8x27.5R French Mle 92	1.44	1.07	.400	120gr	.322	750	'Lebel' revolver
8x18.5mm Roth–Steyr M07	1.14	0.74	.356	116gr	.320	1090	Austrian service
8x27R Rast & Gasser	1.42	1.06	.375	120gr	.318	790	Austrian service
9x19mm Glisenti	1.15	0.75	.393	123gr	.347	1050	Italian service
9x19mm Parabellum	1.15	0.76	.392	115gr	.355	1300	NATO Standard
9x23mm Bergmann-Bayard	1.32	0.91	.392	135gr	.357	1100	Spanish 9mm Largo
9x23mm Steyr	1.30	0.90	.391	115gr	.354	1050	Austrian service
9x20mm Browning Long	1.10	0.80	.404	110gr	.355	1000	
9x17mm Browning Short	0.98	0.69	.374	95gr	.352	955	or 380 Auto
9x18mm Makarov	0.97	0.71	.396	95gr	.364	1100	
9x18mm Police	0.99	0.71	.375	100gr	.354	1040	
9x21mm IMI	1.23	0.83	.391	123gr	.354	1148	
9x22R Japanese Revolver	1.21	0.86	.432	149gr	.351	750	
9x25mm Mauser Export	1.37	0.90	.390	128gr	.356	1350	
357 SIG	1.12	0.86	.418	125gr	.357	1350	
380 Revolver Mark 2	1.23	0.76	.433	178gr	.355	600	Jacketed bullet
380 Revolver Mark 1	1.245	0.76	.433	200gr	.357	550	Lead bullet
38 Long Colt	1.32	1.03	.433	148gr	.346	785	US Govt
38 Special	1.55	1.16	.440	200gr	.355	745	
38 Super Auto	1.28	0.90	.405	130gr	.354	1300	
10mm Auto	1.25	0.98	.422	170gr	.398	1300	
40 Smith & Wesson	1.13	0.85	.424	178gr	.398	935	
41 Action Express	1.15	0.87	.392	200gr	.409	1017	
10.4x21mm Italian service	1.25	0.89	.505	175gr	.425	825	'Bodeo' revolver
10.6x25mm German Service	1.21	0.96	.500	250gr	.428	675	'Reichsrevolver'
45 Auto Colt Pistol	1.17	0.90	.476	230gr	.445	860	US M1911
45 Colt M1909	1.60	1.29	.538	250gr	.445	738	Special US Govt cartridge
455 Webley Revolver	1.23	0.75	.530	265gr	.454	580	Mk 2, lead bullet
	1.23	0.75	.530	265gr	.454	620	Mk 6, jacketed bullet
455 Webley Automatic	1.22	0.91	.500	224gr	.454	710	Service Mk 1
50 Action Express	1.59	1.28	.393	300gr	.500	1378	

Rifle and machine gun ammunition (dimensions in inches)

Type	Round Length	Case length	Rim diameter	Bullet weight	Bullet diameter	Muzzle velocity (fps)	Other
5.45x39.5mm	2.22	1.55	.394	53gr	.221	2950	Soviet AK74 rifle
5.56x45mm	2.26	1.75	.374	55gr	.223	3300	US M193 Ball
	2.26	1.75	.374	54gr	.223	3200	US M196 Tracer
5.56x45mm NATO	2.26	1.76	.377	62gr	.223	3002	Ball SS109
	2.26	1.76	.377	63gr	.223	2920	Tracer SS110
	2.26	1.76	.377	62gr	.223	2965	AP P-112
6mm Lee, US Navy	3.11	2.35	.448	112gr	.239	2560	
6.5x54mm	3.05	2.12	.450	160gr	.262	2225	Greek Mannlicher
6.5mmx54R Mannlicher	3.05	2.11	.527	162gr	.262	2400	Romanian and Dutch
6.5x51SR Arisaka	3.00	2.00	.476	139gr	.261	2500	Japanese Type 38
6.5x55mm Mauser	3.07	2.16	.478	139gr	.263	2600	Norway & Sweden
6.5x52mm Carcano	3.02	2.05	.448	123gr	.265	2450	Italian M1895
6.5x58mm Verguero	3.22	2.28	.465	155gr	.261	2000	Portuguese Mauser
7x43mm	2.53	1.70	.472	140gr	.284	2530	British 280
7.35x51mm	2.98	2.01	.449	130gr	.298	2480	Italian M1938
7.5x55mm	3.05	2.18	.496	174gr	.303	2560	Swiss M1911
7.5x54mm	3.00	2.12	.488	139gr	.308	2700	French Mle 1929
30 M1 Carbine	1.68	1.28	.355	108gr	.308	1900	US Service M1
30-06 Springfield	3.34	2.49	.470	174gr	.308	2675	Ball M1
	3.34	2.49	.470	150gr	—	2500	Ball M2
	3.34	2.49	.470	165gr	—	2715	AP M2
	3.34	2.49	.470	150gr	—	2780	AP/Incendiary M14
	3.34	2.49	.470	140gr	—	2950	Incendiary M1
	3.34	2.49	.470	152gr	—	2700	Tracer M1
	3.34	2.49	.470	108gr	.308	1300	Frangible M22
7.62x45mm	2.47	1.65	.468	130gr	.307	2440	Czech VZ-52
7.62x39mm	2.19	1.52	.445	123gr	.308	2330	Soviet M-43, Ball PS
	2.19	1.52	.445	115gr	.308	2330	Tracer T-45
	2.19	1.52	.445	120gr	.308	2395	AP/Incendiary Type BZ
	2.19	1.52	.445	102gr	.308		Incendiary/ranging Type ZP
7.62x51mm NATO	2.80	2.01	.473	144gr	.308	2700	British L2A2 Ball
	2.80	2.01	.473	135gr	.308	2620	British L5A3 Tracer
	2.80	2.01	.473	150gr	.308	2750	US Ball M59
	2.80	2.01	.473	150gr	.308	2750	US AP M61
7.62x54R	3.02	2.11	.560	149gr	.310	2855	Russian Light Ball LP
	3.02	2.11	.560	185gr	.310	2683	Heavy Ball D
	3.02	2.11	.560	184gr	.310	2790	AP B30
	3.02	2.11	.560	142gr	.310	2800	AP/I/Tracer BZT
	3.02	2.11	.560	187gr	.310	2640	AP/I/Tungsten Core BS40
7.65x53mm Mauser	3.06	2.11	.474	215gr	.311	2035	Belgian Mle 89
7.65x53mm Mauser	3.06	2.09	.474	155gr	.311	2720	Turkish M90

Rifle and machine gun ammunition (dimensions in inches)

Type	Round Length	Case length	Rim diameter	Bullet weight	Bullet diameter	Muzzle velocity (fps)	Other
303 British	3.03	2.15	.530	215gr	.311	1970	Mk 6 Ball
	3.03	2.15	.530	174gr	.311	2400	Mk 7 Ball
	3.05	2.15	.530	175gr	.311	2400	Mk7Z Ball
	3.05	2.15	.530	169gr	.312	2370	G Mk 8 Tracer
	3.05	2.15	.530	166gr	.311	2370	B Mk 7 Incendiary
	3.05	2.15	.530	174gr	.311	2400	O Mk 1 Observing
	3.05	2.15	.530	174gr	.313	2370	W Mk 1 Armor-piercing
	3.05	2.15	.530	174gr	.311	—	Mk 3 Proof; loaded to give a breech pressure of 24 to 26 tons
7.7x58mm	3.14	2.27	.476	179gr	.311	2490	Japan rimless Type 99
7.7x58SR	3.13	2.28	.510	200gr	.311	2400	Japan semi-rim Type 92
7.7x56R	3.02	2.21	.540	174gr	.310	2440	Japan rimmed Type 89
7.92x33mm	1.89	1.29	.467	125gr	.322	2300	'Kurz' M1943
7.92x57mm	3.17	2.24	.473	178gr	.323	2746	German Army Ball SmE
	3.17	2.24	.473	198gr	.323	2510	Heavy Ball SS
	3.17	2.24	.473	156gr	.323	2730	AP/Tracer SmKL
	3.17	2.24	.473	156gr	.323	2730	AP/Incendiary PmK
	3.17	2.24	.473	86gr	.323	3050	Practice Ball
	3.17	2.24	.473	198gr	.323	984	Silenced Ball
7.92x95mm	4.64	3.73	.825	222gr	.323	3545	Anti-tank rifles, German
8x50R Mannlicher	2.99	1.98	.551	244gr	.322	2030	Austrian M1893
8x50R Lebel	2.95	2.00	.629	198gr	.319	2296	French 'Balle D'
8x56R Mannlicher	3.02	2.21	.550	205gr	.328	2280	Hungarian M31
8x58R Krag	2.99	2.28	.575	237gr	.322	1985	Danish M1889
10.15x63R Mauser	3.13	2.46	.592	340gr	.391	1600	Serbian M1 878
11.15x60R Mauser	3.00	2.237	.586	370gr	.440	1430	Germany M1871
12.7x57B	3.78	2.244	.582	665gr	.510	1050	Subsonic
12.7x77mm	4.36	3.00	.800	827gr	.510	1745	US 50 Spotting rifle
12.7x80SR	4.31	3.16	.715	580gr	.514	2540	Vickers 50, also Breda
12.7x99mm	5.42	3.90	.800	759gr	.510	2800	UK 50 Browning Mk 2Z
	5.42	3.90	.800	710gr	.511	2810	US 50 Browning M 2
12.7x108mm	5.76	4.25	.850	681gr	.510	2750	Soviet DSHK &c MG
13x92SR	5.23	3.61	.905	965gr	.522	2600	Mauser Anti-tank rifle 1918
13.2x99mm Hotchkiss	3.90	.800	.791	230gr	.520	2211	also Japan and Italy
55 Boys Anti-tank rifle	5.31	3.95	.797	735gr	.564	2900	AP 'W' Mk 2
14.5x114mm	6.11	4.49	1.058	968gr	.587	3200	Soviet Anti-tank AP/I B32
15x104mm	5.82	4.09	.975	1160gr	.590	2900	UK 15mm Besa AP Mk 1
15x115mm	6.32	4.53	.970	1090gr	.604	3395	FN-BRG (1)
15.2x169mm Steyr AMR	8.15	6.65	1.020	544gr	.216	4557	APFSDS
15.5x106mm	6.92	4.17	1.055	1204gr	.613	3460	FN-BRG (2)
20x105B	6.69	4.13	.984	?	.783	?	Short Solothurn
20x124mm	7.64	4.90	1.122	2052gr	.783	2500	Japan Type 97 Anti-tank rifle
20x138B	8.07	5.42	1.055	2260gr	.783	2950	Long Solothurn

Index